W9-BIQ-481

Introduction to Research in Education

Introduction to Research in Education

FOURTH EDITION

Donald Ary
Northern Illinois University

Lucy Cheser Jacobs
Indiana University

Asghar Razavieh
Shiraz University, Shiraz, Iran

Holt, Rinehart and Winston, Inc.

Fort Worth   Chicago   San Francisco   Philadelphia
Montreal   Toronto   London   Sydney   Tokyo

Publisher	Ted Buchholz
Acquisitions Editor	Jo-Anne Weaver
Production Manager	Kenneth A. Dunaway
Art & Design Supervisor	Impressions Publishing Services, Inc.
Text Designer	Impressions Publishing Services, Inc.
Cover Designer	Impressions Publishing Services, Inc.

Library of Congress Cataloging-in-Publication Data

Ary, Donald.
 Introduction to research in education / Donald Ary, Lucy Cheser Jacobs, Asghar
Razavieh.—4th ed.
  p.   cm.
 Includes bibliographical references.
 ISBN 0-03-032462-9
 1. Education—Research. I. Jacobs, Lucy Cheser. II. Razavieh, Asghar. III. Title.
 LB1028.A7 1990
 370′.7′8—dc20   89-28927
                                                                              CIP

ISBN: 0-03-032462-9

Address for editorial correspondence: Holt, Rinehart and Winston, Inc., 301 Commerce
Street, Suite 3700, Fort Worth, TX 76102

Address for orders: Holt, Rinehart and Winston, Inc., 6277 Sea Harbor Drive, Orlando,
Florida 32887. 1-800-782-4479 or 1-800-433-0001 (in Florida)

PRINTED IN THE UNITED STATES OF AMERICA

0 1 2 3   039   9 8 7 6 5 4 3 2 1

Holt, Rinehart and Winston, Inc.
The Dryden Press
Saunders College Publishing

To Sheila, Marion, and Nasrin

/// CONTENTS

/// PREFACE

In 1972 our goals in preparing the first edition of *Introduction to Research in Education* were to provide a book that would enable readers to master the basic competencies necessary to (1) understand and evaluate the research of others and (2) plan and conduct their own research with a minimum of assistance. The continued acceptance of this book through three editions indicates that we have been successful.

As research in education has evolved and matured, we have adapted each new edition to provide our readers with the knowledge required to keep abreast of these changes.

The sequence of topics discussed in this book begins with a general description of the scientific approach and the relevance of this approach to the search for knowledge in education. We assume that our readers are not familiar with the concepts, assumptions, and terminology of the scientific approach; therefore, these are explained as they are introduced. This is followed by suggestions for translating general problems into specific questions amenable to scientific inquiry through the identification of the population and variables of interest.

Next we describe the role of previous research and theory in the planning of a research project. We have updated the sources of related literature, giving particular emphasis to databases that provide efficient access to relevant research and theory and how these databases can be accessed. We then proceed to investigate the ways in which theory, experience, observations, and related literature lead to hypothesis formation.

Sampling procedures and the more widely used descriptive and inferential statistical procedures are described with emphasis on their role in the research process and on their interpretation. The role of systematic observation and measurement is explored, and examples of useful measurement procedures are included. The chapter on reliability and validity has been revised, updated, and expanded.

Following this, we discuss the various types of research that have proven useful in education, pointing out the advantages and disadvantages of various approaches without espousing any particular one as superior to the others. In this edition we have added a section on qualitative research and have expanded the section on correlational research into a separate chapter.

We conclude by presenting the general rules for interpreting the results of research and the accepted procedures for reporting such results. We have updated the section on the use of computers.

The focus of this edition remains the provision of a text designed for use in an introductory course in educational research. Its aim is to familiarize the beginning researcher with the procedures for conducting an original research project. We focus on the typical and practical problems encountered in research, beginning with the formulation of the question and continuing through the preparation of the final report.

In addition to the study questions at the end of each chapter, multiple-choice questions are available in the instructor's manual.

Although *Introduction to Research in Education* is directed toward the beginning student in educational research, it is hoped that others who wish to learn more about the philosophy, tools, and procedures of scientific inquiry in education will find it useful. The principal criterion used in determining what to include has been the potential usefulness of various aspects of educational research to the educational practitioner.

To all of those teachers who used the first three editions and have made very valuable suggestions for improving and updating the fourth edition, we are deeply grateful. We thank Jon D. Miller for his assistance in preparing the section on ethical and legal considerations and Thomas Schwandt for his contribution in preparing the section on qualitative inquiry. We appreciate Samual Huang for his extensive work in producing a comprehensive and up-to-date related-literature chapter. We thank Wesley Covalt and Jonathan Reich for their assistance in preparing the instructor's manual.

We are grateful to the literary executor of the late Sir Ronald A. Fisher, F.R.S., to Dr. Frank Yates, F.R.S., and the Longman Group Ltd., London, for permission to reprint Tables A2, A4, and A6 from their book *Statistical Tables for Biological, Agricultural and Medical Research* (6th ed., 1974).

// Reviewers

Kevin Crehan, University of Nevada, Las Vegas, NV
Alfredo Cuellar, San Diego State University, San Diego, CA
Gilbert Cuevas, University of Miami, Coral Gables, FL
Charlotte Farr, University of Wyoming, Laramie, WY
Ron Jacobs, San Diego State University, San Diego, CA
Ben Layne, Georgia State University, Atlanta, GA
Edwin Novak, Ohio State University, Columbus, OH
Robert Przybyszewski, Niagara University, Niagara University, NY
David Quist, Worcester State College, Worcester, MA
Bruce Rogers, University of Northern Iowa, Cedar Falls, IA
Dale Shaw, University of Northern Colorado, Greeley, CO
William Ware, University of North Carolina, Chapel Hill, NC
Kinnard White, University of North Carolina, Chapel Hill, NC
Richard Williams, University of Miami, Coral Gables, FL

Introduction to
Research in Education

PART I

Foundations

CHAPTER 1

The Scientific Approach in Education

INSTRUCTIONAL OBJECTIVES

After studying this chapter, the student will be able to

1. List the five major sources of knowledge and comment on each source
2. Describe the characteristics of the scientific approach
3. State the assumptions underlying science and the characteristic attitudes of scientists
4. Specify the purpose and characteristics of scientific theory and distinguish between various approaches to theory construction in behavioral sciences
5. Indicate the limitations involved in the application of the scientific approach in the social sciences
6. Distinguish between the characteristics of basic and applied research
7. Explain the terms *concept, construct,* and *variable*
8. Distinguish between various types of variables: categorical versus continuous, independent versus dependent, and active versus attribute
9. Describe various types of definitions: constitutive vs. operational and measured operational vs. experimental operational
10. Describe the five research methodologies used in educational investigations

Educators are, by necessity, decision makers. Daily, in the course of carrying out the educative process, we are faced with the task of making decisions about how to plan learning experiences, how to teach, how to guide students, how to organize a school system, and myriad other matters.

Unlike unskilled workers who are told what to do and how to do it, professionals must plan for themselves. It is assumed that they have the knowledge and skills necessary to make valid decisions about what to do and how. But how are educators to know what is the right answer in a particular situation? Although there are other sources of knowledge, such as experience, authority, and tradition, it is scientific knowledge about the educational process that makes the most valuable contribution to decision making in education. Educators can turn to this source for reliable information and suggestions to be used in a decision-making situation. This fund of knowledge has been made available to educators as a result of scientific inquiry into educational problems. Education has not always been influenced by the results of such careful and systematic investigations. In fact, it might be said that the development of an educational science is at a comparatively early stage.

/// SOURCES OF KNOWLEDGE

Before we pursue further the role of scientific inquiry in education, let us review the ways in which human beings throughout history have sought answers to their questions. The sources of knowledge may be categorized under five headings: (1) experience, (2) authority, (3) deductive reasoning, (4) inductive reasoning, and (5) the scientific approach.

// Experience

Experience is a familiar and well-used source of knowledge. After trying several routes from home to work, one learns which route takes the least time or is the most free of traffic or is the most scenic. By personal experience one can find the answers to many of the questions one faces. Much of the wisdom that is passed from generation to generation is the result of experience. If we were not able to profit from experience, progress would be severely retarded. In fact, this ability to learn from experience is generally considered a prime characteristic of intelligent behavior.

Yet, for all its usefulness, experience has its limitations as a source of truth. How one is affected by an event depends upon who one is. Two people will have very different experiences in the same situation. The same woods that are a delightful sanctuary to one may be a menacing wilderness to another. Two supervisors observing the same classroom at the same time could truthfully compile very different reports if one focused on and reported the things that went right and the other focused on and reported the things that went wrong.

Another shortcoming of experience is that one so frequently needs to know things that one as an individual cannot learn by experience. A child turned loose to figure out arithmetic alone might figure out the technique of addition but would be unlikely to find an efficient way to compute square roots. A teacher could learn through experience the population of a classroom on a particular day but could not personally count the population of the United States.

// Authority

For those things that are difficult or impossible to know by personal experience, one frequently turns to authority; that is, one seeks the answers to questions from someone who has had experience with the problem or has some other source of expertise. We accept as truth the word of those recognized as authorities. To know the population of the United States, one turns to the U.S. Census Bureau reports. A student looks up the correct pronunciation of a word in the dictionary. The superintendent consults a lawyer concerning a legal problem in the school. A beginning teacher asks an experienced one for suggestions. The new teacher may try a certain technique for teaching reading because the supervisor suggests that it is effective.

Throughout history one can find examples of reliance upon authority for truth, particularly during the Middle Ages when ancient scholars, such as Plato and Aristotle, and the early Fathers of the church were preferred as sources of truth—even over direct observation or experience. Although authority is one of our very useful sources of knowledge, one must not lose sight of the question How does authority know? In earlier days an authority was assumed to be right simply because of the position held, such as that of king, chief, or high priest. Today we are reluctant to rely upon an individual as an authority merely because of position or rank. We are inclined to accept the assertions of an authority only when that authority bases its assertions on experience or other recognized sources of knowledge.

Closely related to authority are custom and tradition, which we depend on for answers to many of the questions related to our professional as well as everyday problems. In other words, one often asks How has this been done in the past? and then uses the answer as a guide for his or her actions. Custom and tradition have been especially prominent influences in the school setting, where educators often rely on past practices as a dependable guide. However, an examination of the history of education reveals that many traditions that had prevailed for years were later found to be erroneous and had to be rejected. It is wise to appraise custom and tradition carefully before one accepts them as truth.

As a source of truth, authority has shortcomings that one must consider. In the first place, authorities can be wrong; they have no claim to infallibility. Also, one may find that authorities are in disagreement among themselves on issues, indicating that their authoritative statements are often more personal opinion than fact.

// Deductive Reasoning

Perhaps the first significant contribution to the development of a systematic approach for discovering truth was made by the ancient Greek philosophers. Aristotle and his followers introduced the use of deductive reasoning, which can be described as a thinking process in which one proceeds from general to specific statements using prescribed rules of logic. It is a system for organizing known facts in order to reach a conclusion. This is done through the use of logical arguments. An argument consists of a number of statements standing in relation to one another. The final statement is the conclusion, and the rest, called premises, comprise supporting evidence. One of the major kinds of deductive reasoning is the syllogism. A syllogism consists of a major premise and a minor premise followed by a conclusion. An example of syllogistic reasoning is: All men are mortal (major premise); the king is a man (minor premise); therefore, the king is mortal (conclusion).

In deductive reasoning, if the premises are true, the conclusion is necessarily true. Deductive reasoning enables one to organize premises into patterns that provide conclusive evidence for the validity of a conclusion. Mystery fans will recall that Sherlock Holmes frequently would say, "I deduce . . ." as he combined previously unconnected facts in such a way as to imply a previously unsuspected conclusion.

However, deductive reasoning does have its limitations. We must begin with true premises in order to arrive at true conclusions. The conclusion of a syllogism can never exceed the content of the premises. Since deductive conclusions are necessarily elaborations on previously existing knowledge, scientific inquiry cannot be conducted through deductive reasoning alone because of the difficulty involved in establishing the universal truth of many statements dealing with scientific phenomena. Deductive reasoning can organize what is already known and can point up new relationships as one proceeds from the general to the specific, but it is not sufficient as a source of new truth.

In spite of its limitations, deductive reasoning is useful in the research process. It provides a means for linking theory and observation. It enables researchers to deduce from existing theory what phenomena should be observed. Deductions from theory can provide hypotheses, which are a vital part of scientific inquiry.

// **Inductive Reasoning**

The conclusions of deductive reasoning are true only if the premises on which they are based are true. But how is one to know if the premises are true? In the Middle Ages dogma was often substituted for true premises, with the result that invalid conclusions were reached. It was Francis Bacon (1561–1626) who first called for a new approach to knowing. He held that thinkers should not enslave themselves by accepting premises handed down by authority as absolute truth. He believed that an investigator should establish general conclusions on the basis of facts gathered through direct observation. Bacon advised the seeker of truth to observe nature directly and to rid the mind of prejudice and preconceived ideas, which he called "idols." For Bacon, obtaining knowledge required that one observe nature itself, gather particular facts, and formulate generalizations from these findings. The importance of observation is seen in the following anecdote attributed to Bacon.

> In the year of our Lord 1432, there arose a grievous quarrel among the brethren over the number of teeth in the mouth of a horse. For 13 days the disputation raged without ceasing. All the ancient books and chronicles were fetched out, and wonderful and ponderous erudition, such as was never before heard of in this region, was made manifest. At the beginning of the 14th day, a youthful friar of goodly bearing asked his learned superiors for permission to add a word, and straightway, to the wonderment of the disputants, whose deep wisdom he sore vexed, he beseeched them to unbend in a manner coarse and unheard-of, and to look in the open mouth of a horse and find an answer to their questionings. At this, their dignity being grievously hurt, they waxed exceedingly wroth; and, joining in a mighty uproar, they flew upon him and smote him hip and thigh, and cast him out forthwith. For, said they, surely Satan hath tempted this bold neophyte to declare unholy and unheard-of ways of finding truth contrary to all the teachings of the fathers. After many days more of grievous strife the dove of peace sat on the assembly, and they as one man, declaring the problem to be an everlasting mystery because of a grievous dearth of historical and theological evidence thereof, so ordered the same writ down.[1]

The youth in this story was calling for a new way of seeking truth, namely, to seek the facts rather than depend upon authority or upon sheer speculation. This was to become the fundamental principle of all science.

In Bacon's system, observations were made on particular events in a class, and then, on the basis of the observed events, inferences were made about the whole class. This approach is known as inductive reasoning, which is the reverse of the processes employed in the deductive method. The

---

[1]Mees, C. E. K. (1934). Scientific thought and social reconstruction. *General Electric Review, 37,* 113–119.

difference between deductive and inductive reasoning may be seen in the following examples:

    A. Deductive: Every mammal has lungs.
                     All rabbits are mammals.
                     Therefore, every rabbit has lungs.
    B. Inductive: Every rabbit that has ever been observed has lungs.
                     Therefore, every rabbit has lungs.

Note that in deductive reasoning the premises must be known before a conclusion can be reached, but in inductive reasoning a conclusion is reached by observing examples and generalizing from the examples to the whole class. In order to be absolutely certain of an inductive conclusion, the investigator must observe all examples. This is known as perfect induction under the Baconian system; it requires that the investigator examine every example of a phenomenon. In the example above, to be absolutely sure that every rabbit had lungs, the investigator would have to have observations on all rabbits currently alive as well as all past and future rabbits. In practice this is usually not feasible; therefore, one generally must rely on imperfect induction based on incomplete observation.

Inductive conclusions can be absolute only when the group about which they are asserted is small. For example, one might observe that all the red-haired pupils in a particular class make above-average grades in spelling and legitimately assert that the red-haired children currently enrolled in the class have above-average spelling grades. But one could not draw legitimate conclusions concerning the spelling grades of red-haired children in other classes or in future classes.

Since one can make perfect inductions only on small groups, we commonly use imperfect induction, a system in which one observes a sample of a group and infers from the sample what is characteristic of the entire group. An example of a conclusion based on imperfect induction is the present thinking concerning the physical characteristics of very intelligent children. For many years it was generally believed that exceptionally bright children were prone to be poor physical specimens. Even today cartoonists usually portray the bright child as a scrawny creature with thick spectacles. Terman, a pioneer in the field of mental testing, was interested in the characteristics of exceptionally bright youngsters.[2] He made an intensive study of over 1000 California children who scored above 140 on the Stanford-Binet Intelligence Test. He found the average height, weight, and general physical health of these children to be slightly above average for children of their age. From this study it has been concluded that bright children, far from being the

---

[2]Terman, L. M. (1926). The mental and physical traits of a thousand gifted children. *Genetic Studies of Genius* (vol. 1). Stanford, CA: Stanford University Press.

traditionally expected scrawny specimens, are a little more likely to be above average in physical development than children with average IQ scores.

Note that this conclusion has not been positively proved. It is simply highly probable that it is true. To be positively sure about this conclusion, one would have to have physical measures for all children with IQ scores of 140 or more on the Stanford-Binet. Even then one could only be positive about the characteristics of such children today and could not be 100 percent sure that the same would be true of such children in the future. Although imperfect induction does not enable us to reach infallible conclusions, it can provide reliable information upon which one can make reasonable decisions.

// The Scientific Approach

Exclusive use of induction often resulted in the accumulation of isolated knowledge and information that made little contribution to the advancement of knowledge. Furthermore, it was found that many problems could not be solved by induction alone. It was inevitable that scholars would soon learn to integrate the most important aspects of the inductive and deductive methods into a new technique, namely, the inductive-deductive method, or the scientific approach. Charles Darwin, in the development of his theory of evolution, is generally recognized as the first to apply this method in the pursuit of knowledge. Darwin reports that he spent a long time making biological observations, hoping to establish some generalizations concerning evolution. He describes how he arrived at a new approach:

> My first note-book (on evolution) was opened in July 1837. I worked on true Baconian principles, and without any theory collected facts on a wholesale scale, more especially with respect to domesticated productions, by printed enquiries, by conversation with skillful breeders and gardeners, and by extensive reading. When I see the list of books of all kinds which I read and abstracted, including whole series of Journals and Transactions, I am surprised at my industry. I soon perceived that selection was the keystone of man's success in making useful races of animals and plants. But how selection would be applied to organisms living in a state of nature remained for some time a mystery to me.
>
> In October 1838, that is, fifteen months after I had begun my systematic enquiry, I happened to read for amusement "Malthus on Population," and being well prepared to appreciate the struggle for existence which everywhere goes on from long-continued observation of the habits of animals and plants, it at once struck me that under these circumstances favourable variations would tend to be preserved, and unfavourable ones to be destroyed. The result of this would be the formation of new species. Here then I had at last got a theory by which to work.[3]

---

[3]Darwin, F. (ed.) (1899). *The Life and Letters of Charles Darwin* (vol. 1, p. 68). New York: Appleton.

Darwin's procedure, involving only observation, was unproductive until reading and further thought led him to formulate a tentative hypothesis to explain the facts that he had gathered through observation. He then proceeded to test this hypothesis by making deductions from it and gathering additional data to determine whether these data would support the hypothesis. From this method of inquiry, Darwin was able to develop his theory of evolution. This use of both inductive and deductive reasoning is characteristic of modern scientific inquiry, which is regarded as the most reliable method for obtaining knowledge.

The scientific approach is generally described as a process in which investigators move inductively from their observations to hypotheses and then deductively from the hypotheses to the logical implications of the hypotheses. They deduce the consequences that would follow if a hypothesized relationship is true. If these deduced implications are compatible with the organized body of accepted knowledge, they are then further tested by the gathering of empirical data. On the basis of the evidence the hypotheses are accepted or rejected.

The use of the hypothesis is a principal difference between the scientific approach and inductive reasoning. In inductive reasoning one makes observations first and then organizes the information gained. In the scientific approach one reasons what one would find if a hypothesis is true and then makes systematic observations in order to confirm or fail to confirm the hypothesis.

// An Example of the Scientific Approach

Robert Pirsig provides a vivid and succinct description of the scientific approach by comparing it to the process of maintaining a motorcycle in good working order:

> Two kinds of logic are used, inductive and deductive. Inductive inferences start with observations of the machine and arrive at general conclusions. For example, if the cycle goes over a bump and the engine misfires, and then goes over another bump and the engine misfires, and then goes over another bump and the engine misfires, and then goes over a long smooth stretch of road and there is no misfiring, and then goes over a fourth bump and the engine misfires again, one can logically conclude that the misfiring is caused by the bumps. That is induction: reasoning from particular experiences to general truths.
>
> Deductive inferences do the reverse. They start with general knowledge and predict a specific observation. For example, if, from reading the hierarchy of facts about the machine, the mechanic knows the horn of the cycle is powered exclusively by electricity from the battery, then he can logically infer that if the battery is dead the horn will not work. That is deduction.
>
> Solution of problems too complicated for common sense to solve is achieved by long strings of mixed inductive and deductive inferences

that weave back and forth between the observed machine and the mental hierarchy of the machine found in the manuals. The correct program for this interweaving is formalized as scientific method.

Actually I've never seen a cycle-maintenance problem complex enough really to require full-scale formal scientific method. Repair problems are not that hard. When I think of formal scientific method an image sometimes comes to mind of an enormous juggernaut, a huge bulldozer—slow, tedious, lumbering, laborious, but invincible. It takes twice as long, five times as long, maybe a dozen times as long as informal mechanic's techniques, but you know in the end you're going to *get* it. There's no fault isolation problem in motorcycle maintenance that can stand up to it. When you've hit a really tough one, tried everything, racked your brain and nothing works, and you know that this time Nature has really decided to be difficult, you say, "Okay, Nature, that's the end of the *nice* guy," and you crank up the formal scientific method.

For this you keep a lab notebook. Everything gets written down, formally, so that you know at all times where you are, where you've been, where you're going and where you want to get. In scientific work and electronics technology this is necessary because otherwise the problems get so complex you get lost in them and confused and forget what you know and what you don't know and have to give up. In cycle maintenance things are not that involved, but when confusion starts it's a good idea to hold it down by making everything formal and exact. Sometimes just the act of writing down the problems straightens out your head as to what they really are.

The logical statements entered into the notebook are broken down into six categories: (1) statement of the problem, (2) hypotheses as to the cause of the problem, (3) experiments designed to test each hypothesis, (4) predicted results of the experiments, (5) observed results of the experiments, and (6) conclusions from the results of the experiments. This is not different from the formal arrangement of many college and high-school lab notebooks but the purpose here is no longer just busy-work. The purpose now is precise guidance of thoughts that will fail if they are not accurate.

The real purpose of scientific method is to make sure Nature hasn't misled you into thinking you know something you don't actually know. There's not a mechanic or scientist or technician alive who hasn't suffered from that one so much that he's not instinctively on guard. That's the main reason why so much scientific and mechanical information sounds so dull and so cautious. If you get careless or go romanticizing scientific information, giving it a flourish here and there, Nature will soon make a complete fool out of you. It does it often enough anyway even when you don't give it opportunities. One must be extremely careful and rigidly logical when dealing with Nature: one logical slip and an entire scientific edifice comes tumbling down. One false deduction about the machine and you can get hung up indefinitely.

In Part One of formal scientific method, which is the statement of the problem, the main skill is in stating absolutely no more than you are positive you know. It is much better to enter a statement "Solve Problem: Why doesn't cycle work?" which sounds dumb but is correct, than it is to enter a statement "Solve Problem: What is wrong with the electrical system?" when you don't absolutely *know* the trouble is *in* the electrical system. What you should state is "Solve Problem: What is wrong with cycle?" and *then* state as the first entry of Part Two: "Hypothesis Number One: The trouble is in the electrical system." You think of as many hypotheses as you can, then you design experiments to test them to see which are true and which are false.

This careful approach to the beginning questions keeps you from taking a major wrong turn which might cause you weeks of extra work or can even hang you up completely. Scientific questions often have a surface appearance of dumbness for this reason. They are asked in order to prevent dumb mistakes later on.

Part Three, that part of formal scientific method called experimentation, is sometimes thought of by romantics as all of science itself because that's the only part with much visual surface. They see lots of test tubes and bizarre equipment and people running around making discoveries. They do not see the experiment as part of a larger intellectual process and so they often confuse experiments with demonstrations, which look the same. A man conducting a gee-whiz science show with fifty thousand dollars' worth of Frankenstein equipment is not doing anything scientific if he knows beforehand what the results of his efforts are going to be. A motorcycle mechanic, on the other hand, who honks the horn to see if the battery works is informally conducting a true scientific experiment. He is testing a hypothesis by putting the question to nature. The TV scientist who mutters sadly, "The experiment is a failure; we have failed to achieve what we had hoped for," is suffering mainly from a bad scriptwriter. An experiment is never a failure solely because it fails to achieve predicted results. An experiment is a failure only when it also fails adequately to test the hypothesis in question, when the data it produces don't prove anything one way or another.

Skill at this point consists of using experiments that test only the hypothesis in question, nothing less, nothing more. If the horn honks, and the mechanic concludes that the whole electrical system is working, he is in deep trouble. He has reached an illogical conclusion. The honking horn only tells him that the battery and horn are working. To design an experiment properly he has to think very rigidly in terms of what directly causes what. This you know from the hierarchy. The horn doesn't make the cycle go. Neither does the battery, except in a very indirect way. The point at which the electrical system *directly* causes the engine to fire is at the spark plugs, and if you don't test here, at the output of the electrical system, you will never really know whether the failure is electrical or not.

To test properly, the mechanic removes the plug and lays it against the engine so that the base around the plug is electrically grounded, kicks the starter lever and watches the spark-plug gap for a blue spark. If there isn't any he can conclude one of two things: (a) there is an electrical failure or (b) his experiment is sloppy. If he is experienced he will try it a few more times, checking connections, trying every way he can think of to get that plug to fire. Then, if he can't get it to fire, he finally concludes that *a* is correct, there's an electrical failure, and the experiment is over. He has proved that his hypothesis is correct.

In the final category, conclusions, skill comes in stating no more than the experiment has proved. It hasn't proved that when he fixes the electrical system the motorcycle will start. There may be other things wrong.

But he does know that the motorcycle isn't going to run until the electrical system is working and he sets up the next formal question: "Solve Problem: What is wrong with the electrical system?"

He then sets up hypotheses for these and tests them. By asking the right questions and choosing the right tests and drawing the right conclusions the mechanic works his way down the echelons of the motorcycle hierarchy until he has found the exact specific cause or causes of the engine failure, and then he changes them so that they no longer cause the failure.

An untrained observer will see only physical labor and often get the idea that physical labor is mainly what the mechanic does. Actually the physical labor is the smallest and easiest part of what the mechanic does. By far the greatest part of his work is careful observation and precise thinking. That is why mechanics sometimes seem so taciturn and withdrawn when performing tests. They don't like it when you talk to them because they are concentrating on mental images, hierarchies, and not really looking at you or the physical motorcycle at all. They are using the experiment as part of a program to expand their hierarchy of knowledge of the faulty motorcycle and compare it to the correct hierarchy in their mind. They are looking at underlying form.[4]

/// THE NATURE OF SCIENCE

It might also be mentioned at this point that all sciences, though they may differ from one another in material or in specialized techniques, have in common this general method for arriving at reliable knowledge. It is this method of inquiry that determines whether a discipline is a science. Perhaps science is best described as a *method* of inquiry that permits investigators to examine the phenomena of interest to them. In addition to the method followed by scientists as they seek reliable knowledge, there are certain other aspects of the scientific approach, which we will examine briefly. These are (1) assumptions made by scientists, (2) attitudes of scientists, and (3) formulation of scientific theory.

// Assumptions Made by Scientists

A fundamental assumption made by scientists is that the events they investigate are lawful or ordered—no event is capricious. Science is based upon the belief that all natural phenomena have antecedent factors. This assumption is sometimes referred to as universal determinism. Primitive people proposed supernatural causes for most of the events they observed. Modern science did not develop until people began to look beyond super-

---

[4]Pirsig, R. M. (1974). *Zen and the Art of Motorcycle Maintenance: An Inquiry into Values* (pp. 107–111). New York: Morrow. (Reprinted by permission of William Morrow & Company.)

natural explanations and began to depend upon the observation of nature itself to provide answers.

This assumption underlies any statement that declares that under specified conditions certain events will occur. For example, the chemist is able to state that when a mixture of potassium chlorate and manganese dioxide is heated, oxygen will be produced. Behavioral scientists likewise assume that the behavior of organisms is lawful and predictable.

Related to this first assumption is the belief that the events in nature are, at least to a degree, orderly and regular and that this order and regularity of nature can be discovered through the scientific method.

A second assumption is that truth can ultimately be derived only from direct observation. Reliance upon empirical observation differentiates science from nonscience. The scientist does not depend upon authority as a source of truth but insists upon studying empirical evidence. In the history of science we find many examples of scientists who rejected the prevailing notions of their day and proceeded with their observations and experimentation. Galileo's early experiments with falling bodies resulted in new knowledge that contradicted notions held by the authorities of his day.

A corollary of this assumption is the belief that only phenomena that can actually be seen to exist are within the realm of scientific investigation.

// Attitudes of Scientists

Scientists recognize certain characteristic attitudes that they acquire as they pursue their work.

1. Scientists are essentially doubters, who maintain a highly skeptical attitude toward the data of science. Findings are regarded as tentative and are not accepted by scientists unless they can be verified. Verification requires that others must be able to repeat the observations and obtain the same results. Scientists want to test opinions and questions concerning the relationships among natural phenomena. Furthermore, they make their testing procedures known to others in order that they may verify, or fail to verify, their findings.

2. Scientists are objective and impartial. In conducting observations and interpreting data, scientists are not trying to prove a point. They take particular care to collect data in such a way that any personal biases they may have will not influence their observations. They seek truth and accept the facts even when they are contrary to their own opinions. If the accumulated evidence upsets a favorite theory, then they either discard that theory or modify it to agree with the factual data.

3. Scientists deal with facts, not values. They do not indicate any potential moral implications of their findings; they do not make decisions for us about what is good or what is bad. Scientists provide data concerning the relationship that exists between events, but we must go beyond these scientific data if we want a decision about whether a certain consequence is

desirable. Thus, while the findings of science may be of key importance in the solution of a problem involving a value decision, the data themselves do not furnish that value judgment.

4. Scientists are not satisfied with isolated facts but seek to integrate and systematize their findings. They want to put the things known into an orderly system. Thus, scientists aim for theories that attempt to bring together empirical findings into a meaningful pattern. However, they regard these theories as tentative or provisional, subject to revision as new evidence is found.

// Scientific Theory

The last aspect of the scientific approach to be considered is the construction of theory. Scientists, through empirical investigation, gather many facts. But as these facts accumulate, there is need for integration, organization, and classification in order to make the isolated findings meaningful. Significant relationships must be identified in the data and explained. In other words, theories must be formulated. A theory may be defined as "a set of interrelated constructs (concepts), definitions, and propositions that presents a systematic view of phenomena by specifying relations among variables, with the purpose of explaining and predicting the phenomena."[5]

Theories knit together the results of observations, enabling scientists to make general statements about variables and the relationships among variables. For example, it can be observed that if pressure is held constant, hydrogen gas expands when its temperature is increased from 20° C to 40° C. It can be observed that if pressure is held constant, oxygen gas contracts when its temperature is decreased from 60° C to 50° C. A familiar theory, Charles's law, summarizes the observed effects of temperature changes on the volumes of all gases: When pressure is held constant, as the temperature of a gas is increased, its volume is increased; and as the temperature of a gas is decreased, its volume is decreased. The theory not only summarizes previous information but predicts other phenomena by telling us what to expect of any gas under any temperature change.

The ultimate goal of science is theory formation. This statement will sound strange to those who think of theory as vague conjecture or impractical speculation. However, a scientific theory is a tentative explanation of phenomena. From such explanations we can proceed to prediction and, finally, to control. As soon as a statement (theory) could be made about the relationship between the *Anopheles* mosquito and malaria in humans, we could (1) explain why malaria was endemic in some areas and not in others, (2) predict how changes in the environment would be accompanied by changes

---

[5]Kerlinger, F. N. (1986). *Foundations of Behavioral Research* (3d ed., p. 9). New York: Holt, Rinehart and Winston.

in the incidence of malaria, and (3) control malaria by making changes in the environment.

/ Purposes of Theories

There are several purposes to be served by theory in the development of a science. In the first place, theory summarizes and puts in order the existing knowledge in a particular area. A theory of learning, for instance, brings together in a consistent manner the results of many separate investigations into the learning process. Furthermore, a theory clarifies and gives meaning to the previously isolated empirical findings.

Theory provides a provisional explanation for observed events and relationships. It does so by showing what variables are related and how they are related. A theory of learning would explain the relationships among the speed and efficiency of learning and such variables as motivation, reward, practice, and so on. On the basis of the explanatory principles embodied within the theory, deductions from the theory permit prediction of the occurrence of phenomena, some as yet unobserved. For example, from theory astronomers predicted the existence of the outermost planets long before they were actually observed.

Theory stimulates the development of new knowledge by providing leads for further inquiry. From the theory the scientist makes deductions about what will happen in certain situations under specified conditions. From reinforcement theory one could make a deduction concerning the effects of rewarding a response regularly versus occasionally. These deductions provide hypotheses for scientific studies, the outcome of which leads to acceptance, rejection, or modification of the theories they were designed to test. In this way scientists use what they know as a springboard for new advances.

/ Approaches to Theory Construction

Melvin Marx[6] has identified four major approaches to theory construction: (1) *the model*, in which emphasis is strictly on conceptualization, (2) *the deductive approach*, which incorporates both conceptual and empirical elements with primary emphasis on formal conceptualization, (3) *the functional approach*, in which equal emphasis is given to conceptual and empirical elements, and (4) *the inductive approach*, which strictly attempts to unify empirical knowledge.

The Model Marx defines *model* as a "conceptual analog, generally of a physical or mathematical nature, which is used to suggest empirical research." Models are useful ways of thinking about complex phenomena. They provide

---

[6]Marx, M. (1966). *Theories in Contemporary Psychology* (p. 43). New York: Macmillan.

a simple representation of the complex and make it more readily understood. Models are not modified as empirical data are accumulated; they are either retained if the data confirm them or abandoned if the data do not confirm them.

In the behavioral sciences numerous examples can be found of the use of analogy in formulating models. An old example is G. Stanley Hall's famous recapitulation theory of human development,[7] which states that social growth in individuals recapitulates the history of mankind. That is, in the early stages of development children behave like savages, gradually progressing through barbarian and semicivilized stages on their way to becoming civilized. Although this theory is abandoned now, in the early decades of this century it played a major role in stimulating research in the area of child and adolescent development. Computer models are now widely used to help researchers develop more specific theories of how children learn, solve problems, think, and so on. Computer models can be developed that "learn" more or less the same way that a child does, so that our understanding of how and what children might be learning is increased.

The Deductive Approach   The deductive approach generates theory by beginning with known facts and proceeding through deductive reasoning to arrive at a highly formalized conceptual system. The deductive approach is based on the assumption that to explain phenomena within a field one should go beyond what is currently known to develop an integrating logical system, even though uncertainty exists as to the validity of many of the assumptions and deductions within the system.

In the deductive approach a great deal of emphasis is placed on conceptualization. That is, first a highly formalized theoretical system is developed, then hypotheses are drawn from this theory for testing. New factual information obtained through empirical testing is used for modifying the theory.

The deductive approach, although criticized for its subjectivity and for the building of an elaborate theoretical system on limited factual information, has led to contributions in the advancement of the behavioral sciences by stimulating numerous research investigations.

The Functional Approach   Many scientists believe that preoccupation with highly formalized theoretical systems at a stage when empirical data are unavailable or limited may lead to premature fixation on certain potential explanations and thus jeopardize the search for alternative explanations of phenomena. They prefer the functional approach, which is characterized by a high degree of informality and flexibility. Tentative, often rudimentary theories are put forward to explain phenomena. Hypotheses based on these

---

[7]Hall, G. S. (1904). *Adolescence* (vols. 1 and 2). New York: Appleton

tentative theories are then formulated and tested empirically. If the results of this testing do not entirely confirm the theory, the theory is revised and new hypotheses are deduced from the revised theory, tested empirically, and so on. A functional approach can be pictured as a stage in the back-and-forth interplay between conceptualization and empirical hypothesis testing.

Some maintain that the eclectic nature of the functional approach tends to limit the scope of new research. However, the functional approach has played a major role in the advancement of behavioral sciences.

The Inductive Approach   The inductive approach attempts only to provide statements integrating and summarizing the known empirical relationships among phenomena. Deductive reasoning and formal logic have minimal roles in the inductive approach. Even the formulation of a research hypothesis prior to experimentation is considered an unnecessary step by those favoring inductive theory because it introduces risk of bias to scientific endeavors. For these scientists theory is the end product of all scientific inquiry and should be obtained only through induction.

The works of B. F. Skinner and his followers in experimental psychology are examples of this approach to theory formation. These scientists avoid using any kind of deduction and formal logic in their scientific investigations. B. F. Skinner's behavioral theory assumes that only observable behavior can be used to build a science of human behavior and that internal states of a human being, such as motives, values, and cognitive knowledge, do not need to be addressed.

This extreme view has been criticized for rejecting the processes that many consider inevitable in scientific work. Critics of the strictly inductive approach also maintain that the choice of a given research question, research design, and research procedure involves at least informal theorizing and deductive reasoning.

/ Characteristics of Theories

A theory, if it is to serve its purpose in science, should satisfy certain criteria. The following are some of the characteristics of a sound theory:

1. A theory should be able to explain the observed facts relating to a particular problem; it should be able to propose the "why" concerning the phenomena under consideration. This explanation of the events should be in the simplest form possible. A theory that has fewer complexities and assumptions is favored over a more complicated one. This statement is known as the *principle of parsimony*.

2. A theory should be consistent with observed facts and with the already established body of knowledge. We look for the theory that provides the most probable or the most efficient way of accounting for the accumulated facts.

3. A theory should provide means for its verification. This is achieved for most theories by making deductions in the form of hypotheses stating the consequences that one can expect to observe if the theory is true. The scientist can then investigate or test these hypotheses empirically in order to determine whether the data support the theory. It must be emphasized that it is inappropriate to speak of the truth or falsity of a theory. The acceptance or rejection of a theory depends primarily upon its *utility*. A theory is useful or not useful, depending upon how efficiently it leads to predictions concerning observable consequences, which are then confirmed when the empirical data are collected. Even then any theory is considered tentative and subject to revision as new evidence accumulates.

4. A theory should stimulate new discoveries and indicate further areas in need of investigation.

The goal of theory formation has been achieved to a far greater extent in the physical sciences than in the social sciences, which is not surprising because they are older sciences. In the early days of a science the emphasis typically is upon empiricism. Scientists are concerned with collecting facts in particular problem areas. Only with maturity does science begin to integrate the isolated knowledge into a theoretical framework.

Education in particular has suffered from an absence of theoretical orientations; the main emphasis has been upon empiricism. Educators have been criticized for their continued concern with "getting the facts" rather than finding out the "why." This concern is reflected in the vast numbers of facts that have been accumulated through educational studies, but without the accompanying integration into theories to help explain educational phenomena. Education needs to focus more attention on theory development in order to obtain more perspective into educational problems as well as to guide its efforts at the empirical level.

Although there are marked differences in the number and power of the theories that have been established in the physical and social sciences, theory has the same role to play in the progress of any science. Regardless of the subject matter, theory works in essentially the same way. It serves to summarize existing knowledge, to explain observed events and relationships, and to predict the occurrence of unobserved events and relationships. It can be said that theories represent our best efforts to understand the basic structure of the world in which we live.

// Limitations of the Scientific Approach in the Social Sciences

In spite of their use of the scientific approach and accumulation of a large quantity of reliable knowledge, education and the other social sciences have not attained the scientific status typical of the natural sciences. The social sciences have not been able to establish generalizations equivalent to the theories of the natural sciences in scope of explanatory power or in capacity to yield precise predictions. Frequently there is a lack of agreement among researchers in the social sciences as to what the established facts are or what explanations are satisfactory for the assumed facts. Perhaps the social sciences will never realize the objectives of science as completely as the natural sciences. Certainly it must be stressed that the use of the scientific approach is not in itself a sufficient condition for scientific achievement. There are several limitations involved in the application of the scientific approach in education and the other social sciences.

/ Complexity of Subject Matter

A major obstacle is the inherent complexity of subject matter in the social sciences. Natural scientists deal with physical and biological phenomena. A limited number of variables that can be measured precisely are involved in the explanation of many of these phenomena, and it is possible to establish universal laws. For example, Boyle's law on the influence of pressure on the volume of gases, which deals with relatively uncomplicated variables, formulates relations between phenomena that are apparently unvarying throughout the universe.

On the other hand, social scientists deal with the human subject. They are concerned with the subject's behavior and development both as an individual and as a member of a group. There are so many variables, acting independently and in interaction, that must be considered in any attempt to understand complex human behavior. Each individual is unique in the way he or she develops, in mental equipment, in social and emotional behavior, and in total personality. The behavior of humans in groups and the influence of the behavior of group members on an individual must also be dealt with by social scientists. A group of first-graders in one situation will not behave like first-graders in another situation. There are learners, teachers, and environments, each with variables that contribute to the behavioral phenomena observed in a setting. Thus, researchers must be extremely cautious about making generalizations, because the data obtained in one group situation may not be valid for other groups and other settings.

/ Difficulties in Observation

Observation, the *sine qua non* of science, is more difficult in the social sciences than in the natural sciences. Observation in the social sciences is more subjective because it more frequently involves interpretation on the part of the observers. For example, the subject matter for investigation is often a person's responses to the behavior of others. Motives, values, and attitudes are not open to inspection. Observers must make subjective interpretations when they decide that behaviors observed indicate the presence of any particular motive, value, or attitude. The problem is that social scientist's *own* values and attitudes may influence both the observations and the assessment of the findings on which they base their conclusions. Natural scientists study phenomena that require less subjective interpretation.

/ Difficulties in Replication

The chemist can objectively observe the reaction between two chemicals in a test tube. The findings can be reported and the observations can be easily replicated by others. This replication is much more difficult to achieve in the social sciences. An American educator cannot reproduce the conditions of a Russian educator's experimental teaching method with the same precision of replication as that with which an American chemist can reproduce a Russian chemist's experiment. Even within a single school building one cannot reproduce a given situation in its entirety and with precision. Social phenomena are singular events and cannot be repeated for purposes of observation.

/ Interaction of Observer and Subjects

An additional problem is that mere observation of social phenomena may produce changes that might not have occurred otherwise. Researchers may think that X is causing Y, when in fact it may be their observation of X that causes Y. For example, in the well-known Hawthorne experiments, changes in the productivity of workers were found to be due not to the varying working conditions but to the mere fact that the workers knew they had been singled out for investigation. Investigators are human beings, and their presence as observers in a situation may change the behavior of their human subjects. The use of hidden cameras and tape recorders may help minimize this interaction in some cases, but much of social science research includes the responses of human subjects to human observers.

/ Difficulties in Control

The range of possibilities for controlled experiments on human subjects is much more limited than in the natural sciences. The complexities involved in research on human subjects present problems in control that are unparalleled in the natural sciences. In the latter, rigid control of experimental conditions is possible in the laboratory. Such control is not possible with human subjects; the social scientists must deal with many variables simultaneously and must work under conditions that are much less precise. They try to identify and control as many of these variables as possible, but the task is sometimes very difficult.

/Problems of Measurement

Experimentation must provide for measurement of the factors involved. The tools for measurement in the social sciences are much less perfect and precise than the tools of the natural sciences. We have nothing that can compare with the precision of the ruler, the thermometer, or the numerous laboratory instruments. We have already pointed out that an understanding of human behavior is complicated by the large number of determining variables acting independently and in interaction. The multivariate statistical devices available for analyzing data in the social sciences take care of relatively few of the factors that obviously are interacting. Furthermore, these devices permit one to attribute the variance only to factors operating at the time of measurement. Factors that have influenced development in the past are not measurable in the present, and yet they have significantly influenced the course of development.

Since social science research is complicated by these factors, researchers must exercise caution in making generalizations from their studies. It will often be necessary to conduct several studies in an area before attempting to formulate generalizations. If initial findings are consistently confirmed, then one would have more confidence in making broad generalizations.

Despite the handicaps, education and the social sciences have made great progress, and their scientific status can be expected to increase as scientific investigation and methodology become more systematic and rigorous.

/// THE NATURE OF RESEARCH

At this point we might do well to ask the question What is research? Research may be defined as "the application of the scientific approach to the study of a problem." It is a way to acquire dependable and useful information. Its purpose is to discover answers to meaningful questions through the application of scientific procedures. An investigation must involve the scientific approach that has been described in the previous section in order to be classified as research. Although it may take place in different settings and may utilize different methods, research is universally a systematic and objective search for reliable knowledge.

// Educational Research

When the scientific approach is applied to the study of educational problems, educational research is the result. Educational research is the way in which one acquires dependable and useful information about the educative process. Its goal is to discover general principles or interpretations of behavior that can be used to explain, predict, and control events in educational situations—in other words, scientific theory.

The acceptance of the scientific approach in education and the other social sciences has lagged far behind its acceptance in the physical sciences. In 1897 Rice, a pioneer in educational research, found himself in a situation similar to that described in the quotation attributed to Bacon earlier in this chapter. Rice asked the educators at the annual meeting of the Department of Superintendence if it would be possible to determine whether students who are given forty minutes of spelling each day learn more than students given ten minutes each day. He reports:

> . . . to my great surprise, the question threw consternation into the camp. The first to respond was a very popular professor of psychology engaged in training teachers in the West. He said, in effect, that the question was one which could never be answered; and he gave me a rather severe drubbing for taking up the time of such an important body of educators in asking them silly questions.[8]

Rice did, in fact, collect empirical evidence on his question and found that the differences in achievement between those spending ten minutes a day and those spending forty minutes a day were negligible. He also pointed out that many of the words children had to learn to spell were of little practical value. His work led other investigators, such as Edward L. Thorndike, to use documentary analysis to determine the frequency of use of words in our language. Their work in turn led to improvements in our language arts texts and curricula.

However, although educational research is a young science, it has made progress since its beginnings in the late nineteenth century. As a science, educational research uses investigative methods that are consistent with the basic procedures and operating conceptions of science. As such, research involves a number of stages.

// Typical Stages in Research

/ Selecting a Problem

Researchers begin with a question that they believe deals with an issue of sufficient consequence to warrant investigation. It must be a question for which the answer is not already available, but for which the means for finding answers through observation and experimentation are available. Consider the question Do children who are taught reading through the whole-language approach score higher on reading achievement than children who are taught

---

[8]Rice, J. M. (1912). *Scientific Management in Education* (pp. 17–18). New York: Hinds, Noble and Eldredge.

reading through the sight method? This could be investigated empirically by comparing scores on a criterion of reading achievement for two groups who are equivalent except that one group is introduced to reading through the whole-language approach and the other through sight reading.[9]

There are meaningful questions that cannot be answered through the use of scientific procedures. For example, Is training with the whole-language approach good for students? could not be investigated scientifically without knowing what *good for students* means or how to observe or measure *goodness*. Value judgments should not be included in the statement of the problem.

/ Formulating a Hypothesis

After the problem has been identified, a thorough study of all previous research that may have been done on the problem follows. This review of related research is necessary to give insight into the problem and to provide a background for formulating the hypothesis of the study. The best guide to an intelligent hypothesis is a careful analysis of the available data bearing on the problem. Using the example above, after a careful review of literature one might hypothesize: "The whole-language approach produces greater reading achievement than introducing reading through the sight method." The hypothesis is employed in research investigating relationships. In other kinds of research one may initiate research by asking a question. This is true especially in most survey research.

In addition to the formulation of a hypothesis, in this stage the researchers also crystallize the definitions of the terms they will use in the study.

/ Selecting Research Strategy and Developing Instruments

Through the process of deductive reasoning, the implications of the suggested hypothesis—that is, what should be observed if the hypothesis is true—are determined. *If* it is true that teaching reading through the whole-language approach produces greater reading achievement than teaching reading through the sight method, *then* one should observe higher reading achievement scores among those students who are taught reading through the whole-language approach than among equivalent students who are introduced to reading through the sight method.

This is followed by the choice of a relevant research method. Certain problems require experimentation; others may be attacked with one of the descriptive strategies. Choice of the research method then influences the details of the design of the study and of the procedures for measuring var-

---

[9]Goodman, K. (1986). *What's Whole in Whole Language?* Portsmouth, NH: Heinemann.

iables. Instruments for measuring variables may already be available as standardized instruments, or they may have to be developed by the researcher.

/ Collecting and Interpreting the Data

The deduced consequences of the hypotheses of the study must be tested. This stage therefore involves data collection, which includes the routine aspects of administering instrument(s), keeping records, scheduling, and so on. Contrary to popular belief, this stage usually takes much less time than the previous planning stages of the study.

After collection, data are analyzed—usually statistically—to determine whether the investigation has produced evidence that supports the hypothesis. In the scientific approach one does not claim to prove the hypothesis—this would be dealing in terms of absolute truth, which is not characteristic of this approach—one merely concludes that the evidence does or does not support the hypothesis.

/ Reporting the Results

Researchers must make their procedures, findings, and conclusions available in an intelligible form to others who may be interested. This involves a clear, concise presentation of the steps in the study in sufficient detail so that another person can replicate it.

Each of the foregoing stages of a research study is discussed in detail in later chapters. It is probably rare for researchers to follow such a rigid sequence as described in the preceding paragraphs. These activities overlap continuously, and there may be a moving back and forth from one stage to another.

// Questions Asked by Educational Researchers

The specific question chosen for research will, of course, depend upon the area that interests the researchers, their background, and the particular problem confronting them. However, we may classify questions in educational research as theoretical, having to do with fundamental principles, or as practical, designed to solve immediate problems of the everyday situation.

/ Theoretical Questions

Questions of a theoretical nature are those asking What is it? or How does it occur? or Why does it occur? In educational research the "what" questions are formulated more specifically as What is intelligence? or What is creativity? Typical "how" questions are How does the child learn? or How does personality develop? "Why" questions might ask Why does one forget? or Why are some children more achievement-oriented than other children?

Research with a theoretical orientation may be directed toward either developing theories or testing existing theories. The former involves a type of study in which researchers attempt to discover generalizations about behavior with the aim of clarifying the nature of the relationships existing among variables. They may believe that certain variables are related and thus conduct their research in order to describe the nature of the relationship. From the findings they may begin to formulate a theory about the phenomenon. Theories of learning have been developed in this way as investigators have been able to show the relationships among certain methods, individual and environmental variables, and the efficiency of the learning process.

Probably more common in educational research are studies that aim to test already existing theories. It may be overly ambitious, especially for beginning researchers in education, to have as a goal the development of a theory. It is usually more realistic to attempt to deduce hypotheses from existing theories of learning, personality, motivation, and so forth, and to test these hypotheses. If the hypotheses are logical deductions from the theory, and the empirical tests provide evidence that supports the hypotheses, then this evidence also provides support for the theory itself.

/ Practical Questions

Many questions in educational research are of a directly practical nature, aimed at solving specific problems that may be encountered by educators in their everyday activities. They are relevant questions for educational research because they deal with actual problems at the level of practice. Such questions are How effective is peer tutoring in the elementary school classroom? or What is the effect of teaching children cognitive strategies on their reading comprehension? or What is the relative effectiveness of the problem-discussion method as compared with the lecture method in teaching high school social studies? The answers to such questions may be quite valuable in helping teachers make practical decisions.

These practical questions can be investigated just as scientifically as the theoretical problems. The two types of questions are differentiated primarily on the basis of the goals they help to achieve rather than the level of sophistication of the study.

// Basic and Applied Research

Another system of classification is sometimes used for the research dealing with these two types of questions. The classification is based on the objective of the research. The first type of research—which has as its aim obtaining the empirical data that can be used to formulate, expand, or evaluate theory—is called basic research. This type of study is not oriented in design or purpose toward the solution of practical problems. Its essential aim is to expand the frontiers of knowledge without regard to practical application. Of course, the findings may eventually be applied to practical problems that have social value. For example, advances in the practice of medicine are dependent upon basic research in biochemistry and microbiology. Likewise, progress in educational practice has been related to progress in the discovery of general laws through basic psychological, educational, and sociological research.

The primary concern of basic research, however, is the discovery of knowledge solely for the sake of knowledge. Its design is not hampered by considerations of the social usefulness of the findings.

The second type of research, which aims to solve an immediate practical problem, is referred to as applied research. It is research performed in relation to actual problems and under the conditions in which they are found in practice. Through applied research, educators are often able to solve their problems at the appropriate level of complexity, that is, in the classroom teaching-learning situation. We may depend upon basic research for the discovery of the more general laws of learning, but applied research must be conducted in order to determine how these laws operate in the classroom. This approach is essential if scientific changes in teaching practices are to be effected. Unless educators undertake to solve their own practical problems of this type, no one else will. It should be pointed out that applied research also uses the scientific method of inquiry. We find that there is not always a sharp line of demarcation between basic and applied research. Certainly applications are made from theory to help in the solution of practical problems. We attempt to apply the theories of learning in the classroom. On the other hand, basic research may depend upon the findings of applied research to complete its theoretical formulations. A classroom learning experiment could shed some light on learning theory. Furthermore, observations in a practical situation serve to test theories and may lead to the formulation of new theories.

/// THE LANGUAGE OF RESEARCH

Any scientific discipline has need for a specific language for describing and summarizing the observations in that area. Scientists need terms at the empirical level in order to describe particular observations; they also need terms at the theoretical level for referring to hypothetical processes that may not be subject to direct observation. Scientists may use words taken from everyday language, but they often ascribe to them new and specific meanings not commonly found in ordinary usage. Or perhaps they must introduce new technical terms that are not a part of everyday language. The purpose of this section is to introduce the reader to some of the general terms used in educational research.

The terms that scientists use at both the descriptive and theoretical levels are labels for concepts and constructs.

// Concepts and Constructs

A concept is an abstraction from observed events; it is a word that represents the similarities or common aspects of objects or events that are otherwise quite different from one another. Words such as *chair, dog, tree, liquid,* and thousands of others in our language represent common aspects of otherwise diverse things. The purpose of a concept is to simplify thinking by including a number of events under one general heading. Some concepts are quite close to the events they represent. Thus, for example, the meaning of the concept *tree* may be easily illustrated by pointing to specific trees. The concept is an abstraction of the characteristics all trees have in common—characteristics that are directly observable.

However, terms such as *motivation, justice,* and *problem-solving ability* cannot be easily illustrated by pointing to specific objects or events. These higher-level abstractions are referred to as constructs. People have put together or constructed more complex abstractions from their concepts. In the same way that we construct a house by putting together wood and other materials in a purposeful pattern, we create constructs by combining concepts and less complex constructs into purposeful patterns. For example, such concepts as visual acuity, symbol discrimination, left-to-right orientation, listening vocabulary, and others are combined in a purposeful manner to produce the construct *reading readiness.* Constructs are useful in interpreting empirical data and in building theory. They are used to account for observed regularities and relationships.

Constructs are created in order to summarize observations and to provide explanations. A construct is abandoned when a better way of explaining and summarizing observations replaces it. For example, the observations that (1) some materials burn and others do not and (2) some materials burn more intensely than others were once summarized by the construct *phlogiston,* which was believed to be a necessary constituent of all combustible materials that was released in the burning process. This construct was abandoned when more useful explanations of the process of burning were developed.

// Specification of Meaning

The further removed one's concepts or constructs are from the empirical facts or phenomena they are intended to represent, the greater the possibility for misunderstanding and the greater the need for precise definitions. The meaning of the words in the scientist's vocabulary must be established. Concepts must be defined both in abstract terms, which give the general meaning they are supposed to have, and in terms of the operations by which they will be measured or manipulated in a particular study. Kerlinger[10] calls the former type of definition a constitutive definition; the latter is known as an operational definition.

/ Constitutive Definition

A constitutive definition is a formal definition in which a term is defined by using other terms. For example, intelligence is defined as the ability to think abstractly. This type of definition helps to convey the general nature of the phenomenon in which the investigator is interested, as well as to show its relation to other studies using similar concepts and to theory. A constitutive definition elucidates a term and perhaps gives one some insight into the phenomenon described by the term. However, if one is to carry out research, one must translate concepts into observable events.

/ Operational Definition

An operational definition is one that ascribes meaning to a concept or construct by specifying the operations that must be performed in order to measure or manipulate the concept. This type of definition is essential in research because data must be collected in terms of observable events. Scientists may deal on a theoretical level with such constructs as learning, motivation, anxiety, or achievement, but before they can study them empirically, they have to decide on some kinds of observable events to represent those constructs. When defining a concept or construct operationally, scientists choose discriminable events as indicators of the abstract concept and devise operations to obtain data relevant to the concept.

There are two types of operational definitions: measured and experimental. A measured operational definition refers to the operations by which investigators may measure a concept. For example, intelligence quotient may be defined operationally as the scores on the Stanford-Binet Test of Intelligence, or creativity may operationally refer to the scores made on the Minnesota Test of Creativity. An experimental operational definition refers to the steps taken by a researcher to produce certain experimental conditions. For example, the operational definition of frustration in a research study may take the form of preventing subjects from reaching a goal, or cognitive dissonance may refer operationally to requiring the subjects of a study to make public statements contrary to their private beliefs.

Although investigators are guided by their own experience and knowledge and the reports of other investigators, the operational definition of a

---

[10]Kerlinger, F. N. *op. cit.*, pp. 28–32.

concept is to some extent an arbitrary procedure. Often we choose from a variety of possible operational definitions those that best represent our approach to the problem. Certainly an operational definition does not exhaust the full scientific meaning of any concept. It is very specific in meaning; its purpose is to delimit a term, to ensure that everyone concerned understands the particular way in which a term is being used. Operational definitions are considered adequate if their procedures gather data that constitute acceptable indicators of the concepts they are intended to represent. Often it is a matter of opinion whether this result has been achieved.

Operational definitions are essential to research because they permit investigators to measure abstract concepts and constructs and permit scientists to move from the level of constructs and theory to the level of observation, upon which science is based. By using operational definitions, researchers are able to proceed with investigations that might not otherwise be possible. It is important to remember that, although researchers report their findings in terms of abstract constructs and relate these to other research and to theory, what they have actually found is a relationship between two sets of observable and measurable data that were selected to represent the constructs. An investigation of the relation of the construct creativity and the construct intelligence in practice will relate scores on an intelligence test to scores on a measure of creativity.

// Variables

A variable reflects or expresses some concept or construct. A variable takes on different values. Height is one example of a variable; it can vary in an individual from one time to another, between individuals at the same time, between the averages for groups, and so on. Social class, sex, vocabulary level, intelligence quotient, and spelling test scores are other examples of variables. Educational researchers are interested in determining how such variables are related to one another. In a study concerned with the relation of vocabulary level to science achievement among eighth-graders, the variables of interest would be the measures of vocabulary and the measures of science achievement. We contrast variables with *constants,* which take on only fixed values. The concept of grade level, although by definition a variable, is in this study a constant because all subjects are eighth-graders.

/ Types of Variables

There are several ways to classify variables. Variables can be categorical or they can be continuous. When subjects are classified by sorting them into groups, the attribute on which the classification is based is termed a *categorical variable.* Home language, county of residence, father's principal occupation, and school in which enrolled are examples of categorical variables. The simplest type of categorical variable has only two classes and is called a *dichotomous variable.* Male-female, citizen-alien, pass-fail are dichotomous variables. Some categorical variables have more than two classes; some examples are educational level, religious affiliation, and state of birth.

When an attribute has an infinite number of values within a range, it is called a *continuous variable.* As a child grows in height from 40 inches to 41 inches, he or she passes through an infinite number of heights. Height, weight, age, and achievement test scores are examples of continuous variables.

The most important classification of variables is on the basis of their *use* within the research under consideration, when they are classified as independent variables or dependent variables.

Some variables are antecedent to other variables. We may know this empirically or we may hypothesize on the basis of some theory that one variable is antecedent to another. For instance, to be able to read, it is presumed, an individual needs to have some degree of intelligence. That is, the variable *intelligence* is antecedent to the variable *reading.* To a certain extent reading ability is a consequence of the variable *intelligence;* it is dependent upon the individual's intelligence level. In research, variables that are a consequence of or dependent upon antecedent variables are called *dependent variables.* Variables that are antecedent to the dependent variable are called *independent variables.* For example, a child's height (dependent variable) would be dependent to a certain extent upon his or her age (independent variable). We often use these terms even in the absence of empirical or theoretical reasons for considering one to be the antecedent and the other to be the consequence. They are used to indicate the direction of prediction— from the individual's position on the independent variable to his or her position on the dependent variable.

The dependent variable is the phenomenon that is the object of study and investigation. The independent variable is the factor that is measurably separate and distinct from the dependent variable, but it may relate to the dependent variable. Many factors that may function as independent variables—such as social class, home environment, and classroom conditions—are discriminable aspects of the environment. In addition, such personal characteristics as age, sex, intelligence, and motivation may be independent variables that can be related to the dependent variable.

Later, when we discuss the experimental methods of research, we will define the independent variable as the variable that is manipulated or changed by the experimenters. The variable upon which the effects of the manipulation are observed is called the dependent variable. It is so named because its value depends upon and varies with the value of the independent variable. For example, to study the effect of computer-based drill on math achievement, the investigators manipulate the method of instruction, the independent variable, and then observe the effect upon math achievement, the dependent variable. After the relationship between the variables has been established through research, one may predict *from* an independent variable *to* the dependent variable. In educational research, teaching methods and procedures are probably the most frequently used independent variables. Others include age, sex, social class, attitudes, intelligence, and motivation. The most common dependent variable is school achievement or learning.

It is possible for a variable to be an independent variable in one study and a dependent variable in another. Whether a variable is considered independent or dependent is determined by the purpose of the study. If the effect of motivation on achievement is investigated, then motivation is considered the independent variable. However, if one wished to determine the effect of testing procedures, classroom grouping arrangements, or grading procedures on students' motivation, then motivation becomes the dependent variable. Intelligence is generally treated as an independent variable because we are interested in its effect on learning, the dependent variable. However, in studies investigating the effect of nursery school experience on the intellectual development of children, intelligence is the dependent variable.

A classification of independent variables can be made on the basis of whether the independent variable is one that can be manipulated by the investigators. According to this classification, there are two types of independent variables, *active* and *attribute.*

An active variable is defined as one that can be directly manipulated by the researchers. For instance, method of teaching, method of grouping, and reinforcement procedures are all variables that can be manipulated and are thus called active variables.

An attribute variable is one that cannot be actively manipulated by the researchers. Such variables, sometimes called *assigned variables,* are characteristics of individuals that cannot be manipulated at will. For example, aptitude, sex, race, age, and social class are typical attribute variables. Investigators can incorporate attribute variables into their research by assigning subjects to groups on the basis of such preexisting variables.

In some situations it is not possible to tell which variable is exerting an effect on the other. For example, when the relationship between dogmatism and political attitude is being investigated, one cannot determine which one of the variables is independent and which dependent. This kind of situation does not lend itself to experimentation. The relationship between such variables is usually investigated in correlational studies.

/// RESEARCH METHODOLOGIES IN EDUCATION

Research method refers to the general strategy followed in gathering and analyzing the data necessary for answering the question at hand. It is the plan of attack for the problem under investigation. Five generally used categories for classifying educational research are

1. Experimental: The researcher manipulates one or more independent variables in a controlled setting in order to determine the effect on the dependent variable(s).

   Examples:
   Effects of Logo Computer-Programming Experience on Problem Solving and Spatial-Relations Ability
   The Effect of Outlines and Headings on Readers' Recall of Text

2. Causal-comparative: This category is similar to the experimental method, except that the investigator cannot directly manipulate the independent variables.

   Examples:
   Relationship of Self-Confidence and Academic Performance to Persistency
   Association of Timing of Puberty on Spatial Ability and Lateralization in Adult Women

3. Descriptive: Its major purpose is to tell what is. There are several subcategories of descriptive research: (*a*) surveys, (*b*) developmental studies, (*c*) follow-up studies, (*d*) documentary analysis, (*e*) trend studies, and (*f*) correlational studies.

   Examples:
   A Survey of Secondary Science Teachers' Needs
   Patterns of Change in SAT Scores among Academically Talented Adolescents

4. Qualitative research: The researcher observes persons or events in their natural setting. Its major purpose is to understand the influence of the particular context on the events. This methodology includes case studies and other naturalistic approaches.

   Examples:
   A Participation Observation Study of a Fourth-Grade Music Classroom
   Kindergarten Readiness and Retention: A Qualitative Study of Teachers' Beliefs and Practices

5. Historical: This category involves the collection of data from the past in order to understand past events and their implications for present events. Its major purpose is to tell what was.

Examples:
Shaker Education in Nineteenth-Century America
Education Policies of the Nixon Administration

/// SUMMARY

Human beings have attempted to answer questions through experience, authority, deductive reasoning, inductive reasoning, and the scientific approach. Each method requires certain assumptions. The correctness of the answers depends upon the correctness of the assumptions underlying the method employed.

The scientific approach rests on two basic assumptions: (1) truth can be derived from observation and (2) phenomena conform to lawful relationships.

Scientific inquirers seek not absolute truth but rather theories that explain and predict phenomena in a reliable manner. They seek theories that are parsimonious, testable, and consistent, as well as theories that are themselves stimuli for further research. The scientific approach incorporates self-correction, inasmuch as every theory is considered tentative and may be set aside if a new theory better fits the criteria.

The scientific approach has been employed to explain, predict, and control physical phenomena for centuries but has only recently been employed in education. The complexity of educational variables and the difficulties encountered in making reliable observations have impeded scientific inquiry in education. However, since the beginning of the movement at the turn of the century scientific inquiry in education has enjoyed increasing acceptance and increasing success both in theoretical and practical research.

The typical steps in educational research are (1) selection of a problem, (2) formulation of a hypothesis, (3) selection of research strategy and development of instruments, (4) collection, analysis, and interpretation of data, and (5) communication of the findings by reporting the results of the study.

Educational research could be classified into two major categories: basic and applied. The primary concern of basic research is to expand the frontiers of knowledge and to discover general laws. The main goal of applied research is to solve immediate practical problems.

At a theoretical level, educational scientists use terms like *intelligence, creativity, problem-solving ability,* and *motivation,* which are abstractions from observation of certain behaviors. These are referred to as *constructs.* In research, constructs are quantified and take on different values. Thus, they are referred to as *variables.* There are two major types of variables: independent and dependent. If a variable is antecedent to another variable, it is called an *independent variable;* but if it is the consequence of another variable, it is referred to as the *dependent variable.*

In research, it is essential that variables be operationally defined. There are two ways of defining variables operationally: (1) by applying some kind of measurement or (2) by listing the steps taken in an experiment to produce certain research conditions. The first type is referred to as a *measured operational definition*, and the second is called an *experimental operational definition*.

// Key Concepts

active independent variable
applied research
attribute independent variable
basic research
categorical variable
concept
constant
constitutive definition
construct
continuous variable
deductive reasoning
dependent variable
dichotomous variable

experimental operational definition
hypothesis
imperfect induction
independent variable
inductive reasoning
measured operational definition
model
operational definition
parsimony principle
scientific approach
theory
variable

/// EXERCISES

1. Identify the source of knowledge—*deductive reasoning, inductive reasoning,* or the *scientific approach*—most prominently utilized in the following examples:
    a. After extensive observation of reactions, Lavoisier concluded that combustion is a process in which a burning substance combines with oxygen. His work was the death blow to the old phlogiston theory of burning.
    b. Dalton, after much reflection, concluded that matter must be composed of small particles called atoms. His early assumptions were the basis for the atomic theory.
    c. Later scientists took Dalton's assumptions, made deductions from them, and proceeded to gather data that confirmed these assumptions. Support was found for the atomic theory.
    d. Knowing that radioactive substances constantly give off particles of energy without apparently reducing their mass, Einstein developed the formula $E = mc^2$ for converting matter into energy.
    e. Accepting Einstein's theory, Fermi carried on experimentation that resulted in the splitting of the atom.

    f. After studying reinforcement theory, a teacher hypothesizes that using a tutorial computer program will lead to superior achievement in arithmetic. She devises a study in which the tutorial is used with two sixth-grade classes, while conventional materials are used with two other sixth-grade classes.

2. What is the role of theory in scientific inquiry?

3. What is the difference between an inductive theory and a deductive theory?

4. Based on the title of the study, classify the following research as *basic* or *applied:*
    a. The Effect of RNA (Ribonucleic Acid) Injections on the Transfer of Skills from Trained Animals to Untrained Animals
    b. Outcomes of a Remedial Arithmetic Program
    c. Conditioning as a Function of the Interval between the Conditioned and Original Stimulus
    d. Teaching Geometry to Cultivate Reflective Thinking: An Experimental Study

5. Using the designations *active, attribute,* or *may be either,* classify the following variables:
    a. amount of drug administered   c. socioeconomic background
    b. anxiety   d. teaching method

6. Which characteristic attitudes of scientists are violated in the following statements?
    a. This study was undertaken to prove that the use of marijuana is detrimental to academic achievement.
    b. It proved conclusively that this is the case.
    c. The results show that marijuana is evil.

7. What are the characteristics of a useful theory?

8. In a study designed to determine the effect of varying amounts of sleep deprivation on the learning of nonsense syllables,
    a. What is the independent variable?
    b. What is the dependent variable?

9. Classify the following variables as *categorical* or *continuous:*
    a. achievement
    b. phonics method of reading versus look-say method of reading
    c. Spanish-speaking, English-speaking, French-speaking
    d. muscle prowess
    e. music aptitude

10. What are the characteristics of operational definitions?

11. Which kind of operational definition (*measured* or *experimental*) is better suited for each of the following variables?
    a. reinforcement
    b. achievement
    c. attitude
    d. teaching method

12. You are a teacher who has been concerned about the amount of aggressive behavior you observe among the children. You have interviewed parents about their child-rearing practices (use of punishment, rewards, and the like) and the amount of TV viewing the children engage in. You have collected much data, but you feel that there is no unifying theme. According to the scientific approach, what would your next step most likely be?

13. Which research method (experimental, causal-comparative, or survey) would most effectively give you answers to each question?
    a. Do children who eat breakfast make better grades in school?
    b. Does a unit on proper nutrition change children's breakfast-eating habits?
    c. How many children in school report that they do not have breakfast at home?
    d. Does the institution of a free breakfast program at school make a difference in the achievement of students?

14. Based on the titles, classify each of the following studies according to the research methodology most likely used:
    a. Gender-Based Differential Item Performance in Mathematics
    b. Effects of "On-Line" Test Feedback on the Seriousness of Subsequent Errors
    c. College Students' Views and Ratings of an Ideal Professor
    d. Effect of Early Father Absence on Scholastic Aptitude
    e. An Alternative High School: An In-Depth Study

15. Give examples of the use of authority and experience as sources of knowledge.

16. Give an example of how basic research in the biological sciences has improved the practice of medicine.

17. Give an example of how basic research in learning has improved the practice of teaching.

18. Give an example of applied research completed in your field of interest. List other areas where additional research needs to be done in your field. What variables might be investigated in such studies?

/// ANSWERS

1. a. inductive reasoning
   b. deductive reasoning

    c. scientific approach
    d. deductive reasoning
    e. scientific approach
    f. scientific approach

2. Theory integrates findings, summarizes information, provides leads for new research, and enables us to explain and predict phenomena.

3. An inductive theory serves to explain previous observations, whereas a deductive theory is developed before extensive observations have been made.

4. a. basic
   b. applied
   c. basic
   d. applied

5. a. active
   b. may be either
   c. attribute
   d. active

6. a. The scientist is objective and impartial.
   b. The scientist is skeptical and regards findings as tentative.
   c. The scientist deals with facts, not values.

7. A useful theory explains the phenomena in the simplest form possible, is consistent with observation and the established body of knowledge, provides means for its verification, and stimulates new investigation.

8. a. amount of sleep deprivation
   b. number of nonsense syllables learned

9. a. continuous
   b. categorical
   c. categorical
   d. continuous
   e. continuous

10. Acceptable definitions state a clear-cut procedure for determining the existence of the phenomenon and its extent.

11. a. experimental
    b. measured
    c. measured
    d. experimental

12. Try to formulate a theory of aggression in children.

13. a. causal-comparative
    b. experimental
    c. survey
    d. experimental

14. a. causal-comparative
    b. experimental
    c. descriptive
    d. causal-comparative
    e. qualitative

15. Answers will vary.

16. Answers will vary.

17. Answers will vary.

18. Answers will vary.

PART II

Research
Background

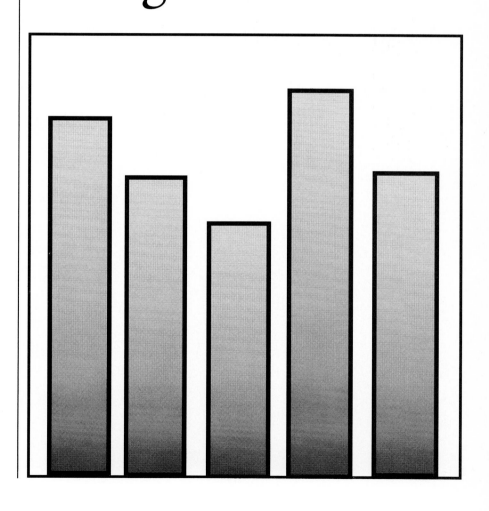

CHAPTER 2

The Research Problem

INSTRUCTIONAL OBJECTIVES

After studying this chapter, the student will be able to
1. Define a research problem
2. Identify potential sources of problems for educational research
3. State the criteria to use for evaluating a research problem
4. Evaluate a given problem for research using the accepted criteria
5. Take a general problem in one's area of interest in education and state it in a specific form ready for empirical investigation
6. Define terms such as *population* and *variables* as used in a research study
7. Identify the population and the variables in a given study

Systematic research begins with a problem. John Dewey[1] spoke of the first step in the scientific method as the recognition of a felt difficulty, an obstacle or problem that puzzles the researchers.

Selecting and formulating a problem is one of the most important aspects of doing research in any field. Beginning researchers are often surprised to find that this initial stage often takes up a large part of the total time invested in a research project. There is no way to do research until a problem is recognized, thought through, and formulated in a useful way.

A researcher must first decide on the general problem area. The researcher must have knowledge or experience in the area in order to ask questions that can be answered through research. We often hear students in difficult courses say, "I don't know enough to ask questions." Similarly, unless a researcher has knowledge or experience in an area, he or she does not know what additional knowledge is needed or how it could be obtained through empirical investigation. Furthermore, the problem area chosen for investigation should be one that holds deep interest or about which there is real curiosity. The choice must necessarily be very personal or else the motivation to carry the research through to its end may be difficult to muster. An elementary school teacher may be interested in finding a more effective way to teach reading. A high school English teacher may want to know if the use of word processors would improve the writing of his/her students.

Once chosen, the general subject is then narrowed down to a specific statement of the research problem. Most beginning researchers find this task of formulating a researchable problem or question a difficult one. The difficulty is not due to a shortage of researchable problems in education. In fact, there are so many questions begging for answers that researchers usually have trouble choosing among them. One common difficulty is that a problem must be selected and a question formulated very early, when the beginner's understanding of how to do research is most limited. In addition, uncertainties about the nature of research problems, the isolation of a problem, the criteria for acceptability, and how to solve the problem often seem overwhelming. Even experienced researchers usually find it necessary to make several attempts before arriving at a research problem that meets generally accepted criteria. A first selection or formulation may on closer examination be found to be unfeasible or not worth doing. Skill in doing research is to a large extent a matter of making wise choices about what to investigate. The skill takes time and repeated effort to develop but can be developed by the willing beginner.

The statement of a problem should clearly indicate what is to be investigated. The actual statement may be in a declarative or question form. Either way, the statement should indicate the variables of interest and the specific relationship between the variables that is to be studied. For example,

---

[1]Dewey, J. (1933). *How We Think* (pp. 106–118). Boston: Heath.

the above high school teacher's research problem may be stated: "The problem to be investigated in this study is the effect of using word processors on the writing of high school English students"; or "What is the effect of using word processors on the writing of high school English students?" Many researchers prefer the question form because it seems to orient one more directly to the task of finding the answer, but either is acceptable.

Unlikely as it may seem, once a problem area is selected and a question or statement clearly formulated, one of the most difficult phases of the research process is accomplished.

/// THE NATURE OF PROBLEMS

Although there are different types of research problems in education, all involve a search for knowledge that is needed in the field. The problem clarifies what one wants to know and determines the method of attack that will be used to obtain the knowledge.

Experimental research addresses questions concerning relationships among variables over which the researcher can have control. In experimental research the investigator manipulates the independent variable (the "cause") while controlling all other variables and observes any subsequent changes in the dependent variable (the "effect"). The control in an experiment makes it possible for the researcher to eliminate alternative explanations for the observed results. If one wanted to investigate the effect of the method of instruction on the learning of addition combinations by elementary school children, one should manipulate the method of instruction while controlling all other factors that might contribute to the learning of the combinations and then observe the effect of the method on learning.

Causal-comparative research also seeks to determine the relationships among two or more variables, but in this type of research manipulation of the independent variable is not possible. The independent variable has already occurred; hence, the researcher cannot decide how to apply the independent variable. If a researcher wanted to investigate the effect of divorce of parents on the achievement of children, he or she would have to compare the achievement of preexisting groups: one of children whose parents are divorced, the other of children whose parents live together.

Descriptive research asks questions about the nature, incidence, or distribution of educational variables and/or the relationships among these variables. No manipulation of variables is attempted—only descriptions of variables and their relationships as they occur naturally. An example of this type of research problem is the question What do high school seniors know about the process through which political parties select candidates for President? or What is the relationship between number of years of French in high school and students' course placement in French at the university?

/// THE SOURCES OF PROBLEMS

The first question most students ask is How do I find a research problem? Although there are no set rules for locating a problem, certain suggestions have been found to be helpful. Three important sources of problems are experience, deductions from theory, and related literature.

// Experience

Among the most fruitful sources for beginning researchers are their own experiences as educational practitioners. Decisions must be made daily about the probable effects of educational practices on pupil behavior. If these decisions are to be sound, educators must make critical inquiry into the validity of their assumptions concerning the relationship between learning experiences and pupil change.

There are decisions to be made about teaching methods. Certainly teaching methods are susceptible to and in need of scientific investigation. The scientific approach to educational practice holds that decisions about how to do things in education should be based on empirical evidence rather than upon hunches, impressions, feelings, or dogma. For instance, primary teachers may question the effectiveness of their methods of teaching reading. They may want to evaluate their usual methods or any of several other well-known methods in order to decide what is the most effective approach to use. Secondary teachers might ask whether the problem-discussion method or the lecture method is more effective in the teaching of high school economics. Biology teachers may want to investigate the effect of computer-based simulations on the development of students' problem-solving skills. Are the computer simulations more effective than alternative methods?

Observations of certain relationships for which no satisfactory explanations exist are yet another source of problems for investigation. A teacher may notice an increase in overt signs of anxiety in students at certain times. To investigate this, the teacher can structure various tentative explanations of the origin of the anxiety and then proceed to test them empirically. This investigation may not only solve the immediate problem but also make some small contribution to an understanding of the causes of classroom anxiety.

Similarly, there are decisions to be made about practices that have become routine in the school situation and are in some instances based mainly upon tradition or authority with little or no support from scientific research. Why not evaluate some of these practices—for instance, the annual testing program? Are there alternative tests that would be more valid for the purpose intended than those now being used?

Educators' everyday experiences can yield worthwhile problems for investigation, and, in fact, most of the research ideas developed by beginning educational researchers tend to come from their personal experiences. They may have hunches about new relationships or about alternative ways of accomplishing certain objectives and thus, through a kind of intuitive process, arrive at ideas for research. These studies will be mainly of a type leading to the solution of an immediate problem, but sometimes such problems are nevertheless more appropriate and meaningful for beginning researchers than those arrived at through a process of logical deduction from theory. In addition, such studies can often be justified on the basis of their contribution to the improvement of educational practice.

// Deductions from Theory

The deductions that can be made from various educational and behavioral theories with which the researcher is familiar provide an excellent source of problems. Theories involve general principles whose applicability to specific educational problems is only hypothetical until they are empirically confirmed. It is only through research that one determines whether the generalizations embodied in theories can be translated into specific recommendations for educational practice.

From a theory, the researcher can generate hypotheses stating the expected findings in a particular practical situation. That is, the researcher asks, What relationships between variables will be observed if the theory correctly summarizes the state of affairs? and then conducts systematic inquiry to ascertain whether the empirical data support the hypothesis and hence the theory.

There are learning theories, personality theories, sociological theories, theories of social development, and many others whose validity, scope, and practicality might be profitably tested in educational situations. Reinforcement theory might be a particularly useful starting point for classroom research. Consider the implications for classroom testing that could be deduced from just one postulate of reinforcement theory, namely, that reinforcement of responses leads to an increment in response rate and strength. We know that this theory has stimulated a great deal of research already, but there are still many deductions to be made and tested under classroom conditions. For instance, there has not been sufficient research concerning the effect of a lack of overt reinforcement or of nonreinforcement on correct student responses in classroom situations. We know from experimental laboratory studies with animals that each withholding of reinforcement decreases the probability of that response and eventually results in its extinction. Can this finding be extrapolated to the classroom? That is, can the teacher assume that correct student responses that are not overtly reinforced will weaken and become extinct? At the present time we do not have sufficient classroom research testing the applicability of this principle.

Among other theories that appear to be fruitful sources of hypotheses for investigation are Sarason's test anxiety theory,[2] Festinger's cognitive dissonance theory,[3] the various self-theories, theories of achievement motivation, social-judgment theory, role theory, and phenomenological theory.

Kipnis, for example, used Festinger's theory of social-comparison processes as the basis for research on the relationship between perception of others and the process of changing self-concept.[4] Festinger's theory postulates that self-evaluations are formulated through comparison between the self and others.[5] A number of hypotheses were deduced from the theory stating the expected changes in self-concept in relation to perception of and comparison with important others. The subjects of the study were eighty-seven students living together in a university dormitory. Their evaluations of their own personality traits were examined in relation to their perceptions of their best friends. All the hypotheses were supported by the data, and Kipnis concluded that interpersonal perception and self-perception are closely related.

This approach to research problems results in studies that are easily integrated because they are all based on a common theory. Such interrelated research is especially productive as a means for expanding knowledge in a particular area.

// Related Literature

Another valuable source of problems is the literature in one's own area of interest. In reading about previous research, we are exposed to examples of research problems and the way in which research is conducted. There are several ways in which the review of previous research can help in the formulation of new research problems.

1. Review of previous research helps us formulate research questions that are the next logical step from previous investigations. The outcomes of one piece of research very often lead to new questions. In some cases, researchers in the concluding section of their research reports describe new questions that have arisen. A productive way of extending studies is introducing new variables for further control and for detecting interaction effects between variables. Many multivariate studies are extensions of earlier single-variable investigations.

2. Review of previous research may stimulate a researcher to see whether the procedures employed can be adapted to solving other problems, or whether a similar study could be conducted in a different field or subject

---

[2]Sarason, I. (1980). Introduction to the study of test anxiety. In I. G. Sarason (ed.), *Test Anxiety: Theory, Research, and Applications.* Hillsdale, NJ: Erlbaum.
[3]Festinger, L. (1957). *A Theory of Cognitive Dissonance.* New York: Harper & Row.
[4]Kipnis, D. M. (1961). Change in self-concepts in relation to perceptions of others. *Journal of Personality, 29,* 449–465.
[5]Festinger, L. (1954). A theory of social comparison process. *Human Relations, 7,* 117–140.

area or with different groups of subjects. For example, one reads a study investigating the effectiveness of a multimedia approach in teaching chemistry. Perhaps a similar study could be conducted in biology or in another subject area. Or a study involving secondary school students might serve as a guide to the elementary teacher who is interested in determining whether the same relationships between variables prevail at the elementary level.

3. Reviewing previous research may suggest the desirability of replication to confirm previous findings. One of the essential characteristics of a scientific research study is that it should be replicable, so that the findings can be verified. Replication of a study with or without variation may be a profitable activity for a beginning researcher. Repeating a study increases the extent to which the research findings can be generalized and provides additional evidence of the validity of the findings. In many educational experiments it is not possible to select subjects at random, but rather we must use classroom groups as they are already organized. Of course this limits the extent to which the findings can be generalized. However, as experiments are repeated at different times and in different places with the expected relations supported in each study, the confidence that can be placed in the scientific validity of the findings increases. Mere repetition of other studies is not the most challenging of research activities, but with educational problems there is frequently need for confirmation and extension of the findings.

In most cases replications of previous studies are not exact ones. Variation is introduced in order to clarify some aspect of the findings, to test how far the findings can be generalized, or to investigate factors not included in the original study. For example, numerous replications of Piaget's studies of the development of moral judgment in children have been conducted in other countries.[6] These studies have used Piaget's basic approach but have investigated the development of moral judgment in children of different socioeconomic classes, in children of the same chronological age but differing in intelligence level, in children differing in the extent of their participation in their own age groups, in children differing in the nature of parental discipline, and in both boys and girls. Recently other investigators have used techniques that were different from Piaget's in their attempts to confirm his findings and conclusions. In general, the large body of research originating from Piaget's investigations has supported his original conclusions. Thus, a single research study, if it deals with a significant problem and if its findings are exciting, can be the inspiration for many other studies.

4. Reviewing research studies previously undertaken may raise the question of the applicability of their findings to other cultures. Conclusions from research done in a given culture cannot automatically be applied to other cultures. This is one reason why in recent decades considerable emphasis has been placed on cross-cultural research. In such areas as child and ado-

---

[6]Piaget, J. (1932). *The Moral Judgment of the Child.* Glencoe, IL: Free Press.

lescent psychology, social learning, cognitive and language development, achievement motivation, personality development, and educational practices, numerous examples can be found of cross-cultural research. The growing number of international students in American universities has both increased interest in this kind of research and facilitated the collection of cross-cultural data. A number of theses and dissertations by these students are of this type and provide basis for further cross-cultural studies.

5. Reviewing previous research may result in detecting inconsistencies and contradictions or in dissatisfaction with the conceptualization, methodology, measuring instruments, and statistical analysis used. Researchers can often find something to improve on in previous research. For example, in 1928 Hartshorne and May challenged the existing theory that honesty was a unified character trait.[7] They correlated the behavior of several thousand schoolchildren in various temptation situations. They concluded from the low correlations among the temptation measures that honesty was not a general inner trait; rather it was specific and influenced by the situation in which individuals were placed.

Burton replicated this study in 1963 because he questioned Hartshorne and May's emphasis on situational factors in honesty behavior.[8] Burton used a factor analysis approach and found evidence for intraindividual consistency across the tasks presented to the children. He concluded that there probably was an underlying trait of honesty that a person shows in resisting temptation situations, but he agreed with Hartshorne and May in rejecting an "all-or-none" formulation about a person's character.

In 1965 Hunt replicated Burton's study but used analysis of variance instead of factor analysis as the statistical technique.[9] Hunt argued that personality differences, situations, and the interaction between persons and situations should be considered as sources of variation in honesty behavior and found support for the interaction hypothesis.

Nelsen, Grinder, and Mutterer replicated and extended all of the above studies in 1969.[10] They compared the alternative methodological approaches to the problem and concluded that temptation behavior is only moderately consistent across a variety of tasks. Thus, their findings agree with the early Hartshorne and May study in spite of a time difference of over forty years in the data collection periods of the two studies and in spite of different populations, tasks, and methodological procedures.

Another example of research inspired by previous studies is the research that investigates the effects of ability grouping on student achievement. Since

---

[7]Hartshorne, H., and M. A. May (1928). *Studies in the Nature of Character: Studies in Deceit* (vol. 1). New York: Macmillan.

[8]Burton, R. V. (1963). Generality of honesty reconsidered. *Psychological Review, 70,* 481–499.

[9]Hunt, J. McV. (1965). Traditional personality theory in the light of recent evidence. *American Scientist, 53,* 80–96.

[10]Nelsen, E. A., R. E. Grinder, and M. L. Mutterer (1969). Sources of variance in behavioral measures of honesty in temptation situations: Methodological analysis. *Developmental Psychology, 1,* 265–279.

the early years of this century hundreds of studies have been done on this problem. Yet it is still a topic for research.[11, 12, 13]

Often one is aware of obvious gaps in the organized knowledge in an area. Research could be planned that would help to fill these gaps and result in more-reliable knowledge. For students, conferences with professors in their major field of study may be helpful with this step. Thus, with some critical analysis of published research in their field and a bit of creativity, students should be able to find several potentially researchable problems. An understanding of the theoretical and empirical aspects of the subject area enables them to read critically and choose a good problem.

// Noneducation Sources

Our experiences and observations in the world at large, as well as our professional activities, can be fruitful sources of research problems. Theories or procedures encountered in other fields might be adapted to apply to education. Often movements that originate outside our profession lead us to new paths of research. The women's movement has led us to study sex stereotyping in educational materials, the influence of schools on the learning of sex roles, sex differences in personality, and so forth. The civil rights movement led to many studies about the education of minority children. The prevalence of the AIDS epidemic in this country has stimulated a great deal of research on the best procedures and materials to use to acquaint young people in school with the danger of the disease and how best to protect themselves from it. The inspiration for much valuable research in education has come from such noneducation sources.

/// EVALUATING THE PROBLEM

After a problem has been tentatively selected, it must be evaluated. The researcher must be confident that the problem area is of sufficient importance to warrant investigation, although this is not always easy to determine. Judging the worth of a problem is often a matter of individual values and subjective opinion. However, there are certain criteria that should be used in this process of evaluating the significance of a problem.

1. *Ideally the problem should be one whose solution will make a contribution to the body of organized knowledge in education.* The researcher should show

---

[11]Slavin, R. E. (1987). Ability grouping and student achievement in elementary schools: A best-evidence synthesis. *Review of Educational Research, 57,* 293–335.

[12]Hiebert, E. (1987). The context of instruction and student learning: An examination of Slavin's assumptions. *Review of Educational Research, 57,* 337–340.

[13]Gamoran, A. (1987). Organization, instruction, and the effects of ability grouping: Comment on Slavin's "best-evidence synthesis." *Review of Educational Research, 57,* 341–345.

that the study is likely to fill in gaps in present knowledge or help resolve some of the inconsistencies in previous research. Perhaps the study can improve upon earlier studies in such a way that more reliable knowledge would be made available. Most scholars agree that the problems that are rooted in theory have greater potential for satisfying this criterion. The investigator might ask whether the study will yield knowledge about new relationships or will replicate previously established findings.

Certain studies may make contributions to both theory and practice. However, if the problem lacks apparent theoretical implications, then it must at least have some practical implications. Researchers should be able to answer the question So what? with respect to their studies. Would the solution of the problem make any difference to educational practice? Would other educators be interested in the findings? Would the findings be useful in an educational decision-making situation? Since there are so many problems with theoretical or practical implications in need of solution, there is little justification for spending time and effort on problems that lack one of these two important aspects.

Sometimes in their effort to locate a problem, students will select a question involving rather trivial relationships. For example, What is the relationship between popularity with one's peers and reading speed? would be considered a trivial problem because it has little or no significance for educational practice, has little relationship to other studies, and has no consequences for theory. The answers to some questions are obvious. A question such as What is the correlation between intelligence and reading achievement? would also be considered trivial because we already have sufficient data on this relationship and thus additional research is probably unnecessary. There is no need to "reinvent the wheel."

Many proposed studies should be rejected because their methodology would contribute little to either educational theory or practice. For example, a researcher seeking to evaluate the comparative merits of phonics and sight reading in beginning reading instruction might propose to survey the attitudes of primary teachers on this question. Such a survey would not yield a meaningful answer concerning the relative merits of the two systems because it would provide only the opinions of a sample of teachers who may be just as ignorant of the answer as the researcher. A superior approach would involve a controlled experiment comparing the progress of students taught under one system with that of students of equivalent ability taught under the other system. The ease of surveying opinion tempts many to use this procedure when it is inappropriate for answering the question being asked.

2. *The problem should be one that will lead to new problems and so to further research.* If researchers begin by linking their problem to organized knowledge and give some consideration to the type of study that might logically follow their own, they are much more likely to satisfy this criterion. A good study, while arriving at an answer to one question, usually generates

a number of other questions that need investigation. This has been true of the studies dealing with reinforcement theory in the classroom. In contrast, much descriptive research fails to satisfy this second criterion.

In connection with this criterion, we suggest that the beginning student in research might give some consideration to the selection of a problem that could possibly be expanded or followed up later in a master's thesis or even a doctoral study.

3. *The problem must be one that is researchable.* Although this criterion would seem self-evident, in practice many problems do not involve questions that can be subjected to scientific investigation. To be researchable, a problem must be one that can be attacked empirically. Many interesting questions in education cannot be subjected to empirical research but must be investigated through philosophic inquiry. Such questions as Is it good to have sex education in the elementary schools? or Should we teach about communism in the high school? are philosophical issues and cannot be answered by scientific investigation. Although these questions as worded cannot be attacked empirically, they might be reformulated into workable research questions. For instance, we might restate the first question above as What is the effect of sex education in the elementary schools on the attitudes of junior high school students toward premarital sex? A study could be designed to obtain information on this type of question. Although philosophical questions as such are not appropriate for scientific research, the information provided by research can be used in developing solutions to philosophical and ethical questions. That is, the data arrived at through scientific research on a problem can be useful to educators as they make decisions involving rights and values.

The researcher must also give some attention to the definition and measurement of the variables involved in the question. A problem such as What is the effect of changes in national priorities on the future of American education? would not be appropriate for research. Defining the terms *changes in national priorities* and *the future of American education* in such a way that they could be measured would be difficult.

4. *The problem must be suitable for the particular researcher.* The problem may be excellent from the point of view of the criteria mentioned but inappropriate for the individual. Some of the personal aspects to be considered here are:

a. The problem should be one in which you, the researcher, have a genuine interest and about which you can be enthusiastic. It should be a problem whose solution is personally important because of the contribution it could make to your own knowledge in an area or to the improvement of your performance as an educational practitioner. Unless the problem is meaningful and interesting, it is doubtful whether you would be willing to expend the time and energy to do a thorough job.

b. The problem should be in an area in which you have both knowledge and some experience. You need to be familiar with the existing theories, concepts, and established facts in order to identify a worthwhile problem. Furthermore, you need to consider whether you have the necessary skills that may be required to carry the study through to completion. Instruments may have to be developed and validated, or complex statistical analyses may be required.

c. The problem must be one that is feasible in the situation in which you find yourself. You must ascertain whether the data necessary to answer the question are or will be available. You must make sure that the necessary subjects will be available or that the appropriate school records will be accessible. School administrators are quite often opposed to the conduct of research in their schools. So unless you are employed in a school situation at the time, you are quite likely to be left without the means to solve the research problem. One of the authors found it necessary to visit four school systems before permission could be obtained to conduct an educational experiment.

d. The problem must be one that can be investigated and completed in the allotted time. You should not select a problem that is too big or too involved, and you should allow adequate time for constructing the instruments, administering the instruments, analyzing the data, and writing the report.

/// STATING THE PROBLEM

After the problem has been selected and its significance decided, there is still the task of formulating or stating the problem in a form amenable to investigation. A good statement of the problem must (1) clarify exactly what is to be determined or solved and (2) restrict the scope of the study to a specific question. We cannot overemphasize the importance of a clear, concise statement of the question. Beginning researchers often have a general idea of the problem but have trouble formulating it as a workable research question. They find that their initial general ideas, although adequate for communication and understanding, are not sufficiently specific to permit an empirical attack on the problem. They cannot make progress until they can state a concrete question amenable to research.

To illustrate, a beginning researcher states that he or she is interested in studying the effectiveness of the new science curriculum in the secondary schools. As the problem is stated, one could understand in a broad sense what he or she wants to do and could communicate about it in a general way. But the researcher must specify the problem with much greater clarity if a method for investigating it is to be found.

An essential step involves a definition of the terms involved. What is meant by *effectiveness, science curriculum,* and *secondary schools?* The definitions required for research will not usually be supplied by a dictionary. For example, effectiveness is defined as "producing the intended or expected result." This definition describes the general construct effectiveness but is not sufficiently precise for research purposes. One needs to be able to specify exactly what indicator of effectiveness one will use or what one will do to assess the presence or absence of the phenomenon denoted by the concept *effectiveness*. The same is true for the other terms. In other words, one must define the variables of the problem operationally. To define concepts operationally, one must designate some kind of overt behavior or event that is directly observable and measurable by oneself and others to represent those concepts. As mentioned in Chapter 1, an operational definition is one that defines a concept in terms of the operation or processes that will be used to measure or to manipulate the concept.

In this study the researcher might choose to define effectiveness as the improvement made in scores on a test of critical thinking or on a standardized science test. The term *curriculum* would be defined as the computer-assisted biology course offered to high school sophomores. *Secondary schools* might refer to those high schools that have certain specified characteristics such as size, type, and so on. The original problem now might become What is the effect of the computer-assisted biology course on the comprehension of biological concepts in beginning biology students at the sophomore level? The operational definitions serve to focus the scope of a general question to specific observable variables.

Now that the work is indicated with some clarity and focus, the researcher can proceed to design an experimental study that compares the scores made on pretests and posttests of comprehension of biological concepts by students having the computer-assisted biology course with those of similar students having an alternative biology curriculum. The researcher can now begin to gather some objective evidence concerning a particular curriculum in a particular situation that will shed light on the more general original question.

Furthermore, in stating the problem, the researcher must strive for a balance between generality and specificity. If the stated problem is too broad and too general, one is faced with a vague area with no clear indication of the direction the research is to take. For instance, a question such as What is the effect of computer-assisted instruction on math achievement? is too general. It would be much better to ask What is the effect of the use of computer-assisted algebra programs on algebra achievement of bright junior high school students? This statement indicates immediately the population to be included, the variables involved, and the type of data that will be gathered.

On the other hand, the problem must not be so narrow that it becomes trivial and meaningless. One wants a problem that is broad enough to be significant according to the criteria discussed, yet specific enough to be feasible in one's particular situation.

While research problems focus on the relationship among two or more variables, this does not mean that the *exact* words *What is the relationship between* ————and ————? have to appear in the statement. The statement *may* appear in that form, or the relationship may only be implied. Neither does the problem have to be stated in the form of a question. Students are often confused on this point. For instance, (1) the declarative statement This study examines the relative effectiveness of Reading Methods A and B in teaching slow learners and (2) the question What is the relative effectiveness of Reading Method A as compared with Method B in teaching slow learners? both inquire about the *relationship between variables* but without using those precise words, and both are acceptable ways to present the research problem. As mentioned earlier, some authors prefer the question form simply because it is straightforward and psychologically seems to orient the researcher to the task at hand—namely, to plan a method of finding the answer to the question. In some cases both a declarative statement and a question are presented: A more general declarative statement may be followed by one or more very specific questions.

You should state the problem in such a way that research into the question is possible. Avoid philosophical issues, as well as value or judgmental questions that cannot be answered by scientific investigation.

Once a potential question is formulated, it should be assessed for its clarity and feasibility. The development of a workable problem is an evolutionary process involving many attempts to sharpen concepts, define operations, and consider ways of collecting data.

/// IDENTIFYING POPULATION AND VARIABLES

A good strategy for shaping a felt problem—or a vague notion of what one wants to investigate—into a researchable problem is to think in terms of population and variables.

For example, let us consider Ms. Burke, an elementary principal whose felt difficulty is *Does individual tutoring by upper-grade students have a positive effect on below-average readers?*

It is usually easiest to identify the population, that is, those people about whom one wishes to learn something. The population is below-average readers. Reading ability is not a variable in this question because all the children being considered have been diagnosed as below-average readers. Having identified below-average readers as the population in the original statement, Ms. Burke should now ask herself if that is really the population she wants. She will probably decide that "below-average readers" is too broad a category and she should confine herself to a particular age: below-average second-grade readers.

Now she is ready to look for variables in the remainder of her original statement. *Individual tutoring* can be made into a variable either by varying the type of tutoring used or by varying the amount of tutoring time or by having some children receive the tutoring while others do not. Ms. Burke decides that the last alternative concerns what she really wants to know, so she rewrites the relevant part of the question to Does receiving a specified amount of individual tutoring versus no tutoring . . . ? Thus, tutoring is the independent variable because it is antecedent to reading achievement, and the principal is predicting that the tutoring will have an effect on reading achievement, the dependent variable.

Now it becomes obvious that the word *tutoring* is too general. Unless all subjects receive the same type and amount of tutoring, the results of the study will be meaningless. Ms. Burke decides to use word flash drill as the specific type of tutoring and to specify 15 minutes per day as the amount of time.

The phrase *have a positive effect on* seems quite vague until she looks at it in terms of her independent variable. Does word flash drill have an effect on . . . what? She knows it has an effect on word flash recall, but she wants to study its effects on other aspects of reading behavior that might be observed: expressive oral reading, silent reading, positive feelings toward reading, number of books read, comprehension, and so forth. But she is afraid that teachers might rate good word callers as comprehending more and being more positive toward reading while they view the poorer word callers as more inferior on these variables than they really are. She wants a dependent variable that is independent of teacher judgment and decides to use reading scores from the California Achievement Test (CAT) as the dependent variable.

Ms. Burke's revised statement of the problem now reads: *Among below-average second-grade readers, is there a difference in CAT reading scores between those who have received 15 minutes per day of individual word flash drill by upper-grade students and those who have received no word drill?* This question tells whom she is studying, what will be done differently for some than for others, and what she expects differential treatment to influence. Note also that the value judgment *positive effect* has dropped out of the question.

It is often useful to follow this procedure in a formal manner similar to that used for diagramming a sentence. One can begin by drawing a vertical line and writing *Population* to the left and *Variables* to the right. These elements in the study are then listed below the horizontal line. In our example the diagram would be as follows:

Population	Variables
Below-average second-grade readers	Word flash drill for 15 minutes daily by upper-grade students versus no word flash drill
	Reading scores on CAT

Let us take another question: What is the effect of having experienced or not having experienced a preschool program on the reading achievement of first-graders?

Population	Variables
First-graders	Having experienced or not having experienced a preschool program (independent)
	Reading achievement (dependent)

This question is complete in that it has an identified population and two variables. Since *preschool program* precedes *reading achievement of first-graders,* the former can be identified as an independent variable and the latter as a dependent variable.

Let us look at another example: Does high school driver education do any good? As it stands, the question has neither a population nor variables. An investigator starting with this question might first decide to compare 19-year-old drivers who have had high school driver education with those who have not. We now have a population statement and an independent variable. Now we can turn our attention to selecting a dependent variable. What effect might having or not having driver education have on 19-year-old drivers? It is decided that *accident rate* would be a suitable dependent variable. Putting these elements into a diagram, we have:

Population	Variables
19-year-old drivers	Have had or have not had high school driver education (independent)
	Accident rate (dependent)

A complete question can now be stated: Do 19-year-old drivers who have had high school driver education have a lower accident rate than 19-year-old drivers who have not had high school driver education?

The question What is the relationship of dogmatism to political attitudes among college freshmen? illustrates another point.

Population	Variables
College freshmen	Dogmatism
	Political attitudes

This question is complete with a population and two variables. But we cannot label the variables as independent and dependent since it cannot be determined which is antecedent to the other.

If a study is conducted to investigate status quo rather than a relationship between variables, it may be complete with only one variable. For example, one might study the opinions of college seniors concerning legalization of marijuana. In this case the population is college seniors and the single variable is their opinions on the subject.

Different methods are employed to answer the different types of research questions. Whenever an independent variable can be manipulated by the researcher, the experimental method is the appropriate one to use (see Chapter 9). The first example in this section involving the influence of word flash drill on CAT reading scores is experimental research. Many variables in education cannot be manipulated, and thus the experimental method cannot be used in research on these variables. The research problem involving a comparison of the accident rate of 19-year-old drivers who had had or had not had driver training would require the causal-comparative method (see Chapter 10). The independent variable (driver education or lack of driver education) was not manipulated by the researcher.

For some research problems either the experimental or the causal-comparative method is appropriate depending upon how the study is designed. The research example above on the effect of preschool programs on reading achievement could employ either method, depending upon whether the investigator chose to manipulate the independent variable of preschool programs or to select subjects who already had or had not had preschool training.

Other research problems are concerned with describing the nature or incidence of one or more educational variables. The descriptive method is the appropriate one for this type of problem (see Chapter 11). The example involving the question of the relationship between dogmatism and political attitudes among college freshmen is descriptive research. Surveys seeking opinions on issues such as legalization of marijuana also represent descriptive research.

// The Journal Article

Identifying the population and the independent and dependent variables provides a framework for analyzing published research reports. The following journal article by Marsh illustrates the elements usually found in a report of an experiment.[14] The introduction gives the rationale for the study and briefly summarizes previous thought and research on the topic. The methods section has several elements: (1) The sample (ten classes from five universities) is drawn to represent the population of interest (university students); (2) The independent variable (take-home versus in-class exams) is described and operationally defined; (3) The dependent variables (responses to a survey

---

[14]Marsh, R. (1984). A comparison of take-home versus in-class exams. *Journal of Educational Research, 78,* 111–113.

asking students how much they were motivated to study and learn in preparation for each type of exam and scores on a surprise test of comprehension and application of the course material) are described and operationally defined; (4) The procedures are described in sufficient detail to enable another researcher to replicate the experiment with a different sample. The results section gives the data generated by the experiment and the results of the statistical tests. The conclusion section gives the authors interpretation of these results.

A Comparison of Take-Home Versus In-Class Exams

This study was an effort to determine whether the take-home test was as good a vehicle or a better one for learning than the traditional in-class test. The results of this experiment are important because instructors are increasingly deleting the in-class tests (Gay and Gallagher, 1976), and there seems to be no empirical basis for the belief that the take-home test is as effective. Thus, the current trend toward eliminating formal written tests may actually operate against one of education's major goals: student retention of learned concepts.

Probably the major concern over classroom exams is that they cause debilitating anxiety. However, research on this claim is inconsistent. For example, it has been demonstrated that in a test situation anxiety has a negative effect (Sarason, Davidson, Lighthall, Waite, and Ruebush, 1960), a positive effect (Castaneda, McCandless, and Palermo, 1964), and no effect (Denny, Paterson, and Feldhusen, 1964) on test performance.

Some authors have hypothesized that it is the amount of anxiety that affects test performance. Anastasi (1976) argues that testing has a total positive effect if accomplished properly. She states that the relationship between anxiety and test performance is probably nonlinear and that some anxiety is good, while too much is detrimental. Many practices have been designed to dispel anxiety in the classroom test environment, but she points out that "the examiner's own manner and a well-organized, smoothly running testing operation will contribute toward the same goal" (Anastasi, 1976).

Although students experience different levels of anxiety before exams, it is probably not a good idea to eliminate testing for that reason alone. Our aim should not be to completely avoid stress, which is not possible in our world, but to learn how to recognize our typical response to stress and then try to adjust our coping style accordingly (Selye, 1978).

There is a paucity of specific literature comparing take-home and in-class exams. There is evidence that oral and written testing are equally effective and that either method is better than no testing at all (Calhoun, 1962). Also, studies show that academic achievement of undergraduate students is lower under a pass/fail grading system than under the standard grading system (Bain, Hales, and Rand, 1973; Gold, Reilly, Silbeman, and Lehr, 1971).

In 1976 a study (Gay and Gallagher, 1976) was performed in which a large basic class of undergraduates was randomly divided into three sections. One section was given periodic take-home exercises; the second section was given periodic tests; and the third group was given a choice.

It is interesting to note that no one in the third group elected to take tests. Except for these different treatments, all students were treated as equally as possible. At the end of the course a surprise exam was given, identical in all three sections. The results of the tests showed that the group that was given tests scored significantly higher than the other two.

This study differs from the preceding one in several ways. First, it included a variety of classes in the arts and behavioral and applied fields of study. Therefore, the results are likely to be generalizable to a wider audience. The study attempted to measure specific levels of learning as defined by the Bloom Hierarchy of Cognitive Learning (Bloom, Engelhart, Furst, Hill, and Krathwohl, 1956). Finally, an attempt was made to identify causality with regard to the results of the experiment.

Methods

Ten classes from five different universities were recruited as participants. There were 258 students in the total sample, which included classes in psychology, statistics, education, research, and history. Early in the academic semester each participating instructor was given a full verbal briefing on the procedures and a packet with instructions to be given verbatim. The students were told that one half would receive a take-home exam, that this was a scientific experiment, no one would be hurt by its results, and anyone who was not satisfied with his or her grade would have the option of taking another exam. It was expected that this procedure would have a neutralizing effect on the anxiety factor.

About two weeks before the midterm, the classes were randomized into two equal groups, A and B. In each class, randomly selected members of Group A were given a take-home test to be returned one week later. Members of Group B were given an identical in-class test. All tests used in this study were the multiple-choice type. The A Group submitted their completed exams at the same time that the B Group took their test in class. One week later a surprise exam was given to both groups during the regular class period. The latter covered the same material upon which they had been tested the previous week. Since members of both groups were taught by the same teachers under identical conditions, the experimental and control subjects received as equivalent an exposure as was possible with a classroom type of experiment. Only the treatment (type of test) differed for each class.

The surprise test had 50 multiple-choice questions, 25 of which measured knowledge and 25 measured a combination of comprehension and application of the course material. The latter categories included the first three levels of cognitive learning in Bloom's Hierarchy (Bloom et al., 1956). A survey was also attached to assist in determining the extent to which the students were motivated to study and learn in preparation for each type of exam. There was a 96.1 percent response rate to the questionnaire. Finally, a two-way analysis of variance was used. Because there were two groups in ten different classes, it was a 2×10 design (Ary and Jacobs, 1976).

Results

Group B (in-class exam) scored significantly higher than did Group A (take-home exam) in all categories of the surprise test. The subjects exhibited significantly more total learning, more knowledge, and more comprehension and application of the subject matter. The statistical analysis for each category thus revealed that the independent variable (type of test) and the dependent variable (learning) were highly related.

On the survey that was attached to the surprise test, one of the questions asked, "If you were a teacher and you wanted your students to really learn the subject matter, which type of test would you give?" participant response was that 25.8 percent would give a take-home exam, 59.1 percent would give an in-class exam, and 15.1 percent were not sure. They appeared to say that the in-class exam was more effective, by a better than two-to-one margin.

Two questions were devised to determine participant attitudes toward preparing for a particular type of exam. The first question asked the student to place him-/herself on a continuum of one through ten, indicating the amount of effort put into studying the material covered on the teacher-made test given the week prior to the surprise test. The second question, also with a continuum of one through ten, asked how much study effort the student would have made had the other type of test (take-home or in-class) been assigned.

The A Group scored significantly lower on the first question. Thus, in effect, the students said that they would have studied harder had they been given an in-class exam. Conversely, the B Group scored significantly lower on the second question. One can interpret this as saying that they would have studied less had they been given a take-home exam. One conclusion that would explain the difference in learning between the groups is that those students who had the in-class test expended more effort, by their own admission.

Conclusion

These data present evidence in favor of an in-class test as opposed to a take-home test for a variety of college students enrolled in psychology, statistics, research, education, and history courses. In this experiment the type of test utilized had an effect on the amount of learning by the student on the first three levels of Bloom's Hierarchy of Cognitive Learning: knowledge, comprehension, and application. Clearly the in-class test was the superior treatment, and the students seemed to agree.

But, for many reasons, one cannot say that the classic in-class exam is the only valid method by which to promote effective learning. More research is needed, with emphasis on the goals and purposes of exams and on ways to measure and compare levels of learning in the affective domain.

/// SUMMARY

The first task facing researchers is the selection and formulation of a problem. A research problem is a question or statement about the relationship between variables. In attempting to find a researchable problem, investigators may look to their personal experiences, to theories from which questions may be deduced, or to the current literature in some area of interest. They must evaluate the significance of the proposed problem in terms of specific criteria, asking the questions: Will the problem contribute to the present body of knowledge? Does it have potential for leading to further research? Is it testable—that is, can the variables be observed and measured? How appropriate is the problem with respect to my interests, experience, and knowledge in the area? Do I have access to the data required by the problem, and are instruments available, or could they be constructed, to measure the variables? Can the data be analyzed and interpreted within the time available? The question should not directly involve philosophical issues nor should it be so general that a research undertaking is impossible. The statement of the question should identify the population of interest and the variables to be investigated.

// Key Concepts

criteria for research problem
   statements
dependent variable
independent variable

population
research problem
sources of research problem

/// EXERCISES

1. Find a research report published in a journal, and answer the following questions based on your reading:
    a. What problem is investigated in the study?
    b. What is (are) the hypothesis(es)?
    c. What are the independent and dependent variables?
    d. Where did you find the problem and hypothesis(es) stated in the report?
    e. Were the problem and hypothesis(es) stated with sufficient clarity so that you knew exactly what was being investigated in the study?

2. Select a broad area in which you might be interested in doing research. Choose a particular aspect of this broad area and then identify a research problem that you would be interested in pursuing. State this problem in a form for research.

3. The following examples are inadequate statements of research problems. Restate each so that it becomes a specific question suitable for research.
    a. effects of different ways of learning science concepts
    b. anxiety and academic achievement
    c. attitudes of culturally disadvantaged children
    d. counseling and underachievers
    e. effectiveness of the Cuisenaire method of teaching elementary arithmetic

4. Evaluate the following research problems:
   a. Has the permissive child-rearing philosophy of Dr. Spock had an adverse effect on American education?
   b. What is the relationship between the preferred method of leg-crossing and the intelligence of American college women?
   c. Considering recent empirical studies on math achievement, should "modern" mathematics be abandoned in the elementary school and replaced by traditional math?
   d. How do students perceive the role of the principal at Central Middle School?

5. State the most likely independent and dependent variables in the following studies:
   a. Lane, S., and J. Bergan (1988). Effects of instructional variables on language ability of preschool children. *American Educational Research Journal, 25,* 271–284.
   b. Linn, R., and C. Hastings (1984). The validity of predictors of performance in law school. *Journal of Educational Measurement, 21,* 245–258.
   c. Hativa, N. (1988). Computer-based drill and practice in arithmetic: Widening the gap between high- and low-achieving students. *American Educational Research Journal, 25,* 366–397.
   d. Chapman, J. (1988). Learning disabled children's self-concepts. *Review of Educational Research, 58,* 347–366.
   e. Ware, N., and V. Lee (1988). Sex differences in choice of college science majors. *American Educational Research Journal, 25,* 593–614.

6. List sources of research problems used by researchers and give an example of each.

7. What is the effect of children's reading of good books on their reading skills? Is this question researchable? If not, how would you suggest changing it so that it could be investigated empirically?

/// ANSWERS

1. Answers will vary.

2. Answers will vary.

3. a. Is there a difference between the Science Research Associates (SRA) science achievement scores of sixth-graders who have had one year of the Elementary Science Study (ESS) science program and the scores of those who have had one year of a textbook-centered science course?

    b. Among high school students, is there a relationship between composite Stanford Achievement Test scores and Manifest Anxiety Scale scores?

    c. One needs to specify which attitudes of children are being investigated and then compare these with attitudes of a suitable control group (perhaps nondisadvantaged children), or hypothesize the relationship between types of attitudes and other behavior. For example, do culturally disadvantaged children with positive attitudes toward school have higher grades than those with negative attitudes toward school?

    d. What is the effect of a counseling program on the attitudes of middle school underachievers toward school?

    e. Do the math achievement scores of third-graders who have had one year of the Cuisenaire method of teaching elementary arithmetic differ from the scores of those who have had an alternative method of teaching?

4. a. This question involves a value judgment that is impossible to investigate empirically.

    b. This question is trivial, and answering it would make little contribution to knowledge.

    c. Research cannot answer questions of value; it can only provide information on which decisions can be based.

    d. Though the question could be researched, it is too local in scope to be generalized to other situations.

5. a. independent: instructional methods
      dependent: some measures of language ability

    b. independent: various predictors (test scores, etc.)
      dependent: some measure of performance in law school (perhaps GPA)

    c. independent: use of computer-based drill in arithmetic
      dependent: achievement in math for high- and low-achieving students

    d. independent: the condition of being learning-disabled
      dependent: some measure of self-concept

    e. independent: sex
      dependent: choice of science major in college

6. educators' everyday experience
    deductions from theory
    related literature
    noneducation sources

7. The terms *good books* and *reading skills* need to be defined. Restate as What is the effect of children's reading of four designated classics on their vocabulary growth?

CHAPTER 3

Related Literature

INSTRUCTIONAL OBJECTIVES

After studying this chapter, the student will be able to
1. List the seven main functions served in research by the review of the literature
2. Describe major reference sources in education
3. Name the ERIC indexes, explaining their similarities and differences
4. Outline a general approach to using periodical indexes in research
5. Name at least three non-ERIC indexes, giving examples of the type of information found in each
6. Relate in detail how *SSCI* can be used in a review of the literature, explaining the function of each of the four indexes
7. Describe use of the *Mental Measurement Yearbooks* as a source of information on tests and measuring devices
8. Describe procedures for a computer search of the related literature
9. Detail a systematic progression of steps in organizing the literature, explaining the purpose of each step

---

[1]This chapter was revised and updated with the assistance of Samuel T. Huang, Founders Library, Northern Illinois University.

Once a topic has been selected, the investigator is naturally eager for action. However, it is a mistake to rush headlong into planning and carrying out the study before making a thorough survey of what is already known in the area of interest. The topic must be related to relevant knowledge in the field. It is as important for educators as it is for others engaged in research to know how to locate, organize, and use the literature in their field.

This chapter discusses (1) the role of related literature in a research project, (2) reference sources in education, and (3) the task of organizing the related literature for presentation in the report.

/// THE ROLE OF RELATED LITERATURE IN A RESEARCH PROJECT

The search for related literature should be completed before the actual conduct of the study begins. This stage serves several important functions:

1. *A knowledge of related research enables investigators to define the frontiers of their field.* To use an analogy, an explorer might say, "We know that beyond this river there are plains for 2000 miles west and beyond those plains a range of mountains, but we do not know what lies beyond the mountains. I propose to cross the plains, go over the mountains, and proceed from there in a westerly direction." So the researcher in a sense says, "The work of A, B, and C has discovered this much about my question; the investigations of D have added this much to our knowledge. I propose to go beyond D's work in the following manner."

2. *A thorough review of related theory and research enables researchers to place their questions in perspective.* One should determine whether one's endeavors would be likely to add to knowledge in a meaningful way. Knowledge in any given area consists of the accumulated outcomes of numerous studies conducted by generations of researchers and the theories designed to integrate this knowledge and to explain the observed phenomena. One should review the literature for the purpose of finding a link between one's study and the accumulated knowledge in one's field of interest. Studies with no link to the existing knowledge seldom make significant contributions to the field. Such studies tend to produce isolated bits of information that are of limited usefulness.

3. *Reviewing related literature helps researchers to limit their question and to clarify and define the concepts of the study.* A research question may be too broad to be carried out or too vague to be put into concrete operation. A careful review of the literature can help researchers to revise their initial question so that it can be investigated. It also helps in clarifying the concepts involved in the study and in translating these concepts into operational definitions. Many educational and behavioral constructs—such as stress, creativity, frustration, aggression, achievement, motivation, and adjustment—

need to be clarified and operationally defined. These constructs, as well as many other educational and behavioral concepts, do not lend themselves to scientific research until they can be quantified. In reviewing literature, one becomes familiar with previous efforts to clarify these concepts and to define them operationally. Successful reviews often result in the formation of hypotheses regarding the relationships between variables in one's study. Studies in which hypotheses are tested are usually more useful than those without hypotheses.

4. *A critical review of related literature often leads to insight into the reasons for contradictory results in an area.* Contradictory results are not uncommon. The reasons for inconsistencies may be found in the kinds of approaches adopted for solving the problem or the kinds of instruments employed, methodologies used, or analyses made. A comparison of the procedures of these studies may explain the inconsistent findings. To resolve such contradictions is a challenge, but it can also provide a significant contribution to the knowledge in one's field of interest.

5. *Through studying related research, investigators learn which methodologies have proved useful and which seem less promising.* As one proceeds through the related literature and develops increasing sophistication, one may soon find oneself seeing better ways in which some of the studies could have been done. Of course, hindsight is always better than foresight, so perhaps it is inevitable that early studies in a field often seem crude and ineffective. Many research projects fail because of the use of inappropriate procedures, instruments, research designs, or statistical analyses. A thorough examination of the methodologies of previous studies often results in finding the reason for the failure of past studies, as well as insight into the selection of an appropriate methodology for one's own research. Both the successes and failures of past work provide insight for designing one's own study. By building on past investigations, we can develop increasing sophistication in our knowledge about educational research.

6. *A thorough search through related research avoids unintentional replication of previous studies.* Frequently a researcher develops a worthwhile idea only to discover that a very similar study has already been made. In such a case the researcher must decide whether deliberately to replicate the previous work or to change the proposed plans and investigate a different aspect of the problem.

7. *The study of related literature places researchers in a better position to interpret the significance of their own results.* Becoming familiar with theory in the field and with previous research prepares researchers for fitting the findings of their research into the body of knowledge in the field.

/// REFERENCE SOURCES IN EDUCATION

It is clearly essential for scholars and researchers to know how to find previous work in their areas. To do this, one should know (1) the sources of previous work, (2) what agencies collect such information and organize it into databases, (3) what form these databases take, and (4) efficient ways of finding the information one needs. In order to use these sources, one must become familiar with available library facilities and services. Many libraries have printed guides describing their services and regulations or will schedule orientation tours. It is especially important to learn how the card catalog is organized. Many libraries use an online catalog through the library computer system. If your library system has been computerized, you may want to learn how to use this system efficiently. In the meantime, you should find out whether the library can obtain books and other materials—such as dissertations and periodical articles—from other institutions by using an interlibrary loan service.

// Basic Guides

To begin a search of research studies, it is useful to consult basic guides to the research literature. One of these helpful guides is Berry's *A Bibliographic Guide to Educational Research.*[2] This guide is intended "as a concise guide to assist the student in education courses to make effective use of the resources of the library of his/her college or university." It is an annotated listing of over 700 major research sources arranged by types of materials, such as periodicals, research studies, government publications, reference materials, and tests. The reference materials include yearbooks, directories, biographical sources, and handbooks on the methodology of educational research and on form and style for writing research papers.

Current Bibliographical Sources in Education,[3] published in a trilingual (English, French, and Spanish) edition, is based mainly on the reference collection at the Unesco International Bureau of Education Documentation Centre in Paris. It includes current bibliographies, indexes of periodicals, and registers of research and is arranged by country, with separate listings for the publications of international and regional organizations.

Woodbury's *A Guide to Sources of Educational Information*[4] is a comprehensive guide for locating information in education. It selects, describes, and in many cases evaluates the major print, nonprint, and institutional sources for educational research. Arrangement is basically by type of publications, with chapters on finance and government, special education, instructional materials, and tests and assessment instruments. An explanation of the steps in effective research and a guide for researchers are also included.

---

[2]Berry, D. M. (1980). *A Bibliographic Guide to Educational Research* (2d ed.). Metuchen, NJ: Scarecrow Press.
[3]Unesco (1984). *Current Bibliographical Sources in Education* (2d ed.). Paris: Unesco, International Bureau of Education.
[4]Woodbury, M. (1982). *A Guide to Sources of Educational Information* (2d ed.). Arlington, VA: Information Resources Press.

Sheehy's *Guide to Reference Books*[5] briefly describes and evaluates several thousand reference sources from various subject fields, including education. It is updated by means of biennial supplements. *American Reference Books Annual*[6] covers the reference book output (including reprints) of the previous year in all subjects and provides descriptive and evaluative notes.

// Reviews of Education-Related Literature

Reviews that integrate and summarize research studies on specific topics can help to get one started on a literature search. There are several basic reviews that one can consult. Mitzel's *Encyclopedia of Educational Research*,[7] designed to present "a critical synthesis and interpretation of reported educational research," contains signed articles with bibliographies providing well-documented discussions of recent trends and developments as well as traditional topics. Approximately 164 topics are included in this four-volume encyclopedia. It is a good basic source to research preliminary topics related to education. The *Encyclopedia of Educational Evaluation*[8] attempts to present the major concepts and techniques for evaluating education training programs in a single alphabetical arrangement of articles. *American Educator's Encyclopedia*[9] comprises about 2000 short entries for names and terms frequently found in the literature of professional education. *The International Encyclopedia of Education: Research and Studies*[10] presents "an up-to-date overview of scholarship brought to bear on educational problems, practices, and institutions all over the world." It covers scholarly and professional work in education in the broad sense, surveying the state of the art in the various branches of education, the availability of scientifically sound and valid information relating thereto, and the types of further research needed. *The International Encyclopedia of Higher Education*[11] includes 282 articles on contemporary topics in higher education written by educational leaders all over the world.

Another useful review source is the *Handbook of Research on Teaching*.[12,13,14] Three different editions have been published about ten years apart. They list, summarize, and critically analyze research in the field of teaching.

[5]Sheehy, E. P. (1986). *Guide to Reference Books* (10th ed.). Chicago: American Library Association.

[6]Wynar, B. S. (ed.) (1970–   ). *American Reference Books Annual.* Littleton, CO: Libraries Unlimited.

[7]Mitzel, H. E. (ed.) (1982). *Encyclopedia of Educational Research* (5th ed., vols. 1–4). New York: Free Press.

[8]Anderson, S. B., *et al.* (1975). *Encyclopedia of Educational Evaluation.* San Francisco: Jossey-Bass.

[9]Dejnozka, E. L., and D. E. Kapel (1982). *American Educators' Encyclopedia.* Westport, CT: Greenwood Press.

[10]*The International Encyclopedia of Education: Research and Studies* (1985). (10 vols.) Oxford: Pergamon.

[11]Knowles, A. S. (ed.). *The International Encyclopedia of Higher Education* (1978). (10 vols.). San Francisco: Jossey-Bass.

[12]Gage, N. L. (ed.) (1963). *Handbook of Research on Teaching.* Chicago: Rand McNally.

[13]Travers, R. (ed.) (1973). *Second Handbook of Research on Teaching* (2d ed.). Chicago: Rand McNally.

[14]Wittrock, M. C. (ed.) (1985). *Handbook of Research on Teaching* (3d ed.). Chicago: Rand McNally.

Each edition contains authoritative articles by specialists on selected topics in the field. Comprehensive bibliographies are included under selected topics. Among the topics in the third edition are "Measurement of Teaching," "Quantitative Methods in Research on Teaching," "Qualitative Methods in Research on Teaching," "Observation as Inquiry and Method," "Syntheses of Research on Teaching," "The Teaching of Learning Strategies," "Teacher Behavior and Student Achievement," "Research on Teaching Arts and Aesthetics," and many other empirical research studies on teaching. The *Encyclopedia of Special Education*[15] provides basic information for many disciplines and professions concerned with the education of exceptional children and with their special characteristics, needs, and problems. This three-volume encyclopedia contains more than 2000 topics. Although the arrangement of this book is alphabetical, the various subjects can be grouped conceptually into seven major areas: biographies, educational and psychological tests, interventions and service delivery, handicapping conditions, related services, legal issues, and miscellaneous.

Four editions of *Review of Special Education*[16] as well as *Advances in Special Education*[17] present comprehensive examinations of major fields and brief, more restricted evaluations of special areas in special education. *Review of Educational Research*,[18] a quarterly publication of the American Educational Research Association (AERA), publishes "integrative reviews and interpretation of educational research literature on both substantive and methodological issues." From 1931 until 1970 the review concentrated in sequence on one of 15 broad areas in education in each issue. In June 1970 the periodical abandoned this policy and began publishing unsolicited reviews; since then each issue covers an assortment of topics. In an attempt to provide summaries of research within broad subject areas in the profession, AERA launched publication of the series *Review of Research in Education*,[19] which has been published annually since 1973. This series attempts to identify what research has been done, is being done, and needs to be done in the field. For instance, Volume 13 of *Review of Research in Education* includes reviews of advances in research and in practice in four major areas: early reading instruction, the development of writing skills, the teaching force, and meta-analysis of education experimentation.

Psychological studies play an important role in education research. The *Annual Review of Psychology*,[20] published annually since 1950, employs subject

[15]Reynolds, C. R., and L. Mann (eds.) (1987). *Encyclopedia of Special Education: A Reference for the Education of the Handicapped and Other Exceptional Children and Adults* (3 vols.). New York: John Wiley.
[16]Mann, L., and D. Sabatino (eds.) (1973–1980). *Review of Special Education* (1st–4th eds.) Philadelphia: JSE Press.
[17]Keogh, B. K. (1981). *Advances in Special Education: A Research Annual*. Greenwich, CT: JAI Press.
[18]*Review of Educational Research* (1931–). Washington: American Educational Research Association.
[19]*Review of Research in Education* (1973–). Washington: American Educational Research Association.
[20]*Annual Review of Psychology* (1950–). Palo Alto: Annual Reviews.

specialists to report on and evaluate research literature, spot trends and new developments in all aspects of psychology for each year, and indicate neglected areas. The *Handbook of General Psychology*[21] is another useful review source dealing with the broad areas of history, theory, and methodology; the human organism; perception; learning; language, thought and intelligence; motivation and emotion; personality; and other special areas. It includes bibliographic references of the existing research studies.

// Periodical Indexes, Abstract Journals, and Citation Indexes

Having established a broad base of relevant research, theory, and opinion on a particular topic of interest, one can begin to locate additional material not cited in the basic review sources. Various periodical indexes, abstract journals, and citation indexes enable one to locate this information. These publications, which are issued in successive parts at regular intervals, serve as guides for finding information that is widely dispersed in journals and other sources. The publishers of these indexes employ professional readers who survey and classify papers in published and unpublished sources. These papers are then grouped by subject, sometimes with annotations, so that researchers are presented with a fairly comprehensive and reasonably up-to-date listing of work in their areas.

/ The ERIC Indexes

Two of the most important indexes are produced by the Educational Resources Information Center (ERIC), which was established by the U.S. Office of Education (USOE) to collect, store, and disseminate information on education.

Before the ERIC system was established, reports submitted to USOE by its contractors and grantees received an initial scattered distribution and disappeared, as did reports from other sources. ERIC was intended to correct this chaotic situation, to collect and preserve unpublished "fugitive" materials of interest to educators, and to make this store of information available to the public.

The ERIC system, now funded by the National Institute of Education (NIE), gathers, evaluates, indexes, and abstracts information for inclusion in the ERIC indexes through a network of 16 clearinghouses located at various universities and professional organizations across the country and a central processing facility. Each clearinghouse is responsible for a specific educational area. A guide entitled *Directory of ERIC Information Service Providers*[22]

[21]Wolman, B. B. (1973). *Handbook of General Psychology*. Englewood Cliffs, NJ: Prentice-Hall.
[22]Brandhorst, T., and J. Eustace (eds.) (1986). *Directory of ERIC Information Service Providers*. Washington: U.S. Government Printing Office.

lists these clearinghouses and every organization that provides its users and clients with access to the ERIC database and its related resources.

The three most important periodicals produced by ERIC are *Current Index to Journals in Education (CIJE)*,[23] *Resources in Education (RIE)*,[24] and *Exceptional Child Education Resources (ECER)*.[25] A carefully developed system of indexing is used for providing access to ERIC documents. This system is described in the *Thesaurus of ERIC Descriptors*,[26] which is available in most libraries.

/ Current Index to Journals in Education

The monthly journal *Current Index to Journals in Education (CIJE)* is compiled from the work of the specialists of the ERIC clearinghouses. Articles from over 700 journals are classified and indexed according to the system developed in the ERIC thesaurus. Over 350,000 articles are indexed in *CIJE,* and approximately 18,000 are added each year.

CIJE is divided into four sections: (1) subject index, (2) author index, (3) main entry section, and (4) journal contents index. One can find articles of interest by first looking in the subject index for the titles and numbers of relevant articles, then using these numbers to find the entries in the main entry section. If you cannot find your topic of interest in the subject index, look for synonyms for the topic. The vocabulary of the ERIC thesaurus is deliberately limited to provide a more systematic indexing system. The separate author index is useful to those wishing to find the work of a particular researcher. The journal contents index indicates the journals covered and the contents of each issue.

Figure 3.1 is a typical article description taken from the main entry section, with an explanation of its various parts, as provided by *CIJE* to illustrate the type of information in each entry.

The annotation is particularly useful because it gives a brief description of the article. Note that in the example in Figure 3.1 the title alone gives only a partial idea of what the article is about. Before January 1970, when *CIJE* began including annotations, researchers endured extensive frustration in their search for articles whose titles were misleading or insufficiently revealing and that on inspection proved to be unrelated to the topic of interest. If the title of an article is considered sufficient to convey the main thrust of the article, the abstractors do not include an annotation. Publication of *CIJE* was begun in 1969. The journal is cumulated semiannually and annually.

An efficient approach to the use of *CIJE* falls into six stages:

---

[23]*Current Index to Journals in Education* (1969–). Phoenix: Oryx Press (1979–).
[24]*Resources in Education* (1968–). Washington: U.S. Government Printing Office.
[25]*Exceptional Child Education Resources* (1969–). Reston, VA: Council for Exceptional Children.
[26]Houston, J. E. (ed.) (1987). *Thesaurus of ERIC Descriptors* (11th ed.). Phoenix: Oryx Press.

FIGURE 3.1 Example of a *CIJE* Entry

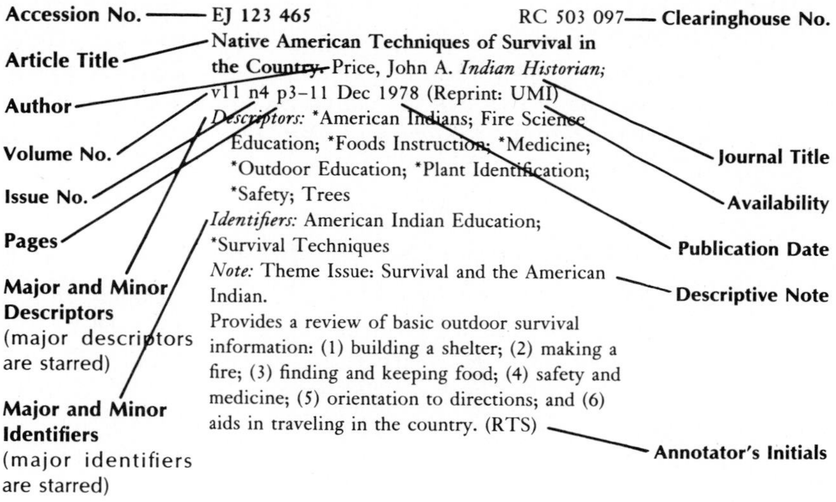

Accession No. ——— EJ 123 465   RC 503 097—— Clearinghouse No.

Article Title — Native American Techniques of Survival in
the Country—Price, John A. *Indian Historian;*

Author — v11 n4 p3–11 Dec 1978 (Reprint: UMI)

Descriptors: *American Indians; Fire Science

Volume No. — Education; *Foods Instruction; *Medicine;   — Journal Title
*Outdoor Education; *Plant Identification;

Issue No. — *Safety; Trees   — Availability

Identifiers: American Indian Education;

Pages — *Survival Techniques   — Publication Date

Note: Theme Issue: Survival and the American

Major and Minor Indian.   — Descriptive Note
Descriptors
(major descriptors   Provides a review of basic outdoor survival
are starred)   information: (1) building a shelter; (2) making a
fire; (3) finding and keeping food; (4) safety and
medicine; (5) orientation to directions; and (6)

Major and Minor   aids in traveling in the country. (RTS)
Identifiers
(major identifiers   — Annotator's Initials
are starred)

1. Determine the key words under which articles relevant to your study might be listed. These key words will typically include the population and the variables you have identified in your problem statement.
2. Check the *Thesaurus of ERIC Descriptors* to find which of your key words are used as descriptors. You may need to find synonyms for the key words you have listed.
3. Begin your search with the most recent issues of *CIJE* and work back through earlier issues.
4. Copy from *CIJE* the entire reference given for any title that may be useful. This procedure simplifies the task of finding the original articles.
5. Search out the articles in their journals. If your library does not have the journal, the librarian may be able to obtain a photocopy of the article through interlibrary loan.
6. Read the abstract first—if one accompanies the journal article—to determine whether it will be useful to read the entire article. If there is no abstract, start with the summary and conclusion sections.

/ Exceptional Child Education Resources

This quarterly publication (formerly *Exceptional Child Education Abstracts*) contains abstracts stored in the computer file of the Council for Exceptional Children Information Center as part of the ERIC program.

Abstracts related to education of the handicapped and gifted children and youth are indexed. Its arrangement is similar to *CIJE* and *RIE*. Indexes were cumulative within each volume through 1975; beginning in 1976 there are cumulative author, title, and subject indexes in the final issue of the year. The coverage of *ECER* includes books, journal articles, government documents, and so on.

/ Resources in Education

Abstracts of research reports from sources other than journals are indexed and published monthly by ERIC in *Resources in Education* (*RIE*). A semiannual cumulative edition of the index sections is also published. Each clearinghouse collects materials related to its field of specialization and then catalogs the documents and prepares indexes and abstracts. The original documents, together with the abstracts prepared by each clearinghouse, are sent on a regular basis to the Processing Facility, where they become part of the central database on which users of the ERIC system can draw. The Processing Facility is responsible for collecting the input of all clearinghouses and publishing the combined abstracts monthly in *RIE*.

The sources covered by the specialized clearinghouses include reports of all federally funded educational research, abstracts, pamphlets, curriculum guides, significant papers from the proceedings of learned societies and institutes, bibliographies, exemplary course-related materials, teachers' guides and program outlines, as well as various other research proposals and project reports. With such a far-ranging coverage it is clear that the documents in the ERIC collections are of vital interest to practitioners as well as researchers in education. Over 350,000 documents are now included, and the collection is growing at a rate of about 18,000 documents per year.

Each abstract is assigned its own accession number for the purpose of identification and for ordering copies of the original documents. Three indexes are provided: author, institution, and subject. Using the appropriate index, one finds the titles of documents and their accession numbers, which one then uses to locate the individual abstracts.

The procedure for using *RIE* is similar to that used for *CIJE*. One typically begins with the most recent copy and works backward, looking under the subject or subjects of interest.

Figure 3.2 is an example of an entry in the main entry section of *RIE*.

/ The ERIC Document Collection

Microfiche copies of most of the original documents can be obtained as required, or a standing order may be placed with ERIC to receive all documents as they become available. Many libraries have such an arrangement

FIGURE 3.2 Example of an RIE Entry

ERIC Accession Number— identification number sequentially assigned to documents as they are processed

Author(s)

Title

Organization where document originated

Date Published

Contract or Grant Number

Alternate source for obtaining document

Language of Document— documents written entirely in English are not designated, although "English" is carried in their computerized records

Publication Type—broad categories indicating the form or organization of the document, as contrasted to its subject matter. The category name is followed by the category code.

ERIC Document Reproduction Service (EDRS) Availability—"MF" means microfiche; "PC" means reproduced paper copy. When described as "Document Not Available from EDRS," alternate sources are cited above. Prices are subject to change; for latest price code schedule, see section "How to Order ERIC Documents" in the most recent issue of *RIE*

ED 654 321   CE 123 456
Smith, John D.   *Johnson, Jane*
Career Planning for Women
Central Univ., Chicago, IL
Spons Agency—National Inst. of Education (ED), Washington, DC
Report No.—CU-2081-S
Pub Date—May 83
Contract—NIE-C-83-0001
Note—129p.; Paper presented at the National Conference on Career Education (3rd, Chicago, IL, May 15–17, 1983).
Available from—Campus Bookstore, 123 College Ave., Chicago, IL 60690 ($3.25).
Language—English, French
Pub Type—Speeches/Meeting Papers (150)
EDRS Price—MF01/PC06 plus postage.
Descriptors—Career Guidance, *Career Planning, Careers, *Demand Occupations, *Employed Women, *Employment Opportunities, Females, Labor Force, Labor Market, *Labor Needs, Occupational Aspiration, Occupations
Identifiers—Consortium of States, *National Occupational Competency Testing Institute Women's opportunities for employment will be directly related to their level of skill and experience and also to the labor market demands through the remainder of the decade. The number of workers needed for all major occupational categories is expected to increase by about one-fifth between 1980 and 1990, but the growth rate will vary by occupational group. Professional and technical workers are expected to have the highest predicted rate (39 percent), followed by service workers (35 percent), clerical workers (26 percent), sales workers (24 percent), craft workers and supervisors (20 percent), managers and administrators (15 percent), and operatives (11 percent). This publication contains a brief discussion and employment information concerning occupations for professional and technical workers, managers and administrators, skilled trades, sales workers, clerical workers, and service workers. (SB)

Clearinghouse Accession Number

Sponsoring Agency— agency responsible for initiating, funding, and managing the research project

Report Number—assigned by originator

Descriptive Note (pagination first)

Descriptors—subject terms found in the *Thesaurus of ERIC Descriptors* that characterize substantive content. Only the major terms, preceded by an asterisk, are printed in the subject index

Identifiers—additional identifying terms not found in the *Thesaurus*. Only the major terms, preceded by an asterisk, are printed in the subject index

Informative Abstract

Abstractor's Initials

with ERIC, thus making available to their users the entire document collection in a convenient location.

Most documents are available in two forms, hard copy and microfiche. In most libraries microfiche is preferred, as it is less expensive and requires less storage space. The entire ERIC collection in microfiche occupies the space of a few file cabinets. A machine called a microfiche reader is used to enlarge the images of the pages onto a built-in screen and to allow the user to proceed from page image to page image. Most libraries and universities have such equipment available. The cost of each ERIC document is listed in *RIE* for both microfiche and hard copy.

All projects funded by the USOE are automatically included in the ERIC system, and complete copies of reports of these projects are available through ERIC. When publication is first made under copyright privileges, reference is made to the source; however, copies are usually not available through ERIC. The same is true for books and other materials prepared for sale. ERIC is invaluable to the field of education because it collects and abstracts, from a wide range of sources, relevant material for educational researchers, much of which was previously almost impossible to obtain.

The ERIC clearinghouses prepare annotated bibliographies on selected topics. Before preparing your own bibliography, it is a good idea to write to the clearinghouse dealing with your field of interest to see if their staff already has a bibliography that will be of value to you in preparing your own.

A more complete description of the ERIC system and how to use it will be found in the booklet *ERIC: What It Can Do for You, How to Use It,* which is available in many libraries.[27]

The clearinghouses of the ERIC network wish to make their collections as comprehensive as possible and ask educators to submit relevant materials. If you have prepared a report, speech, or paper that you would like to have considered for national dissemination through ERIC, send a copy to the ERIC Processing and Reference Facility, 4833 Rugby Avenue, Bethesda, MD 20814 or to the individual clearinghouse responsible for collecting in the relevant subject area.

/ Computer Access to the ERIC System

A generation ago a thorough search of 500 journals and 100,000 other documents for material relevant to a given research problem was a task of major proportions. Today computerized access to the ERIC system makes it possible to conduct such searches by means of a personal computer or telephone communication.

---

[27]Brown, J. W., M. K. Setts, and J. Yarborough (1977). *ERIC: What It Can Do for You, How to Use It.* Stanford, CA: ERIC Clearinghouse on Information Sources.

The contents of *CIJE* and *RIE* are available on computer tapes, and computer searches of the ERIC system can be made with these tapes. For example, to identify journal articles and *RIE* documents that deal with the use of programmed materials to teach French, the computer is instructed to identify all documents and journal articles that have been given both the descriptor *programmed instruction* and the descriptor *French*. Some computer programs print out only the ED and EJ accession numbers, but most programs print out complete *CIJE* entries (see Figure 3.1) and complete *RIE* entries (see Figure 3.2) for every article and document that has both descriptors.

Over 900 institutions have the ERIC tapes and can run online computer searches. Most of the state departments of education have the ERIC tapes and will run free computer searches for educators within their state. Most of these departments also have information retrieval specialists who will work with clients to translate general requests for help into the form needed for the computer to retrieve the desired information from the ERIC system. Many universities provide similar services to their students and other users.

Some libraries also have ERIC and other databases on CD-ROM (Compact Disc–Read-Only Memory), a new method for accessing ERIC and other databases. Silver Platter[28] has published the complete ERIC database from 1966 to the present on three CD-ROM discs. Each record contains the bibliographic citation, abstract, and descriptors. Unlike the printed ERIC indexes, these CD-ROM discs can be carried in a small briefcase with plenty of room to spare. To use CD-ROM requires a personal computer with 512 K of memory and a CD-ROM disc drive. In addition to the ERIC online database, there are about 500 other databases dealing with various subjects, including *Psychological Abstracts, Dissertation Abstracts International, Sociological Abstracts,* and *Social Sciences Citation Index.* New databases are being produced to the online searching system through vendors almost everyday. *Education Index* is one of the many databases included in the online computer system Wilsonline. This service is also available in many libraries.

A search of the ERIC system is an important step in the quest for related literature, but one *cannot* assume that when this step is finished the quest is completed. Material relevant to one's question may not have entered the ERIC system.

/ Other Periodical Indexes

There are many other periodical indexes in the field of education that are useful for locating up-to-date information on research as well as contemporary opinion in education. One of the standard indexes for the field

---

[28]Silver Platter Information, Inc., 37 Walnut St., Wellesley Hills, MA 02181.

is the *Education Index,*[29] which has been published regularly since 1929 by the H. W. Wilson Company. This index lists articles in about 350 periodicals, yearbooks, bulletins, proceedings, and monographic series. *Education Index* is the best source for locating journal articles prior to the establishment of *Current Index to Journals in Education* in 1969, as well as for very recent articles, as it typically lists articles about six months before *CIJE* does. A disadvantage of the *Education Index* is that it has no annotations.

In addition to these general indexes a number of useful specialized indexes are available to the researcher. *Psychological Abstracts*[30] lists the world's literature in psychology and related disciplines. This index includes books, doctoral dissertations, and periodical articles, with a summary of each, enabling the reader to determine the relevance of the material. *Child Development Abstracts and Bibliography*[31] provides an author and subject approach to the areas of infancy, clinical medicine and public health, developmental and comparative psychology, and experimental psychology, including learning phenomena, personality and educational psychology, and counseling. *Sociology of Education Abstracts,*[32] an international publication, lists by subject and author periodical articles, books, and dissertations in its field, with a summary for each. *Educational Administration Abstracts*[33] provides an author and subject approach to specialized journals in the field of educational administration. *Higher Education Abstracts*[34] (formerly *College Student Personnel Abstracts*) is a compilation of abstracts from journals, conference proceedings, and research reports relating to college students and student services. Topics covered include counseling and housing, financial aid, and testing and measurement. *Social Science Index*[35] lists, by author and subject, journal articles in the social sciences, covering education journals as well as journals from the fields of psychology, sociology, political science, anthropology, law, and economics.

Every discipline has its specialized indexes, such as business education, industrial arts, and medicine, to name only a few. Consulting the basic guides to the literature will give readers the names of the specialized indexes in other fields that they may need.

/ Indexes of Dissertations and Theses

Master's theses and doctoral dissertations are useful sources of information for researchers. In addition to the periodical indexes and abstract

---

[29]*Education Index* (1929–   ). New York: H. W. Wilson.

[30]*Psychological Abstracts* (1927–   ). Lancaster, PA: American Psychological Association.

[31]*Child Development Abstracts and Bibliography* (1927–   ). Lafayette, IN: Purdue University, Society for Research in Child Development.

[32]*Sociology of Education Abstracts* (1965–   ). Abbington, England: Carfax Publishing Co.

[33]*Educational Administration Abstracts* (1966–   ). Beverly Hills: Sage Publications.

[34]*Higher Education Abstracts* (1984–   ). Claremont, CA: Claremont Institute for Administrative Studies.

[35]*Social Sciences Index* (1974–   ). New York: H. W. Wilson.

journals that list some dissertations and theses, such as ERIC's *RIE* and *Psychological Abstracts,* several specialized guides and indexes are very useful.

Comprehensive Dissertation Index[36] attempts to cover all dissertations accepted at U.S. universities during 1961–1972. This index contains 37 volumes in 17 major subject categories, with full bibliographic citations in both the author and subject listings. An annual supplement is published to bring this index up-to-date. *Dissertation Abstracts International* (*DAI*),[37] published monthly, contains abstracts of doctoral dissertations submitted to University Microfilms International by cooperating universities (about 370 in 1984). *DAI* is divided into three sections: humanities and social sciences, the sciences and engineering, and European universities. Computerized searches of *DAI* are available through several major online database vendors, including Dialog,[38] BRS,[39] and CompuServe.[40] Most libraries provide online database searching to assist researchers.

Another publication, similar to *DAI,* is *American Doctoral Dissertations.*[41] It consolidates into one list the dissertations for which doctoral degrees were granted in the United States and Canada during the academic year covered, as well as those available on microfilm from University Microfilms. It includes a number of dissertations that are not included in *DAI. American Doctoral Dissertations* is arranged by subject category and institution and has an author index, but no abstracts are provided.

Black's *Guide to Lists of Master's Theses*[42] contains two main sections: lists of master's theses in special fields, with annotations, and lists of master's theses of specific institutions. *Masters Abstracts: Abstracts of Selected Masters Theses on Microfilm*[43] contains abstracts of a selected list of master's essays, from various U.S. universities and colleges, available on microfilm. Silvey's *Master's Theses in Education*[44] is an annual listing of master's theses in education from U.S. colleges and universities. For each thesis listed, bibliographical information is given, but abstracts are not included.

/ Social Sciences Citation Index (SSCI)

A relevant article found by consulting one of these indexes will itself provide references to earlier work in the area. When one has found relevant and important articles, a citation index can be used to move forward in time. For example, if you have read a particularly useful article published in 1976,

[36]*Comprehensive Dissertation Index* (1861–1972). (37 vols.) Ann Arbor: University Microfilms.
[37]*Dissertation Abstracts International* (1938–   ). Ann Arbor: University Microfilms.
[38]Dialog Information Services, Inc., 3460 Hillview Avenue, Palo Alto, CA 94304.
[39]BRS Information Technologies, 1200 Route 7, Latham, NY 12110.
[40]CompuServe Information Service, Inc., 5000 Arlington Centre Boulevard, Columbus, OH 43220.
[41]*American Doctoral Dissertations* (1957–   ). Ann Arbor: University Microfilms.
[42]Black, D. (ed.) (1965). *Guide to Lists of Master's Theses.* Chicago: American Library Association.
[43]*Masters Abstracts: Abstracts of Selected Masters Theses on Microfilm* (1962–1985); *Masters Abstracts International* (1986–   ). Ann Arbor: University Microfilms.
[44]Silvey, H. M. (1951–   ). *Master's Theses in Education.* Cedar Falls, IA: Research Publications.

through subsequent indexes you can identify articles that cite the article of interest in their bibliography. Many of these articles will describe continuations, expansions, or modifications of the original work of interest.

Social Sciences Citation Index (*SSCI*),[45] published in three volumes a year by the Institute for Scientific Information, can tell you which authors have been cited during the year in all areas of social science, including education, and what has been written in various areas, with the necessary bibliographic information for both cited and citing authors. This information is made available by way of four indexes:

1. The *Source Index* provides an alphabetical list of all authors published during the year, with complete bibliographic information, including an alphabetical list of the references provided by the source author's bibliography. This index is cross-referenced to secondary authors.

2. The *Citation Index* takes the names cited by the authors in the *Source Index* and presents them alphabetically so that the researcher can find where a particular paper has been cited. Bibliographic references are provided for each cited item. A corporate-author citation index and an index for anonymously authored papers are also provided. This index enables one to follow ideas forward in time.

3. The *Permuterm Subject Index* takes every significant word and pairs it with every other significant word in each title. Each word in a title is then listed as a primary term combined with each of the other terms as coterms. An alphabetical listing of the names of authors whose titles contain the words is provided for each pair of primary term and coterm. Bibliographic information can then be found for each author in the *Source Index*.

4. The *Corporate Address Index* is an alphabetical listing of organizations to which authors publishing during the year are affiliated. Under each corporate entry is a list of authors with complete bibliographic information.

// Government Publications

The federal government, a major source of education information, sponsors more research, conducts more surveys, and collects more statistics of all kinds than any other organization in the United States. The Department of Education, as well as the National Center for Educational Statistics, disseminates a vast number of publications, including research reports, surveys, administrative actions, and descriptive programs.

---

[45] *Social Sciences Citation Index* (1973–). Philadelphia: Institute for Scientific Information.

For locating specific U.S. government publications, the *Monthly Catalog of U.S. Government Publications*[46] is the prime index to consult. It includes a main section that lists, by agency, documents published and title, author, subject, and title-keyword indexes. Annual compilations by title and subject were included in the December issue until 1975; since 1976 there are six-month compilations. There are also five-year cumulative indexes for faster searching back through the years.

Publications of state departments of education and other state agencies can be located through the *Monthly Checklist of State Publications.*[47]

// Test Sources

In conducting research a test or measuring device is often required. Buros's *Mental Measurement Yearbooks*[48] are the major reference sources that list and critically review tests. These books are specifically designed to assist users in education, psychology, and industry to make more intelligent use of standardized tests. Each yearbook is arranged in the same pattern and is meant to supplement rather than supersede the earlier volumes. Tests are grouped by subject, and descriptions of each test are followed by critical reviews and references to studies in which the test has been used. Each volume has cross-references to reviews, excerpts, and bibliographic references in earlier volumes. The volumes include aptitude and achievement tests in various subject areas, personality and vocational tests, and intelligence tests. Complete information is provided for each test, including cost and ordering instructions. *Tests in Print III*[49] serves as an index and supplement to the first eight *Mental Measurement Yearbooks.* Buros also organized the material in the *Mental Measurement Yearbooks* into specialized monographs on tests of personality, reading, intelligence, vocational and business skills, English, foreign languages, mathematics, science, and social studies.

The Buros Institute also offers an online computer database, with monthly updates through BRS Information Technologies. Full-text features allow users to search and print the complete text of each document or to browse and print selected portions of retrieved records. It is an excellent information retrieval system for keeping up-to-date in between yearbooks.

A standard reference work *Tests: A Comprehensive Reference for Assessments in Psychology, Education and Business*[50] and its supplement includes

---

[46]U.S. Superintendent of Documents (1895–). *Monthly Catalog of U.S. Government Publications.* Washington: U.S. Government Printing Office.

[47]U.S. Library of Congress, Exchange and Gift Division (1910–). *Monthly Checklist of State Publications.* Washington: U.S. Government Printing Office.

[48]Buros, O. K. (ed.) (1938–). *Mental Measurement Yearbooks.* Lincoln: Buros Institute of Mental Measurements, University of Nebraska.

[49]Mitchell, J. V., Jr. (ed.) (1983). *Tests in Print III: An Index to Tests, Test Reviews, and the Literature on Specific Tests.* Lincoln: Buros Institute of Mental Measurements, University of Nebraska.

[50]Sweetland, R. C., and D. J. Keyser (eds.) (1983). *Tests: A Comprehensive Reference for Assessments in Psychology, Education and Business.* Kansas City, MO: Test Corporation of America.

over 3000 tests available in English. Each test has been given a primary classification and described in detail in one of the sections and may be cross-referenced in a second category.

Since 1984, *Test Critiques*[51] has provided general descriptions and critiques of measurement instruments. A useful cumulative subject index of tests by type of variables is also included. Specialized guides to tests include *Measures of Social Psychological Attitudes*,[52] *Reading Tests and Reviews*,[53] *A Guide to 65 Diagnostic Tests for Special Education*,[54] *An International Directory of Spatial Tests*,[55] *Assessing the Learning Disabled: Selected Instruments*,[56] *Tests in Microfiche: Annotated Index*,[57] and *The Educational Testing Service Test Collection Catalog*.[58]

Information about tests may also be found in periodical indexes, including *Current Index to Journals in Education (CIJE)*, *Education Index*, *Exceptional Child Education Resources (ECER)*, and *Psychological Abstracts*, where tests are listed under their specific name in the subject index. You can also search under such subject headings as "Tests" and "Test Reviews."

// Computer Searching

Most academic libraries provide computer searching under such names as computer searching, online database searching, computer reference services, and the like. In most libraries this service is provided by appointment, and walk-in service is sometimes restricted. Some libraries may require your presence when the information specialist is conducting the computer searching. This not only offers you an opportunity to view the sample results of information retrieved, it also gives you a chance to give additional input and refine your search strategies.

Many of the sources cited in this chapter have been incorporated into online databases, including *Education Index*, ERIC indexes, *Exceptional Child Education Resources*, *Psychological Abstracts*, *Social Sciences Citation Index*, *Dissertation Abstracts International*, and *Mental Measurements Yearbooks*. In addition, there are other databases, such as the Acquired Immune Deficiency Syndrome Database (AIDS), Medical Science Research databases, Resources

---

[51]Keyser, D. J., and R. C. Sweetland (eds.) (1984–   ). *Test Critiques* (Vol. 1–   ). Kansas City, MO: Test Corporation of America.

[52]Robinson, J. P., and P. R. Shaver (1973). *Measures of Social Psychological Attitudes*. Ann Arbor: Survey Research Center, Institute for Social Research.

[53]Buros, O. K. (ed.) (1968–1975). *Reading Tests and Reviews* (2 vols.). Lincoln: Buros Institute of Mental Measurements, University of Nebraska.

[54]Compton, C. (1980). *A Guide to 65 Diagnostic Tests for Special Education*. Belmont, CA: Fearon Education.

[55]Eliot, J., and I. Macfarlane (1983). *An International Directory of Spatial Tests*. New York: Humanities Press.

[56]Mauser, A. J. (1977). *Assessing the Learning Disabled: Selected Instruments* (2d ed.). Navato, CA: Academic Therapy Publications.

[57]*Tests in Microfiche: Annotated Index* (1975–   ). Princeton: Educational Testing Service.

[58]*The Educational Testing Service Test Collection Catalog* (1986–   ). Phoenix: Oryx Press.

in Vocational Education (RIVE), Educational Testing Service Test Collection (ETSF), and *Sociological Abstracts* (*SOCA*). For detailed listings of most of the databases available, consult the two database catalogs published by Dialog Information Services and BRS Information Technologies.[59] Many institutions employ professional librarians who are adept in online database searching and who can assist you in using the various services.

Among the advantages of computer researching are: (1) Time Saving: When there are several synonymous or analogous terms that could be used for the concept(s) involved, in minutes the computer can retrieve and print information that may help you bypass hours or even days of a manual search; (2) Currency: Online databases generally are more up-to-date than printed indexes. Most databases are updated weekly or biweekly; (3) Linkage: When the research topic involves the combination of two or more subjects, the computer can search more than one topic at a time; (4) Precision: When a subject cannot be easily identified in printed indexes, the computer may provide access to materials in a variety of ways: titles, keywords, subject codes, or additional subject headings that conventional indexes do not offer. Online computer searching can also limit your results by certain parameters, such as date and type of publication, author's name, or language; (5) Unique Sources: Some databases provide information that is not available in printed sources; and (6) Sorting: Online searches can sort retrieved information by publication date (in descending or ascending order) or alphabetically by author or by title.

For most researchers computer searching is the method of choice. In a "manual" search one must examine numerous periodical indexes for a particular topic, follow it through the indexes, and find a few relevant entries that combine the selected term with another of interest. Computer searching, however, can search for many topics at the same time and combine them, using logical concepts known as Boolean operators (from the logic system developed by the nineteenth-century English mathematician George Boole).

Figure 3.3 illustrates ways different concepts or terms can be linked by using Boolean logical operators.

A AND B asks for those items that have *both* key terms. For example, in March 1989 the ERIC system had 1047 items with the key term *adult students* and 2502 items with the key term *mathematics education.* Using the Silver Platter program, four items that have both key terms were identified.

A OR B asks for those items that have *either or both* ("nonexclusive or") of the terms. In the same example a request for *mathematics education* or *mathematics achievement* would yield those that have either or both key terms.

---

[59]*1988 Dialog Database Catalog* (1988). Palo Alto: Dialog Information Services, Inc.; *1988 BRS Database Catalog* (1988). Latham, NY: BRS Information Technologies.

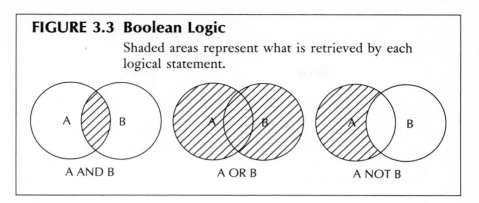

FIGURE 3.3 Boolean Logic

Shaded areas represent what is retrieved by each logical statement.

| A AND B | A OR B | A NOT B |

A typical search will use both these strategies. An adult educator interested in mathematics education would use OR statements to include various key terms that might cover the domain of adult education and OR statements to include various statements that might cover the domain of mathematics education, together with an AND statement to link the two domains (factors).

Adult Education Factors	Mathematics Education Factors
adult basic education	mathematics achievement
OR	OR
adult education	mathematics education
OR	OR
adult learning	mathematics skills
OR	
adult programs	
OR	
adult students	
OR	
continuing education	
OR	
nontraditional students	

Using these factors, the Silver Platter program revealed that 15,316 items had one or more of the key terms in the first factor and 3009 had one or more of the key terms in the second factor. Only 94 items had at least one key term in both factors, of which 73 were ERIC documents and 21 were articles in journals covered by *CIJE*. (All of this information was obtained from the computer in less than four minutes!)

At this stage, one can choose to further restrict the number of items by such strategies as introducing another factor, excluding items that are not in English, or limiting the search to specific dates. Or one can have various pieces of information about each item displayed on the computer screen in order to decide which are relevant. Finally, one can have this information printed out for the remaining items. Figure 3.4 reproduces a printout for one of the 21 journal articles the search identified, including the ERIC document number, author, title, journal (including title, volume and part numbers, page numbers, and date), the descriptors, and the abstract.

The previous example illustrates the most common uses of Boolean logic. Other operators are sometimes employed. For instance, NOT could ask for "adult education" items that do not also have the descriptor "adult basic education."

// Dictionaries

Almost every academic discipline can be said to have its own specialized vocabulary. It is the function of a subject dictionary to explain briefly the words, whether terms or names, that make up a particular subject's jargon. There are several basic dictionaries in the field of education. Good's *Dictionary of Education,*[60] is a scholarly dictionary of words and terms that have special meaning in the educational field. Nearly 200 coordinators, associates, and reviewers are listed in the third edition, which contains over 33,000 entries. Educational terms used in Canada and in England and Wales are

---

FIGURE 3.4 Example of an ERIC-search Printout

```
AN: EJ293655
AU: Dolan,-Lawrence
TI: Affective Characteristics of the Adult Learner: A Study of Mas-
tery-Based Instruction.
JN: Community/Junior-College-Quarterly-of-Research-and-Practice;
v7 n4 p367-78 Jul-Sep 1983
DE: Affective-Behavior; Community-Colleges; Remedial-Mathematics; Two-
Year-Colleges
DE:  *Adult-Learning;  *Mastery-Learning;  *Mathematics-Achievement;
*Mathematics-Instruction; *Reentry-Students; *Student Characteristics
AB: Presents an investigation of the benefits of mastery learning
strategies for adults with mathematics skill deficiencies. Examines
which student types benefit most from mastery learning, centering on
affective characteristics. Demonstrates that students with low self-
concept, control, and instructional mastery skills had higher achieve-
ment in mastery than nonmastery classes. (DMM)
```

---

[60]Good, C. V. (ed.) (1973). *Dictionary of Education* (3d ed.). New York: McGraw-Hill.

defined in separate sections at the end of the dictionary. The *International Dictionary of Education*[61] includes more than 10,000 entries covering expressions and terms, international organizations, major national institutions and associations, educators, and the like.

The *Dictionary of Education*,[62] edited by Hill, provides brief essays on 15 areas of education followed by an alphabetical listing of terms (primarily British terms). The first volume of the *International Encyclopedia of Higher Education*[63] also provides brief definitions for acronyms and a glossary of terms. In the area of special education, Bush's *Dictionary of Reading and Learning Disabilities*[64] and Davis's *Educator's Resource Guide to Special Education: Terms-Laws-Tests-Organizations*,[65] and *A Dictionary of Special Education Terms*[66] are three practical basic dictionaries.

// Interlibrary Loan

Interlibrary loan services can also be extremely helpful. If you find references to research studies in periodicals, books, or theses that are not available in the library you are using, it may be possible to borrow those materials from other libraries through interlibrary loan service.

/// ORGANIZING THE RELATED LITERATURE

Once one is satisfied that a reasonably comprehensive study of the literature in the field has been carried out, one can proceed to the task of organizing it. A useful approach is to arrange the studies by topic and determine how each of these topics relates to one's own study.

The literature should be presented in such a way as to justify carrying out one's study by showing what is known and what remains to be investigated in the topic of concern. The hypotheses provide a framework for such organization. Like an explorer proposing an expedition, the researcher maps out the known territory and points the way to the unknown territory to be explored. If the study includes several facets or investigates more than a single hypothesis, the organization process is done separately for each one.

[61]Page, G. P., J. B. Thomas, and A. R. Marshall (1977). *International Dictionary of Education*. New York: Nicholas Publishing.

[62]Hill, P. J. (ed.) (1982). *A Dictionary of Education*. Boston: Kegan Paul.

[63]Knowles, A. S. (ed.) (1977). *The International Encyclopedia of Higher Education* (10 vols.). San Francisco: Jossey-Bass.

[64]Bush, C. L., and R. C. Andrews (1978). *Dictionary of Reading and Learning Disabilities*. Los Angeles: Western Psychological Services.

[65]Davis, W. E. (1980). *Educator's Resource Guide to Special Education: Terms-Laws-Tests-Organizations*. Boston: Allyn & Bacon.

[66]Moore, B. C., W. Abraham, and C. R. Laing (1980). *A Dictionary of Special Education Terms*. Springfield, IL: Thomas.

One should avoid the temptation to present the literature as a series of abstracts. Rather, it should be presented in such a way as to lay a systematic foundation for the study.

It is almost inevitable that a number of the reports one has carefully studied and included in one's notes will, on reflection, prove to be only peripherally related to the topic. It is neither necessary nor desirable to include in a proposal every study encountered in a search through the literature. One's readers will not be impressed by mere quantity. Relevance and organization of the material are of prime importance.

The researcher who fails to approach the task of assembling the related literature in a systematic manner from the beginning can become very disorganized. The following suggestions may be of assistance.

1. *Begin with the most recent studies in your field and then work backward through earlier volumes.* One obvious advantage of this approach is that you start with studies that have already incorporated the thoughts and findings of previous research. Earlier misunderstandings have been corrected, and unprofitable approaches have been avoided. Another advantage is that these studies will include references to earlier works and, therefore, will direct you to sources you might not otherwise encounter. Obviously, limits must be set to the process of gathering related research. On the one hand, laying meaningful groundwork for a study entails including all the important works in the field. On the other hand, devoting excessive time to this endeavor could result in boring the readers of your own report with superfluous detail. Make sure that the related literature serves, but does not dominate, your own work.

2. *Read the abstract or summary sections of a report first to determine whether it is relevant to your question.* Doing so can save much time that might be wasted reading unhelpful articles.

3. *Before taking notes, skim the report quickly to find those sections that are related to your question—*another way to save reading time.

4. *Make notes directly on file cards, as they are easier to sort and organize than sheets of paper, backs of envelopes, and so on.* Many prefer 4-by-6-inch file cards, which provide a reasonable space for notes but are small enough to fit in a pocket or book bag.

5. *Write out a complete bibliographic reference for each work.* If you know which style manual will be used in the finished report, you can save time by using that reference form while taking notes. Add the library call number to facilitate finding the work again, should it be necessary.

6. *To facilitate sorting and organizing, do not put more than one reference on each card.* It is not possible to arrange your references alphabetically or in any other way unless you record them singly.

7. *Be sure to indicate which parts of the notes are direct quotations from the author and which are your own paraphrases.* Failure to make this distinction

TABLE 3.1. Sources of Related Literature in Education

Source	Content
Child Development Abstracts and Bibliography	Abstracts of journal articles in the field of child development.
Current Index to Journals in Education	Titles, authors, and journal citations of journal articles related to education, with annotations where needed. Classification by subject, by author, and by journal. No abstracts.
DATRIX II	Computerized sorting system for finding relevant dissertations listed in *Dissertation Abstracts International.*
Dissertation Abstracts International	Abstracts of doctoral dissertations in the United States, Canada, and Europe.
Education Index	Titles, authors, and journal citations of journal articles related to education. Indexed by subject and title. No abstracts.
Encyclopedia of Educational Research	Summaries and evaluations of research in education, published at the end of each decade.
ERIC Microfiche Collection	Complete documents, the abstracts of which are in *Resources in Education.*
Exceptional Child Education Resources	Abstracts of journal articles and other sources in special education.
Mental Measurement Yearbooks	Information and evaluations of commercially available tests.
Monthly Catalog of Government Publications	Subject listing of U.S. federal government publications.
Psychological Abstracts	Abstracts of journal articles in psychology.
Readers' Guide to Periodical Literature	Titles, authors, and journal citations of articles in popular journals. Indexed by subject and title. No abstracts.
Resources in Education	Abstracts of research reports and other documents acquired by ERIC clearinghouses.
Review of Educational Research	Reviews on various topics in each quarterly issue.
Social Sciences Citation Index	Bibliographic information for cited authors and topics.
Test Critiques	Reviews of measurement instruments, including general description, practical applications/uses, critiques, and technical aspects.
Tests in Print III	Index and supplement to the first eight *Mental Measurement Yearbooks.*
Thesaurus of ERIC Descriptors	System for classifying and indexing ERIC documents.

can lead to inadvertent plagiarism. It is also wise to clearly separate an author's evaluation of his research from your own.

8. *If online database searching has been conducted, keep your search strategies on file.* This information will help you to retrieve precise information and to reduce your cost in case an update is needed.

/// SUMMARY

If the researcher covers the avenues to information in the area as suggested, a reasonably complete picture of the place the study occupies within the field should result.

Table 3.1 summarizes the most important sources and contents of related literature in education.

// Key Concepts

bibliographic guides
Boolean logic
computer searching
databases
ERIC system

guides to government documents
indexes to dissertations and theses
periodic reviews
specialized dictionaries
test sources

/// EXERCISES

1. State three important roles of related literature in a research project.

2. Compare the merits of *CIJE* and *Education Index*.

3. What is DATRIX II and how might it be useful in research projects?

4. At what point during the research project should the researcher survey the literature and research concerning the chosen question?

5. What is an annotation?

6. Explain the importance of Buros's *Mental Measurement Yearbooks* in locating test sources.

7. Why is ERIC such a useful source to consult in a search of the literature?

8. Explain the use of *Social Sciences Citation Index* in a literature search.

9. What are the typical steps employing the ERIC system in a literature review?

10. What are the advantages of using computerized access to professional literature databases?

11. How is Boolean logic used in accessing databases?

12. Which of the sources of related literature in Table 3.1 are available in libraries that are accessible to you?

/// ANSWERS

1. A knowledge of related research enables the researcher to define the frontiers of the field, place the question in perspective, and avoid unintentional replication of previous studies.

2. *Education Index* provides a means of locating articles published from 1929 to the present. *CIJE* covers more journals and provides annotations, whereas *Education Index* lists articles more quickly than *CIJE*.

3. DATRIX II is a computer search service for dissertations offered by University Microfilms. It is an efficient means of finding dissertations on topics related to the researcher's area of interest.

4. The researcher surveys the related literature as soon as the research problem has been selected and delineated.

5. An annotation is a brief description of an article. It can aid the researcher in selecting articles on his topic.

6. They provide the most comprehensive listing and description of standardized tests available. The critical reviews of the tests assist one in selecting an appropriate test.

7. ERIC is very comprehensive in its coverage of the many subject areas in education. Each of the clearinghouses is assigned to a specific subject area to collect and input information and materials into the system. ERIC also provides coverage of a wide variety of materials: research studies and projects, curriculum guides, significant papers from proceedings of learned societies and institutes, bibliographies, and course-related materials. Many of these materials are unpublished and would not be available anywhere else. ERIC not only lists the materials but also provides most of them on microfiche.

8. Through the *Citation Index* one can pursue a line of inquiry forward in time by locating articles that have cited a particular work. Its *Permuterm Subject Index* enables one to locate articles with specific pairs of words in their titles.

9. a. Identify the key words in your study.
   b. Find your key words or their synonyms in the *Thesaurus of ERIC Descriptors*.

    c. Employ a computer-access program to find which journal articles and ERIC documents have your key terms or descriptors, *or* hand-search through *CIJE* and *RIE* to find accession numbers of articles and documents with your key terms. Begin with the most recent issues of *CIJE* and *RIE* and work backward in time.

    d. Read abstracts or annotations to eliminate articles and documents of no interest.

    e. Locate remaining articles and ERIC documents.

    f. Read abstract, summary, and conclusions first.

10. Computer searchers can rapidly search database systems. They are particularly useful for identifying articles and other materials with specific combinations of key words. They can access in a variety of ways, for example, title, date, authors, key words, or subject codes. Online databases are more up to date than printed indexes, and some include information not available elsewhere.

11. An A-AND-B search will identify only documents with both descriptors. An A-OR-B search will identify all documents with either descriptor. An A-NOT-B search will identify all documents with the A descriptor *unless* they also include the B descriptor.

12. Answers will vary.

CHAPTER 4

The Hypothesis

INSTRUCTIONAL OBJECTIVES

After studying this chapter, the student will be able to
1. Define *hypothesis*
2. State the purposes of the hypothesis(es) in a research study
3. Distinguish between an inductive and a deductive hypothesis
4. State the criteria used to evaluate hypotheses for research
5. Define an operational definition and give an example
6. Identify a testable hypothesis from given examples
7. Define a null hypothesis and explain its purpose in a research study
8. Write a research hypothesis and a null hypothesis for a research study
9. Distinguish between a directional and a nondirectional hypothesis
10. Describe the steps in testing a hypothesis
11. State the purpose(s) served by a pilot study
12. List the elements that are to be included in a research plan

The hypothesis is a powerful tool in scientific inquiry. It enables us to relate theory to observation and observation to theory. Today the use of hypotheses enables us, in our search for knowledge, to employ both the ideas of the inductive philosophers, with their emphasis on observation, and the logic of the deductive philosophers, with their emphasis on reason. The use of hypotheses has united experience and reason to produce a powerful tool for seeking truth.

After finding and stating the problem and examining the literature, the researcher is ready to structure a hypothesis. A hypothesis may be precisely defined as a tentative proposition suggested as a solution to a problem or as an explanation of some phenomenon. It presents in simple form a statement of the researcher's expectations relative to a relationship between variables within the problem. It is then tested in a research study. Hence, it is presented only as a suggested solution to the problem, with the understanding that the ensuing investigation may lead either to its retention or to its rejection.

For instance, one may begin with the question What is the role of children's perceptions of themselves in the process of learning to read? One might then hypothesize that there is a positive relationship between children's perceptions of themselves and their achievement in reading in the first grade. Or one may begin with a question such as What is the effect of preschool training upon the achievement of culturally disadvantaged children in first grade? The hypothesis might read: Culturally disadvantaged children who have had preschool training achieve at a higher level in first grade than culturally disadvantaged children who have not had preschool training. In both examples it can be seen that the hypothesis is a proposition relating two variables. In the first hypothesis the variables are self-perception and reading achievement; in the second they are having or not having preschool training and achievement in first grade.

Although hypotheses are recommended and, as we will see, serve several important purposes, they are not absolutely essential in all research studies. Hypotheses are tools in the research process, not ends in themselves. Studies are often undertaken in areas where there is little accumulated background information. If an investigator lacks insight into the scope of a problem, the major variables that influence a phenomenon, or the settings in which the variables occur, then it is very difficult to state a meaningful hypothesis. For example, surveys that attempt to describe the characteristics of particular phenomena or seek to ascertain the attitudes and opinions of groups often proceed without hypotheses. The empirical data upon which hypotheses could be based are not yet available to the researcher. A statement of the research problem suffices in such studies. Hypotheses are most important for research in which causal relationships between variables are being investigated.

The hypothesis must be structured before the data-gathering phase of the study for two reasons: (1) a well-grounded hypothesis indicates that the researcher has sufficient knowledge in the area to undertake the investigation; and (2) the hypothesis gives direction to the collection and interpretation of the data; it tells the researcher what procedure to follow and the type of data to gather and thus may prevent a great deal of wasted time and effort on the part of the researcher.

The purposes served by the hypothesis are:

1. *The hypothesis provides a tentative explanation of phenomena and facilitates the extension of knowledge in an area.* In order to arrive at reliable knowledge about education problems, one must go beyond a mere gathering of isolated facts to seek generalizations and interrelations existing among those facts. These interrelations and generalizations provide the patterning significant for an understanding of the problem. Such patterning is not likely to become apparent as long as data gathering is without direction. Well-planned hypotheses provide direction and propose explanations. Because they can be tested and validated through scientific inquiry, they permit us to extend knowledge.

2. *The hypothesis provides the investigator with a relational statement that is directly testable in a research study.* Questions cannot be tested directly. An investigation begins with a question, but only the proposed relationship between the variables can be tested. For instance, one does not test the question Do teachers' comments on students' papers cause a significant improvement in student performance? Instead, one tests the hypothesis that the question implies: Teachers' comments on students' papers result in a significant improvement in performance; or more specifically: The performance scores of students who have had teacher comments on previous papers will exceed those of students who have not had teacher comments on previous papers. One then proceeds to investigate the relationship between the two variables: teachers' comments and student performance.

3. *The hypothesis provides direction to the research.* The hypothesis represents a specific objective and thus determines the nature of the data needed to test the proposition. Very simply, the hypothesis tells the researcher what to do. Facts must be selected and observations made because they have relevance to a particular question, and it is the hypothesis that determines the relevancy of these facts. The hypothesis provides a basis for selecting the sample and the research procedures to be used and suggests the statistical analysis needed and the relationship to be tested. Furthermore, the hypothesis helps to keep the study restricted in scope, preventing it from becoming too broad or unwieldy.

For example, consider again the hypothesis concerning preschool training of culturally disadvantaged children and their achievement in first grade. This hypothesis indicates the research method required and the sample to use, and it even directs the researcher to the statistical test that would be necessary for analyzing the data. It is clear from the statement of the hypothesis that the researcher will conduct a causal-comparative study that compares the first-grade achievement of a sample of culturally disadvantaged children who went through a preschool program and a similar group of children who did not have preschool training. Any difference in the mean achievement of the two groups could be analyzed for statistical significance by the *t*-test or analysis-of-variance technique. (These procedures are discussed in Chapter 6).

4. *The hypothesis provides a framework for reporting the conclusions of the study.* The researcher will find it very convenient to take each hypothesis separately and state the conclusions that are relevant to it. That is, the researcher can organize this section of the written report around the provision of answers to the original hypotheses, thereby making a more meaningful and readable presentation.

/// SUGGESTIONS FOR DERIVING HYPOTHESES

How does the researcher go about deriving a hypothesis? As explained in Chapter 2, one's study might have its origin in a practical problem, in some observed behavioral situation in need of explanation, in previous research, or even more profitably in some educational, psychological, or sociological theory. Thus, hypotheses are derived inductively from observations of behavior or deductively from theory or from the findings of previous research.

// Inductive Hypotheses

In the inductive procedure the researcher formulates a hypothesis as a generalization from observed relationships. That is, the researcher makes observations of behavior, notices trends or probable relationships, and then hypothesizes an explanation for this observed behavior. Of course, this reasoning process should be accompanied by an examination of previous research to determine what findings other investigators have reported on the question. The inductive procedure is a particularly fruitful source of hypotheses for classroom teachers. Teachers observe student behavior every day and attempt to relate it to their own behavior, to the behavior of other students, to the teaching methods used, to changes in the school environment, and so on. On the basis of their experience and knowledge of behavior in a school situation, teachers may inductively formulate a generalization that attempts to explain the observed relationship. The validity of this explanation must be determined, however, and thus it can become the hypothesis for a scientific investigation.

Perhaps a teacher has observed a high degree of anxiety that is aroused by classroom tests and believes that this has an adverse effect on students' performance. Furthermore, the teacher has noted that when students are given an opportunity to write comments about objective questions, their test performance seems to improve. The teacher reasons that this freedom to make comments must somehow serve to reduce anxiety and, as a result, the students make better scores. This observation suggests a hypothesis: Students who are encouraged to write comments about test items on their answer sheets will make higher test scores than students who have no opportunity to make comments. Our teacher could then design an experiment to test the validity of this hypothesis. Note that the hypothesis expresses the teacher's belief concerning the relationship between the two variables: writing comments about test items and the performance on the test. Note also that the variable *anxiety* that was part of the deductive chain leading to the hypothesis is not part of the final hypothesis. Therefore, the results of the investigation would provide information concerning only the relation between writing comments and test performance. The relationships between anxiety and comments, and anxiety and test performance, could be subjects for subsequent hypotheses to be investigated. Frequently one will find that an original idea involves a series of relationships that cannot be directly observed. One then reformulates the question in order to focus on relationships that are amenable to direct observation.

The following are some other examples of hypotheses that might result from a teacher's observations: There is a positive relationship between math anxiety and computer anxiety among high school students; Students' learning of computer programming in the middle grades increases their growth in logical thinking skills; The use of advance organizers increases high school students' learning from computer-assisted instruction in chemistry; Teaching the commutative property increases the speed with which addition combinations are learned; Children make higher scores on final measures of first-grade reading achievement when they are taught in small groups rather than large groups; and The cognitive and affective development of first-grade children is influenced by the amount of prior kindergarten experience. In the inductive process, the researcher makes observations, thinks about the problem, turns to the literature for clues, makes additional observations, and then formulates a hypothesis that attempts to account for the observed behavior. The hypothesis is then tested under controlled conditions in order to examine scientifically the teacher's assumption concerning the relationship between the variables.

The investigation of inductive hypotheses that derive from everyday problems can often be helpful in indicating solutions to such problems. Because they are generated from specific local problems, however, the results of such hypotheses often lead to a series of findings that, although worthwhile, have limited explanatory power.

// Deductive Hypotheses

In contrast to hypotheses that are formulated as generalizations from observed relationships, there are those that are derived by deduction from theory. These hypotheses have the advantage of leading to a more general system of knowledge, as the framework for incorporating them meaningfully into the body of knowledge already exists within the theory itself. A science cannot develop efficiently if each study remains an isolated effort. It becomes cumulative by building on the existing body of facts and theories. A hypothesis derived from a theory is known as a deductive hypothesis.

Perhaps it will be helpful to distinguish between theory and hypothesis. A theory includes a set of concepts along with statements about the how and why of the interrelationships that exist among these concepts. Theories are proposed as general explanations that apply to a wide range of phenomena. Within a theory the statements are often nothing more than hypotheses assumed to be true, hypotheses that may be tested in subsequent studies. From the interrelationships proposed in the theory, one can state specific consequences that could logically be assumed to follow. These assumed consequences are the bases for hypotheses. A scientific theory must imply conclusions that can be verified through empirical investigation; that is, from the theory one should be able to predict certain events that will be observed or will not be observed. These deduced consequences become the hypotheses that are subjected to empirical investigation.

As the hypotheses derived from a theory receive support in research, then the theory also receives support. Hypotheses thus provide the evidence that supports, expands, contradicts, or leads to revision of the theories from which they were derived. It should be emphasized that while research can disprove a theory, it cannot ever prove that the theory is true. This is because theories are generalizations that apply to all possible instances of the phenomena they are trying to explain; it is not possible to test a theory against all possibilities. But the more support the theory gets in a variety of research studies, the more confidence we have that the theory is valid and useful.

Theories are more general in content than hypotheses, and one theory may give rise to a number of hypotheses to be investigated in several separate studies. One may begin a study by selecting one of the theories in one's own area of interest. The particular theory that one chooses in his/her research is determined, of course, by the purpose of the research and the contribution that the theory can make to the understanding of the problem. Once the theory has been chosen, one proceeds to derive a hypothesis from this theory by using deductive reasoning to arrive at the logical consequences of the theory. These deductions then become the hypotheses in the research study. A researcher interested in studying the achievement motive in children might read McClelland's classic theory of achievement motivation. One of the postulates of McClelland's theory is that "the intensity of the achievement motive is a directly proportional function of the education to independence and self-sufficiency."[1] From this theory one would predict that the children

---

[1] McClelland, D. (1953). *The Achievement Motive* (p. 288). New York: Appleton.

of parents who urge independence and self-sufficiency in their children would exhibit greater motivation to achieve in the classroom. The researcher then proceeds to use deductive reasoning to arrive at a logical consequence of the theory that could be empirically verified. This deduction is the hypothesis in this hypothetical research study. The problem and hypothesis might be stated as follows:

> *Problem:* What is the relationship between child-rearing practices in the home and the motivation to achieve in elementary school children?
> *Hypothesis:* Children whose parents greatly restrict their freedom, when compared with children whose parents do not restrict their freedom, make lower scores on a task where the amount of work done is a function of their motivation.

The researcher would then proceed to design a study, most likely a causal-comparative one, to test this hypothesis. If the predicted results are observed, McClelland's theory about achievement motivation receives support. If no difference is observed in the two groups of children, one might question the theory or at least its application in this situation.

One interested in the development of logical thinking in children might look at Piaget's theory. Piaget has suggested that children pass through various stages in their mental development, one of which is the stage of concrete operations, which begins at age 7 or 8 and marks the transition from dependence on perception to an ability to use some logical operations. These operations are on a concrete level but do involve symbolic reasoning.[2] Using this theory as a starting point, one might therefore hypothesize: The proportion of 9-year-old children who will be able to answer correctly the transitive inference problem "Frank is taller than George; George is taller than Robert; who is the tallest?" will be greater than the proportion of 6-year-olds who are able to answer it correctly.

In a study designed to test a deduction from a theory, it is extremely important to check for any logical gaps intervening between theory and hypothesis. The researcher must ask, Does the hypothesis logically follow from the theory? If the hypothesis does not really follow from the theory, then the researcher cannot reach valid conclusions about the adequacy of the theory. If the hypothesis is supported, but not rigorously deduced from the theory, the researcher cannot say that the findings furnish credibility to the theory. Conversely, if the hypothesis is not supported by the data, the theory from which it originated will not necessarily be any less credible.

It is true that many of the hypotheses that can be deduced from the better-known theories have already been tested, but many such deductions remain to be made and tested. Also, a previously researched deduction could

---

[2]Piaget, J. (1968). *Six Psychological Studies* (pp. 61–62). New York: Vintage Books.

be used to generate hypotheses in more widely varied circumstances in order to extend the application of the theory.

/// CHARACTERISTICS OF THE USABLE HYPOTHESIS

After the hypothesis has been tentatively formulated, but before any actual empirical testing is attempted, the potential of the hypothesis as a research tool must be assessed. A hypothesis must meet certain criteria of acceptability. The final worth of a hypothesis cannot be judged prior to empirical testing, but there are certain criteria that characterize worthwhile hypotheses, and the researcher should use them to judge the adequacy of the proposed hypothesis.

// A Hypothesis Must Have Explanatory Power

A hypothesis must be a possible explanation of what it is attempting to explain. This is an obvious but important criterion. To illustrate, suppose you attempt to start your car and nothing happens. A hypothesis stating that the car will not start because you left the water running in the bathroom sink is not a possible explanation. A hypothesis stating that the battery is dead is a possible explanation and should be worth testing.

// A Hypothesis Must State the Expected Relationship between Variables

A hypothesis should conjecture the relationship between two or more variables. In our example, it would be unprofitable to state "The car will not start and it has a wiring system" because no relationship between variables is specified, and, consequently, there is no proposed relationship to test. A fruitful hypothesis would be: The car will not start because of a fault in the wiring system. This criterion may seem patently obvious, but consider the following statement: If children differ from one another in self-concept, they will differ from one another in social studies achievement. The statement appears to be a hypothesis until you note that there is no statement of an expected relationship. An expected relationship could be described as: Higher self-concept is a likely antecedent to *higher* social studies achievement. This hypothesis would then be stated: There will be a *positive* relationship between self-concept and social studies achievement. If the opposite is predicted, that is, higher self-concept leads to *lower* social studies achievement, then the hypothesis would be: There will be a *negative* relationship between self-concept and social studies achievement. Either statement would meet our second criterion.

// A Hypothesis Must Be Testable

It is said that the most important characteristic of a "good" hypothesis is testability. A testable hypothesis is verifiable; that is, deductions, conclusions, or inferences can be drawn from the hypothesis in such a way that empirical observations can be made that will either support or not support the hypothesis. If the hypothesis is true, then certain predictable results should be manifest. A testable hypothesis enables the researcher to determine by observation whether those consequences that are deductively implied actually do occur. Otherwise, it would be impossible either to confirm or not to confirm the hypothesis. In our example, the hypothesis "The car's failure to start is a punishment for my sins" is apparently untestable in this world.

Many hypotheses or propositions as they may initially be stated are essentially untestable. For instance, the hypothesis "Preschool experience promotes the all-around adjustment of the preschool child" would be hard to test because of the difficulty of defining and measuring all-around adjustment. Another example of an untestable hypothesis is The use of ditto work in school art stifles the child's artistic creativity. In this case, the problem would be one of defining and measuring artistic creativity as well as setting up the criteria to determine whether a stifling of creativity has occurred.

To be testable, a hypothesis must relate variables that are capable of being measured. If there are no means available for measuring the variables, then it would be impossible to gather the data necessary to test the validity of the hypothesis. This cannot be emphasized too strongly. Unless it is possible to define specifically the indicators of each variable and subsequently to measure these variables, then the hypothesis is not testable.

The indicators of the variables are referred to as *operational definitions*. An operational definition, as explained earlier, is one that defines a variable by stating the "operations," or procedures, necessary to measure that variable. For instance, consider the hypothesis There is a positive relationship between a child's self-esteem and his reading achievement in first grade. In order for this hypothesis to meet the criteria of acceptability, it is necessary to define the variables operationally. Self-esteem might be defined as the scores made on the Coopersmith Self-Esteem Scale[3] and reading achievement, as scores on the California Reading Test, or as first-grade teachers' ratings of reading achievement.

A primary consideration in formulating a hypothesis is to make sure that the variables can be given operational definitions. Avoid the use of constructs for which it would be difficult or impossible to find adequate measures. Constructs such as creativity, authoritarianism, democracy, and

[3]Coopersmith, S. (1981). *The Antecedents of Self-Esteem*. San Francisco: Consulting Psychology.

the like have acquired such diverse meanings that agreement on operational definitions of such concepts would be difficult, if not impossible. Remember that the variables must be defined in terms of identifiable and observable behavior.

It is important to avoid value statements in hypotheses. A statement such as "A counseling program in the elementary school is desirable" cannot be investigated in a research study. However, one could test the hypothesis Elementary pupils who have had counseling will verbally express greater satisfaction with their school than those who have not had counseling. One can measure verbal expressions of satisfaction, but whether they are desirable or not is a value judgment.

// A Hypothesis Should Be Consistent with the Existing Body of Knowledge

Hypotheses should not contradict previously well-established hypotheses, theories, and laws. The hypothesis "My car will not start because the fluid in the battery has changed to gold" satisfies the first three criteria but is so contrary to what is known about the nature of matter that one would not pursue it. The hypothesis "The car will not start because the fluid in the battery has evaporated to a low level" is consistent with previous knowledge and therefore is worth pursuing. It would probably be unprofitable to hypothesize an absence of relationship between the self-concept of adolescent boys and girls and their rate of physical growth because the preponderance of evidence supports such a relationship.

In the history of science it is found that people such as Einstein, Newton, Darwin, and Copernicus developed truly revolutionary hypotheses that conflicted with what was accepted knowledge in their time, but it must be remembered that the work of such pioneers was not really so much a denial of previous knowledge as it was a reorganization of the knowledge into more satisfactory theory. In most cases, and especially for the beginning researcher, it is safe to suggest that the hypothesis should be in agreement with the knowledge already established in the field. Again, this points up the necessity for a thorough review of the literature so that hypotheses will be formulated on the basis of previously reported research in the area.

// A Hypothesis Should Be Stated as Simply and Concisely as Possible

Stating the hypothesis in a simple manner not only makes testing of the hypothesis much easier, but also provides a basis for a clear and easily comprehended report at the conclusion of the study. It is often necessary to break a broad general hypothesis into several specific ones in order to allow for testability and clarity. For instance, Tuma and Livson considered these very general hypotheses: The socioeconomic status of the family plays a part in determining the degree of conformity experienced by an adolescent in various social contexts, and The various components of this social status differ in the extent of their effects upon his attitudes to authority. To promote clarity and testability, they broke these general hypotheses into specific ones, such as the following: (1) There is a significant negative relationship between the attitude toward authority experienced by the male adolescent at home and the socioeconomic status of his family; (2) There is a significant negative relationship between the attitude toward authority experienced by the male adolescent at school and the socioeconomic status of his family; (3) There is a significant negative relationship between the attitude toward authority experienced by the male adolescent when with peers and the socioeconomic status of his family; (4) There is a significant negative relationship between adolescent boys' attitudes toward authority and fathers' education; (5) There is a significant negative relationship between adolescent boys' attitudes toward authority and mothers' education; and so on.[4] These hypotheses would need to be restated to reflect expectations as far as female adolescents are concerned. Stating the hypotheses in this very specific form also facilitates a reporting of the findings and conclusions. The experimenter can consider each hypothesis separately and can indicate the findings and conclusions relevant to each.

Thus, it can be seen that several hypotheses may be needed in any one study. Generally, it is recommended that the researcher state a hypothesis for every subaspect of the problem or for every data-gathering device that will be used. For example, an investigator might begin with the hypothesis Students taught mathematics by means of PLATO (a specific computer-assisted instruction package) will show greater learning and retention of mathematical concepts than those using traditional textbooks. Since it will be necessary to report results for both learning and retention, the original hypothesis must be restated as two separate hypotheses. These hypotheses would read: (1) Students taught mathematics by means of PLATO will show greater learning of mathematical concepts than those using traditional text-books, and (2) Students taught mathematics by means of PLATO will show greater retention of mathematical concepts than those using traditional text-books. In this way, it is possible to show whether the data obtained support for each particular aspect of the general question. The data may indicate the effectiveness of the computer-assisted instruction for original learning but not for retention. One need not worry about the verbal redundancy obvious in stating multiple hypotheses. Remember that the goals of testability and clarity will be served better by the more specific hypotheses.

---

[4]Tuma, E., and N. Livson (1960). Family socioeconomic status and adolescent attitude to authority. *Child Development, 31,* 387–399.

It is also recommended that the terms used in the hypothesis be the simplest that would be acceptable for the purpose of conveying the intended meaning; the use of vague constructs must be avoided. Use terms in the way that is generally accepted for referring to the phenomenon. When two hypotheses are of equal explanatory power, the simpler one is to be preferred because it will provide the necessary explanation with fewer assumptions and variables to be defined. Remember that this principle of parsimony is important in evaluating hypotheses.

Many of the hypotheses that are formulated are rejected after empirical testing. They are predictions that are not supported by the data. In the history of scientific research, hypotheses that failed to be supported have greatly outnumbered those that have been supported. Experienced researchers realize that unconfirmed hypotheses are an expected and useful part of the scientific experience. They can lead to reconsideration of theory and often bring us closer to a correct explanation of the state of affairs. "I have steadily endeavored," Darwin wrote, "to keep my mind free so as to give up any hypothesis, however much beloved (and I cannot resist forming one on every subject), as soon as facts are shown to be opposed to it. Indeed, I have had no choice but to act in this manner, for with the exception of the Coral Reefs, I cannot remember a single first-formed hypothesis which had not after a time to be given up or greatly modified."[5] Even an unsupported hypothesis can be useful in that it points up the need to consider other aspects of a problem and thus may bring the investigator a step closer to an acceptable explanation. In formulating a hypothesis, one's chief concern should be the avoidance of vagueness or ambiguity.

Even though one finds support for a hypothesis, except in cases of perfect induction, the hypothesis is not *proved* to be true. A hypothesis is never proved or disproved; it is only supported or not supported. Hypotheses are essentially probabilistic in nature; empirical evidence can lead one to conclude that the explanation is probably true or that it is reasonable to accept the hypothesis, but it never proves the hypothesis.

An example of a study with hypotheses deduced from a theory is shown below.

The Effect of Time of Day of Instruction on Achievement[6]

Research Problem

What is the effect of time of day of instruction on eighth-grade students' English and mathematics achievement?

---

[5]Darwin F. (ed.) (1919). *Life and Letters of Charles Darwin.* New York: Appleton.
[6]Davis, Z. T. (1988). The effect of time-of-day of instruction on eighth-grade students' English and mathematics achievement. *The High School Journal, 71,* 78–80.

Theory

A theory involving short-term memory (STM) and long-term memory (LTM) suggests that tasks that involve mainly the use of STM are learned and performed better in the morning; tasks that involve mainly the use of LTM are learned and performed better in the afternoon. Two physiological factors account for time-of-day differences in learning: (*a*) basal arousal rises from a low level in the morning to a peak in the evening, and the use of STM and LTM are associated with it, respectively; (*b*) diurnal rhythms in plasma and hormone levels influence the way people encode, store, and retrieve information and are associated with better LTM processing later in the day and better STM processing earlier in the day.

Hypothesis

Because reading involves connecting the printed information to prior knowledge and experience, it was hypothesized: Students will achieve more in reading when instruction is provided in the afternoon. And because instruction in math skills involves more mental manipulation of data and use of STM, it was hypothesized: Students will achieve more in arithmetic when instruction is provided in the morning than in the afternoon.

Methods

Eighty eighth-grade students were randomly assigned to the following treatment groups: (1) first-period English, (2) last-period English, (3) first-period math, (4) last-period math. The same English teacher and the same math teacher taught the first-period and last-period sections of the courses using the same methods and materials. The Comprehensive Test of Basic Skills (CTBS) was administered at the beginning (pretest) and the end of the school year (posttest) to measure achievement. The tests were given on the same day for each content area, as well as during the middle of the school day for all groups in order to control the potential influence of time of day of output effects.

Analysis

The respective sets of English and math scores were each analyzed through the analysis of covariance (ANCOVA), with the pretest scores serving as the covariate. ANCOVA takes into account the variation that exists between pupils' pretest scores and adjusts the posttest scores in relation to them so that valid comparisons can be made.

Results

The afternoon English group achieved at a significantly higher level than the morning English group. There was no significant difference in the math achievement of the morning and afternoon math groups.

Conclusions

It was concluded that learners would benefit more from afternoon instruction than from morning instruction in eighth-grade English. Time of day of instruction made no difference in eighth-grade math achievement. The researcher concluded that the hypothesis concerning math be subjected to further investigation. Perhaps the STM and LTM functions found in previous research are not very representative of those required in math reasoning; or perhaps math reasoning involves a fairly balanced use of STM and LTM.

/// TYPES OF HYPOTHESES
// Research Hypothesis

The hypotheses we have discussed thus far are called *research,* or substantive, *hypotheses.* They are the hypotheses developed from observation, the related literature, and/or the theory described in the study. A research hypothesis is a statement about the relationship one expects to find as a result of the research. It may be a statement about the expected *relationship* or the expected *difference* between the variables in the study. A hypothesis about children's IQ and anxiety in the classroom could be stated: There is a positive relationship between IQ and anxiety in elementary school children, or Children classified as having high IQs will exhibit more anxiety in the classroom than children classified as having low IQs. Research hypotheses may be stated in a *directional* or *nondirectional* form. A directional hypothesis specifies the nature of the relationship or difference that is predicted. The above two hypotheses about IQ and anxiety are directional. A nondirectional hypothesis, on the other hand, states that a relationship or difference exists but without specifying the nature of the expected finding—for example, There is a relationship between IQ and anxiety in children.

// Null Hypothesis

Research hypotheses cannot be tested directly by available statistical procedures. In empirical investigations where statistical tests are to be performed, the research hypothesis must be translated into another type of hypothesis known as a *null hypothesis* (symbolized as H_0). It is called null because it states that there is "no difference" or "no effect" or that there is "no relationship." A null hypothesis states a negation of what the experimenter expects or predicts. A researcher may hope to show that, after an experimental treatment, two populations have different means, but the null hypothesis would state that the populations' means are not different.

A null hypothesis is used because it enables researchers to compare their findings with chance expectations through statistical tests. The null hypothesis assumes that observed differences occurred because of chance alone and hence do not represent real differences at all. Statistical tests are used to determine the probability that the null hypothesis is true. If the tests indicate that observed differences had a very slight probability of occurring by chance, the null hypothesis becomes a very unlikely assumption. Therefore, it can be rejected in favor of an alternative hypothesis. The evidence is sufficient for tentatively concluding that the difference is real. If the observed differences could easily be a function of chance, the evidence is insufficient and the null hypothesis is retained. Testing a null hypothesis is analogous to the prosecutor's work in a criminal trial. In order to establish guilt, the prosecutor (in the U.S. legal system) must provide sufficient evidence to enable a jury to reject the presumption of innocence beyond reasonable doubt. It is not possible for a prosecutor to prove guilt conclusively, nor can a researcher obtain unequivocal support for a research hypothesis. The defendant is presumed to be innocent until there is sufficient evidence to indicate that he or she is not, and the null hypothesis is presumed to be true until there is sufficient evidence to indicate otherwise.

Let us go back to the hypothetical study of anxiety levels in children of high and low IQ. The research hypothesis might be stated: Children with high IQs will exhibit more anxiety than children with low IQs. The null hypothesis is stated: The anxiety level of high-IQ children is *not* different from the anxiety level of low-IQ children.

The null hypothesis would be tested using one of the various statistical techniques to be discussed in Chapter 6. If, when the study is completed, the empirical data indicate that the difference between the sample groups is large enough that it is not likely to be due to chance, then the null hypothesis can be rejected. Rejection of the null hypothesis indicates that the anxiety level of the two groups of children is not likely to be equal. The researcher then adopts an *alternative* hypothesis (symbolized as H_1) which states: The mean anxiety scores of the two populations are not equal. The alternative hypothesis is said to be *nondirectional* because it does not state which group's average score will be larger. Probably most research in education begins with nondirectional hypotheses. In some situations, however, the researcher may have a definite reason for stating a *directional* hypothesis, which, as the name implies, specifies the direction of the expected findings. An example of a directional hypothesis is as follows: The mean anxiety scores of children with high IQs will be higher than the anxiety scores of children with low IQs.

/// TESTING THE HYPOTHESIS

A study begins with a research hypothesis, which should be a simple, clear statement of the expected relationship between the variables. We have explained earlier that hypotheses must be testable, which means that they are amenable to empirical verification. When researchers speak of testing a hypothesis, however, they are referring to the null hypothesis. Only the null hypothesis can be directly tested by statistical procedures. Testing a hypothesis involves the following steps:

1. State, in operational terms, the relationships that should be observed if the research hypothesis is true.

2. State the null hypothesis.
3. Select a research method that will permit the observation and/or experimentation necessary to show whether or not these relationships exist.
4. Gather and analyze the empirical data.
5. Determine whether the evidence is sufficient to reject the null hypothesis.

// An Example of Testing a Hypothesis

An example may help to illustrate better this process of empirically testing a hypothesis. Assume that a teacher is interested in investigating reinforcement theory in the classroom. From her understanding of reinforcement theory, this teacher might hypothesize that praise or encouragement will result in heightened motivation on the part of students. If this hypothesis is correct, it is logical to assume that teachers' encouraging comments on test papers (praise) would be followed by improvement in student performance, which implies the assumption that heightened motivation is indicated by improved test performance.

(Step 1) This deduced implication is stated as follows: Teachers' comments on students' papers result in an improvement in pupils' performance on tests. It is the relationship between the two variables, teachers' comments and pupil performance, that will be investigated.

(Step 2) For statistical testing, the above research hypothesis must be transformed into a null hypothesis. The null hypothesis is stated: Teachers' comments on students' papers will not result in an improvement in pupils' performance on tests.

(Step 3) This type of hypothesis can be investigated by means of an experiment. The researcher could randomly select a number of classes to use in the study. Within each class, students would be randomly assigned to two groups: For those students assigned to Group A, their teachers would write encouraging comments concerning their test performance. (These comments would simply be words of encouragement to the student, such as "Excellent," "Keep up the good work," or "You're doing better." These comments should have nothing to do with content or the correction of particular student errors; otherwise, the improvement could be attributed to the educational usefulness of such comments rather than to increased motivation.) The students assigned to Group B would receive no comments at all on their test papers.

(Step 4) The teachers would administer an objective test covering a certain unit of content. The tests would be scored and the experimental treatment introduced as described above. Then the teachers would administer a second test covering a unit comparable in difficulty to the previous unit and taught after the first test and the experimental treatment. The change from the first test to the second test would be ascertained for each student as well as the average gain for the group. It would then be possible through analysis of the data to determine whether average gains on the second test were related to the experimental treatment (teacher comments on papers).

(Step 5) If it is found that, as a group, the students who had received comments, Group A, achieved statistically significantly higher gains than the group that did not receive comments, Group B, then the null hypothesis can be rejected. Rejection of the null hypothesis would mean that the effects of the two methods are not equal. The researcher would tentatively conclude that teachers' comments on students' papers result in an improvement in students' performance on tests.

// Pilot Study

Before the research plan is prepared, it may be helpful to try out the proposed procedures on a few subjects. This trial run, or pilot study, will, first of all, help the researcher to decide whether the study is feasible and whether it is worthwhile to continue. It provides an opportunity to assess the appropriateness and practicality of the data collection instruments. It permits a preliminary testing of the hypothesis, which may give some indication of its tenability and suggest whether further refinement is needed.

The pilot study will also demonstrate the adequacy of the research procedures and the measures that have been selected for the variables. Unanticipated problems that appear may be solved at this stage, thereby saving time and effort later. A pilot study is well worth the time required and is especially recommended for the beginning researcher.

/// THE RESEARCH PLAN

After the question and the hypothesis have been formulated, one is ready to complete the tentative research plan. One needs to write out in detail what one proposes to do and just how one plans to do it.

Developing the research plan is essential. It forces one to set down ideas in a concrete form. Many initial ideas seem promising until one has to spell them out in black and white; then the difficulties or the inadequacies become obvious.

The written form can also be given to others for their comments and criticism. It is much easier for another to detect flaws and errors in a proposal when it is written out than when it is communicated orally.

Typically the research plan is at this stage only a preliminary proposal, and many changes will probably be needed before the final, formal proposal is written. However, it is helpful to keep in mind that the more complete and detailed this initial proposal is, the more useful it will be to the researcher and the more time will be saved later.

The research plan includes the following elements.

// The Problem

The plan begins with a clear statement of the research problem. The statement asks about the relationship between variables and specifies the population of interest. A brief description of the background of the problem in theory and related research should also be included in this section.

// The Hypothesis

The question is followed by a concise statement of the hypothesis or hypotheses to be tested. The hypothesis gives the research its direction. All subsequent plans for the research project depend on the statement of the hypothesis. It is imperative that the researcher state the hypothesis and the supporting rationale with the greatest clarity. This section of the plan should include operational definitions of the variables involved.

// The Research Design

The next section of the plan presents a description of the research design—that is, a description of the procedures to be followed in testing the hypotheses. It is very important that an appropriate testing method be chosen. An experimental question cannot be answered by using descriptive methods and vice versa. This section should also include a listing of the measures or instruments to be used in gathering the data. Investigators must locate appropriate tests, scales, and other tools required to measure the variables and must assess the reliability and validity of these operations. The aim is to choose measures that are as objective and reliable as possible, without sacrificing the adequacy of their "fit" with the concepts they are supposed to represent.

// The Sample

The plan must include a description of the population of concern in the study—that is, the type of subjects to be included. The researcher must have given some attention to the availability of these subjects. It is also necessary to describe the sampling procedures to be followed. The universe to be sampled must be specified, as well as the techniques to be followed in drawing the sample and the proposed sample size.

// The Statistical Analysis

This section will include the researcher's plan for the statistical analysis of the data. Before one begins to collect data, one must identify the statistical procedure that will permit an answer to the research question or a test of the hypothesis. First one will need to describe or summarize the data collected from the sample studied. Then one must be able to estimate the reliability or accuracy of the inferences and generalizations made from the sample findings to the total populations. Statistical methods serve both of these functions. The function of summarizing the obtained data is accomplished by descriptive statistics. Inferential statistics enables one to make inferences from sample data.

Many experienced researchers, as well as those who are just learning the process, find it necessary to consult with an expert in statistics before completing their research plan. A brief discussion of the role statistical analysis plays in testing hypotheses is presented in Chapter 6.

/// SUMMARY

In order to proceed with the confirmatory phase of a research study, it is important to have one or more clearly stated hypotheses. The hypothesis is the researcher's prediction about the outcome of the study. Hypotheses are derived inductively from observation or deductively from a known theory. Experience and knowledge in the area and familiarity with previous research are important factors in the formulation of a satisfactory hypothesis.

The hypothesis serves a multipurpose function in research. Since it proposes an explanation that can be empirically tested, it serves to extend knowledge. The hypothesis provides direction to the researcher's efforts because it determines the research method and the type of data relevant to the solution of the problem. It also provides a framework for interpreting the results and for stating the conclusions of the study.

A good hypothesis must satisfy certain criteria: (1) it must have explanatory power; (2) it must be testable, which means that it relates variables that can be measured; (3) it must be in agreement with the preponderance of existing data; (4) it must be stated as clearly and concisely as possible; and (5) it must state the expected relationship between the variables.

After the formulation of the hypothesis, the next step is to write out a plan for the research, including a statement of the problem and the hypothesis and a description of the research design, the sample, and the statistical analysis to be applied. This initial written plan affords an opportunity for both the investigator and others to determine whether a feasible program for testing the hypothesis can be implemented.

Once formulated and evaluated in terms of the above criteria, the research hypothesis is ready to be subjected to an empirical test. The null hypothesis—the negation of what the researcher expects—is stated. It is important to remember that a hypothesis cannot be proved or disproved, only supported or not supported. Even if it is not supported, a hypothesis may still serve a useful purpose because it can lead the researcher to reevaluate his or her rationale and procedures and to consider other approaches to the problem.

// Key Concepts

criteria for evaluating hypotheses
deductive hypothesis
directional hypothesis
functions of hypotheses
inductive hypothesis

nondirectional hypothesis
null hypothesis
testing hypotheses
theory

/// EXERCISES

1. What is the purpose of hypotheses?

2. What is the difference between an inductive and a deductive hypothesis?

3. State a hypothesis based on each of the research questions listed below:
   a. What would be the effect of using the Cuisenaire method in teaching elementary arithmetic?
   b. Is there a relationship between the sex of the tutor and the gains made in reading achievement by black male elementary students?
   c. Does living in interracial housing affect one's attitude toward members of another race?
   d. Is there any relationship between the type of reinforcement (tangible or intangible) and the amount of learning achieved by socioeconomically disadvantaged children?
   e. Does preschool training reduce the educational gap separating advantaged and disadvantaged children before they enter first grade?
   f. Do teacher expectations of children's intellectual performance have any effect on their actual performance?

4. Rewrite the following hypothesis in null form: Children who read below grade level will express less satisfaction with school than those who read at or above grade level.

5. Evaluate the adequacy of each of the following hypotheses. If a hypothesis is inadequate, state the reason for the inadequacy and write an adequate hypothesis.

    a. Teachers deserve higher pay than administrators.

    b. Students who take a middle school government course will be capable of more enlightened judgments concerning local political affairs than will those who do not take the course.

    c. Traditional math is better than new math for slow learners.

    d. If students differ in their socioeconomic status, they will differ in their English proficiency scores.

    e. Children who show high achievement motivation will show high anxiety as measured by the Children's Manifest Anxiety Scale.

    f. Positive verbal reinforcement of student responses by the teacher will lessen the probability of future responses.

6. Write a directional and a nondirectional hypothesis based on the research question *What is the relationship between the rate of maturation of adolescent boys and their self-concepts?*

7. Why should a hypothesis be clearly stated before research is initiated?

8. Label the following hypotheses as research hypotheses or null hypotheses.

    a. Students will receive lower scores on achievement tests that measure the higher levels of Bloom's taxonomy.

    b. There is no difference in the performance of students taught mathematics by Method A and those taught mathematics by Method B.

    c. The mean retention scores of children receiving experimental Drug X will not differ from the scores of children who did not receive Drug X.

    d. Students taught by *laissez-faire* teachers will show higher problem-solving skills than students taught by authoritarian teachers.

9. Locate a research study stating a hypothesis, and try to identify the theory from which the hypothesis originated.

10. Criticize the following hypothesis: Using the discussion method in high school social studies class will result in better adult citizens than using the lecture method.

/// ANSWERS

1. The purpose of the hypotheses is to provide a tentative proposition suggested as a solution to a problem or as an explanation of some phenomenon.

2. With an inductive hypothesis, the researcher makes observations of relationships and then hypothesizes an explanation for the observed behavior. With a deductive hypothesis, the researcher formulates a hypothesis based on known theory, accompanied by a rationale for the particular proposition.

3. a. Elementary students taught by the Cuisenaire method will score higher on an arithmetic test than students not taught by the Cuisenaire method.

   b. Black male elementary students tutored by another male will achieve higher reading scores than will black male elementary students tutored by a female.

   c. People living in interracial housing will express more favorable attitudes toward those of another race than will people living in segregated housing.

   d. Lower-class children reinforced with tangible rewards will exhibit greater learning achievement than will lower-class children reinforced with intangible rewards.

   e. Advantaged and disadvantaged children of preschool age receiving preschool training will be separated by a smaller educational gap than will advantaged and disadvantaged children of preschool age not receiving preschool training.

   f. Children whose teachers evidence high expectations of their intellectual performance will perform at a higher level than will children whose teachers evidence low expectations of their intellectual performance.

4. There is no difference in the satisfaction with school expressed by children who read below grade level and children who read at or above grade level.

5. a. The hypothesis is inadequate because it is a value statement and cannot be investigated in a research study. A legitimate hypothesis would be: Teachers who receive higher pay than their administrators will express greater job satisfaction than will teachers who do not receive higher pay than their administrators.

   b. The hypothesis is inadequate because *enlightened judgments* is a value term. An acceptable hypothesis would be: Students who take a middle school government course will evidence more knowledge concerning local political affairs than will students who do not take a middle school government course.

   c. The hypothesis is inadequate because it is a value statement and lacks clear and concise operational definitions. A testable hypothesis would be: Those students performing below grade level in math who receive instruction in traditional math will score higher on a math test than will those performing below grade level in math who receive instruction in the new math.

   d. The hypothesis is inadequate because there is no statement of an expected relationship between variables. An acceptable hypothesis would be: There is a positive relationship between socioeconomic status and scores on an English proficiency exam.

e. The hypothesis is inadequate because there are no independent or dependent variables. An acceptable hypothesis would be: Children who show high achievement motivation will have higher scores on the Children's Manifest Anxiety Scale than children with low achievement motivation.

f. The hypothesis in inadequate because it is inconsistent with the existing knowledge of positive reinforcement and its effect on student responses.

6. Directional hypothesis: Early-maturing boys will exhibit more-positive self-concepts than late-maturing boys. Nondirectional hypothesis: There is a difference in the self-concepts of early- and late-maturing adolescent boys.

7. It gives direction to the collection and interpretation of data. Clearly stating the hypothesis may point to flaws that were not apparent while developing the vague idea of the study in mind.

8. a. research
   b. null
   c. null
   d. research

9. Answers will vary.

10. The hypothesis is not testable within a reasonable time period. Furthermore, it would be difficult to define and measure *better adult citizens.*

PART III

Statistical
Analysis

CHAPTER 5

Descriptive Statistics

INSTRUCTIONAL OBJECTIVES

After studying this chapter, the student will be able to

1. Identify the characteristics and limitations of four types of measurement scales: nominal, ordinal, interval, and ratio
2. Organize research data into frequency distributions and present them as frequency polygons and histograms
3. Distinguish between the measures of central tendency and the situations in which each should be used and calculate the mean, the median, and the mode for any given data
4. Describe appropriate applications of measures of variability and compute variance, standard deviation, quartile deviation, and range for any given set of data
5. Transform raw scores into standard scores and determine the relative position of z-scores in a normal curve
6. Identify appropriate applications of various correlation indexes for describing the relationship between variables
7. Compute the coefficient of correlation between two sets of interval or ratio data
8. Compute the coefficient of correlation between two sets of ranked data
9. Describe the meaning of *coefficient of determination* and its application in interpreting the coefficient of correlation
10. Identify the meaning, characteristics, and applications of meta-analysis

Statistical procedures are basically methods of handling quantitative information in such a way as to make that information meaningful. These procedures have two principal advantages. First, they enable us to organize, summarize, and describe our observations. Such techniques are called *descriptive statistics*. Second, they help us determine how reliably we can infer that those phenomena observed in a limited group, a *sample*, will also occur in the unobserved larger population of concern, from which the sample was drawn—in other words, how accurately we can employ inductive reasoning to infer that what we observe in the part will be observed in the whole. For problems of this nature we will need to employ *inferential statistics*.

A knowledge of some basic statistical procedures is essential for those proposing to carry out research, so that they can analyze and interpret their data and communicate their findings to others. In addition, it is desirable that educators who need to keep abreast of research and to make use of research findings be familiar with statistical procedures in order that they can understand and evaluate research studies conducted by others. The proper administration and interpretation of tests used in our schools also require some understanding of statistical procedures. Teachers who are unfamiliar with these procedures may have difficulty in evaluating their students' abilities and achievement. They also find it difficult to review research in their areas of specialization and to acquire up-to-date information.

/// SCALES OF MEASUREMENT

A fundamental step in the conduct of research is measurement: the process through which observations are translated into numbers. S. S. Stevens stated, "In its broadest sense, measurement is the assignment of numerals to objects or events according to rules."[1] Researchers begin with variables, then use rules to determine how these variables will be expressed in numerical form. The variable *religious preference* may be measured according to the numbers indicated by students who are asked to select one among (1) Catholic, (2) Jewish, (3) Protestant, or (4) other. The variable *weight* may be measured as the numbers observed when subjects step on a scale. The variable *social maturity* may be measured as scores on the Vineland Social Maturity Scale.

The nature of the measurement process that produces the numbers determines the interpretation that can be made from them and the statistical procedures that can be meaningfully used with them. The most widely quoted taxonomy of measurement procedures is Stevens's[2] Scales of Measurement, in which he classifies measurement as nominal, ordinal, interval, and ratio.

[1]Stevens, S. S. (1951). Mathematics, measurement, and psychophysics. In S. S. Stevens, (ed.). *Handbook of Experimental Psychology* (p. 1). New York: Wiley.
[2]*Ibid.*, pp. 1–49.

// Nominal Scale

The most primitive scale of measurement is the nominal scale. Nominal measurement involves the placing of objects or individuals into categories that are qualitatively rather than quantitatively different. Measurement at this level requires only that one be able to distinguish two or more relevant categories and know the criteria for placing individuals or objects into one or another category. The required empirical operation at this level involves recognizing that a given object or individual belongs in a given mutually exclusive category or that it does not. The only relationship between the categories is that they are *different* from each other; there is no suggestion that they represent "more" or "less" of the characteristic being measured. Classifying students according to gender would constitute nominal measurement.

Numbers are often used at the nominal level, but only in order to identify the categories. The numbers arbitrarily assigned to the categories serve merely as labels. All the members of a category are assigned the same number, and no two categories are assigned the same number. For example, in preparing data for a computer, the numeral 0 might be used to represent a male and the numeral 1 to represent a female. There is no empirical relationship among the numbers used in nominal measurement that corresponds to the mathematical relation between the numbers. The 1 does not indicate more of something than the 0. The numbers could be interchanged without affecting anything but the labeling scheme used.

The numbers used in a nominal scale do not represent absolute or relative amounts of any characteristic. They merely serve to identify the members of a given category. For example, the numbers assigned to football players constitute a nominal scale. We would not say that the player with number 48 on his jersey is necessarily a better player than the one with 36 on his jersey. Nor could we say that the difference in playing ability between players with the numbers 40 and 48 is equal to the difference between players with the numbers 50 and 58.

The identifying numbers in a nominal scale can never, of course, be arithmetically manipulated through addition, subtraction, multiplication, or division. One may use only those statistical procedures based on mere counting, such as reporting the number of observations in each category.

// Ordinal Scale

The next highest scale of measurement is ordinal, in which one determines the relative position of objects or individuals with respect to some attribute, but without indicating the distance between positions. The essential requirement for measurement at this level is an empirical criterion for ordering objects or events with respect to the attribute—that is, some procedure for determining, for each thing being measured, whether that individual or object has more, the same amount, or less of the attribute in question. Ordinal measurement occurs, for example, when teachers rank students on certain characteristics, such as their social maturity, leadership abilities, cooperativeness, and so on. Students are frequently ranked according to their academic achievement or according to their performance in a music or athletic contest.

In ordinal measurement, the empirical procedure used for ordering objects must satisfy a criterion known as the *transitivity postulate*. This postulate is written: If $(a > b)$ and $(b > c)$, then $(a > c)$; it means that the relationship must be such that if object a is greater than object b, and object b is greater than object c, then object a is greater than object c. Of course, other words may be substituted for *greater than*; these might include *stronger than, precedes, has more of some attribute,* and so on.

The empirical operation in ordinal measurement involves only direct comparison of the objects or individuals in terms of the extent to which they possess the attribute in question. Thus, when numbers are assigned to the objects, the only information considered is the *order* of the objects. Consequently, the only characteristic of the numbers having meaning is their order. The numbers assigned in ordinal measurement indicate only the order of position and nothing more. Neither the difference between the numbers nor their ratio has meaning. When the numbers 1, 2, 3, and so on, are used in ordinal measurement, there is no implication that rank 1 is as much higher than rank 2 as 2 is than 3, and so on. The distance between the child with a rank of 1 and the child with a rank of 2 may be the same, less than, or greater than the distance between children with rankings of 2 and 3. There is simply no basis for interpreting the magnitude of differences between the numbers or the ratio of the numbers. In an untimed footrace, we may know who came in first, second, third, and so on, but we would not know how much faster one runner was than another. The difference between the first and second would not necessarily be the same as the difference between the second and third, or the third and fourth. Neither could one say that the runner who came in second was twice as fast as the runner who came in fourth.

A good example of an ordinal scale is the scale of hardness of minerals. Minerals are arranged according to their ability to scratch one another. If mineral A can scratch mineral B, then mineral A is said to be harder than mineral B. On this basis a diamond is ranked as the hardest, since it can scratch all other known minerals but cannot be scratched by any others. A set of ten minerals ranging in hardness from the softest to the hardest was selected as a standard and assigned the numbers from 1 to 10, with 1 indicating the softest mineral and 10 the hardest. Other minerals are assigned numbers on the basis of the scratch test. Thus, we know the order of hardness of minerals, but we do not know how much harder one mineral is than another. We may not assume that a mineral assigned a value of 4 is twice as hard as a mineral with a value of 2, or that the difference in hardness between minerals 2 and 4 is the same as the difference in hardness between minerals with values 1 and 3.

The statistics appropriate for an ordinal scale are limited. Since the size of the interval between the categories is unknown, one cannot use any statistical procedure that assumes equal intervals. Statistics that indicate the points below which certain percentages of the cases fall are appropriate with an ordinal scale.

// Interval Scale

An interval scale is one that provides equal intervals from an arbitrary origin. An interval scale not only orders objects or events according to the amount of the attribute they represent but also establishes equal intervals between the units of measure. Equal differences in the numbers represent equal differences in the attribute being measured. The Fahrenheit and Centigrade thermometers are examples of interval scales.

On an interval scale, both the order and distance relationships among the numbers have meaning. We may assert that the difference between 50 and 51 degrees Centigrade is equal to the difference between 30 and 31 degrees Centigrade. We could not say, however, that 50 degrees is twice as hot as 25 degrees. This is because there is no true zero point on an interval scale. A zero point is established by convention, as in the Centigrade scale, which assigns the value 0 degrees to the freezing point of water.

Likewise, the zero point on a psychological or educational test is arbitrary. For example, there is no zero intelligence; there is no way in our standardized intelligence tests to identify an individual of zero intelligence. A student may occasionally receive a score of zero on a statistics test, but this does not mean that he has zero knowledge of statistics. If we had three students who made scores of 15, 30, and 45 on a statistics test, we could not say that the score of 30 represents twice as much knowledge of statistics as the score of 15 or that the score of 45 represents three times as much knowledge as the score of 15. To understand the reason why this is so, let us assume that 15 very simple items are added to the test so that all three students are able to answer them correctly. The three scores would now become 30, 45, and 60 for the three students. If we attempted to form ratios between the values on this interval-type scale, we would mistakenly report that the student with a score of 60 had twice as much knowledge of statistics as the student with a score of 30, whereas in the earlier ratio we had incorrectly assumed that the same student had three times as great a knowledge of statistics as the other student.

Thus, because the zero is arbitrary, multiplication and division of the numbers are not appropriate; as we have seen, ratios between the numbers on an interval scale are meaningless. However, the difference between positions on an interval scale may be reported or the numbers may be added. Any statistical procedures based on adding may be used with this level scale along with the procedures appropriate for the lower-level scales. These include most of the common statistical procedures.

It is important to point out that in most of the cases where we use interval scales, the intervals are equal in terms of the measuring instrument itself but not necessarily in terms of the ability we are measuring. To illustrate, consider a spelling test with the following words: *cat, dish, ball, loquacious, schizophrenia, and pneumonia*. Here the distance between 1 correct and 3 correct is the same as the distance between 3 correct and 5 correct. However, when considered in terms of spelling ability, the difference between 3 and 5 correct suggests a greater difference in ability than does the difference between 1 and 3 correct. Unless one can say that the distance between 3 and 5 on the spelling test represents the same amount of spelling ability as does the distance between 1 and 3, then these scores indicate only the rank order of the students.

However, through careful construction one can produce an instrument where the intervals observed between scores on the test give a reasonable approximation of ability intervals. The better intelligence tests are an example of this. The difference in ability between an IQ of 90 and an IQ of 95 may not be precisely the same as the difference between an IQ of 105 and an IQ of 110, but we will not be greatly misled if we assume that the two differences are approximately equal.

// Ratio Scale

A ratio scale, the highest level, is one that provides a true zero point as well as equal intervals. Ratios can be formed between any two given values on the scale. A yardstick used to measure length in units of inches or feet is a ratio scale, for the origin on the scale is an absolute zero corresponding to no length at all. Thus, it is possible to state that a stick 6 feet long is twice as long as a stick 3 feet long. With a ratio scale, it is possible to multiply or divide each of the values by a certain number without changing the properties of the scale. For example, we can multiply 2 pounds by 16 to change the unit of measurement to 32 ounces or we can multiply 6 feet by 12 to change the unit to inches. We can multiply and maintain the same ratio as before the multiplication. For example, we can multiply 4 quarts of milk and 2 quarts of milk by 2 and change the unit of measurement to pints. In pints, 8 pints is still twice as much as 4 pints.

Only a few variables of interest in education are ratio in nature. These are largely confined to motor performance and other physiological measures. While we can say that a person 6 feet tall is twice as tall as a person 3 feet tall, because heights are ratio data, we cannot say that a person with an IQ of 150 is twice as intelligent as a person with an IQ of 75 because IQ scores are interval data.

All types of statistical procedures are appropriate with a ratio scale.

/// ORGANIZING RESEARCH DATA

Describing data that have not been arranged in some kind of order is very difficult, if not impossible. Therefore, organizing research data is a fundamental step in descriptive statistics. Two frequently used ways of organizing data are (1) arranging the measures into frequency distributions and (2) presenting them in graphic form.

// Frequency Distributions

A systematic arrangement of individual measures from lowest to highest is called a frequency distribution. The use of this technique merely involves making a list of the individual measures in a column, with the highest measure at the top, the next highest second from the top, and continuing down until the lowest measure is recorded at the bottom of the column. It is often found that several identical scores will occur in a distribution. Instead of listing these scores separately, it is customary to add a second column where the frequency of each measure is recorded. In Table 5.1 the scores of a group of 105 students in a statistics test are shown. In Section A of the table the scores are listed in an unorganized form. In Section B the same scores are arranged into a frequency distribution.

From a frequency distribution it is possible to examine the general "shape" of the distribution. With the scores so organized, one can determine their spread, whether they are distributed evenly or tend to cluster, and where clusters occur in the distribution. For example, looking over the frequency distribution of the scores presented in Table 5.1, it is easy to see that they range from 21 to 35, that 29 is the most frequent score, and that there is a tendency for scores to cluster more near the top of the distribution than the bottom. None of this would be apparent if the scores had not been organized. Organizing data into frequency distributions also facilitates the computation of various useful statistics.

// Graphic Presentation of Data

It is often helpful and convenient to present research data in graphic form. Among various types of graphs, the most widely used are the *histogram* and the *frequency polygon*. The initial steps in constructing the histogram and the frequency polygon are identical:

TABLE 5.1 The Test Scores of 105 Students in a Statistics Test

A. Unorganized Scores

33,	29,	30,	30,	33,	29,	33,	32,	28,	24,	34,	31,	27,	29,	23,
25,	29,	24,	27,	26,	33,	33,	26,	30,	28,	26,	29,	32,	32,	31,
28,	34,	30,	31,	33,	21,	29,	31,	30,	32,	35,	30,	31,	27,	29,
26,	29,	33,	32,	29,	28,	28,	30,	28,	27,	30,	31,	34,	33,	22,
30,	29,	27,	29,	24,	30,	21,	31,	31,	33,	28,	21,	31,	29,	31,
31,	33,	22,	29,	31,	32,	32,	31,	28,	29,	30,	22,	33,	30,	30,
32,	33,	31,	33,	28,	29,	27,	33,	27,	21,	30,	29,	28,	27,	33,

B. Frequency Distribution

Scores (X)	Tallies	Frequencies (f)
35	/	1
34	///	3
33	ﬀﬀﬀ ﬀﬀﬀ ﬀﬀﬀ	15
32	ﬀﬀﬀ ///	8
31	ﬀﬀﬀ ﬀﬀﬀ ////	14
30	ﬀﬀﬀ ﬀﬀﬀ ////	14
29	ﬀﬀﬀ ﬀﬀﬀ ﬀﬀﬀ /	16
28	ﬀﬀﬀ ﬀﬀﬀ	10
27	ﬀﬀﬀ ///	8
26	////	4
25	/	1
24	///	3
23	/	1
22	///	3
21	////	4
		N = 105

1. Lay out the score points on a horizontal dimension (abscissa) from the lowest value on the left to the highest on the right. Leave enough space for an additional score at both ends of the distribution.
2. Lay out the frequencies of the scores (or intervals) on the vertical dimension (ordinate), numbering up from zero.
3. Place a dot above the center of each score at the level of the frequency of that score.

From this point one can construct either a histogram or a polygon.

In constructing a histogram, one should draw through each dot a horizontal line equal to the width representing a score, as shown in Figure 5.1.

To construct a polygon, the adjacent dots are connected and the two ends of the resulting figure are connected to the base (zero line) at the points representing one less than the lowest score and one more than the highest score, as shown in Figure 5.2.

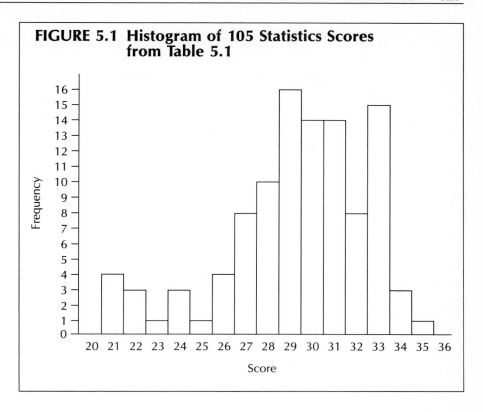

FIGURE 5.1 Histogram of 105 Statistics Scores from Table 5.1

/// MEASURES OF CENTRAL TENDENCY

A convenient way of summarizing data is to find a single index that can represent a whole set of measures. For example, finding a single score that can give an indication of the performance of a group of 300 students on an IQ test would be useful for comparative purposes. In statistics three indices are available for such use. They are called *measures of central tendency,* or *averages.* To most laymen the term *average* means the sum of the scores divided by the number of scores. To a statistician the average can be this measure, known as the *mean,* or one of the other two measures of central tendency, known as the *mode* and the *median.* Each of these three can serve as an index to represent a group as a whole.

// The Mode

The mode is that value in a distribution that occurs most frequently. It is the simplest to find of the three measures of central tendency because

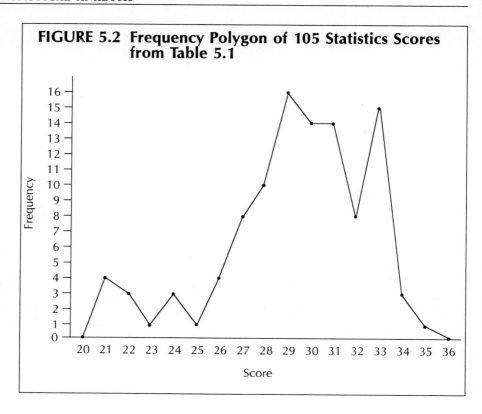

FIGURE 5.2 Frequency Polygon of 105 Statistics Scores from Table 5.1

it is determined by inspection rather than by computation. Given the distribution of scores

14   16   16   17   18   19   19   19   21   22

one can readily see that the mode of this distribution is 19 because it is the most frequent score.

Sometimes there is more than one mode in a distribution. For example, if the scores had been

14   16   16   16   18   19   19   19   21   22

we would have two modes: 16 and 19. This kind of distribution with two modes is called *bimodal*. Distributions with three or more modes are called *trimodal* or *multimodal*, respectively.

The mode is not often a useful indicator of central value in a distribution for two reasons. In the first place, it is unstable. For example, two random samples drawn from the same population may have quite different modes. In the second place, a distribution may have more than one mode. In published research the mode is seldom reported as an indicator of central tendency.

Its use is largely limited to inspectional purposes. A mode may be reported for any of the scales of measurement, but it is the only measure of central tendency that may legitimately be used with nominal scales.

// The Median

The median is defined as that point in a distribution of measures below which 50 percent of the cases lie (which means that the other 50 percent will be above this point). For example, given the distribution of scores

14   16   16   17   18   19   19   19   21   22

the point below which 50 percent of the cases fall is halfway between 18 and 19. Thus, the median of this distribution is 18.5. To find this value, we first placed the ten scores of the distribution in rank order (that is, from the lowest to the highest) and then found the point below which one half of the scores lie. This point, 18.5, which exactly separates the two values 18 and 19, is called in statistical terminology the *upper limit* of the score 18 and the *lower limit* of the score 19. In computing the median, each score is thought of as representing a range, or interval, from halfway between that score and the next lowest score up to halfway between that score and the next highest score. Thus, in the example, 18 is thought of as representing an interval from 17.5 to 18.5, while 19 represents an interval from 18.5 to 19.5.

It is important to note that the median does not always fall on the border line between two values. In fact it is often located somewhere between the upper limit and the lower limit of an interval. For the purpose of establishing the median, we must picture a recorded score as representing the range between its lower and upper limits rather than a single point. Consider the following example:

23   24   25   26   26   26   26   27

In this distribution, the median falls between two of the scores of 26. Note the frequency of the score 26. There are four of these scores in the distribution, one of which is located below the midpoint and three above the midpoint. In this case, to find the median we must subdivide the interval 25.50–26.50 into four parts. The distance between each of these four scores would thus be 0.25 of the interval. Each of these scores is therefore thought of as representing a range covering 0.25 of the distance between 25.50 and 26.50, which are the lower and upper limits of the score 26. The following is an illustration of this concept showing the position and value of the median:

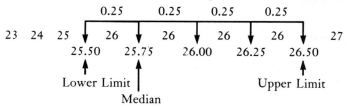

It is easier to use the following formula for finding the median rather than go through this process each time.

$$Md = L + \left(\frac{\frac{N}{2} - cfb}{fw}\right)i \qquad (5.1)$$

where

Md = the median
L = the lower limit of the interval within which the median lies
N = the number of cases in the distribution
cfb = the cumulative frequency in all intervals below the interval containing the median
fw = the frequency of cases within the interval containing the median
i = the interval size

In the foregoing example, L is 25.50, N is 8, cfb is 3, fw is 4, and i is 1.

$$\underbrace{23 \quad 24 \quad 25}_{cfb = 3} \Big| \underbrace{26 \quad 26 \quad 26 \quad 26}_{\substack{fw = 4 \\ L = 25.50}} \quad \underset{0}{27}$$

Putting these values in the formula, we obtain

$$Md = 25.50 + \left(\frac{\frac{8}{2} - 3}{4}\right)1 = 25.75$$

The value i becomes necessary only when the size of the interval is other than 1. For example, if we are working with achievement-test grade-level scores that are expressed in decimal units such as 3.4 and 5.9, the interval size is 0.1.

A frequency distribution can be used to compute the median efficiently. Table 5.2 shows the same data as Table 5.1 and includes an additional column labeled *cumulative frequencies* (*cf*), which is used for locating the median. Cumulative frequencies show the frequencies of the values up to and including any given interval in a distribution. For example, the frequency of scores up to and including the interval of the score 30 in Table 5.2 is 64, as shown in the *cf* column. This column enables us to locate the interval within which the median lies. Because the median is that point in the distribution below which 50 percent of the cases fall, the interval containing the median will be the one with a cumulative frequency containing the value of $N/2$. In other words, we divide the N of the distribution by 2 and look for the interval that contains this value.

In the distribution of scores shown in Table 5.2, the number of cases, or N, equals 105, and thus the value of $N/2$ is 52.50. Looking in the *cf*

TABLE 5.2 Computation of the Median with a Frequency Distribution of Scores of 105 Students in a Statistics Test

Scores (X)	Frequencies (f)	Cumulative Frequencies (cf)
35	1	105
34	3	104
33	15	101
32	8	86
31	14	78
30	14 *fw*	64
29	16	50
28	10	34
27	8	24
26	4	16
25	1 *cfb* = 50	12
24	3	11
23	1	8
22	3	7
21	4	4

$$Md = 29.50 + \left(\frac{\frac{105}{2} - 50}{14} \right)1 = 29.678$$

column, we see that there are 50 cases up to and including the score 29 and 64 cases up to and including the score 30; thus, the median is located within the interval represented by the score of 30. It is possible now to apply formula 5.1 and find the median of the distribution. The value of L in this example is 29.50 because the interval that contains the median represents a range from 29.50, the lower limit, to 30.50, the upper limit. The value of *cfb* (that is, the cumulative frequency of the values below the interval that contains the median) is 50. The frequency of the values within the interval represented by the score 30 (that is, the value of *fw*) is 14. The interval size, or the value of i, in this distribution is 1 because each score represents an interval width of 1. Applying the formula 5.1, we find that the median of the distribution is 29.678.

  Notice that the median does not take into account the size of individual scores. In order to find it we arrange our data in rank order and find the point that divides the distribution into two equal halves. The median is an ordinal statistic because it is based on rank. We can compute a median from interval or ratio data, but in such cases the interval characteristic of the data is not being used.

  One circumstance in which the median may be the preferred measure of central tendency arises when there are some extreme scores in the distribution. In this case the use of a measure of central tendency that takes into account the size of each score results in either overestimation or under-estimation of the typical score. The median, because of its insensitivity to extreme scores, is the appropriate index to be applied when one wants to find the typical score. For illustration consider the following distribution:

$$49 \quad 50 \quad 51 \quad 53 \quad 54 \quad 55 \quad 56 \quad 70 \quad 89$$

The score of 54, which is the median of this distribution, is the most typical score. An index that takes into account the individual values of the scores 70 and 89 will certainly result in an overestimation of the typical score.

// The Mean

The most widely used measure of central tendency is the mean, which is popularly known as the average or *arithmetic average.* It is the sum of all the values in a distribution divided by the number of cases. In terms of a formula it is

$$\bar{X} = \frac{X_1 + X_2 + X_3 + \ldots + X_n}{N} \tag{5.2}$$

which is usually written as

$$\bar{X} = \frac{\Sigma X}{N} \tag{5.3}$$

where

$$\bar{X} = \text{the mean}$$
$$\Sigma = \text{the sum of}$$
$$X = \text{raw score}$$
$$N = \text{the number of cases}$$

Applying formula 5.3 to the following IQ scores, we find that the mean is 111.

IQ Scores: 112   121   115   101   119   109   100

$$\bar{X} = \frac{112 + 121 + 115 + 101 + 119 + 109 + 100}{7} = \frac{777}{7} = 111$$

Note that in this computation the scores were not arranged in any particular order. That is unnecessary when the mean of a set of measures is to be found.

Because the mean is an arithmetic average, it is classified as an interval statistic. Its use is appropriate for interval or ratio data but not for nominal or ordinal data.

/ Computing the Mean from a Frequency Distribution

If the data have been arranged into a frequency distribution, the sum of the scores can be computed by multiplying each score by its frequency, summing these products and then dividing the results by the number of cases. The formula for computing the mean from a frequency distribution is

$$\bar{X} = \frac{\Sigma fX}{N} \qquad (5.4)$$

Table 5.3 shows the computation of the mean for the data presented in Table 5.1. It is obvious that applying formula 5.4 to that frequency distribution has simplified the computation of the mean of that distribution.

// Comparison of the Three Indices of Central Tendency

Since the mean is an interval or ratio statistic, it is generally a more precise measure than the median (an ordinal statistic) or the mode (a nominal statistic). It takes into account the value of *every* score. It is also the most stable of the three measures of central tendency in that if a number of samples are randomly drawn from a parent population, the means of these samples will vary less from one another than will their medians and their modes. For these reasons the mean is more frequently used in research than the other two measures.

TABLE 5.3 Computation of the Mean for Frequency Distribution of Scores of 105 Students in a Statistics Test

X	f	fX
35	1	35
34	3	102
33	15	495
32	8	256
31	14	434
30	14	420
29	16	464
28	10	280
27	8	216
26	4	104
25	1	25
24	3	72
23	1	23
22	3	66
21	4	84
	$N = 105$	$\Sigma fX = 3076$

$$\bar{X} = \frac{3076}{105} = 29.295$$

The mean is the best indicator of the combined performance of an entire group. However, the median is the best indicator of *typical* performance. Consider, for example, a school board whose members have the following annual incomes: $70,000, $30,000, $25,000, $20,000, $20,000. The mean, $33,000, indicates the total income in relation to the number of members, but it is higher than all but one of the board members' incomes. The median, $25,000, gives a better picture of the typical income in the group.

/ Shapes of Distributions

Frequency distributions can have a variety of shapes. A distribution is symmetrical when the two halves are mirror images of each other. In a symmetrical distribution the values of the mean and the median coincide. If such a distribution has a single mode, rather than two or more modes, the three indices of central tendency will coincide, as shown in Figure 5.3.

If a distribution is not symmetrical, it is described as being *skewed*. In skewed distributions the values of the measures of central tendency differ. In such distributions the value of the mean, because it is influenced by the size of extreme scores, is pulled toward the end of the distribution in which the extreme scores lie, as shown in Figures 5.4 and 5.5. The effect of extreme values is less on the median because this index is influenced not by the size

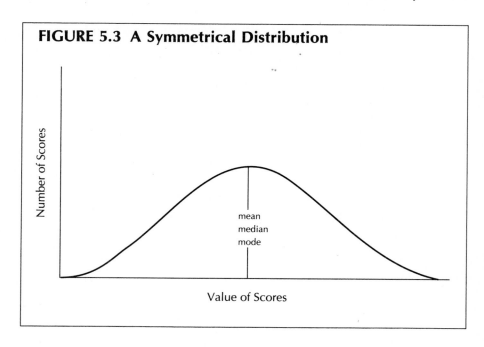

FIGURE 5.3 A Symmetrical Distribution

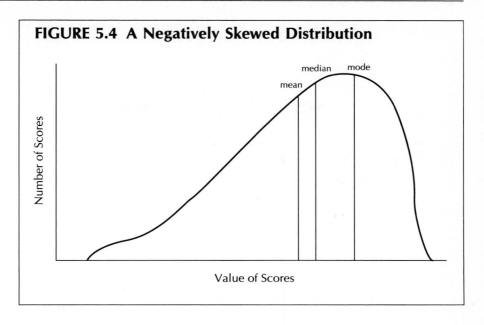

FIGURE 5.4 A Negatively Skewed Distribution

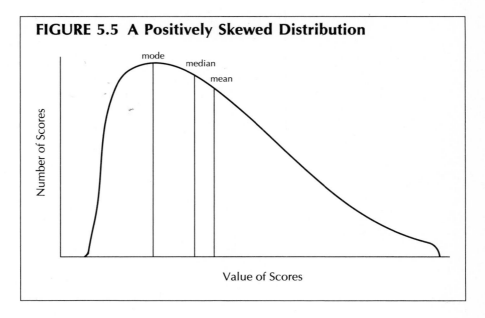

FIGURE 5.5 A Positively Skewed Distribution

of scores but by their position. Extreme values have no impact on the mode because this index has no relation with either of the ends of the distribution. When the distribution is skewed toward the lower end, or negatively skewed, the mean is *always* smaller than the median and the median is *usually* smaller than the mode (Figure 5.4). When a distribution is skewed toward the higher end, or positively skewed, the mean is *always* greater than the median and the median is *usually* greater than the mode (Figure 5.5). The skew of a distribution can be identified by comparing the mean and the median without necessarily constructing a histogram or polygon.

/// MEASURES OF VARIABILITY

Although indices of central tendency help us describe data in terms of average value or typical measure, they do not give us the total picture of a distribution. The mean values of two distributions may be identical, while the degree of dispersion, or variability, of their scores might be different. In one distribution the scores might cluster around the central value; in the other they might be scattered. For illustration consider the following distributions of scores:

$$(a) \ 24, 24, 25, 25, 25, 26, 26 \quad \bar{X} = \frac{175}{7} = 25$$

$$(b) \ 16, 19, 22, 25, 28, 30, 35 \quad \bar{X} = \frac{175}{7} = 25$$

The value of the mean in both of these distributions is 25, but the degree of scattering of the scores differs considerably. The scores in distribution (a) are obviously much more homogeneous than those in distribution (b). There is clearly a need for an index that can describe distributions in terms of *variation* of scores. In statistics several indices are available for this purpose. The four most commonly used are *range, quartile deviation, variance,* and *standard deviation.*

// Range

The simplest of all indices of variability is the range. It is the difference between the highest and the lowest scores in a distribution, and it is found by subtracting the smallest value from the highest. In formula form it is

$$R = X_h - X_l \tag{5.5}$$

where

R = the range
X_h = the highest value in a distribution
X_l = the lowest value in a distribution

For example, the ranges in the following distributions are 14 and 6, respectively.

$$2 \quad 10 \quad 11 \quad 12 \quad 13 \quad 14 \quad 16$$
$$9 \quad 10 \quad 11 \quad 12 \quad 13 \quad 14 \quad 15$$

The range is an unreliable index of variability in that it is based on only two values, the highest and the lowest. As can readily be seen from the above distributions, it is not a stable indicator of the nature of the spread of the measures around the central value. For this reason the use of the range is mainly limited to inspectional purposes. In some research reports, reference is made to the range of distributions, but such references are usually used in conjunction with other measures of variability, such as quartile deviation and standard deviation.

// Quartile Deviation

The quartile deviation (QD) is half the difference between the upper and lower quartiles in a distribution. The upper quartile (Q_3) is the point in a distribution below which 75 percent of the cases lie. The lower quartile (Q_1) is the point below which 25 percent of the cases lie. The upper quartile is also referred to as the 75th percentile and the lower quartile as the 25th percentile.

The procedure for finding Q_1 and Q_3 is similar to that used for finding the median. The median is, in fact, the second quartile. In the case of Q_3 the formula becomes

$$Q_3 = L + \left(\frac{\frac{3N}{4} - cfb}{fw} \right) i \qquad (5.6)$$

and for Q_1 the formula is

$$Q_1 = L + \left(\frac{\frac{N}{4} - cfb}{fw} \right) i \qquad (5.7)$$

where

Q_3 = the upper quartile
Q_1 = the lower quartile
L = the lower limit of the interval within which the quartile lies
N = the number of cases in the distribution
cfb = the cumulative frequency below the interval containing the quartile
fw = the frequency of cases within the interval containing the quartile
i = the interval size

Once the values of the first and third quartiles have been found, the quartile deviation can be computed as follows:

$$QD = \frac{Q_3 - Q_1}{2} \qquad (5.8)$$

For example, if the upper and the lower quartiles in a distribution of scores are 35 and 15, respectively, the value of the quartile deviation would be 10.

$$QD = \frac{35 - 15}{2} = 10$$

The quartile deviation provides a measure of one half of that range of scores within which lie the middle 50 percent of the cases. If the spread of scores is great, the value of the quartile deviation will be higher than it will be if the spread is small. Although quartile deviation, like the range, is based on only two values in a distribution (Q_1 and Q_3), it is a more useful measure of variability than the range. This is because Q_1 and Q_3 are much more stable than the highest and the lowest values on which the range is based.

The quartile deviation belongs to the same statistical family as the median because it is an ordinal statistic. It is most often used in conjunction with the median. It is also called the *semi-interquartile range*. Like the median, it is especially useful when we want a measure that is not influenced by a few extreme scores. If the quartile deviation for family incomes in village A is $10,000 and in village B it is $8000, we know the family incomes in A are more heterogeneous as measured by the spread through the middle of the distribution. If one family in village B won a huge lottery, it would make little or no change in the median or quartile deviation. However, it would considerably increase the mean and the standard deviation.

// Variance and Standard Deviation

Variance and standard deviation are the most useful measures of variability. They are both based on *deviation scores*—scores that show the difference between a raw score and the mean. The formula for a deviation score is: $x = X - \bar{X}$. Raw scores below the mean will have negative deviation scores, and raw scores above the mean will have positive deviation scores. By definition, the sum of the deviation scores in a distribution is always 0. Thus, if one is to use deviation scores in calculating measures of variability, one must find a way to get around the fact that $\Sigma x = 0$. The technique used is to square each deviation score so that they all become positive numbers. If we then sum the squared deviations and divide by the number of scores, we have the mean of the squared deviations from the mean, or the *variance*. In mathematical form variance is

$$\sigma^2 = \frac{\Sigma x^2}{N} \tag{5.9}$$

where

$\sigma^2 =$ the variance
$\Sigma =$ the sum of
$x =$ the deviation of each score from the mean $(X - \bar{X})$, otherwise known as the deviation score
$N =$ the number of cases in the distribution

Because each of the deviation scores is squared, the variance is necessarily expressed in units that are squares of the original units of measure. For example, we might find the variance of the heights of children in a class is 9 square inches. This would tell us that this class is more heterogeneous in height than a class with a variance of 4 square inches and more homogeneous than a class with a variance of 16 square inches.

In many cases educators prefer an index that summarizes the data in the same unit of measurement as the original data. *Standard deviation* (σ), the square root of variance, provides such an index. It is by far the most commonly used measure of variability. By definition the standard deviation is the square root of the mean of the squared deviation scores. Rewriting this definition using symbols, we obtain

$$\sigma = \sqrt{\frac{\Sigma x^2}{N}} \tag{5.10}$$

For an illustration, consider Table 5.4. Column (1) in this table shows

TABLE 5.4 Computation of the Standard Deviation

(1) X	(2) $x = X - \bar{X}$	(3) $x^2 = (X - \bar{X})^2$
10	+4	+16
9	+3	+9
9	+3	+9
8	+2	+4
7	+1	+1
6	0	0
5	−1	+1
3	−3	+9
2	−4	+16
1	−5	+25
$\Sigma X = 60$		$\Sigma x^2 = 90$

$$\bar{X} = \frac{60}{10} = 6 \qquad \sigma = \sqrt{\frac{90}{10}} = \sqrt{9} = 3$$

the distribution of the test scores of ten individuals. The mean of this distribution is 6. Column (2) presents the deviations for each of the scores. For example, the deviation of the score 8 from the mean is $+2$, the deviation of the score 5 from the mean is -1, and so forth. Column (3) shows the squares of each of these deviation scores. The sum of these squared deviation scores is 90. Putting this value in the formula and dividing by 10, the number of cases, we arrive at 9, which is the mean of the squared deviation scores. The square root of this value is 3, which is the standard deviation of this distribution.

The foregoing procedure is convenient when the mean of the distribution is a round number, which it is not in most cases. Therefore, the following formula has been developed to eliminate the tedious task of working with fractional deviation scores. The use of this formula gives the same result with much less labor. Thus, it is recommended that students always use this formula for the computation of standard deviation.

$$\sigma = \sqrt{\frac{\Sigma X^2 - \frac{(\Sigma X)^2}{N}}{N}} \qquad (5.11)$$

where

σ = the standard deviation

ΣX^2 = the sum of the squares of each score (that is, each score is first squared, then these squares are summed)

$(\Sigma X)^2$ = the sum of the scores squared (the scores are first summed, then this total is squared)

N = the number of cases

Table 5.5 shows the computation of the standard deviation of the data

TABLE 5.5 Computation of the Standard Deviation Using Formula 5.11

X	X^2	
10	100	
9	81	$\sigma = \sqrt{\dfrac{450 - \dfrac{(60)^2}{10}}{10}}$
9	81	
8	64	
7	49	
6	36	$= \sqrt{\dfrac{450 - 360}{10}}$
5	25	
3	9	
2	4	$= \sqrt{9}$
1	1	
$\Sigma X = 60$	$\Sigma X = 450$	$= 3$

in Table 5.4 using formula 5.11. The first column in this table shows the scores and their sum. The second column shows the square of each score and the sum of these squares. The rest of the table shows the application of formula 5.11 to find the value of the standard deviation. Note that the resulting value is the same as that found by applying formula 5.10 to the same data.

The standard deviation belongs to the same statistical family as the mean; that is, like the mean, it is an interval or ratio statistic and its computation is based on the size of individual scores in the distribution. It is by far the most frequently used measure of variability and is used in conjunction with the mean.

/// STANDARD SCORES

We often wish to make a comparison between the relative positions of one individual on two different tests. It is only possible to do this meaningfully if the two tests have the same means and the same standard deviations, but this seldom happens in practice. To overcome this difficulty we can translate measures into standard scores. A widely used standard score that plays an important role in statistical analyses is the z-score, which is defined as the distance of a score from the mean, as measured by standard deviation units. The formula for finding a z-score is

$$z = \frac{X - \bar{X}}{\sigma} = \frac{x}{\sigma} \qquad (5.12)$$

where

$X =$ the raw score
$\bar{X} =$ the mean of the distribution
$\sigma =$ the standard deviation of the distribution
$x =$ the deviation score ($X - \bar{X}$)

Applying this formula, a score exactly one standard deviation above the mean becomes a z of $+1$, a score exactly one standard deviation below the mean becomes a z of -1, and so on. A score with the same numerical value as the mean will have a z-score value of 0. For illustration, suppose a student's score on a psychology test is 72 where the mean of the distribution is 78 and the standard deviation equals 12. Suppose also that the same student has made a score of 48 on a statistics test where the mean is 51 and the standard deviation is 6. If we substitute these figures for the appropriate symbols in formula 5.12, we can derive a z-score for each test.

$$
\begin{array}{cc}
\textit{Psychology} & \textit{Statistics} \\
z_1 = \dfrac{72 - 78}{12} = -0.50 & z_2 = \dfrac{48 - 51}{6} = -0.50
\end{array}
$$

Both these standard scores belong to the z-distribution, where by definition the mean is 0 and the standard deviation is 1, and therefore they are directly comparable. It is apparent in this example that the score of 72 on the psychology test and the score of 48 on the statistics test are equivalent—that is, both scores are indicative of the same relative level of performance. In other words, the standing of the student who has obtained these scores is the same in both tests when compared with the performance of the other students. It would be very difficult to make such a comparison without employing the z-score technique.

Let us use another example: Suppose a student who has taken the same tests has obtained a score of 81 on the psychology test and a score of 53 on the statistics test. As before, it is difficult to compare these raw scores to show on which test this student has done better. Converting the scores to z-scores makes the comparison easy. Using formula 5.12, we find the values of z_1 and z_2 in this case to be

$$\textit{Psychology} \qquad\qquad\qquad \textit{Statistics}$$
$$z_1 = \frac{81 - 78}{12} = +0.25 \qquad\qquad z_2 = \frac{53 - 51}{6} = +0.33$$

This rather surprising result shows that the score of 53 on the statistics test actually indicates a slightly better relative performance than the score of 81 on the psychology test. Compared with the other students, this student has done somewhat better in statistics than in psychology.

A disadvantage of z-scores is that we have to deal with negative values and decimal fractions. To overcome these difficulties we can transform the z-scores into another standard-score scale that does not involve negative numbers or decimals. One of the most common is the Z-score distribution that has a mean of 50 and a standard deviation of 10. To transform z-scores to Z-scores we multiply the z-value by 10 and add 50. The Z-score formula is

$$Z = 10z + 50 = 10\left(\frac{X - \bar{X}}{\sigma}\right) + 50 \qquad (5.13)$$

Suppose a student's score on a Spanish test is 21. Given that the mean of the scores in this test is 27 and the standard deviation is 6, the z-score will be $(21-27)/6$, which can be inserted directly into the Z-score formula as follows:

$$Z = 10\left(\frac{21 - 27}{6}\right) + 50 = 40$$

The transformation of z-scores into Z-scores not only enables one to work with whole numbers, but it also avoids the adverse psychological implications of describing subjects' performances with negative numbers.

Teachers who wish to compare the standings of their students on successive tests, or to add all the scores obtained on different tests in the same course to make a general distribution, can convert the students' raw scores to z-scores or Z-scores in order to give equal weight to each set of scores. Adding and averaging scores that belong to different distributions and have different means and different standard deviations, without converting them to some kind of standard score, is not statistically justified.

In addition to Z, there are other transformed standard-score distributions. To transform a distribution of scores to a new standardized distribution, it is only necessary to multiply the z-score by the desired standard deviation and add the desired mean. The general formula is:

$$A = \mu_A + \sigma_A(z) \qquad\qquad (5.13a)$$

where

A = the standard score on the new scale
μ_A = the mean for the new standard scale
σ_A = the standard deviation for the new standard scale

For example, each part of the Graduate Record Examination (GRE) has a mean of 500 and a standard deviation of 100 for its transformed distribution. If you were 1.5 standard deviations above the mean ($z = 1.5$) on the verbal section of the GRE, your score would be reported as 650 [500 + 100(1.5) = 650]. If your quantitative score is 500, you have scored exactly at the mean.

The Stanford-Binet Intelligence Scale is a standard-score scale with a mean of 100 and a standard deviation of 16. So to convert a raw score on the Stanford-Binet to the standard scale, one would first determine its z-value, then multiply by 16 and add 100.

Transforming a set of scores to standard scores does not alter the shape of the original distribution. If a distribution of scores is skewed, the derived standard scores will also produce a skewed distribution. Only if the original distribution is normal will the standard scores produce a normal distribution.

/// THE NORMAL CURVE

It has been found that the distribution of many physical and psychological measures takes the shape of a bell when plotted as a frequency polygon. For example, if we measure American boys on their tenth birthday, we will find many boys whose height is near the mean and slightly fewer boys who are a bit above or below the mean. The further we get from the mean, the fewer boys we will find at each height. A polygon showing this distribution closely resembles a theoretical polygon known as the normal curve. Tables of the ordinate and the areas of the normal curve have already been computed. The areas are shown in Table A.2 in the Appendix.

This hypothetical polygon indicates the expected (that is, theoretical) frequencies of all possible z-scores. It indicates that z-scores near 0 will be expected to occur more frequently than other z-score values, and the farther from 0 a z-score is, the less frequently it will be expected to occur.

Inasmuch as so many naturally occurring distributions resemble the normal curve, this theoretical model has proved to be highly useful. Whenever actual data are known or believed to resemble the normal curve in distribution, we can deduce many useful estimates from the theoretical properties of the normal curve.

The normal curve is a symmetrical distribution of measures with the same number of cases at specified distances below the mean as above the mean. Its mean is the point below which exactly 50 percent of the cases fall and above which the other 50 percent of the cases are located. The median and the mode in such a distribution are identical values and coincide with the mean. In a normal curve most of the cases concentrate near the mean. The frequency of cases decreases as we proceed away from the mean in either direction. Approximately 34 percent of the cases in a normal distribution fall between the mean and one standard deviation above or below the mean. The area between one and two standard deviations from the mean on either side of the distribution contains about 14 percent of the cases. Only about 2 percent of the cases fall between two and three standard deviations from the mean, and only about 0.1 percent of the cases fall above or below three standard deviations from the mean. This is illustrated in Figure 5.6. It is possible to determine the percentage of the cases below and above each z-score in the normal distribution by consulting Table A.1 in the Appendix,

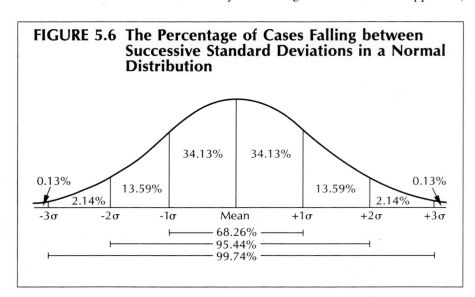

FIGURE 5.6 The Percentage of Cases Falling between Successive Standard Deviations in a Normal Distribution

which gives the areas of the normal curve. Column (1) of the table contains different z-values. Column (2) gives the area under the curve between the mean and each z-value. Column (3) shows the remaining area from each z-score to the end of the curve. Therefore the areas in column (2) and column (3) add up to .5000. Take as an example the z-value of +0.70. The area between this z-value and the mean can be found in column (2); it is .2580. This figure indicates that about 26 percent of the cases fall between this z-value and the mean of the distribution. Because the mean of the normal distribution coincides with the median, 50 percent of the cases lie below the mean. We add .50 to the .2580, and the result tells us that we can expect 75.8 percent of the cases to fall below the z-value of +0.70. Column (3) indicates that 24.2 percent of the cases fall above the z-value of +0.70.

This procedure is reversed when the z-value is negative. Suppose we want to find the percentage of cases below the z-value of −0.70. The area between the mean and a z-score of −0.70 is .2580 or, in terms of percentage, 25.8 percent of the cases. Subtracting 25.8 from 50, we obtain 24.2. This result would indicate that only about 24 percent of the scores lie below a z-value of −0.70 in a normal distribution. This value can also be found in column (3) of the table, which gives a value of .2420 for a z-score of 0.70. The percent of scores above −0.70 is 24.2 plus 50.0 or 74.2 percent.

The areas under the normal curve between two z-scores apply exactly only to a normal distribution. The application of the characteristics of a normal curve to skewed distributions yields, at best, only approximations. Thus, it is necessary that one examine the shape of the distribution before applying these characteristics.

/// CORRELATION

Our discussion of statistical techniques so far has been concerned with describing single distributions of scores. We want now to discuss a method of indicating the relationship between pairs of scores.

Statistical techniques for determining relationships between pairs of scores are known as *correlational procedures*. Typically measurements on two variables are available for each member of a group and one determines if there is a relationship between these paired measurements. Correlational procedures show the extent to which change in one variable is associated with change in another variable. For example, we know that achievement and intelligence are related and so we would expect students with high IQs to earn above-average scores on achievement tests. A simple way of showing this relationship is to plot the intelligence test scores and achievement test scores of a number of individuals in a two-dimensional table called a *scattergram*. Scores on one variable are plotted on the horizontal axis, with the lowest number on the left and the highest on the right. Scores on the other variable are plotted on the vertical axis, with the lowest at the bottom and the highest at the top. The position of each individual on the two tests is then indicated by a single point in the scattergram. The achievement test scores of 30 tenth-graders are plotted against their intelligence test scores in Figure 5.7. An examination of this figure reveals that there is a tendency for achievement scores to be high when the intelligence tests scores are high.

Plotting a scattergram enables us to see both the *direction* and the *strength* of a relationship. Direction refers to whether the relationship is positive or negative. In Figure 5.7 the dots form a pattern going from lower left to upper right as low scores on one variable (intelligence) are associated with low scores on the other variable (achievement) and high scores on one variable are associated with high scores on the other. (By convention, scores of the independent variable [X] are plotted along the horizontal axis and scores of the dependent variable [Y] are plotted on the vertical axis.) Such a relationship between variables is said to be positive because high scores are associated with high scores and low scores with low scores.

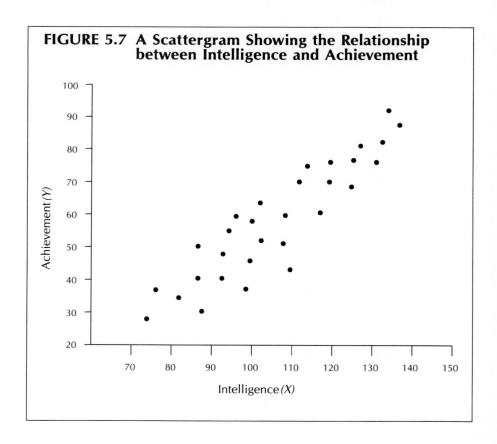

FIGURE 5.7 A Scattergram Showing the Relationship between Intelligence and Achievement

The relationship between two variables is not always positive. Some variables are negatively related. For example, birthrate and socioeconomic level have been found to be negatively related; that is, birthrate decreases as the socioeconomic level increases. With a negative relationship high scores on one variable are associated with low scores on the other variable and the dots on the scattergram go from upper left to lower right.

A scattergram of z-scores also reveals the strength of the relationship between variables. If the dots in the scattergram form a narrow band, so that when a straight line is drawn through the band the dots will be near the line, there is a strong relationship between the variables. However, if the dots in the z-score scattergram scatter widely, the relationship between the variables is relatively weak. The scattergrams in Figure 5.8 show various positive and negative and strong and weak relationships.

/// CORRELATION COEFFICIENTS

Statistical indices have been developed that indicate both the direction (negative or positive) and the strength of a relationship between variables. These indices are called *correlation coefficients*. Calculation of a correlation coefficient between two variables results in a value that ranges from −1.00 to +1.00. A correlation coefficient of −1.00 indicates a perfect negative relationship, a value of +1.00 indicates a perfect positive relationship, and the midpoint of this range, 0, indicates no relationship at all. A perfect positive correlation results when each individual's z-score on one variable is identical in size and sign to the z-score on the other variable. A perfect negative correlation, on the other hand, results when each individual's z-scores are the same in size but opposite in sign. A 0 correlation results when no such trends are present, that is, when positions on one variable are not associated with positions on the other. A coefficient of correlation near unity, either −1.00 or +1.00, indicates a high degree of relationship. Such high relationships enable one to make accurate predictions about one variable on the basis of information about the other. A negative correlation coefficient is just as good for prediction as a positive correlation.

In Figure 5.8 the coefficient of correlation for each of the sets of data in z-score form is given. Note that where the correlation is perfect all the scores fall on a straight line. The nearer to 0 the coefficient of correlation is, the greater the deviation of the scores from a straight line. In the example with 0 correlation (F), the scores are scattered over the surface of the graph and do not take any shape in any direction.

Correlation coefficients in educational and psychological measures, because of the complexity of these phenomena, seldom reach the maximum points of +1.00 and −1.00. For these measures, any coefficient that is greater than plus or minus .90 is usually considered to be very high.

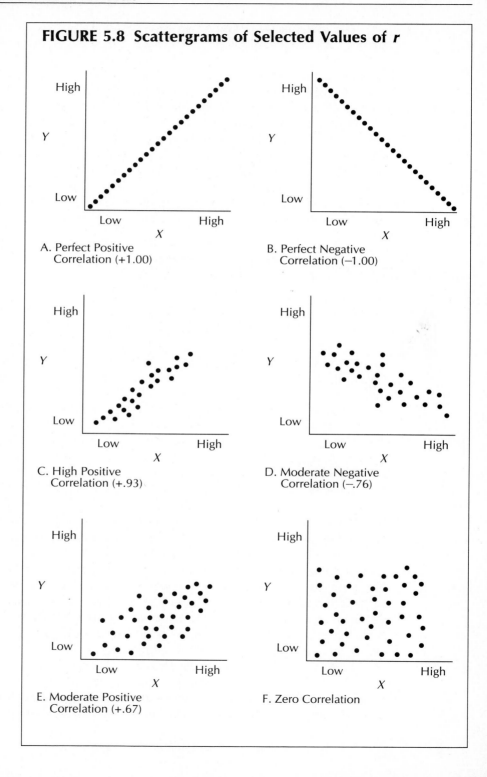

FIGURE 5.8 Scattergrams of Selected Values of *r*

A. Perfect Positive
Correlation (+1.00)

B. Perfect Negative
Correlation (−1.00)

C. High Positive
Correlation (+.93)

D. Moderate Negative
Correlation (−.76)

E. Moderate Positive
Correlation (+.67)

F. Zero Correlation

// The Product Moment Correlation

The product moment coefficient of correlation, developed by the English statistician Karl Pearson and called Pearson r, is the most commonly used correlation index. This coefficient is used when the scale of measurement is of either the interval or the ratio type. It is defined as the mean of the z-score products; that is, each individual's z-score on one variable (X) is multiplied by his or her z-score on the other variable (Y). These paired z-score products are added, and the sum is divided by the number of pairs. The definition formula for Pearson r is:

$$r = \frac{\Sigma z_x z_y}{N} \qquad (5.14)$$

where

$r =$ the Pearson product moment coefficient of correlation
$\Sigma z_x z_y =$ the sum of the z-score products
$N =$ the number of paired scores

Because of the way z-scores are defined mathematically, when each individual has the same z-score on X that he has on Y, the sum of the $z_x z_y$ products will be equal to the number of pairs and the mean z-score product (the Pearson product moment correlation) will be $+1.00$. If there is a perfect positive correspondence between z-scores, the product moment correlation will be $+1.00$. If the z-scores are numerically identical but of opposite sign, the product will be negative and the Pearson product moment correlation will be -1.00. In both cases all the scores will fall along a straight line when plotted on a scattergram. Let us now use formula 5.14 to compute the correlation between the scores of 14 subjects on two tests, X (descriptive statistics) and Y (inferential statistics), as shown in Table 5.6.

Columns (2) and (3) present the subjects' raw scores (X) and deviation scores (x), respectively, on the descriptive statistics test. Columns (5) and (6) present the subjects' raw scores (Y) and deviation scores (y) on the inferential statistics test. Columns (4) and (7) show the squared deviation scores used for calculating the standard deviations. Columns (8) and (9) present the z-scores of the X- and Y-scores computed using formula 5.12. Column (10) shows the products of $z_x z_y$ values. The sum of these products is 11.50. It is now possible to find the Pearson product moment coefficient of correlation between the two sets of scores by applying formula 5.14.

$$r = \frac{11.50}{14} = +.82$$

The process of converting scores to z-scores becomes tedious when a large number of cases is being used. It is possible to eliminate this step and

TABLE 5.6 Computation of Pearson r between Two Sets of Scores (X and Y)

(1) Subjects	(2) X-scores	(3) x	(4) x^2	(5) Y-scores	(6) y	(7) y^2	(8) z_x	(9) z_y	(10) $z_x z_y$
1	18	+3	9	28	4	16	+1.5	+1	+1.50
2	18	+3	9	30	6	36	+1.5	+1.5	+2.25
3	17	+2	4	30	6	36	+1	+1.5	+1.50
4	17	+2	4	26	2	4	+1	+0.5	+0.50
5	16	+1	1	28	4	16	+0.5	+1	+0.50
6	16	+1	1	24	0	0	+0.5	0	0
7	15	0	0	22	−2	4	0	−0.5	0
8	15	0	0	20	−4	16	0	−1	0
9	14	−1	1	26	2	4	−0.5	+0.5	−0.25
10	14	−1	1	22	−2	4	−0.5	−0.5	+0.25
11	13	−2	4	24	0	0	−1	0	0
12	13	−2	4	18	−6	36	−1	−1.5	+1.50
13	12	−3	9	20	−4	16	−1.5	−1	+1.50
14	12	−3	9	18	−6	36	−1.5	−1.5	+2.25
	210		56	336		224			11.50

$$\bar{X} = \frac{\Sigma X}{N} = \frac{210}{14} = 15 \qquad \bar{Y} = \frac{\Sigma Y}{N} = \frac{336}{14} = 24$$

$$\sigma_x = \sqrt{\frac{\Sigma x^2}{N}} = \sqrt{\frac{56}{14}} = 2 \qquad \sigma_y = \sqrt{\frac{\Sigma y^2}{N}} = \sqrt{\frac{224}{14}} = 4$$

work directly with the raw scores by using a computation formula that is mathematically equivalent to formula 5.14:

$$r = \frac{\Sigma XY - \dfrac{(\Sigma X)(\Sigma Y)}{N}}{\sqrt{\left[\Sigma X^2 - \dfrac{(\Sigma X)^2}{N}\right]\left[\Sigma Y^2 - \dfrac{(\Sigma Y)^2}{N}\right]}} \qquad (5.15)$$

where

r = Pearson r
ΣX = the sum of scores in X-distribution
ΣY = the sum of scores in Y-distribution
ΣXY = the sum of the products of paired X- and Y-scores
ΣX^2 = the sum of the squared scores in X-distribution
ΣY^2 = the sum of the squared scores in Y-distribution
N = the number of paired X- and Y-scores (subjects)

Using the same raw-score data as before, let us use formula 5.15 to compute the Pearson product moment coefficient of correlation. The necessary figures and calculations are provided in Table 5.7. Substituting the values from this table in formula 5.15, we can calculate Pearson r:

TABLE 5.7 Computation of Pearson *r* Using the Raw-Score Formula

(1) Subjects	*(2)* X	*(3)* Y	*(4)* X²	*(5)* Y²	*(6)* XY
1	18	28	324	784	504
2	18	30	324	900	540
3	17	30	289	900	510
4	17	26	289	676	442
5	16	28	256	784	448
6	16	24	256	576	384
7	15	22	225	484	330
8	15	20	225	400	300
9	14	26	196	676	364
10	14	22	196	484	308
11	13	24	169	576	312
12	13	18	169	324	234
13	12	20	144	400	240
14	12	18	144	324	216
$N = 14$	$\Sigma X = 210$	$\Sigma Y = 336$	$\Sigma X^2 = 3206$	$\Sigma Y^2 = 8288$	$\Sigma XY = 5132$

$$r = \frac{5132 - \dfrac{(210)(336)}{14}}{\sqrt{\left[3206 - \dfrac{(210)^2}{14}\right]\left[8288 - \dfrac{(336)^2}{14}\right]}} = +.82$$

Note that by applying this formula not only was it unnecessary to convert the scores to z-scores, but also computation of the means and standard deviations of the two distributions was eliminated.

The product moment coefficient of correlation belongs to the same statistical family as the mean. Its computation takes into account the size of each score in both distributions, X and Y. Like the mean and the standard deviation, it is an interval statistic that can also be used with ratio data.

An assumption underlying the product moment coefficient of correlation is that the relationship between the two variables (X and Y) is a linear one; that is, a straight line provides a reasonable expression of the relationship of one variable to the other. If a curved line is needed to express this relationship, the relationship is said to be curvilinear.

A practical way of finding out whether the relationship between two variables is linear or curvilinear is to examine the scattergram of the data. Figure 5.9 shows two diagrams, one of which (A) indicates a linear relationship and the other (B), a curvilinear one.

If the relationship between the variables is curvilinear, the computation of the Pearson r will result in a misleading underestimation of the degree of relationship. In this case another index, such as the correlation ratio (eta),

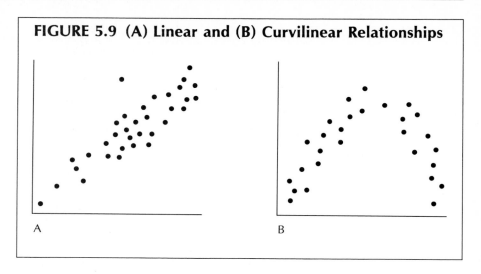

FIGURE 5.9 (A) Linear and (B) Curvilinear Relationships

should be applied. A discussion of the correlation ratio can be found at the end of this chapter.

// Interpretation of Pearson *r*

We have seen that when two variables are highly related in a positive way the correlation between them approaches +1.00. When they are highly related in a negative way, the correlation approaches −1.00. When there is little relation between variables, the correlation will be near 0. Pearson *r* provides a meaningful index for indicating relationship, with the sign of the coefficient indicating the direction of the relationship, and the difference between the coefficient and 0 indicating the degree of the relationship.

However, in interpreting the coefficient of correlation one should keep the following points in mind.

1. *Correlation does not necessarily indicate causation.* When two variables are found to be correlated, this indicates that relative positions in one variable are *associated* with relative positions in the other variable. It does not necessarily mean that changes in one variable are *caused* by changes in the other variable. In our example we found a correlation of +.82 between scores in a test on descriptive statistics and another test on inferential statistics. This correlation coefficient tells us that a person with an above-average score on one test will probably obtain an above-average score on the other test. We cannot say that a high performance on one test *causes* a high performance on the other. Scores on both tests may be the result of other causes, such as the numerical aptitude of the persons who take these tests.

Using another example, suppose we find a high positive correlation between the wealth of families and intelligence of the children of those families. Such high correlation is by no means indicative of a cause-and-effect relationship between these two variables. Wealth does not necessarily result in intelligence, nor does intelligence necessarily create wealth for these individuals.

2. *The size of correlation is in part a function of the variability of the two distributions to be correlated.* Restricting the range of the scores to be correlated reduces the observed degree of relationship between two variables. For example, it has been observed that success in playing basketball is related to height: that is to say, the taller an individual is, the more probable it is that that person will do well in this sport. This statement is true about the population at large, where there is a wide range of heights. However, within a basketball team whose members are all tall, there may be little or no correlation between height and success because the range of heights is restricted.

In a college that accepts students with a wide range of scores on a scholastic aptitude test, we would expect a correlation between the test scores and college grades. In a college that accepts only students with very high scholastic aptitude scores, we would expect very little correlation between the test scores and grades because of the restricted range of the test scores in this situation.

3. *Correlation coefficients should not be interpreted in terms of percentage of perfect correlations.* Since correlation coefficients are expressed as fractions, individuals who are not trained in statistics sometimes interpret correlation coefficients as a percentage of perfect correlation. An r of .80 does *not* indicate 80 percent of a perfect relationship between two variables. This interpretation is erroneous because, for example, an r of .80 does not express a relationship that is twice as great as an r of .40. One way of determining the degree to which one can predict one variable from the other is to calculate an index called the *coefficient of determination*. The coefficient of determination is the square of the correlation coefficient. It gives the percentage of variance in one variable that is associated with the variance in the other. For example, if we find a correlation of $+.80$ between achievement and intelligence, 64 percent of the variance in achievement is associated with variance in intelligence test scores. Probably the best way to give meaning to the size of the correlation coefficient is to picture the degree of scatter implied by correlations of different sizes (as illustrated in Figure 5.8) and to become familiar with the size of correlations commonly observed between variables of interest.

4. *Avoid interpreting the coefficients of correlation in an absolute sense.* In interpreting the degree of correlation, keep in mind the purpose for which it is being used. For example, a coefficient of correlation equal to $+.50$ might be satisfactory when predicting the future performance of a group of individuals, but it might not be wise to use this coefficient of correlation for predicting the performance of one person in a future task. That is, the

coefficient of +.50 is not an absolute value with the same implication in both cases.

// The Rank Correlation Coefficient

The Pearson product moment coefficient of correlation is the statistical index used for finding the relationship between two sets of linearly distributed interval data. In research we sometimes wish to find the coefficient of correlation between two sets of measures that are rank-ordered, that is, ordinal rather than interval data. For example, we might want to correlate the ranks assigned by two teachers to a group of students with respect to originality. The index employed in such cases is the Spearman rho (rank) correlation coefficient (ρ), which is calculated by means of the formula

$$\rho = 1 - \frac{6\Sigma D^2}{N(N^2 - 1)} \tag{5.16}$$

where

ρ = the Spearman rho correlation coefficient
ΣD^2 = the sum of the squares of the differences between ranks
N = the number of cases

For illustration, consider Table 5.8, which shows the ranking of 11 students by two teachers. Columns (2) and (3) of Table 5.8 present the rankings of teacher one and teacher two, respectively. Column (4) shows the differences between these ranks. For example, the difference between the ranking of student A by these teachers is -3, of student B is -1, and so forth. The sum of the values in this column is always zero. Column (5) gives the square of these differences. The sum of the D^2 values is 26, and the number of cases is 11. When these values are substituted into formula 5.16, the computation gives a Spearman rank correlation of +.88.

When ranking individuals or objects for the purpose of finding a correlation between two sets of ranks, you are likely to find that two or more will have been assigned to the same rank. For example, when two individuals are tied for rank 3, they are in fact the third and fourth in the series and it is necessary to assign to both the average position—in this case, 3.5. The next person will be assigned rank 5.

Sometimes one wants to find the relationship between a set of ranks and a set of interval measures, such as a group of test scores. It is not possible to upgrade the ranks from ordinal to interval data; therefore, one first converts the scores into ranks and then applies the Spearman rho formula. Consider, as an example, Table 5.9. Column (2) of the table shows a teacher's prediction of the ranks of a group of students in an examination prior to the administration of the test. Column (3) shows the actual scores of these students on the examination. To determine the relationship between predicted ranks and actual ranks, the teacher will have to convert the students'

**TABLE 5.8 The Computation of the Correlation Coefficient
between Two Sets of Ranks**

(1)	(2)	(3)	(4)	(5)
	First Teacher's Rank	Second Teacher's Rank	Difference	
Student	R_1	R_2	D	D^2
A	1	4	-3	9
B	2	3	-1	1
C	3	1	$+2$	4
D	4	2	$+2$	4
E	5	5	0	0
F	6	6	0	0
G	7	8	-1	1
H	8	9	-1	1
I	9	7	$+2$	4
J	10	11	-1	1
K	11	10	$+1$	1
			0	26

$$\rho = 1 - \frac{(6)(26)}{11(121 - 1)} = +.88$$

test scores to ranks. Column (4) shows the ranking of the students on the basis of their test scores. Note that both Linda and Dick made scores of 17 and thus tied for the third and fourth places; consequently, they are given an equal rank of 3.5, which is the average of ranks 3 and 4. The situation is similar for Tom, John, and David, who all made a score of 15 and share the fifth, sixth, and seventh places. A rank of 6, which is the average for ranks 5, 6, and 7, is assigned to each of the three. The procedure for finding the values for D and D^2 is exactly like that shown in Table 5.8. The coefficient of correlation between these sets of data is $+.95$.

The Spearman rank correlation is a special case of the Pearson product moment correlation, and its formula has been derived from the Pearson r formula. Thus, it is possible to use formula 5.15 for computation of the correlation between two sets of ranks. For example, if we apply formula 5.15 to the ranks of Table 5.8, an identical correlation coefficient, that is, $+.88$, will be obtained. An exception to this is the case of tied ranks. With tied ranks, such as those in Table 5.9, the use of the Pearson r formula will no longer result in a coefficient identical with the one obtained by applying Spearman rank formula.

The Spearman rho rank correlation coefficient is part of the same statistical family as the median. It is an ordinal statistic designed for use with ordinal data. Like the Pearson product moment coefficient of correlation, it

TABLE 5.9 The Computation of Rank Correlation between a Set of Ordinal and a Set of Interval Data

(1) Students	(2) Rank 1	(3) Scores	(4) Rank 2	(5) D	(6) D^2
Jack	1	19	1	0	0
Linda	2	17	3.5	−1.5	2.25
Lucy	3	18	2	+1	1
Dick	4	17	3.5	+0.5	0.25
Tom	5	15	6	−1	1
Marsha	6	14	8	−2	4
John	7	15	6	+1	1
David	8	15	6	+2	4
Joan	9	12	10	−1	1
Ann	10	13	9	+1	1
George	11	8	11	0	0
Sue	12	5	12	0	0
				$\overline{0}$	$\overline{15.5}$

$$\rho = 1 - \frac{(6)(15.5)}{12(144 - 1)} = +.95$$

ranges from −1.00 to +1.00. When each individual has the same rank on both variables, the rank correlation will be +1.00, and when their ranks on one variable are exactly the opposite of their ranks on the other variable, rho will be −1.00. If there is no relationship at all between the rankings, the rank correlation coefficient will be 0. Spearman rho is interpreted in the same way as Pearson r.

// Other Indices of Correlation

In addition to the Pearson and Spearman indices, there are several other indices of correlation appropriate for finding the strength of relationship among different types of variables. The following section introduces some of these other indices and their applications but without going into computational details. Interested students are advised to consult statistics books for the computational procedures.[3]

// Biserial and Point Biserial Correlation

Biserial and point biserial correlation techniques have been developed for instances when one wants to find the relationship between a continuous

---

[3]For further discussion and computational details of correlation indices, see (1) G. A. Ferguson (1981). *Statistical Analysis in Psychology and Education* (5th ed.). New York: McGraw-Hill. (2) A. L. Edwards (1976). *An Introduction to Linear Regression and Correlation*. San Francisco: Freeman. (3) J. D. Wynne (1982). *Learning Statistics*. New York: Macmillan.

interval or ratio variable and a dichotomous nominal variable. The use of biserial correlation requires the assumption that the variable underlying the dichotomy is continuous and normal. In other words, the dichotomy is artificially created from a continuous variable. For example, one may categorize individuals as below and above average in creativity on the basis of their scores on a test of creativity. If intelligence test scores (the continuous variable) were correlated with creativity measured as above and below average (the artificial dichotomy), the biserial correlation coefficient would be the appropriate measure of relationship.

Point biserial correlation is used when the dichotomy is a genuine one, for example, when studying the relationship between sex and scores on a reasoning test. The dichotomy is assigned numerical values of 1 or 0, and these values are correlated with the values on the continuous variable. Other truly dichotomous variables are U.S. citizen/noncitizen, left-handed/right-handed, graduate/undergraduate, smoker/nonsmoker, and so on. The point biserial correlation is a mathematical simplification of the Pearson r.

// The Tetrachoric Correlation and the Phi Coefficient

The tetrachoric correlation and the phi coefficient are used to find the relationship between variables when both are dichotomous. The nature of the dichotomy determines the specific index to be used. If both variables are really continuous but have been artificially dichotomized, the tetrachoric correlation coefficient is the appropriate index. If one wishes to find the correlation between two genuine dichotomies, then the phi coefficient is the index to use. The tetrachoric correlation would be used, for example, to find the relationship between creativity and intelligence when both variables have been dichotomized into below-average and above-average measures. It is not a widely used correlation index. Too much information is lost by reducing the continuous variables to dichotomies. The phi coefficient would be applied in order to describe the relationship between the sex of a group of high school seniors and whether they win a college scholarship. Sex is dichotomized as male-female and "winning a scholarship" as yes-no, both genuine dichotomies. Numerical values (1 and 0) are assigned to the dichotomies, and the phi coefficient is calculated. The phi coefficient is also a mathematical simplification of the Pearson r. Table 5.10 summarizes the correlation coefficients used with different types of scales.

// The Correlation Ratio

An assumption underlying the product moment correlation coefficient is that the relationship between the two variables is linear. Sometimes, however, the relationship between the variables is curvilinear; that is, the relationship is described by a curved rather than a straight line. In such cases

TABLE 5.10 Types of Correlation Coefficients and Corresponding Types of Scales

Correlation Coefficient	Type of Scale
1. Pearson product moment	1. Interval or ratio scale characteristic of both variables
2. Spearman rank	2. Ordinal scale characteristic of both variables
3. Point biserial	3. One variable on interval scale; the other a genuine dichotomous variable on a nominal scale
4. Biserial	4. One variable on interval or ratio scale; the other an aritifical dichotomy*
5. Tetrachoric	5. Artificial dichotomy (nominal scale) used with both variables; both have underlying continuous distributions
6. Phi coefficient	6. Genuine dichotomy (nominal scale) characteristic of both variables

*An artificial dichotomy arbitrarily divides a continuous variable into two classes—for example, test scores divided into pass and fail categories—through the use of a cutoff point. Examples of genuine dichotomies are male-female and alive-dead.

the Pearson r formula is not appropriate because it results in an underestimation of the degree of relationship. Another index, the correlation ratio, eta, is used when the relationship between variables X and Y is curvilinear. It involves a correction for nonlinearity and therefore gives a more accurate estimation of the extent of association between the variables.

Suppose, for example, that one wants to find the correlation between age and physical strength. We know that physical strength is positively related with age up to a certain point, after which increase in age is accompanied by a decrease in physical strength. The correlation ratio would be an appropriate index to use in such a case.

// Partial and Multiple Correlation

The correlation techniques discussed so far are appropriate for use with two variables only. There are situations, however, when one must deal with more than two variables. *Partial correlation* is a technique used to determine what correlation remains between two variables when the effect of another variable is eliminated. Correlation between two variables may occur because both of them are correlated with a third variable. Partial correlation controls for this third variable. For example, assume one is interested in the correlation between mental age and psychomotor skills. Both of these variables are related to a third variable, chronological age. For example, 12-year-old children are in general more mentally mature than 8-year-old children, and they also have more highly developed physical skills. Scores on mental age and a psychomotor test will correlate with each other because both are correlated with chronological age. Partial correlation would be used with such data in order to obtain a measure of correlation with the effect of age removed. The remaining correlation between two variables when their correlation with a third variable is removed is called a first-order partial correlation. Partial correlation may be used to remove the effect of more than one variable. However, because of the difficulty of interpretation, partial correlation involving the elimination of more than one variable is not often used.

Multiple correlation also involves more than two variables. This technique enables researchers to find the best possible weighting of two or more independent variables to yield a maximum correlation with a single dependent variable. For example, researchers have used high school percentile rank (HSPR), Scholastic Aptitude Test (SAT) scores, and personality test scores to predict subsequent college grade-point average. Results have shown that (1) HSPR is the best single predictor, (2) an appropriately weighted composite of HSPR and SAT is a better predictor of college grade-point average than any of the independent variables alone, and (3) personality test scores do not provide a useful addition to the predictive utility of the HSPR-SAT composite.[4] Multiple correlation will be discussed in greater detail in Chapter 11.

// Calculators and Computer Programs for Statistics

Many pocket calculators have built-in programs for the statistical procedures described in this and the next chapter. A description of canned statistical programs for mainframe and microcomputers is included in Chapter 15.

/// META-ANALYSIS

Meta-analysis, a method for systematically combining quantitative data from a number of studies, focusing on the same question and using similar variables, is defined by Glass as an analysis of analyses.[5] Using the statistics reported from original studies comparing experimental groups receiving treatment and control groups, one derives a common metric that is interpreted as an overall statement of outcomes for the selected studies.

For each study, the difference between control and experimental means is translated into standard deviation units by dividing this difference by the standard deviation of the control group. This ratio in standard deviation units is labeled as effect-size.

---

[4] A complete discussion of multiple correlation can be found in E. J. Pedhazur (1982), *Multiple Regression in Behavioral Research* (2d ed.), New York: Holt, Rinehart and Winston.

[5] Glass, G. V., B. McGaw, and M. L. Smith (1981). *Meta-analysis in Social Research*. Beverly Hills: Sage Publications.

For each study

$$ES = \frac{\bar{X}_E - \bar{X}_C}{\sigma_C} \tag{5.17}$$

where

ES = estimated effect size
$\bar{X}_E$ = mean of experimental group
$\bar{X}_C$ = mean of control group
σ_C = standard deviation of the control group

If one assumes normality for this distribution of effect-size values, each value may then be interpreted as a z-score with a mean of 0 and a standard deviation of 1, the reference, or 0, point being $\bar{X}_c$. The average of the effect-size values from all the studies describes the overall effect for the experimental variables.

For example, Smith and Glass used meta-analysis to investigate the broad question Does psychotherapy make a difference?[6] A standard literature search located 1000 experiments. Experiments selected as appropriate for a complete analysis yielded a total of 833 effect sizes. The selected studies included ego, dynamic, behavioral, and humanistic treatment strategies, related experimentally to such outcome variables as self-esteem, adjustment, fear-anxiety, and school performance. The average effect size was .68, that is, the posttreatment mean for treated subjects was equivalent to a score .68 of a standard deviation above the mean for untreated subjects. Smith and Glass concluded that the typical outcome of psychotherapy is a gain on the dependent variable equivalent to a move from the mean to the 75th percentile of the control group. (See Figure 5.10.)

Meta-analysis can be used not only with studies that compared means but with studies of correlation, proportion, and other measures. Glass, McGaw, and Smith give a full explanation of meta-analysis techniques and their uses.[7]

/// SUMMARY

Descriptive statistics serve to describe and summarize observations. The descriptive technique to be employed is selected according to the purpose the statistic is to serve and the scale of measurement used in recording the data.

Scales of measurement are means of quantifying observations and are of four types: nominal scales classify observations into mutually exclusive

---

[6]Smith, M. L., and G. V. Glass (1977). Meta-analysis of psychotherapy outcome studies. *American Psychologist, 32,* 752–760.
[7]Glass, McGaw, and Smith, *op. cit.*

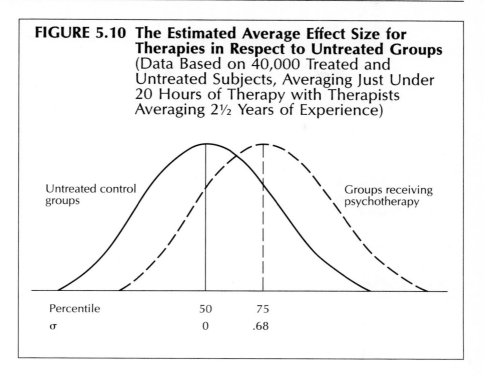

FIGURE 5.10 The Estimated Average Effect Size for Therapies in Respect to Untreated Groups (Data Based on 40,000 Treated and Untreated Subjects, Averaging Just Under 20 Hours of Therapy with Therapists Averaging 2½ Years of Experience)

Untreated control groups

Groups receiving psychotherapy

| Percentile | 50 | 75 |
| σ | 0 | .68 |

categories; ordinal scales sort objects or classes of objects on the basis of their relative standing; interval scales use equal intervals for measurement and indicate the degree to which a person or an object possesses a certain quality; ratio scales use equal intervals for measurement and measure from an absolute zero point.

Once observations are quantified, the data—either raw or grouped—can be arranged into frequency distributions and shown graphically in histograms or polygons.

Measures of central tendency—the mode, the median, and the mean—provide a single index to represent the average value of a whole set of measures. The mode, which is a nominal statistic, is the least stable and least useful measure in educational research. The median is an ordinal statistic that takes into account the ranks of scores within a distribution and not the size of the individual scores. The mean, which is an interval (or ratio) statistic, is the most stable and most widely used index of central tendency.

Another way of describing observations is to indicate the variation, or spread, of the values within a distribution. The range, the quartile deviation, and the standard deviation are three indices used for this purpose. The range gives the distance between the highest and the lowest values in a distribution. It is a nominal statistic. Quartile deviation gives the half-distance between

TABLE 5.11 Summary of Descriptive Statistics Presented in This Chapter

	Nominal	Ordinal	Interval
Indices of central tendency	mode	median	mean
Indices of variability	range	quartile deviation	variance and standard deviation
Indices of location	label or classification	percentile rank	z-score, Z-score, and other standard scores
Correlation indices	phi	Spearman rho	Pearson *r*

the upper and the lower quartiles. It is an ordinal statistic. The standard deviation is the square root of the mean of the squared deviations of values from the mean. It is an interval (or ratio) statistic and is the most widely used index of variability.

Standard scores are used to indicate the position of a single score in a distribution. The most widely used is the z-score, which converts values into standard-deviation units. Using the characteristics and the areas of the normal curve, we can approximate the percentage of cases below and above each z-score in a normal distribution.

Correlation techniques enable us to describe the relationship between two sets of measures. Product moment correlation (Pearson *r*) and rank correlation (Spearman rho) are two widely used indices of relationship. Pearson *r* is used with interval or ratio data, and for ordinal data Spearman rho is used to find the relationship between two sets of ranks. Table 5.11 summarizes these statistics.

// Key Concepts

biserial correlation
central tendency
coefficient of correlation
coefficient of determination
correlation
correlation ratio (eta)
cumulative frequency
curvilinear relationship
descriptive statistics
frequency distribution
frequency polygon

histogram
inferential statistics
interval scale
linear relationship
mean
median
meta-analysis
mode
negative correlation
negatively skewed curve
nominal scale

normal curve
ordinal scale
Pearson product moment coefficient
phi coefficient
point biserial correlation
positive correlation
positively skewed curve
quartile deviation (semi-interquartile range)
range
ratio scale

scattergram
Spearman rank correlation
standard deviation
standard score
symmetric distributions
tetrachoric coefficient
variability
variance
z-score
Z-score

/// EXERCISES

1. Identify the type of measurement scale—*nominal, ordinal, interval,* or *ratio*—suggested by each statement:
    a. John finished the math test in 35 minutes, while Jack finished the same test in 25 minutes.
    b. Jack speaks French, but John does not.
    c. Jack is taller than John.
    d. John is 6 feet, 2 inches tall.
    e. John's IQ is 120, while Jack's IQ is 110.

2. Draw a histogram and a frequency polygon for the following frequency distribution:

X	f	X	f	X	f	X	f
80	1	76	6	73	20	70	7
79	2	75	15	72	17	69	3
78	3	74	22	71	9	68	1
77	10						

3. Given the following distribution, 15, 14, 14, 13, 11, 10, 10, 10, 8, 5:
    a. Calculate the mean.
    b. Determine the value of the median.
    c. Determine the value of the mode.

4. Briefly explain the relationship between the skewness of a distribution of scores and the resulting values of the mean, median, and mode.

5. Identify the measure—*mode, mean,* or *median*—that best suits each type of scale:
    a. ordinal   b. nominal   c. interval

6. Identify the measure—*mode, mean,* or *median*—that each term defines:
   a. the middle score
   b. the arithmetic average
   c. the most frequently occurring score

7. The scores below represent the vocabulary test scores from a seventh-grade class of 20 pupils. Calculate the range, standard deviation, and quartile deviation, and discuss the benefits and disadvantages of each as a measure of the variability of the scores.

X	f	fX	X^2	fX^2
16	1	16	256	256
15	0	0	225	0
14	0	0	196	0
13	0	0	169	0
12	2	24	144	288
11	0	0	121	0
10	2	20	100	200
9	1	9	81	81
8	1	8	64	64
7	1	7	49	49
6	4	24	36	144
5	2	10	25	50
4	1	4	16	16
3	1	3	9	9
2	4	8	4	16

8. To minimize the effect of an extreme score, should one choose the *quartile deviation* or *standard deviation* as the index of variability? Why?

9. The mean score on a test is 40, and the standard deviation is 4. Express each of the following raw scores as a *z*-score:
   a. 41   b. 30   c. 48   d. 36   e. 46

10. In a normal distribution what percent of the scores would fall below a *z*-score of −1.0? a *z*-score of 0? a *z*-score of +.67?

11. Describe the relationship shown by these scattergrams. Then estimate the correlation coefficients.

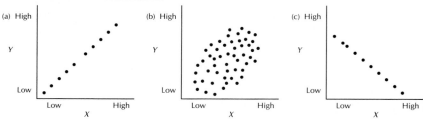

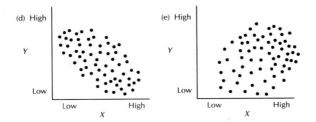

12. The following data are scores obtained by ten students on an Abstract Reasoning Test and their cumulative grade-point averages in philosophy. Calculate the Pearson *r* for these data.

Student	Abstract Reasoning	Grade-Point Average
A	15	1.5
B	20	2.5
C	30	3.0
D	35	2.0
E	25	3.0
F	40	3.5
G	35	4.0
H	5	1.0
I	12	2.0
J	10	2.5

13. A researcher is interested in anxiety and how it might affect performance on intelligence tests. He has a clinical psychologist assess the anxiety of subjects by ranking them from 1 through 20. Then he administers a standardized intelligence test to each of the 20 subjects and converts their IQ scores to ranks. Which correlation coefficient should the researcher calculate for the data? Explain your answer.

14. A researcher demonstrated a correlation of +.60 between principals' rating of teacher attire and student academic performance across 150 grade schools in his state. He concluded that encouraging teachers to be properly attired will increase academic performance. Comment on his conclusion.

15. Determine the kind of index of correlation appropriate for use in solving each of the following problems:
    a. We want to find the coefficient of correlation between intelligence and creativity when we have scores of a group of subjects on both variables.
    b. We want to find the coefficient of correlation between the performances of a group of subjects on two tests when we have scores of subjects on one test and their standing as above or below average on the other.

    c. We want to find the correlation between sex and qualification for a job when we have pass and fail information for 60 men and 60 women on a qualifying test for that job.

    d. We want to find the correlation between the responses of 180 students to two test items when we know the right and wrong responses of these students on both test items.

    e. We want to find the relationship between intelligence and achievement motivation when we have the intelligence test scores of 200 subjects on the Stanford-Binet test of intelligence and their standing in a test of achievement motivation as above or below average.

    f. We want to find the relationship between gender and mechanical ability when we have the scores of 60 boys and 60 girls on a test of mechanical ability.

    g. We want to find the relationship between sociometric scores of a group of students and their academic rank in a high school class.

16. Which statistical technique has been called analysis of analyses?

/// ANSWERS

1. a. ratio b. nominal c. ordinal d. ratio e. interval

2. Answers will vary.

3. a. mean $= 11$ b. median $= 10.5$ c. mode $= 10$

4. The three measures are not equal in a skewed distribution. The mean is pulled in the direction of the skewed side. Thus, in a positively skewed distribution the mean is always higher than the median and the mode is usually lowest in value. In a negatively skewed distribution the mean is always lower than the median and the mode is usually highest in value.

5. a. median b. mode c. mean

6. a. median b. mean c. mode

7. range $= 16 - 2 = 14$

$$\sigma = \sqrt{\frac{1173 - \frac{(133)^2}{20}}{20}} = \sqrt{14.4275} = 3.798$$

$$QD = \frac{Q_3 - Q_1}{2} = \frac{9.5 - 3.5}{2} = \frac{6}{2} = 3$$

8. quartile deviation because extreme scores do not influence the quartile deviation

9. a. .25 b. −2.5 c. 2 d. −1 e. 1.5

10. 16%, 50%, 75%

11. a. perfect positive, +1 b. positive, +.75 c. perfect negative, −1. d. negative, −.75 e. no correlation, 0

12.

X	Y	XY	X^2	Y^2
15	1.5	22.5	225	2.25
20	2.5	50.0	400	6.25
30	3.0	90.0	900	9.00
35	2.0	70.0	1225	4.00
25	3.0	75.0	625	9.00
40	3.5	140.0	1600	12.25
35	4.0	140.0	1225	16.00
5	1.0	5.0	25	1.00
12	2.0	24.0	144	4.00
10	2.5	25.0	100	6.25
Σ 227	25.0	641.5	6469	70.00

$$ r = \frac{\Sigma XY - \dfrac{(\Sigma X)(\Sigma Y)}{N}}{\sqrt{\left[\Sigma X^2 - \dfrac{(\Sigma X)^2}{N}\right]\left[\Sigma Y^2 - \dfrac{(\Sigma Y)^2}{N}\right]}} $$

$$ \frac{641.5 - \dfrac{(227)(25)}{10}}{\sqrt{\left[6469 - \dfrac{(227)^2}{10}\right]\left[70 - \dfrac{(25)^2}{10}\right]}} = +.74 $$

13. Because the researcher has ordinal or rank-order data, he should calculate the Spearman rank correlation coefficient.

14. The researcher has no justification for inferring a causal relationship merely on the basis of correlational evidence. Principals' rating of teacher attire and student academic performance could very well be functions of some other variable.

15. a. Pearson product moment b. biserial c. tetrachoric d. phi coefficient e. biserial f. point biserial g. Spearman rho

16. Meta-analysis

6

Sampling and Inferential Statistics

INSTRUCTIONAL OBJECTIVES

After studying this chapter, the student will be able to

1. Describe the meaning, rationale, and steps involved in sampling and distinguish between probability and nonprobability sampling
2. List the characteristics, uses, and limitations of each kind of probability and nonprobability sampling
3. Explain the meaning of *sampling error* and its relationship to making statistical inferences
4. Explain the meaning of *statistical significance*
5. Explain the meaning of *null hypothesis* and its use in scientific research
6. Describe Type I and Type II errors
7. Explain the difference between directional and nondirectional tests of significance and the appropriate use of each of these tests
8. Apply the *t*-test to find the significance of the difference between correlated and noncorrelated means
9. Apply the *F*-test for finding the significance of the differences between groups in one-way and two-way analysis of variance
10. Apply the chi-square test for finding the significance of the differences between proportions in one-way and two-way classifications
11. Describe the purpose of the *t*-test for the Pearson *r* and determine if any given correlation coefficient is significant
12. Select the kind of inferential statistical procedures appropriate for use in testing a given research hypothesis
13. Demonstrate comprehension of the basic technical statistical terms used in reporting research results

The statistics discussed in the previous chapter are used for organizing, summarizing, and describing data. In research, however, we often need to go further than describing data. After making observations of a sample, we employ induction or inference to generalize our findings to the entire population from which the sample was drawn. To do this we need techniques that enable us to make valid inferences from samples to whole populations.

/// SAMPLING

An important characteristic of inferential statistics is the process of going from the part to the whole. For example, we might study a randomly selected group of 500 students attending a university in order to make generalizations about the entire student body of that university.

The small group that is observed is called a *sample,* and the larger group about which the generalization is made is called a *population.* A *population* is defined as all members of any well-defined class of people, events, or objects. For example, in a study where American adolescents constitute the population of interest, one could define this population as all American boys and girls within the age range of 12–21. A sample is a portion of a population. For example, the students of Washington High School in Indianapolis constitute a sample of American adolescents. They are a portion of the large population in that they are both American citizens and within the age range of 12–21.

Statistical inference is a procedure by means of which one estimates *parameters,* characteristics of populations, from *statistics,* characteristics of samples. Such estimations are based on the laws of probability and are best estimates rather than absolute facts. In any such inferences a certain degree of error is involved. As we shall see later, inferential statistics are also used to test hypotheses about populations.

// Rationale of Sampling

Inductive reasoning is an essential part of the scientific approach. The inductive method involves making observations and then drawing conclusions from these observations. If one can observe all instances of a population, one can with confidence base conclusions about the population on these observations (perfect induction). On the other hand, if one observes only some instances of a population, then one can do no more than infer that these observations will be true of the population as a whole (imperfect induction). This is the concept of sampling, which involves taking a portion of the population, making observations on this smaller group, and then generalizing the findings to the larger population.

Sampling is indispensable to the researcher. Usually the time, money, and effort involved do not permit a researcher to study all possible members of a population. Furthermore, it is generally not necessary to study all possible cases to understand the phenomenon under consideration. Sampling comes to our aid by enabling us to study a portion of the population rather than the entire population.

Because the purpose of drawing a sample from a population is to obtain information concerning that population, it is extremely important that the individuals included in a sample constitute a representative cross section of individuals in the population. That is, samples must be representative if one is to be able to generalize with confidence from the sample to the population. For example, the researcher might assume that the students at Washington High School are representative of American adolescents. However, this sample might not be representative if the individuals who are included have some characteristics that differ from the parent population. The location of their school, their socioeconomic backgrounds, their family situations, their prior experiences, and many other characteristics of this group might make them unrepresentative of American adolescents. This type of sample would be termed a *biased sample*. The findings of a biased sample in a research study cannot legitimately be generalized to the population from which it is taken.

/ Steps in Sampling

The first step in sampling is the identification of the population to be represented in the study. If the researcher is interested in learning about the teachers in the St. Louis school system, all those who teach within that system constitute the target population. In a study of the attitudes and values of American adolescents, the target population would be all American boys and girls in the age range of 12–21, given that *adolescence* is operationally defined as the period between ages 12 and 21.

However, since it is usually not possible to deal with the whole of the target population, one must identify that portion of the population to which one can have access—called the *accessible population*—and it is from this group that the researcher will take the sample for the study. The nature of the accessible population is influenced by the time and resources of the researcher. In a typical attitude study, for example, a researcher might designate all adolescent boys and girls in California or just those in San Francisco as the accessible population.

From the accessible population, one selects a sample in such a way that it is representative of that population. For example, the researcher would have to sample from adolescents all over the state of California if California adolescents are identified as the accessible population. Or if adolescents living in San Francisco are the accessible population, then the sample would be drawn from this particular group.

How safely can one generalize from a sample to the target population? If the sample selected is truly representative of the accessible population, then there is little difficulty in making this first step in the generalization process. The general principle is: If a sample has been selected so that it is representative of the accessible population, findings from the sample can be generalized to that population. For example, if one has selected a representative sample of California adolescents, then one could make generalizations concerning the attitudes and values of all adolescent boys and girls in California.

However, generalizing from the accessible population to the target population typically involves greater risk. The confidence that one can have in this step depends upon the similarity of the accessible population to the target population. In the example above, a researcher could have more confidence making generalizations about American adolescents if adolescents in several states throughout the country are designated as the accessible population rather than those in California alone. In this way all sections of the United States would be represented and a more adequate sampling of attitudes and values would be possible.

It is true that one must make an inferential "leap of faith" when estimating population characteristics from sample observations. The likelihood that such inferences will be correct is largely a function of the sampling procedure employed.

There are two major types of sampling procedures available to researchers: *probability* and *nonprobability sampling*. Probability sampling involves sample selection in which the elements are drawn by chance procedures. The main characteristic of probability sampling is that every member or element of the population has a known probability of being chosen in the sample. Nonprobability sampling includes methods of selection in which elements are not chosen by chance procedures. There is no way of estimating the probability that each element has of being included in the sample. Its success depends on the knowledge, expertise, and judgment of the researcher. Nonprobability sampling is used when the application of probability sampling is not feasible. Its advantages are convenience and economy.

// Probability Sampling

Probability sampling is defined as the kind of sampling in which "every element in the population has a nonzero chance of being selected."[1] The

---

[1]Stuart, A. (1984). *The Ideas of Sampling* (3d ed.). New York: Macmillan.

possible inclusion of each population element in this kind of sampling takes place by chance and is attained through randomization. When probability sampling is used, inferential statistics enable researchers to estimate the extent to which the findings based on the sample are likely to differ from what they would have found by studying the whole population. The four types of probability sampling most frequently used in educational research are simple random sampling, stratified sampling, cluster sampling, and systematic sampling.

/ Simple Random Sampling

The best known of the probability sampling procedures is simple random sampling. The basic characteristic of simple random sampling is that all members of the population have an equal and independent chance of being included in the sample. That is, for every pair of elements X and Y, X's chance of being selected equals Y's chance, and the selection of X in no way affects Y's probability of selection. The steps in simple random sampling are

1. Define the population
2. List all members of the population
3. Select the sample by employing a procedure where sheer chance determines which members on the list are drawn for the sample

The most systematic procedure for drawing a random sample is to refer to a *table of random numbers,* which is a table containing columns of digits that have been mechanically generated, usually by a computer, to assure a random order. Table A.6 in the Appendix is an example. The first step in drawing a random sample from a population is to assign each member of the population a distinct identification number. Then the table of random numbers is used to select the identification numbers of the subjects to be included in the sample.

Let us illustrate the use of this table to obtain a sample of adolescents from the population of students attending Washington High School. First it is necessary to enumerate all of the individuals included in the population. The principal's office could supply a list of all students enrolled in the school. One would then assign a number to each individual in the population for identification purposes. Assuming there were 800 students in the school, one might use the numbers 000, 001, 002, 003, . . . , 799 for this purpose. Then one would enter a table of random numbers to obtain numbers of three digits each, using only those numbers that are less than or equal to 799. For each number chosen, the corresponding element in the population falls in the sample. One continues the process until the desired number for the sample has been chosen. It is customary in using a table of random numbers to determine by chance the point at which the table is entered. One way is to touch the page blindly and begin wherever the page is touched.

The generally understood meaning of the word *random* is "without purpose or by accident." However, random sampling is purposeful and methodical. It is apparent that a sample selected randomly is not subject to the biases of the researcher. When researchers employ this method, they are committing themselves to selecting a sample in such a way that their biases are not permitted to operate. They are pledging themselves to avoid a deliberate selection of subjects who will confirm the hypothesis. They are allowing chance alone to determine which elements in the population will be in the sample.

One would expect a random sample to be representative of the parent population sampled. However, a random selection, especially with small samples, does not absolutely guarantee a sample that will represent the population well. Random selection does guarantee that any differences between the sample and the parent population are only a function of chance and not a result of the researcher's bias. The differences between random samples and their parent population are not systematic. For example, the mean reading achievement of a random sample of sixth-graders may be higher than the mean reading achievement of the parent population, but it is equally likely that the mean for the sample will be lower than the mean for the parent population. In other words, with random sampling the sampling errors are just as likely to be negative as they are to be positive.

Furthermore, statistical theorists have shown, through deductive reasoning, how much one can expect the observations derived from random samples to differ from what would be observed in the population. All of the statistical procedures described in this chapter have this aim in mind. Remember that characteristics observed in a small sample are more likely to differ from population characteristics than are characteristics observed in a large sample. When random sampling is used, the researcher can employ inferential statistics to estimate how much the population is likely to differ from the sample. The inferential statistics in this chapter are all based on random sampling and apply only to those cases in which the sampling has been random.

Unfortunately, simple random sampling requires an enumeration of all the individuals in a finite population before the sample can be drawn—a requirement that often presents a serious obstacle to the use of this method in practice.

/ Stratified Sampling

When the population consists of a number of subgroups, or strata, that may differ in the characteristics being studied, it is often desirable to use a form of probability sampling called stratified sampling. For example, if one were conducting a poll designed to assess opinions on a certain political issue, it might be advisable to subdivide the population into groups on the basis of age or occupation because one would expect opinions to differ systematically among various age or occupational groups. In stratified sampling one first identifies the strata of interest and then randomly draws a specified number of subjects from each stratum. The basis for stratification may be geographical or it may involve characteristics of the population, such as income, occupation, sex, age, year in college, or teaching level. In the study of adolescents, for example, one may be interested not merely in surveying the attitudes of adolescents toward certain phenomena, but also in comparing the attitudes of adolescents who reside in small towns with those who live in medium-size and large cities. In such a case one would divide the adolescent population into three groups, based on the size of the towns or cities in which they reside, and then randomly select independent samples from each stratum.

An advantage of stratified sampling is that it improves representativeness and it enables the researcher to study the differences that might exist between various subgroups of a population. In this kind of sampling one may either take equal numbers from each stratum or select in proportion to the size of the stratum in the population. The latter procedure is known as *proportional stratified sampling,* which is applied when the characteristics of the entire population are the main concern in the study. The stratum is represented in the sample in exact proportion to its frequency in the total population. For example, if 10 percent of the voting population are college students, then 10 percent of one's sample of voters to be polled would be taken from this stratum.

In some research studies, however, the main concern is with differences among various strata. In these cases the researcher chooses samples of equal size from each stratum. For example, if one is investigating the difference between the study habits of graduate and undergraduate students, one includes equal numbers in both groups and then studies the differences that might exist between them. The procedure used will be chosen according to the nature of the research question. If the emphasis is on the types of differences among the strata, one selects equal numbers of cases from each. If the characteristics of the entire population are the main concern, proportional sampling is more appropriate.

When applicable, stratified sampling may give us a more representative sample than simple random sampling. In simple random sampling certain strata may by chance be over- or underrepresented in the sample. For example, in the simple random sample of high school students it would be theoretically possible (though highly unlikely) to obtain female subjects only. This could not happen, however, if males and females are listed separately and a random sample is then chosen from each group.

The major advantage of stratified sampling is that it guarantees representation of defined groups in the population.

/ Cluster Sampling

As mentioned earlier, it is very difficult, if not impossible, to list all the members of a target population and select the sample from among them. The population of American high school students, for example, is so large that one cannot list all its members for the purpose of drawing a sample. In addition, it would be a very expensive undertaking to study a sample that is scattered all around the United States. In this case it would be more convenient to study subjects in naturally occurring groups, or clusters. That is, the researcher would choose a number of schools randomly from a list of schools and then include all the students in those schools in the sample. This kind of probability sampling is referred to as *cluster sampling* because the unit chosen is not an individual but a group of individuals who are naturally together. These individuals constitute a cluster insofar as they are alike with respect to characteristics relevant to the variables of the study. Let us assume a public opinion poll is being conducted in Atlanta. The investigator would probably not have access to a list of the entire adult population; thus, it would be impossible to draw a simple random sample. A more feasible approach would involve the selection of a random sample of, say, 50 blocks from a city map and then the polling of all the adults living on those blocks. Each block represents a cluster of subjects, similar in certain characteristics associated with living in proximity.

It is essential that the clusters actually included in the study be chosen at random from a population of clusters. If only a single cluster were used—for example, one elementary school in a large city—one could not generalize to the population. Another procedural requirement is that once a cluster is selected, *all* the members of the cluster must be included in the sample. The sampling error in a cluster sample is much greater than in true random sampling.

/ Systematic Sampling

Still another form of probability sampling is called *systematic sampling*. This procedure involves drawing a sample by taking every kth case from a list of the population.

One first decides how many subjects one wants in the sample (n). Because one knows the total number of members in the population (N), one simply divides N by n and determines the sampling interval (k) to apply to the list. The first member is randomly selected from the first k members of the list, and then every kth member of the population is selected for the sample. For example, let us assume a total population of 500 subjects and a desired sample size of 50; $k = N/n = 500/50 = 10$.

One would start near the top of the list so that the first case could be randomly selected from the first ten cases; and then every tenth case thereafter would be selected. Let's say the third name or number on the list was the first to be selected. One would then add the sampling interval *k*, or 10, to 3—and thus the 13th person falls in the sample, as does the 23rd, and so on—and would continue adding the constant sampling interval until the end of the list is reached.

Systematic sampling differs from simple random sampling in that the various choices are not independent. Once the first case is chosen, all subsequent cases to be included in the sample are automatically determined.

If the original population list is in random order, systematic sampling would yield a sample that could be statistically considered a reasonable substitute for a random sample. However, if the list is alphabetical, for example, it is possible that every *k*th member of the population might have some unique characteristic that would affect the dependent variable of the study and thus yield a biased sample. Systematic sampling from an alphabetical list would probably not give a representative sample of various national groups because certain national groups tend to cluster under certain letters and the sampling interval could omit them entirely or at least not include them to an adequate extent.

It should be noted that the various types of probability sampling that have been discussed are not mutually exclusive. Various combinations may be used. For example, one could use cluster sampling if one is studying a very large and widely dispersed population. At the same time, one may be interested in stratifying the sample to answer questions regarding its different strata. In this case one would stratify the population according to the predetermined criteria and then randomly select the clusters of subjects from among each stratum.

// Nonprobability Sampling

In many research situations the enumeration of the population elements, a basic requirement in probability sampling, is difficult if not impossible. In these instances the researcher uses nonprobability sampling. The major forms of nonprobability sampling are accidental sampling, purposive sampling, and quota sampling.

/ Accidental Sampling

Accidental sampling, which is regarded as the weakest of all sampling procedures, involves using available cases for a study. Interviewing the first individuals one encounters on campus, using the students in one's own classroom as a sample, or taking volunteers to be interviewed in survey research are various examples of accidental sampling. There is no way (except by repeating the study using probability sampling) of estimating the error introduced by the accidental sampling procedures. If one does use accidental sampling, one must be extremely cautious in the interpretation of the findings.

/ Purposive Sampling

In purposive sampling, also referred to as judgment sampling, sample elements judged to be typical, or representative, are chosen from the population. The assumption underlying this type of sampling is that erroneous judgments in the selection of the elements from the population will counterbalance one another.

Purposive sampling is often used for forecasting national elections. In each state a number of small districts whose returns in previous elections have been typical of the entire state are chosen. All the eligible voters in these districts are interviewed, and the results are used to predict the voting patterns of the state. Using similar procedures in all states, the pollsters forecast the national results.

The critical question in purposive sampling is the extent to which judgment can be relied on to arrive at a typical sample. The assumption that errors in judgment would necessarily counterbalance one another is not always credible. Furthermore, there is no reason to assume that the units judged to be typical of the population will continue to be typical over a period of time. Consequently, the results of a study using purposive sampling may be misleading.

Because of its low cost and convenience, purposive sampling has been useful in attitude and opinion surveys. One should be aware of the limitations, however, and use the method with extreme caution.

/ Quota Sampling

Quota sampling involves the selection of typical cases from diverse strata of a population. The quotas are based on known characteristics of the population to which one wishes to generalize. Elements are drawn so that the resulting sample is a miniature approximation of the population with respect to the selected characteristics. For example, if census results show that 25 percent of the population of an urban area lives in the suburbs, then 25 percent of the sample should come from the suburbs.

The steps in quota sampling are

1. Determine a number of variables, strongly related to the question under investigation, to be used as bases for stratification. Variables such as sex, age, education, and social class are frequently used.
2. Using census or other available data, specify the size of each segment of the population.
3. Compute quotas for each segment of the population that are proportional to the size of each segment.

4. Select typical cases from each segment, or stratum, of the population to fill the quotas.

The major weakness in quota sampling lies in step 4, the selection of individuals from each stratum. One simply does not know whether the individuals chosen are representative of the given stratum. The selection of elements is likely to be based on accessibility and convenience. If one is selecting 25 percent of the households in the inner city for a survey, one is more likely to go to houses that are attractive rather than dilapidated, to those that are more accessible, to those where people are at home during the day, and so on. Such procedures automatically result in a systematic bias in the sample, because certain elements are not going to be represented. Furthermore, there is no basis for calculating the error involved in quota sampling.

Despite these shortcomings, quota sampling has been used in many research projects that might otherwise not have been possible. Many feel speed of data collection outweighs the disadvantages. Moreover, years of experience with quota samples have made it possible to identify some of the pitfalls and to take steps to avoid them.[2]

// The Size of the Sample

One of the first questions to be asked concerns the number of subjects that need to be included in the sample. Technically, the size of the sample depends upon the precision the researcher desires in estimating the population parameter at a particular confidence level. There is no single rule that can be used to determine sample size. An estimation of required sample size can be calculated algebraically if one defines precisely the variance of the population, the expected difference, and the desired probabilities of Type I and Type II errors (see pp. 185–186). A number of statistics texts describe this procedure.

The best answer to the question of size is to use as large a sample as possible. Other things being equal, a larger sample is much more likely to be representative of the population. Furthermore, with a large sample the data are likely to be more accurate and precise—which is to say, the larger the sample, the smaller the standard error. In general, the standard error of a sample mean is inversely proportional to the square root of n. Thus, in order to double the precision of one's estimation, one must quadruple the sample size.

Apart from this general statement, the size of the sample depends on the homogeneity of the population from which it is to be selected. If the

---

[2]For further discussion of sampling techniques see W. C. Cochran (1985), *Sampling Techniques* (2d ed.), New York: Wiley; L. Kish (1965), *Survey Sampling*, New York: Wiley; and S. Sudman (1976), *Applied Sampling*, New York: Academic Press.

population under study is homogeneous, a small sample could represent it. But with increasing variability of the population, a larger sample will be needed. For example, if the population of interest is first-graders, a smaller sample is needed than when elementary school children constitute the population under study.

Most authors suggest that one include at least 30 subjects in a sample because this number permits the use of large-sample statistics. Therefore, in experimental research one should select a sample that will permit at least 30 in each group. In descriptive research, however, the use of larger samples is desirable, particularly when the population of interest is heterogeneous.[3]

It must be emphasized, however, that size alone will not guarantee accuracy. Representativeness is the most important consideration in selecting a sample. A sample may be large and still contain a bias. The latter situation is well illustrated by the *Literary Digest* poll of 1936, which predicted the defeat of President Roosevelt. Although the sample included approximately 2½ million respondents, it was not representative of the voters; thus, an erroneous conclusion was reached. The bias resulted from the selection of respondents for the poll from automobile registrations, telephone directories, and the magazine's subscription lists. These subjects would certainly not be representative of the total voting population in 1936. Also, since the poll was conducted by mail, the results were biased by differences between those who responded and those who did not. Therefore, the researcher must recognize that sample size will not compensate for the bias that may be introduced through faulty sampling techniques. Representativeness must remain the prime goal in sample selection.

// The Concept of Sampling Error

When an inference is made from a sample to a population, a certain amount of error is involved because even samples that are random can be expected to vary from one to another. The mean intelligence score of one random sample of fourth-graders may be different from the mean intelligence score of another random sample of fourth-graders from the same population. Such differences, called sampling errors, result from the fact that one has observed a sample and not the entire population.

Sampling error is defined as "the difference between a population parameter and a sample statistic." For example, if one knows the mean of the entire population (symbolized μ) and also the mean of a random sample (symbolized $\bar{X}$) from that population, the difference between these two, $\bar{X} - \mu$, represents sampling error (symbolized e). Thus, $e = \bar{X} - \mu$. For example, if we know that the mean intelligence score for a population of

---

[3]For further discussion of the size of the sample see A. L. Edwards (1974), *Statistical Methods* (4th ed.), Fort Worth: Holt, Rinehart and Winston.

10,000 fourth-graders is $\mu = 100$ and a particular random sample of 200 has a mean of $\bar{X} = 99$, then the sampling error is $\bar{X} - \mu = 99 - 100 = -1$. Because we usually depend on sample statistics to estimate population parameters, the notion of how samples are expected to vary from populations is a basic element in inferential statistics. However, instead of trying to determine the discrepancy between a sample statistic and the population parameter (which is not often known), the approach in inferential statistics is to estimate the variability that could be expected in the statistics from a number of different random samples drawn from the same population. Because each of the sample statistics is considered to be an estimate of the same population parameter, then any variation among sample statistics must be attributed to sampling error.

// The Lawful Nature of Sampling Errors

Given that random samples drawn from the same population will vary from one another, is using a sample to make inferences about a population really any better than just guessing? Yes, it is, because sampling errors behave in a lawful and predictable manner. The laws concerning sampling error have been derived through deductive logic and have been confirmed through experience.

Although we cannot predict the nature and extent of the error in a single sample, we can predict the nature and extent of sampling errors in general. Let us illustrate this with reference to sampling errors connected with the mean.

/ Sampling Errors of the Mean

Some sampling error can always be expected when a sample mean $\bar{X}$ is used to estimate a population mean μ. Although, in practice, such an estimate is based on a single sample mean, assume that one drew several random samples from the same population and computed a mean for each sample. We would find that these sample means would differ from one another and would also differ from the population mean (if it were known). This variation among the means is due to the sampling error associated with each random sample mean as an estimate of the population mean. Sampling errors of the mean have been studied carefully, and it has been found that they follow known laws.

The Expected Mean of Sampling Errors Is Zero Given an infinite number of random samples drawn from a single population, the positive errors can be expected to balance the negative errors so that the mean of the sampling errors will be 0. For example, if the mean height of a population of college freshmen is 5 feet 9 inches and several random samples are drawn from that population, we would expect some samples to have mean heights greater than 5 feet 9 inches and some to have mean heights less than 5 feet 9 inches. In the long run, however, the positive and negative sampling errors will balance. If we had an infinite number of random samples of the same size, calculated the mean of each of these samples, then computed the mean of all these means, the mean of the means would be equal to the population mean.

Since positive errors equal negative errors, a single sample mean is as likely to underestimate a population mean as to overestimate it. Therefore, we can justify saying that a sample mean is an unbiased estimate of the population mean and is a reasonable estimate of the population mean.

Sampling Error Is an Inverse Function of Sample Size   As the size of a sample increases, there is less fluctuation from one sample to another in the value of the mean. In other words, as the size of a sample increases, the expected sampling error decreases. Small samples are more prone to sampling error than large ones. One would expect the means based on samples of 10 to fluctuate a great deal more than the means based on samples of 100. In our height example it is much more likely that a random sample of 4 will include 3 above-average freshmen and 1 below-average freshman than that a random sample of 40 would include 30 above average and 10 below. As sample size increases, the likelihood that the mean of the sample is near the population mean also increases. There is a mathematical relationship between sample size and sampling error. We will show later how this relationship has been incorporated into inferential formulas.

Sampling Error Is a Direct Function of the Standard Deviation of the Population   The more spread, or variation, we have among members of a population, the more spread we expect in sample means. For example, the mean weights of random samples of 25, each selected from a population of professional jockeys, would show relatively less sampling error than the mean weights of samples of 25 selected from a population of schoolteachers. The weights of professional jockeys fall within a narrow range, the weights of schoolteachers do not. Therefore, for a given sample size, the expected sampling error for teachers' weights would be greater than the expected sampling error for jockeys' weights.

Sampling Errors Are Distributed in a Normal or Near-Normal Manner around the Expected Mean of Zero   Sample means near the population mean will occur more frequently than sample means far from the population mean. As we move farther and farther from the population mean, we find fewer and fewer sample means occurring. Both theory and experience have shown that the means of random samples are distributed in a normal or near-normal manner around the population mean.

Since a sampling error in this case is the difference between a sample mean and the population mean, the distribution of sampling errors is also normal or near-normal in shape. The two distributions are by definition identical, except that the distribution of sample means has a mean equal to the population mean while the mean of the sampling errors is 0.

The distribution of sample means will resemble a normal curve even when the population from which the samples are drawn is not normally distributed. For example, in a typical elementary school we find about equal numbers of children of various ages included, so a polygon of the children's ages would be basically rectangular. If we took random samples of 40 each from a school with equal numbers of children aged 6 through 11, we would find many samples with a mean age near the population mean of 8.5, sample means of about 8 or 9 would be less common, and sample means as low as 7 or as high as 10 would be rare.

/ Standard Error of the Mean

Since the extent and the distribution of sampling errors can be predicted, we can use sample means with predictable confidence to make inferences concerning population means. However, we need an estimate of the magnitude of the sampling error associated with the sample mean when it is used as an estimate of the population mean. An important tool for this purpose is the *standard error of the mean.*

It has been stated that sampling error manifests itself in the variability of sample means. Thus, if one calculates the standard deviation of a collection of means from random samples from a single population, one would have an estimate of the amount of sampling error. It is possible, however, to obtain this estimate on the basis of only one sample. We have seen that two things affect the size of sampling error: the size of the sample and the standard deviation in the population. When these two things are known, one can predict the standard deviation of sampling errors. This expected standard deviation of sampling errors of the mean is called the *standard error of the mean* and is represented by the symbol $\sigma_{\bar{x}}$. It has been shown through deductive logic that the standard error of the mean is equal to the standard deviation of the population (σ) divided by the square root of the number in each sample ($\sqrt{n}$). In formula form:

$$\sigma_{\bar{x}} = \frac{\sigma}{\sqrt{n}} \qquad (6.1)$$

where

$\sigma_{\bar{x}}$ = standard error of the mean
σ = standard deviation of the population
n = number in each sample

In Chapter 5 we saw that standard deviation (σ) is an index of the degree of spread among individuals in a population. In the same way, standard error of the mean $(\sigma_{\bar{x}})$ is an index of the spread expected among the means of samples drawn randomly from a population. As we will see, the interpretation of σ and $\sigma_{\bar{x}}$ is very similar.

Because the means of random samples have approximately normal distributions, we can also use the normal-curve model to make inferences concerning population means. Given that the expected mean of sample means is equal to the population mean, that the standard deviation of these means is equal to the standard error of the mean, and that the means of random samples are distributed normally, one can compute a z-score for a sample mean and refer that z to the normal-curve table to approximate the probability of a sample mean occurring through chance that far or farther from the population mean. The z is derived by subtracting the population mean from the sample mean and then dividing this difference by the standard error of the mean.

$$ z = \frac{\bar{X} - \mu}{\sigma_{\bar{x}}} \qquad (6.2) $$

To illustrate, let us consider a college admissions officer who wonders if her population of applicants is average or below average on the College Board examination. The national mean for College Board scores is 500, and the standard deviation is 100. She pulls a random sample of 64 from the population and finds the mean of the sample to be 470. She asks the question How probable is it that a random sample of 64 with a mean of 470 would be drawn from a population with a mean of 500? Using formula 6.1, the admissions officer calculates the standard error of the mean as 12.5:

$$ \sigma_{\bar{x}} = \frac{\sigma}{\sqrt{n}} $$
$$ = \frac{100}{\sqrt{64}} $$
$$ = 12.5 $$

Calculating the z-score for her sample mean with formula 6.2, she obtains

$$ z = \frac{\bar{X} - \mu}{\sigma_{\bar{x}}} $$
$$ = \frac{470 - 500}{12.5} $$
$$ = -2.4 $$

Thus, the sample mean deviates from the population mean by 2.4 standard-error units. What is the probability of having a sample mean that deviates by this amount $(-2.4\sigma_{\bar{x}})$ or more from the population mean? It is only necessary to refer to the normal curve in order to express this deviation (z)

in terms of probability. Referring to the normal-curve table, one finds that the probability of a $z = -2.4$ or lower is .0082. This means that a z-score that low or lower would occur by chance only about 8 times in 1000. Because the probability of getting a sample mean that far from the population mean is remote, she concludes that the sample mean probably did not come from a population with a mean of 500 and therefore the mean of her population, applicants to her college, is probably less than 500.

/// THE STRATEGY OF INFERENTIAL STATISTICS

Inferential statistics is the science of making reasonable decisions with limited information. We use what we observe in samples and what is known about sampling error to reach fallible but reasonable decisions about populations. The statistical procedures performed before these decisions are made are called *tests of significance*. A basic tool of these statistical tests is the null hypothesis.

// Null Hypothesis

Suppose we have 100 fourth-graders available to participate in an experiment concerning the teaching of certain number concepts. Further suppose that our research hypothesis is that Method B of teaching results in a higher mastery of these concepts than Method A. We randomly assign 50 students to be taught these concepts by Method A and the other 50 to be taught by Method B. We arrange their environment in such a way that the two groups differ only in method of instruction. At the end of the experiment we administer an examination that is considered to be a suitable operational definition of mastery of the number concepts of interest. We find that the mean for those students taught by Method B is higher than the mean for those taught by Method A. How do we interpret this difference?

Assuming we have been careful to make the learning conditions of the two groups equivalent except for the method of teaching, we could account for the difference by declaring that (1) the method of teaching caused the difference or (2) the difference occurred by chance. Even though the subjects were randomly assigned to the treatments, it is possible that through chance the Method B group had students who were more intelligent, more highly motivated, or for some other reason were more likely to learn the number concepts than the students in the Method A group, no matter how they were taught.

The difference between the groups therefore could be a result of a relationship between the variables—method of teaching and mastery of the concepts—or it could be the result of chance alone (sampling error). How are we to know which explanation is correct? In the ultimate sense we cannot know. What we do, then, is estimate the likelihood of chance alone being responsible for the observed difference and determine which explanation to accept as a result of this estimate.

The chance explanation is known as the null hypothesis, which, as you will recall from Chapter 4, is a statement that there is *no* actual relationship between variables and that any observed relationship is only a function of chance. In our example the null hypothesis would state that there is no relationship between teaching method and mastery of the number concepts.

Another way of stating the null hypothesis in our example is to declare that the mean for all fourth-graders taught by Method A is equal to the mean for all fourth-graders taught by Method B. In formula form, using the symbol μ for population mean, this statement becomes

$$H_0 : \mu_A = \mu_B$$

where

H_0 = the null hypothesis
μ_A = the mean of all fourth-graders taught by Method A
μ_B = the mean of all fourth-graders taught by Method B

Note that the assumption is made that the 50 pupils taught by Method A are a sample of all fourth-graders who might be taught by Method A and the 50 pupils taught by Method B are a sample of all those who might be taught by Method B. The investigator hopes to use the data from the experiment to infer what would be expected when other fourth-graders are taught by Method A or B.

In interpreting the observed difference between the groups, the investigator must choose between the chance explanation (null hypothesis) and the explanation that states that there is a relationship between variables (research hypothesis)—and must do so without knowing the ultimate truth concerning the populations of interest. This choice is based on incomplete information and is therefore subject to possible error.

// Type I and Type II Errors

The investigator will either retain or reject the null hypothesis. Either decision may be right or wrong. If the null hypothesis is true, the investigator is correct in retaining it and in error in rejecting it. The rejection of a true null hypothesis is labeled a *Type I error*.

If the null hypothesis is false, the investigator is in error in retaining it and correct in rejecting it. The retention of a false null hypothesis is labeled a *Type II error*. The four possible states of affairs are summarized in Table 6.1.

Let us consider some possible consequences of the two types of errors in our example.

TABLE 6.1 Schematic Representation of Type I and Type II Errors

		Real Situation in the Population	
		H_0 is true	H_0 is false
Investigator's Decision after Making Test of Significance	Rejects H_0	Type 1 error	Correct
	Retains H_0	Correct	Type II error

/ Type I Error

The investigator declares that there is a relationship between teaching method and the mastery of the numerical concepts and therefore recommends Method B as the better method. Schools discard textbooks and other materials based on Method A and purchase materials based on Method B. In-service training is instituted to train teachers to teach by Method B. After all this expenditure of time and money the schools do not observe an increase in mastery of the numerical concepts. Subsequent experiments do not produce the results observed in the original investigation. Although the ultimate truth or falsity of the null hypothesis is still unknown, the evidence supporting it is overwhelming. The original investigator is embarrassed and humiliated.

/ Type II Error

The investigator concludes that the difference between the two groups may be attributed to chance and that the null hypothesis is probably true. She declares that there is insufficient evidence for concluding that one method is better than the other.

Subsequent investigators conclude that Method B is better than Method A, and schools that change from Method A to Method B report impressive gains in student mastery. Although the ultimate truth still remains unknown, a mountain of evidence supports the research hypothesis. The original investigator is embarrassed (but probably not humiliated).

Type I errors typically lead to changes that are unwarranted. Type II errors typically lead to a maintenance of the status quo when a change is warranted. The consequences of a Type I error are generally considered more serious than the consequences of a Type II error, although there are certainly exceptions to this.

/// LEVEL OF SIGNIFICANCE

Recall that all scientific conclusions are statements that have a high probability of being correct, rather than statements of absolute truth. How high must the probability be before an investigator is willing to declare that a relationship between variables exists? In other words, how unlikely must the null hypothesis be before one rejects it? The consequences of rejecting a true null hypothesis, a Type I error, vary with the situation. Therefore, investigators usually weigh the relative consequences of Type I and Type II errors and decide, before conducting their experiments, how strong the evidence must be before they would reject the null hypothesis. This predetermined level at which a null hypothesis would be rejected is called the *level of significance*. The probability of a Type I error is directly under the control of the researcher, who sets the level of significance according to the type of error he/she wishes to guard against.

Of course one could avoid Type I errors by always retaining the null hypothesis or avoid Type II errors by always rejecting it. Neither of these alternatives is productive. If the consequences of a Type I error would be very serious but a Type II error would be of little consequence, the investigator might decide to risk the possibility of a Type I error only if the estimated probability of the observed relationship's being due to mere luck is one chance in a thousand or less. This is called testing the hypothesis at the .001 level of significance and is considered to be a quite conservative level. In this case the investigator is being very careful not to declare that a relationship exists when there is no relationship. However, this decision means the acceptance of a high probability of a Type II error, declaring there is no relationship when in fact a relationship does exist.

If the consequences of a Type I error are judged to be not serious, the investigator might decide to declare that a relationship exists if the probability of an observed relationship's being due to mere luck is one chance in ten or less. This is called testing the hypothesis at the .1 level of significance. Here the investigator is taking only moderate precautions against a Type I error, yet is not taking a great risk of a Type II error.

The level of significance is the probability of a Type I error that an investigator is willing to risk in rejecting a null hypothesis. If an investigator sets the level of significance at .01, it means that the null hypothesis will be rejected if the estimated probability of the observed relationship's being a chance occurrence is one in a hundred. If the level of significance is set at .0001, the null hypothesis will be rejected only if the estimated probability of the observed relationship's being a function of mere chance is one in 10,000 or less. The most commonly used levels of significance in the field of education are the .05 and the .01 levels.

Traditionally, investigators determine the level of significance after weighing the relative seriousness of Type I and Type II errors, but before running the experiment. If the data derived from the completed experiment indicate that the probability of the null hypothesis being true is equal to or less than the predetermined acceptable probability, the null hypothesis is rejected and the results are declared to be statistically significant. If the probability is greater than the predetermined acceptable probability, the results are described as nonsignificant—that is, the null hypothesis is retained.

The familiar meaning of the word *significant* is "important" or "meaningful." In statistics this word means "less likely to be a function of chance than some predetermined probability." Results of investigations can be statistically significant without being inherently meaningful or important.

// Directional and Nondirectional Tests

In testing a null hypothesis, we are not usually concerned with the direction of the differences. Rather, we are interested in knowing about the possible departure of sample statistics from population parameters. In the previous example of the admissions officer, our main interest was to determine if the difference between the mean of the sample and the mean of the population exceeded the amount that could happen by chance. The kind of test performed was called *nondirectional* because the investigator was interested in differences in either direction. The investigator states only that there will be a difference. Note in Figure 6.1 that the region of rejection is equally divided between the two tails of the distribution. Thus, if a sample mean is observed that is *either* much greater or much less than the hypothesized value, the null hypothesis would be rejected. The direction of the difference is not important. If on the basis of experience, previous research, or theory the researcher is able to state the direction of possible differences, however, then she/he would perform a *directional* test. A directional hypothesis would state either that the parameter is greater than *or* less than the hypothesized value. Thus, in directional tests the critical region is located in only one of the two tails of the distribution. This region in a normal curve is the point equal to $z = 1.645$. That is, we do not, as we do in nondirectional tests, divide the 5 percent between the two sides of the curve. Rather, we place all the 5 percent of chance error on one side of the curve. It is obvious that for rejecting a null hypothesis at a given level a directional test requires a smaller z-value than a nondirectional test (compare $z = 1.645$ with $z = 1.96$). So a directional test makes it easier to reject the null hypothesis and thus increases the probability that the null hypothesis will be rejected.

In statistical terminology a nondirectional test is often referred to as a two-tailed test of significance, a directional test as a one-tailed test. The decision to use either a one-tailed test or a two-tailed test should be made early in the study, before any statistical tests are performed. One does not wait to see what the data look like and then select a one-tailed or two-tailed test.

There are numerous ways of testing a null hypothesis. Among the most widely used procedures are the *t*-test, analysis of variance, and the chi-square test.

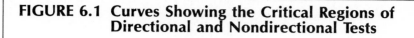

FIGURE 6.1 Curves Showing the Critical Regions of Directional and Nondirectional Tests

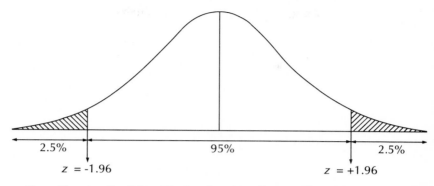

2.5%   95%   2.5%

$z = -1.96$ $z = +1.96$

a. Curve Showing the Critical Region for a Nondirectional Test (Two-Tailed Test)

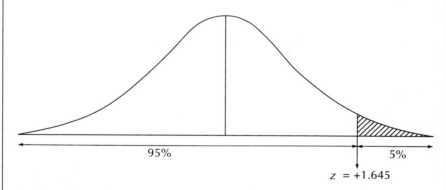

95%   5%

$z = +1.645$

b. Curve Showing the Critical Region for a Directional Test (One-Tailed Test)

/// THE *T*-TEST

We have shown that it is possible to make use of the normal probability curve to compare the mean of a sample with the population mean by using the z-score to see whether or not the sample mean is representative of the population mean. In our example the college admissions officer found the standard error of the mean for the sample distribution, then used the formula $(\bar{X} - \mu)/\sigma_{\bar{x}}$. Implied in using this procedure is the appropriateness of the normal probability curve.

However, it has been shown mathematically that the normal curve is appropriate for hypothesis testing only when the population standard deviation is known, as is the case with College Board scores. In most research situations the population standard deviation is not known and must be estimated by the formula

$$s = \sqrt{\frac{\Sigma x^2}{n - 1}} \qquad (6.3)$$

where

s = estimated population standard deviation
Σx^2 = sum of the squared deviations scores,
$\Sigma (X - \bar{X})^2$
n = number in the sample

When this estimate (s) is substituted for the population standard deviation (σ) in the calculation of the standard error of the mean, it is customary to express formula 6.1 as

$$s_{\bar{x}} = \frac{s}{\sqrt{n}} \text{ instead of } \sigma_{\bar{x}} = \frac{\sigma}{\sqrt{n}}$$

When $s_{\bar{x}}$ is used instead of $\sigma_{\bar{x}}$, each finite sample size has its own unique probability distribution. These distributions are known as the *t*-curves. These distributions become more and more similar to the normal curve as the size of the sample increases. A series of distributions called *t*-distributions has been developed for testing hypotheses concerning the population mean using small samples. When the sample size is infinite, the *t*-distribution is the same as the normal distribution. As the sample size becomes smaller, the *t*-distribution becomes increasingly different from the *z*-distribution. For our purposes it is not necessary to know how to calculate *t*-distributions because the most frequently needed results of these calculations are to be found in Table A.2 in the Appendix. The *t*-curve does not approach the baseline as rapidly as does the normal curve. Some of the *t*-curves are shown in Figure 6.2 along with the normal curve, the solid line labeled $df = \infty$.

The *t*-curves are labeled according to their degrees of freedom, abbreviated *df*. Before further discussion of the characteristics of *t*-curves, let us turn our attention to the concept of degrees of freedom.

/ Degrees of Freedom

The number of degrees of freedom refers to the number of observations free to vary around a constant parameter. To illustrate the general concept of degrees of freedom, suppose a teacher asks a student to name any five numbers that come into his or her mind. The student would be free to name any five numbers he or she chooses, so we would say that the student has five degrees of freedom. Now suppose the teacher tells the student to name

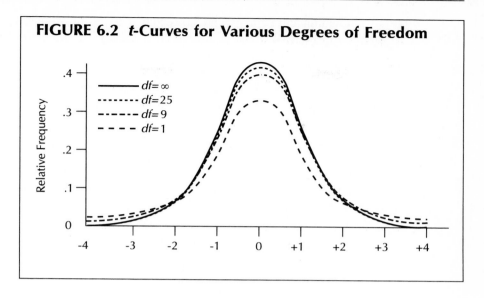

FIGURE 6.2 *t*-Curves for Various Degrees of Freedom

five numbers but to make sure that the mean of these five numbers is 20. The student now is free to name any numbers for the first four, but for the last number must name the number that will make the total for the five numbers 100 in order to arrive at a mean of 20. If the student names, as the first four numbers, 10, 16, 20, and 35, then the fifth number must be 19. The student has five numbers to name and one restriction, so his or her degrees of freedom are $5 - 1 = 4$. We can show this in formula form as

$$df = n - 1$$
$$= 5 - 1$$
$$= 4$$

Now suppose the teacher asks the student to name seven numbers in such a way that the first three have a mean of 10 and all seven have a mean of 12. Here we have seven numbers and two restrictions, so

$$df = n - 2$$
$$= 7 - 2$$
$$= 5$$

When the unknown population standard deviation is estimated from the sample standard deviation $\left(s_{\bar{x}} = \dfrac{s}{\sqrt{n}}\right)$, one degree of freedom is lost. The one *df* is lost because the sample statistic (*s*) is derived from the deviations about the sample mean that must always sum to 0. Thus, all but one of the deviations is free to vary, or $df = N - 1$.

The concept of degrees of freedom is involved in most of the procedures in inferential statistics. There is an appropriate method of computing the degrees of freedom associated with each procedure. In general, the number of degrees of freedom on which a sample statistic is based depends on the sample size (N) and the number of sample statistics used in its calculation.

/ The *t*-Test for Independent Samples

Research workers often draw two random samples from a population and assign a specific experimental treatment to each group. After being exposed to this treatment, the two groups are compared with respect to certain characteristics in order to find the effect of the treatments. A difference might be observed between the two groups after such treatments, but this difference might be statistically nonsignificant—that is, attributable to chance. The index used to find the significance of the difference between the means of the two samples in this case is called the t-*test for independent samples.* These samples are referred to as independent because they are drawn independently from a population without any pairing or other relationship between the two groups.

Let us use an example. Suppose a researcher is interested in finding out whether stress affects problem-solving performance. The first step is to randomly assign the students in a course to two groups. Because the members of the two groups are assigned randomly, the mean performances of the two groups in a problem-solving task should not significantly differ prior to the treatment. After the treatment, however, the mean performance of the two groups should differ significantly if stress is actually related to problem-solving performance.

Table 6.2 shows the posttreatment, problem-solving scores (X), deviation scores (x), and squared deviation scores (x^2) of the members of the two groups, one of which worked under stress conditions and the other under relaxed (nonstress) conditions. The mean performance score of the subjects in the stress group is 10 and the mean performance score of the nonstress group is 14. Clearly there is a difference. Now we need to determine whether this difference could easily occur by chance. In order to do this we must estimate how much difference between the groups would be expected through chance alone under a true null hypothesis. An appropriate procedure for doing this is to calculate the *standard error of the difference between two means* ($s_{\bar{x}_1 - \bar{x}_2}$). The formula for this in the case of independent samples is

$$s_{\bar{x}_1 - \bar{x}_2} = \sqrt{\frac{\Sigma x_1^2 + \Sigma x_2^2}{n_1 + n_2 - 2}\left(\frac{1}{n_1} + \frac{1}{n_2}\right)} \qquad (6.4)$$

TABLE 6.2 The Computation of the *t*-Value for Two Sample Means

Group 1 Nonstress Condition			Group 2 Stress Condition		
X_1	x_1	x_1^2	X_2	x_2	x_2^2
18	+4	16	13	+3	9
17	+3	9	12	+2	4
16	+2	4	12	+2	4
16	+2	4	11	+1	1
16	+2	4	11	+1	1
15	+1	1	11	+1	1
15	+1	1	10	0	0
15	+1	1	10	0	0
14	0	0	10	0	0
14	0	0	10	0	0
13	−1	1	9	−1	1
12	−2	4	9	−1	1
11	−3	9	8	−2	4
10	−4	16	7	−3	9
8	−6	36	7	−3	9

$$\frac{\Sigma X_1}{n_1} = \frac{210}{15} \qquad \Sigma x_1^2 = 106 \qquad \frac{\Sigma X_2}{n_2} = \frac{150}{15} \qquad \Sigma x_2^2 = 44$$

$$\bar{X}_1 = 14 \qquad\qquad \bar{X}_2 = 10$$

where

$s_{\bar{x}_1 - \bar{x}_2}$ = the standard error of the difference between two means

n_1 = the number of cases in Group 1

n_2 = the number of cases in Group 2

Σx_1^2 = the sum of the squared deviation scores in Group 1

Σx_2^2 = the sum of the squared deviation scores in Group 2

The standard error of the difference between two means is sometimes referred to as the *error term for the* t-*test*. In our example this would be calculated as follows:

$$s_{\bar{x}_1 \bar{x}_2} = \sqrt{\frac{106 + 44}{15 + 15 - 2}\left(\frac{1}{15} + \frac{1}{15}\right)}$$

$$= \sqrt{\frac{150}{28}\left(\frac{2}{15}\right)}$$

$$= \sqrt{0.714}$$

$$= 0.84$$

This calculation tells us the difference that would be expected through chance alone if the null hypothesis were true. In other words, the value 0.84 is the difference we would expect between the mean performance scores for our two groups if they were drawn at random from a common population and were *not* subjected to different treatments. Given an infinite number of samples in such circumstances, we would expect to observe a difference of less than 0.84 in 68 percent of the calculations of the differences between such random groups and a value of more than 0.84 in the other 32 percent. (It is beyond the scope of this text to discuss the reason why the application of the formula for the standard error of the difference between means yields the appropriate estimated difference that would be due to chance.)[4]

In our example for the data in Table 6.2 we should expect a difference of 0.84 through chance under a true null hypothesis. We observed a difference of 4.0. Is the observed difference sufficiently greater than the expected difference to enable us to reject the null hypothesis?

To answer this question we first make a ratio of the two numbers. This ratio is called the t-*ratio*. Its formula is

$$t = \frac{\bar{X}_1 - \bar{X}_2}{s_{\bar{x}_1 - \bar{x}_2}} \tag{6.5}$$

where

$$t = \text{the } t\text{-ratio}$$
$$\bar{X}_1 - \bar{X}_2 = \text{the observed difference between two means}$$
$$s_{\bar{x}_1 - \bar{x}_2} = \text{the standard error of the difference between two means}$$
$$\text{(expected difference between the two means}$$
$$\text{when the null hypothesis is true)}$$

We can write the t-ratio formula in more complete form by including the formula for the standard error for the difference between two means:

$$t = \frac{\bar{X}_1 - \bar{X}_2}{\sqrt{\left(\dfrac{\Sigma x_1{}^2 + \Sigma x_2{}^2}{n_1 + n_2 - 2}\right)\left(\dfrac{1}{n_1} + \dfrac{1}{n_2}\right)}} \tag{6.6}$$

In our example the value of the t-ratio is

$$\frac{14 - 10}{0.84} = 4.76$$

Our observed difference is 4.76 times as large as the difference expected under a true null hypothesis. Is this large enough to reject the null hypothesis at the .05 level? To answer this we need only calculate the degrees of freedom and consult the t-table.

The degrees of freedom for an independent t-test are the number of cases in the first group plus the number of cases in the second group minus 2.

$$df = n_1 + n_2 - 2$$

In our example we have $15 + 15 - 2 = 28$ degrees of freedom. We can now use Table A.2 in the Appendix to determine the significance of our

---

[4]For a discussion of the rationale of this procedure see D. Ary and L. C. Jacobs (1976), *Introduction to Statistics*, New York: Holt, Rinehart and Winston.

results. The first column in this table is labeled *df* (degrees of freedom). One finds the appropriate row in the table by locating the degrees of freedom in one's study. For our example we would consult the row for 28 degrees of freedom. The remaining columns show the *t*-values associated with certain probabilities for directional and nondirectional tests. Because the independent variable in our example could affect problem solving in either a positive or negative direction, we need to perform a nondirectional test. In the row for 28 degrees of freedom we find 1.701 in the column labeled .10 for a nondirectional test, which tells us that with a true null hypothesis and 28 degrees of freedom a *t*-ratio of +1.701 or more or −1.701 or less will occur by chance one time in ten. The number 2.048 in the column labeled .05 indicates that under a true null hypothesis and 28 degrees of freedom a *t*-ratio of ±2.048 or more will occur by chance 5 percent of the time.

Our observed ratio of 4.76 is greater than 2.048, which means that the difference between our groups is greater than the value required to reject the null hypothesis at the .05 level of significance. The estimated probability of the null hypothesis being true is less than 5 percent ($p < .05$). Although we do not know for certain that the variables *stress* and *problem-solving performance* are related, the evidence is significant enough according to our previously set criteria to enable us to conclude that the observed relationship is probably not just a chance occurrence. If the observed *t*-ratio had been less than 2.048, we would have concluded that the evidence was not good enough to lead us to declare that a relationship exists between the variables. In other words, we would have retained the null hypothesis.

Notice that as we proceed from left to right in the *t*-table we find the *t*-values required for rejecting the null hypothesis at increasingly rigorous levels of significance. For 28 degrees of freedom a value of 2.763 or greater would lead to the rejection of a null hypothesis at the .01 level. A value of 3.674 or greater would lead to the rejection of the null hypothesis at the .001 level. So our value of 4.76 is significant not only at the .05 level ($p < .05$) but also at the .01 level ($p < .01$) and the .001 level ($p < .001$).

/ The Logic of the *t*-Test

The numerator of the *t*-test is the actual difference that has been observed between two groups. The denominator ($s_{\bar{x}_1 - \bar{x}_2}$) is an estimate of how much these two groups would be expected to differ by chance alone; that is, it indicates the difference to be expected between two groups selected by a random procedure from a single parent population. This denominator is based on (1) the number in the samples, $n_1 + n_2$ (the larger the number, the fewer random differences to be expected between sample means), and (2) the variation within the groups, s_1 and s_2 (the greater the variation *within* groups, the greater the random differences to be expected between groups).

Because the denominator is a measure of how much apparent difference can be expected through chance alone, it is called the *error term* of the *t*-test.

If the ratio of observed difference (numerator) divided by error term (denominator) equals or exceeds the value indicated in the Table of *t*-Values, the null hypothesis can be rejected at the indicated level of significance.

/ The *t*-Test for Nonindependent Samples

So far, our discussion has centered on comparing the means obtained from two independent samples. In an independent sample each member is chosen randomly from the population and the composition of one group has no bearing on the composition of the other group. Sometimes, however, investigators may wish to match the subjects of their two groups on some qualities that are important to the purpose of their research, or they may wish to compare the means obtained by the same group under two different experimental conditions. In such cases the groups are no longer independent, inasmuch as the composition of one group is related to the composition of the other group. We would expect the dependent variable scores to be correlated. Therefore, the *t*-test for nonindependent, or correlated, means must be used. This test is also known as the correlated, or dependent, *t*-test. The measure to be analyzed by the nonindependent *t*-test is the difference between the paired scores.

Let us consider an example. Suppose we wish to know whether taking a research course affects the attitudes of the students toward research. To investigate this we select a research class and obtain attitude measures toward research from the students on the first and last days of class. Let us suppose we have collected such data and the results are as presented in Table 6.3. Columns (2) and (3) show the scores of each student in the first and second measures. Column (4) presents the difference between the first and second scores of each student. The sum of these differences amounts to $+30$. The mean of the differences, $+2$, is found by dividing $+30$ (ΣD) by n, the number of paired observations, or 15. Column (5) shows the squares of the differences.

The formula for the nonindependent *t*-test is

$$t = \frac{\bar{D}}{\sqrt{\dfrac{\Sigma D^2 - \dfrac{(\Sigma D)^2}{N}}{N(N-1)}}} \tag{6.7}$$

where

$$
\begin{aligned}
t &= \text{the } t\text{-value for nonindependent (correlated) means} \\
\bar{D} &= \text{the mean of the differences} \\
D &= \text{the difference between the paired scores} \\
\Sigma D^2 &= \text{the sum of the squared difference scores} \\
N &= \text{the number of pairs}
\end{aligned}
$$

TABLE 6.3 Before-and-After Attitude Scores of 15 Students in an Introduction to Research Class

(1) Subject Number	(2) Pretest	(3) Posttest	(4) D	(5) D²
1	10	12	+2	+4
2	9	13	+4	+16
3	8	12	+4	+16
4	11	9	−2	+4
5	10	8	−2	+4
6	7	9	+2	+4
7	10	12	+2	+4
8	9	11	+2	+4
9	8	10	+2	+4
10	6	10	+4	+16
11	10	12	+2	+4
12	7	13	+6	+36
13	10	6	−4	+16
14	9	13	+4	+16
15	10	14	+4	+16
			$\Sigma D = +30$	$\Sigma D^2 = +164$

Substituting the values from Table 6.3, we obtain

$$t = \frac{\dfrac{30}{15}}{\sqrt{\dfrac{164 - \dfrac{(30)^2}{15}}{15(15-1)}}} = \frac{2}{\sqrt{\dfrac{164 - 60}{210}}} = \frac{2}{\sqrt{\dfrac{104}{210}}} = \frac{2}{\sqrt{0.4952}} = \frac{2}{0.704} = 2.84$$

The t-ratio tells us that the observed difference is 2.84 times as great as the difference that would be expected under a true null hypothesis. We must now consult the Table of t-Values (Appendix Table A.2) to determine the statistical significance of our observed ratio.

The number of degrees of freedom for the nonindependent t-test equals $N - 1$, N being the number of pairs of observations. In our example we have $15 - 1 = 14$ degrees of freedom. In the Table of t-Values we find that with 14 degrees of freedom a t-value of 2.145 is needed for the t to be significant at the .05 level and a t-value of 2.977, for significance at the .01 level when a nondirectional test is performed. Our obtained value of 2.84 exceeds the given value for the .05 level but does not reach the given value for the .01 level. This means that the difference between the two means is significant at the .05 level but not at the .01 level. If we had set our level of significance at .05, we could conclude that the attitude of the students toward research has changed.

/ The *t*-Test for Pearson *r* Correlation Coefficients

Another important use for the *t*-test is in testing hypotheses concerning a population correlation (ρ). A test of significance of the relationship between variables is needed before one can draw conclusions about population correlations from sample data. The most common null hypothesis in such cases is that the population correlation is 0 and that the correlation observed in the sample (*r*) is a function of chance. For example, an investigator might draw a sample of 30 college freshmen, administer vocabulary and spatial orientation tests to them, and find a Pearson *r* of .20 between the two measures. The next step would be to decide whether this observed correlation coefficient could easily be a result of chance in a population where the true correlation (ρ) is 0.

The *t*-distribution is an appropriate model for testing the null hypothesis that the population correlation coefficient is 0. The *t*-statistic may be calculated using the following formula:

$$t = r\sqrt{\frac{N - 2}{1 - r^2}} \tag{6.8}$$

where

$t =$ the *t*-value
$r =$ the obtained correlation coefficient
$N =$ the number of paired observations

Applying Forumula 6.8 to the above example, we find that the *t* is 1.08:

$$t = .20\sqrt{\frac{30 - 2}{1 - (.20)^2}} = 1.08$$

The calculated *t*-value is compared to the tabled *t* with $N - 2$ degrees of freedom. A significant relationship exists if the observed value equals or exceeds the tabled value at the specified level of significance. Table A.2 indicates that a *t*-value of 2.048 is needed for significance at the .05 level with 28 *df* when a nondirectional test is performed. Because the calculated *t* of 1.08 is less than the tabled value, the investigator must conclude that there is insufficient evidence to state that there is a correlation between the two variables in the population from which the sample was drawn.

Tables have been constructed that indicate the critical value of the correlation coefficient *r* needed to reject the null hypothesis at various levels of significance (see Appendix Table A.5). A significant *r* is one equal to or larger than the tabled value with $N - 2$ degrees of freedom, where $N =$ the number of *pairs* of scores. Table A.5 indicates that with $df = 28$ when a two-tailed test is performed, an observed Pearson *r* above $+ .36$ or less than $-.361$ is required to reject the null hypothesis.[5] Thus, the correlation

---

[5]A one- or two-tailed test may be used. A one-tailed test is used if the investigator is interested only in a positive or in a negative coefficient. If, however, *either* a positive or a negative coefficient is of interest, a two-tailed test is used.

of .20 obtained in the above study involving college freshmen is not significant.

With a reasonably large number of cases, a coefficient of correlation may be low in value and yet be statistically significant. Because it is the value of correlation that indicates the degree of relationship between the variables, a low correlation always indicates a low relationship even when the correlation is statistically significant. For example, Jackson and Lahaderne, with a sample of 144 sixth-grade girls, found a correlation of +.25 between the students' response on a questionnaire measuring students' satisfaction with school and their teachers' prediction of how these students would respond to the questionnaire.[6] Because the sample size was large, the correlation, though low, was statistically significant at the .01 level. The findings indicate that in the population that was represented by the sample, the correlation is not likely to be 0. However, the low observed correlation suggests that, although teachers can predict student satisfaction at greater than chance level, the teachers' predictions of satisfaction have only a weak relationship with actual student satisfaction.

The *t*-test can also be used to test hypotheses about population correlations other than 0. It can also be used to test the hypothesis that the correlations observed in two samples could have arisen from the same population. Because this is an introductory text, we have chosen not to include such tests here. A useful description of these tests may be found in Glass and Hopkins[7] and in various other texts.

/// ANALYSIS OF VARIANCE

In *analysis of variance* (ANOVA), as in the *t*-test, a ratio of observed differences/error term is used to test hypotheses. This ratio, called the F-*ratio,* employs the variance (σ^2) of group means as a measure of observed differences among groups. This means that ANOVA is a more versatile technique than the *t*-test. A *t*-test can be used only to test a difference between *two* means. ANOVA can test the difference between *two or more* means. Some statisticians never use the *t*-test because ANOVA can be used in any situation where a *t*-test can be used and, moreover, can do many things the *t*-test cannot do.

The general rationale of ANOVA is that the *total variance* of all subjects in an experiment can be subdivided into two sources, *variance between groups* and *variance within groups.*

Variance between groups is incorporated into the numerator in the F-ratio. Variance within groups is incorporated into the error term or denom-

---

[6]Jackson, P. W., and H. M. Lahaderne (1967). Scholastic success and attitude toward school in a population of sixth graders. *Journal of Educational Psychology, 58,* 15–18.
[7]Glass, Gene V., and K. D. Hopkins (1984). *Statistical Methods in Education and Psychology* (2d ed.). Englewood Cliffs, NJ: Prentice-Hall.

inator, as it is in the *t*-test. As variance between groups increases, the *F*-ratio increases. As variance within increases, the *F*-ratio decreases. The number of subjects influences the *F*-ratio; the larger the number, the larger the numerator becomes. When the numerator and denominator are equal, the differences between group means are no greater than would be expected by chance alone. If the numerator is greater than the denominator, one consults the table of *F*-values (in the Appendix) to determine whether the ratio is great enough to enable one to reject the null hypothesis at the predetermined level.

// Computation of *F*-Ratio (Simple Analysis of Variance)

Suppose we have the three experimental conditions of high stress, moderate stress, and no stress, and we wish to compare the performance of three groups of individuals, randomly assigned to these three conditions, on a simple problem-solving task. Assume that the data presented in Table 6.4 summarize our observations of the performance of these three groups and we are now to test the null hypothesis that there is no significant difference among these observations at the .01 level.

The means can be seen to differ from one another and from the overall mean for all 30 subjects ($\bar{\bar{X}}$, the *grand mean*). Are the differences among these means great enough to be statistically significant, or is it likely that they occurred by chance? To answer this we compute the *F*-ratio.

TABLE 6.4 Measures Obtained in Three Random Samples after Performance of a Task under Conditions of High Stress, Moderate Stress, and No Stress

Group 1 High Stress		Group 2 Moderate Stress		Group 3 No Stress	
X_1	$X_1{}^2$	X_2	$X_2{}^2$	X_3	$X_3{}^2$
19	361	22	484	15	225
18	324	20	400	14	196
17	289	19	361	14	196
16	256	18	324	13	169
15	225	17	289	13	169
15	225	16	256	12	144
14	196	16	256	12	144
13	169	15	225	11	121
12	144	14	196	11	121
11	121	12	144	10	100
$\Sigma X_1 = 150$	$\Sigma X_1{}^2 = 2310$	$\Sigma X_2 = 169$	$\Sigma X_2{}^2 = 2935$	$\Sigma X_3 = 125$	$\Sigma X_3{}^2 = 1585$

$\bar{X}_1 = 15.0$ $\bar{X}_2 = 16.9$ $\bar{X}_3 = 12.5$ $\bar{\bar{X}} = 14.8$

$\Sigma X_t = 444$ $\Sigma X_t{}^2 = 6830$

The first step is to find the sum of the squared deviation of each of the individual scores from the grand mean. This index is called the *total sum of squares* and reflects all treatment effects and sampling error.

$$SS_t = \Sigma x_t^2 = \Sigma X_t^2 - \frac{(\Sigma X_t)^2}{N} \tag{6.9}$$

In our example this value is

$$SS_t = 6830 - \frac{(444)^2}{30} = 258.8$$

Then we find the part of the total sum of squares that is due to the deviations of the group means from the grand mean. This index is called the *sum of the squares between groups*. (To be grammatically correct, we should say the sum of squares *among* groups when more than two groups are involved. However, it is a long-standing tradition to use the term *sum of squares between groups*, and in order to be consistent with other texts, we are retaining this usage here.) This index is found by applying the formula

$$SS_b = \Sigma x_b^2 = \frac{(\Sigma X_1)^2}{n_1} + \frac{(\Sigma X_2)^2}{n_2} + \ldots - \frac{(\Sigma X)^2}{N} \tag{6.10}$$

In our problem this value is

$$SS_b = \Sigma x_b^2 = \frac{(150)^2}{10} + \frac{(169)^2}{10} + \frac{(125)^2}{10} - \frac{(444)^2}{30} = 97.4$$

Then we find the part of the total sum of squares that is due to the deviations of each individual score from its own group mean. This index is called the *sum of the squares within groups* and is found by applying the raw-score formula for the sum of squared deviations to each group and then summing across groups ($SS_w = SS_1 + SS_2 + SS_3$).

$$SS_w = \Sigma x_w^2 = \Sigma X_1^2 - \frac{(\Sigma X_1)^2}{n_1} + \Sigma X_2^2 - \frac{(\Sigma X_2)^2}{n_2} + \ldots \tag{6.11}$$

In our problem this value is

$$SS_w = \Sigma x_w^2 = 2310 - \frac{(150)^2}{10} + 2935 - \frac{(169)^2}{10} + 1585 - \frac{(125)^2}{10} = 161.4$$

The sum of the squares within groups could also be found by subtracting the sum of squares between groups from the total sum of the squares, that is,

$$SS_w = SS_t - SS_b \quad \text{or} \quad \Sigma x_w^2 = \Sigma x_t^2 - \Sigma x_b^2 \tag{6.12}$$

In our case

$$SS_w = 258.8 - 97.4 = 161.4$$

/ The *F*-Test of Significance

Table 6.5 summarizes the results of our calculations so far, together with the results of further calculations. Column (1) of the table lists the

TABLE 6.5 Summary of the Analysis of Variance of the Three Groups

(1) Source of Variance	(2) SS	(3) df	(4) MS	(5) F	(6) Level of Significance
Between groups	97.4	2	48.70	8.14	0.01
Within groups	161.4	27	5.98		
Total	258.8	29			

three sources of variance: between-groups variance, within-groups variance, and total variance. Column (2) contains the sums of squares, which we have already calculated. Column (3) lists the number of degrees of freedom associated with each source of variance. The number of degrees of freedom for between-groups variance is equal to $(G - 1)$, G being the number of groups. In our example this value is $3 - 1 = 2$. The degrees of freedom for within-groups variance is $n_1 - 1 + n_2 - 1 + \cdots$ (or $[n - G]$, total number of scores $[n]$ minus the number of groups $[G]$). In our example this value is $10 - 1 + 10 - 1 + 10 - 1 = 27$, or $30 - 3 = 27$. The number of degrees of freedom for total variance equals $N - 1$; in our example $30 - 1 = 29$. This last value could also be obtained by adding the between-groups and within-groups degrees of freedom.

The next step, then, is to calculate the two variance estimates known as the *between-groups mean square* and the *within-groups mean square*. These values are obtained by dividing the between-groups and within-groups sums of squares by their respective degrees of freedom. The resulting values are the mean squares. In our example the mean square between groups is $97.4/2 = 48.7$ and the mean square within groups is $161.4/27 = 5.98$. The mean square within groups is the error term for our F-ratio. By applying the following formula, we finally arrive at the end product of the analysis-of-variance procedure, the F-ratio:

$$F = \frac{MS_b}{MS_w} = \frac{SS_b/df_b}{SS_w/df_w} \tag{6.13}$$

In our example this value is

$$F = \frac{48.70}{5.98} = 8.14$$

We now consult Table A.3 in the Appendix to determine whether the F-ratio we have obtained is statistically significant. We find the column headed by the between-groups (numerator) degrees of freedom of our experiment and go down this column to the row entry corresponding to the number of our within-groups (denominator) degrees of freedom. At this point in the column we find two values, one in lightface type and one in boldface type. If our *F*-ratio is equal to or greater than the value given in lightface, our *F*-ratio is significant at the .05 level. If our obtained *F*-ratio is equal to or greater than the value given in boldface, it is also significant at the .01 level. In our example, with 2 and 27 degrees of freedom, we need an *F*-ratio of 3.35 to reject the null hypothesis at the .05 level and an *F*-ratio of 5.49 to reject the null hypothesis at the .01 level. Because our obtained *F*-ratio is greater than both of these values, it is significant at the .01 level and the null hypothesis is rejected at that level.

The assumption underlying the analysis-of-variance procedure is that if the groups to be compared are truly random samples from the same population, then the between-groups mean square should not differ from the within-groups mean square by more than the amount we would expect from chance alone. Thus, under a true null hypothesis we would expect the *F*-ratio to be approximately equal to 1.0. On the other hand, if the null hypothesis is false, the difference among group means should be greater than what is expected by chance, so the mean square between would exceed the mean square within. In such cases the *F*-ratio, the mean square between divided by the mean square within, will have a value greater than 1.0. We then consult the table of *F*-values (Table A.3) to determine whether the ratio for our data is sufficiently greater than 1.0 to enable us to reject the null hypothesis at our predetermined level. As the difference between these mean squares increases, the *F*-ratio increases and the probability of the null hypothesis being correct decreases.

When the null hypothesis is rejected as a result of this analysis-of-variance procedure, we cannot say more than that the measures obtained from the groups involved differ and the differences are greater than one would expect to exist by chance alone.

A significant *F*-ratio does not necessarily mean that all groups differ significantly from all other groups. The significant *F* may be a result of a difference existing between one group and the rest of the groups. For instance, in our problem it might be that Group 3 is significantly different from Group 1 and Group 2, but Groups 1 and 2 do not differ significantly from each other. There are several statistical tests that can be applied to find the location of significant differences. Those developed by Tukey and by Scheffé are particularly useful.[8]

In our example we selected our three groups randomly from the same population and thus we can assume that they did not differ beyond the chance expectation prior to our experimental treatments. The significance of the *F*-ratio indicates that the differences found between these groups *after* treatment are beyond chance expectation. We attribute this to our experimental treatment and conclude that the level of stress affects the performance of indi-

---

[8] See Glass and Hopkins, *op. cit.*

viduals in simple problem-solving tasks. This is as far as we can go in our interpretation of this *F*-ratio. If we need further statistical analysis, we can use Tukey's, Scheffé's, or other tests to determine the significance between specific groups or combinations of groups. These techniques can tell us how specific stress conditions affect the performance and can answer such questions as: Is there a significant difference in performance scores under conditions of moderate and high stress? moderate and no stress? and high and no stress?

// Multifactor Analysis of Variance

We may wish to investigate the combined effect of stress level and achievement need on performance in a problem-solving task. To investigate this problem we will vary both the level of stress and the achievement need. The layout for an experiment investigating the combined effects of two or more independent variables is called a *factorial design,* and the results are analyzed by means of a *multifactor analysis of variance.*

Let us assume that we have carried out this experiment using five subjects in each group and that the data shown in Table 6.6 represent a summary of our observations of the performance of the subjects. Applying multifactor analysis of variance will enable us to find (1) whether there is a significant difference between the performance of the subjects under a high-stress condition and under a low-stress condition, (2) whether there is a

TABLE 6.6 Measures on Problem-Solving Tasks of Subjects with Low and High Achievement Need under High and Low Conditions of Stress

	Stress		
	High	Low	
High	20 20 Group 1 19 19 $\bar{X} = 19$ 17 ΣX 95	23 22 Group 3 21 20 $\bar{X} = 21$ 19 ΣX 105	$\Sigma X_{r_1} = 200$ $\bar{X}_{r_1} = 20.0$
Achievement Need			
Low	22 21 Group 2 20 19 $\bar{X} = 20$ 18 ΣX 100	18 16 Group 4 15 14 $\bar{X} = 15$ 12 ΣX 75	$\Sigma X_{r_2} = 175$ $\bar{X}_{r_2} = 17.5$

$\Sigma X_{c_1} = 195$ $\Sigma X_{c_2} = 180$ ΣX Total $= 375$
$\bar{X}_{c_1} = 19.5$ $\bar{X}_{c_2} = 18.0$ $\bar{\bar{X}}$ (Grand mean) $= 18.75$

significant difference between the performance of the subjects with high achievement need and those with low achievement need, and (3) whether the two variables, stress and achievement need, have a combined effect on the performance of the subjects. The effects investigated by the first and second analyses are called *main effects,* whereas the third is referred to as the *interaction effect.* The end products of these analyses will be three *F*-ratios, two of which indicate the significance of the two main effects and the third, that of the interaction effect.

The computation of these *F*-ratios involves the following steps:

1. Find the total sum of squares, the sum of squares between groups, and the sum of squares within groups, using the same procedures and formulas applied in simple analysis of variance. These values, derived from the data in Table 6.6 are

$$SS_t = 7181 - \frac{(375)^2}{20} = 149.75$$

$$SS_b = \frac{(95)^2}{5} + \frac{(105)^2}{5} + \frac{(100)^2}{5} + \frac{(75)^2}{5} - \frac{(375)^2}{20} = 103.75$$

$$SS_w = 149.75 - 103.75 = 46.00$$

2. Break down the sum of the squares between groups into three separate sums of squares: (*a*) the sum of squares between columns, (*b*) the sum of squares between rows, and (*c*) the sum of squares for interaction between columns and rows:

a. The between-columns sum of squares represents the sum of the squared deviations due to the difference between the column means and the grand mean. It is found by using the formula

$$SS_{bc} = \frac{(\Sigma X_{c1})^2}{n_{c_1}} + \frac{(\Sigma X_{c_2})^2}{n_{c_2}} + \ldots - \frac{(\Sigma X)^2}{N} \tag{6.14}$$

Using this formula, the sum of squares between the columns for the data shown in Table 6.6 is

$$SS_{bc} = \frac{(195)^2}{10} + \frac{(180)^2}{10} - \frac{(375)^2}{20} = 11.25$$

b. The between-rows sum of squares is the sum of the squared deviations due to the difference between the row means and the grand mean. It is found by applying the formula

$$SS_{br} = \frac{(\Sigma X_{r1})^2}{n_{r_1}} + \frac{(\Sigma X_{r_2})^2}{n_{r_2}} + \ldots - \frac{(\Sigma X)^2}{N} \tag{6.15}$$

For the data presented in Table 6.6 this value is

$$SS_{br} = \frac{(200)^2}{10} + \frac{(175)^2}{10} - \frac{(375)^2}{20} = 31.25$$

c. The sum-of-squares interaction is the part of the deviation between the group means and the overall mean that is due neither to row differences nor to column differences. In other words, this is the difference between the total of the sum of squares between groups and the sum of squares between rows, that is,

$$SS_{int} = SS_b - (SS_{bc} + SS_{br}) \qquad (6.16)$$

Expressed in words, the interaction sum of squares is equal to the between-groups sum of squares minus the sum of the between-columns sum of squares and the between-rows sum of squares.

For the data presented in Table 6.6, this interaction value is

$$SS_{int} = 103.75 - (11.25 + 31.25) = 61.25$$

3. Determine the number of degrees of freedom associated with each source of variation. They are found as follows:

df for between-columns sum of squares $= C - 1$
df for between-rows sum of squares $= R - 1$
df for interaction $= (C - 1)(R - 1)$
df for between-groups sum of squares $= G - 1$
df for within-groups sum of squares $= N - G$
df for total sum of squares $= N - 1$

where

$C =$ the number of columns
$R =$ the number of rows
$G =$ the number of groups
$N =$ the number of subjects in all groups

4. Find the mean-square values by dividing each sum of squares by its associated number of degrees of freedom.

5. Compute the F-ratios for the main and the interaction effects by dividing the between-groups mean squares by the within-groups mean square for each of the three components.

6. The results of the calculations based on the data presented in Table 6.6 are summarized in Table 6.7. Three F-ratios are listed in this table. To find the significance of each of these values we consult the Table of F-Values as before. To enter this table we use the number of degrees of freedom associated with each F-ratio (df for the numerator) and the number of degrees of freedom associated with the within-groups mean square (df for the denominator). For example, our between-columns F-ratio is 3.913. Consulting the table, we see that, with 1 and 16 degrees of freedom, an F-ratio of 4.49 or more is needed for significance at the .05 level. Since our F-ratio is smaller than the value shown in the table, it is not significant.

To be significant, the F-ratio for between rows, with 1 and 16 degrees of freedom, should reach 4.49 (.05 level) or 8.53 (.01 level). Since our

TABLE 6.7 Summary of a 2 × 2 Multifactor Analysis of Variance

Source of Variance	SS	df	MS	F	Level of Significance
Between columns (stress)	11.25	1	11.25	3.913	—
Between rows (achievement need)	31.25	1	31.25	10.869	.01
Columns by rows (interaction)	61.25	1	61.25	21.304	.01
Between groups	103.75	3	34.583		
Within groups	46.00	16	2.875		
Total	149.75	19			

obtained value of F, 10.869, exceeds both of these values, it is significant at the .01 level.

For the interaction between columns and rows, with 1 and 16 degrees of freedom, an F-ratio of 4.49 (.05 level) or 8.53 (.01 level) is needed. Our obtained value of $F = 21.304$, exceeds both of these values and thus is significant at the .01 level.

/ Interpretation of the F-Ratios

The first F-ratio (between columns) in Table 6.7 is not significant and shows that the stress conditions do not differ significantly from one another in their effect on the performance of the subjects in the experiment. This analysis is a comparison of the combined performance of Groups 1 and 2 with the combined performance of Groups 3 and 4. We could have arrived at the same conclusion by using the t-test procedure.

The second F-ratio (between rows), which is significant at the .01 level, is based on the comparison of the performance of the subjects in groups 1 and 3 with those in Groups 2 and 4. From the significance of this F-ratio we can infer that the difference between the performance of those subjects with high achievement need and those with low achievement need is beyond chance expectation. Examining the data presented in Table 6.7, we see that those groups with high achievement need have obtained a combined mean of 20 as compared with a mean of 17.5 for those groups with low achievement need. Since we have a significant F-ratio for the difference, we conclude that under conditions similar to those of our experiment, a higher level of task performance can be expected from persons with higher achievement need.

The third F-ratio shows the interaction effect between the two variables: stress level and the achievement need. The significance of the F-ratio in this case means that the effect of stress level on performance in a problem-solving task depends on the degree of achievement need. We can see this phenomenon more clearly if we compare the observed results with the results that would be expected if there had been no interaction between the two independent variables.

Let us calculate what we would expect the means of the four groups to be if there had been no interaction. The mean for all subjects is 18.75. The mean for the ten subjects under high stress, 19.5, is .075 greater than this figure, whereas the mean of the ten subjects under low stress is 0.75 less. The mean for the ten subjects with high achievement need, 20, is 1.25 greater than the mean for all subjects, whereas the mean for the ten subjects with low achievement need is 1.25 less.

For each group we can calculate the mean that would be expected for this group if there had been no interaction. We do this by adding to the grand mean the difference for the column that group is in and the difference for the row that group is in. If there had been no interaction, what would we expect the mean of Group 1 to be? Beginning with the total mean, 18.75, we would add 0.75 because the subjects were under high stress and another 1.25 because they had high achievement need. This gives a total of 20.75.

Following this procedure for each of the four groups, we would obtain the following expected values:

	Overall Mean	+	Stress Difference	+	Achievement Need Difference	=	Expected Value
Group 1	18.75		+0.75		+1.25		20.75
Group 2	18.75		+0.75		−1.25		18.25
Group 3	18.75		−0.75		+1.25		19.25
Group 4	18.75		−0.75		−1.25		16.75

Now compare the actual group means with these expected group means:

	Actual High	Actual Low			Expected High	Expected Low	
High	Group 1 $\bar{X} = 19$	Group 3 $\bar{X} = 21$	$\bar{X} = 20$	**High**	Group 1 $\bar{X} = 20.75$	Group 3 $\bar{X} = 19.25$	$\bar{X} = 20$
Low	Group 2 $\bar{X} = 20$	Group 4 $\bar{X} = 15$	$\bar{X} = 17.5$	**Low**	Group 2 $\bar{X} = 18.25$	Group 4 $\bar{X} = 16.75$	$\bar{X} = 17$
	$\bar{X} = 19.5$	$\bar{X} = 18.0$	$\bar{\bar{X}} = 18.75$		$\bar{X} = 19.5$	$\bar{X} = 18.0$	$\bar{\bar{X}} = 18$

(Note that we could use the differences between expected and observed values to compute the sum of squares for interaction directly. Each group differs from its expected mean by 1.75. Square this value and multiply by the number of cases to get $1.75^2 \times 20 = 61.25$.)

We see that Group 1 actually did less well than we would expect, knowing they were under high stress and had high achievement need. Group 2, having low achievement need and being under high stress, did better than we would expect. Considering the groups under low stress, we find that Group 3, with high achievement need, did better than expected, whereas Group 4, with low achievement need, did less well than expected. Since our *F*-test indicated that the interaction was significant, we conclude that high stress produces higher scores when combined with low achievement need than when combined with high achievement need, whereas low stress produces higher scores when combined with high achievement need than when combined with low achievement need.

The use of multifactor analysis has been of great value in educational research because many of the questions that educators need to investigate are inherently complex in nature. These techniques enable us to analyze the combined effects of two or more independent variables in relation to a dependent variable. For example, a simple comparison of the dependent variable means of two groups of pupils taught by different methods might yield insignificant results. But if intelligence is incorporated into the experiment as a measured independent variable, we might find that one method works better with the less-intelligent pupils while the other works better with the more-intelligent pupils.

Multifactor analysis of variance is not limited to two independent variables as in our example. Any number of independent variables may be incorporated in this technique. Several intermediate statistics books, including Edwards',[9] explain the computation and interpretation of these procedures.

/// THE CHI-SQUARE TEST OF SIGNIFICANCE

Sometimes we need to find the significance of differences among the *proportions* of subjects, objects, events, and so forth, that fall into different categories. A statistical test used in such cases is called the *chi-square* (χ^2) test.

In the chi-square test two sets of frequencies are compared: *observed frequencies* and *expected frequencies*. Observed frequencies, as the name implies, are the actual frequencies obtained by observation. Expected frequencies are theoretical frequencies, which are used for comparison.

Consider the hypothesis that the proportion of male to female students in statistics courses is different from that of male to female students in a school of education as a whole. If we know that 40 percent of the total

---

[9]Edwards, A. L. (1984). *Experimental Designs in Psychological Research* (5th ed.; ch. 11 and 12). New York: Harper & Row.

enrollment in the school is male and that 300 students are enrolled in statistics courses, our expected frequencies will be

Male students   120
Female students   180 $\Big\} \ 300$

Now suppose that our observed frequencies are found to be

Male students   140
Female students   160 $\Big\} \ 300$

We want to determine whether the difference between our expected and observed frequencies is statistically significant. To determine this we apply the chi-square formula, which is

$$\chi^2 = \sum \left[\frac{(f_o - f_e)^2}{f_e} \right] \tag{6.17}$$

where

$\chi^2 =$ the value of chi-square
$f_o =$ the observed frequency
$f_e =$ the expected frequency

Applying this formula to our data, we obtain

$$\chi^2 = \frac{(140 - 120)^2}{120} + \frac{(160 - 180)^2}{180} = 5.55$$

To determine whether this chi-square value is significant we consult the table of χ^2 values in the Appendix (Table A.4). The first column in this table shows the number of degrees of freedom involved in any given chi-square problem. The remaining columns present the values needed for different levels of significance. The number of degrees of freedom, as we have discussed previously, is based on the number of observations that are free to vary once certain restrictions are placed upon the data. When we have a fixed number of observations divided into only two categories, as soon as the number falling into one category has been determined, the other is fixed. Thus, when we find that the number of male students is 140, the number of female students in the total of 300 must be 160. In this example there is only one degree of freedom. In problems such as this the number of degrees of freedom equals $K - 1$, where K is the number of categories used for classification. By consulting the Table of χ^2 we find that our observed value of 5.55 is statistically significant at the .05 (and .02) level.

Interpreting this result, we can now state that the proportion of males who take statistics courses within our school is significantly greater than that of females at the .05 level of confidence. The significance level of .05 means that there are less than five chances in a hundred of observing such a difference between the proportions of male and female students through chance alone. Thus, the data lend support to our research hypothesis that the proportion of male students who take statistics courses is greater than that of female students.

The use of the chi-square test is not limited to situations in which there are only two categories of classification; this test can also be used to test a null hypothesis that there is no significant difference between the proportion of the subjects falling into any number of different categories. Suppose, for example, we have asked a sample of 120 undergraduate students to indicate whether they prefer to live in a dormitory or in town or have no preference, with the results shown in Table 6.8.

If there were no difference between the three categories of response, we would have 40 responses in each category. These would be our expected frequencies, as shown in Table 6.9.

A comparison of the two sets of frequencies presented in Tables 6.8 and 6.9 shows that there are differences between our expected and observed data. To determine whether they are significant, we apply the chi-square test. The value of χ^2 for these data, using formula 6.20, would be

$$\chi^2 = \frac{(40 - 40)^2}{40} + \frac{(50 - 40)^2}{40} + \frac{(30 - 40)^2}{40} = 5.00$$

The degrees of freedom, again, equal the number of categories minus 1 $(K - 1)$ or, in this case, $3 - 1 = 2$. Referring to the Table of χ^2 we see that with 2 degrees of freedom a χ^2 value of 5.991 or greater is required for significance at the .05 level. However, our obtained χ^2 value is smaller than this value and therefore is not statistically significant. This means that the observed differences between categories could easily have happened by chance. Consequently, the null hypothesis that there is no significant difference between the frequencies of the three categories cannot be rejected. In other words, if the proportions of preferences for the three categories in

TABLE 6.8 The Observed Frequencies of Responses of 120 Undergraduate Students as to Their Preference with Respect to Living Accommodations

Subjects	Dormitory	Town	No Preference	Total
Undergraduate students	40	50	30	120

TABLE 6.9 The Expected Frequencies of Responses of 120 Undergraduate Students as to Their Preference with Respect to Living Accommodations

Subjects	Dormitory	Town	No Preference	Total
Undergraduate students	40	40	40	120

the entire undergraduate population were equal, we would expect to observe sample differences as great as those in our sample more often than five times in a hundred through chance.

// The Chi-Square Test of Independence

So far we have only considered examples in which observations were classified along a single dimension. Sometimes, however, we wish to use more than one dimension for classification. Suppose, for example, we add another dimension to the previous problem and ask both graduate and undergraduate students to state their preferences as to their living accommodations. Assume the frequencies as shown in Table 6.10 were the result.

In this case our null hypothesis is that the preference for living accommodations is the same for graduates as it is for undergraduates—that is, the variables *student status* and *preference for living accommodations* are unrelated, or independent. The null hypothesis in this chi-square test of independence is always that the variables are independent in the population. Our observations show that 30 percent of all students prefer dormitories, 45 percent prefer town, and 25 percent state no preference. If the null hypothesis is true, we would expect to find identical proportions among both graduates and undergraduates, as shown in Table 6.11. We can compute expected cell frequencies by multiplying the row frequency associated with a cell by the column frequency associated with that cell, then dividing this

TABLE 6.10 The Observed Frequencies of Responses of 200 Undergraduate and Graduate Students as to Their Preference with Respect to Living Accommodations

Subjects	Dormitory	Town	No Preference	Total
Undergraduate students	40	50	30	120
Graduate students	20	40	20	80
Total	60	90	50	200

TABLE 6.11 The Expected Frequencies of Responses of 200 Undergraduate and Graduate Students as to Their Preference with Respect to Living Accommodations

Subjects	Dormitory	Town	No Preference	Total
Undergraduate students	36	54	30	120
Graduate students	24	36	20	80
Total	60	90	50	200

product by the grand total ($E = f_r f_c / N$). For example, the expected frequency of response for undergraduate students who want to live in a dormitory is $120 \times 60 \div 200 = 36$; for those undergraduate students who prefer to live in town it is $120 \times 90 \div 200 = 54$; and for graduate students who want to live in a dormitory it is $80 \times 60 \div 200 = 24$. Using this approach, we find the expected frequencies for each cell.

Note that all the row and column totals in Table 6.11 are exactly the same as those shown in Table 6.10. We now ask if the observed frequencies differ enough from the expected frequencies to enable us to reject the likelihood that these differences could have occurred merely by chance. Applying the formula, we obtain

$$\chi^2 = \frac{(40 - 36)^2}{36} + \frac{(50 - 54)^2}{54} + \frac{(30 - 30)^2}{30} + \frac{(20 - 24)^2}{24} + \frac{(40 - 36)^2}{36} + \frac{(20 - 20)^2}{20}$$

$$\chi^2 = 1.8518$$

The number of degrees of freedom for a two-way table is found by applying the formula

$$df = (C - 1)(R - 1) \tag{6.18}$$

where

$df =$ the number of degrees of freedom
$C =$ the number of columns
$R =$ the number of rows

Applying this formula to the problem under consideration, we obtain

$$df = (3 - 1)(2 - 1) = 2$$

Referring to Table A.4 we see that with 2 degrees of freedom a χ^2 value of 5.991 is needed for significance at the .05 level. But our obtained χ^2 value of 1.8518 is smaller than this table value and is therefore not significant. This means that the differences between expected and observed frequencies are not beyond what would be expected by chance. In other words, we do not have reliable evidence that there is a relationship between the variables *student status* and *living-accommodation preference* in the population from which our sample was drawn. The null hypothesis cannot be rejected.

/ Assumptions of Chi Square

Chi square is so easy to use that one may forget that there are assumptions that must be met if valid interpretations are to be made.

1. Observations must be independent—that is, the subjects in each sample must be randomly and independently selected.

2. The categories must be mutually exclusive; each observation can appear in one and only one of the categories in the table.
3. The observations are measured as frequencies.

/// SUMMARY

Investigators hope to form generalizations about populations by studying groups of individuals selected from the populations. These generalizations will be sound only if the selected groups—the samples—used in these studies are representative of the larger groups—the populations—from which they are chosen.

Distinction is made between two major types of sampling procedures: probability sampling and nonprobability sampling. Probability sampling is characterized by the use of randomization in selection of population elements. In nonprobability sampling, the judgment of the researcher takes the place of random selection. Simple random sampling, stratified sampling, cluster sampling, and systematic sampling are forms of probability sampling. In simple random sampling, all the members of a population have an equal chance of being included within the sample. In stratified sampling, independent samples are selected from different subgroups, or strata, of a population. In cluster sampling, naturally occurring groups, or clusters, are selected from a population, then all individuals within the selected clusters are used as the sample. Finally, in systematic sampling, every kth case from a list of the population is taken as the sample. Forms of nonprobability sampling are accidental sampling, purposive sampling, and quota sampling. In accidental sampling, the available cases are used as the sample. In purposive sampling, cases judged as typical of the population of interest constitute the sample. Finally, in quota sampling, quotas are assigned to various strata of a population; then judgment is used to select cases within each stratum judged to be typical of that stratum.

Inferential statistics provide tools by means of which researchers are able to estimate how confident they can be in inferring that phenomena observed in samples would also be observed in the populations from which the samples were drawn. In other words, inferential statistics enable us to estimate how reliable our observations may be.

A basic strategy in inferential statistics is to compute the extent of difference among observations that would be likely to arise by chance alone. The result of this computation is often called the *error term*. Then the observed differences among observations are compared with the error term. If the observed differences are similar to the differences that could arise by chance, the researcher cannot reject the likelihood that the observed differences were merely a function of chance. If the observed differences are greater than the error term, the researcher consults the tabled values of the statistic to determine whether the ratio of observation to error is great enough to reject the chance explanation at a predetermined level of significance.

The indices most commonly used in inferential statistics are the *t*-test, analysis of variance, and the chi-square test. The *t*-test is used to determine whether the difference between two sample means is statistically significant. There are two types of *t*-tests: (1) the *t*-test for independent groups, which is used to compare two sample means when the samples have been drawn independently from a population, and (2) the *t*-test for nonindependent groups, which is employed with two samples in which the subjects are matched or with two repeated measures obtained from the same subjects.

Analysis of variance is used to compare the means of two or more samples and to test the null hypothesis that no significant differences exist between the means obtained from these samples. Multifactor analysis of variance enables us to test the effect of more than one independent variable and the interaction effect of such variables.

The chi-square statistic is an index employed to find the significance of differences between proportions of subjects, objects, events, and so forth that fall into different categories, by comparing observed frequencies and expected frequencies.

// Key Concepts

accessible population	null hypothesis
accidental sampling	observed frequency
analysis of variance (ANOVA)	one-tailed test
biased sample	parameter
chi square	population
cluster sampling	probability sampling
degrees of freedom	purposive sampling
directional test (one-tailed)	quota sampling
expected frequency	random sample
factorial design	sampling error
F-test	standard error of the mean
interaction	statistic
level of significance	stratified sampling
main effect	systematic sampling
multifactor analysis of variance	table of random numbers
nondirectional test	target population
nonprobability sampling	test of significance

t-test for dependent samples   Type I error
t-test for independent samples   Type II error
two-tailed test   *z*-test

/// EXERCISES

1. Does the accuracy of a sample in representing the characteristics of the population from which it was drawn always increase with the size of the sample? Explain.

2. You have been asked to determine whether teachers in the Central School District favor the "year-round school" concept. Because the district is rather large, you are asked to contact only 500 teachers. Determine the number you would choose from each of the following levels to draw a proportioned stratified random sample:

Level	Total Number
Elementary	3500
Middle School	2100
High School	1400
Total	7000

3. You are asked to conduct an opinion survey on a college campus with a population of 15,000 students. How would you proceed to draw a representative sample of these students for your survey?

4. A national magazine has one million subscribers. The editorial staff wants to know which aspects of the magazine are liked and which are not. The staff decides that a personal interview is the best method to obtain the information. For practical and economic reasons only 500 people in five cities will be surveyed. In this situation, identify
   a. the target population
   b. the accessible population
   c. the sample

5. Which of the following are probability samples? Which are nonprobability samples?
   a. random sample
   b. accidental sample
   c. cluster sample
   d. stratified sample
   e. purposive sample
   f. quota sample
   g. systematic sample

6. Investigators wish to study the question Do blondes have more fun?
   a. What is the null hypothesis in this question?
   b. What would be a Type I error in this case?
   c. What would be a Type II error in this case?
   d. If one investigator uses a .05 level of significance in investigating this question and another investigator uses a .001 level of significance, which would be more likely to make a Type I error?
   e. If one investigator uses a .05 level of significance in investigating this question and another investigator uses a .001 level of significance, which would be more likely to make a Type II error?

7. Inferential statistics enable researchers to
   a. reach infallible conclusions
   b. reach reasonable conclusions with incomplete information
   c. add an aura of legitimacy to what is really sheer guesswork

8. What two conditions are necessary for a Type I error to occur?

9. Which of the following statements describes the role of the null hypothesis in research?
   a. It enables us to determine the probability of an event occurring through chance alone when there is no real relationship between variables.
   b. It enables us to prove there is a real relationship between variables.
   c. It enables us to prove there is no real relationship between variables.

10. A Type II error occurs when one
    a. rejects a false null hypothesis
    b. rejects a true null hypothesis
    c. has already made a Type I error
    d. retains a false null hypothesis
    e. retains a true null hypothesis

11. The phrase *level of significance* refers to
    a. the probability of an event being due to chance alone, which is calculated after the data from an experiment are analyzed
    b. the probability of a Type I error that an investigator is willing to accept
    c. the actual probability of a Type II error
    d. the probability of a Type II error that an investigator is willing to accept

12. How does one determine the level of significance to use in an experiment?

13. A cigarette manufacturer has employed researchers to compare the rate of occurrence of lung cancer among smokers and nonsmokers. Considering the results of previous research on this question, the manufacturer would probably urge the researchers to be especially careful to avoid making

    a. a Type I error

    b. a Type II error

14. What is indicated when the results of a study are not statistically significant?

15. Compare stratified sampling with quota sampling.

16. Find the chi-square value for the following set of data. Then indicate if the obtained value of chi square is significant at the .05 level of significance.

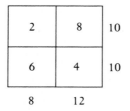

17. We have the responses of two groups of students (education and noneducation majors) to an item in a Likert-type attitude scale. Find the chi-square value for this problem and indicate whether your obtained chi-square value is statistically significant.

	Strongly Agree	Agree	Undecided	Disagree	Strongly Disagree
Education students	7	8	10	9	6
Noneducation students	8	10	7	8	7

18. Which of the following statistical procedures are appropriate for testing hypotheses *a* through *g*?

    t-test for independent means

    t-test for nonindependent means

    factorial analysis of variance

    chi square

    a. The proportion of doctoral students in the class who receive A's will be greater than the proportion of master's-level students who receive A's.

    b. The mean score of the 1 p.m. section on the final examination will be significantly higher than the mean score of the 7 p.m. section.

    c. Attending the evening class is an advantage grade-wise for female students and a disadvantage for male students.

    d. If the same statistics quiz that was given to students on the first day of class were administered on the last day of class, students would show a significant gain in achievement.

e. There is a relationship between passing or failing the class and whether one expresses satisfaction or dissatisfaction with the course.

f. Any differences among the mean scores of the fall semester classes and the summer session classes of the same instructor can easily be accounted for by chance.

g. There is a significant interaction effect between teaching experience and research experience and success in a research course.

19. A directional test is different from a nondirectional test in that in a directional test the researcher is interested in changes that take place
   a. only in a positive direction
   b. only in a negative direction
   c. in both positive and negative directions
   d. either in a positive or a negative direction

20. Two randomly selected groups have been used in an experiment in which Group I has received treatment and Group II has received no treatment. The researcher's hypothesis is that the mean performance of Group I will be higher than the mean performance of Group II. Apply the *t*-test to the following information and state if the researcher's hypothesis could be confirmed.

	X	N	Σx^2
Group I	45.32	30	382.02
Group II	41.78	30	264.32

21. A researcher wants to test the hypothesis that the correlation between variable A and variable B is significantly greater than 0. He has obtained an $r = .21$ between the two variables using 22 subjects. Use Table A.5 to find if the hypothesis can be rejected at the .05 level (one-tailed).

22. The following are data for a 2 × 3 experimental design. Apply the multifactor analysis of variance to test the significance of the main effects and the interaction effect.

		Columns		
		A	B	C
Rows	A	25, 23, 20, 17, 15	22, 20, 18, 16, 14	20, 18, 16, 14, 12
	B	16, 14, 12, 10, 8	18, 16, 14, 12, 10	19, 18, 16, 14, 13

Provide a table in which the sums of squares (*SS*), degrees of freedom (*df*), mean squares (*MS*), and *F*-values are shown. Then answer the following questions:

a. Which *F*-values are significant and at what level?

    b. How many null hypotheses are being tested in this problem?

    c. How many of these hypotheses can we reject?

23. You have a list of high school pupils who have been assigned a number from 1 to 1000. Use the table of random numbers in the Appendix to select a sample of 50 from the hypothetical list. List the numbers selected for the sample.

/// ANSWERS

1. A larger *randomly* drawn sample is more likely to be representative of the population than is a smaller *random* sample. A large sample obtained with a method that permits systematic bias will not be any more representative than a small biased sample.

2. To obtain a proportional stratified sample, divide the 500 teachers in proportion to their representation in the population, as follows:

Elementary	$3500/7000 \times 500 =$	250
Middle school	$2100/7000 \times 500 =$	150
High school	$1400/7000 \times 500 =$	100
Total sample		500

3. Number a list of all students, then select a random sample of a given number by using a table of random numbers. Starting at a random point in the table, go up or down the column and include those students whose numbers are drawn.

4. a. all subscribers to the magazine
   b. the subscribers in the five cities
   c. 500 individuals who are interviewed

5. Probability samples: a, c, d, g
   Nonprobability samples: b, e, f

6. a. There is no relationship between hair color and how much fun one has.
   b. The investigators make a Type I error if they declare that blondes have more fun than nonblondes or that blondes have less fun than nonblondes, when in fact the two groups have an equal amount of fun.
   c. The investigators make a Type II error if they fail to conclude that blondes have more fun or less fun, when in fact they do.
   d. the investigator with the .05 level of significance
   e. the investigator with the .001 level of significance

7. b

8. The null hypothesis must be true, and the investigator must reject it.

9. a

10. d

11. b

12. by weighing the consequences of Type I and Type II errors

13. a

14. The results could easily be a function of chance; the evidence is insufficient to justify a conclusion.

15. In stratified sampling, representativeness in each stratum is achieved through the use of randomization, while in quota sampling representativeness in various strata is attained by way of judgment.

16. 3.33—nonsignificant

17. 0.954—nonsignificant

18. a. chi square
    b. t-test for independent means
    c. factorial analysis of variance
    d. t-test for nonindependent means
    e. chi square
    f. t-test for independent means
    g. factorial analysis of variance

19. d

20. $t = 4.11$, $df = 58$, significant at .001

21. With 22 degrees of freedom, an r of .4227 or greater is needed to reject the null hypothesis. Therefore, the null hypothesis is retained.

22.

Source of Variance	SS	df	MS	F
Between columns	0	2	0	0
Between rows	120	1	120	11.34
Interaction	80	2	40	3.78
Between groups	200	5	40	3.78
Within groups	254	24	10.58	—

a. Between rows at .01 and interaction at .05
b. 3
c. 2

PART IV

Fundamentals
of Measurement

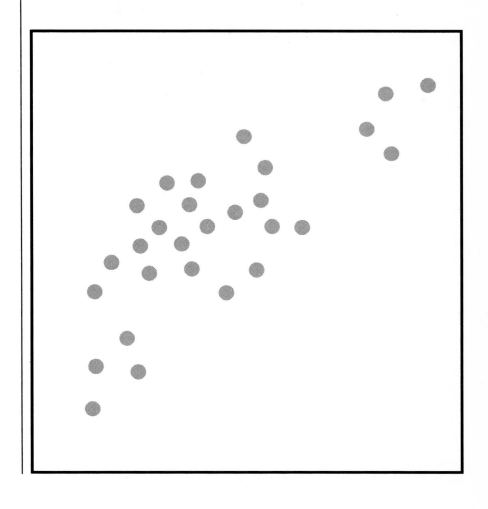

CHAPTER 7

Tools
of Research

INSTRUCTIONAL OBJECTIVES

After studying this chapter, the student will be able to

1. Explain the role of measurement in research
2. Use Buros' *Mental Measurements Yearbooks* to obtain data necessary in evaluating standardized tests and other measuring instruments
3. State the difference between a test and a scale
4. Distinguish between norm-referenced and criterion-referenced tests
5. Distinguish between measures of aptitude and achievement
6. Describe the steps to be followed in the preparation of a Likert scale for measuring attitudes
7. Describe the steps to be followed in the preparation of a Thurstone scale
8. Compare the characteristics of a Likert and a Thurstone scale
9. Describe a Guttman scale and list its advantages
10. Describe the characteristics of a semantic differential scale
11. State the kinds of errors that are common to rating scales
12. State advantages and disadvantages of self-report personality measures
13. List at least five guidelines that a researcher should follow when using direct observation as a data-gathering technique
14. Define a situational test and tell when it might be used in research
15. State the essential characteristic of a projective technique and name at least two well-known projective techniques

One of the aims of educational research is to obtain greater understanding of relationships among variables in populations. For example, one might ask What is the relationship between intelligence and creativity among six-year-olds? We cannot directly observe either intelligence or creativity. Nor can we directly observe all six-year-olds. But this does not mean that we must remain in ignorance about this and similar questions. We have indicators that approximate the constructs of intelligence and of creativity; that is, there are observable behaviors that are accepted as being valid indices of these constructs. The use of indicators to approximate constructs is the measurement aspect of research.

One of the researcher's most important tasks is to select or develop scales and instruments that can measure such characteristics as intelligence, achievement, personality, motivation, attitudes, aptitudes, interests, self-concept, and so on. Different types of devices are used for quantifying different qualities. There are two basic ways to obtain these measures: (1) use one that has already been developed or (2) construct one's own.

To select a measuring instrument, the researcher should look at the research that has been published on his/her problem. See what other researchers have used to measure the construct of interest. These writers will generally indicate whether the instrument worked well or whether other procedures might be better. Other useful sources for identifying published instruments for one's research purposes are Buros' *Mental Measurements Yearbooks* and *Tests in Print III*, described in Chapter 3. Another good source of information about tests is the Educational Testing Service (ETS) Test Collection. The ETS Test Collection is a library of more than 16,000 commercial and research tests and other measuring devices designed to provide up-to-date test information to educational researchers. Unlike Buros, it indexes both published and unpublished tests. A recent addition to this series is *The Cumulative Index to Tests in Microfiche, 1975–87*, which indexes the research tests by author, title, and subject. In the subject index, there are more than 750 headings, covering everything from abstract reasoning to work attitudes.

If researchers cannot find a previously developed instrument, then they must develop their own. The procedure involves identifying and using behavior that can be considered an indicator of the presence of the construct. In order to locate these indicators, researchers should turn first to the theory behind the research. A good theory will generally suggest how the construct will manifest itself and the changes that can be observed; that is, it suggests ways to measure the construct(s). Researchers can also use their own experience and expertise to decide on the appropriate indicators of the construct. In the following section we will discuss briefly some of the kinds of measuring instruments that are used in educational research.

/// MEASURING INSTRUMENTS
// Tests

Tests are valuable measuring instruments for educational research. A test is a set of stimuli presented to an individual in order to elicit responses on the basis of which a numerical score can be assigned. This score, based on a representative sample of the individual's behavior, is an indicator of the extent to which the examinee possesses the characteristic being measured. Two essential requirements for tests are validity and reliability, characteristics that will be discussed in Chapter 8.

Another essential requirement for a test is objectivity, shown by a maximum level of agreement among scorers. Once the scoring key is prepared for an objective test, the scoring can be accomplished by an untrained person or by a machine.

/ Achievement Tests

In most research concerned with the effectiveness of instructional methods the dependent variable is achievement. Therefore, achievement tests are widely used in educational research, as well as in school systems. They measure the mastery and proficiency of individuals in different areas of knowledge.

Achievement tests are generally classified as standardized and teacher- or researcher-made. Standardized tests are published tests that have resulted from careful and skillful preparation and cover broad academic objectives common to a large number of school systems. These are tests for which comparative norms have been derived, their validity and reliability established, and directions for administering and scoring prescribed. The directions are contained in the manuals provided by the test publishers.

In order to establish the norms for these tests, their originators administer them to a relevant and representative sample. The norm group may be chosen to represent the nation as a whole or the state, city, district, or local school. The mean for a particular grade level in the sample becomes the norm for that grade level. The skills measured are not necessarily what "ought" to be taught at any grade level, but the use of norms does give educators a basis for comparing their groups with an estimate of the mean for all children at that grade level.

Standardized tests are available for individual school subjects, such as mathematics and chemistry, and also in the form of comprehensive batteries measuring several areas of achievement. For example, the California Achievement Test (CAT) contains tests in the areas of reading, language, and arithmetic. The Sequential Tests of Educational Progress (STEP) include tests in seven areas.

In selecting an achievement test, researchers must be careful to choose one that is reliable and is appropriate (valid) for measuring the aspect of achievement in which they are interested. The test must also be valid and reliable for the type of subjects included in the study. Sometimes a researcher will not be able to select the test but will have to use what the school system has already selected. *The Mental Measurement Yearbooks* present a comprehensive listing, together with reviews of the different achievement tests available.

If an available test measures the desired behavior and if the reliability and the norms are adequate for the purpose, then there are advantages in the use of a standardized instrument. In addition to the time and effort saved, investigators will realize an advantage from the continuity of testing procedures. That is, the results of their studies can be compared and interpreted with respect to those of other studies using the same instrument.

When the use of standardized tests of achievement is not deemed suitable for the specific objectives of a research study, research workers may construct their own tests. It is much better to construct one's own test than to use an inappropriate standardized one just because it is available. In this case one should take great care in preparing the test, particularly with respect to determining the validity and reliability of the test before employing it. For suggestions on test construction one may refer to specialized texts in measurement, such as those by Gronlund; Sax; and Thorndike and Hagen.[1]

On the basis of the type of interpretation made, standardized and teacher-made tests may be further classified as norm-referenced or criterion-referenced.[2] Norm-referenced tests permit one to compare individuals' performance on the test to the performance of other individuals. An individual's performance is interpreted in terms of his or her relative position in a specified group known as the normative group. Performance is reported in terms of percentiles, standard scores, and so on.

On the other hand, criterion-referenced tests enable one to describe just what an individual can do, without reference to the performance of others. Performance is reported in terms of the level of mastery of some defined content/skill domain. Typically, the level of mastery is indicated by the percentage of items answered correctly. Predetermined cutoff scores are used in interpreting the individual's performance.

Before measuring instruments are designed, one must know the type of interpretation that is to be made. In norm-referenced tests, items are selected that will yield a wide range of scores. One must be concerned with

[1]Gronlund, N. E, and R. L. Linn (1990). *Measurement and Evaluation in Teaching* (6th ed.). New York: Macmillan; Sax, G. (1980). *Principles of Educational and Psychological Measurement and Evaluation* (2d ed.). Belmont, CA: Wadsworth; Thorndike, R. L., and E. Hagen (1977). *Measurement and Evaluation in Psychology and Education* (4th ed.). New York: Wiley.
[2]For more discussion of criterion-referenced measures see R. A. Berk (1984), *A Guide to Criterion-Referenced Test Construction*, Baltimore: Johns Hopkins University Press; and W. J. Popham (1981), *Modern Educational Measurement*, Englewood Cliffs, NJ: Prentice-Hall.

the difficulty of the items and the power of the items to discriminate among individuals. In criterion-referenced tests, items are selected solely on the basis of how well they measure a specific set of instructional objectives. The tests may be easy or difficult, depending upon what is being measured. The major concern is to have a representative sample of items measuring the stated objectives so that individual performance can be described directly in terms of the specific knowledge and skills that these persons are able to achieve.

Sometimes grade-point averages (GPA's) of the subjects in their schools are used as indicators of success and academic achievement. Caution is in order when the GPA's of students of different school systems are being used. Letter grades in different schools do not necessarily mean the same thing and cannot be relied on to indicate the same degree of mastery and proficiency.

/ Intelligence Tests

Intelligence tests differ from achievement tests in that the former attempt to measure general performance, whereas the latter attempt to measure performance in specific areas. Intelligence tests attempt to measure the subject's ability to perceive relationships, solve problems, and apply knowledge in a variety of contexts.

Intelligence tests should *not* be considered as measures of innate, or "pure," intelligence. Performance on such tests is partly dependent on the background and schooling of the subject. Because of the controversy over the meaning of the concept of intelligence and because of people's tendency to associate intelligence with inherited ability, the use of the term *intelligence* to describe these tests has declined in recent years. *Intelligence* is being replaced by *scholastic aptitude*—a more descriptive term because it points out specifically the main function of these tests, which is to predict school performance.

Educators have found these tests useful and generally valid for the purpose of predicting school success. Researchers also use these tests extensively. Intelligence is an independent variable that must usually be controlled in educational experiments. To control this variable the researcher uses the scores from some scholastic aptitude test. Of the many tests available some have been designed for use with individuals and others for use with groups.

Individual Intelligence Tests   The most widely used of this type are the Stanford-Binet and the three Wechsler tests. The Stanford-Binet currently in use is the outcome of several revisions of the device first developed by Alfred Binet in France to identify those children who were not likely to benefit from normal classroom instruction. This test was originally used for measuring an individual's *mental age*. Later the concept of *intelligence quotient* was introduced. This quotient is derived by dividing mental age (MA) by chronological age (CA) and multiplying the result by 100. The present revision of the Stanford-Binet yields mental ages but does not employ the MA/CA ratio for determining IQ. Instead the IQ is found by comparing an individual's performance (score) with norms obtained from his or her age group through the use of standard scores (see Chapter 5). A major characteristic of the Stanford-Binet test is that it gives a general measure of intelligence. It does not attempt to measure separate abilities, as do some other tests.

The tests David Wechsler developed to measure intelligence now come in several forms: the Wechsler Intelligence Scale for Children (WISC), which was revised in 1974 and is now the WISC-R; the Wechsler Adult Intelligence Scale (WAIS); and the Wechsler Preschool and Primary Scale of Intelligence (WPPSI), which was introduced for the 4–6½ age group.

An important characteristic of the Wechsler tests is that they are divided into subtests, which enable the examiner to obtain two scores for each subject, one for verbal IQ and the other for nonverbal IQ. These subtests are further divided into subscales, which indicate the examinee's performance on specific tasks.

Group Tests of Intelligence   A Stanford-Binet or Wechsler test must be given by a trained psychometrician to an individual subject, a procedure expensive in both time and money. They are impractical when intelligence measures for large groups of individuals are desired. In this situation group tests of intelligence are used. The first group test of mental capacity was developed during World War I for the purpose of measuring the intelligence of men in military service. One form of this test, the Army Alpha, was released for civilian use after the war and became the model for a number of group tests. Today there are many group tests of intelligence available. For further discussion of intelligence tests see the text by Anastasi.[3]

// Measures of Personality

Obtaining measures of personality is another area of concern to educational research workers. There are several different types of personality measures, each reflecting a different theoretical point of view. Some reflect trait and type theories, whereas others have their origins in psychoanalytic and motivational theories. Researchers must know precisely what they wish to measure and then select the instrument, paying particular attention to the evidence of its validity. The two most widely used types of personality measures in research are inventories and projective techniques.

---

[3]Anastasi, A. (1988). *Psychological Testing* (6th ed.). New York: Macmillan.

/ Inventories

In an inventory, subjects are presented with an extensive collection of statements describing behavior patterns and are asked to indicate whether or not each statement is characteristic of their behavior by checking *yes, no,* or *uncertain.* Their score is computed by counting the number of responses that agree with a trait the examiner is attempting to measure. For example, paranoids would be expected to answer *yes* to the statement "People are always talking behind my back" and *no* to the statement "I expect the police to be fair and reasonable." Of course such responses to just two items would not indicate paranoid tendencies. However, such responses to a large proportion of such items could be considered an indicator of paranoia.

Some of the self-report inventories measure only one trait, such as the *California F-Scale,* which measures authoritarianism. Others, such as Cattell's *Sixteen Personality Factor Questionnaire,* measure a number of traits. Other well-known inventories in research are the *Minnesota Multiphasic Personality Inventory,* the *Guilford-Zimmerman Temperament Survey,* the *Mooney Problem Check List,* the *Edwards Personal Preference Schedule,* the *Myers-Briggs Type Indicator,* and the *Strong Interest Inventory.*

Inventories have been used in educational research to obtain trait descriptions of certain defined groups, such as underachievers, dropouts, members of minority groups, and so forth. They have also been used in research concerned with interrelationships between personality traits and such variables as intelligence, achievement, and attitudes.

Inventories have the advantages of economy, simplicity, and objectivity. Most of the disadvantages are related to the problem of validity. Their validity depends in part upon the respondents' being able to read and understand the items, their understanding of themselves, and especially their willingness to give frank and honest answers. As a result, the information obtained from inventories may be superficial or biased. This possibility must be taken into account when using results obtained from such instruments.

/ Projective Techniques

Projective techniques are measures in which an individual is asked to respond to an ambiguous or unstructured stimulus. They are called *projective* because a person is expected to project into the stimulus his or her own needs, wants, fears, anxieties, and so forth. On the basis of the subject's interpretation and responses, the examiner attempts to construct a comprehensive picture of the individual's personality structure.

Projective methods are used mainly by clinical psychologists for the study and diagnosis of persons with emotional problems. They are not frequently used in educational research because of the necessity of specialized training for administration and scoring and the expense involved in individual administration. Furthermore, many researchers feel that their validity has not been satisfactorily established.

The two best-known projective techniques are the Rorschach and the Thematic Apperception Test (TAT). The Rorschach uses ink blots as the stimulus, and in the TAT the respondent is shown pictures and asked to tell a story about each one. Further discussion of these tests and the methods of interpreting them can be found in Anastasi's book.[4]

The following is an example of a research study that used inventories to measure the variables.

The Relationship between Myers-Briggs Type Indicator Scale Scores and Advising-Style Preferences of College Freshmen

Background

Prior research has shown that academic advising in higher education is an important strategy for retaining students and that improving the quality of advising can increase student retention. Research has also shown that students' advising needs and preferences vary in relation to specific student personality profiles. In order to explore further the relationship between student characteristics and advising-style preferences, instruments had to be located to measure both of these variables. A review of the literature indicated that the Myers-Briggs Type Indicator (MBTI) was a widely used and well-established research instrument.[5] An instrument known as the Academic Advising Inventory was selected to assess academic advising-style preferences.[6]

Question

(1) Is there a relationship between the MBTI scale scores and advising-style preferences? (2) Is there a relationship between age, race, sex, or English entry level and advising-style preferences?

Sample

The 201 entering freshmen at a large Southern university who completed both inventories were included in the study. The inventories were administered in freshman English classes.

Instruments

The MBTI is an inventory based on Carl Jung's theory of preferences and types. Individuals are asked to indicate their preference between pairs of items, and a personality assessment is based on these responses. This study used the ratings on four scales: Extraversion-Introversion (EI), which measures a preference for focusing on the outer world of people and things or on the inner world of ideas; Sensing-Intuition (SN), which assesses a preference for gathering information through the senses or through insight; Thinking-Feeling (TF), which measures a preference for making decisions on the basis of logic and analysis of facts or on

---

[4]Anastasi. *op. cit.*, ch. 19.

[5]Briggs, K. C., and I. B. Myers (1983). *Myers-Briggs Type Indicator, Form G*. Palo Alto: Consulting Psychologists Press.

[6]Winston, R. B., and J. A. Sandor (1984). *Academic Advising Inventory*. Athens, GA: Student Development Associates.

the basis of feelings and personal values; and Judgment-Perception (JP), which measures a preference for coming to a conclusion and organizing life (judgment) or remaining open to incoming information and change.

The Academic Advising Inventory has a theory-based perspective of academic advising that assumes that preferences for advising exist along a continuum ranging from highly prescriptive to highly developmental. Prescriptive advising is the traditional type where the advisor takes the major responsibility for the decisions. Developmental advising has a broader scope and encompasses students' total campus experiences; the advisor collaborates, but the student takes responsibility for the decisions. This study selected 14 paired statements from the inventory and asked the students to indicate their preference for each member of the pair. Scores were obtained on three scales: (1) Personalizing Education, which measures the scope of advising activities, (2) Academic Decision-Making, which measures the way in which responsibility for making decisions is divided between advisor and student, and (3) Selecting Courses, which assesses how courses are selected.

Method

Correlational and multiple regression analyses were made using the scores on the MBTI and AAI and data on the demographic variables (race, age, sex, and English entry level).

Results

Developmental advising was strongly favored by all the students in this study. It was found that scores on the SN and TF scales of the Myers-Briggs were positively and significantly related to the advising-style preferences of freshmen. Students who were more intuitive and feeling had higher preferences for developmental advising. English entry level was the only significant demographic variable related to advising-style preference.

// Attitude Scales

A scale is a set of numerical values assigned to subjects, objects, or behaviors for the purpose of quantifying and measuring qualities. Scales are used to measure attitudes, values, and other characteristics. They differ from tests in that the results of these instruments, unlike those of tests, do not indicate success or failure, strength or weakness. They measure the degree to which an individual possesses the characteristic of interest. For example, we may use a scale to measure the attitude of college students toward religion or any other topic.

Researchers often develop their own scales for measuring attitudes. In the following discussion we will attempt to introduce some of the techniques used in the scaling of attitudes.

Attitude may be defined as "a positive or negative affect toward a particular group, institution, concept, or social object." The measurement of attitudes presumes the ability to place individuals along a continuum of favorableness-unfavorableness toward the object.

There are four main types of attitude scales: summated rating scales (Likert scales), (2) equal-appearing interval scales (Thurstone scales), (3) cumulative scales (Guttman scales), and (4) semantic differential scales.

/ Likert Scales: Method of Summated Ratings

The Likert scale (see Figure 7.1) has been one of the most widely and successfully used techniques to measure attitudes.[7] A Likert scale assesses attitudes toward a topic by asking respondents to indicate whether they strongly agree, agree, are undecided, disagree, or strongly disagree with each of a series of statements about the topic.

FIGURE 7.1 Example of a Likert Scale

Social Responsibility Scale (SRS)

1. It is no use worrying about current events or public affairs; I can't do anything about them anyway.
   Strongly agree   Agree   Undecided   *Disagree   *Strongly disagree

2. Every person should give some of his time for the good of his town or country.
   *Strongly agree   *Agree   Undecided   Disagree   Strongly disagree

3. Our country would be a lot better off if we didn't have so many elections and people didn't have to vote so often.
   Strongly agree   Agree   Undecided   *Disagree   *Strongly disagree

4. Letting your friends down is not so bad because you can't do good all the time for everybody.
   Strongly agree   Agree   Undecided   *Disagree   *Strongly disagree

5. It is the duty of each person to do his job the very best he can.
   *Strongly agree   *Agree   Undecided   Disagree   Strongly disagree

6. People would be a lot better off if they could live far away from other people and never have to do anything for them.
   Strongly agree   Agree   Undecided   *Disagree   *Strongly disagree

7. At school I usually volunteered for special projects.
   *Strongly agree   *Agree   Undecided   Disagree   Strongly disagree

8. I feel very bad when I have failed to finish a job I promised I would do.
   *Strongly agree   *Agree   Undecided   Disagree   Strongly disagree

*Asterisks indicate responsible replies. They did not appear on the scale given to the subjects.

Source: From L. Berkowitz and K. Lutterman (1968). The traditionally socially responsible personality. *Public Opinion Quarterly, 32,* pp. 169–185. Copyright by The University of Chicago Press.

---

[7]Likert, R. (1932). A technique for the measurement of attitudes. *Archives of Psychology,* no. 140. This is Likert's original monograph.

A Likert scale is constructed by assembling a number of statements about an object, about half of which express a clearly favorable attitude and half of which are clearly unfavorable. It is important that these statements constitute a representative sample of all the possible opinions or attitudes about the object. It may be helpful to think of all the subtopics relating to the attitude object and then write items on each subtopic. In order to generate this diverse collection of items the researcher may find it helpful to ask people who are known to have knowledge about and definite attitudes toward the particular object to write a number of positive and negative statements. Editorial writings about the object are also good sources of potential statements for an attitude scale.

The statements, along with response categories (typically five) on an agreement-disagreement continuum, are presented to the subjects. The statements should be arranged in random order so as to avoid any response set on the part of the subjects. The subjects are directed to select the response category that best represents their reaction to each statement: strongly agree (SA), agree (A), undecided (U), disagree (D), or strongly disagree (SD).

In order to score the scale, the response categories must be weighted. For favorable or positively stated items the numerical values 5, 4, 3, 2, 1, respectively, are assigned to the response categories beginning at the favorable end. For example, *strongly agree* with a favorable statement would receive a weight of 5, *agree* would receive a 4, and *strongly disagree* a weight of 1. For unfavorable or negatively stated items the weighting is reversed, because disagreement with an unfavorable statement is psychologically equivalent to agreement with a favorable statement. Thus, for unfavorable statements *strongly agree* would receive a weight of 1 and *strongly disagree* a weight of 5. (The weight values do not appear on the attitude scale presented to respondents.)

Consider these examples selected from a scale measuring attitudes toward mathematics:

	SA	A	U	D	SD
Mathematics is my favorite subject in school.	5	4	3	2	1
I dislike mathematics in any form.	1	2	3	4	5

A person with a favorable attitude toward mathematics would agree with the positive item and disagree with the negative item; a person who disliked mathematics would agree with the negative item and disagree with the positive item. If the subject marked A for the first statement above and D for the second, the summated score would be 8 (4 + 4) for these two items. The sum of all the items' weights checked by the subject on the entire scale would represent the individual's total score.

The above weighting system means that a high scale score (SA to favorable items; SD to unfavorable items) indicates a positive attitude toward the object. The highest possible scale score is $5 \times N$ (the number of items); the lowest possible score is $1 \times N$.

Item Analysis   After the attitude scale has been administered to a preliminary group of respondents, an item analysis is done in order to identify the best items. The item analysis typically yields three statistics for each item: (1) an item discrimination index, (2) the number and/or percentage of respondents marking each choice to each item, and (3) the item mean and standard deviation. The item discrimination index shows the extent to which each item discriminates among the respondents in the same way as the total score discriminates. If high scorers on an item have high total scores and if low scorers on an item have low total scores, then the item is discriminating in the same way as the total score. The item discrimination index is calculated by correlating item scores with total-scale scores, a procedure usually done by computer. Each item should correlate at least .25 with the total score. Items that have very low correlation or negative correlation with the total score should be eliminated because they are not measuring the same thing as the total scale and hence are not contributing to the measurement of the attitude. The researcher will want to examine those items that are found to be nondiscriminating. The items may be ambiguous or double-barreled (containing two beliefs or opinions in one statement), or they may be factual statements not really expressing feelings about the object. Revisions of the items may make them usable.

The other statistics from the item analysis (2 and 3 above) indicate the extent to which the respondents have used the various options. Items on which the respondents are spread out among the response categories are preferred over items on which the responses are clustered in one or two categories.

After selecting the good items as indicated by the item analysis, the researcher should then try out the revised scale with a different group of subjects and again check the items for discrimination. The reliability of the new scale must also be determined (see Chapter 8).

Validity   It is somewhat more difficult to locate criteria to be used in establishing the validity of attitude scales. Some researchers have used observations of actual behavior as the criterion for the attitude being measured, but this procedure is not often used because of the difficulty of determining what behavior would be the best criterion for the attitude and also because of the difficulty of securing measures of the behavior.

One of the easiest ways to gather validity evidence is to determine the extent to which the scale is capable of discriminating between two groups whose members are known to have different attitudes. To validate a scale measuring attitudes toward organized religion one would determine if the scale discriminated between active church members and people who do not attend church and have no church affiliation. A valid scale measuring attitudes toward abortion should discriminate between members of "pro-life" groups and members of "pro-choice" groups. That is, the two groups would be expected to have significantly different mean scores on the scale. Another method of determining validity is to correlate scores on the attitude scale with those obtained on another attitude scale measuring the same construct and whose validity is well established.

/ Thurstone Scales: Method of Equal-Appearing Intervals

Thurstone developed a method for assigning specific scale values to attitude items.[8] While Likert scales assess attitudes by asking respondents to indicate degree of agreement-disagreement with each of a series of statements, Thurstone scales assess attitude by presenting statements about a topic that range from very favorable through neutral to very unfavorable and asking respondents to select from these statements those that most nearly correspond to their own attitude. Creating a Thurstone scale involves the following steps:

Collect a large number of statements (50 to 100) that express widely differing degrees of favorableness-unfavorableness toward the attitude object, including neutral statements. The statements are given to a large number of people (50 or more) who know enough about the object to be able to sort the statements into 11 categories along a favorable-unfavorable dimension. Category A contains those statements judged to be most favorable, Category B those statements next most favorable, and so on. The sixth category (F) represents the neutral position with respect to the attitudes, and the last category (K) contains those statements that are most unfavorable.

```
A   B C D E F G H I J K
1   2 3 4 5 6 7 8 9 10 11
favorable    neutral unfavorable
```

The classification of the statements into categories should have nothing to do with the judges' own attitudes toward the psychological object, but reflect only their perceptions of the favorableness or unfavorableness of the statements.

After the judges have rated all items, a distribution of the judges' ratings is prepared for each item. The distribution will show the number of judges who placed an item into each of the 11 categories. For example, assume a statement about the church was placed in Category A by 4 judges, in Category

---

[8]Thurstone, L., and E. Chave (1929). *The Measurement of Attitude*. Chicago: University of Chicago Press.

B by 28 judges, in C by 32, and in D by 16 judges. Two values, the median and *Q*, are calculated from this distribution.

Category	Category Value	Judges
D	4	16
C	3	32
B	2	28
A	1	4
		80

$$\text{Median} = 2.5 + (8/32)\ 1$$
$$= 2.5 + .25$$
$$= 2.75 \qquad \text{(see Formula 5.1)}$$

The median of the ratings is 2.75. This becomes the scale value assigned to that item. The scale value indicates the item's position on the positive-negative continuum. In order to address the extent of agreement among the judges, a variability index is also computed for each item. The measure of variability used is *Q*, the quartile deviation, which is equal to half the difference between the 75th and the 25th percentiles (see Chapter 5). *Q* is preferred over the standard deviation because it is not affected by extreme scores. The quartile deviation for the above example is $(3.38 - 2.07)/2 = .65$. High agreement among judges concerning how favorable-unfavorable a statement is will result in a low *Q* value. Poor agreement among judges will result in a high *Q* value. Items that have too high a *Q* value are usually rejected as being too ambiguous to include in the scale.

After the scale values (medians) and the *Q* values have been computed for each statement, the next step is to select statements to represent points on the favorable-unfavorable continuum that are as evenly distributed from 1 to 11 as possible. To the extent that these scale values represent equal increments, one has attained interval measurement. If two or more items have essentially the same scale value, the item having the lowest *Q* value is chosen.

Items are placed in random order on the final form, and, of course, the scale values are not shown on the form itself. The following items with their scale values are taken from Thurstone's scale measuring attitudes toward the church.

Scale Value	Statement
1.5	I believe church membership is almost essential to living life at its best.
2.3	I find the services of the church both restful and inspiring.
3.3	I enjoy my church because there is a spirit of friendliness there.
4.5	I believe in what the church teaches, but with mental reservations.

Scale Value	Statement
5.6	Sometimes I feel that the church and religion are necessary, and sometimes I doubt it.
6.7	I believe in sincerity and goodness without any church ceremonies.
7.4	I believe the church is losing ground as education advances.
8.3	I think the teaching of the church is altogether too superficial to have much social significance.
9.6	I think the church is a hindrance to religion, for it still depends upon magic, superstition, and myth.
11.0	I think the church is a parasite on society.[9]

In administering a Thurstone scale, the researcher instructs the respondents to check *only* the statements with which they agree. The subject's attitude score is the average scale value (mean or median) of the statements checked.[10] That average score places the individual on the favorable-unfavorable continuum with respect to the attitudinal object. If, for example, a respondent agreed with statements having scale values of 1.5, 2.3, 3.3, and 4.5 in the Thurstone scale above, his or her attitude score would be 2.9 (the mean), which indicates a favorable attitude toward the church.

The amount of spread in the scale values of the attitude items checked by any respondent may be taken as a measure of the extent to which that respondent has a clearly defined attitude. That is, an individual with a well-defined attitude toward some object would be expected to check only items very close in scale value. If the responses of an individual scatter widely over noncontiguous items, then it is likely that the respondent has an ambiguous or poorly defined attitude.

/ Comparison of Likert and Thurstone Scales

There are advantages to both the Likert and Thurstone scales.[11] The Likert scales are much simpler to construct, and several studies have found that they are somewhat more reliable even with fewer items.

The main advantage of the Thurstone scale is that it permits a more absolute interpretation of the scale scores, whereas the Likert scale permits scores to be interpreted on a relative basis only. The Likert scale permits the ranking of individuals in terms of the favorableness of their attitude toward a certain object, but it provides only limited information for saying how much more favorable one person is than another.

---

[9]Thurstone and Chave, *op. cit.*, pp. 61–63.

[10]Thurstone, on the assumption that the scales constructed by his method were interval scales, recommended the use of the mean. Other researchers who cautiously assume that the intervals may not be truly equal, recommend that the median be used.

[11]Edwards, A. L., and K. C. Kenney (1946). A comparison of the Thurstone and Likert techniques of attitude scale construction. *Journal of Applied Psychology, 30*, pp. 72–83.

The biggest disadvantage of the Thurstone scale is the amount of work involved in constructing the scale. Also, judges may have difficulty rating the statements independently of their own attitudes toward the object.

Many Likert and Thurstone scales are available on a wide variety of topics.[12] Researchers should first seek a published scale before attempting to construct their own.

/ Guttman Scales: Cumulative Technique

Critics of the Thurstone and Likert attitude scales pointed out that these scales contained heterogeneous statements concerning various dimensions of an attitude object. For example, in Thurstone's scale measuring attitudes toward war no attempt was made to separate ethical statements from statements concerning the economic results of war or those reflecting other possible aspects of attitudes toward war. As a result of this combination of several dimensions on one scale, it may be difficult to make any clear interpretation of the scores obtained.

Guttman developed a technique to attempt to overcome this problem. His technique, characterized as a unidimensional scale, aims to determine if the attitude being studied actually involves only a single dimension. An attitude is considered unidimensional *only* if it yields a cumulative scale—one in which the items are related to one another in such a way that a subject who agrees with item 2 also agrees with item 1; one who agrees with item 3 also agrees with items 1 and 2; and so on. Thus, individuals who agree with a particular item in this type of scale will have a higher score on the total scale than those who disapprove of that item. For example, consider the following items with which respondents are asked either to disagree or agree:

1. The PTA is worth the time spent on it.
2. The PTA is a strong influence for improving schools.
3. The PTA is the most important organization in the United States for improving schools.

If this is a cumulative scale, it should be possible to arrange all the responses of the respondents into the type of pattern shown in Table 7.1. Thus, if we know an individual's score, it should be possible to tell exactly which items he or she approved. For example, all individuals with a score of 2 believe that the PTA is worth the time spent on it and that it is a strong influence for improving schools, but do *not* believe that it is the most important organization in the United States for improving schools. Subjects can be ranked according to their scale responses.

---

[12]Shaw, M. E., and J. M. Wright (1967). *Scales for the Measurement of Attitudes*. New York: McGraw-Hill; and Miller, D. C. (1983). *Handbook of Research Design and Social Measurement* (4th ed.). New York: Longman.

TABLE 7.1 Example of Cumulative Technique*

Score	Agrees with Item			Disagrees with Item		
	3	2	1	3	2	1
3	X	X	X	0	0	0
2	0	X	X	X	0	0
1	0	0	X	X	X	0
0				X	X	X

*The respondent scores 1 for each agreement.

When constructing a cumulative scale, one must determine first of all whether the items form a unidimensional scale.[13] To do this, one analyzes the *reproducibility* of the responses—that is, the proportion of responses that actually fall into a pattern as shown in Table 7.1. On the basis of the total score a prediction is made of the pattern of responses to particular items. Then the actual pattern of responses is studied and a measure is made of the extent to which the responses were reproducible from the total score. One technique is to divide the total number of errors by the total number of responses and subtract from 1. Guttman suggests .90 as the minimum reproducibility coefficient necessary for a series of items to be recognized as forming a unidimensional or cumulative scale.

Many maintain that the Guttman scale has more theoretical than practical significance because it is difficult to assemble items satisfying the reproducibility criterion. The technique is criticized also because it does not suggest ways to prepare or select the items. Only after items have been selected can one judge their reproducibility.

/ Semantic Differential Scales

Another approach to measuring attitudes is the Semantic Differential technique developed by Osgood, Suci, and Tannenbaum.[14] The Semantic Differential is based on the assumption that objects have two different types of meaning for individuals, *denotative* and *connotative*, which can be rated independently. Denotative meaning refers to the dictionary meaning of a word, while connotative meaning refers to the associations or suggestions that a word calls up. One can more easily state the denotative meaning of an object than its connotative meaning. It is possible, however, to measure the connotative meaning of objects indirectly by asking individuals to rate the object using a number of bipolar adjectives. Thus, the meaning of an

[13]For a detailed discussion, see A. L. Edwards (1952), *Techniques of Attitude Scale Construction,* New York: Irvington.

[14]Osgood, C. E., G. J. Suci, and P. H. Tannenbaum (1967). *The Measurement of Meaning.* Urbana: University of Illinois Press.

object for an individual would be the pattern of his or her ratings of that object on the bipolar adjective scales.

Osgood and associates have found, through factor analysis, three clusters of adjectives: *evaluative*, consisting of such adjectives as *good* and *bad* or *valuable* and *worthless*; *potency*, consisting of such adjectives as *strong* and *weak* or *heavy* and *light*; and *activity*, consisting of such adjectives as *active* and *passive* or *fast* and *slow*. Among the three clusters, the evaluative dimension appears to have the most significance for attitude measurement.

Attitude scales are constructed by selecting pairs of adjectives representing the evaluative dimension. The adjective pairs are presented along with seven response scale categories, and the respondent is directed to place an X in one of the seven spaces to indicate the extent to which each adjective describes the object. For example, suppose one wanted to measure secondary school students' attitudes toward school.

	School	
Bad	__:__:__:__:__:__:__:	Good
Active	__:__:__:__:__:__:__:	Passive
Sharp	__:__:__:__:__:__:__:	Dull
Pleasant	__:__:__:__:__:__:__:	Unpleasant
Worthless	__:__:__:__:__:__:__:	Valuable
Hard	__:__:__:__:__:__:__:	Soft
Heavy	__:__:__:__:__:__:__:	Light
Weak	__:__:__:__:__:__:__:	Strong
Fast	__:__:__:__:__:__:__:	Slow

Notice in the above scale that the adjective pairs are listed in both directions in order to minimize a *response set,* that is, a tendency to favor certain positions in a list of options. An individual might have a tendency to choose the extreme right end and would check that position for each item. However, if the direction of the scale is changed in a random way so that the right end is not always the more favorable response, then the individual is forced to read each item and respond in terms of its content rather than in terms of a positional preference. In scoring the Semantic Differential scale, however, the points are assigned on a 1-to-7 scale with 7 representing the most positive response. Thus, on the first item above, the first position, *bad,* would receive a score of 1, the next position a 2, and *good,* the last position, would receive a score of 7. On item 2, the scoring would be reversed, with *active* receiving 7 points and *passive* 1 point. Ratings over all the items would be totaled and an average score reported.

// Rating Scales

One of the most widely used measuring instruments is the rating scale. Rating scales involve assessments by one person of another's behavior or performance. Typically the rater is asked to place the person being rated at some point on a continuum or in a category that describes his or her characteristic behavior. A numerical value is attached to the point or category. It is assumed that the raters are familiar with the individual's typical behavior. Ratings have been used in research on children's development and on many other aspects of behavior.

There are several different types of rating scales. One of the most widely used is the *graphic scale*, in which the rater simply places a check at the appropriate point on a horizontal line that runs from one extreme of the behavior in question to the other. Figure 7.2 is a typical example of a graphic scale. The rater can check any point on the continuous line. On some graphic scales the test constructor assigns numerical values to the descriptive points. Such scales are referred to as *numerical rating scales*. The speaking-skills item in Figure 7.2 could look like this in a numerical scale:

1	2	3	4	5	6	7
one of the poorest speakers			an average speaker			one of the very best speakers

A second type of rating scale is the *category scale*, which consists of a number of categories that are arranged in an ordered series. Five to seven categories are most frequently used. The rater picks the one that best characterizes the behavior of the person being rated. Suppose a student's abilities are being rated and one of the characteristics being rated is creativity. A category item might be

How creative is this person? (check one)

exceptionally creative
very creative
creative
not creative
not at all creative

Brief descriptive phrases sometimes make up the categories in this type of scale. For example:

How creative is this person? (check one)

FIGURE 7.2 Example of a Graphic Scale

	Low	Medium	High
Personal Appearance	_____		
Social Acceptability	_____		
Speaking Skills	_____		

always has creative ideas
has many creative ideas
sometimes has creative ideas
rarely has creative ideas

In using the graphic and category scales, raters make their judgments without directly comparing the person being rated to other individuals or groups. In *comparative rating scales,* on the other hand, raters are instructed to make their judgments with direct reference to the positions of others with whom the individual might be compared. The positions on the rating scale are defined in terms of a given population with known characteristics. A comparative rating scale is shown in Figure 7.3. Such a scale might be used in selecting applicants for admission to graduate school. Raters are asked to judge the applicant's ability to do graduate work as compared with all the students the rater has known. If the rating is to be valid, the judge must have an understanding of the range and distribution of the abilities of the total group of graduate students.

All techniques of rating are subject to considerable error, which reduces their validity and reliability. Among the most frequent systematic errors in rating people is the *halo effect,* which occurs when raters allow a generalized

FIGURE 7.3 Example of a category scale						
Area of Competency (to be rated)	Unusually low	Poorer than most students	About average among students	Better than most	Really superior	Not able to judge
1. Does this person show evidence of clear-cut and worthy professional goals?						
2. Does this person attack problems in a constructive manner?						
3. Does he or she take well-meant criticism and use it constructively?						

impression of the subject to influence the rating given on very specific aspects of behavior. This general impression carries over from one item in the scale to the next. For example, a teacher might rate a student who does good academic work as also being superior in intelligence, popularity, honesty, perseverance, and all other aspects of personality. Or if one has a generally unfavorable impression of a person, one is likely to rate the person low on all aspects.

Another type of error is the *generosity error,* which refers to the tendency to give the subject the benefit of any doubt. That is, when raters are not sure, they are likely to speak favorably about the person they are rating. In contrast, there is the *error of severity,* which is a tendency to rate all individuals too low on all characteristics. Another source of error is the *error of central tendency,* which refers to the tendency to avoid either extreme and rate all individuals in the middle of the scale.

One way of reducing such errors is to train the raters thoroughly before they are asked to make ratings. They should be informed about the possibility of making these types of errors. It is absolutely essential that raters have adequate time to observe the individual and his or her behavior before making a rating. Another way to minimize error is to make certain that the behavior to be rated and the points on the rating scale are clearly defined. The points on the scale should be described in terms of overt behaviors that can be observed rather than in terms of behaviors that require inference on the part of the rater. The reader is referred to Guilford for an excellent discussion of ways of dealing with rater error.[15]

The reliability of ratings is usually increased by having several raters make independent ratings of an individual. These independent ratings are pooled, or averaged, to obtain a final score.

// Sociometric Techniques

Sociometric techniques are used for studying the organization of social groups. The basic procedure, though it may be modified in several ways, involves requesting the members of a particular group to indicate their first, second, and subsequent choices for companions on the basis of a specific criterion, usually for some particular activity. For example, each of the children in a reading group might be asked to choose two other children whom they would like to study with, sit next to, eat lunch with, or play with after school. The sociometric method is essentially a study of choices made by each person in a group. The choices obtained are plotted on what is called a *sociogram,* which shows the pattern of interpersonal relations in a group. In the sociogram shown in Figure 7.4, Fred, the most frequently chosen member, might be referred to as the "star." Notice that Pat, Ann, and John

---

[15]Guilford, J. P. (1954). *Psychometric Methods* (ch. 11). New York: McGraw-Hill.

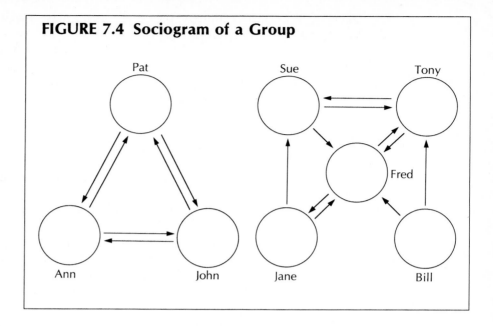

FIGURE 7.4 Sociogram of a Group

choose one another. This represents a clique; that is, three or more individuals who mutually choose one another. Bill received no choices; he is an *isolate*. The choices revealed in a sociogram can be quantified and used for research purposes.

Sociometric methods have been widely used for research in social psychology and in educational research, where sociometric status may be studied in its relationship to other variables, such as mental ability, achievement, and teachers' preferences for children.[16]

// Direct Observation

In many cases, systematic direct observation of behavior is the most desirable measurement method. An investigator identifies the behavior of interest and devises a systematic procedure for identifying, categorizing, and recording the behavior in either a natural or a contrived situation. Systematic observation has been used extensively in research on infants and preschool children.

Urban's study "Behavior Changes Resulting from a Study of Communicable Diseases" is an excellent example of the use of direct observation

---

[16]For further discussion see G. Lindzey (1968), *Handbook of Social Psychology* (vol. 1), Reading, MA: Addison-Wesley.

in a natural setting.[17] Observers recorded the number of instances of undesirable behavior, such as putting fingers or other objects in the mouth, and the number of desirable behaviors, such as using one's handkerchief when coughing or sneezing. Following this, an experimental group was selected and taught a six-week course on communicable diseases that was designed to change their overt behavior as well as to provide them with factual information and understanding. At the end of the course the undesirable behaviors were again recorded. It was found that they had been dramatically reduced and the desirable behaviors dramatically increased in the experimental group, while there was little change in the control group, which had not had the course. Observations 12 weeks later found these differences between the control and experimental groups persisting.

There are five important preliminary steps to be taken when using direct observation.

1. *The aspect of behavior to be observed must be selected.* Because it is not possible to observe everything that happens, the investigator must decide beforehand which behaviors to record and which to ignore.

2. *The behaviors falling within the chosen category must be clearly defined.* The observers must understand what actions will be classified as, for instance, cooperative behavior or selfish behavior.

3. *The people who will carry out the observations must be trained.* Training and opportunity for practice are necessary in order that the investigator can rely on the observers to follow an established procedure in observing and in interpreting and reporting observations.

4. *A system for quantifying observations must be developed.* The investigator must decide on a standard method for counting the observed behaviors. For instance, it must be established beforehand whether an action and the reaction to it are to be counted as a single incident of the behavior observed or as two incidents. A suggested approach is to divide the observation period into brief time segments and to record for each period—say, 30 seconds—whether the subject showed the behavior.

5. *Detailed procedures for recording the behavior must be developed.* The memory of most observers is usually not reliable enough for meaningful research. The best solution is a coding system that allows the immediate recording of what is observed using a single letter or digit, rather than a narrative system, which takes too much of the observers' time and attention.

Another application of direct observation is in the study of classroom behavior. Flanders studied verbal interaction in the classroom and developed

---

[17]Urban, J. (1943). Behavior changes resulting from a study of communicable diseases. *Teachers College Contributions to Education*, no. 896. New York: Teachers College Press, Columbia University.

a coding plan for recording observations, as can be seen in Figure 7.5. Flanders' system provides exhaustive and mutually exclusive categories, each of which can be recorded as a single digit. Trained observers are able to record a digit every 3 seconds. The chain of digits produced can easily be analyzed to provide not only a record of the proportions of verbal behavior falling into each category but also a picture of which behaviors preceded or followed which other behaviors.

Flanders divided teacher talk into *response,* which he termed *indirect influence,* and *initiation,* which he termed *direct influence.* In an investigation using his observation categories, Flanders studied the effect of the indirect-influence form of teacher talk as compared with the direct-influence talk.[18] Social studies and mathematics classes were observed, and classes with the most-indirect teachers were compared with those classes with the most-direct teachers on achievement in a unit of instruction taught during the observation time as well as on attitudes toward the teacher. Flanders found that the classes of the most-indirect teachers performed better on both the attitude and achievement measures. The implication was that teachers' work in the classroom can be improved by training them to make greater use of the indirect categories of verbal behavior.

In another classroom study, Rollins and others used systematic observation before and after a training period during which teachers learned and were encouraged to use positive reinforcement procedures.[19] Observations were made to ascertain the extent to which teachers used positive reinforcement and the effect of the positive reinforcement on the behavior of pupils. Observation was carried out in 5-minute cycles: During the first cycle a count was made of the positive and negative reinforcing behaviors of the teacher; during the second, a count of disruptive behaviors by pupils was made; during the third, the attentive behaviors of pupils were observed. Rollins found that teachers who had been trained showed approximately four times as many positive reinforcements per student as teachers in control classes and had to use far fewer punishments. Observations of the pupils showed a marked decrease in disruptive behaviors and an increase in attentive behaviors. Furthermore, the students in the experimental classes made a greater average gain in reading test grade equivalent over an 8-month period. In this study, systematic observation was used very effectively to document the changes in classroom behaviors that were associated with marked changes in pupil achievement.

---

[18]Flanders, N. A. (1965). *Teacher Influence, Pupil Attitudes, and Achievement.* U.S. Office of Education Cooperative Research Monograph. Washington: U.S. Government Printing Office.

[19]Rolling, H. A., B. R. McCandless, and M. Thompson (1974). Project success environment: An extended application of contingency management in inner-city schools. *Journal of Educational Psychology, 66,* pp. 167–178.

FIGURE 7.5 Flanders' Interaction Analysis Categories (FIAC)*

Teacher Talk:

1. *Accepts feelings:* accepts and clarifies an attitude or the feeling tone of a pupil in a nonthreatening manner. Feelings may be positive or negative. Predicting and recalling feelings are included.

2. *Praises or encourages:* praises or encourages pupil action or behavior. Tells jokes that release tension, but not at the expense of another individual; nodding head or saying "Um hm?" or "Go on" are included.

Response

3. *Accepts or uses ideas of pupils:* clarifies, builds, or develops ideas suggested by a pupil. Teacher extensions of pupil ideas are included, but, as the teacher brings more of his own ideas into play, they shift to category 5.

4. *Asks questions:* asks a question about content or procedure, based on teacher ideas, with the intent that a pupil will answer.

5. *Lectures:* gives facts or opinions about content or procedures; expresses own ideas, gives own explanation, or cites an authority other than a pupil.

6. *Gives directions:* gives directions, commands, or orders to which a pupil is expected to comply.

Initiation

7. *Criticizes or justifies authority:* makes statements intended to change pupil behavior from nonacceptable to acceptable pattern; bawls someone out; states why he is doing what he is doing; extreme self-reference.

Pupil Talk:
Response

8. *Pupil-talk—response:* talk by pupils in response to teacher. Teacher initiates the contact, solicits pupil statement, or structures the situation. Freedom to express own ideas is limited.

Initiation

9. *Pupil-talk—initiation:* talk by pupils that they initiate. They express their own ideas; initiate a new topic; have freedom to develop opinions and a line of thought, like asking thoughtful questions; go beyond the existing structure.

Silence

10. *Silence or confusion:* short periods of silence and periods of confusion in which communication cannot be understood by the observer.

*This is a nominal scale. Each number is classificatory; it designates a particular kind of communication event. To write these numbers down during observation is to categorize, not to judge a position on a scale.
Source: From N. A. Flanders (1970). *Analyzing Teaching Behavior* (p. 34). Boston: Addison-Wesley.

/ Evaluation of Direct Observation

In direct observation we are able to obtain a record of individuals' actual behavior in naturally occurring situations. It is an especially valuable technique to use with very young children who cannot communicate through language.

Direct observation, however, is an expensive procedure because of the observer time required. Furthermore, there is always the possibility that the presence of the observer will change the individual's behavior. One-way-vision screens may be used in some situations to overcome this problem. In many cases it is found that after an initial reaction the subjects being observed will come to pay little attention to the observer, especially one who operates unobtrusively. Observers require extensive training to become competent in knowing what to observe and just how the observations are to be reported.

/ Contrived Observations

In contrived observations, the researcher arranges for the observation of subjects in simulations of real-life situations. The circumstances have been arranged so that the desired behaviors are elicited.

One form of contrived observation is the *situational test*. A classic example of a situational test—although it was not labeled as such at the time—was used in a series of studies by Hartshorne and May for the Character Education Inquiry (CEI).[20] These tests were designed for use in the study of the development of such behavior characteristics as honesty, self-control, truthfulness, and cooperativeness. Hartshorne and May made observations of children in routine school activities but also staged some situations in order to focus on specific behavior. For example, they gave vocabulary and reading tests to the children, collected the tests, and without the children's knowledge made duplicate copies of their answers. Later the children were given answer keys and were asked to score their original papers. The difference between the scores the children reported and the actual scores obtained from scoring the duplicate papers provided a measure of cheating.

Another test asked the children to make a mark in each of ten small, irregularly placed circles, while keeping their eyes shut. Previous control tests under conditions that prevented peeking indicated that a score of more than 13 correctly placed marks in three trials was highly improbable. Thus, a score above 13 was recorded as evidence that the child had peeked.

Hartshorne and May found practically no correlation between cheating in different situations, such as on a test and in athletics. They concluded that children's responses were situationally specific. That is, whether students

---

[20]Hartshorne, H., M. A. May, and F. K. Shuttleworth. *Studies in the Organization of Character*. New York: Macmillan.

cheated depended on the specific activity, the teacher involved, and other situations rather than on some general character trait.

/// SUMMARY

An important task of researchers in the behavioral sciences is the selection of dependable measuring instruments for the purpose of quantifying research information. In educational research, tests are widely used measuring instruments. A test is defined as a set of stimuli presented to an individual in order to elicit responses on the basis of which a numerical score can be assigned. Achievement tests are prime examples of this kind of instrument. There are a variety of achievement tests available that provide norms that can be used as a basis for comparison. Intelligence tests are tools for assessing an individual's verbal and nonverbal capacities. Personality inventories are designed to measure the subject's personal characteristics and typical performance.

Attitude scales are tools for measuring individuals' beliefs, feelings, and reactions to certain objects. The major types of attitude scales are Likert-type scales, Thurstone scales, Guttman scales, and the semantic differential.

Sociometric techniques are means of assessing individuals' standings among their peers. Through these techniques it is possible to locate popular members of groups (stars), isolates, and cliques.

A number of methods for systematically observing the behavior of subjects have been developed as direct observation and contrived observation methods.

// Key Concepts

achievement test
attitude scale
contrived observation
cumulative scale
direct observation
error of central tendency
error of severity
generosity error
Guttman scale

halo effect
intelligence test
inventory
Likert scale
projective technique
scale
scholastic aptitude test
semantic differential scale
sociogram

standardized test   test
summated rating scale   Thurstone scale

/// EXERCISES

1. What is the meaning of the term *standardized* when applied to measuring instruments?

2. What is the difference between comparative rating scales and graphic and category scales?

3. List some of the common sources of bias in rating scales.

4. Why is a Guttman scale considered unidimensional as compared with the Thurstone and Likert scales?

5. What is the main measurement use of the semantic differential scale?

6. What are some procedures for increasing the accuracy of direct-observation techniques?

7. Construct a five-item Likert scale for measuring teachers' attitudes toward foreign-language instruction in the elementary school.

8. What are the major advantages of the Likert scale over the Thurstone scale?

9. Construct a five-item graphic rating scale that would be useful for evaluating a research program.

10. The following data represent the ratings assigned to an item by 200 judges in the Thurstone procedure. What scale value would be assigned to this item?

Category	Number of Judges
11	0
10	0
9	0
8	30
7	50
6	60
5	34
4	16
3	10
2	0
1	0
	200

11. The following are the scale values of five items checked by two students on a Thurstone scale. Calculate their attitude scores, and interpret the scores in terms of how favorable and clearly defined the attitudes are.

Jane	Jon
5.5	10.5
4.6	8.2
4.1	7.1
3.8	3.9
3.1	2.8

/// ANSWERS

1. *Standardized* refers to instruments for which comparative norms have been derived, their reliability and validity have been established, and directions for administration and scoring prescribed.

2. In judging an individual on graphic and category scales, raters do not make a direct comparison of the subject with other persons. In judging an individual on a comparative rating scale, the rater must have knowledge of the group with which the individual is being compared.

3. Raters may be less than objective in judging individuals when influenced by such tendencies as the halo effect, the generosity error, the error of severity, or the error of central tendency.

4. The Thurstone and Likert scales may contain statements on various dimensions of the attitude object. A Guttman scale is considered uni-dimensional because it asks questions about degrees of reaction to a single topic. Therefore, it is cumulative; that is, a person who agrees with a given item on the scale can be predicted to agree on all items below that item on the scale.

5. The semantic differential scale is used to measure the connotative meaning that a person attaches to an object.

6. The behaviors to be observed must be specified; behaviors falling within a category must be defined; a system for quantification must be developed; and the observers must be trained to carry out the observations according to this established procedure.

7. Answers will vary.

8. The main advantage is that the Likert scale is easier to construct. It is also likely to be more reliable than the Thurstone scale having the same number of items.

9. Answers will vary.

10. 5.17

11. With a mean of 4.2 and a median of 4.1, Jane shows a moderately favorable attitude. Her choices are near each other in scale value, indicating consistency. Jon's mean of 6.5 and median of 7.1 indicate a slightly unfavorable position. The wide spread of scale values indicates an attitude that is not clearly defined.

CHAPTER 8

Validity and Reliability

INSTRUCTIONAL OBJECTIVES

After studying this chapter, the student will be able to
1. Distinguish between validity and reliability
2. Describe the three major types of validity and the methods used in assessing them
3. Explain the type of validity that is appropriate for different measurement purposes
4. Distinguish between convergent and discriminant validity
5. Explain the relationship between reliability and the concept of random errors of measurement
6. State the different sources of error in educational and psychological measures
7. Describe the different procedures (test-retest, equivalent forms, split-half, Kuder-Richardson, and others) for estimating the reliability of a measure
8. Compute reliability coefficients from given data
9. Apply the Spearman-Brown formula to determine the effect of lengthening a test on test reliability
10. Explain the factors affecting the size of a reliability coefficient
11. Interpret the standard error of measurement and explain its relationship to test reliability
12. Compute the standard error of measurement and interpret score bands
13. Compute indices to show the reliability of a criterion-referenced test

Research is always dependent upon measurement. There are two important characteristics that every measuring instrument should possess: *validity* and *reliability*. Validity refers to the extent to which an instrument measures what it is intended to measure. Reliability, on the other hand, is the extent to which a measuring device is consistent in measuring whatever it measures. Strictly speaking, validity and reliability refer to the information produced by a measuring instrument rather than to the instrument itself. For the sake of convenience, we speak of the validity and reliability of a test, but it is more accurate to speak of the validity and reliability of the test scores. Whereas the test is static, the results (scores) change according to the situation. A researcher must inquire into the validity and reliability of the instruments used in a study and must include this information in the research report. If a researcher's data are not obtained with valid and reliable instruments, one would have little faith in the results obtained or in the conclusions based on the results.

Evidence of validity and reliability is especially important in educational research because most of the measurements attempted in this area are obtained indirectly. One needs to assess to what extent an educational or a psychological measuring instrument measures precisely and dependably what it is intended to measure.

/// VALIDITY

The validity question is concerned with the extent to which an instrument measures what one thinks it is measuring. It is absolutely essential that the researcher ask this question. Educational and psychological testing instruments are designed for the purpose of appraising constructs such as achievement, intelligence, creativity, aptitude, attitudes, motivation, and the like. However, there are no direct means of measuring these constructs such as exist in the physical sciences for the measurement of characteristics like length, volume, and weight. Researchers must develop indirect means to measure complex attributes. These indirect means involve tests and scales consisting of a number of tasks that are selected to serve as indicators of the complex constructs. One asks how well these indirect procedures measure what they are supposed to be measuring. Researchers must ask the following kinds of questions: Does this test really measure achievement motivation? Does this test measure other qualities as well? Can this creativity test really separate highly creative persons from less creative persons? Could one make useful predictions based on scores on this aptitude test? Is it an appropriate instrument for use with all pupils, or should it be used only with certain groups? For example, how appropriate are aptitude tests for predicting academic achievement of minority students? These questions all concern the meaningfulness and usefulness of the inferences that will be made from the scores, that is, the test's validity.

Validity is always specific to the particular purpose for which the instrument is being used. For example, a test that has validity in one situation and for one purpose may not be valid in a different situation or for a different purpose. For example, a standardized history test that emphasizes understanding and interpretation may have validity for one history teacher, but would not be valid for another teacher who has stressed the learning of dates and factual knowledge. The purpose for which the test is being used is also a major factor in validity. A standardized chemistry test may be used to measure end-of-the-year achievement in chemistry. In this case one would have questions about just what the test measures and how well it does so. The same test might be used to predict achievement in college chemistry. In this case one would be interested in how well the test can predict future achievement. These different purposes of tests require different types of evidence to support the validity of that particular use.

Although validity is a unitary concept, there are different types of evidence that can be gathered to support the inferences being made from the scores of a measuring instrument. The joint committee of the American Psychological Association (APA), American Educational Research Association (AERA), and National Council on Measurement in Education (NCME) classifies the means of accumulating validity evidence into the following categories: content-related, criterion-related, and construct-related evidence of validity.[1]

// Content-Related Evidence

Classroom tests are generally used for the purpose of assessing students' knowledge and skills in a defined content area. The ideal way to accomplish this would be to use an examination that would include all the questions that could possibly be asked about that content. Obviously such a procedure is not feasible. The useful alternative is to prepare a sample of the total content area and then to use this sample as a basis for inferences about students' knowledge of the entire universe of content. Because inferences are to be made on the basis of only a sample, it is very important that that sample be representative of the total content universe, that is, that it be a valid sample.

This brings us to the question of content-related evidence. This type of evidence shows the extent to which the sample of items on a test are representative of some defined universe, or domain of content. The evidence is gathered by careful and critical examination by expert judges of the test's content to determine the relationship between the test and the defined uni-

---

[1]American Psychological Association (1985). *Standards for Educational and Psychological Testing.* Washington: APA.

verse. This procedure is carried out from the point of view of a specific use for the test results.

Such a content universe is theoretical, of course. If one were to prepare a test, one would prepare an outline of the topics, skills, and abilities that make up the content area being measured along with an indication of the importance of each. A large number of test items could be written using this outline as a guide. From each category of the outline, test items could be randomly drawn with the number of items reflecting the proportionate weight of that category in the whole. The resulting sample of items should be representative of the content universe. For example, the universe of content for a test on the Civil War might be defined as a knowledge and understanding of such topics as the causes, the military strategies and campaigns, important personalities, economic impact, effects on subsequent history, and so on. The test items written on each of these topics should measure not only knowledge of the topic but also understanding, interpretation, analysis, and any other cognitive objectives emphasized in the course. The number of items covering each topic and each type of objective should reflect the emphasis given that topic and that objective in the total course. Assume a teacher of English literature has emphasized an understanding of the ideas of selected authors and the relevance of those ideas in the twentieth century. If this teacher's test contained mostly items asking students to match authors' names with their works and to recall their birth dates, the teacher has failed to obtain a representative sample of the content area, and the test would have little validity for its intended purpose: to measure understanding of authors' ideas.

Content-related evidence is not usually expressed in numerical form. Gathering such evidence is essentially and of necessity based on judgment, and such judgment must be made separately for each purpose. It involves a careful and critical examination to determine if the content and objectives measured by the test are representative of those that constitute the content domain. One should determine whether the items in the test represent the course and objectives as stated in curriculum guides, syllabi, and texts. In order to obtain an external evaluation of content validity, the test maker should ask a number of teachers or other experts to examine the test content systematically and evaluate its relevancy to the specified universe. If all agree that the test items represent the content domain adequately, the test can then be said to have content validity. It should also be established that the test is free from the influence of factors that are irrelevant to the purpose of the measurement. For example, performance on a mathematics test should not be influenced by reading speed and vocabulary. The presence of these factors in a mathematics test would lower its validity because the test would be measuring something other than what it was intended to measure. Content-related evidence is especially important in evaluating the validity of achievement tests.

The researcher must always gather content-related evidence for the validity of any self-constructed or standardized achievement test to be used in a study. Test publishers generally provide extensive validity evidence of this type. However, it must be stressed again that an achievement test that has high validity for the test constructor may not have validity for another user, who may define the content universe in a different way. Only the user of an achievement test can ultimately judge its validity for his or her own purpose.

// Criterion-Related Evidence

Criterion-related evidence shows the extent to which the scores on a measuring instrument are related to an independent external variable (criterion) believed to measure directly the behavior or characteristic in question. When one investigates the relationship between the scores on a scholastic aptitude test and college grade-point average (GPA), one is gathering criterion-related evidence for the validity of the test. The extent to which scores on the aptitude test are related to success in college as measured by GPA is the extent to which the aptitude test has validity for the purpose of predicting GPA.

As the name indicates, the emphasis in this type of evidence is on the criterion and the measurement procedures used to obtain criterion scores. The choice of the criterion is thus crucial to the success of this type of investigation. There are several characteristics that a criterion measure should possess. Of these the most important is *relevance*. One must judge whether the criterion chosen really represents successful performance on the behavior in question. If the criterion does not reflect the attribute under study, it would be meaningless to use it as a basis for validating another instrument. GPA is considered a relevant measure of success in college and is generally chosen as the criterion for validating aptitude tests constructed for the selection of college applicants. To validate a test designed to select salespersons, the relevant criterion might be dollar value of sales made in a specified time. In some cases it may be difficult to find relevant criteria. For example, it has been difficult to locate criteria for use in validating measures to be used for predicting teacher effectiveness. With neither an agreed-upon description of teacher effectiveness nor an effective method of measuring that variable, it is practically impossible to establish the validity of any instrument designed to identify promising teacher candidates.

A second characteristic is that a criterion must be *reliable*. This means that the criterion must be a consistent measure of the attribute over time or from situation to situation. If the criterion itself is not consistent, one would not expect it to relate consistently to any predictors.

A criterion should be *free from bias*. That is, the scoring of a criterion measure should not be influenced by any factors other than actual performance on the criterion. Assume that a supervisor's rating is the criterion used to validate a test to select applicants for a certain job. If the supervisor lets a general opinion of the individual or any factor other than actual performance influence the rating, then the criterion score will be biased. In order to avoid bias when the criterion is a rating, one should give explicit instructions on the characteristics to be rated and how the rating is to be done. The more objective the rating procedure, the less bias there will be in the criterion. Another possible source of bias in a criterion is *contamination*. Contamination occurs when an individual's score on the criterion is influenced by the scorer's knowledge of the subject's predictor score. For example, assume that one has an art aptitude test that is to be validated by using grades in art class as the criterion. If the teachers who grade the students' works are aware of the students' scores on the aptitude test, such awareness may influence the teachers' evaluation of the students. Contamination of the criterion can be prevented by not permitting the person who grades or rates the criterion to see the predictor scores.

Once the external criterion has been defined, empirical data are gathered in order to assess the relationship between scores on the measuring instrument (X) and on the criterion (Y). The instrument to be validated is administered to a group of individuals representative of those on whom the measure will be used. The scores made by these subjects on the predictor (X) are put aside and are not used to make any decisions that might influence subsequent events for this particular group in order to avoid contamination of the criterion scores. When the criterion data (Y) become available at a later time, the original tests are retrieved and the scores on the tests are then correlated with the scores on the criterion. The resulting coefficient of correlation between the two sets of measures is called a *validity coefficient* (r_{xy}) and indicates how accurately the test scores (X) can predict the criterion (Y). The larger the r_{xy}, the more accurately the test predicts.

An example of this procedure occurred in the validation of the Scholastic Aptitude Test (SAT). In numerous studies, the SAT was administered to a large number of high school seniors, and the tests were filed away until the students completed the freshman year of college. At that time the SAT scores were correlated with the first-year GPA (the criterion) in order to obtain the validity coefficient of the test. Because the SAT was found in repeated studies to have useful criterion-related validity, it is now routinely used to predict performance in college. High school students usually take the SAT during their senior year and submit the scores to colleges. College admissions officers, aware of the predictive validity of the SAT, examine the scores and make admissions decisions based, at least in part, on the SAT scores. The higher the score on the SAT, the greater the probability of success in college. In most cases prediction is based on a combination of SAT scores and some measure of high school achievement, such as rank in high school class. The combination of SAT score and high school rank predicts college GPA more accurately than either measure alone.

Criterion-related evidence is essential for tests that are used for selection and classification purposes. Before a test can be used for selection, one must have evidence that the test can in fact predict performance on the specified criterion. The fundamental question is How accurately can criterion performance be predicted from scores on the test? Whether high or low, useful or not useful, depends on the context in which the test is to be used. A correlation coefficient of .40 could be very helpful in cases for which no predictive instrument has previously been available. In other cases a correlation of .65 might be considered low and unsatisfactory if other predictors are available that have a higher relationship with the criterion. In general an instrument has "good" validity as a selection device if the evidence shows that it has a higher correlation with the criterion than do competing instruments. Accumulating criterion-related evidence for a test's validity requires time and patience. In some cases it is necessary to wait for several years to determine whether performance on a measure is useful for predicting success on a criterion.

Two designs for obtaining criterion-related evidence can be distinguished: *predictive* studies and *concurrent* studies. Both are concerned with the empirical relationship between test scores and a criterion, but a distinction is made on the basis of the time when the criterion data are collected. A predictive study gathers information about the correlation between test scores and a criterion that occurs at a future time. A concurrent study gathers information about the correlation between test scores and a criterion measure available at the same time. For example, a concurrent study of a reading test administered at the end of fourth grade would look at the relationship between subjects' scores on the test and the grades teachers assigned the same subjects in fourth-grade reading; a predictive study would correlate these same test scores with the grades the students subsequently received in fifth-grade reading. Predictive evidence is generally preferred in the validation of selection tests in education or industry; concurrent studies are generally preferred for achievement tests, tests designed to measure constructs, or tests used for certification or diagnosis.

Because a validity coefficient is a correlation coefficient, its size will be influenced by the same factors that influence any correlation coefficient, namely, the linearity of the relationship between test and criterion and the range of individual differences in the group.

// Construct-Related Evidence

Construct-related evidence focuses on the test scores as a measure of a psychological trait or construct. Recall from Chapter 1 that the term *construct* refers to something that is not itself directly measurable but that explains observable effects. The construct *social maturity* was "constructed" to account for observed behavior patterns. Social maturity cannot itself be measured directly, but many of the behaviors that we believe to be aspects of this construct can be described and measured and the sum of these measures can give us an indirect measure of the abstract construct social maturity. Some other common examples of constructs are anxiety, intelligence, motivation, reasoning ability, critical thinking, aptitude in various areas, reading comprehension, and self-concept.

Throughout history people have put together, or constructed, more-complex abstractions from their concepts. Just as a child puts together Tinkertoy pieces and labels them "horse" or "man," so people create constructs by combining concepts and less complex constructs in purposeful patterns. The impetus for construct validation came from personality theory and the researchers' need for a method of validating the instruments used in theory development. Neither content nor criterion-related evidence directly focuses on the construct being measured by a test. The objective in gathering construct evidence is to determine what psychological construct is being measured by a test and how well it is being measured.

Construct studies combine both a logical and an empirical approach. One aspect of the logical approach is to ask if the elements the test measures are the elements that make up the construct. For example, when Doll originated the Vineland Social Maturity Scale in 1935,[2] he defined the construct *social maturity* as a combination of interrelated elements of self-help, self-direction, locomotion, occupation, communication, and social relations. Those who reviewed the first revised version of the test in Buros' *Mental Measurements Yearbook*[3] tended to agree that these elements are aspects of the construct that should be incorporated in a test of social maturity. Sometimes there is disagreement on what the elements of a construct are. For example, if one thinks of the construct *intelligence* as primarily a combination of skills that enable an individual to cope with an academic environment, one will expect such skills to be measured in an intelligence test. If one defines *intelligence* as a set of skills that are no more related to school environments than to other environments, one will not want school-specific skills incorporated into the test.

Another aspect of the logical approach is to inspect the items to determine if they seem appropriate for assessing the elements in the construct. In the Vineland scale, for example, the parent of a six-year-old is asked if the subject uses skates, sled, wagon (occupation); goes to bed unassisted (self-help); prints simple words (communication); plays simple table games

---

[2]Doll, E. A. (1935, 1949, 1965). *Vineland Social Maturity Scale.* Circle Pines, MN: American Guidance Service. The scale was revised in 1984 by S. S. Sparrow, D. A. Balla, and D. V. Cicchetti as the *Vineland Adaptive Behavior Scales.*
[3]Buros, O. K. (1949). *Mental Measurements Yearbook* (vol. 4). Lincoln: University of Nebraska Press.

(locomotion); and is trusted with money (self-direction). These questions seem appropriate for measuring elements of social maturity. If the original test had included questions concerning the child's preference for certain foods or whether he or she is right-handed, these items would have been deleted, as they are not directly related to the elements in the construct.

There are also empirical data gathered as evidence: Internally, relationships within the test should be as predicted by the construct; and externally, relationships between scores on the test and other observations should be consistent with the construct. Doll was able to show that Vineland scores for occupation, self-help, and so forth were positively correlated with one another. These observations provided internal support for the theory that the construct *social maturity* consists of interrelated elements and provided evidence that the Vineland scale was successful in measuring these interrelated elements.

If the relationships of elements within a test are not what were predicted by the construct, then either the construct itself is inappropriate or the test is failing to measure the elements within the construct.

For example, one might propose to measure the construct *sociobiological instinct* by first positing that the construct consisted of interrelated elements: (1) a will to survive, (2) a will to reproduce, (3) a desire to select healthy mates, and (4) a willingness to sacrifice in order to promote the survival only of one's own children and near relatives. If—when the test is constructed and administered—one finds that these elements are not positively related, one would conclude that the measure lacked validity and that either the test or the construct itself should be revised.

Scores on a test should be related to external measures in a manner consistent with the construct. Doll and others have shown that scores on the Vineland scale do correlate with chronological age, mental age, and with independent assessments of social maturity. Therefore, it can be said that scores on the Vineland scale show the relationships with external measures that should be expected in a scale of social maturity that has validity for measuring the construct.

A measure of a particular construct should be as independent as possible of measures of other constructs. For example, if we develop a test designed to measure arithmetic problem-solving skills and find scores on this test are very highly correlated with scores on reading tests, we would conclude that we have developed another test of reading rather than an arithmetic problem-solving test per se. It is probably not possible to develop a test of arithmetic problem solving that is completely unrelated to reading. However, if we have two competing arithmetic problem-solving tests that are both correlated with an arithmetic computation test ($r = .7$), but one correlates with a reading test ($r = .8$) and the other correlates with the reading test ($r = .6$), we would judge the latter to have greater validity for measuring arithmetic problem solving because it is more independent of reading.

/ Methods Used in Gathering Construct-Related Evidence

There is no single method used to gather evidence for the construct interpretations of a test. Any evidence that bears on the meaning or usefulness of the scores is relevant. Some of the most common procedures used to gather construct-related evidence are presented below.

Correlation with Other Measures   One of the simplest procedures is to show that scores on a new test correlate with scores on an established test that is considered to be a valid measure of the construct. For example, a newly developed intelligence test could be correlated with a well-established test of intelligence such as the Stanford-Binet or the Wechsler. If the correlation is high, one assumes that the new test is measuring the same construct (intelligence) as the established test.

Data relevant to construct interpretations are also provided by validity coefficients. Scores on a scholastic aptitude test should correlate highly with grades in school, with achievement test scores, or with teachers' ratings of aptitude. A test of spatial relations should predict success in mechanical drawing. Confirmation of such predictions provides support for one's beliefs in the test as a measure of the construct.

Messick discusses the use of a convergence of indicators of the construct as well as discriminability from other constructs.[4] Convergence means that the measure is related to other measures presumed to be valid indicators of the same construct. One looks for a convergence of indicators of the construct by seeking out the other measures with which the construct should theoretically be correlated and then showing how they are correlated. A mathematical reasoning test should correlate with grades in mathematics. If, in fact, the test does correlate highly with mathematics grades, this would be evidence of convergence.

Convergence of indicators, however, is not sufficient evidence. Messick points to the need for evidence that the construct could be empirically distinguished from other constructs. To establish discriminability one seeks evidence that the construct is not substantially correlated with instruments known to measure different constructs. That is, one identifies measures with which the construct should not be substantially correlated. A mathematical reasoning test should have a very low and insignificant correlation with a reading test because reading is an irrelevant variable in a mathematical reasoning test. If a low and insignificant correlation is found between the math test and the reading test, this would be evidence of discriminability. Of course, a low or zero correlation with just *any* construct would not be appropriate evidence. The construct used should be one that at least represents some potential aspect of the construct under investigation. While it

---

[4]Messick, S. (1989). Validity. In R. Linn (ed.). *Educational Measurement* (pp. 13–103). New York: American Council on Education and Macmillan.

would be reasonable to choose reading as a measure with which a mathematical reasoning test should not correlate substantively, it would be meaningless to correlate the mathematics scores with football throwing to provide construct-related evidence. It might be helpful to think of the construct measure in question as representing a point on a continuum of related constructs and the convergence and discriminability constructs as other points on the same continuum. For example, a measure of sociability would be expected to correlate positively with a measure of extraversion (convergence), but negatively with a measure of introversion (discriminability). For a more complete discussion of the role of convergence and discriminability as evidence of the construct being measured, the reader is referred to the classic article by Campbell and Fiske.[5]

Another aspect of the correlational approach to gathering evidence is factor analysis. Factor analysis is a statistical method for studying the intercorrelations among a set of test scores in order to determine the number of factors (constructs) needed to account for the intercorrelations. The method also provides information on what factors determine performance on each test as well as the percentage of variance in the test scores accounted for by the factors. One starts with a large number of different measures; but by examining the intercorrelations among them and finding which measures seem to go together (correlate), one may reduce the large number of measurement outcomes to a smaller number of factors that are actually measured.[6] The intercorrelations indicate not only which tests measure the same factor but also the extent to which they measure the factor. By examining the content of the tests that load on the same factor,[7] one can infer the nature of the construct being measured.

Experimental Studies It may be hypothesized that test scores would change when certain types of experimental treatments are introduced. For example, in validating an anxiety scale, one might hypothesize that scores on the scale would change when individuals are put into an anxiety-provoking situation. If anxiety is manipulated in a controlled experiment and the resulting scores on the anxiety scale do change in the predicted way, one would have some evidence that the scale does measure anxiety.

Comparison of Scores of Defined Groups One can use groups already known to be different and hypothesize that scores on the instrument in question would discriminate one group from another. One would expect that scores on a musical aptitude test would discriminate between students cur-

---

[5]Campbell, D. T., and D. W. Fiske (1959). Convergent and discriminant validation by the multitrait-multimethod matrix. *Psychological Bulletin, 56,* 81–105.
[6]See, for example, J. Kim and C. Mueller (1978), *Introduction to Factor Analysis: What It Is and How To Do It,* Beverly Hills: Sage Publications.
[7]The term *loading* refers to the correlation between the test and the factor. A high loading indicates that the test is a good measure of the factor (construct).

rently enrolled in music school and an unselected group of college students. Similarly, if mechanics and nonmechanics could be discriminated on the basis of their scores on a mechanical aptitude test, this would provide support for the validity of the test as a measure of mechanical aptitude. If an inventory measures psychological adjustment, then scores on the inventory could be expected to discriminate between groups previously identified as adjusted and those previously identified as neurotic. The different groups used for comparison in validity studies may be age groups, sex groups, groups with different amounts of training in some area related to the construct, groups known to be normal and those known to be maladjusted, and so on. If the predicted differences in test scores are confirmed, one has support for the validity of the test as a measure of the construct in question.

The Intratest Analysis   The intratest analysis method examines the test itself and gathers information about the content of the test, the processes used in responding to the items of the test, and correlations among items of the test. Data from content-related studies may provide relevant information about the construct being measured by a test. When the behavioral universe being sampled by a test is specified, one has some insight into the nature of the construct being measured by the test. For example, if one were to define the behavior universe of a reasoning test by describing the abilities that are being sampled by the test (such as the ability to reason with quantitative and verbal analogies), one would gain some insight about the validity of the test.

One might also investigate the mental processes and skills that individuals use when responding to the items of a test. For example, students might be asked to "think aloud" as they work through a verbal reasoning test. Such a procedure may reveal that the test is measuring this reasoning ability as it claims, or it may reveal that other factors, such as vocabulary or reading comprehension, are being measured.

One should also investigate the homogeneity of the test content in order to ascertain if the test measures a single trait or quality. Measures of internal consistency, such as coefficient alpha or a Kuder-Richardson coefficient, provide evidence of homogeneity. These measures will be discussed in a later section of this chapter. Measures of homogeneity provide relevant construct-related evidence because they help describe the extent to which a single trait or construct is being measured. However, intratest data are never sufficient to validate a test. We need external data in order to determine what a test measures.

/ Contribution of Construct-Related Studies

Construct-related investigations are the most comprehensive because they subsume content relevance and representativeness as well as criterion-related evidence. The construct-related approach for test validity is important because it has focused attention on the role of theory in test construction and the need to formulate hypotheses that can be investigated as part of the validation process.

Even when a specific theory is not directly involved, this approach has stressed the need to anchor the construct of interest for a particular test in a conceptual framework that specifies the meaning of the construct, distinguishes it from other constructs, and indicates how measures of the construct should relate to other variables. Thus, the researcher can gather data from a variety of sources to provide support for the test's validity.

// Comparison of the Sources of Evidence for Validity

The varieties of evidence for validity supplement one another; they all essentially are concerned with valid interpretations of the meaning of the scores and how they can be used. This is the main reason that validity is recognized as a unitary concept.

Assume that a teacher wants to construct a reading test to be used with a sixth-grade class. What kinds of evidence should the teacher gather to support the validity of the uses of the test? If the test is to be used to make inferences about reading achievement, the teacher would first decide on the universe of content to be sampled. Specifically, the textbooks, outside reading materials, class exercises, and so on would be identified. Samples from this universe would be selected in such a way that the test comprises a representative sample of all the content and the objectives of the course. Other teachers would be asked to make a judgment concerning the adequacy of the content for the intended purpose.

Evidence would be gathered on the relationship between students' scores on the test and their performance on some appropriate criterion. A follow-up study could be carried out to determine if there is a correlation between these test scores and reading achievement in seventh grade. A high correlation would provide evidence that the reading test has validity for predicting reading achievement in the seventh grade. Additional evidence could be gathered by correlating the scores on the test with the students' grades in reading class or with scores on a valid standardized reading test.

To gather construct-related evidence of validity, the teacher would attempt to determine whether hypotheses made about the nature of reading proficiency are supported by the test performance of the students. Differences in the performance of high scorers versus low scorers would be studied, and an attempt would be made to determine whether test performance is related to a theory of instruction in reading, and so on. Another method would involve a study of the convergence of reading scores with other variables. A measure of internal consistency would indicate whether the test was measuring a single construct. A summary of all the above types of evidence would indicate how appropriate or meaningful the inferences from the reading test scores would be, hence the validity of the test. Table 8.1 summarizes the type of validity evidence relevant to different purposes of tests.

// Application of the Validity Concept

Although we define *validity* in a general way as "the extent to which a test measures what it is intended to measure," validity is *not* some general characteristic that a test has. Validity is specific to the particular job that one wants a test to do. A test or scale should be constructed with only a single purpose in mind. A measure intended for multiple purposes will usually not achieve any of them very well. One must know the purpose of the test and the setting in which it will be used in order to assess the test's validity for those particular circumstances.

/// RELIABILITY

The reliability of a measuring instrument is the degree of consistency with which it measures whatever it is measuring. This quality is essential in any kind of measurement. A post office will soon take action to repair a scale if it is found that the scale sometimes underestimates and sometimes overestimates the weight of packages. Psychologists and educators are equally concerned about the consistency of their measuring devices when they attempt

TABLE 8.1 Validation of a Reading Test for Different Purposes

Purpose	Type of Evidence	Questions to Be Asked
Achievement test in 6th-grade reading	Content	How well does the test sample what has been learned?
Aptitude test to predict performance in 7th-grade reading	Criterion-related: predictive study	How well does the test predict achievement in 7th-grade reading?
Diagnostic test to identify reading problems	Criterion-related: concurrent study	How well does the test diagnose current reading difficulties?
A test to measure reading comprehension	Construct	How well does the test measure reading comprehension? Do the data support hypotheses about reading comprehension?

to measure such complex traits as scholastic aptitude, achievement, motivation, anxiety, and the like. They would not consider a scholastic-aptitude test worthwhile if it yields markedly different results each time it is used on the same subject. People who use such measuring instruments must identify and utilize techniques that will help them to determine to what extent their measuring instruments are consistent and reliable.

// Theory of Reliability

As a way of distinguishing the reliability concept from the validity concept, it is useful to identify *random errors of measurement* and *systematic errors of measurement*. Random error refers to error that is a result of pure chance. Random errors of measurement may inflate or depress any subject's score in an unpredictable manner. For example, one element in the President's Physical Fitness Test for elementary students is the baseball throw. Subjects are instructed to throw a baseball as far as they can, and the distance of the throw is measured. Although the object of the test is to get a score that is typical of a subject's performance, certainly if we have a single subject throw a baseball on several occasions, we would find that the child does not throw it the same distance every time.

Assume we have each student make a throw on two consecutive days. If we then compare the two scores (distance thrown) for each student, we would find that they are almost never exactly the same. Most of the differences would be small, but some would be moderately large and a few, quite large. The results are inconsistent from one day's throw to the next. One throw is not completely reliable as a measure of a student's throwing ability.

There are three types of chance, or random, influences that lead to inconsistency between scores achieved on the two days:

1. *The student may actually change from one day to the next.* On one day he or she may feel better than on the other. On one day the student may be more motivated or less fatigued. Perhaps the student's father, hearing about the task, begins coaching the child in throwing a baseball.

2. *The task itself may change* for the two measurements. For example, the ball used one day may be firm, whereas on the second day it may be wet and soggy. One day perhaps the examiner permits the students to take a running start up to the throwing line, whereas on the second day they are permitted only a couple of steps. These changes may help some students more than others.

3. *The limited sample* of behavior results in an unstable score. A small sample of behavior is subject to many kinds of chance influences. Maybe there is a gust of wind as the ball is thrown. Maybe the

student loses balance when starting to throw the ball, or maybe his or her fingers slip while gripping the ball.

Reliability is concerned with the effect of such random errors of measurement on the consistency of scores.

On the other hand, some errors involved in measurement are predictable or systematic. Using the example of the baseball throw, imagine a situation in which the instructions for the throw are given in English but not all the subjects understand English. The scores of the non-English-speaking subjects could be systematically depressed because the subjects do not comprehend what they are expected to do. Such systematic errors of measurement are a validity problem. The validity of a test is lowered whenever scores are systematically changed by the influence of anything other than what we are attempting to measure. In this instance we are measuring not only baseball-throwing ability but also, in part, English comprehension.

To decide whether we are dealing with reliability or validity, we determine whether we are considering random errors or systematic errors. If a class is being given the baseball-throw test and two balls are being employed, one firm and one soggy, and it is purely a matter of chance who gets which ball, the variation due to the ball used is a reliability problem. The variation due to the ball represents random error that affects the consistency of the measurements. If class members are called to take the test in alphabetical order and it is a rainy day and the one baseball provided gets wetter with each successive throw, the variation due to the increasing wetness of the ball is a validity problem. Scores in this case are increased for those near the beginning of the alphabet and decreased for those near the end. The validity of the baseball-throw scores is lessened because the scores reflect not only baseball-throwing prowess but alphabetical order as well. This is an instance of systematic error that affects the validity of the measurement.

Reliability is concerned with how consistently we are measuring whatever we are measuring. It is not concerned with whether we are measuring what we intend to measure: that is the validity question. It is possible for a measuring instrument to be reliable without being valid. However, it cannot be valid unless it is first reliable. For example, someone could decide to measure intelligence by determining the circumference of the head. The measures might be very consistent from time to time (reliable), but this method would not be considered a valid measure of intelligence because circumference of the head does not correlate with any other criteria of intelligence nor is it predicted by any theory of intelligence.

Reliability is affected by random errors, which are any factors that will result in discrepancies between scores in repeated administrations of a measuring instrument.

Random errors arise from a number of sources. Errors may be inherent in the instrument itself. For example, if a test is very short, those subjects who happen to know the few answers required will get higher scores than they deserve, whereas those who do not know those few answers get lower scores than they deserve. For example, if a test is given to assess how well students know the capitals of the 50 states, but only five questions are asked, it is possible that a student who knows only ten capitals could get all five correct, whereas a student who knows 40 could get none correct. In a short test luck is more of a factor than it is in a long test. If a test is so easy that everyone knows most of the answers, the subjects' relative scores again depend upon only a few questions and luck is a major factor. If questions are ambiguous, "lucky" subjects respond in the way the examiner intended, whereas "unlucky" subjects respond in another equally correct manner, but their answers are scored as incorrect. The scoring procedure also affects reliability. Precise scoring procedures enhance reliability, whereas vague scoring procedures depress it.

Errors may be inherent in the administration of the instrument. An inexperienced person may depart from standardized procedures in administering or scoring the test. Testing conditions such as light, heat, and ventilation may affect performance. Instructions for taking the test may be ambiguous.

There is also pupil error, that is, fluctuations in motivation, interest, fatigue, physical condition, anxiety, and other mental and emotional factors affect the test results. A pupil's breaking a pencil point on a timed test would increase the error component in the results.

// Equations for Reliability

It is generally accepted that all measurements of human qualities contain some error. Reliability procedures are concerned with determining the degree of inconsistency in scores due to random error.

When one administers a test to a student, one secures a score, which can be called the *observed score*. If one had tested this student on some other occasion with the same instrument, one probably would not have obtained exactly the same observed score. The observed score contains an error of measurement. Therefore, one concludes that every test score consists of two components: the *true score* plus some *error of measurement*. As noted above, this error component may be due to any one, or a combination, of a number of factors associated with variations within the subject from time to time or with the administration of the test to that subject.

The reliability of a test is expressed mathematically as the best estimate of what proportion of the total variance of scores on the test is true variance. As explained in Chapter 5, variance is an index of the spread of a set of scores. If we administer a test to a group of students, some of the spread (variance) is due to true differences among the group and some of the spread (variance) is due to errors of measurement.

The idea of error component and true component in a single test score may be represented mathematically by formula 8.1.

$$X = T + E \tag{8.1}$$

where

X = the observed score
T = the true-score component
E = the error-of-measurement component

The true-score component may be defined as the score an individual would make under conditions in which a perfect measuring device is used. The error-of-measurement component can be either positive or negative. If it is positive, the individual's true score will be overestimated by the observed score; if it is negative, the person's true score will be underestimated. Because it is assumed that an error of measurement is just as likely to be positive as it is to be negative, then it can be concluded that the sum of the errors and the mean of the errors would both be 0 if the same measuring instrument or an equivalent form of the instrument were administered an infinite number of times to a subject. Under these conditions, the true component would be defined as the individual's mean score on an infinite number of measurements. The true score is a theoretical concept, since an infinite number of administrations of a test to the same subject is not feasible.

In the usual research situation, the investigator has one measure on each of a group of subjects. In other words, the researcher has a single set of test scores to consider. Each observed score has a true-score component and an error-score component. It has been shown mathematically that the variance of the observed scores of a large group of subjects (σ_x^2) is equal to the variance of their true scores (σ_t^2) plus the variance of their errors of measurement (σ_e^2) or

$$\sigma_x^2 = \sigma_t^2 + \sigma_e^2 \tag{8.2}$$

Reliability may be defined theoretically as the ratio of the true-score variance to the observed-score variance in a set of scores. That is, reliability is equal to

$$r_{xx} = \frac{\sigma_t^2}{\sigma_x^2} \tag{8.3}$$

where

r_{xx} = the reliability of the test
σ_t^2 = the variance of the true scores
σ_x^2 = the variance of the observed scores

Reliability is the proportion of the variance in the observed scores that is free of error. This notion can be expressed in the following formula derived from formulas 8.2 and 8.3.

$$r_{xx} = 1 - \frac{\sigma_e^2}{\sigma_x^2} \tag{8.4}$$

The *coefficient of reliability* (r_{xx}) can range from 1, when there is no error in the measurement, to 0, when the measurement is all error. (When there is no error in the measurement, σ_e^2 in the preceding equation is 0 and $r_{xx} = 1$. If measurement is all error, $\sigma_e^2 = \sigma_x^2$ and $r_{xx} = 0$.) This degree of error is indicated by the degree of departure of the correlation coefficient from 1. Thus, the greater the error, the more the reliability coefficient is depressed below 1 and the lower the reliability. Conversely, if the reliability coefficient is near 1, the instrument has relatively little error and high reliability.

// Approaches to Reliability

A test is reliable to the extent that the scores made by an individual remain nearly the same in repeated measurements. There are two approaches to expressing the reliability of a set of measurements.

1. One approach indicates the amount of variation to be expected within a set of repeated measurements of a *single* individual. If it were possible to weigh an individual on 200 scales, we would get a frequency distribution of scores to represent his or her weight. This frequency distribution would have an average value, which we could consider the "true" weight. It would also have a standard deviation, indicating the spread. This standard deviation is called the *standard error of measurement* because it is the standard deviation of the "errors" of measuring the weight for one person. With psychological or educational data, we do not often make repeated measurements on an individual. Time would not permit such repeated measurements for each individual. In addition, the practice and fatigue effects associated with repeated measurement would have an influence on the scores. Thus, instead of measuring one person many times, we measure a large, diverse group on two occasions. Using the pair of measurements for each individual, we can estimate what the spread of scores would have been for the average person had the measurement been made again and again.

2. Reliability of measurement also tells the extent to which each individual maintains the same relative position in the group. The person who scores highest on a test today should also be one of the highest scorers the next time the test is given. Each person in the group should stay in the same position. We can compute a coefficient of correlation between two administrations of the same test to determine the extent to which the individuals maintain the same relative position. This coefficient is called a *reliability coefficient* (r_{xx}). Thus, reliability of a measure is indicated by a low standard error of measurement or by a high reliability coefficient.

// The Reliability Indices

Reliability can be estimated by correlating the scores obtained by the same individuals on different occasions or with different sets of equivalent items. These procedures require two administrations of a test. Other procedures examine the internal consistency of the test.

/ Test-Retest Reliability

An obvious way to estimate the reliability of a test is to administer it to the same group of individuals on two occasions and correlate the paired scores. The correlation coefficient obtained by this procedure is called a *test-retest reliability coefficient*. For example, a physical fitness test may be given to a class during one week and the same test given again the following week. If the test is reliable, each individual's relative position on the second administration of the test will be near his or her relative position on the first administration of the test. The reliability coefficient (r_{xx}) will be near 1. Any change in relative position from one occasion to the next is considered as error. If the test contains considerable error, the r_{xx} will be nearer 0. As explained earlier, a reliability coefficient is an estimate of the proportion of observed variance in test scores that is true variance. The difference between the value of the reliability coefficient and 1 is an unbiased estimate of the proportion of error variance in a test. For example, a test-retest reliability of .80 on the physical fitness test indicates that our best estimate is that 80 percent of the observed variance is true variance and 20 percent is error variance.

The test-retest reliability coefficient, because it is indicative of the consistency of subjects' scores over time, is sometimes referred to as a *coefficient of stability*. It tells us whether we can generalize from the score a person receives on one occasion to a score that person would receive if the test had been given at a different time.

A test-retest coefficient assumes that the characteristic being measured by the test is stable over time, so any change in scores from one time to another is due to random error. The error may be due to the condition of the subjects themselves or to testing conditions. The test-retest coefficient also assumes that there is no practice effect or memory effect. For example, students may learn something just from taking a test and thus will react differently on the second taking of the test. These practice effects from the first testing will not likely be the same across all students, thus lowering the reliability estimate. If the interval of time is short, there may also be a memory effect. That is, students may mark a question the same way they had previously just because they remember marking it that way the first time. This memory effect tends to inflate the reliability estimate. The memory effect can be controlled somewhat by increasing the time between the first test and the retest. On the other hand, if the time between testings is too long, differential learning may be a problem. That is, students will learn different amounts during the interval, which would affect the reliability coefficient.

Because of the problems discussed above, the test-retest procedure is not usually appropriate for tests in the cognitive domain. The use of this procedure in schools is largely restricted to measures of physical fitness and athletic prowess.

/ Equivalent-Forms Reliability

The equivalent-forms technique of estimating reliability, which is also referred to as the *alternate-* or *parallel-forms technique,* is used when it is probable that subjects will recall their responses to the test items. Here, rather than correlating the results of two administrations of the same test to the same group, one correlates the results of equivalent forms of the test administered to the same individuals. If the two forms are administered at essentially the same time (in immediate succession), the resulting reliability coefficient is called the *coefficient of equivalence.* This measure reflects variations in performance from one specific set of items to another. It indicates whether we can generalize a student's score to what the student would receive if another form of the same test had been given. The question is to what extent does the student's performance depend upon the particular set of items used in the test?

If subjects are tested with one form on one occasion and with another form on a second occasion and their scores on the two forms are correlated, the resulting coefficient is called the *coefficient of stability and equivalence.* This coefficient reflects two aspects of test reliability: variations in performance from one time to another as well as variations from one form of the test to another. This is the most demanding and the most rigorous measure available for determining the reliability of a test.

Designing alternate forms of a test that are truly equivalent is the major problem with this technique of estimating reliability. If this is not successfully achieved, then the variation in scores from one form to another could not be considered as error variance. Equivalent forms of a test are independently constructed tests that must meet the same specifications; that is, they must have the same number of items, form, instructions, time limits, format, content, range, and level of difficulty, but the actual questions are not the same. Ideally one should have pairs of equivalent items and assign one of each pair to each form. The distribution of the test scores must also be equivalent.

The equivalent-forms technique is recommended when one wishes to avoid the problem of recall or practice effect and in cases when one has available a large number of test items from which to select equivalent samples. It is generally considered that the equivalent-forms procedure provides the best estimate of the reliability of academic and psychological measures.

// Internal-Consistency Measures of Reliability

There are other reliability procedures that are designed to determine whether all the items in a test are measuring the same thing. These are called the *internal-consistency procedures* and require only a single administration of one form of a test.

/ Split-Half Reliability

The first of these procedures, known as the *split-half,* artificially splits the test into two halves and correlates the individuals' scores on the two forms. The test is administered to a group, and later the items are divided into two halves, scores are obtained for each individual on the two forms, and a coefficient of correlation is calculated. This split-half reliability coefficient is like a coefficient of equivalence because it reflects fluctuations from one sample of items to another. If each subject has a very similar position on the two forms, the test has high reliability. If there is little consistency in positions, the reliability is low. The method requires only one form of a test, there is no time lag involved, and the same physical and mental influences will be operating on the subjects as they take the two sections.

A problem with this method is in splitting the test to obtain two comparable halves. If, through item analysis, one establishes the difficulty level of each item, one can place each item into one of the two halves on the basis of equivalent difficulty and similarity of content. The most common procedure, however, is to correlate the scores on the odd-numbered items of the test with the scores on the even-numbered items.

The correlation coefficient computed between the two halves will systematically underestimate the reliability of the entire test. Longer tests are more reliable than shorter tests if everything else is equal. Therefore, the correlation between the odd 50 and even 50 items on a 100-item test is a reliability estimate for a 50-item test, not a 100-item test. To transform the split-half correlation into an appropriate reliability estimate for the entire test, the Spearman-Brown prophecy formula is employed:

$$r_{xx} = \frac{2r_{1/2\,1/2}}{1 + r_{1/2\,1/2}} \qquad (8.5)$$

where

r_{xx} = the estimated reliability of the entire test

$r_{1/2\,1/2}$ = the Pearson r correlation between the two halves

For example, if we find a correlation coefficient of .65 between two halves of a test, the estimated reliability of the entire test, using the Spearman-Brown formula, would be

$$r_{xx} = \frac{(2)(.65)}{1 + .65} = .79$$

The Spearman-Brown procedure is based on the assumption that the two halves are parallel. As this assumption is seldom exactly correct, in practice the split-half technique with the Spearman-Brown correction tends to overestimate the reliability that would be obtained if test-retest or equivalent-forms procedures are used. This should be borne in mind when evaluating the reliabilities of competing tests.

Split-half reliability is an appropriate technique to use when time-to-time fluctuation in estimating reliability is to be avoided and when the test is relatively long. For short tests the other techniques, such as test-retest or equivalent-forms, are more appropriate.

The split-half procedure is not appropriate to use with speed tests because it yields spuriously high coefficients of equivalence in such tests. A speed test is one that purposefully includes easy items so that the scores are mainly dependent upon the speed with which subjects can respond. Errors are minor, and most of the items are correct up to the point where time is called. If a student responds to 50 items, his split-half score is likely to be 25–25; if another student marks 60 items, his split-half score is likely to be 30–30, and so on. Since individuals' scores on odd- and even-numbered items are very nearly identical, within-individual variation is minimized and the correlation between the halves would be nearly perfect. Thus, other procedures are recommended for use with speed tests.

/ Homogeneity Measures

Other internal-consistency measures of reliability do not require splitting the test into halves and scoring each half separately. These procedures assess the inter-item consistency, or homogeneity, of the items. They reflect two sources of error: (1) the content sampling as in split-half and (2) the heterogeneity of the behavior domain sampled. The more heterogeneous the domain, the lower the inter-item consistency and, conversely, the more homogeneous the domain, the higher the inter-item consistency.

Kuder-Richardson Procedures   Probably the best-known index of homogeneity is the Kuder-Richardson formula 20, which is based on the proportion of correct and incorrect responses to each of the items on a test.[8]

$$r_{xx} = \frac{K}{K - 1} \left(\frac{s_x^2 - \Sigma_{pq}}{s_x^2} \right) \qquad \text{K-R 20 (8.6)}$$

where

K = number of items on the test
s_x^2 = variance of scores on the total test (squared standard deviation)
p = proportion of correct responses on a single item
q = proportion of incorrect responses on the same item

The product pq is computed for each item, and the products are summed over all items to give Σ_{pq}. Kuder-Richardson 20 is applicable to tests whose

---

[8]Kuder, G. F., and M. W. Richardson (1937). The theory of estimation of test reliability. *Psychometrika, 2,* 151–160.

items are scored dichotomously, that is, as either right or wrong. Many machine-scoring procedures for tests routinely provide a K-R 20 coefficient along with a split-half coefficient.

Another formula (Kuder-Richardson 21) is computationally simpler but requires the assumption that all items in the test are of equal difficulty. This assumption is often unrealistic.

$$r_{xx} = \frac{Ks_x^2 - \bar{X}(K - \bar{X})}{s_x^2(K - 1)} \qquad \text{K-R 21 (8.7)}$$

where

$r_{xx} =$ the reliability of the whole test
$K =$ the number of items in the test
$s_x^2 =$ the variance of the scores
$\bar{X} =$ the mean of the scores

This method is by far the least time-consuming of all the reliability estimation procedures. It involves only one administration of a test and employs only easily available information. As such, it can be recommended to teachers for classroom use.

For example, suppose a teacher has administered a 50-item test to a class and has computed the mean as 40 and the standard deviation as 6. Applying formula 8.7, the reliability could be estimated as follows:

$$r_{xx} = \frac{(50)6^2 - 40(50 - 40)}{6^2(50 - 1)} = \frac{1800 - 400}{1764} = .79$$

Because the Kuder-Richardson procedures stress the equivalence of all the items in a test, they are especially appropriate when the intention of the test is to measure a single trait. For a test designed to measure several traits, the Kuder-Richardson reliability estimate will usually be lower than reliability estimates based on a correlational procedure.

It has been shown through deductive reasoning that the Kuder-Richardson reliability for any test is mathematically equivalent to the mean of the split-half reliability estimates computed for every possible way of splitting the test in half. This fact helps explain the relationship between the two procedures. If a test is of uniform difficulty and is measuring a single trait, any one way of splitting that test in half is as likely as any other to yield similar half scores. Therefore, the Spearman-Brown and Kuder-Richardson methods will yield similar estimates. If a test has items of varying difficulty and is measuring various traits, the Kuder-Richardson estimate is expected to be lower than the split-half estimate. For example, suppose a secretarial-skills test samples typing, shorthand, spelling, and English grammar skills. In applying the split-half method the test maker would assign equal numbers of items from each subtest to each half of the test. If the test is doing a good job of measuring this combination of skills, the split-half reliability will be high. The Kuder-Richardson method, which assesses the extent to which all the items are equivalent to one another, would yield a considerably lower reliability estimate.

Coefficient Alpha Another widely used measure of homogeneity is Cronbach's coefficient alpha.[9] The formula for alpha is

$$\alpha \text{ or } r_{xx} = \left(\frac{K}{K-1}\right)\left(\frac{s_x^2 - \Sigma s_i^2}{s_x^2}\right) \tag{8.8}$$

where

K = number of items on the test
Σs_i^2 = sum of the variances of the item scores
s_x^2 = variance of the test scores (all K items)

The formula for alpha is similar to the K-R 20 except that the Σ_{pq} is replaced by Σs_i^2, the sum of the variances of item scores. To calculate, one determines the variance of all the scores for *each* item and then adds these variances across all items to get Σs_i^2. Alpha and K-R 20 are equivalent for dichotomously scored items.

Cronbach alpha is used when measures have multiply scored items, such as attitude scales or essay tests. For example, on a Likert attitude scale the individual may receive a score from 1 to 5 depending on which option was chosen. Similarly, on essay tests a different number of points may be assigned to each answer. Many computer programs for reliability, such as the one included in SPSS, will provide a coefficient alpha as the index of reliability.

If the test items are heterogeneous—that is, they measure more than one trait or attribute—the reliability index as computed by either coefficient alpha or K-R 20 will be lowered. Furthermore, these formulas are not appropriate for timed tests, since item variances will be accurate only if each item has been attempted by every person.

Table 8.2 presents a summary of the different types of reliability coefficients arranged according to the number of forms and number of administrations required.

/ Interpretation of Reliability Coefficient

The interpretation of a reliability coefficient should be based on a number of considerations. There are certain factors that affect reliability coefficients, and unless these factors are taken into account, any interpretation of reliability will be superficial.

The reliability of a test is in part a function of the length of the test. The longer the test, the greater its reliability. A test usually consists of a number of sample items that are, theoretically, drawn from a universe of test items. We know from what we have studied about sampling that the greater the

---

[9]Cronbach, L. J. (1951). Coefficient alpha and the internal structure of tests. *Psychometrika, 16*, 297–334.

TABLE 8.2 Summary of Reliability Coefficients

Number of Administrations Required	Number of Test Forms Required	
	One	Two
One	Split-half K-R 20 Cronbach alpha	Equivalent Forms (no time lapse)
Two	Test-Retest	Equivalent Forms (time lapse)

of sample items that are, theoretically, drawn from a universe of test items. We know from what we have studied about sampling that the greater the sample size, the more representative it is expected to be of the population from which it is drawn. This is true also of tests. If it were possible to use the entire universe of items, the score of a person who takes the test would be his or her true score. A theoretical universe of items consists of an infinite number of questions and is obviously not a practical possibility. One therefore constructs a test that is a sample from such a theoretical universe. The greater the length of this test (that is, the greater the number of items included in the test), the more representative it should be of the true scores of the persons who take it. Because reliability is the extent to which a test represents the true scores of individuals, the longer test, the greater its reliability, provided that all the items in the test belong in the universe of items.

Reliability is in part a function of group heterogeneity. The reliability coefficient increases as the spread, or heterogeneity, of the subjects who take the test increases. Conversely, the more homogeneous the group is with respect to the trait being measured, the lower will be the reliability coefficient. One explanation of reliability is that it is the extent to which we can place individuals, relative to others in their groups, according to certain traits. Such placement is easier when one is dealing with measures that fall in a large range rather than those that fall in a small range. It does not take a sensitive device to determine the placement of children in a distribution according to their weights when the age range of these children is from 5 to 15. In fact, this placement is possible with some degree of accuracy even without using any measuring device. It does take a sensitive device, however, to carry out the same placement if all those who are to be compared and placed in the distribution are 5 years old. Thus, the heterogeneity of the group with whom a measuring instrument is used is a factor that affects the reliability of that instrument. The more heterogeneous the group used in the reliability study, the higher the reliability coefficient.

This fact should be kept in mind when you are selecting a standardized test. The publisher may report a high reliability coefficient based on a sample with a wide range of ability. However, when the test is used with a group having a much narrower range of ability, the reliability will be lower.

The reliability of a test is in part a function of the ability of the individuals who take that test. A test may be reliable at one level of ability but unreliable at another level. The questions in a test might be difficult and beyond the ability level of those who take it, or the questions might, on the other hand, be easy for the majority of the subjects. This difficulty level affects the reliability of the test. When a test is difficult, the subjects are guessing on most of the questions and a low reliability coefficient will result. When it is easy, all subjects have correct responses on most of the items and only a few more-difficult items are discriminating among subjects. Again we would expect a low reliability.

There is no simple rule by which one can determine how difficult, or how easy, a test should be. It depends on the type of test, the purpose, and the population for which it is being constructed.

Reliability is in part a function of the specific technique used for its estimation. Different procedures for estimating the reliability of tests result in different coefficients of reliability. The equivalent-forms technique gives a lower estimation of reliability than either test-retest or split-half procedures because in the equivalent-forms technique form-to-form as well as time-to-time fluctuation is present. The split-half method, on the other hand, results in higher reliability coefficients than do its alternatives because in most tests some degree of speed is involved and to that extent the reliability coefficient is overestimated. Thus, in evaluating the reliability of a test, one would give preference to a test whose reliability coefficient has been estimated by the equivalent-forms technique, rather than other techniques, when the reported reliabilities are similar. The same generalization would be true when comparing test-retest reliability with split-half. The same coefficient is more satisfactory if it results from the test-retest procedure rather than from the split-half method.

Reliability is in part a function of the nature of the variable being measured. Some variables of interest to researchers yield consistent measures more often than do other variables. For instance, most established tests of academic achievement have quite high reliabilities, whereas tests of personality variables have only moderate reliabilities.

What is the minimum reliability that is acceptable for an instrument? Perhaps the best response to this question is that a good reliability is one that is as good as or better than the reliability of competing measures. A spelling achievement test with a reliability of .80 is unsatisfactory if competing tests have reliability coefficients of .90 or better. A coefficient of .80 for a test of creativity would be judged excellent if other tests of the same construct have reliabilities of .60 or less.

The degree of reliability needed in a measure depends to a great extent on the use that is to be made of the results. If the measurement results are to be used for making a decision about a group or even for research purposes, a lower reliability coefficient (in the range of .30 to .50) might be acceptable. But if the results are to be used as a basis for making decisions about individuals, especially important or irreversible decisions, only instruments with the highest reliability are acceptable.

/ Interrater Reliability

There is another type of reliability that is important in measuring instruments that require ratings or observations of individuals by other individuals. *Interrater,* or *interobserver, reliability* is an index of the extent to which different judges/observers give similar ratings to the same behavior. One must show that the ratings assigned are not influenced by the observers' own values, attitudes, and other personality characteristics. The procedure to assess this type of reliability requires that two or more raters observe, or rate, the same behavior. The judges' ratings are then correlated to determine the extent of agreement among the judges; the resulting correlation is the interrater reliability index. Assuming that the behaviors to be observed are well defined and the judges well trained, the correlation coefficient (reliability) should be positive and quite high.

// Standard Error of Measurement

As explained earlier in this chapter, the reliability, stability, or dependability of a test may also be expressed in terms of the standard error of measurement, which provides an estimate of the range of variation in a set of repeated measurements of the same thing. Returning to our example of the baseball throw, we would expect with repeated administration, by chance, to obtain a number of different scores for the same individual. We would have a frequency distribution of scores. This frequency distribution has a mean, which is the best approximation of the true score. The distribution also has a standard deviation, indicating the extent of the variation in the scores. Because this standard deviation is the standard deviation of the errors of measurement, it is called the *standard error of measurement*. If one were to construct a frequency polygon showing this distribution of scores, its shape would approximate that of the normal curve. Measurement errors are normally distributed; there may be many small errors, but there will be few large ones. The standard deviation of this distribution of errors (standard error of measurement, s_M) would give us an estimate of how frequently errors of a given size might be expected to occur when the test is used.

In many situations, one does not have repeated measures, but one can get an estimate of the standard error of measurement by using the reliability coefficient:

$$s_M = s_x \sqrt{1 - r_{xx}} \qquad (8.9)$$

where

s_M = the standard error of measurement
s_x = the standard deviation of test scores
r_{xx} = the reliability coefficient

If an intelligence test has a reliability coefficient of .96 and a standard deviation of 15, then $s_M = 15\sqrt{1 - .96} = 15\sqrt{.04} = 3$.

The standard error of measurement is an index of the expected variability of obtained scores around the true score. The s_M can be interpreted as the standard deviation of the error score associated with an observed score and can be interpreted like any other standard deviation. Given a student's obtained score, we use the s_M to determine the range of score values that will, with a given probability, include the true score. This range of scores is referred to as a *confidence interval.* If it can be assumed that the errors of measurement are normally distributed about a given score and equally distributed throughout the score range, one could be 68 percent confident that a person's true score lies within one s_M on either side of the observed score. For example, if a subject has an observed score of 110 on the intelligence test where the standard error of measurement is 3, one could infer at the 68-percent confidence level that the subject's true score lies somewhere between 107 and 113. Or we can state at the 95-percent confidence level that the true score will fall within $\pm 1.96 s_M$ of the obtained score (between 104 and 116). We can also use the standard error of measurement to determine how much variability could be expected on retesting the individual. If the subject could be retested on the same intelligence test a number of times, one could expect in about two-thirds of the retests the scores would fall within a range of 6 points and in 95 percent of retest scores they would fall within a range of 12 points.

The standard error of measurement and the reliability coefficient are alternative ways of expressing test reliability. How precise an estimate of the true score any obtained score will be is indicated by the size of the standard error of measurement and the reliability coefficient. One looks for a low standard error of measurement or a high reliability coefficient as indicators of a test's reliability.

The standard error of measurement is recommended for use when interpreting individual scores and the reliability coefficient for use when comparing the consistency of different tests.

/ Reliability of Criterion-Referenced Tests

Developing satisfactory methods for assessing the reliability of criterion-referenced tests has been more difficult. Recall that criterion-referenced tests are used to determine an individual's status with respect to a well-defined set of content objectives. Reliability of this type of test is concerned with the consistency with which this status is estimated. Does the individual have the same level of proficiency on the two administrations of the test? The traditional reliability procedures, such as correlation and K-R 20, are not considered appropriate for criterion-referenced tests because these procedures are dependent on the variability of the individuals for which they are computed. On criterion-referenced tests, there is typically little or no variability in scores because training continues until the skill is mastered or nearly mastered. The restricted variability, or spread, of scores will result in low or near-zero estimates of reliability, even though the test may be internally consistent and highly stable.

Several procedures have been suggested for estimating the reliability of criterion-referenced tests. A relatively simple procedure involves administering two equivalent forms of the test or the same test on two occasions and finding the consistency of the decisions reached. The consistency of the results is determined by finding the percentage of persons for whom the same decision (mastery or nonmastery) is made on both administrations. This index is referred to as the *agreement coefficient* (p_0).

For example, the results displayed in Table 8.3 were obtained when two equivalent forms of a criterion-referenced test were administered to a sample of 100 students. In this situation, 70 students were consistently classified as masters and 14 students were consistently classified as nonmasters. The agreement coefficient is the percentage of the total subjects consistently classified on the two administrations of the test.

$$p_0 = \frac{a + d}{N} = \frac{70 + 14}{100} = \frac{84}{100} = .84$$

where

a = number classified as masters on both administrations
d = number classified as nonmasters on both administrations
N = total number of subjects
p_0 = agreement coefficient

Thus, 84 percent of the subjects were classified consistently and .84 is the reliability index of this test. If classifications as master or nonmaster are consistent for all examinees on both administrations, the agreement coefficient = 1, the maximum value.

Some agreement in classifications as master-nonmaster between two administrations is expected merely by chance. That is, even if classifications were made randomly, some individuals would be expected to fall in cells (a) and (d) in the example. Some writers have therefore suggested using coefficient kappa, κ, a statistic that takes *chance agreement* into consideration. The kappa coefficient refers to the proportion of consistent classifications observed *beyond* that expected by chance.

TABLE 8.3 Decisions Based on Forms 1 and 2

		Form 1 Master	Form 1 Nonmaster	
Form 2	Master	(a) 70	(b) 10	80
	Nonmaster	(c) 6	(d) 14	20
		76	24	100 (N)

The rationale of kappa coefficient is straightforward. One first calculates the percentage of cases expected to have consistent classification even if there were no statistical relationship between the tests, that is, if the classification on the two administrations was completely independent. This index is referred to as the *expected chance agreement*, p_c. The expected chance agreement is subtracted from the observed agreement ($p_0 - p_c$) to obtain the actual increase over chance consistency; this quantity is then divided by $1 - p$, the maximum possible increase in decision consistency beyond chance, to yield κ, the kappa coefficient.

$$p_c = \frac{(a + b)(a + c) + (c + d)(b + d)}{N^2}$$

where

p_c = percentage of agreement expected by chance

$$\kappa = \frac{p_o - p_c}{1 - p_c}$$

where

κ = percentage of agreement *above* that expected by chance

p_o = observed agreement coefficient

p_c = chance agreement

Using the data in the above example,

$$p_c = \frac{(80)(76) + (20)(24)}{100^2}$$

$$= \frac{6080 + 480}{10,000}$$

$$= .66$$

$$\kappa = \frac{.84 - .66}{1 - .66}$$

$$= \frac{.18}{.34}$$

$$= .53$$

It can be seen that the kappa coefficient (.53) provides a somewhat lower estimate of reliability than the agreement coefficient (.84). Both are often calculated because the information provided by the two indices is different. For further discussion of the factors affecting these measures of reliability for criterion-referenced tests, the reader is referred to a book by Crocker and Algina.[10]

The agreement coefficient and kappa require two administrations of a test. Techniques have been developed by Huynh and by Subkoviak for estimating these coefficients from a single test administration. The reader is referred to discussions by these writers.[11, 12] The simplest procedure, however, is to use tables developed by Subkoviak that permit one to read directly the approximate value of the agreement coefficient or the kappa coefficient after just one administration of a criterion-referenced test. These tables are presented in an article by Subkoviak.[13]

// Validity and Reliability Compared

Validity is a more important and comprehensive characteristic than reliability. It is also more difficult to determine. Published research studies often report much more reliability data than validity data. That is because validity is not obtained so directly as reliability. Much more subjective judgment is required in assessing the validity of a measuring instrument. One must answer questions about the appropriateness of test content, the adequacy of criteria, the definitions of human traits, the specification of the behavioral domain, the theory behind the test content, and so forth. All of these matters involve judgment and the gathering of data from many sources.

Reliability, on the other hand, can be investigated directly from the test data; no data external to the measure are required. The basic issues of reliability lend themselves easily to mathematical analysis, and reasonable conclusions about the amount of error can be stated in mathematical terms.

If a measure is valid, one should get the same results from one measurement to another; that is, a measure that has validity will also have reliability. The reverse, however, is not necessarily true. Remember that a measure can have reliability without having validity; it can consistently measure the wrong thing. Feldt and Brennan emphasize the primacy of validity in the evaluation of the adequacy of an educational measure by stating: "No body of reliability data, regardless of the elegance of the methods used to analyze it, is worth very much if the measure to which it applies is irrelevant or redundant."[14]

---

[10]Crocker, L., and J. Algina (1986). *Introduction to Classical and Modern Test Theory* (pp. 197–203). New York: Holt, Rinehart and Winston.
[11]Huynh, H. (1976). On the reliability of decisions in domain-referenced testing. *Journal of Educational Measurement, 13,* 253–264.
[12]Subkoviak, M. J. (1976). Estimating reliability from a single administration of a mastery test. *Journal of Educational Measurement, 13,* 265–276.
[13]Subkoviak, M. J. (1988). A practitioner's guide to computation and interpretation of reliability indices for mastery tests. *Journal of Educational Measurement, 25,* 47–55.
[14]Feldt, L. S., and R. L. Brennan (1989). Reliability. In R. Linn (ed.). *Educational Measurement* (p. 143). New York: American Council on Education and Macmillan.

/// SUMMARY

The multiplicity of measuring instruments available to the researcher requires the use of criteria for the evaluation of these instruments. The two most important criteria for measuring devices are validity and reliability.

Validity refers to the appropriateness, meaningfulness, and usefulness of the specific inferences made from test scores. In the process of validating a test, one gathers evidence to support the inferences.

There are various procedures used to gather evidence about test validity. Content-related evidence shows how well the content of the test samples the subject matter domain about which conclusions are to be drawn. Criterion-related evidence shows how the scores on the test correlate with appropriate criteria. Criterion-related evidence shows what psychological or educational constructs the test measures.

It is important to know what use is to be made of test scores. A test may be valid for one use but invalid for other uses. A test designed to measure scholastic aptitude may be a valid measure of scholastic aptitude but not valid as a measure of art aptitude.

We must also ask How consistently does the test measure whatever it does measure? This is the problem of reliability. No test can have validity unless it measures accurately and consistently—that is, unless it is reliable. Reliability refers to the extent to which the test is consistent in measuring whatever it does measure. Specifically, reliability refers to the extent to which an individual remains nearly the same in repeated measurements as indicated by a high reliability coefficient or by a low standard error of measurement. Reliability coefficients can be computed in various ways, depending upon the source of error being considered. The reliability coefficient shows the extent to which random errors of measurement influence scores on the test. The standard error of measurement enables us to employ the normal curve to estimate the limits within which a subject's true score can be expected to lie.

Different types of reliability coefficients are required for norm-referenced and criterion-referenced tests. Establishing reliability of the latter is more problematic, but two procedures that have been used for criterion-referenced tests were presented in this chapter.

// Key Concepts

agreement coefficient
equivalent-forms reliability
construct evidence for test validity
content evidence for test validity

criterion-related evidence for test
  validity
internal-consistency reliability
interrater reliability

reliability   standard error of measurement
Spearman-Brown formula   test-retest reliability
split-half reliability   validity

/// EXERCISES

1. Compare *validity* and *reliability* with respect to
   a. the meaning of each concept
   b. the relative importance of each concept
   c. the extent to which one depends on the other

2. Explain the statement: A measuring device may be reliable without being valid, but it cannot be valid without being reliable.

3. How would you propose to validate a new scholastic aptitude test that had been developed for use with high school seniors?

4. You have been asked to validate an instrument designed to measure a student's academic self-concept, that is, the way he sees himself as a student. How would you go about establishing the validity of this instrument?

5. Which of the three types of evidence for validity is indicated in each situation?
   a. The high school language proficiency test scores of college dropouts and college persisters are compared in order to determine whether the test data correlated with the subjects' college status.
   b. A new scholastic aptitude test is found to have a correlation of .93 with the SAT that has been used to predict college success.
   c. A new intelligence test has been developed. The author argues that the mental processes required by the test are congruent with the Z theory of intelligence. Furthermore, he shows that the average score on the test increases with each year of age.
   d. A teacher carefully examines a standardized achievement test to see if it covers the knowledge and skills that are emphasized in the class.
   e. The mean difference between the rankings of members of the Ku Klux Klan and members of the Americans for Democratic Action on the liberalism scale was found to be highly significant.
   f. A mathematics test is judged by a group of teachers to be an adequate and representative sample of the universe of test items.

6. Identify the type of procedure for estimating reliability that is illustrated in each of the following:
   a. The same test was given twice to a certain group. The correlation between the scores on the two administrations of the test was .90.

b. The group's scores on the odd items of a test were correlated with their scores on the even items of the same test: $r_{xx} = .95$.

c. Parallel forms of the test were administered after one month, and results of the two administrations were correlated: $r_{xx} = .85$.

d. The variance, the mean, and the number of items are used to estimate reliability.

7. How would you account for the differences in the reliability coefficients in question 6, assuming that the groups tested were the same?

8. How would you validate a reading readiness test?

9. What can one do to increase reliability when constructing a test?

10. Indicate the type of evidence that would be most important for validating the following types of tests:
a. a classroom spelling test
b. an instrument to measure achievement motivation
c. A measure designed to identify potential dropouts

11. Explain how a mathematics test could have high validity in one mathematics class and low validity in another mathematics class.

12. Criticize the following statement: The reliability of the intelligence test is .90. Therefore, one can assume that the test is really measuring intelligence.

13. Determine the standard error of measurement for a test with a standard deviation of 16 and a reliability coefficient of $r_{xx} = .84$. How would you interpret this standard error of measurement?

14. Select a standardized achievement test that you might use in a research study and obtain the necessary validity data on this test. (You may use Buros and the manual that accompanies the test you select.)

15. Check the test manual for the achievement test being used in your school. What type of reliability data is reported there?

16. The following data were obtained when two forms of a criterion-referenced test in mathematics were given to a group of elementary school children. There were 50 items on each form. In order to pass, a student had to get 80 percent correct on each form. Express the reliability of this test in terms of the agreement coefficient (p) and the kappa coefficient (κ).

Examinee	Form 1	Form 2
1	45	47
2	43	48
3	45	31
4	39	39
5	39	48
6	34	37
7	46	46
8	48	49
9	43	38
10	36	46
11	45	48
12	38	39
13	44	45
14	31	34
15	42	48

17. Criticize the following validation procedures:
    a. A high school English teacher developed a writing test for identifying talented high school students and administered the test to her senior English classes. On the basis of high scores students were permitted to enroll in an English class at the local university. At the end of the semester the teacher correlated the original test scores with the grades the students earned in the college English class. The teacher was surprised to find a negligible correlation. What was the problem?
    b. A school counselor developed a scale to measure need for academic achievement in elementary school children. The scale was administered to two classes of elementary school children, and the results were given to the teachers of these children. The teachers were asked to observe these children carefully for one semester, after which they were asked to rate the children on their need for achievement. The teachers' ratings were then correlated with the scores the children received on the scale. The correlation was quite high, so the counselor concluded that the scale had high validity for measuring need for achievement. Do you agree with the counselor's conclusion?

18. Assume that you wanted to investigate teacher "burnout." Suggest some indicators of this construct that you might use to measure the construct.

19. A true-false test was administered to ten students. A 1 indicates a correct answer; a 0 indicates an incorrect answer. The results are as follows:

Students	1	2	3	4	5	6	7	8	9	10	Total
A	1	1	1	1	1	1	1	1	0	0	8
B	1	1	1	1	0	1	0	1	0	0	6

Items

Students	1	2	3	4	Items 5	6	7	8	9	10	Total
C	1	1	1	1	1	0	0	0	0	0	5
D	1	1	1	0	0	0	0	1	1	0	5
E	1	1	1	1	1	1	1	1	0	0	8
F	1	1	1	1	1	1	1	1	1	1	10
G	1	1	1	1	1	1	1	1	1	0	9
H	1	1	1	0	0	0	0	0	0	0	3
I	1	1	1	1	0	0	0	0	0	0	4
J	1	1	1	1	0	1	1	1	1	1	9

    a. Calculate the split-half reliability coefficient of this test by dividing the test into odd- and even-item subtests.

    b. What is the reliability for the full-length test?

20. What type of reliability estimate would be most appropriate for the following measuring instruments?

    a. A multiple-choice achievement test will be used as the dependent variable in an experimental study.

    b. A researcher will study changes in attitude and will administer one form of an attitude scale as both the premeasure and the postmeasure.

    c. A researcher has two forms of an achievement test; she administered one form at the beginning of the study and the other at the conclusion of the study. She wants to determine the reliability of the test.

21. A 100-item test was split into two halves, and the split-half coefficient of correlation was found to be .60. Calculate the reliability coefficient for the full-length test.

/ ANSWERS

1. Validity refers to the extent to which an instrument measures what it is designed to measure. Reliability is the extent to which an instrument is consistent in measuring. Validity is considered a more important aspect than reliability because lack of validity implies lack of meaning. However, an instrument cannot be valid without first being reliable.

2. A measure may give consistent scores when made repeatedly on a given group of subjects, yet may bear no relationship to other accepted measures of the construct or not be able to predict behavior associated with the construct. Scores on a test with 0 reliability are entirely random and therefore cannot correlate with any criterion.

3. To determine the construct validity, one first must define what is meant by *aptitude*. If one wishes to measure general academic ability, then content validity could be determined by examining the test items for representativeness. Do they assess the basic academic skills of reading, spelling, math, and so on? Criterion-related validity would be assessed by the correlation coefficients between the test scores and senior-year GPA, freshman-college GPA, and other criteria. Correlation with other validated aptitude test scores could also be done

4. The items of the scale or questionnaire would need to cover aspects of the student behavior that would logically be a part of the construct, academic self-concept (for example, I intend to go to college). Criterion measures could be personal interviews with students or independent assessment by teachers. Assuming academic self-concept is related to achievement, self-concept scores could be correlated with GPA and/or achievement test scores.

5. a. criterion-related
   b. criterion-related
   c. construct-related
   d. content-related
   e. construct-related
   f. content-related

6. a. test-retest reliability
   b. split-half reliability
   c. equivalent-forms reliability
   d. rational equivalence (Kuder-Richardson formula 21)

7. Split-half reliabilities tend to be higher than test-retest reliabilities because subject variability due to maturation, increase in testing skill, and other random factors are less. Equivalent-forms reliability is lower than same-test reliability because (a) it is impossible to construct exactly equivalent forms and (b) there is an added source of variability when non-identical forms are used. The rational equivalence reliability will be depressed if the test is not homogeneous.

8. One would first identify which specific skills (for example, letter recognition, left-to-right orientation) comprise reading readiness and then determine if the test incorporated these skills in appropriate proportions. When subjects who have taken the test have begun their reading programs, one would determine how scores on the test and on subtests correlate with reading test scores, teachers' ratings, and other criteria.

9. Rewriting ambiguous items and clarifying instructions will increase reliability. Making a test longer by including additional items drawn from the same universe increases reliability, as does testing on a more heterogeneous group.

10. a. content
    b. construct
    c. criterion-related

11. A mathematics test that covered only computation would have little validity in a class that stressed concepts and reasoning. If content and emphasis of a different class match the content and emphasis of the test, the test will have high validity in that class.

12. A test can be reliable without measuring what it intends to measure. To determine validity, one needs to look at content, constructs, and relations with other measures of the same construct as well as relations with measures of behavior assumed to be correlated with the construct.

13. By the formula 8.5,

$$\sigma_M = \sigma_x\sqrt{1 - r_{xx}}$$
$$= 16\sqrt{1 - .84}$$
$$= (16)(.4)$$
$$= 6.4$$

one interprets the standard error of measurement as a standard deviation. Thus, one can say that there are two chances in three that the individual's true score will fall in the range of the actual score ±6.4 score points from the observed score.

14. Answers will vary.

15. Answers will vary.

16. A score of 40 represents mastery ($50 \times .80 = 40$).

		Form 1		
		Master	Nonmaster	
		(a)	(b)	
Form 2	Master	7	2	9
		(c)	(d)	
	Nonmaster	2	4	6
		9	6	15

$$p_o = \frac{7 + 4}{15} = \frac{11}{15} = .73 \text{ (73\% of the students were classified consistently)}$$

$$p_c = \frac{(9)(9) + (6)(6)}{15^2} = \frac{81 + 36}{225} = \frac{117}{225} = .52$$

$$\kappa = \frac{.73 - .52}{1 - .52} = \frac{.21}{.48} = .44$$

17. a. Selecting just high scorers restricted the variability. The restricted variability lowered the coefficient of correlation.

b. There was criterion contamination. Letting the teachers see the results of the original measurement of need for achievement contaminated their ratings of the children on need for achievement.

18. There are a number of possible indicators of teacher burnout. One could look at absenteeism from school, lower evaluations by supervisors, incidences of hostility toward students or supervisors, and incidences of challenging of school policies. One might also develop a scale to measure attitudes toward their work; from teachers' own responses to appropriate questions, one might infer the presence of burnout.

19.

Student	Odd	Even	Total
A	4	4	8
B	2	4	6
C	3	2	5
D	3	2	5
E	4	4	8
F	5	5	10
G	5	4	9
H	2	1	3
I	2	2	4
J	4	5	9

a. The split-half reliability coefficient is $r = .72$. (Calculate the coefficient of correlation, r, using the raw-score formula with N in the denominator.)

b. The reliability estimate for the full-length test is .84.

20. a. One would be interested in the internal consistency of this one form of the test. A split-half reliability coefficient would be appropriate.

b. With one form to be used as both a pre- and postmeasure, one would compute a coefficient of stability.

c. With two forms and two administrations, one would compute the coefficient of stability and equivalence.

21. $$r_{xx} = \frac{2(.60)}{1 + .60} = .75$$

V
Research
Methods

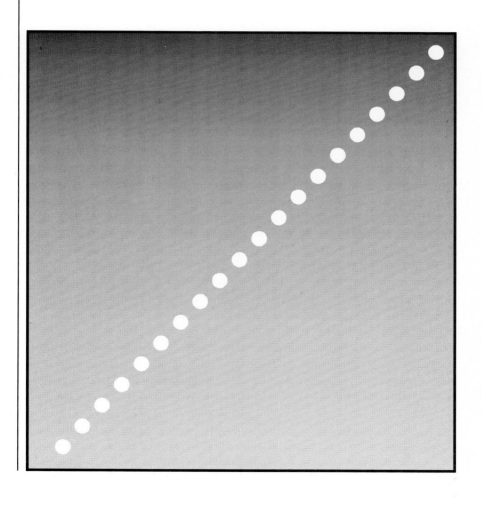

CHAPTER 9

Experimental Research in Education

INSTRUCTIONAL OBJECTIVES

After studying this chapter, the student will be able to
1. Describe characteristics of experimental research
2. Define internal and external validity
3. Identify threats to internal validity and strategies for avoiding or minimizing them
4. Identify internal-validity problems in research proposals and reports
5. Identify threats to external validity and strategies for avoiding them
6. Identify external-validity problems in research proposals and reports
7. Describe the difference between random sampling and random assignment and show how they are related to internal and external validity
8. Describe single-subject experimental research and its uses

An experiment is a scientific investigation in which the experimenter controls one or more independent variables and observes the effects of these manipulations on the dependent variable or variables. The researcher advances one or more hypotheses stating the nature of the expected relationship. The experiment is planned and carried out by the researcher to gather evidence relevant to the hypotheses. The experimenter deliberately and systematically introduces changes into natural phenomena and then observes the consequences of those changes. The hypotheses express expectations as to the findings that will result from the changes that are introduced. In conducting an experiment the researcher devotes great care to the manipulation and control of variables and to the observation and measurement of results. It is through such a research method that the researcher can obtain the most convincing evidence of the effect that one variable has on another.

Early scientists learned the value of observation in the study of our environment but soon realized that nature's complexity could not always be understood through simple observation of its many events. They found that events occurring in their "natural" state were often so complicated by irrelevant factors that the operation of the factor they wished to study was obscured. The difficulty was solved by controlling the conditions under which it occurred so that the irrelevant factors were eliminated. Then they could deliberately manipulate the independent variables of interest and measure the changes in the dependent variables that result from changes in the independent variables. In other words, they began to perform experiments.

Because the application of experimental methods was fruitful in the investigation of the physical world, these methods were applied to other fields. The nineteenth century saw these methods introduced into the biological sciences, and great advances were made in zoology, physiology, and medicine. Toward the end of the nineteenth century, scholars began to apply the same methods to psychological problems, thus beginning experimental psychology. In the 1890s the experimental method was first used to study an educational problem. Rice's investigation of spelling achievement in the schools marks the first attempt at educational field experimentation.[1] Thorndike and other early investigators extended the experimental method to education.[2]

In its simplest form an experiment has three characteristics: (1) an independent variable is manipulated, (2) all other variables except the independent variable are held constant, and (3) the effect of the manipulation of the independent variable on the dependent variable is observed. Thus, in an experiment the two variables of major interest are the independent variable and the dependent variable. The independent variable is manipulated

[1]Rice, J. M. (1987). The futility of the spelling grind. *Forum, 23*, 163–172, 409–419.
[2]Thorndike, E. L. (1924). Mental discipline in high school subjects. *Journal of Educational Psychology, 15*, 1–22, 83–98.

(changed) by the experimenter. The variable upon which the effects of the changes are observed is called the *dependent variable*, which is observed but not manipulated by the experimenter. The dependent variable is so named because its value is hypothesized to depend upon, and vary with, the value of the independent variable. For example, to examine the effect of different teaching methods upon achievement in reading, an investigator would manipulate method, the independent variable, by using different teaching methods in order to ascertain their effect upon achievement, the dependent variable.

/// CHARACTERISTICS OF EXPERIMENTAL RESEARCH

There are three essential ingredients with which the scientist is actively involved in the conduct of an experiment: control, manipulation, and observation.

// Control

Control is the essence of the experimental method. Without control it is impossible to evaluate unambiguously the effects of an independent variable. Let us examine briefly this concept of control in experimentation.

Basically the experimental method of science rests upon two assumptions regarding variables: (1) If two situations are equal in every respect except for a variable that is added to or deleted from one of the situations, any difference appearing between the two situations can be attributed to that variable. This statement is called the *law of the single independent variable*.[3] (2) If two situations are not equal but it can be demonstrated that none of the variables is significant in producing the phenomenon under investigation, or if significant variables are made equal, any difference occurring between the two situations after the introduction of a new variable to one of the systems can be attributed to the new variable. This statement is called the *law of the only significant variable*.

The purpose of control in an experiment is to arrange a situation in which the effect of variables can be investigated. The conditions underlying the law of the single variable are more likely to be fulfilled in the physical sciences than in education. Since educational research is concerned with human beings, there are always many variables present. To attempt to reduce educational problems to the operation of a single variable is not only unrealistic but perhaps even impossible. Fortunately such rigorous control is not absolutely essential because many aspects in which situations differ are irrelevant to the purpose of the study and thus can be ignored. It is sufficient

---

[3]Mill, J. S. (1846). *A System of Logic* (p. 224). New York: Harper & Brothers.

to apply the law of the single *significant* independent variable. For example, in a study of the different effects of two methods of teaching arithmetic, one would wish to have two groups of children who are identical in every respect except the way in which they are taught arithmetic. Because it is impossible to have two absolutely identical groups of children, the experimenter seeks to establish two groups that are as similar as possible in respect to those variables that are related to arithmetic achievement, such as reading ability, motivation, general intelligence, and the like. Other variables that are highly unlikely to be related to arithmetic, such as athletic ability, height, or color of hair, are ignored. Although the law of the single variable cannot be followed absolutely, the experiment endeavors to approximate it as closely as possible in all relevant variables. Therefore, in experimental studies in education we need procedures that permit us to compare groups on the basis of significant variables. A number of methods of control have been devised to make such comparisons possible.

Let us assume that we wish to test the hypothesis that children taught by the inductive method (Group A) show greater gains in learning scientific concepts than children taught by the deductive method (Group B). In other words, we wish to study the relationship between teaching method (independent variable) and the learning of scientific concepts (dependent variable). In order for us to draw a conclusion concerning the relationship of the independent variable and the dependent variable, we must control for the effects of any *extraneous* variables. An extraneous variable is a variable that is not related to the purpose of the study but may affect the dependent variable. *Control* is the term used to indicate an experimenter's procedures for eliminating the differential effects of all variables extraneous to the purpose of the study. If a variable is known to be unrelated to the dependent variable, then it could not influence the dependent variable and we do not need to control for its effects.

In the experiment mentioned above, intelligence is a factor that certainly affects the learning of scientific concepts; therefore, it would be considered an extraneous variable and must be controlled. Otherwise, if the children in Group A were more intelligent than those in Group B, the greater gains in learning by Group A could be attributed to intelligence and therefore we could not properly evaluate the effects of the teaching method on learning. In other words, intelligence has confounded the relationship between the variables in which we are interested. The term *confounding* refers to the "mixing" of the variables extraneous to the research problem with the independent variable(s) of the research study in such a way that their effects cannot be separated. It could not be clearly stated whether the relation found is (1) between the independent variable and the dependent variable of the study or (2) between the extraneous variables and the dependent variable or (3) a combination of (1) and (2). Confounding is eliminated by controlling for the effect of relevant extraneous variables.

Where there is no known relationship, as between the size of a ten-year-old's shoes and his or her ability to learn science concepts, there would be no need for the experimenter to control for the extraneous variable—shoe size, in this case.

Our first efforts must be directed toward controlling for any relevant preexisting differences between subjects used in an experiment. Only in this way can one be fairly confident that any postexperimental differences can be attributed to the conditions of the experiment rather than to preexisting subject differences. There are five basic procedures that are commonly used to increase equivalence among the groups that are to be exposed to the various experimental situations. These procedures for controlling intersubject differences are (1) random assignment, (2) randomized matching, (3) homogeneous selection, (4) analysis of covariance, and (5) use of subjects as their own controls.

// Controlling Intersubject Differences

/ Random Assignment

Let us consider the experimenter's task. There is an available supply of subjects who for experimentation must be divided into two groups that will be treated differently and then compared. In assigning subjects to groups for the experiment, the experimenter needs a system that operates independently of personal judgment and of the characteristics of the subjects themselves. For example, the known high scorers must not all be assigned to Group A and the low scorers to Group B. A system that satisfies these requirements is *random assignment*. Random assignment is the assignment of subjects to groups in such a way that, for any given placement, every member of the population has an equal probability of being assigned to any of the groups. The term *randomization* is often used as a synonym for random assignment.

Random assignment is not the same thing as random selection. Random selection (see Chapter 6) is the use of a chance procedure to select a sample from a population. Random assignment is the use of a chance procedure to assign subjects to treatments. For example, Ms. Brown has 1000 subjects available for an experiment but only has sufficient facilities to include 100 in her experiment. By randomly selecting the 100 to include in the experiment, she avoids creating systematic differences between the subjects in the experiment and the population from which they were selected. By randomly assigning 50 of the 100 subjects to Treatment A and 50 to Treatment B, she avoids systematic pretreatment differences between the two groups.

To obtain randomized groups, the experimenter could number all the available subjects and then draw from a table of random numbers the number needed for the two groups. A coin flip could then determine which of the two groups is to get Treatment A and which is to get Treatment B.

When subjects have been randomly assigned to groups, the groups can be considered *statistically equivalent*. Statistically equivalent does not mean that the groups are absolutely equal, but it does mean that any difference between the groups is a function of chance alone and not a function of experimenter bias, subjects' choices, or any other factor. A subject with high intelligence is as likely to be assigned to Treatment A as to Treatment B. The same is true for a subject with low intelligence. For the entire sample the effects of intelligence on the dependent variable will tend to balance or randomize out. In the same manner, subjects' differences in political viewpoints, temperament, motivation, and other characteristics will tend to be approximately equally distributed between the two groups.

When random assignment has been employed, any pretreatment differences between groups are a function of chance alone. When this is the case, inferential statistics can be employed to determine how likely it is that posttreatment differences are due to chance alone.

Note that not only known extraneous variables, but also other relevant extraneous variables unknown to or unimagined by the experimenter, can be expected to randomize out.

/ Randomized Matching

An alternative procedure for assigning subjects to groups is to match individual subjects on as many extraneous variables as one thinks might affect the dependent variable and then to use some random procedure to assign one member of each matched pair to Treatment A and the other to Treatment B. If the groups are adequately matched on these variables, then there is reasonable assurance that any postexperimental differences can be attributed to the experimental treatment.

Although matching is a method for providing partial control of intersubject differences, there are several difficulties one may encounter. The first of these is to determine what variable(s) to use for matching. Variables such as IQ, MA, socioeconomic status (SES), age, gender, reading score, or pretest score may be used. The variables on which subjects are matched must be substantially correlated to the dependent variable or else the matching is useless. As a general rule, we suggest that unless the variable correlates .50 or higher with the dependent variable, it should not be employed for the matching procedure because it would do little to increase the precision of the study. Ideally we would like to match on two or more variables that correlate well with the dependent variable and do *not* correlate significantly with each other. However, when we try to match on more than two variables, it becomes almost impossible to find subjects who are well matched on these several variables. Subjects are lost because no match can be found for them.

Another question that arises is how closely to match the subjects on the variable(s). Matching closely increases the precision of the method, but it also increases the number of subjects who cannot be matched. This, of course, reduces the sample size and introduces sampling bias into the study.

Procedures for Matching   The researcher must decide what matching procedure is feasible in each particular situation. The usual method is to use a person-to-person procedure, in which an effort is made to locate two persons from among the available subjects who score within the limits decided upon. For example, if the matching variable is IQ, then the researcher locates two subjects who are within, say, 5 points of each other on the IQ scale and then randomly assigns one subject to Treatment A and the matching subject to Treatment B. It would not be too difficult to match subjects on just the IQ variable. But if gender and social class were also relevant variables, then it would become extremely difficult to find pairs who match on all three variables. Those subjects for whom no match can be found are lost to the experimenter.

Another method of matching is to place all subjects in rank order on the basis of their scores on the matching variable. The first two subjects are selected from the rank order list (regardless of the actual difference in their scores) to constitute the first pair. One subject of this pair is then randomly assigned to Treatment A and the other to Treatment B. The next two subjects on the list are selected, and again one is randomly assigned to A and the other to B. This process is continued until all subjects have been assigned. It is somewhat simple to match according to this procedure, but it is less precise than the person-to-person method. Note that randomized matching requires that the subjects be matched first and then randomly assigned to treatments. A study where subjects who are already experiencing one treatment are matched with subjects who are already experiencing another treatment cannot be classified as an experimental study. Such studies (discussed in Chapter 10) where matching is present, but random assignment to groups is not present, can lead researchers to erroneous conclusions.

/ Homogeneous Selection

Another method that can be used to make groups comparable on an extraneous variable involves selecting samples that are as homogeneous as possible on that variable. If the experimenter suspects that age is a variable that might affect the dependent variable, only children of a particular age would be selected. By selecting only six-year-old children, for instance, the experimenter would control for the effects of age as an extraneous independent variable. Similarly, if intelligence is likely to be a variable affecting the dependent variable of the study, then subjects would be selected from children within a restricted range of IQ, say, 100–110. By this procedure the effects of IQ have been controlled. Then the experimenter randomly assigns individuals to groups from the resulting homogeneous population and can be confident that they were comparable on IQ. Beginning with a group that is homogeneous on the relevant variable eliminates the difficulty of trying to match subjects on that variable.

Although homogeneous selection is an effective way of controlling extraneous variables, it has the disadvantage of decreasing the extent to which the findings can be generalized to other situations. If a researcher investigates the effectiveness of a particular method with such a homogeneous sample, say, of children with average IQs, the results could not be generalized to children of other IQ ranges. The effectiveness of the method with children of low intelligence or very high intelligence would not be known, and the experiment would have to be repeated with subjects from different IQ strata.

As is the case with matching, a true experiment requires that the subjects be selected first and then assigned randomly to treatments.

/ Analysis of Covariance

Analysis of covariance (ANCOVA) is a statistical procedure that improves the precision of a research design by employing a preexisting variable that is correlated with the dependent variable.[4] For example, consider an experiment to study the effects of two methods of teaching reading. At the beginning of the semester a pretest is administered and half of the subjects are randomly assigned to Method A and half to Method B. The independent variable is the method of reading instruction, and the dependent variable is the reading posttest. The reading pretest is the *covariate*, the variable related to the dependent variable, which is used to add precision to the design.

Those subjects who are good readers will tend to score well on both the pretest and the posttest, and those who are poor readers will tend to score poorly on both tests; therefore, there will be a positive correlation between pretest and posttest scores. The ANCOVA technique removes the portion of each subject's posttest score that is in common with his or her pretest score.

Using this technique we are not considering a subject's posttest score per se. We are able to analyze the difference between posttest scores and what we would expect the posttest score to be, given the score on the pretest and the correlation between pretest and posttest.

By removing that portion of the dependent-variable score variance that is systematically associated with pretest variance, the precision of the experiment is improved. With part of the variance in the posttest scores that

---

[4]The computation of analysis of covariance is beyond the scope of this text. For an explanation of the process see Gene V. Glass and Kenneth D. Hopkins (1984), *Statistical Methods in Education and Psychology* (2d ed.; ch. 20), Englewood Cliffs, NJ: Prentice-Hall.

is not due to treatment removed, difference that is due to treatment stands out more clearly. The use of a covariate that is related to the dependent variable reduces the likelihood of Type II error.

Other measures besides pretest scores can be used as covariates. In our example, measures such as intelligence test scores or grade-point average could be used. To be useful, a covariate must be correlated with the dependent variable. In the example, baseball throw scores or shoe sizes would not be useful covariates, as they would be expected to have negligible correlation with the reading posttest.

/ Use of Subjects as Their Own Controls

Still another procedure involves assigning the same subjects to all experimental conditions and then obtaining measurements of the subjects, first under one experimental treatment and then under another. The experimental treatment generally consists of selected values of an independent variable. For instance, the same subjects might be required to learn two different lists of nonsense syllables, one list with high association value and the other with low association value. The difference in learning time between the two lists is found for each subject, and the average difference in learning time for all subjects then can be tested for significance.

This is an efficient method of control when feasible, but there are circumstances in which it cannot be used. In some types of studies exposure to one experimental condition would make it impossible to use the subjects for the other experimental condition. We cannot teach children how to divide by fractions one way and then erase their memory and teach it another way.

In the foregoing experiment, where one group of subjects was used to investigate the relative ease of learning high-association and low-association nonsense syllables, there could be a "learning to learn" effect, and thus whichever list appeared second would have an advantage over the first. Conversely, fatigue or interference effects might result in poorer performance on the second list. In either case we cannot separate the effect of the independent variable and the effect of order on the dependent variable. A useful strategy is to randomly divide the subjects into two groups: one group learning the high-association syllables first, the other learning the low-association syllables first. This would "balance out" the effects of learning to learn or fatigue. However, if learning high-association syllables first helps subjects to learn low-association syllables later, while the reverse is not true, this can confound the interpretation of the results.

// Controlling Situational Differences

In addition to intersubject differences it is also necessary to control any extraneous variables that might operate in the experimental situation itself. If situational variables are not controlled in an experiment, one cannot be sure whether it is the independent variable or these incidental differences operating in the groups that are producing the difference in the dependent variable.

For instance, let us assume that an experimenter is interested in the effectiveness of a film in producing changes in attitude toward some issue. One group of children is selected at random from a classroom and sent off to see the film, leaving a comparable group in the classroom. Unknowingly the experimenter may have set in motion a large number of forces. The children in the control group may be resentful or feel rejected or inferior to the others. Any of these factors could have an effect on the outcome of the study. The difference that the experimenter wants to attribute to the use of the film could really be due to one of these incidental features. In this case steps must be taken to ensure that the control subjects also see a film of some sort and that both groups, or neither of the groups, know that they are taking part in an experiment. This precaution is necessary in order to control what is known as the Hawthorne effect, which refers to the observation, first made at the Hawthorne plant of the Western Electric Company, that almost any change, any extra attention, any experimental manipulation, or even the absence of manipulation but the knowledge that an experiment is being done, is enough to cause subjects to change. In short, any type of attention may lead subjects to respond.

In an experiment to study the effect of a drug on the performance of a manipulative skill, all groups must think that they are taking the drug. Therefore, the experimenter must give every subject the same kind of substance as far as quantity, taste, and color are concerned. For some subjects this will be the drug under investigation and for the remainder, an inert chemical known as a *placebo*. Otherwise, just the knowledge that they had been given a drug might act by suggestion on the experimental subjects and lead them to be either extra cautious or quite reckless, and the experimenter would not know whether it was the effect of the drug or the subjects' attitude or both that produced the result.

There are three methods commonly used to control potentially contaminating situational variables. One can (1) hold them constant, (2) randomize them, or (3) manipulate them systematically and separately from the main independent variable.

Holding extraneous variables constant means that all subjects in the various groups are treated exactly alike except for their exposure to the independent variable. For instance, in a reading experiment it would be necessary to control for the size of the groups because size of group is known to be a factor affecting reading achievement. One must see that the experimental and control groups have the same number of subjects. The teacher variable must be controlled because teacher efficiency and enthusiasm are factors that may affect the outcome of any learning experiment. Thus, the same teacher should be used with two teaching methods that are to be compared.

In an experiment, the various assistants must follow the same procedures: use the same instructions, apparatus, and tests and try to assume the same attitudes with all groups. All groups should meet at the same time of day and in the same room. One would not want the experimental group to meet during the first period in the morning of a school day and the control group during the last period of the day. Environmental conditions—such as temperature, light intensity, humidity, furniture in the room, and the presence or absence of distracting noises—should be the same for all groups.

If conditions cannot be held constant, the experimenter must attempt to randomize or balance out certain situational variables. For instance, if it is not possible to have the same teacher for both treatments, an experimenter might randomly assign half of the Method A subjects and half of the Method B subjects to each teacher. The same could be done with other experimental conditions, such as apparatus. In this way situational variables are randomized; a variety of extraneous conditions is represented but is not allowed to affect the dependent variable systematically.

It is possible to control extraneous situational variables by manipulating them systematically. In many educational experiments it is necessary to use a sequence of experimental and control conditions in order to control progressive effects, like those of practice and fatigue. This is done by controlling the order in which experimental conditions are presented through a counterbalancing; half the subjects may receive an AB order and the other half a BA order. In this case an extraneous variable is being systematically manipulated. This procedure not only controls the potentially contaminating effect of order but can also provide an estimate of the size of the order effect by determining whether the average A and B values obtained in the two sequences are different.

It should be mentioned here that other types of variables, such as those associated with the subjects themselves, can be built into an experimental design and thus controlled. For example, if gender is to be controlled in an experiment and it is not possible to use any of the methods for controlling intersubject differences, then one could add gender as another independent variable with a two-way analysis of variance. This not only controls the extraneous variable but also yields information about the effect of this variable on the dependent variable, as well as its possible interaction with the other independent variables.

This method for controlling extraneous variables amounts to the same thing as adding more independent variables to the experiment. Although it increases the complexity of the study, it has the advantage of furnishing additional information about the effect of relevant variables on the dependent variable and their interaction with the main independent variables. The use of this method of control has been increasing since the introduction of electronic computers to handle the analysis of data in complex studies. Two-way analysis-of-variance designs and more-complex analysis-of-variance designs permit the simultaneous investigation of a number of variables considered singly and in interaction—the latter often being the most significant aspect of the study.

// Manipulation

The manipulation of a variable refers to a deliberate operation performed by the experimenter. In educational research and other behavioral sciences the manipulation of a variable takes a characteristic form in which the experimenter imposes a predetermined set of varied conditions on the subjects. The set of varied conditions is referred to as the *independent variable*, the *experimental variable*, or the *treatment variable*. The different conditions are designed to represent two or more values of the independent variable; these may be differences in degree or differences in kind. We may manipulate a single variable or a number of variables simultaneously.

// Observation

In experimentation we are interested in the effect of the manipulation of the independent variable on a response variable. Observations are made with respect to some characteristic of the behavior of the subjects employed in the research. These observations, which are quantitative in nature, if possible, are the dependent variable.

The dependent variable in educational research is often achievement of some type, such as learning. We are often interested in explaining or predicting achievement. Note that we cannot measure learning directly. We can only estimate learning through such measures as scores on a test. Therefore, strictly speaking, the dependent variable is scores or observations rather than achievement per se.

/// EXPERIMENTAL COMPARISON

For the simplest experiment two groups of subjects are required: the *experimental group* and the *control group*. The original definitions designated the experimental group as the one receiving a specific treatment, while the control group receives no treatment. In a pharmaceutical experiment the experimental group receives the drug, while the control group receives no treatment or a placebo. The use of a control group enables the researcher to discount many alternative explanations for the effect of treatment. For example, a fertilized field might yield a bumper crop because of benign weather or for other reasons. If equivalent adjacent unfertilized fields yield less, the effect of fertilizer on yield becomes credible.

It should be noted that the majority of educational experiments study the difference in the results of two or more treatments rather than the difference in the results of one particular treatment versus no treatment at all. For example, it would be pointless to compare the spelling achievement of an experimental group taught by Method A with a control group that had no spelling instruction at all. Instead, a comparison is made between groups receiving Method A and Method B treatment. Comparison of groups receiving two treatments provides the same control over alternative explanations as does comparison of treated and untreated groups. In order to simplify subsequent discussions, we will use the term *control group* to refer to either groups with no treatment or groups with alternative treatments. Comparisons are essential in scientific investigation. Comparing a group receiving treatment with either an equivalent group receiving no treatment or an equivalent group or groups receiving alternative treatment makes it possible to draw well-founded conclusions from the results.

The experimental and control groups must be equivalent in all variables that may affect the dependent variable; they differ only in exposure to the independent variable. After the experimenter has imposed the different conditions on the subjects, each subject is measured on the dependent variable.

Measurement is followed by evaluation. Is there a difference between the two groups? Is the effect of Treatment A different from that of Treatment B? This question implies and requires a comparison of the measures of the dependent variable in the one group with the measures of response in the other group. The comparison should tell the experimenter whether differences on the dependent variable are associated with differences on the independent variable as represented by the two conditions, A and B.

// Laboratory Experiments and Field Experiments

Experiments in education may be conducted in either a laboratory or in a field situation. The control of extraneous variables, which is so crucial to the experimental method, can usually be handled most adequately in the laboratory. In a laboratory experimenters can control the environment in such a way that the independent variables of interest can be isolated. They can thus be very specific in the operational definition of variables. For these reasons, laboratory experiments can be replicated with a high degree of precision.

Field experiments can be conducted in classrooms, playgrounds, interest-club meetings, or other natural settings. The experimenter controls the extraneous variables as much as possible while manipulating the independent variables, but in a field experiment control is inevitably less complete. However, field experiments have certain advantages. First, experimental variables can be much stronger in field experiments than in laboratory experiments. It is difficult to implement a treatment in a laboratory situation for more than a short period of time, whereas a field experiment can encompass daily sessions for an entire school year. Second, because field experiments are conducted in a more realistic setting, their results are more likely to provide solutions to the actual daily problems of educators.

Laboratory experiments are generally preferred for theoretical problems and field experiments for pragmatic problems. There are two general types of experimentation conducted under classroom conditions: (1) the *methods study*, in which two or more ways of doing something are compared in an unbiased fashion, and (2) *fundamental research*, the purpose of which is to derive general principles applicable beyond the immediate situation. Both types of classroom research are greatly needed.

/// EXPERIMENTAL DESIGN

Experimental design refers to the conceptual framework within which the experiment is conducted. An experimental design serves two functions: (1) It establishes the conditions for the comparisons required by the hypotheses of the experiment, and (2) it enables the experimenter through statistical analysis of the data to make a meaningful interpretation of the results of the study. If a design is to accomplish these functions, the experimenter, when selecting it, must keep in mind certain general criteria. Detailed descriptions of the various types of experimental design follow the discussion of these general criteria.

The most important criterion is that the *design be appropriate* for testing the particular hypotheses of the study. The mark of a sophisticated experiment is neither complexity nor simplicity but rather appropriateness. A design that will do the job it is supposed to do is the right design. Thus, the first task for the experimenter is to select the design that best arranges the experimental conditions to meet the needs of the particular experimental problem.

If the research hypothesis is an interaction hypothesis, then it can be tested adequately only by means of a factorial type of design. Unfortunately, one often finds that educational researchers have tried to test an interaction hypothesis by performing two or more separate experiments. The latter type of design would be incapable of testing the hypothesis. Let us assume that a researcher is interested in the effects of computer-assisted instruction on the learning of basic scientific concepts in elementary school science, believing that there may be a differential effect of this method based on class size and the intelligence level of the students. This problem calls for a factorial type of design. The researcher could not answer the question by performing two or three separate experiments, each with a single independent variable.

Another example of an inadequate design is the attempt to use a matched-subjects design in cases when it is impossible for the experimenter to match the subjects on all the relevant extraneous variables. Even though matching may be successful on one or two variables, it cannot be assumed that the groups are equivalent on all relevant variables. A randomized-subjects design would be superior in these circumstances.

A second criterion is that the design must provide *adequate control* so that the effects of the independent variable can be evaluated as unambiguously as possible. Unless the design controls extraneous variables, one can never be confident of the relationship between the variables of the study. As we have mentioned earlier, *randomization* is the single best way to achieve the necessary control. Therefore, the best advice is to select a design that utilizes randomization in as many aspects as possible.

// Validity of Research Designs

A very significant contribution to the evaluation of research designs has been made by Campbell and Stanley, who suggest that there are two general criteria of research designs: *internal validity* and *external validity*.[5]

/ Internal Validity

Internal validity is concerned with such questions as: Did the experimental treatment really bring about a change in the dependent variable? and Did the independent variable really make a difference? These questions of internal validity cannot be answered positively by the experimenter unless the design provides adequate control of extraneous variables. That is, if the design provides control of variables, one is able to eliminate alternative explanations of the observed outcome and interpret it as showing some kind of intrinsic relationship between variables. Internal validity is essentially a problem of control. The design of appropriate controls is a matter of finding ways to eliminate extraneous variables—that is, variables that could lead to alternative interpretations. Anything that contributes to the control of a design contributes to its internal validity.

Campbell and Stanley have identified eight extraneous variables that frequently represent threats to the internal validity of a research design. These variables must be controlled or else they might very well produce an effect that could be mistaken for the effect of the experimental treatment.

---

[5]Campbell, D. T., and J. C. Stanley (1966). *Experimental and Quasi-experimental Designs for Research* (p. 5). Skokie, IL: Rand McNally. The authors are indebted to the work of Campbell and Stanley for the terminology and designs used in this section of the chapter.

1. *History.* Specific events or conditions, other than the experimental treatment, may occur between the first and second measurements of the subjects to produce changes in the dependent variable. For example, during an experiment to measure the effectiveness of a unit on how the stock market works, the stock market drops precipitously and the newspapers and television devote considerable attention to the stock market. The investigator cannot determine whether the students' greater knowledge is due to the unit or to the students' exposure to the media coverage. The effects of the unit and of the students' exposure to the media coverage are confounded, mixed inextricably, and it is impossible to know how much of the students' learning is due to the unit and how much is due to history as an internal-validity problem.

2. *Maturation.* Processes that operate within the subjects simply as a function of the passage of time may produce effects that could mistakenly be attributed to the experimental variable. Subjects may perform differently on the dependent-variable measure simply because they are older, hungrier, more fatigued, or less motivated than they were at the time of the first measurements. For example, it can be difficult to assess the effects of treatments for articulation problems among preschoolers because young children naturally outgrow such problems.

3. *Pretesting.* Exposure to a pretest may affect the subjects' performance on a second test, regardless of the experimental treatment. Subjects may learn subject matter from a pretest. They may do better on a posttest because they have become familiar with the format of the tests and the testing environment, have developed a strategy for doing well on the tests, or are less anxious about the test the second time around. Such practice effects can cause higher posttest scores when the independent variable makes no difference at all. With attitude and personality inventories, taking a pretest may prompt subjects to subsequently think about the questions and issues raised in the pretest and to give different responses on the posttest.

4. *Measuring instruments.* Changes in the measuring instruments, in the scorers, or in the observers used may produce changes in the obtained measures. If the posttest is more difficult or if different observers are used for pre- and post-measures, these factors may account for observed differences in the two scores. If observers recording a dependent variable know which subjects have received treatment and which have not, they may unconsciously overestimate the performance of the treatment group and underestimate it for the control group.

5. *Statistical regression.* If groups are selected on the basis of extreme scores, statistical regression may operate to produce an effect that could be mistakenly interpreted as an experimental effect. This regression effect refers to the tendency for extreme scores to regress, or move toward, the common mean on subsequent measures. For example, let us assume that the lowest fourth of the scorers on an English proficiency test are selected for a special

experimental program in English. The mean of this group will tend to move toward the mean of the population on a second test whether or not an experimental treatment is applied. Similarly, high initial means would tend to go down toward the population mean on a second testing.

Let us illustrate regression with a scattergram (Figure 9.1) that shows the pattern we would get if the correlation of fourth-grade reading test scores and fifth-grade reading test scores is $r = .7$. Each dot represents both z-scores for an individual. If we select individuals with a particular z-score (X) on the fourth-grade reading test and look at their scores on the fifth-grade reading test, we find that few have the same z-score on both tests. If the fourth-grade z-score for this subgroup is above the mean, we find that

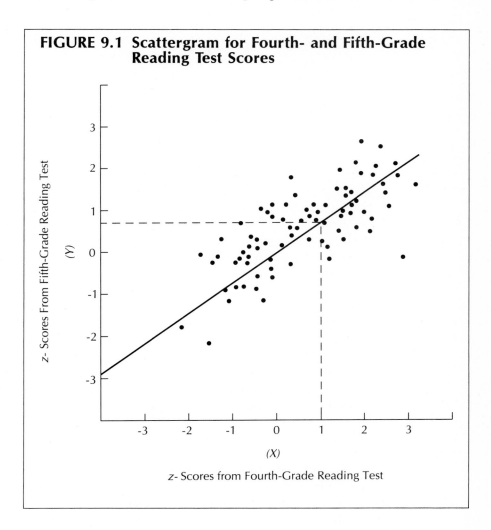

FIGURE 9.1 Scattergram for Fourth- and Fifth-Grade Reading Test Scores

a minority of the students score further above the mean in fifth grade than they did in fourth grade, but the majority of them have z-scores closer to the mean and some even fall below the mean.

For the subgroup with a z-score one standard deviation above the mean on X, the mean on Y is $+.7$; for the subgroup with z-scores two standard deviations below the mean on X, the mean on Y is -1.4; the group with a z-score of $+2$ on X has a mean z-score of $+1.4$ on Y, and so forth. The slanted line on the scattergram connects these means on Y for various scores on X. Note that for each group with scores above the mean on the fourth-grade reading test, the mean score on Y is *lower* on the fifth-grade reading test. For each group with scores below the mean on the fourth-grade reading test, the mean score is *higher* on the fifth-grade reading test. In other words, the average scores for each group move closer to the mean—which is the result of regression.

Regression inevitably occurs when the correlation between two variables is less than perfect. Since practically none of the variables of interest in education are perfectly correlated, we must always be aware of the effect of regression in the design of our experiments. An aspect of regression is captured in the old adages "When you are at the bottom, you have nowhere to go but up" and "When you are on top, you have nowhere to go but down."

For example, a school establishes a remedial mathematics program and assigns those middle school students who score 2 years or more below grade level on a standardized mathematics test to this program. After a semester the students are given an equivalent form of the standardized test. The majority of them score nearer their grade equivalent and appear to have benefited from the remedial program. Before attributing the gains to the program, we must remember that when you are at the bottom you have nowhere to go but up. The lowest scorers on the pretest include those whose scores were depressed because of temporary ill health, emotional problems, inattention, or other problems. It will also include those whose scores were depressed by measurement error. The majority of these cases would be expected to score better in a subsequent test.

Conversely, if those who score highest on any measure are assigned to a special treatment, such as an enrichment program, a posttreatment measure may make it appear that the treatment had a deleterious effect. Those on top have nowhere to go but down.

6. *Differential selection of subjects.* There may be important differences between the groups even before the application of the experimental treatment. For example, if the experimental group in a learning experiment is more intelligent than the control group, the former may perform better on the dependent-variable measure even if this group does not receive an experimental treatment.

7. *Experimental mortality attrition.* There may be differential loss of respondents from the comparison groups. If a particular type of subject drops out of one group during the course of the experiment, this differential loss may affect the outcome of the study. If, for example, several of the lowest scorers on a pretest gradually drop out of the experimental group, this group will have a higher mean performance on the final measure, not because of the experimental treatment but because the low-scoring subjects are absent when the posttest is administered.

For example, a church counselor wanted to compare the effectiveness of two different marital-counseling procedures. She administered a pretreatment measure of marital adjustment to couples who had enrolled in her program, then randomly assigned them to Procedure A and Procedure B. With Procedure A, which involved considerable soul-searching and confrontation, only 11 of 20 couples persisted in the program and were available for the posttreatment measure. With Procedure B, which was relaxed and less demanding, 18 of 20 couples persisted and were available for the posttreatment measure. The posttreatment mean of Procedure A was higher than the mean of the Procedure B group. This may be evidence that Procedure A is more effective, but it may also be evidence that only those couples who were highly motivated to improve their marriage persisted in the program, while the posttreatment scores for Procedure B included less-motivated couples.

8. *Selection-maturation interaction.* This type of interaction may occur in a quasi-experimental design where the experimental and control groups are not randomly selected but instead are preexisting intact groups, such as classrooms. Even though a pretest may show that the groups are equivalent, the experimental group may happen to have a higher rate of maturation than the control group and it is the increased rate of maturation that accounts for the observed effect. More-rapidly-maturing students are "selected" into the experimental group, and it is the selection-maturation interaction that may be mistaken for the effect of the experimental variable.

For example, a group who elected to take an honors freshman English class might show more vocabulary growth than a group in a regular freshman English class because their vocabulary growth was at a higher rate both before and during their freshman year. A comparison of pretest and posttest differences of the honors and the regular classes might lead one to conclude erroneously that the independent variable was responsible for a difference in gain that is due only to selection-maturation interaction. This problem also frequently arises when volunteers are compared with nonvolunteers. The volunteers may be more motivated to make gains on the dependent variable than are the nonvolunteers, and this difference in gains may be mistakenly attributed to the independent variable—as can happen even when the groups are equivalent on a pretest.

All the methods of control discussed earlier in this chapter are designed to control those extraneous variables that pose a threat to the internal validity of a design.

/ External Validity

External validity refers to the generalizability or representativeness of the findings. The experimenter asks the question To what populations, settings, experimental variables, and measurement variables can these findings be generalized?

Any single study is necessarily performed on a particular group of subjects, with selected measuring instruments and under conditions that are in some respects unique. Yet the researcher wants the results of the study to furnish information about a larger realm of subjects, conditions, and operations than were actually investigated. In order to make generalizations from the observed to the unobserved, we need to assess how well the sample of events actually studied represents the larger population to which results are to be generalized. To the extent that the results of an experiment can be generalized to different subjects, settings, and measuring instruments, the experiment possesses external validity.

Smith and Glass have identified three types of external validity: *population external validity*, *ecological external validity*, and *external validity of operations*.[6]

Population external validity is concerned with the identification of the population to which the results of an experiment are generalizable. It asks the question What population of subjects can be expected to behave in the same way as did the subjects in the sample? Ecological validity is concerned with generalizing experimental effects to other environmental conditions. It asks the question In what settings can the same results be expected? External validity of operations is concerned with how well the operational definitions and the experimental procedures represent the constructs of interest: Would the same relationships be seen if a different researcher were investigating the same question with different operations?

Population Validity   It is the researcher's hope that findings can be generalized from the experimental group of subjects to a much larger population, as yet unstudied. For example, let us assume that a researcher, having discovered an effective new method of teaching reading to a sample of first-graders, would like to conclude that this method is superior for other groups of first-graders, perhaps all first-graders in the United States. In order to be able to make valid inferences from the experimental results to larger pop-

---

[6]Smith, M. L., and G. V. Glass (1987). *Research and Evaluation in Education and the Social Sciences* (pp. 143–153). Englewood Cliffs, NJ: Prentice-Hall.

ulations, the researcher must correctly identify the populations to which the results would be generalizable. Relevant to this problem is Kempthorne's distinction between the *experimentally accessible population* and the *target population*, referred to in Chapter 6.[7] The experimentally accessible population refers to the population of subjects that is accessible or available to the researcher for his study. The target population is the total group of subjects to whom the researcher wants to apply the conclusions from the findings. In the foregoing example, the experimentally accessible population would likely be all the first-graders in the local school district. The target population would be all first-grade students in the United States. The researcher's generalizations would occur in two stages: (1) from the sample to the experimentally accessible population and (2) from the accessible population to the target population.

If the researcher has randomly selected the sample from the experimentally accessible population (all first-graders in the school district), then the findings can be generalized to this larger group with no difficulty. Inferential statistics indicate the likelihood that what was true of the sample is also true of the population from which it was drawn.

In the second stage, the researcher wants to generalize from the accessible to the target population (all first-graders in the United States). This type of generalizing cannot be made with the same degree of confidence as the former type. To make such an inference requires a thorough knowledge of the characteristics of both populations. The more nearly similar the accessible and target populations are, the more confidence one has in generalizing from the one to the other. Generalizing from the accessible population to the target population cannot be done statistically. It is a matter of judgment. The researcher must describe the accessible population as thoroughly as possible and point out any ways this population differs from the target population. Then the researcher and the readers of the research report can make intelligent judgments about how likely the results are to generalize to the target population or to other populations.

Another aspect of population external validity is the possibility of *interaction of subject characteristics and treatment*. When two experimentally accessible populations are not representative of the same target population, seemingly similar studies can lead to entirely different results. That is, a relationship between the treatment and the dependent variable may occur with one group that would not occur in another group with different characteristics. Thus, it would not be possible to generalize the findings from one group to another. Counseling Method A may produce better results than Method B in inner-city schools, while Method B is superior in affluent

---

[7]Kempthorne, O. (1961). The design and analysis of experiments with some reference to educational research. In R. O. Collier, Jr., and S. M. Elam (eds.). *Research Design and Analysis: Second Annual Phi Delta Kappa Symposium on Educational Research* (pp. 97–126). Bloomington, IN: Phi Delta Kappa.

suburban schools. The best method for teaching quantitative reasoning among second-graders may be the worst method among eighth-graders. As the old saying goes, "One man's meat is another man's poison." Again, a thorough description of the accessible population will assist other educators in judging whether a particular treatment is likely to be "meat or poison" for their populations of interest.

Researchers can often strengthen the external validity of a study by dividing subjects on relevant characteristics and employing a factorial design (see Chapter 6). For example, with an accessible middle school population for a study comparing the effectiveness of two teaching methods one could do a $2 \times 3 \times 2$ (methods by grade levels by gender) factorial design. The results would not only enable one to compare the effectiveness of the two methods but to see how consistent the results were among sixth-, seventh-, and eighth-graders, as well as between boys and girls.

Ecological Validity　Experimenters must also be concerned with ecological external validity; that is, they want to be able to say that the same findings will be obtained in other settings. To have ecological validity, a design must provide assurance that the experimental effect is independent of the particular experimental environment.

Obviously the first requirement for ecological validity is that the experimenter furnish a complete description of the experimental *setting* involved in the study. Only then could a reader judge to what extent the results can be generalized to other settings. For example, would results found in a spacious, well-equipped classroom generalize to a crowded, ill-equipped classroom? Here again, the researcher should give a sufficient description of the setting to enable readers to make a reasonable judgment concerning the generalizing of the results. Experiments are often done in settings where variables such as lighting, noise, and other distractions can be tightly controlled. Such control is desirable for enhancing internal validity. However, to the extent that such control makes the setting unrepresentative of the subjects' natural environment, the external validity of the experiment is lessened. It may be desirable to first try a treatment in a setting that has sufficient control to yield high internal validity and, if the treatment works there, try it again in a more natural setting.

There may be a *reactive effect* due to the experimental arrangements. Subjects' knowledge that they are participating in an experiment may alter their responses to the treatment. The presence of observers of equipment during an experiment may so alter the normal responses of subjects participating in the experiment that one could not generalize about the effect of the experimental variable upon persons exposed to it in a nonexperimental setting.

When subjects are aware that they are part of an experiment, they often alter their behavior to be "good subjects" rather than display their typical behavior.

A special case of the reactive effect as an external validity problem is the *Hawthorne effect,* named for the productivity studies conducted at Western Electric's Hawthorne plant in Cicero, Illinois. First, the investigators' hypothesis that increasing lighting in the plant would increase productivity appeared to be supported. However, subsequent investigation revealed that any change, including lowered lighting, also increased productivity. The investigators concluded that the workers' productivity had increased simply because they knew they were in a study and were receiving special attention.

A new instructional method may appear to be more successful than an old one, when, in fact, they are equally effective because teachers and students in the new program may feel they are special and develop enthusiasm for what they are doing, while those in the control group feel left out. On the other hand, the new method may appear less effective than the old one because teachers and students are using unfamiliar materials and procedures and haven't yet learned to employ them effectively by the time the dependent variable measure is taken. For example, when Schoen[8] summarized the outcomes of prior research comparing the results of individualized versus group instruction in elementary school mathematics, he found 17 studies with statistically significant results favoring group instruction, 11 that retained the null hypothesis, and only eight with statistically significant differences favoring individualized instruction. Most of the investigators had hypothesized that individualized instruction would be more effective. This may be evidence that for most populations group instruction is more effective. However, it is also possible that students with group instruction did better because they and their teachers already knew how to cope with group instruction, whereas with individualized instruction they had to learn a new way of proceeding, as well as the content of the arithmetic unit.

Certain interaction effects may threaten the generalizability of experimental findings. For instance, a pretest may increase or decrease the experimental subjects' sensitivity or responsiveness to the experimental variable and thus make the results that are obtained for this pretested population unrepresentative of the effects of the experimental variable for the unpretested population from which the experimental subjects are selected. In this case one could generalize to pretested groups but not to unpretested ones.

External Validity of Operations   Individual investigators conduct research with specific operational definitions of the independent and dependent variables and specific procedures. The external-validity-of-operations question asks if similar results would be expected from different investigators and with different operational definitions and/or different procedures.

---

[8]Schoen, H. L. (1976). Self-paced mathematics instruction: How effective has it been? *The Arithmetic Teacher, 23,* 90–96.

Experimenter effect can be an external-validity problem. Those conducting an experiment are often very committed to what they are doing and enthused about it. Subjects may be caught up in this enthusiasm and perform better than they would under normal circumstances. Sometimes, without thinking about it, experimenters will do more, provide more help, than is specified by the operational definition of the treatment. Also, an experimenter's expectation of results can be subtly, even unconsciously, communicated to subjects. Because of what is expected of them, experimental-group subjects may do better and control-group subjects may do less well than they would in normal circumstances.

Another aspect of external validity is the *operational definitions of the independent and dependent variables.* In some experiments anxiety has been induced by electric shock, in others by verbal instructions to the subjects. How much can findings from a study with the one definition generalize to another? Is frustration produced by barring children from desirable toys the same as frustration produced by giving them unsolvable problems?

If an objective test is used to measure the dependent variable, can the experimenter say that the same effect would be observed if an essay test were used as the measuring instrument? How well do scores on the Torrance Test of Creative Thinking represent the construct of creativity as an English or art teacher would define it?

The reader of a research report assesses this aspect by first asking how explicitly the independent and dependent variables have been defined. For all practical purposes, reports with vague definitions are worthless. Next, the reader must assess the reliability and validity of these definitions and make a judgment concerning how well the operational definitions fit the definitions of the constructs that have meaning for him or her.

Another potential external-validity problem is *pretest sensitization.* The administration of a pretest may alert, or sensitize, subjects to respond to treatment in a different way than they would if they had not been pretested. For example, a group of seventh-graders is given a questionnaire concerning their dietary habits and randomly divided into experimental and control groups. The experimental group is exposed to a series of film presentations concerning good eating habits, while the control group see a series of health films unrelated to eating habits (placebo). The dependent variable is derived by observing the children's food selections in an actual free-choice situation. If the experimental group shows a significantly greater preference for healthful foods, the investigator would like to conclude that the films are effective. Before reaching a conclusion, the investigator must consider the possibility that the pretest caused the students to think about their eating habits and "set them up" to respond to the films. The same effect might not have been observed in an unpretested group. Later we will discuss ways of isolating or avoiding pretest-treatment interaction (including not pretesting and trusting randomization to yield groups that would have been approximately equal on a pretest if one had been given). Note that pretest sensitization differs from testing as a threat to internal validity. The latter refers to testing per se making a difference on the dependent variable. The former means the pretests and treatments in combination produce an effect that treatment alone might not produce.

Although internal validity is the *sine qua non*, the experimenter wants to select a design that is strong in both internal and external validity. However, in some cases obtaining one type of validity tends to threaten the other types. For instance, as we arrange for more rigorous control in an educational experiment, we may increase its artificiality and cut down on the applicability of the findings to an actual classroom setting. In practice we try to reach a compromise between internal and external validity, which amounts to choosing a design that provides sufficient control to make the results interpretable, while preserving some realism, so that the findings will generalize to the intended settings.

/// CLASSIFICATION OF EXPERIMENTAL DESIGNS

In the discussion of experimental designs that follows, designs are classified as *preexperimental, true experimental,* or *quasi-experimental,* depending upon the degree of control provided. Comments are made about the internal and external validity of the designs as they are presented. Before we begin the discussion of the experimental designs, it is necessary to introduce the reader to the terms and symbols that will be used.

1. X represents the independent variable, which is manipulated by the experimenter; it will also be referred to as the experimental variable or the treatment.
2. Y represents the measure of the dependent variable. Y_1 represents the dependent variable *before* the manipulation of the independent variable X; it is usually a pretest of some type administered before the experimental treatment. Y_2 represents the dependent variable *after* the manipulation of the independent variable X; it is usually a posttest administered to subjects after the experimental treatment.
3. S represents the subject or respondent used in the experiment; the plural is Ss.
4. E group refers to the experimental group: the group that is given the independent-variable treatment.
5. C group refers to the control group: the group that does not receive the experimental treatment.
6. R indicates random assignment of subjects to the experimental groups and the random assignment of treatments to the groups.

7. M_r indicates that the subjects are matched and then members of each pair are assigned to the comparison groups at random.

In the paradigms for the various designs, the Xs and Ys across a given row are applied to the same persons. The left-to-right dimension indicates the temporal order, and the Xs and Ys vertical to one another are given simultaneously. A dash (—) indicates that the control group does *not* receive the X treatment.

// Preexperimental Designs

This section presents two designs that have been classified as preexperimental because they provide little or no control of extraneous variables. Unfortunately one finds that these designs are still being used in educational research. It will be helpful to begin our discussion with these poor designs because they illustrate quite well the way that extraneous variables may operate to jeopardize the internal validity of a design. If readers become aware of these sources of weakness in a design, they should be able to avoid them.

/ Design 1. One-Group Pretest-Posttest Design

The one-group design usually involves three steps: (1) administering a pretest measuring the dependent variable, (2) applying the experimental treatment X to the subjects, and (3) administering a posttest, again measuring the dependent variable. Differences attributed to application of the experimental treatment are then determined by comparing the pretest and posttest scores.

DESIGN 1 One-Group Pretest-Posttest Design

Pretest	Independent Variable	Posttest
Y_1	X	Y_2

To illustrate the use of this design, let us assume that an elementary teacher wants to evaluate the effectiveness of a new technique for teaching fourth-grade social studies. At the beginning of the school year the students are given a standardized test that appears to be a good measure of the achievement of the objectives of fourth-grade social studies. The teacher then introduces the new teaching technique and at the end of the year administers the standardized test a second time, comparing scores from the first and second administrations of the test in order to determine what difference the exposure to the new teaching method, X, has made.

Since Design 1 involves only one group and one teacher, it would seem to control intersubject differences and situation variables. The control is only superficial however.

The major limitation of the one-group design is that, because no control group is used, the experimenter cannot assume that the change between the pretest and posttest is brought about by the experimental treatment. There is always the possibility that some extraneous variables account for all or part of the change. Thus, this design is lacking in internal validity.

What are some of the extraneous variables that could operate to produce the change noted between the pretest and posttest scores? Two extraneous variables that are not controlled in this design are *history* and *maturation*. History as a source of extraneous variance refers to the specific events that can occur between the pretest and the posttest, other than the experimental treatment. In the social studies example widespread community interest in an election, increased emphasis on social studies in the school, or the introduction of a particularly effective teacher could increase student achievement in this area. An epidemic causing increased absences could decrease achievement. Maturation refers to changes in the subjects themselves that occur with the passage of time. Between pretest and posttest, children are growing mentally and physically, and they may have learning experiences that could affect the dependent variable. History and maturation become increasingly influential sources of extraneous variance when the time interval between Y_1 and Y_2 is long.

Another shortcoming of Design 1 is that it affords no way of assessing the effect of the pretest itself. We know that there is a practice effect when subjects take a test a second time or even take an alternate form of the test. That is, subjects do better the second time even without any instruction or discussion during the interval. This is true not only for achievement and intelligence tests but also for personality tests. In the case of personality tests a trend toward better adjustment is generally observed.

This test-retest gain is an aspect of the larger problem of the *reactivity* of measuring instruments. Reactivity refers to the fact that there is often a reaction between the subject and the pretest measure, and it is this reaction rather than the manipulation of X that produces the change in the Y_2 measure. Measures that cause the subject to react are called *reactive measures*. For example, in a study of attitude change, the measurement of the attitude itself may function as a stimulus; that is, the subject may react to the content of the measurement scale, and it is this reaction that brings about the observed change in attitudes, even without any experimental treatment. This effect is most obvious when the pretest has novel or controversial content or when it has a particular motivating effect on the subjects.

Design 1 has little to recommend it. Without a control group to make a comparison possible, the results obtained in a one-group design are basically uninterpretable.

/ Design 2. Static Group Comparison

Design 2 utilizes two or more groups, only one of which is exposed to the experimental treatment. The groups are assumed to be equivalent in all relevant aspects and to differ only in their exposure to X. The dependent-variable measures for the groups are compared to determine the effect of the X treatment.

This design has been used in much of the methods research in education. The achievement of students taught by a new method is compared with that of a similar class taught by the old method.

Design 2 has a control group or groups, which permits the comparison that is required for scientific respectability. However, there is a basic flaw in this design. Since neither randomization nor even matching is used to assign subjects to the experimental and control groups, we cannot assume that the groups are equivalent prior to the experimental treatment. They may differ on certain relevant variables, and it may be these differences rather than X that are responsible for the observed change. Because we cannot be sure that the groups are equal in respect to all factors that may influence the dependent variable, this design is considered to be lacking in the necessary control and must be classified as preexperimental.

DESIGN 2 Static Group Comparison

Group	Independent Variable	Posttest
E	X	Y_2
C	—	Y_2

// True Experimental Designs

The designs in this category are the most highly recommended designs for experimentation in education because of the control that they provide.

/ Design 3. Randomized Subjects, Posttest-Only Control Group Design

Design 3 is one of the simplest yet one of the most powerful of all experimental designs. It requires two randomly assigned groups of subjects, each assigned to a different condition. No pretest is used; the randomization controls for all possible extraneous variables and assures that any initial differences between the groups are attributable only to chance and therefore will follow the laws of probability.

After the subjects are assigned to groups, only the experimental group is exposed to the experimental treatment. In all other respects the two groups are treated alike. Members of both groups are then measured on the dependent variable Y_2. Scores are compared to determine the effect of X. If the obtained means of the two groups are significantly different (that is, more different than would be expected on the basis of chance alone), the experimenter can be reasonably confident that the experimental conditions are responsible for the observed result.

The main advantage of Design 3 is randomization, which assures statistical equivalence of the groups prior to the introduction of the independent variable. Recall that as the number of subjects is increased, the likelihood that randomization will produce equivalent groups is increased. Design 3 controls for the main effects of history, maturation, and pretesting; because no pretest is used, there can be no interaction effect of pretest and X. This design is especially recommended for situations in which pretest reactivity is likely to occur. It is also useful in studies in which a pretest is either not available or not appropriate—as, for example, in studies with kindergarten or primary grades, where it is impossible to administer a pretest because the learning is not yet manifest. Another advantage of this design is that it can be extended to include more than two groups if necessary.

DESIGN 3 Randomized Subjects, Posttest-Only Control Group Design

	Group	Independent Variable	Posttest
(R)	E	X	Y_2
(R)	C	—	Y_2

Design 3 does not permit the investigator to assess change. If such an assessment is desired, then a design (such as Design 5) that utilizes both a pretest and a posttest should be used.

/ Design 4. Randomized Matched Subjects, Posttest-Only Control Group Design

This design is similar to Design 3, except that it uses a matching technique, rather than random assignment, to obtain equivalent groups. Subjects are matched on one or more variables that can be measured conveniently, such as IQ or reading score. Of course the matching variables used are those that presumably have a significant correlation with the dependent variable. Although a pretest is not included in Design 4, if pretest scores on the dependent variable are available, they could be used very effectively for the matching procedure. The measures are paired so that opposite members' scores are as close together as possible; one member of each pair is randomly assigned to one treatment, and the other, to the second treatment. The flip of a coin can be used to achieve this random assignment.

DESIGN 4 Randomized Matched Subjects, Posttest-Only Control Group Design

(M_r)	Group	Independent Variable	Posttest
	E	X	Y_2
	C	—	Y_2

Matching is most useful in studies where small samples are to be used and where Design 3 is not appropriate. Design 3 depends completely upon random assignment to obtain equivalent groups. With small samples the influence of chance alone may result in a situation in which random groups are initially very different from each other. Design 3 provides no assurance that small groups are really comparable before the treatments are applied. The matched-subjects design, however, serves to reduce the extent to which experimental differences can be accounted for by initial differences between the groups; that is, it controls preexisting intersubject differences on variables highly related to the dependent variable that the experiment is designed to affect. The random assignment of the matched pairs to groups adds to the strength of this design.

Design 4 is subject to the difficulties that we mentioned earlier in connection with matching as a means of control. The matching of all potential subjects must be complete, and the assignment of the members of each pair to the groups must be determined randomly. If one or more subjects should be excluded because an appropriate match could not be found, this would bias the sample. When using Design 4 it is essential to match every subject, even if only approximately, before random assignment. Design 4 can be used with more than two groups by creating matched sets and randomly assigning one member of each set to each group.

/ Design 5. Randomized Subjects, Pretest-Posttest Control Group Design

In Design 5, subjects are assigned to the experimental and control groups by random methods and are given a pretest on the dependent variable, Y. The treatment is introduced only to the experimental subjects for a specified time, after which the two groups are measured on the dependent variable. The average difference between the pretest and posttest $(Y_2 - Y_1)$ is found for each group, and then these average difference scores are compared in order to ascertain whether the experimental treatment produced a greater change than the control situation.

The significance of the difference in average changes (found when the average change for the control group is subtracted from the average change for the experimental group) is determined by an appropriate statistical test, such as the *t*-test or *F*-test. Another, more precise, statistical procedure is to do an analysis of covariance with posttest scores as the dependent variable and pretest scores as the covariate.

DESIGN 5 Randomized Subjects, Pretest-Posttest Control Group Design

	Group	Pretest	Independent Variable	Posttest
(R)	E	Y_1	X	Y_2
(R)	C	Y_1	—	Y_2

The fact that the control group does not receive the experimental treatment does not mean that control subjects receive no experience at all. In research on teaching methods the control group is generally taught by the traditional or usual procedure. In certain learning experiments it is common practice to give the control group some kind of irrelevant activity between the pre- and posttest while the experimental group is receiving specific training for the task. In an experiment on the effects of a particular drug, one would administer a placebo (such as a sugar pill) to the control group without letting them know that they were being treated differently from the experimental group.

The before-and-after measures in Design 5 permit the investigator to study change, and it is often referred to as the classical design for change experiments. The main strength of this design is the initial randomization, which assures statistical equivalence between the groups prior to experimentation; also the fact that the experimenter has control of the pretest can provide an additional check on the equality of the two groups on the dependent variable, *Y*. Design 5, with its randomization, thus controls most of the extraneous variables that pose a threat to internal validity. For example, the effects of history, maturation, and pretesting are experienced in both groups; therefore, any difference between the groups on the *Y* measure could probably not be attributed to these factors. Differential selection of subjects and statistical regression are also controlled through the randomization procedure. Design 5 can be used with more than two groups.

The main concern in using Design 5 is external validity. Ironically, the problem stems from the use of the pretest, an essential feature of the design. As was mentioned earlier, there may be an interaction between the pretest and the subjects that can change them or sensitize them in certain ways. Although both *E* and *C* groups take the pretest and may experience the sensitizing effect, it can cause the experimental subjects to respond to the *X* treatment in a particular way just because of their increased sensitivity. The crucial question is Would the effect of *X* on the experimental subjects be the same without the exposure to the pretest? This problem has been particularly evident in studies of attitude change. When the first attitude scale is administered as the pretest in a study, it can arouse interest or sensitize subjects to the issues or material included in the scale. Then when the experimental treatment (a lecture, film, or the like) is administered, the subjects may be responding not so much to the X treatment as to a combination of their aroused sensitivity to the issues and the experimental treatment.

Let us consider another example. Suppose that one criterion for the success of a new teaching method in high school social studies is the number of students who report that they get their news from a source like the *Wall Street Journal*. During the course itself no special emphasis is placed on this particular source; but it, along with several other papers of somewhat lower repute, is made available to students. If the study uses a pretest-posttest design, the pretest questionnaire might include such an item as Do you read the *Wall Street Journal* for daily news? This question alone may be enough to sensitize the experimental students to that newspaper, so when it becomes available during the course, they will be more likely to pick it out from the others. But the control group is not exposed to the various news sources; hence, the pretest question does not have an opportunity to exert its sensitizing effect on them. What might happen in such a study, as a result, is that the experimental group shows greater use of the *Wall Street Journal* on the posttest than does the control group, not because of the course content only but because of the combined effect of course content and pretest. A new class taught by the same method, but not pretested and hence not sensitized, may show no greater attentiveness to the *Journal* than the control group.

Such an effect represents an interaction between the pretest and the experimental treatment. Because a pretest might increase (or decrease) the subject's sensitivity or responsiveness to the X manipulation, the results obtained for a pretested sample may be unrepresentative of the effects of the experimental variable for the unpretested population from which the experimental subjects are taken. Thus, we have a problem in generalizability; we may only be able to generalize the experimental findings to pretested groups and not to unpretested ones. This interaction between pretest and treatment is a threat to external validity.

In spite of this shortcoming, Design 5 is widely used because the interaction effect is not a serious problem in most educational research. The pretests used are generally achievement tests of some type and therefore do not have significant sensitizing effect on subjects who are accustomed to such testing. However, if the testing procedures are somewhat novel or motivating in their effect, then it is recommended that the experimenter choose a design not involving a pretest. Alternatively, whenever one suspects that the effect of the pretest might be interactive, it is possible to add a new group or groups to the study—a group that is *not* pretested. Solomon has suggested two designs that overcome the weakness of Design 5 by adding an unpretested group or groups.[9]

---

[9]Solomon, R. L. (1949). On extension of control group design. *Psychological Bulletin, 46,* 137–150.

/ Design 6. Solomon Three-Group Design

The first of the Solomon designs uses three groups with random assignment of subjects to groups.

It can be seen that the first two lines of this design are identical to Design 5. However, this Solomon design has the advantage that it employs a second control group and thereby overcomes the difficulty inherent in Design 5—namely, the interactive effect of pretesting and the experimental manipulation. This second control group, labeled C_2, is *not* pretested but is exposed to the X treatment. Their Y_2 measures are then used to assess the interaction effect.

DESIGN 6 Solomon Three-Group Design

	Group	Pretest	Independent Variable	Posttest
(R)	E	Y_1	X	Y_2
(R)	C_1	Y_1	—	Y_2
(R)	C_2	—	X	Y_2

An assessment of the interaction effect is achieved through a comparison of the Y_2 scores for the three groups. Only the posttest scores are entered into the analysis. Even though the experimental group has a significantly higher mean on Y_2 than does the first control group, we cannot be confident that this difference is due to X. It might have occurred because of the subjects' increased sensitization after the pretest and the interaction of their sensitization and X. However, if the Y_2 mean of the second control group is also significantly higher than that of the first control group, then we can assume that the experimental treatment, rather than the pretest-X interaction effect, has produced the difference because the second control group is not pretested. This group, though receiving the X treatment, is functioning as a control and is thus labeled C_2.

/ Design 7. Solomon Four-Group Design

Design 7 provides still more rigorous control by extending Design 6 to include one more control group. This fourth group receives neither pretest nor treatment. Again the third group, though receiving the X treatment, is functioning as a control group.

DESIGN 7 Solomon Four-Group Design

	Group	Pretest	Independent Variable	Posttest
(R)	E	Y_1	X	Y_2
(R)	C_1	Y_1	—	Y_2
(R)	C_2	—	X	Y_2
(R)	C_3	—	—	Y_2

Design 7 has strength because it incorporates within it the advantages of several other designs along with its own unique contribution. The first two lines (Design 5) control extraneous factors such as history and maturation, and the third line (Design 6) provides control over the pretest-X interaction effect. When the fourth line is added to make Design 7, we have control over any possible contemporary effects that may occur between Y_1 and Y_2. The last two lines represent Design 3, so actually we have a combination of the pretest-posttest randomized-subjects control group design with the randomized-subjects posttest-only control group design. In addition to the strengths of each design taken separately, we also have the replication feature provided by the two experiments. This combination takes advantage of the information provided by the pretest-posttest procedure and at the same time shows how the experimental condition affects an unpretested group of Ss.

In Design 7 one can make several comparisons to determine the effect of the experimental-X treatment. If the posttest mean of the E group is significantly greater than the mean of the first control group, C_1, and if the C_2 posttest mean is significantly greater than that of C_3, we have evidence for the effectiveness of the experimental treatment. The influence of the experimental conditions on a pretested group can be determined by comparing the posttests of E and C_1 or the pre-post changes of E and C_1; the effect of the experiment on an unpretested group is found by comparing C_2 and C_3. If the average differences between posttest scores, $E - C_1$ and $C_2 - C_3$, are about the same, then the experiment must have had a comparable effect on pretested and unpretested groups.

Design 7 actually involves conducting the experiment twice, once with pretests and once without pretests. If the results of these two experiments are in agreement, as indicated above, the investigator can have much greater confidence in the findings.

The main disadvantage of this design is the difficulty involved in carrying it out in a practical situation. More time and effort are required to conduct two experiments simultaneously, and there is the problem of locating the increased number of subjects of the same kind that would be needed.

Another difficulty is with the statistical analysis. There are not four complete sets of measures for the four groups. As noted above, we can make comparisons between E and C_1 and between C_2 and C_3, but there is no single statistical procedure that would make use of the six available measures simultaneously. Campbell and Stanley suggest working only with posttest scores in a two-way analysis-of-variance design. The pretest is considered as a second independent variable, along with X. The design is as follows:

	No X	X
Pretested	Y_2, control 1	Y_2, experimental
Unpretested	Y_2, control 3	Y_2, control 2

From the column means, one can determine the main effect of X; from row means, the main effect of pretesting; and from cell means, the interaction of testing with X.

// Factorial Designs

The designs presented thus far have been the classical single-variable designs in which the experimenter manipulates one independent variable to produce an effect on the dependent variable. However, in the case of complex social phenomena there are generally several variables interacting simultaneously, and to attempt to restrict a study to one variable may impose an artificial simplicity on a complex situation. The X variable alone may not produce the same effect as it might in interaction with another X, so the findings from one-variable design may be meaningless. For instance, the effectiveness of a particular method of teaching may well depend upon a number of variables, such as the intelligence level of the students, the personality of the teacher, the general atmosphere of the classroom, and so on. Computer-assisted instruction, for example, may be more effective with slow students than with bright ones. A classical one-variable design would not reveal this interactive effect of method and intelligence level. The information yield of an experiment can be increased markedly by ascertaining the simultaneous effects of two or more independent variables in a factorial design. In fact, it has been said that the real breakthrough in educational research came with Fisher's development of factorial designs.

A factorial design is one in which two or more variables are manipulated simultaneously in order to study the independent effect of each variable on the dependent variable, as well as the effects due to interactions among the several variables.

Factorial designs are of two types. In the first type of design, one of the independent variables may be experimentally manipulated. In this case the experimenter is primarily interested in the effect of a single independent variable but must take into consideration other variables that may influence the dependent variable. Typically these other variables are attribute variables, such as sex, intelligence, race, socioeconomic status, achievement, and the like. Their influence can be investigated (and at the same time controlled) by building the attribute variable directly into a factorial design. The experimenter assesses the effect of the main independent variable at each of several "levels" of the one or more attribute-independent variables. The different levels of the attribute variable typically represent naturally occurring selected groups of subjects, as when a study uses bright and slow students to determine the effectiveness of an instructional technique. Building the attribute variables into a factorial design not only increases the precision of the experiment but also its generalizability. Because one is able to determine whether the treatment has comparable effects over all levels, the generalizability of the experimental findings is increased.

In the second type of design, all of the independent variables may be experimentally manipulated. Here the experimenter is interested in several active independent variables and wishes to assess both their separate and their combined effects. Both independent variables are experimentally manipulated. For instance, an experiment might compare the effects of class size as well as the introduction of computer-assisted instruction on the learning of science concepts. In this study both variables would be manipulated; there would be two levels of the variable *method of instruction*, namely, computer-assisted versus traditional, and the second variable, *size of class*, namely, large versus small. Such a design permits an analysis of the main effects for both experimental variables as well as an analysis of the interaction between the treatments.

/ Design 8. Simple Factorial Design

Factorial designs have been developed at varying levels of complexity. The simplest factorial design is the 2 × 2. In this design each of two independent variables has two levels.

DESIGN 8 Simple Factorial Design

Attribute Variable (X_2)	Experimental Variable (X_1)	
	Treatment A	Treatment B
Level 1	Cell 1	Cell 3
Level 2	Cell 2	Cell 4

To illustrate, let us assume that an experimenter is interested in comparing the effectiveness of two types of teaching methods—Methods A and B—on the achievement of ninth-grade science students, believing that there may be a differential effect of these methods based on the level of intelligence of the students. The experimenter stratifies the population into high and low IQ scores and randomly selects 60 Ss from the high group and assigns 30 Ss to Method A and 30 Ss to Method B. This process is repeated for the low-IQ group. Teachers are also randomly assigned to the groups.

In our hypothetical experiment we have two experimental treatments and two levels of intelligence. Table 9.1 shows the 2 × 2 factorial design for measuring the effects of the two methods of instruction on the learning of students. Note that a 2 × 2 design requires four groups of subjects; subjects within each of two levels of intelligence are randomly assigned to the two treatments.

The scores in the four cells represent the mean scores of the four groups on the dependent variable, the science achievement test. In addition

TABLE 9.1 Example of a Factorial Design

IQ (X_2)	Instructional Method (X_1)		Mean
	Method A	Method B	
High	75.0	73.0	74
Low	60.0	64.0	62
Mean	67.5	68.5	

to the four cell scores representing the various combinations of treatments and levels, we notice that there are four marginal mean scores: two for the columns and two for the rows. The marginal column means are for the two methods, or treatments, and the marginal row means are for the two levels of intelligence.

From the data given we can first determine the *main effects* for the two independent variables. The treatment mean scores without regard to IQ level indicate the main effect for treatments. If we compare the mean score of the two Method A groups, 67.5, with that of the two Method B groups, 68.5, we find that the difference between these means is only one point. Therefore we might be tempted to conclude that the method used has little effect on the dependent variable.

Now let us examine the mean scores for the levels in order to determine the main effect of X_2, intelligence level, on achievement scores. The main effect for levels does not take into account any differential effect due to treatments. The mean score for the two high-IQ groups is 74, and the mean score for the two low-IQ groups is 62; because this difference is 12 points, we would assume that there is an effect attributable to intelligence level. The high-IQ group has a markedly higher mean score; thus, regardless of treatment, the high-IQ groups perform better than the low-IQ groups.

A factorial design also permits the investigator to assess the interaction between the two independent variables—that is, the different effects of one of them at different levels of the other. If there is an interaction, the effect that the treatment has on learning will differ for the two IQ levels. If there is no interaction, the effect of the treatment will be the same for both levels of intelligence. From an examination of Table 9.1 we can see that the Method A mean is higher than the Method B mean for the high-IQ group, and the Method B mean is higher for the low-IQ group. Thus, some particular combinations of treatment and level of IQ interact to produce greater gains than do some other combinations. This interaction effect between method and intelligence levels is shown graphically in Figure 9.2. If this interaction is statistically significant, we conclude that the effectiveness of the method depends upon the IQ level. One method is more effective at one level of intelligence, and the reverse is true for the other level.

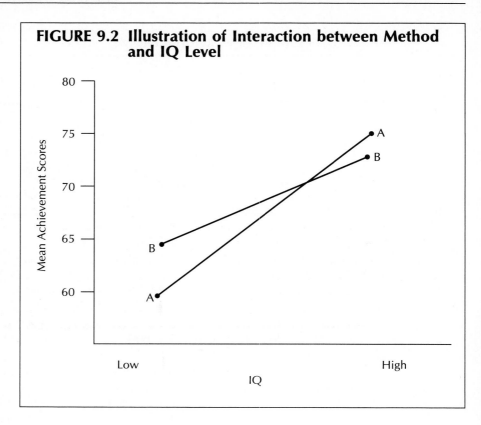

FIGURE 9.2 **Illustration of Interaction between Method and IQ Level**

TABLE 9.2 **Example of a Factorial Design**

IQ (X_2)	Treatment (X_1) Method A	Method B	**Mean**
High	50	58	54
Low	40	48	44
Mean	45	53	

Let us examine another set of data obtained in a hypothetical 2×2 factorial study. Table 9.2 shows the results of a study designed to investigate the effect of two methods of instruction on achievement. Again, because the investigator anticipates that the method may be differentially effective depending on the intelligence level of the subject, the first step is to distinguish two levels of intelligence. Subjects within each level are randomly assigned to the two methods. Following the experimentation period, achievement tests are administered and the scores are recorded for every subject. If we compare the mean score of the two groups taught by Method B, 53, with that of the two groups taught by Method A, 45, we see that the former is somewhat higher. Therefore, Method B appears to be more effective than Method A. The difference between the means for the two IQ levels, on the main effects for intelligence, is 10 (54 − 44). Regardless of treatment, the high-IQ group performs better than the low-IQ group. The data reveal no interaction between treatment and levels. Method B appears to be more effective regardless of the IQ level. In other words, treatments and levels are independent of each other. The lack of interaction is illustrated graphically in Figure 9.3. It is not possible to demonstrate either the presence or absence of such interaction without using a factorial design.

The factorial design can be extended to more-complex experiments, in which there are a number of independent variables; the numerical values of the digits indicate the number of levels for the specific independent variables. For instance, in a 2 × 3 × 4 factorial design there are three independent variables with two, three, and four levels, respectively. Such an experiment might use two teaching methods, three ability levels, and four grades. The-

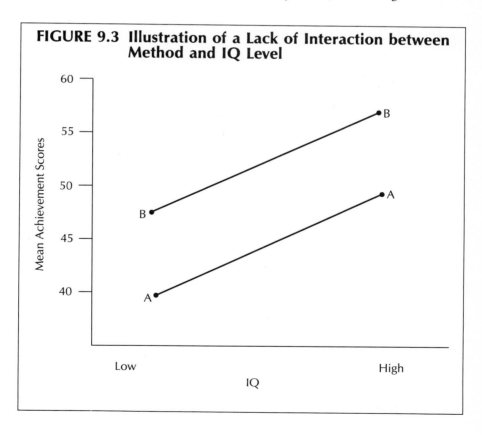

FIGURE 9.3 Illustration of a Lack of Interaction between Method and IQ Level

oretically a factorial design may include any number of independent variables with any number of levels of each. However, when too many factors are manipulated or controlled simultaneously, the study and the statistical analysis become unwieldy and some of the combinations may be artificial. The number of groups required for a factorial design is the product of the digits that indicate the factorial design. In the 2 × 3 × 4 design 24 groups would be required in order to represent all combinations of the different levels of the multiple independent variables. The mere thought of the complexities involved in arranging for large numbers of subjects under large numbers of conditions will perhaps help the reader to understand why most educational researchers attempt to answer their questions with the simplest possible designs, even though the statistical analysis can be easily handled by electronic computers.

The advantages of the factorial design are that it (1) accomplishes in one experiment what otherwise might require two or more separate studies, (2) provides an opportunity to study interactions that are often so important in educational research, and (3) provides a more powerful test of hypotheses.

// Quasi-Experimental Designs

The goal of the experimenter is to use designs that provide full experimental control through the use of randomization procedures. These are the true experimental designs as presented in the previous section (Designs 3 through 8). There are many situations in educational research in which it is not possible to conduct a true experiment. Neither full control over the scheduling of experimental conditions nor the ability to randomize can always be realized. For instance, in research conducted in a classroom setting it may not be possible for the experimenter to assign subjects randomly to groups. In this case one must use designs that will provide as much control as possible under the existing situation. These designs are known as quasi-experimental designs and are used where true experimental designs are not feasible.[10] Because the quasi-experimental design does not provide full control, it is extremely important that the researcher be aware of the sources of both internal and external validity and consider these sources in the interpretation.

/ Design 9. Nonrandomized Control Group, Pretest-Posttest Design

Although randomized assignment of subjects to groups is the ideal, it often is not possible in practice. In a typical school situation, schedules cannot be disrupted nor classes reorganized in order to accommodate the experi-

---

[10]Campbell, D. T., and J. C. Stanley (1966). *Experimental and Quasi-Experimental Designs for Research* (p. 34). Skokie, IL: Rand McNally.

menter's study. In such a case it is necessary to use groups as they are already organized into classes or other intact groups.

DESIGN 9 Nonrandomized Control Group, Pretest-Posttest Design

Group	Pretest	Independent Variable	Posttest
E	Y_1	X	Y_2
C	Y_1	—	Y_2

A researcher might be allowed to conduct an experiment with the four freshman English sections of a high school. Because the sections meet at different times, subjects cannot be randomly assigned to treatments. However, the researcher can use a random procedure to determine which two sections will be experimental and which two will be control. All subjects take the pretest before the experiment begins and the posttest at its conclusion. Since both experimental and control groups take the same pre- and posttest, and the experiment occupies the same time period for all subjects, testing, instrumentation, maturation, and mortality are not internal-validity problems.

If the researcher is in complete charge of treatment, history is not a problem. If the researcher only supervises the regular teachers who deliver the experimental and control treatments, differences among teachers can systematically influence results.

Both Design 9 and Design 5—the randomized subjects, pretest-posttest control group experiment—use the differences between pretest and posttest as the dependent variable. The nonrandomization in Design 9 is responsible for three threats to internal validity that the randomization in Design 5 avoids.

1. Although selection per se is not an internal-validity problem because subjects were not assigned for the purpose of the experiment and the groups to receive experimental and control treatments were chosen randomly, the interaction of selection and maturation may be a serious internal-validity problem. Suppose section one of freshman English meets at the same hour that the remedial mathematics class meets, while section three meets at the same hour as the advanced algebra class. We would expect section one as a group to show the most gain on academic performance because many of the poorer students are in the remedial mathematics class at the same hour. Section three would be expected to show the least gain because many of the best students are in the advanced algebra class at the same time. The timing of the mathematics classes influences the makeup of the English sections, and this affects the gain to be expected, because of the interaction between selection and maturation.

Selection-maturation interaction can be a particularly difficult problem when volunteers are compared with nonvolunteers. For example, an after-school reading improvement program is offered to those who wish it. Pretest reading-test means show no difference between those who volunteer for the after-school program and those who do not. If the posttreatment scores show greater gain for the treatment group than for the control group, we cannot confidently attribute the greater gain to the treatment. It is quite possible that those who were willing to participate in the after-school program were more concerned about their reading and were therefore more likely to show greater gain in reading whether they received treatment or not.

2. Statistical regression is another possible major validity problem for Design 9. This term refers to the tendency for extreme scores to regress (move) toward the common mean on subsequent measurement. Such a regression effect could be introduced into this design if the groups used in the study were drawn from populations having different means. Even though the groups are equivalent on a pretest, the regression effect that occurs could result in a shift (change) from pre- to posttest that is incorrectly interpreted as an experimental effect.

Let us assume that the experimental group in a study has a mean of 75 on a pretest, which is below the mean of its parent population, whereas the control group with a pretest mean of 75 is above the mean of its population. Because each group will regress toward the mean of the parent population when retested, the experimental group will be expected to have a higher mean on the posttest, whether or not X is introduced; on the other hand, the mean of the control group will regress downward. The experimental group would appear to have made more progress during the course of the study than the control group, which would most likely be erroneously attributed to the effect of X.

3. With Design 9 serious internal-validity problems arise with change or "gain" scores because the subjects are not randomly assigned to treatment or control groups. Although it is not possible to go into the problems of change scores in detail in this text, let us point out some of the difficulties. A negative correlation is usually found between pretest scores and the gain made from pretest to posttest. Does this mean that students with low initial scores learn more (as measured by the change scores) than students with high initial scores? Probably not. The negative correlation is most likely due to the peculiar psychometric characteristics of change scores. For one thing, most educational tests have a ceiling, which means that the range of achievement on the test items is limited. If a student answers 92 items correctly on a 100-item pretest, it is only possible for this student to gain 8 points on the posttest. On the other hand, a student with a score of 42 on the pretest could make a gain of 58 points. Because of this ceiling effect, students in the high-achievement group on the pretest are restricted to a low change score on the posttest.

The problems associated with change scores are only threats to internal validity when subjects have not been randomly assigned to treatment. With randomization, any distortions created by use of change scores will in the long run have the same effect on both experimental and control groups. When using Design 9, problems with change scores are especially serious when the mean pretest scores of the experimental and control groups differ substantially, as ceiling effect and regression will probably influence posttest scores of one group more than the other. For example, if Design 9 is used to compare the effects of two methods of spelling instruction in which equivalent forms of a 100-item spelling test are used as pretest and posttest and one group has a pretest mean of 80 and the other a pretest mean of 50, the ceiling effect would restrict the possible gain of the former more than the latter.

The threats to external validity in Design 9 are similar to those encountered with Design 5. An advantage of Design 9, however, is that the reactive effects of experimentation are more easily controlled than they are in Design 5. When intact classes are used, subjects are probably less aware of an experiment being conducted than when subjects are drawn from classes and put into experimental sessions. This contributes to the generalizability of the findings. Incidentally, it might also be noted that an experimenter in a school situation is much more likely to obtain administrative approval to conduct an experiment if intact classes are used, as in Design 9.

The more similar the experimental and the control groups are at the beginning of the experiment and the more this similarity is confirmed by similar group means on the pretest, the more credible the results of the nonrandomized control group pretest-posttest study become. If the pretest scores are similar and selection-maturation interaction and regression can be shown to be unlikely explanations of posttest differences, the results of this quasi-experimental design are quite credible.

Even if the group means are noticeably different before treatment, a nonequivalent control group is better than no control group at all. This design is a better choice than the preexperimental designs, which do not have a control group. Design 9 can be extended to employ more than two groups.

/ Design 10. Counterbalanced Design

Design 10, another design that can be used with intact class groups, rotates the groups at intervals during the experimentation. For example, the *E* group and *C* group might use Methods A and B, respectively, for the first half of the experiment and then exchange methods for the second half. The distinctive feature of Design 10 is that all subjects receive all experimental treatments at some time during the experiment. In effect, this design involves a series of replications; in each replication the *E* groups are shifted so that at the end of the experiment each group has been exposed to each *X*. The order of exposure to the experimental situation differs for each group. The counterbalanced design is usually employed when several treatments are to be tested, but it also may be used with only two treatments.

DESIGN 10 A Sample Counterbalanced Design

Replication	Experimental Treatments			
	X_1	X_2	X_3	X_4
1	Group A	B	C	D
2	Group C	A	D	B
3	Group B	D	A	C
4	Group D	C	B	A
	column mean	column mean	column mean	column mean

Each row in Design 10 represents one replication. For each replication the groups are shifted so that Group A first experiences X_1, then X_2, X_3, and finally X_4. Each cell in the design would contain the mean scores on the dependent variable for the group, treatment, and replication indicated. The mean score for each column would indicate the performance of all four groups on the dependent variable under the treatment represented by the column.

A classroom teacher could use a counterbalanced study to compare the effectiveness of two methods of instruction on learning in science. The teacher could choose two classes and two units of science comparable in difficulty, length, and so on. It is essential that the units be equivalent in the complexity and difficulty of the concepts involved. During the first replication of the design Class 1 is taught Unit 1 by Method A and Class 2 is taught by Method B. An achievement test over Unit 1 is administered to both groups. Then Class 1 is taught Unit 2 by Method B and Class 2 is taught by Method A; both are then tested over Unit 2. The arrangement is shown in Table 9.3.

After the study the column means are computed to indicate the mean achievement for both groups (classes) when taught by the method indicated by the column heading. A comparison of these column mean scores through an analysis of variance indicates the effectiveness of the methods upon achievement in science.

Design 10 overcomes some of the weaknesses of Design 9. That is, when intact classes must be used, counterbalancing provides an opportunity to rotate out any differences that might exist between the groups. Since the

TABLE 9.3 Example of a Counterbalanced Design

Replication	Experimental Treatments	
	Method A	Method B
(Unit) 1	Class 1	Class 2
(Unit) 2	Class 2	Class 1
	column mean	column mean

treatments are administered to all groups, the results obtained for each X cannot be attributed to preexisting differences in the subjects. If one group should be more intelligent on the average than the other, each X treatment would benefit from this superior intelligence.

The main shortcoming of Design 10 is that there may be a carry-over effect from one X to the next. Therefore, it should be used only when the experimental treatments are such that exposure to one treatment will have no effect on subsequent treatments. This requirement may be hard to satisfy in much of educational research. Furthermore, there is the necessity for establishing the equivalence of the learning material used in the various replications. It may not always be possible to locate equivalent units of material. Another weakness of the counterbalanced design is the possibility of boring students with the repeated testings required by this method.

// Time Series Designs

/ Design 11. One-Group Time Series Design

Design 11 involves periodic measurement on one group and the introduction of an experimental treatment into this time series of measurements. As the design indicates, a number of measurements on a dependent variable, Y, are taken. X is introduced, and additional measurements of Y are made. By comparing the measurements before and after X, it is possible to assess the effect of X on the performance of the group on Y. A time series design might be used in a school setting to study the effects of a major change in administrative policy upon disciplinary incidents. Or a study might involve repeated measurements of students' attitudes and the effect produced by the introduction of a documentary film designed to change attitudes.

DESIGN 11 One-Group Time Series Design

Y_1	Y_2	Y_3	Y_4	X	Y_5	Y_6	Y_7	Y_8

Figure 9.4 illustrates some possible patterns from time series studies into which an experimental treatment is introduced. It shows the series of measurements Y_1 through Y_8, with the introduction of the experimental treatment at point X. We can assess the effect of the X by examining the stability of the repeated measurements.

From an examination of the difference between Y_4 and Y_5 in pattern A, perhaps one would be justified in assuming that X has an effect on the dependent variable. Pattern B also indicates the possibility of an experimental effect of X. However, one could not assume that X produces the change in either pattern C or D. Pattern C appears to result from maturation or a similar influence. The erratic nature of pattern D suggests the operation of extraneous factors.

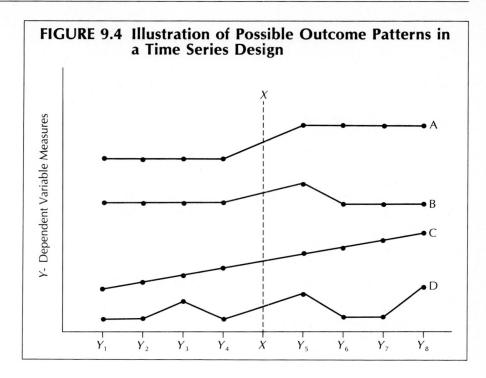

FIGURE 9.4 Illustration of Possible Outcome Patterns in a Time Series Design

Design 11 is similar to Design 1 in that it uses before-and-after measures and lacks a control group. However, it has certain advantages over Design 1 that make it a more useful design in educational research. The multitesting provides a check on some of the common threats to internal validity. Maturation, testing, and regression could be ruled out as plausible explanations of the shift occurring between Y_4 and Y_5, if such shifts do not occur in the previous time periods under observation. It is recommended that no change in measuring instruments be made during the course of the time study. In this way one eliminates changes in instrumentation as a possible explanation of the $Y_4 - Y_5$ difference.

The major weakness of Design 11 is its failure to control history; that is, one has to rule out the possibility that it is not X but some simultaneous event that produces the observed change. Perhaps such factors as seasonal or weather changes or such school agents as examinations could account for the change. In a study designed to assess the effect of a lecture-film treatment on student attitudes toward school integration, to what extent would the attitude measurements be affected by a nationally publicized black riot in a distant city? The extent to which history (uncontrolled contemporary events) is a plausible explanatory factor must be ascertained by the experimenters as they attempt to interpret their findings.

One must also consider the external validity of the time design. Because there are repeated tests, perhaps there is a kind of interaction effect of testing that would restrict the findings to those populations subject to repeated testing. However, as long as the measurements are of a typical, routine type used in school situations, this is not likely to be a serious limitation. Further, a selection-X interaction may occur, especially if one selects some particular group that may not be typical.

Statistical interpretation can be a particular problem with time data. Since individual and mean scores are so variable over the time period, it is tempting to attribute these changes to the X treatment, when they may in fact result from other variables. The usual tests of significance may not be appropriate with a time design. The reader is referred to Campbell and Stanley for a discussion of the statistical tests that may be used with this design.

/ Design 12. Control Group Time Series Design

Design 12 is an extension of Design 11 to include a control group. The control group, again representing an intact class, would be measured at the same time as the E group but would not experience the X treatment. This design overcomes the weakness of Design 11—that is, failure to control history as a source of extraneous variance. The control group permits the necessary comparison. If the E group shows a gain from Y_4 to Y_5 but the C group does not show a gain, then the effect must be due to X rather than any contemporaneous events, which would have affected both groups.

DESIGN 12 Control Group Time Series Design

Group									
E	Y_1	Y_2	Y_3	Y_4	X	Y_5	Y_6	Y_7	Y_8
C	Y_1	Y_2	Y_3	Y_4	—	Y_5	Y_6	Y_7	Y_8

Other variations of the time series design include adding more control groups, more observations, or more experimental treatments.

// Validity Problems with Experimental Designs

Some of the sources of invalidity in the one-variable experimental designs are summarized in Table 9.4. This brief summary must not be depended upon as the sole guide in selecting a design. It must be accompanied by a thorough consideration of the qualified presentation appearing in the text so that the reader understands the particular strengths and weaknesses that characterize each design.

TABLE 9.4 Factors Jeopardizing the Validity of Experimental Designs

| | Designs* | | | | | | | | | | | |
| Sources of Invalidity | Pre-experimental | | | True Experimental | | | | | Quasi-experimental | | | |
	1	2	3	4	5	6	7	8	9	10	11	12
Internal Validity												
Contemporary history†	−	+	+	+	+	+	+	+	+	+	−	+
Maturation processes	−	?	+	+	+	+	+	+	+	+	+	+
Pretesting procedures	−	+	+	+	+	+	+	+	+	+	+	+
Measuring instruments	−	+	+	+	+	+	+	+	+	+	?	+
Statistical regression	?	+	+	+	+	+	+	+	?	+	+	+
Differential selection of *Ss*	+	−	+	+	+	+	+	+	+	+	+	+
Experimental mortality	+	−	+	+	+	+	+	+	+	+	+	+
Interaction of selection and maturation, and the like	−	−	+	+	+	+	+	+	−	?	+	+
External Validity												
Interaction of selection and experimental variable	−	−	?	?	?	?	?	?	?	?	?	−
Interaction of pretesting and experimental variable	−		+	+	−	+	−	+	−	?	−	−
Reactive experimental procedures	?		?	?	?	?	?	?	?	?	?	?
Multiple-treatment interference										−		

*Designs are as follows:
1. One-group pretest-posttest
2. Static group comparison
3. Randomized *Ss*, posttest-only control group
4. Randomized matched *Ss*, posttest-only control group
5. Randomized *Ss*, pretest-posttest control group
6. Solomon, three groups
7. Solomon, four groups
8. Simple factorial
9. Nonrandomized control group, pretest-posttest
10. Counterbalanced
11. One-group time series
12. Control group time series

†A plus sign indicates that the factor is controlled; a minus sign indicates lack of control; a question mark indicates a possible source of concern; and a blank indicates that the factor is not relevant.

// Single-Subject Experimental Designs

The single-subject experimental design almost sounds like a contradiction in terms. How can an experiment be run with a sample size of one? Obviously there can be no random assignment or use of control groups. Yet research involving single subjects has become popular over the past 20 years. Proponents of this particular methodology argue that experimental control can be achieved in other than the traditional ways. After describing the two major approaches to single-subject research and the rationale behind them, we will examine the strengths and limitations of this type of research in comparison with the other more conventional designs.

Study of the individual has always had a place in educational and psychological research. Freud's case studies and Piaget's observations of individual children are notable examples. Although both case studies (see Chapter 11) and single-subject experiments both study the individual, in a single-subject experiment the investigator deliberately manipulates one or more independent variables, while in a case study the observer studies the subjects' interaction with events that occur naturally.

Single-case designs have been particularly useful in clinical applications in which the focus is on the therapeutic value of an intervention for the client. A teacher of severely retarded children, for example, would want information regarding the effectiveness of a specific procedure with an individual child. It is felt by some that studies that report mean or average differences for groups may have little meaning when treating a specific individual.

Single-subject designs are basically extensions of the quasi-experimental one-group time series design (Design 11). The two most common are the ABAB and the multiple-baseline design.

The ABAB design consists of a period of no treatment, or baseline (A), during which the behavior of interest is repeatedly measured. Examples of such behaviors are the number of times a special-education student leaves her seat and the number of times an autistic child bangs his head. This pretreatment assessment serves as a control period with which treatment effects will be compared. After a stable picture of pretreatment behavior has been established, phase B, the treatment, is initiated. In the treatment phase the child might be given tokens (exchangeable for desired privileges) for time periods spent seated, or the child might be mildly shocked following a self-abusive action. The behavior is consistently monitored throughout the treatment phase, usually until the intervention appears to have taken effect and the rate of behavior stabilizes. Further experimental control is achieved by a second A phase. This is usually a withdrawal of treatment, but in some cases the second A phase is actually a reversal of treatment, reinforcing a behavior incompatible with the desired response. Discontinuing the giving of tokens to the retarded girl constitutes a withdrawal of treatment, while giving her tokens when she leaves her seat is a reversal of treatment. In either case removal of treatment is expected to cause the behavior to return to the original (first baseline) level. Ending the experiment with the second A phase has the drawback of leaving the client in the same state as before the experiment started. For ethical reasons and to add strength to the design by replicating the procedure, the treatment phase (B) is again instituted. Many variations on the ABAB design are possible. More than one treatment can be tested—for instance, using an ABCACB format in which A is no treatment and B and C are alternate treatments.

Figure 9.5 illustrates an ABAB design. Mornings were often difficult for the entire family of an 8-year-old mentally retarded boy, Curt, because

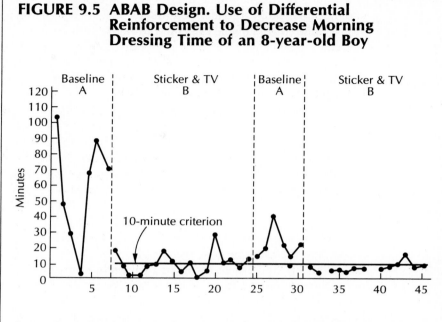

FIGURE 9.5 ABAB Design. Use of Differential Reinforcement to Decrease Morning Dressing Time of an 8-year-old Boy

Source: From W. Heward, J. C. Dardig, and A. Rossett (1979), *Working with Parents of Handicapped Children* (p. 59), Columbus, OH: Charles E. Merrill. Copyright 1979 by Bell & Howell Company. Reprinted by permission.

he took up to 2 hours to get dressed in the morning. Constant reminders, pleadings, and occasional scoldings had not helped. Once during a week of baseline measurement (A) Curt did get dressed in only 4 minutes, so his parents knew he was capable of dressing himself in a reasonable time.

During the treatment (B) phase, each morning Curt's clothes were laid out in the bathroom, he was awakened, and then a kitchen timer was set for 10 minutes. Curt earned a red sticker to put on the chart on his door if he dressed himself before the timer rang. The sticker entitled him to watch TV that evening. If he did not finish within the 10 minutes, he had to stay in the bathroom until dressed and forfeit TV for the day. Curt was praised when he met the criterion, ignored when he didn't.

During the week of baseline, Curt took an average of 59 minutes to get dressed. During 17 days of the first B phase, Curt met the criterion nine times and his average was 10 minutes. On three occasions 0 minutes was recorded because he woke and dressed himself before his parents were awake.

During the following 6 days, Curt's clothes were laid out for him but the timer was omitted and he was allowed to watch TV no matter how long he took to dress. His dressing time averaged 23 minutes during this second

A phase. When treatment was reinstituted for 12 of the next 13 days, Curt's dressing time then averaged 8 minutes.

Because treatment was always accompanied by a change in dressing time, a credible relationship between treatment and dressing time was established. The key element in the ABAB design is the return to former levels of behavior when the baseline condition is reinstated. The assumption that the intervention is the cause of the change can be considerably weakened under certain circumstances. If there is considerable variability during the baseline period, one could argue that posttreatment behavior was not meaningfully different from pretreatment behavior. If the shift from treatment (B) back to baseline (A) is equivocal, much of the power of the ABAB design is gone. The second baseline often will not show the same extreme of behavior as the first, and in some cases there is no return to previous rates. In some cases other factors, such as history or maturation, could cause the observed effect.

Kazdin (1980) has argued that returning to baseline conditions may be unethical under some circumstances.[11] Do you really want the autistic child to return to the previous levels of head-banging just to show that it was the treatment that caused the reduction? Because of these potential problems with the ABAB design, the multiple-baseline design was developed. This design has the clinical advantage of continuing any improvement made without returning to less desired behavior.

In a multiple-baseline design, measures of different behaviors are made simultaneously during the baseline condition. For example, the researcher might record the number of times a student talked in class without permission, the number of worksheets completed, and the number of times the student hit another child. Or the same behavior of several clients, such as amount of eye contact with the teacher, could be recorded for two or more children in a preschool class during the baseline phase. In both cases the treatment (B) is the same across all conditions or students. Experimental control in the multiple baseline results from starting the treatment at a different point in time for each behavior and/or person involved, rather than from returning to baseline. Thus, after the baseline is established, treatment for Behavior 1 is instituted and the baseline is continued for Behaviors 2 and 3. When treatment for Behavior 2 is instituted, treatment for Behavior 1 and baseline for Behavior 3 is continued. Finally, treatment for Behavior 3 is instituted. It is expected that each behavior will change in the desired direction at the point at which treatment is begun, not before or after.

Thus the multiple-baseline design uses the AB as its basic unit. If some outside event other than the treatment was the actual cause of the changes, it should affect all children or all behaviors at the same point in time. One assumption of this design is that treatment affects different behaviors spe-

[11]Kazdin, A. (1980). *Research Design in Clinical Psychology*. New York: Harper & Row.

cifically. Reinforcing one behavior (completing arithmetic problems) is not expected to increase another response (reading rate). The behaviors, or situations, must be independent (uncorrelated) in order for the multiple-baseline study to show interpretable effects. In actuality, independence of behavior may be difficult to attain. Modifying one behavior (such as talking in class) may influence other targeted behaviors (completing assignments on time).[12]

// Comparison of Single-Subject and Group Designs

In both single-subject and group experiments the goal of the experimenter is to establish as unequivocally as possible the connection between the manipulation of the independent variable (treatment) and its effect on the dependent variable (behavior). In group designs, random assignment of subjects to experimental or control groups eliminates many rival explanations of differences observed after treatment. Treatment effects (between groups) can be assessed relative to intersubject variability effects (within group) by the use of appropriate statistical tests. These tests determine whether chance alone is a credible explanation for the results. The single-subject design uses other methods to establish credibility. The experimenter controls the amount of time in which baseline and treatment phases are in effect, and the length of the baseline period can be extended until the behavior stabilizes. For unambiguous interpretation the baseline should be relatively flat or the trend should be in the opposite direction from that expected after treatment. One drawback to experimenter control of the length of treatment phase is the tendency to continue treatment until "something happens." If behavior change does not closely follow upon the beginning of treatment, it is possible that another, nonexperimental variable is the cause of the observed change.

Single-subject experimental designs do bypass a source of error of group designs, namely, intersubject variability. Each individual serves as his or her own control, so comparability is not a problem. The major means of control is replication, a feature seldom incorporated into group designs. The ABAB design involves a single replication using the same subject, whereas the multiple-baseline design replicates more than one treatment. Replication of the multiple-baseline design makes it less likely that effects attributed to treatment were in fact caused by extraneous event or subject variables.[13]

Well-designed single-subject research can meet the criteria for internal validity. However, the question of external validity—the generalizability of experimental findings—is not as easily answered by designs that use only one or a few subjects. One can demonstrate that allowing a behaviorally disordered teenager to listen to rock music contingent on completing assignments

---

[12]Kazdin, A., and S. Kopel (1975). On resolving ambiguities of the multiple baseline design: Problems and recommendations. *Behavior Therapy, 6,* 601–608.

[13]Birnbauer, J., C. Peterson, and J. Solnick (1974). Design and interpretation of studies of single subjects. *American Journal of Mental Deficiency, 79,* 191–203.

will increase the amount of schoolwork done by that particular teenager, but how can we determine whether this treatment will be successful with other teenagers, or all behaviorally disordered teenagers? Although any one particular single-subject study will be low in external validity, a number of similar studies that carefully describe subjects, conditions, and treatments will build the case for wide application of particular treatment effects. For a more complete discussion of single-subject designs see Hersen and Barlow[14] or Kazdin.[15]

/// SUMMARY

Experimentation is the most rigorous and the most desirable form of scientific inquiry. The controlled conditions that characterize the experiment make it possible to identify verified functional relationships among the phenomena of interest to educators. Experimenters who control the conditions under which an event occurs have distinct advantages over observers who simply watch or study an event without control: (1) They can manipulate or vary the conditions systematically and note the variation in results; (2) they can make the event occur at a time when they are prepared to make accurate observations and measurements; and (3) they can repeat their observations under the same conditions, for verification, and can describe these conditions so that other experimenters can duplicate them and make an independent check on the results.

True experimental designs provide the best control for internal validity. With these designs subjects are randomly assigned to treatments. With quasi-experimental designs the investigator can control treatment but cannot randomly assign subjects to treatments. Quasi-experimental designs that study the effect of treatment on a single subject have proven useful in behavioral research.

// Key Concepts

ABAB design	counterbalanced design
analysis of covariance (ANCOVA)	differential selection
confounding variables	ecological validity
control group	experimental design
control group time series design	experimental group
control of variables	experimental research
controlling situational differences	experimenter effect

---

[14]Hersen, M., and D. H. Barlow (1976). *Single-case experimental designs: Strategies for studying behavior.* New York: Pergamon.
[15]Kazdin, A. E. (1982). *Single case research designs: Methods for clinical and applied settings.* New York: Oxford University Press.

external validity
external validity of operations
extraneous variables
factorial designs
field experiments
Hawthorne effect
history as internal-validity problem
homogeneous selection
interaction in factorial design
interaction of subject
    characteristics and treatment
internal validity
laboratory experiments
law of the single significant
    variable
manipulation of independent
    variable
maturation as internal-validity
    problem
measuring instruments as internal-
    validity problem
multiple-baseline design
nonrandomized control group,
    pretest-posttest design
one-group pretest-posttest design

one-group time series design
population validity
preexperimental designs
pretest sensitization
pretesting as internal-validity
    problem
quasi-experimental research
random assignment (randomization)
random sampling
randomized matched subjects,
    posttest-only control group design
randomized matching
randomized subjects, posttest-only
    control group design
randomized subjects, pretest-posttest
    control group design
single-subject experiment
Solomon four-group design
Solomon three-group design
static group comparison
statistical equivalence
statistical regression as internal-
    validity problem
true experimental designs
using subjects as their own controls

/// EXERCISES

1. From a group of students enrolled in social studies in a high school, a researcher randomly selected 60 students. The students were then divided into two groups by random assignment of 30 to Group A, the traditional social studies curriculum, and 30 to Group B, a new program designed to deal with the history of certain ethnic groups. The two groups were compared at the end of the semester on a scale designed to measure attitudes toward ethnic groups. In this study identify
    a. the independent variable
    b. the dependent variable
    c. the control group
    d. the experimental group

    e. the method(s) used to control for differences between the groups

    f. the research design used

2. Consider the following research question: Does teaching the first year of French through an oral-aural approach, rather than the grammar-transformational method, alter pupil performance on a standardized year-end test in grammar, reading, and vocabulary?

    a. Design the *ideal* experiment to answer this question, assuming that there are no administrative or other restrictions.

    b. Design the experiment that would most likely be required in the typical high school setting.

    c. State the relative advantages of the ideal experimental design (*a*) as compared with the design in question *b*.

3. What is the difference between random sampling and random assignment? How are they related to internal and external validity?

4. Evaluate the following research designs with respect to methods used and the control provided. Make suggestions for improvements if needed.

    a. A researcher wanted to ascertain if homogeneous grouping improves learning in a first course in biology. The researcher designated one of two high schools in a small town to serve as the experimental school and the other as the control. Both schools had about the same number of students in each of four sections of science. In the experimental school, pupils were grouped homogeneously on the basis of IQ and scores on achievement tests in science. In the control school, pupils were placed in sections at random. At the end of the year all pupils were given a standardized test in biology. Statistical tests showed the experimental group to be superior on the test. The researcher concluded that homogeneous grouping results in greater learning in biology.

    b. A history teacher was concerned about her students' lack of knowledge of their state and national governments and of current events. She decided to experiment with some new materials and methods to see if she could obtain improvement. In Classes A and B she introduced the new materials and methods. In Classes C and D she used the traditional methods. Classes A and B were administered both the pretest and posttest; Classes C and D were administered only the posttest. When comparisons were made on the posttest, Classes A and B were found to be superior. Their superior performance was attributed to the new materials and methods.

5. Design the *ideal* experiment to test the following hypothesis: Children who view films of harmonious racial interaction will show a more positive attitude toward racial minorities than will children shown films that depict racial conflict.

6. Returning to the research problem in question 2, suppose you also want to know if the two methods of teaching French have differential effects for boys and girls? Outline the experimental design that would permit you to answer this question at the same time.

7. Assume an investigator had used two methods of instruction (A_1 and A_2) with two groups of students (B_1 and B_2) having varying levels of achievement motivation. The groups were compared on an achievement test at the end of the study. The means are presented below. What interpretation would you make of these results?

	A_1	A_2
B_1	35	15
B_2	15	35

8. What must occur to establish credibility of results in a single-subject design?

/// ANSWERS

1. a. type of social studies curriculum
   b. scores on an ethnic attitude scale
   c. Group A, the present curriculum
   d. Group B, curriculum with ethnic history
   e. random selection of the sample from the population and random assignment of the sample to the experimental and control groups
   f. Design 3, the randomized subjects, posttest-only control group design

2. a. Use Design 3, that is, randomly assign first-year French students to either the grammar-transformational (control) or oral-aural (experimental) group. Maintain the same conditions, time spent, teachers, classroom facilities for both groups so that only the teaching method is different. Administer test at the end of the year and compare group achievement.
   b. Randomly assign intact classes of first-year French students to the two teaching methods. Each teacher has an equal number of the two types of classes.
   c. In the ideal design, threats to external and internal validity are better controlled through randomization of individual students. The design in question *b* could have problems with nonequivalence of subjects before treatment is given, so that test score differences could be due to factors other than difference in treatment.

3. Random sampling is using a chance procedure to draw a sample from a population. Because it addresses the question of how well results drawn from a sample can be generalized to the population from which the sample was drawn, it is a strategy for increasing external validity. Random assignment is using a chance procedure to assign the subjects available for an experiment to treatment. It is a strategy for increasing internal validity.

4. a. Because the researcher could not assign students randomly to the high schools, there are several threats to internal validity. Students in the experimental school may have been brighter or have had more background in science than students in the control school. Differences in the quality of teaching biology in the schools have not been controlled. Because the researcher used only schools in a small town, the results of the study could not be generalized to other high schools in different settings.

   The researcher could compare initial science achievement and IQ scores for the schools to see if the groups were equivalent before treatment. Using several high schools, with classes within each high school being randomly assigned to experimental conditions, would control for factors specific to a given school.

   b. Classes not randomly assigned may not be equivalent. Pretesting could have been used to determine equivalence but was only given to the experimental groups. The pretesting of the experimental groups alone may have sensitized the groups and influenced the differences found. Classes should be randomly assigned to treatments, even if individual students cannot be randomly assigned.

5. The ideal experiment would randomly assign students to groups. The results of a posttreatment measure of attitudes toward racial minorities would be used to compare the experimental and control groups.

6. This question requires a factorial design with two groups of boys and two groups of girls assigned randomly to the control and experimental conditions.

7. It appears that there is an interaction between achievement motivation and type of instruction. Students with achievement motivation at level B_1 did better with Method A_1, while those at level B_2 did better with method A_2. The significance of this interaction could be tested with an F-test. There is no overall effect of motivation or instructional method, as the means for A_1 and A_2, and B_1 and B_2 are the same.

8. There must be an unambiguous change in behavior whenever there is a change in treatment.

CHAPTER 10

Causal-Comparative Research

INSTRUCTIONAL OBJECTIVES

After studying this chapter, the student will be able to

1. Describe causal-comparative research and compare it to experimental research
2. State conditions needed to infer a causal relationship
3. Describe alternative explanations in causal-comparative research and identify cases where these are or are not plausible
4. Describe methods of partial control and identify cases where they would be useful
5. Identify questions for which causal-comparative research would be the method of choice

As we probe such educational questions as Why are some children better readers than others? and Why do some youths become delinquent while others do not? we find that only some of our questions can be investigated through experimental research. If we wish to investigate the influence of such variables as home environment, motivation, intelligence, parental reading habits, and so forth, we cannot randomly assign students to different categories of these variables. Independent variables such as these are called *attribute variables*. An attribute variable is a characteristic that a subject possesses before a study begins.

In contrast, an independent variable that an investigator can directly manipulate is an *active variable*. An investigator can determine which students will have access to a shorthand laboratory and which will not, which will use Program A to study a unit in algebra and which will use Program B. When active independent variables are involved, we can employ experimental or quasi-experimental research. When we have attribute independent variables, we must turn to *causal-comparative research* (sometimes called *ex post facto* research).

The designation *ex post facto,* Latin for "from after the fact," serves to indicate that the research in question is conducted after variations in the independent variable have already been determined in the natural course of events. The investigator does not have direct control over the independent variables, either because they are inherently not manipulable or because they have already occurred.

Researchers achieve the variation they want, not by direct manipulation of the variable itself but by selection of individuals in whom the variable is present or absent, strong or weak, and so on. They present brain-damaged and nonbrain-damaged children with the same perceptual task; or they compare the performance of high-IQ and low-IQ children on the same measure of anxiety.

/// CAUSAL-COMPARATIVE AND EXPERIMENTAL APPROACHES COMPARED

In both types of research, interest is focused upon discovery or establishment of relationships among the variables in one's data. Causal-comparative research, as well as experimental research, can test hypotheses concerning the relationship betwen an independent variable, *X,* and a dependent variable, *Y.* In basic logic experimental and causal-comparative approaches are similar. The aim of both is to compare two groups, similar in all relevant characteristics but one, in order to measure the effects of that characteristic. Thus, much of the same kind of information that an experiment provides can also be obtained through a causal-comparative analysis.

However, with an experiment it is possible to obtain much more convincing evidence for causal or functional relationships among variables than can be obtained with causal-comparative studies. The effects of extraneous variables in an experiment are controlled by the experimental conditions, and the presumably antecedent independent variable is directly manipulated in order to ascertain its effect on the dependent variable. If Y is observed to vary concomitantly with the variation in X in this controlled situation, then one has obtained evidence for the validity of the hypothesized antecedent-consequent relationship between X and Y. In a causal-comparative situation, on the other hand, the researcher cannot control the independent variables by manipulation or by randomization. Changes in the independent variable have already taken place; the researcher is faced with the problem of trying to determine the antecedents of the observed consequence. Because of the lack of control, it is more hazardous to infer that there is a genuine relationship between X and Y in a causal-comparative study.

Let us illustrate the difference between a causal-comparative and an experimental approach by examining these two approaches to the same research question. Consider the question of the effect that students' anxiety in an achievement-testing situation has on their examination performance. The causal-comparative approach to this problem would involve measuring the already existing anxiety level at the time of the examination, then comparing the performance of "high-anxious" and "low-anxious" students. The weakness of such an approach is that one could not necessarily conclude that it was the students' anxiety that produced the observed difference in achievement examination performance. Both sets of scores may have been influenced by a third factor, such as general intelligence. General intelligence may be the major cause of both the level of anxiety and the achievement test results.

An experimental approach to the same problem would involve the administration of the examination under two conditions that are identical in every respect except that one is anxiety-arousing and the other is neutral. The experimenter can induce anxiety by telling the subjects that their final grade is dependent upon their performance, that the test is extremely difficult, or that the test will be used to identify the incompetent. The neutral group would merely be told that their cooperation is needed for the experiment. The investigator could randomly assign subjects to the two conditions. Then if the anxious group performed better than the neutral, it could be concluded that the anxiety had a facilitating effect on test performance. Such a conclusion could be legitimately drawn because of the control provided by the random assignment of groups to treatments and by the direct manipulation of the independent variable by the experimenter. Anxiety is one of the few variables that can be either an active or an attribute independent variable. That is, one can manipulate it actively, as described (experimental approach), or one can take subjects and classify them on the basis of their scores on an anxiety measure (causal-comparative approach).

In a sense the causal-comparative study can be viewed as a reverse approach to experimentation. Instead of taking groups that are equivalent and exposing them to different treatments, the causal-comparative study starts with groups that are different and tries to determine the antecedents of these differences. A causal-comparative study begins with a description of a present situation, which is assumed to be an effect of some previously acting factors, and attempts a retrospective search to determine the assumed antecedent factors, which began operating at an earlier time. Such a procedure does not provide the safeguards, typical in experimentation, that are necessary for making inferences about causal relationships. An investigator who finds a relationship between the variables in an *ex post facto* study has secured evidence only of some concomitant variation. Because the investigator has not controlled X or other possible variables that may have determined Y, there is no basis for inferring a causal relationship between X and Y. In order to be able to infer a type of antecedent-consequent relationship between the variables, one must gather evidence to show that Y did not precede X or that the Y effect has not been produced by some other factor that is related to the presumed antecedent factor. For example, if we give children with brain damage and children without damage a perceptual test, the differences in their performance might reflect the effects of brain damage or they might reflect such other factors as differences in anxiety associated with certain types of illness. Or let us consider an early study by Rogerson and Rogerson that reported the finding that a group of children who had been breast-fed during infancy subsequently exhibited a higher level of performance in elementary school than did a group of children who had been bottle-fed.[1] It cannot be concluded from such a finding that performance in school may be improved by breast feeding during infancy. Most likely the relationship observed by these investigators was an outcome of variations in one or more variables that influenced both the type of feeding received by the children studied and the level of performance they subsequently achieved in school. The authors report that the study was conducted at a clinic where breast feeding was encouraged and that failures to do so were often the result of poor health of the infant or the mother or both. Thus, the most reasonable interpretation would probably be that both the type of feeding received by the infants and their subsequent performance in school were influenced by health, good health tending to result more often in successful breast feeding *and* in superior school performance. So despite the observed relationship between these two factors, we certainly would not want to conclude that level of school performance was a direct consequence of type of feeding.

Causal-comparative research, though not a satisfactory substitute for experimentation, does provide a method that can be used in the circumstances

---

[1] Rogerson, B. C. F., and C. H. Rogerson (1939). Feeding in infancy and subsequent psychological difficulties. *Journal of Mental Science, 85,* 1163–1182.

under which much of educational research must be conducted. It remains a useful method that can supply much information of value in educational decision making.

/// CONDITIONS NECESSARY FOR INFERRING CAUSAL RELATIONSHIPS

If one wishes to reach a conclusion that one variable (X) is the cause of another variable (Y,) *three* kinds of evidence are necessary:

1. that a statistical relationship between X and Y has been established
2. that X preceded Y in time
3. that other factors did not determine Y

Because of the safeguards built into an experimental design, experimental studies provide evidence on all of these, so that causal inferences can be made. In causal-comparative studies, however, the safeguards of the experimental situation are lacking and interpretation of causal relationship is much more hazardous.

If one does establish a relationship between two variables in a causal-comparative study, one must proceed to look for evidence on the other two points. The investigator must establish the time sequence; that is, one must consider whether Y might have occurred before X and hence could not be an effect of X. Decisions about the time relationship between X and Y can be made either on a logical basis or as a result of measurements that show the groups did not differ on Y before exposure to X.

It is also extremely important that the investigator consider whether factors other than X might have determined Y. One proceeds to check this possibility by introducing other relevant variables into the analysis and observing how the relationship between X and Y is affected by these additional variables.

One may find that the relationship between X and Y holds up even when the other variables are introduced. In this case one has some evidence to support a causal inference. On the other hand, one may find that the presence of the other variables may change the relationship between X and Y or even eliminate it. In this case one concludes either that X does not determine Y or that the relationship between X and Y is spurious.

// Possibilities for Spurious Results in Causal-Comparative Research

The difference between an active independent variable and an attribute independent variable is exceedingly important. When investigators can control the treatment (X) and then observe the dependent variable (Y), they have reasonable evidence that X influences Y. If they cannot control X, they may be led to inappropriate conclusions because the observed relationship may be a *spurious* one, that is, a relationship that is due to other causes, not to X influencing Y. Among the possible origins of spurious relationships are common cause, reverse causality, and the presence of other independent variables.

/ Common Cause

In a causal-comparative investigation one must consider the possibility that both the independent and dependent variables of the study are merely two separate results of a third variable. For example, if we use average teachers' salary as an independent variable and sales of distilled spirits as a dependent variable for each year since the repeal of Prohibition in the United States, we find a high positive correlation between the two variables. Does this mean that whenever teachers' salaries are raised they spend their money on alcohol? A more plausible explanation is that both teachers' salaries and sales of distilled spirits are the result of increasing affluence and inflation since 1933.

It is well established that the average income of private high school graduates is much higher than the average income of public and parochial high school graduates. Does this mean that private schools better prepare students for financial success? Or is the difference due to the fact that those families with enough money to send their children to private schools are also able to finance their children's professional training, set them up in business, or buy them ambassadorships or seats in the United States Senate?

In city X we find that over the last 20 years an increase in the consumption of electricity has been accompanied by a corresponding increase in cases of mental illness. Does this mean that an increase in the use of electricity leads to an increase in mental illness? A check of census figures shows that the population of city X has increased through the years and that the consumption of electricity and cases of mental illness are both functions of population growth.

A causal-comparative researcher must always consider the possibilities of common cause or causes accounting for an observed relationship. In our examples fairly obvious common causes could be identifed. However, in *ex post facto* research there is always a nagging doubt that there may be common causes that no one has thought of that explain a relationship. It has been shown that the injury rate of drivers who use seat belts is lower than the injury rate of drivers who do not. Is this because the use of seat belts reduces injury or is it that cautious drivers (*a*) use seat belts and (*b*) have fewer injury-causing accidents?

/ Reverse Causality

In interpreting an observed relationship in a causal-comparative study one must consider the possibility that the reverse of the suggested hypothesis could also account for the finding. That is, instead of saying that X causes Y, perhaps it is the case that Y causes X. For instance, it is a fact that the proportion of Episcopalians who are listed in *Who's Who in America* is much greater than the proportion of Episcopalians in the general population. Does this mean that Episcopalianism leads to the kind of success that results in being listed in *Who's Who?* It is just as plausible, or perhaps more so, to hypothesize that successful people tend to gravitate to the Episcopal church.

If we find that college students who drink have a lower GPA than nondrinkers, we cannot automatically conclude that alcohol consumption depresses academic performance. Perhaps bad grades drive students to drink. (Or, of course, there may be any number of common causes that could lead to both drinking and poor grades.)

Investigations on the effects of child-rearing practices have revealed that there is more aggressive behavior on the part of children who are frequently punished. Does this mean that one can conclude that parental punishment leads to aggressive children, or is it that aggressive children are more likely to be punished?

The hypothesis of reverse causality is easier to deal with than the hypothesis of common cause. With the latter there may be numerous common causes in each case that could produce a spurious relationship. With reverse causality there is only one possibility in each case; Y caused X instead of X caused Y.

In any situation when X always precedes Y in time, the very nature of our data rules out the possibility of reverse causality. For example, numerous studies have shown that the average annual income of college graduates is higher than the average annual income of nongraduates. We can rule out the hypothesis of reverse causality because graduation or nongraduation precedes the subsequent annual income. We cannot rule out a variety of possible common causes.

A method of establishing the time order of variables is to obtain measurements of the same subjects at different times. Let us assume that one is interested in the relationship between acceptance of the philosophy of a corporation and promotion within that corporation. If one merely interviewed a sample of the employees and found that those in higher positions held attitudes and opinions more in line with the company's value system, one would not know whether acceptance of company values and objectives was conducive to promotion or whether promotion increased acceptance of the company value system. To rule out reverse causality as an explanation, one could interview a group of new trainees and obtain by means of a questionnaire, rating scale, or the like a measure of their acceptance of the corporation philosophy. Then after a period of time, perhaps 18 months, the investigator could determine from company records which of the employees had been promoted. If the findings showed that a significantly higher proportion of those who had expressed attitudes and opinions consistent with corporation philosophy had been promoted, as compared with those who had not, one would have better evidence that conformity with company philosophy was conducive to promotion. (One is still left with the possibility that some common cause or causes account for differences in both philosophy and promotion.)

/ Other Possible Independent Variables

There may be independent variables other than the one under consideration in the causal-comparative study that could bring about the observed effect on the Y variable. That is, in addition to X_1, other variables, X_2 and X_3, might also be antecedent factors for the variation in the dependent variable.

It is known that the recorded suicide rate in Sweden is among the highest in the world. Does this mean that the Swedish environment causes more people to commit suicide? Does it mean that the Swedish people are more suicide prone than others? Perhaps there is truth in one or both of these hypotheses. It is equally possible, however, that the actual independent variable is the honesty of coroners in Sweden compared with the honesty of coroners in other countries. In countries where great social stigma falls on the families of those who commit suicide, coroners may well use every conceivable means to record a death as accidental rather than suicide. Therefore, the difference between reported suicide rates may be a function of coroner behavior and nothing else.

At a governors' conference Governor X points with pride to the low crime rate in his state. Another governor points out that the police forces in Governor X's state are seriously undermanned and the low crime rate may indicate only that very few crimes there are ever reported. An industrialist asks his personnel manager why he does not hire more Old Siwash graduates, asserting that since so many of them are rapidly moving up the promotion ladder, they are obviously more competent than other graduates. The personnel manager tactfully points out that the phenomenon might not be explained by competence but rather by the fact that the industrialist is himself an Old Siwash graduate and may be subconsciously favoring his fellow alumni in promotion decisions.

An obvious first task for investigators is to make an attempt to list all the possible alternative independent variables. Then by holding the others constant, we can test in turn each of the variables to determine if it is related to Y. If we can eliminate the alternative independent variables by showing that they are not related to Y, we gain support for the original hypothesis of a relationship between X and Y.

In the following report the data show a relationship between automobile use and academic achievement.

Do Automobiles and Scholarship Mix?

No, says Madison HS, Rexburg, Idaho. A study made of the 4-year grade averages of a typical Madison senior class and car drivers showed the following:

No straight-A student had the use of a car.

Only 15% of the B students drove a car to school.

Of C students, 41% brought cars to school.

Of D students, 71% drove to school.

Of E students, 83% drove to school.

Action Program

As a result of the study, Rexburg's Board of Education adopted a resolution on August 11, 1958, which specified that—

1. Junior and senior high school students who drive cars to school must make written application to the School Board showing the reason or need to drive their cars to school. Those granted permission will receive student permits.
2. Students driving cars to school on the student permits must park them in designated areas.
3. Students failing to comply with established rules and regulations will have their student permits revoked. If students persist in non-compliance, they will be subject to expulsion from school by action of the School Board.

Community Cooperation

The entire community has organized to support the Board of Education's regulations. The Citizen's Law Enforcement Council and the Rexburg Youth Conference have enlisted the participation of the Civic Club, Rotary Club, American Legion, newspapers, police department, and parents in their drive for high school traffic safety. Hundreds of citizens have signed a pledge to back the drive and have received membership cards issued by the Council and Conference. Madison's principal, W. G. Nelson, strongly supports the community-wide action against unrestricted car use by high school students. "We believe that restriction on automobile use will make for better attendance and closer attention to studies. We haven't 'arrived' but we certainly are on the way."

A Texas Principal

Commenting on the Rexburg program, [a Texas principal] said, "It has long been my opinion that there is a high correlation between rate of failure, scholarship, and ownership and operation of automobiles freely by high school youth. We are finding it difficult to obtain much interest from able-bodied boys in major athletics. So many of the boys are paying for automobiles or for their maintenance and operation by holding down part-time jobs after school hours that they don't go out for athletics. If they have money to operate their cars, they prefer to ride in them around town after school. There are a few parents who have sufficient control of and influence with their youngsters to prevent the unwise use of their own cars, but they are very scarce."[2]

Is the conclusion that automobile use causes lower academic achievement justified? Let us consider the possible alternative hypotheses.

1. *Common cause.* Are there variables that may influence both auto use and scholarship? We know social class is related to scholarship. If social class also influences auto use, the apparent relationship between grades and auto use would be not a cause-effect relationship but two aspects of social-class differences. Differences in student life-style or values could also account for the apparent relationship. If some students value driving highly and have little interest in scholarship, denying them access to cars would not necessarily increase their scholarship. We could propose a number of credible common-cause hypotheses.

2. *Reverse causality.* Is it possible that poor grades are a cause of car use? We could reasonably hypothesize that students who do poorly in school look for other paths to social acceptance and that car use is one of the possibilities.

3. *Other possible independent variables.* Could it be that teachers perceive car users as disinterested students and assign them lower grades than they deserve?

There are so many credible alternative hypotheses that one should hesitate to interpret the data as indicating a cause-effect relationship. Asher and Schusler investigated the same issue with a design that incorporated more control than had previous studies.[3] Instead of considering only present grades and auto use, they recorded grades of seniors at the end of the first semester and the grades of the same subjects when they were freshmen. If auto use affects scholarship, then the grades of drivers would be expected to drop between the time they were freshmen—and therefore ineligible for driver's licenses—and the time they were seniors. Asher and Schusler used the difference between freshman and senior GPA as their dependent variable. They also co-varied (see Chapter 9) on IQ. They found no significant relation between auto use and change in grades. They concluded, "access to an automobile seems not to cause an established pattern of grades to decline, or for that matter, to go up."

/// PARTIAL CONTROL IN CAUSAL-COMPARATIVE RESEARCH

There are strategies for improving the credibility of causal-comparative research, although none of them can adequately compensate for the inherent

---

[2]National Association of Secondary School Principals (1959). Do automobiles and scholarship mix? *NASSP Spotlight on Junior and Senior High Schools, 36,* 3.
[3]Asher, W., and M. M. Schusler (1967). Students' grades and access to cars. *Journal of Educational Research, 60,* 10.

weakness of such research, namely, lack of control of the independent variable. Among these strategies are change scores, matching, analysis of covariance, partial correlation, homogeneous groups, and building extraneous variables into the design.

// Change Scores

In the car-use examples, we found that the conclusion reached when the difference between subjects' senior grades and freshman grades were used did not agree with the conclusion reached when only grades per se were used. Certainly the former has more credibility than the latter because the latter completely fails to take into account the possibility that car users were poorer students than nonusers before any of them might have had access to cars.

With change scores, one takes into account previous scores on the Y variable rather than just present scores on Y. When one compares how much a treatment group changes in comparison with a control group, one may be somewhat less likely to be misled than when only present scores are used. However, the use of change scores is only a partial solution, and the results of such studies must be treated with caution. For example, Principal A has introduced a new reading program in the fifth grade, and after it has been in use for a year he wants to compare its effectiveness with the effectiveness of the reading program it replaced. In the same district, Principal B's school is still using the old program. Both schools give the same standardized reading test at the end of each school year. Principal A compares the mean grade-equivalent reading scores for fifth-graders in the two schools. He finds the mean grade level equivalent for his fifth-graders is 6.0, while the mean for Principal B's fifth-graders is 4.0. Is this dramatic evidence of the effectiveness of the new method? Principal A realizes that the difference between means could be due to differences between the pupils when they began the fifth grade in the two schools. He obtains scores for the reading test administered when the pupils were finishing fourth grade. He finds that his students had a mean grade level equivalent of 4.8, while Principal B's students had a mean grade level equivalent of only 3.2. Therefore he must make an adjustment for the fact that the two groups were not at the same point when they began fifth grade. For each pupil for whom both scores are available, Principal A subtracts the fourth-grade score from the fifth-grade score. He finds a mean difference of +1.2 for his pupils and +.8 for Principal B's pupils. The difference of .4 between the two groups' mean change scores is less dramatic but more convincing than the difference of 2.0 obtained when only fifth-grade scores were used and no adjustment was made for previous performance.

Can Principal A now conclude that the new method is more effective than the old one? Given the nature of change scores, he cannot. Differences in change scores may be due to the continuation of previous patterns. In order to find the pattern in this case, Principal A divides the final mean grade level equivalent, obtained at the end of the fourth-grade year, by four (the number of years in school). Principal A's pupils with a mean score of 4.8 at the end of their fourth year have had an average grade equivalent gain in reading performance of 1.2 per year, while Principal B's students have averaged a reading grade equivalent gain of .8. In both cases the gains in reading scores during the fifth grade are just what one would expect given the previous gain patterns, and therefore there is no support for the hypothesis that the new method is more effective than the old method. An inherent weakness in change scores is that an apparent greater gain in one group compared with another group may well be a continuation of a previous pattern and not due to the treatment at all.

Consider another example. It is hypothesized that the study of Latin improves high school students' English vocabulary. The investigators have freshman and senior vocabulary scores for both those who took and those who did not take Latin. If we look at Figure 10.1, we see that the gain in the vocabulary scores from grade 9 to grade 12 for the Latin group (from 80 to 95 points) is greater than the gain for the non-Latin group (from 54 to 63 points). However, we see in Figure 10.1 that those who elected to

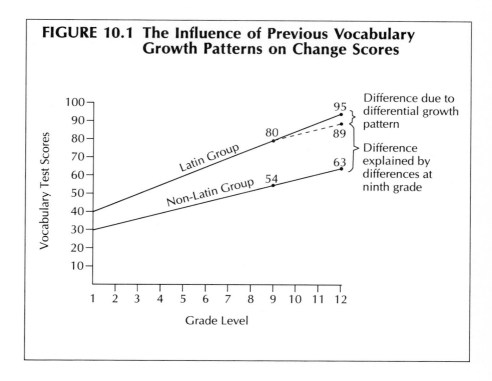

FIGURE 10.1 The Influence of Previous Vocabulary Growth Patterns on Change Scores

take Latin are merely continuing a previous pattern of accelerated vocabulary growth, and those who did not elect to take Latin are continuing their previous pattern. The gain for both groups in the 3 years from grades 9 to 12 is the same as their gain from grades 6 to 9. A very naive investigator, looking at only the senior scores of the two groups and not taking into account their different starting places, might conclude that the difference of 32 points (95 − 63) is due to the Latin experience. A less naive investigator, using change scores from grade 9 to grade 12 for the two groups, attributes only 6 points (15 − 9) to the Latin experience. However, this investigator has also reached the wrong conclusion. Who is the more likely to mislead the unaware? The conclusion of the first investigator is less likely to be accepted because the idea that the two groups may well differ on previous English vocabulary proficiency is a fairly obvious one, and readers are likely to be skeptical of a conclusion based on only senior scores. The use of change scores *seems* to solve the problem of preexisting differences, and the second investigator's conclusion seems more credible. However, the use of change scores is only a partial solution.

Change scores adjust for (*a*) groups beginning at different points. They do *not* adjust for (*b*) preexisting differences in growth rates. Whenever preexisting differences in growth rate do exist, differences in posttreatment scores are due to both (*a*) and (*b*). The use of change scores removes the spurious effect of (*a*) but not the spurious effect of (*b*). Therefore, the change scores are only a partial solution. We can be misled by the underadjustment.

// Matching

A common method of providing partial control in causal-comparative investigations has been to match the subjects in the experimental and control groups on as many extraneous variables as possible. The matching is usually done on a subject-to-subject basis to form matched pairs. For example, if one is interested in the relationship between scouting experiences and delinquency, one could locate two groups of boys classified as delinquent and nondelinquent according to specified criteria. It would be wise in such a study to select pairs from these groups matched on the basis of socioeconomic status, family structure, and other variables known to be related to both choosing the scouting experience and delinquency. Analysis of the data from the matched samples could be made to determine whether scouting characterizes the nondelinquent and is absent in the background of the delinquent. The matching procedure in causal-comparative research presents some of the difficulties described in our discussion of its use in experimentation (Chapter 9). In the first place, utilizing matching in a causal-comparative study assumes that one knows what the relevant factors are—that is, the factors that may have some correlation with the dependent variable. Furthermore, matching is likely to reduce greatly the number of subjects that can actually be used in the final analysis. The loss of cases inherent in the matching process is an even more serious problem in causal-comparative research than in experimentation, where matching precedes the introduction of the independent variable. At least in the experimental approach there may be a possibility (although it is not recommended) of adding new cases to replace the ones that do not match. This cannot be done in causal-comparative research.

One of Chapin's studies shows the loss of subjects that occurs as a result of matching.[4] Chapin was interested in the influence of high school graduation on an individual's success and community adjustment after a 10-year period. The initial data revealed that those who had completed high school were more successful than those who had not. However, an examination of the high school files revealed that those who had graduated also had higher marks in elementary school, younger ages, higher parental occupations, lived in better neighborhoods, and so on. These factors could have been the causative factors for both completion of high school and later success. To partially control these common causes, Chapin examined subgroups of students matched on all these background factors and differing only in completion of high school. Matching reduced the number of cases from 1195 to 46, or 23 graduates and 23 nongraduates—fewer than 4 percent of the number interviewed.

A more serious problem than loss of subjects is the role regression plays in a causal-comparative matched-pairs design. Let us use our reading example to illustrate the point. In order to use matched pairs instead of unmatched change scores, Principal A would take a student from his school with a fourth-grade reading score of 3.1 and match that student with a student from Principal B's school with a fourth-grade reading score of 3.1, a student from his school with a score of 4.8 with a student from B's school with a score of 4.8, and so on. However, since the mean of the B population is lower than the mean of the A population, there will be many low-scoring B students for whom there is no match in A and many high-scoring A students for whom there is no match in the B group. The scores of all the unmatchable students will be excluded from the data analysis. For those who could be matched, the mean score for the fourth-grade reading test for group A and group B will be identical. Therefore, it appears that we have successfully created a group from school B who are the same as the group from school A in reading achievement.

This all sounds very good. Can we now attribute differences in fifth-grade reading scores to a difference in the effectiveness of the old and new methods? Alas, no! Our matched pairs are basically those students with poorer fourth-grade reading scores from population A and those students with higher scores from population B. The matched A students' scores will regress *up*

---

[4]Chapin, F. S. (1947). *Experimental Designs in Sociological Research*. New York: Harper & Row.

toward the total A mean, and the matched B students' scores will regress *down* toward the total B mean. Thus, when we compare the fifth-grade reading scores of the matched groups, we would expect the A mean to be higher than the B mean even if the new method is no more effective than the old method.

Matching looks good because it provides experimental and control groups that are equal on a pretreatment variable or variables. However, when two matched groups are drawn from different populations, regression toward the original population means will be expected to create spurious results whenever the two populations are not equal. Matching pairs from within a *single* population is often a useful strategy. Matching subjects from one population with subjects from another population is a *bad* strategy. As is the case with change scores, matching only partly adjusts for preexisting differences between groups. This underadjustment can mislead us in the same manner that the underadjustment in change scores can mislead us.

// Analysis of Covariance

Analysis of covariance (ANCOVA), like matching, can be used to partially adjust for preexisting differences between groups. An advantage of ANCOVA is that data from all subjects can be used rather than only data from matched pairs. We have seen in Chapter 9 that ANCOVA is an excellent procedure for improving the precision in a randomized experiment. ANCOVA is also sometimes used to partially adjust for initial differences in a causal-comparative design. However, as the adjustment in causal-comparative research is only partial, ANCOVA does not "solve" the problem of initial differences between groups; it only lessens it. When interpreting causal-comparative research, it is inappropriate to assume ANCOVA has satisfactorily adjusted for initial differences.

A well-known example of the dangers of matching and analysis of covariance is the Westinghouse/Ohio University causal-comparative study of the effects of the Head Start program.[5] This study compared the academic achievement of students who had been in the Head Start program with the achievement of those who had not been in the Head Start program. Children who had been in the program were matched with non–Head Start children from the same neighborhoods on gender, racial-ethnic groups, and kindergarten attendance. Analysis of covariance was used to adjust for differences in income per capita, educational level of father, and occupational level of father. The results indicated that the achievement of the non–Head Start

---

[5]Cicirelli, V., *et al.* (1969). *The Impact of Head Start: An Evaluation of the Effects of Head Start on Children's Cognitive and Affective Development.* (A report presented to the Office of Economic Opportunity pursuant to contract B89-4536.) Westinghouse Learning Corporation and Ohio University. (Distributed by the Clearinghouse for Federal Scientific and Technical Information, U.S. Department of Commerce, National Bureau of Standards, Institute for Applied Technology. PB 184 328.)

group was greater than that of the Head Start group even when scores were adjusted for initial differences, suggesting that the effect of the Head Start program was a harmful one.

Campbell and Erlebacher pointed out that because both matching and analysis of covariance underadjust for initial differences between groups, we would expect adjusted posttreatment scores of a disadvantaged group to be less than adjusted posttreatment scores of a less disadvantaged group.[6] Since the extent of the underadjustment is unknown, we cannot safely conclude that the Head Start experience was harmful or beneficial or had no effect.

// Homogeneous Groups

You may recall from the discussion of control in experimentation that it is possible to control for the effects of a variable by selecting samples that are as homogeneous as possible on that variable. A similar procedure can be followed in causal-comparative research. Instead of taking a heterogeneous sample and comparing matched subgroups within it, an investigator may control a variable by including in the sample only subjects who are homogeneous on that variable. If intelligence is a relevant extraneous variable, the investigator could control its effect by using subjects from only one intelligence level. This procedure serves the purpose of disentangling the independent variable in which the investigator may be interested from other variables with which it is commonly associated so that any effects that are found can more justifiably be associated with the independent variable.

Suppose one wishes to investigate whether having a quiet room at home, with desk, books, and so on, in which to study affects the grades of high school students. If one simply selects a cross section of high school students, asks them whether they have a quiet room in which to study, and then compares the grades of those who have a room and those who do not, one may erroneously conclude that having a quiet room in which to study leads to good grades. An alternative explanation is that there are other factors associated with social class that may influence both one's study arrangements and grades received in school. Low-income families, for instance, are more likely to be overcrowded and are less likely to put emphasis on scholastic achievement than are middle- and upper-class families. If one wants to control for the effects of social class, one can limit the study to subjects of only one socioeconomic level. If one finds a relationship between study arrangements and grades within the one social class, one would have somewhat more confidence in the conclusion that the difference in grades is due to study arrangements and not to socioeconomic differences. Of course this procedure

---

[6]Campbell, D. T., and A. Erlebacher (1970). How regression artifacts in quasi-experimental evaluations can mistakenly make compensatory education look harmful. In V. Hellmuth (ed.). *Compensatory Education: A National Debate*, vol. 3: *Disadvantaged Child*. New York: Brunner/Mazel.

limits the generalizability of the findings to the one social class used in the study; one would not know whether the relationship exists in other social classes.

The use of homogeneous samples is only a partial solution to the problems inherent in causal-comparative research. We can control for some common-cause variables by selecting samples who are alike on a suspected common-cause variable. We cannot be sure we have subjects who are homogeneous on all suspected or unsuspected common-cause variables. In our example it is quite possible that *within* middle-class families both having or not having a quiet room and academic achievement are a function of family size or other variables. Regression can also be a problem with homogeneous samples. For example, if Principal A in our earlier example had used only children in the two schools who scored exactly 4.0 on the fourth-grade reading test, regression would cause the A group to regress up and the B group to regress down, as they did when subjects were matched.

// Building Extraneous Variables into the Design

It may be possible to build relevant extraneous independent variables into the causal-comparative design and use a factorial analysis-of-variance technique. For example, assume that intelligence is a relevant extraneous variable and it is not feasible to control it through any other means. In such a case intelligence could be added to the design as another independent variable and the subjects of the study classified in terms of intelligence levels. The dependent-variable measures would then be analyzed through the analysis of variance, and the main and interaction effects of intelligence might be determined. Such a procedure would reveal any significant differences among the groups on the dependent variable, but no causal relationship between intelligence and the dependent variable could be assumed. Other extraneous variables could be operating to produce both the main effect and any interaction effect.

For example, many studies have reported a relationship between birth order and intellectual attainment and occupational achievement: firstborn doing better than secondborn, secondborn doing better than thirdborn, and so forth. After a thorough review of the literature, Schooler concluded: "The most frequently reported differences between birth ranks—the greater occurrence of first-borns among groups marked by unusual intellectual attainment or occupational achievement—seems to be most parsimoniously explained in terms of differences among social class trends in family size.[7] Because there is an inverse relationship between social class and family size, the average social-class standing of fifth children would be lower than the average social-class standing of fourth children, and so forth. As social class

---

[7]Schooler, C. (1972). Birth order effects: Not here, not now! *Psychological Bulletin, 72,* 161–175.

is related to achievement, the apparent relationship between birth order and achievement might be due solely to differences in average social-class standing and not to birth order per se.

Later Belmont and Marolla studied birth order and scores on the Raven Progressive Matrices test (a nonverbal intelligence test) for nearly 400,000 young men in the Netherlands.[8] They found that *within* each family-size intelligence declined with birth order. Since they were comparing scores only within five-child families, within four-child families, and so forth, differences in social class could not account for their results.

Do the Belmont and Marolla results now enable us to say that birth order per se is related to intelligence? We would be wise to treat this as only a tentative conclusion. One reason for our reservation is that there may be variables other than social class that account for the apparent relationship. Certainly the average age of the parents of fourth children is older than the average age of parents of third children and this may have something to do with the phenomenon. Perhaps it is accounted for by something we cannot even imagine.

Building other variables into a causal-comparative design is a partial solution, but we can never be sure that we have selected the right variables or that we have employed *all* the variables that should have been considered.

It has been emphasized throughout this chapter that the major weakness of causal-comparative designs is the lack of control. Because it is not feasible to utilize randomization to assign subjects to groups or to have direct manipulation of the independent variable in a controlled situation, there is always the possibility that there are uncontrolled variables that are responsible for the variations in the dependent variable. Because of this, one cannot assume that the groups are similar at the beginning of a study. Because the researcher has no control over who has been exposed to the experience and who has not, it is quite possible that something else about the people or their environment determines exposure in the first place. Therefore, it may be that it is the "something else" rather than the experience itself that constitutes the critical independent variable.

As a result of the inadequate control in a causal-comparative study, interpretation of the findings may be particularly hazardous. The risk of incorrect interpretation is great. When a relationship between two variables has been established in the course of a causal-comparative study, the analysis has, in a sense, taken only its first step. The investigator must consider and test any plausible alternative hypotheses and, even after doing so, must realize that an apparent relationship may be due to some other unfathomable cause. Procedures such as the use of change scores, matching, analysis of covariance, partial correlation, homogeneous groups, and building extraneous variables

---

[8]Belmont, L., and F. A. Marolla (1973). Birth order, family size, and intelligence. *Science, 182,* 1096–1101.

into a study can help avoid gross errors in causal-comparative studies, but they all underadjust for pretreatment differences among groups. Listing alternative hypotheses (common cause, reverse causality, and alternate independent variables) can help one assess more realistically causal-comparative results.

/// DESIGNING THE CAUSAL-COMPARATIVE INVESTIGATION

The two basic modes of causal-comparative research are (1) Begin with subjects who differ on an independent variable and test hypotheses concerning how they will differ on dependent variables, and (2) Begin with subjects who differ on a dependent variable and test hypotheses concerning possible independent variables. An example of the former would be a study to compare the problem-solving performance of creative and noncreative college students. The hypothesis would read: Creative college students will exhibit greater speed and accuracy on a problem-solving task than will noncreative college students. This hypothesis clearly indicates the need for a causal-comparative design because the investigators can neither manipulate creativity nor assign students randomly to groups. They must start with two groups who already differ on the independent variable, creativity, and compare them on the dependent variable, problem-solving performance.

The investigators must define *creative college student* and *noncreative college student* in precise operational terms. The creative college student might be defined as those undergraduates in the school of education scoring above the upper quartile on both the Guilford Test of Alternate Uses and Consequences and an anagram test. Those students scoring below the first quartile on the tests would be defined as noncreative.

The investigators should try to identify variables other than creativity that could affect the dependent variable of problem-solving performance and take steps to equate the experimental and control groups on these variables by matching or by statistical means. For example, in this study other independent variables that should be controlled are intelligence, gender, and perhaps college major or college year. A bright male sophomore in the creative group might be matched with his counterpart in the noncreative group.

After the formation of the matched groups, both groups would be given a measure of the dependent variable, a problem-solving task. Further analysis of the data by means of a *t*-test would reveal any significant differences in the problem-solving performance of the two groups and perhaps show a relationship between creativity and problem-solving performance. Although one may conclude from such a study that there is a relationship, one cannot assume a causal connection between creativity and problem-solving performance. There may be other uncontrolled variables that singly or in combination could influence problem solving. The alert investigator is aware of the need to examine other plausible alternative explanations of a causal-comparative finding.

Sometimes the independent variable is an attribute that cannot be manipulated, such as gender, socioeconomic status, or ethnicity. For example, Robinson-Awana, Kehle, and Jensen compared the self-esteem of seventh-grade boys and girls.[9] Using the School Short Form of the Coopersmith Self-Esteem Inventory (SEI) as the dependent-variable measure, they found that boys reported significantly higher levels of self-esteem than did girls. Dividing subjects into below-average, average, and above-average achievement groups, they found self-esteem rose as achievement rose. Then the investigators administered the SEI again, asking subjects to respond as they thought a member of the opposite sex but of the same age and grade would respond. Boys at all three achievement levels indicated lower self-esteem for girls. Below-average- and average-achieving girls indicated higher self-esteem for boys, but high-achieving girls indicated lower self-esteem for boys.

Sometimes the independent variable is one that could possibly be manipulated but is typically beyond the control of the investigator for practical or ethical reasons. For example, it would be unethical to randomly assign some students to be retained in school and others to be promoted in order to study the effects of retention on subsequent achievement. However, insight into this question can be gained by matching retained students with nonretained students on as many relevant variables as possible. Peterson, DeGracie, and Ayabe matched first-, second-, and third-grade retainees with same-age students in the same school system who were not retained.[10] Subjects were matched on gender; chronological age; and Total Reading, Total Language, and Total Math scores on the California Achievement Test. In the years following retention, retained students and their nonretained counterparts were compared in terms of their relative standing in class. The relative standing of first- and second-grade retainees was statistically significantly higher than their nonretained counterparts in reading and math but not in language. Differences between third-grade retainees and their matched counterparts, now in the fourth grade, were not significant. The investigators also compared the performance of retainees when they reached the next grade with that of their nonretained counterparts in that grade in the previous year and found that retainees achieved better than their nonretained counterparts in second and third grade but not in first grade.

With the second mode of causal-comparative research, two or more groups differ on a dependent variable and hypotheses are tested concerning

[9]Robinson-Awana, P., T. J. Kehle, and W. R. Jensen (1986). But what about smart girls? Adolescent self-esteem and sex role perceptions as a function of academic achievement. *Journal of Educational Psychology, 78 (3),* 179–183.

[10]Peterson, S. E., J. S. DeGracie, and C. R. Ayabe (1987). A longitudinal study of the effects of retention/promotion on academic achievement. *American Educational Research Journal, 24,* 107–118.

possible independent variables. Consider the ten members of a wrestling team, three of whom become ill when returning from a tournament. To investigate the cause of the illness the doctor asks what they ate when the team stopped for dinner on their way home. She finds that every item the three ill wrestlers chose differed except for creamed chicken. The seven wrestlers who did not have creamed chicken did not become ill. She concludes the creamed chicken is the cause of the illness. The doctor is employing philosopher John Stuart Mill's Joint Method of Agreement and Difference, which rules that

> If two or more instances in which the phenomenon occurs have only one circumstance in common, while two or more instances in which it does not occur have nothing in common save the absence of that circumstance; the circumstance in which alone the two sets of instances differ, is the effect, or cause, or necessary part of the cause, of the phenomenon.[11]

An example of the second mode of causal-comparative research is Benn's study of variables related to the security of attachment of 18-month-old sons and their employed mothers.[12] The quality of the mother-son attachment (dependent variable) was assessed by analyzing videotapes of the boys in structured episodes designed to assess the balance of attachment and exploratory behavior in the presence and absence of their mother and an unfamiliar person. It was found that among securely attached boys the mother-son relationship was characterized by warmth, acceptance, and freedom of emotional expression. The mothers of securely attached boys had also returned to work earlier during the infant's first year of life than did mothers of insecurely attached boys. Socioeconomic class and form of child care were not related to mother-son attachment.

/// THE ROLE OF CAUSAL-COMPARATIVE RESEARCH

Given the hazards involved in interpreting causal-comparative research, there are many in our profession who say we should not engage in this type of research at all. Basically their contention is that it is better to admit that we are ignorant than to risk reaching conclusions that are incorrect.

On the other hand, there are those who contend that many of the variables that are of great interest to us are not amenable to experimental research. We cannot randomly assign children to broken or intact homes, to high or low social class, to achievement-oriented or non-achievement-

---

[11]Mill, J. S. (1846). *A System of Logic* (p. 229). New York: Harper & Brothers.
[12]Benn, R. K. (1986). Factors promoting secure attachment relationships between employed mothers and their sons. *Child Development, 57,* 1224–1231.

oriented peer groups, and so forth. Therefore, if we want to learn anything about relationships between such attribute variables and other variables, the causal-comparative method is our only recourse. If we use appropriate methods of partial control and if we consider alternative hypotheses, perhaps we can be right more often than we are wrong.

Certainly there have been many highly credible causal-comparative studies. The surgeon general's study of the relationship between smoking and lung cancer is a well-known example. It is not possible to designate randomly a group of human subjects who are to smoke and a group who are not to smoke for years, so the study had to be done as causal-comparative research. The reversed-causality hypothesis that lung cancer causes people to smoke is not plausible. None of the common-cause hypotheses offered seem very likely: nervous people are prone to both smoking and lung cancer, some genetic predisposition leads to both, and so forth. The surgeon general controlled for many alternative independent variables by, for example, analyzing separately samples from areas of high air pollution and low air pollution. Experimental evidence with animals who were made to inhale or did not inhale cigarette smoke has produced evidence of a cause-to-effect relationship. Given all this, despite the dangers inherent in causal-comparative research, most of us would conclude that it is better to bet that there is a cause-to-effect relationship between smoking and lung cancer among humans than to bet that there is not such a relationship.

We all can deplore the many instances when causal-comparative research has been employed in situations where true experimental or, at least, quasi-experimental designs could have been used. It is dismaying how often local or state agencies and the federal government have "tested" new programs by entering all eligible subjects into the program and then attempted to evaluate the effects of the program *ex post facto*. Too often governmental agencies, including schools, have responded to pressure to "do something" about a problem by instituting a new program for all eligible subjects. Evans (of the U.S. Office of Education) and Schiller (of the Office of Economic Opportunity) describe the way government agencies have responded to this pressure:

> Attempts to implement the required condition of random assignment will continue to face the objections of program clients on the grounds that such procedures involve an arbitrary deprivation of the program to those designated as controls. Among the dissatisfied, the vocal ones will complain to officials and congressmen. Program directors consequently will want to avoid this procedure and will be on the side of those opposing it.
>
> Our experience leads us to conclude, though reluctantly, that in the actual time-pressured and politically loaded circumstances in which social action programs inevitably arise, the instances when random assignment is practical are rare; and the nature of political and governmental processes makes it likely that this will continue to be the case. Unfortunately,

the political process is not orderly, scheduled, or rational. Crests of public and congressional support for social action programs often swell quickly and with little anticipation. Once legislation is enacted, the pressures on administrators for swift program inplementation are intense. In these circumstances—which are the rule rather than the exception—pleas that the program should be implemented carefully, along the lines of a true experiment with random assignment of subjects so we can confidently evaluate the program's effectiveness, are bound to be ignored.[13]

We contend that any dissatisfaction encountered among clients "deprived" of a new program is a drop compared with the flood of dissatisfaction from taxpayers who discover that millions have been spent on programs that lacked a well-planned method for determining whether these programs actually accomplished anything. There must be ways of handling the public-relations problems in random assignment. Could not the government offer to several schools a fully funded program for a random half of their pupils? If the program is attractive, we would think many communities would be willing to participate in such an experiment, figuring that a random half-a-loaf is better than no loaf at all. Then when the evidence is in, the government could offer all pupils those programs that have shown their worth and quietly drop those that have not.

/// SUMMARY

Causal-comparative research is used when investigators are not in a position to test a hypothesis by assigning subjects to different conditions in which they directly manipulate the independent variable. In causal-comparative research the changes in the independent variable have already taken place and the researchers must study them in retrospect for their possible effects on an observed dependent variable.

Although there are many disadvantages of the causal-comparative approach, it nevertheless is frequently the only method by which educational researchers can obtain necessary information about characteristics of defined groups of students or information needed for the intelligent formulation of programs in the school. It permits researchers to investigate situations in which it is impossible to introduce controlled variation. Attributes such as intelligence, creativity, socioeconomic status, and teacher personality cannot be manipulated and hence must be investigated through causal-comparative research rather than through the more rigorous experimental approach.

---

[13]Evans, V. W., and J. Schiller (1970). How preoccupation with possible regression artifacts can lead to a faulty strategy for the evaluation of social action programs: A reply to Campbell and Erlebacher. In V. Hellmuth (ed.). *Compensatory Education: A National Debate*, vol. 3: *Disadvantaged Child*, New York: Brunner/Mazel.

Many causal-comparative investigations have been notable in their influence on education. Variables such as home background, genetic endowment, brain damage, and early experiences are very important educational variables even though they are beyond the control of educators.

The possibility of spurious relationships is always present in causal-comparative research. Considering the possibilities of common cause, reversed causality, and possible alternate independent variables can help us evaluate such research more realistically. Several partial-control strategies can help us avoid gross errors in causal-comparative designs, but none can entirely solve the problems inherent in those designs. We must always exercise caution in interpreting causal-comparative results.

// Key Concepts

active versus attribute variables
analysis of covariance (ANCOVA)
building extraneous variables into a
   design
causal relationship
change scores
characteristics of causal-comparative
   research

common cause
ex post facto research
homogeneous groups
matching
other independent variables
partial control
reverse causality
spurious results

/// EXERCISES

1. How do attribute variables and active variables differ from each other?

2. Under what conditions does one use causal-comparative research? What is the major weakness of causal-comparative designs?

3. What conditions are necessary to infer that X caused Y?

4. Which of the following research hypotheses call for *experimental research* and which call for *causal-comparative research?*
   a. Young children who are read a story by a stranger will not retain it as long as those who are read the same story by their own mothers.
   b. Creative fifth-grade students have higher achievement motivation than do noncreative fifth-grade students.
   c. Adolescents from single-parent homes more frequently have police records than do adolescents from homes where both parents reside.
   d. First-grade students who learn to spell phonetically will score higher on a spelling test than will those who learn to spell using the whole-word method.

e. Students at Learning University who score above 1200 on the Graduate Record Examination will receive higher grades in the College of Education than will students who do not score above 1200.

f. Handicapped children have lower self-concepts than do nonhandicapped children.

5. Define and give an example of each of the following terms:
   a. common cause
   b. reverse causality
   c. other independent variables

6. What do change scores adjust for and what do they not adjust for?

7. What are the advantages and disadvantages of matching?

8. How can a researcher deal with a relevant extraneous variable that cannot be controlled through matching or other means?

/// ANSWERS

1. An attribute variable is a characteristic that a subject possesses before the study begins; therefore, it cannot be directly manipulated. An active variable is also an independent variable, but it can be directly manipulated by the researcher.

2. Causal-comparative research is used when there are attribute independent variables, that is, when the subjects possess the independent variables before the study begins and therefore those variables are not manipulable. The major weakness of causal-comparative designs is control. Since randomization and manipulation of the independent variables are impossible, uncontrolled variables may be responsible for the variation in the dependent variable.

3. a. a statistical relationship between X and Y must be established
   b. X must precede Y in time
   c. other factors did not determine Y

4. a. experimental
   b. causal-comparative
   c. causal-comparative
   d. experimental
   e. causal-comparative
   f. causal-comparative

5. *Common cause* means that if variables A and B are related, it is possible that neither one caused the other, but both were caused by a third variable, C. For example, if it is shown that high scores on an achievement test and high grades in academic work are related, it is possible that both are caused by a third factor, general intelligence.

   Reverse causality means that the reverse of the suggested hypothesis could account for a relationship. For example, one may observe that there is a relationship between unemployment and excessive drinking and hypothesize that drinking to excess causes a worker to lose his or her job, when in reality it may be that those who lose their jobs tend to drink to excess.

   Other independent variables are variables, other than those observed, that may be responsible for relationships. For example, it is known that the proportion of the population confined to mental hospitals for schizophrenia is greater in the United States than it is in Great Britain, while the proportion of the population in Great Britain confined for depression is greater than the proportion in the United States. This does not necessarily mean that the American environment is more conducive to schizophrenia and the British environment is more likely to produce depression. It may be that the British are more tolerant of schizophrenic symptoms and less likely to hospitalize those with such symptoms, while Americans are more tolerant of the manifestation of the symptoms of depression.

6. Change scores adjust for initial differences between groups. They do not adjust for differential change patterns.

7. Matching provides groups that are equivalent on a particular variable or set of variables before treatment. Statistical regression can be expected to distort results when the matched groups are from different populations. Matching also reduces the number of subjects available.

8. The researcher may build the relevant extraneous variable into the causal-comparative design and use an analysis-of-variance technique. This procedure requires an analysis of the main and interaction effects.

CHAPTER **11**

Descriptive Research

INSTRUCTIONAL OBJECTIVES

After studying this chapter, the student will be able to

1. Explain how descriptive research differs from experimental and causal-comparative methods
2. State the different types of research that are classified as descriptive
3. Identify situations where the longitudinal method would be preferred for a developmental study and cases where the cross-sectional method would be preferred
4. Describe the methods and uses of trend analysis and follow-up studies
5. Describe documentary analysis and give examples of when it would be used
6. State the general purpose of correlational research
7. Describe the design of correlational research
8. Identify some factors that affect the magnitude of a correlation coefficient
9. Test a hypothesis about a correlation coefficient, r
10. Explain the two major purposes of correlational research
11. Define *predictor* and *criterion*
12. Develop a regression equation for predicting one variable, Y, from another variable, X
13. Define *multiple regression* and explain when it is used
14. Explain the phenomenon of shrinkage in multiple regression
15. Define *discriminant analysis*
16. Define *factor analysis*
17. Explain the role of correlation in factor analysis
18. Define *partial correlation* and explain its purpose

Descriptive research studies are designed to obtain information concerning the current status of phenomena. They are directed toward determining the nature of a situation as it exists at the time of the study. As with causal-comparative research, there is no administration or control of a treatment as is found in experimental research. Unlike causal-comparative studies, descriptive research is not generally directed toward hypothesis testing. The aim is to describe "what exists" with respect to variables or conditions in a situation. For example, a school administrator wishes to know how many first-graders are likely to be enrolled in school next year in order to plan the most effective use of school facilities and staff in accommodating the total school population. There is no need to study first-grade enrollment as a variable related to some other variable. In other words, the administrator is not testing a hypothesis but is seeking information to assist in decision making.

The simplest descriptive studies measure a single variable; they may involve no more than reporting the frequency of some event, as in the above example. Often, however, there is more than one variable and efforts are made to see if the variables are related. A researcher may start out to investigate attrition in the freshman year of college; later he or she may want to relate attrition to gender, race, high school preparation, and the like. A researcher who has been investigating high school students' achievement on standardized mathematics achievement tests and on the math part of the Scholastic Aptitude Test (SAT) may also investigate gender differences in their performance.

There are several types of studies that may be classified as descriptive research. These are (1) surveys (see Chapter 12), (2) developmental studies, (3) follow-up studies, (4) documentary analyses, (5) trend analyses, and (6) correlational studies.

/// STEPS IN DESCRIPTIVE RESEARCH

The process of descriptive research may be summarized in the following steps:

1. *Statement of the problem.* As in the case of experimental research, the researcher must start with a clear statement of the problem. This statement identifies the variables to be involved in the study and specifies whether the study is merely seeking to determine the status of these variables or will also investigate relationships between the variables.

2. *Identification of information needed to solve the problem.* The researcher lists the information to be collected, states whether this information is of a qualitative or a quantitative nature, and identifies the form the information will take (counts, test scores, responses to questionnaires or interviews, and so on).

3. *Selection or development of instruments for gathering data.* Questionnaires, interviews, tests, and scales of various types are the most frequently used instruments for descriptive research. If the researcher will be using existing instruments, the reliability of these instruments, their validity for measuring the variables of concern, and their suitability for the population of interest must be investigated. Further insight into their qualities can be gained by reading previous studies in which the same instruments were used.

If the researcher must design his or her own instruments, it would be wise to try them out with a small group as a pilot test in order to evaluate them and make any needed improvements.

As you will recall, the instruments operationally define the variables in the study. Therefore, before proceeding, the researcher must be satisfied that the data that will be obtained with the instruments selected for the study are in fact the information needed to solve the problem.

4. *Sample selection.* The researcher determines the group about which information is being sought. Then she or he decides on the most appropriate procedure for sample selection. Identification of the target population and selection of the samples that would represent it are critical steps in conducting descriptive research. Generalizability of the results in these studies directly depends on how well the sample represents the population of interest. Usually a random selection of the subjects is necessary.

5. *Design of the procedure for data collection.* The researcher lays out the strategies and the practical schedule for obtaining the sample and using the instruments.

6. *Collection of data.*

7. *Analysis of data.*

8. *Preparation of the report.*

// Developmental Studies

It is important for the profession of education to have reliable information about what children are like at various ages, how they vary from one another within age levels, and how they grow and develop. Knowledge of physiological, intellectual, and emotional growth is important for numerous practical as well as theoretical questions. Physical plant, curriculum, and teaching methods must take into consideration the relevant characteristics of the learner, as must any comprehensive theory of learning or instruction. Two complementary techniques have emerged for investigating the characteristics of children and the ways in which these characteristics change with growth. These are generally referred to as the longitudinal method and the cross-sectional method.

/ The Longitudinal Method

In the longitudinal method the same sample of subjects is studied over an extended period of time. Researchers studying the development of quantitative concepts of elementary school pupils, for example, would start by measuring the quantitative skills of a group of first-graders and would continue by making annual measurements of their skills at each successive grade level. Thus, the researchers could assess how these skills develop over a period of time for this group. Because they are dealing with the same individuals, such factors as initial ability will remain constant and the differences observed between two grade levels can be interpreted as changes in quantitative skills related to the growth of the subjects.

Using the longitudinal method, McKinney studied the behavioral characteristics of children with learning disabilities (LD) over a 3-year period, beginning in the first and second grades, and compared their development to that of a randomly selected sample of average achievers.[1] Subsequently a follow-up study was conducted on the academic outcomes for children in the original longitudinal sample who were available when they reached the fifth and sixth grades. He found that children with LD, as a heterogeneous group, displayed a persistent pattern of maladaptive classroom behavior that distinguished them from average-achieving peers and that was associated with continued underachievement over time. The findings confirmed the evidence from previous research that the disparity between most students with LD and same-aged average achievers increases developmentally. Subsequently children with LD in the longitudinal sample were clustered into different subtypes, representing attention problems, conduct and classroom management problems, withdrawn-dependent behavior, and normal behavior. Although no differences in achievement were found initially between behavioral subtypes, children in the attention- and conduct-problem subtypes had poorer academic outcomes 3 years later compared to those in the withdrawn subtype and those who had no significant behavior problems. McKinney concluded that there is a need for a greater focus on behavioral interventions in special education and prevention efforts in the early grades.

The longitudinal method allows for intensive studies of individuals because the investigator accumulates data for the same subjects at various levels. However, longitudinal studies have inherent practical difficulties. To begin with, they demand an extended commitment from an individual or institution willing to spend time, money, and other resources for several years before completing the project. If the sample selected should prove to be a poor one, there is nothing that can be done to remedy it, nor can new longitudinal variables for investigation be introduced after the study has matured. Keeping up with subjects who move may become extremely difficult. In some cases, also, it proves difficult to maintain the cooperation of subjects for an extended period.

---

[1]McKinney, J. D. (1989). Longitudinal research on the behavioral characteristics of children with learning disabilities. *Journal of Learning Disabilities, 22,* 141–150.

/ The Cross-Sectional Method

Many of the practical difficulties of the longitudinal method are not characteristic of the cross-sectional method. This approach studies subjects of different age levels at the same point in time. A cross-sectional study of the development of quantitative skills would employ a different sample from each of the grade levels. It would compare the statistics derived from the samples concurrently and draw conclusions about the growth of children with respect to these skills.

A major disadvantage of the cross-sectional method is that chance differences between samples may seriously bias the results. One may by chance draw a sample of first-graders who are more mature than average and a sample of second-graders who are less mature than average, with the result that the difference between the groups appears to be much smaller than it really is. However, it is usually possible to obtain larger samples for cross-sectional studies than can be obtained for longitudinal studies, and the advantages of these large samples may in many cases outweigh the disadvantages of the cross-sectional approach.

A further disadvantage of the cross-sectional approach lies in the possibility of extraneous variables creating differences between the populations sampled. For example, suppose investigators are studying the vocabulary development of high school students. The seniors will probably be a less diverse group than the freshmen, inasmuch as the less capable students tend to drop out during the high school years in greater proportion than do the more capable students. Consequently, comparisons of vocabulary will tend to reflect this selection factor as well as students' vocabulary growth during high school. Of course subjects can be lost from longitudinal studies for various reasons, with a corresponding lessening of comparability between data from various levels. However, the investigator with longitudinal data will know which subjects have been lost and how they differ from the remaining sample and can then take these differences into account in interpreting the results.

When we want to learn the characteristics of *typical* children at various stages, the cross-sectional method is preferred because of the greater possibility of obtaining large samples with this technique. It would also be preferred if we want to know how contemporary first-graders differ from contemporary sixth-graders, because a longitudinal study would be comparing first-graders of five years ago with sixth-graders of today.

If we want to study *change* per se, the longitudinal method is preferred because it follows the same subjects through their development. Spurts and plateaus of growth, which cannot be observed in a cross-sectional study, can be seen in a longitudinal study. Consider the following hypothetical mental-age scores of three boys tested annually:

Bob	Joe	Paul	$\bar{X}$
6.0	6.0	6.0	6.0
6.5	8.0	6.5	7.0
7.0	8.5	8.5	8.0
9.0	9.0	9.0	9.0

Each has a growth spurt at a different age, but the mean score for the three shows a steady increase.

// Follow-up Studies

The follow-up study somewhat resembles the longitudinal method. Studies of this type are concerned with investigating the subsequent development of subjects after a specified treatment or program. Among the best known are the studies by Terman and his associates of subjects who had been part of an original sample of gifted children in 1921–22.[2] The subjects were studied 6 years later and again in 1936, 1940, and 1945. Among other things, it was found that as adults these subjects had better physical and mental health than the general population. Only four of the 1467 subjects served terms in penal institutions. Approximately 90 percent of the males entered college, and 70 percent of these graduated, 40 percent with honors. About 80 percent of the women entered college, and 67 percent of these graduated, 32 percent with honors. In general, the gifted children matured into gifted and successful adults.

Follow-up studies are frequently conducted to evaluate the success of particular programs. The following titles illustrate this type: "Normal Children at Risk for Suicidal Behavior: A Two-Year Follow-up Study" and "Recurrent Depression in Adolescents: A Follow-up Study."

// Documentary Analyses

Although the discipline of education is primarily concerned with people, many interesting and useful research projects in the field have been concerned with information obtained by examining records and documents. The procedure for systematically analyzing written materials is called *documentary*, or *content, analysis*. One examines documents to investigate specific topics or themes, such as level of difficulty of textbooks, evidence of bias or prejudice, and prevailing practices. The data gathered are generally expressed as frequency counts in various relevant categories. A classic study of this type was Thorndike's documentary analysis to identify the most

---

[2]Burks, B. S., D. W. Jensen, and L. M. Terman. (1930). *The Promise of Youth: Follow-up Studies of a Thousand Gifted Children*, vol. 3. Stanford: Stanford University Press. Terman, L. M., and M. H. Oden (1947). *The Gifted Child Grows Up: Twenty-Five Years' Follow-up Studies of a Superior Group*, vol. 4. Stanford: Stanford University Press.

commonly used words in the English language.[3] His work was a very valuable tool for early developers of elementary language arts texts.

A recent example of a content analysis is Hitchcock and Tompkins' study of sexism in the new editions of six basal reading series for elementary schools.[4] They analyzed the first-, second-, fifth-, and sixth-grade books in the series, a total of 55 books. Each story was read, and the main character was scored as being male, female, or other (animal, talking tree, and so on). A count was also made of the frequency of the occupations portrayed for the female main characters. They compared the results with an earlier study done in 1981.

The researchers concluded that publishers have reduced sexism in basal readers. Males were the main characters in 18 percent of the stories, females in 17 percent, and the "other" category in 65 percent. Since 1981 the percentage of male main characters dropped, while the percentage of female main characters remained about the same. Female main characters were portrayed in 37 different roles; the most frequently occurring were, in order, child, student, author, grandmother, and artist. Hitchcock and Tompkins concluded that publishers of readers appear to be avoiding the question of sexism by creating neutral characters (for instance, animals without sex roles).

"Depictions of Aging and the Elderly in Primary-Grade Reading Instructional Materials," "The Literary Content of Children's Responses to Poetry," and "A Content Analysis of Elementary American History Textbooks" are other examples of content analyses. The last of these was designed to determine the treatment of blacks and race relations in history books.

Content analysis is basically library research. It is very time-consuming and requires a great deal of patience and attention to detail. The more material analyzed, the more valid the conclusions from the study. But one can't analyze every relevant book or document, so obtaining a representative sampling of the material is very important.

A discussion of the conduct of documentary analysis and its uses will be found in a book by Krippendorff.[5]

// Trend Analyses

Trend studies involve specifying a population, drawing a representative sample, and obtaining measures on certain variables. At later times that same population is sampled again and the measures are repeated. This design permits trends (changes) in the variables to be identified. The National As-

---

[3]Thorndike, E. L. (1932). *A Teacher's Book of the Twenty Thousand Words Found Most Frequently and Widely in General Reading for Children and Young People.* New York: Teachers College Press, Columbia University.

[4]Hitchcock, M. E., and G. E. Tompkins (1987). Basal readers: Are they still sexist? *Reading Teacher, 41,* 288–292.

[5]Krippendorff, K. (1980). *Content Analysis: An Introduction to Its Methodology.* Beverly Hills: Sage Publications.

sessment of Educational Progress (NAEP) gathered data to study national trends in mathematics achievement.[6] They measured performance of 13-year-olds and 17-year-olds in the late 1970s, in 1982, and again in 1986. The study showed that the performance of 13-year-olds, which had increased in the late 1970s and early 1980s, had not changed between 1982 and 1986. For 17-year-olds the downtrend that had characterized mathematics performance in the 1970s was reversed; they made significant gains between 1982 and 1986. There were also signs of improvement for blacks and Hispanic students, and the gap in achievement between 17-year-old males and females narrowed somewhat.

// Correlational Studies

Correlational studies are concerned with determining the relationship(s) existing among variables. In correlational research one collects measures on at least two variables for the same group of subjects and then calculates a coefficient of correlation between the measures. A correlation coefficient is an index of the direction and magnitude of the relationship.[7] Correlational research is not typically used to establish cause-and-effect relationships. You may recall from Chapter 5 that a correlation between X and Y can mean that X causes Y, Y causes X, or that a third variable causes both X and Y. Correlation alone is not sufficient evidence of causation. Causal relationships are investigated in experimental or causal-comparative research.

The purposes of correlational research are (1) to describe relationships that exist among variables and/or (2) to use the known correlation to predict from one variable to another.

/ Relationship Studies

One type of correlational study is mainly exploratory, that is, a researcher attempts to identify the pattern of relationships existing between two or more variables. Information gained from such correlational studies is especially useful when one is trying to understand a complex construct or is building a theory about some behavioral phenomenon. The variables selected for study should be based on a theory, on previous research, or on the researcher's observations. The "shotgun" approach, in which one correlates a number of variables just to see what might show up, is not recommended. In some correlational studies the researcher may be able to state a hypothesis about the expected relationship. For example, from phenomenological theory one might hypothesize that there is a positive relationship

---

[6]Silver, E. A., *et al.* (1988). The fourth NAEP mathematics assessment: Performance trends and results and trends for instructional indicators. *Mathematics Teacher, 81,* 720–727.
[7]The computation and interpretation of coefficients of correlation are explained in Chapter 5.

between first-grade children's perceptions of themselves and their achievement in reading. In other instances the researcher lacks the information necessary to state a hypothesis.

A study by Bourke illustrates the use of the correlational method in understanding why larger class size is related to lower student achievement.[8] He hypothesized that it was the implementation of different teaching practices in classes of different sizes that resulted in variations in achievement. Bourke's first step was to investigate the simple correlations between class size and certain teaching practices. Table 11.1 shows the variables that had significant correlations with class size.

Table 11.1 shows that there were more student questions in larger classes (usually seeking help or explanation), but more teacher follow-up of questions in smaller classes. A greater use of homework and assignments was typical of smaller classes. The amount of time teachers spent directly interacting with students was greater in small classes. Although the study is more involved than this example illustrates, it is possible to see how a researcher starts with correlations to help understand a complex phenomenon, in this case the possible explanations of the relationship between class size and achievement.

Often when researchers have investigated a number of bivariate relationships in a single study, they summarize these in a *correlation matrix*, which shows the coefficient of correlation between all possible pairs of variables. Table 11.2 shows a correlation matrix of 21 hypothetical correlations that might result when seven different types of aptitude measures were administered to a group of students and correlations computed between all possible pairs of measures. Notice that the dashes (—) are used to indicate

TABLE 11.1 Relationships of Teaching-Practice Variables with Class Size

Variable	Correlation with Class Size
Use of whole-class teaching	−.24
Number of groups used in class	.33
Teacher directly interacting with students	−.27
Amount of noise tolerated	.34
Teacher probes after a question	−.25
Student questions	.32
Teacher waits for a response	−.20
Homework and assignments assessed	−.28
Nonacademic management	.29

[8]Bourke, S. (1986). How smaller is better: Some relationships between class size, teaching practices, and student achievement. *American Educational Research Journal, 23,* 558–571.

TABLE 11.2 Aptitude Scores: Intercorrelations for High School Students

Aptitude Measure	1.	2.	3.	4.	5.	6.	7.
1. Vocabulary	—	.42	.40	.65	.29	.45	.74
2. Numerical		—	.34	.26	.35	.66	.23
3. Spatial			—	.29	.74	.81	.20
4. Analogies				—	.15	.56	.85
5. Hidden Figures					—	.74	.35
6. Similarities						—	.39
7. Synonyms							—

a correlation of a variable with itself, which, of course, would be 1.00. The data in the correlation matrix could perhaps be used to better understand the construct, intelligence.

Typically, correlational studies do not require extremely large samples. It can be assumed that if a relationship exists it will be evident in a sample of moderate size, for instance, 50–100. It is good to recall at this point that the variability in the scores that are being correlated affects the size of the coefficient of correlation. A restricted range of the scores on one or both variables will result in a smaller coefficient than would be obtained with a wider range of scores.

It is important to select or develop measures that are appropriate indicators of the variables to be correlated. It is especially important that these instruments have reliability and are valid for measuring the variables under consideration. The size of a coefficient of correlation is influenced by the adequacy of the measuring instrument for its intended purpose. For instance, an instrument that is too easy or too difficult for the subjects of a study would not discriminate among them and would result in a smaller correlation coefficient. Studies using instruments with low reliability and questionable validity are unlikely to produce results acceptable to researchers.

/ Prediction

Correlation is basic to prediction. If one knows that there is a correlation between two variables, then one can predict from one variable to the other. Because we know that IQ and GPA are positively correlated, we can predict with some degree of accuracy that an individual with a high IQ will probably have a high GPA. To be valuable for prediction, the extent of correlation between two variables must be substantial, and, of course, the higher the correlation, the more accurate the prediction.

Let us illustrate prediction with a very simple set of data. Figure 11.1 shows a graph of the correlated data. In such graphs the predictor, *X*, is

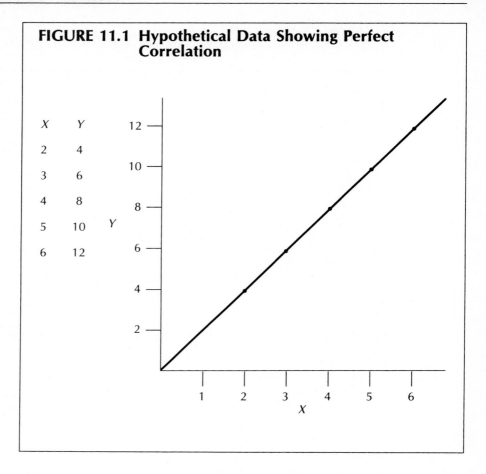

FIGURE 11.1 Hypothetical Data Showing Perfect Correlation

X	Y
2	4
3	6
4	8
5	10
6	12

always plotted on the horizontal axis and the criterion, Y, on the vertical axis. The variables X and Y in this example are perfectly correlated ($r = 1.00$); thus, all the points fall exactly on the diagonal line, known as the regression line. We could use the line later to predict from known X values to Y values. For example, one can see that a score of 12 on the Y variable would be predicted for persons with an X score of 6.

Instead of drawing a graph for prediction, it is more convenient to develop a prediction equation. The equation is a special case of the mathematical equation for a straight line.

$$Y' = bX + a \tag{11.1}$$

where

$Y' =$ predicted score on Y
$b =$ slope of the regression line
(the amount of change in Y for each unit change in X)
$a =$ intercept (where the line crosses the Y axis;
the score value of Y when $X = 0$)

In the example above, it can be seen that b (the slope) is 2. For each unit change in X, Y changes by 2: $b = \dfrac{Y_2 - Y_1}{X_2 - X_1}$. When X changes from 3 to 4, Y changes from 6 to 8. $b = \dfrac{8 - 6}{4 - 3} = 2.$

The intercept, a, can be determined by inspection of the graph; the line crosses the Y axis at 0. So by substituting in the equation $Y' = bX + a$, one can predict the Y corresponding to any value of X. If X is 5, then the predicted Y score is 10: $Y' = 2(5) + 0 = 10.$

In the above example, X and Y were perfectly correlated and it was easy to determine b and a. But in most prediction situations X and Y are not perfectly correlated. Let us consider another simple example in Figure 11.2. It can be seen in Figure 11.2a that not all the points fall on a straight line. But a regression line can be drawn through the points that represent the best-fitting line for those data. We must first develop the regression equation. The values of a and b in the equation are determined according to the criterion of *least squares*. This criterion results in a regression line drawn so that the average squared deviations of the actual points (scores achieved) from the predicted scores on the line is at a minimum. When we use a Pearson r for prediction, the slope of the regression line (b) is equal to the Pearson r multiplied by the standard deviation of the predicted scores (σ_y) divided by the standard deviation of the predictor scores (σ_x):

$$b = r\frac{\sigma_y}{\sigma_x} \tag{11.2}$$

In the above example,

$$b = .84\left(\frac{2.07}{1.58}\right) = 1.10$$

The intercept (a) is the mean of the predicted scores ($\bar{Y}$) minus the product of the slope (b) and the predictor mean ($\bar{X}$):

$$a = \bar{Y} - b\bar{X} \tag{11.3}$$

In the above example,

$$a = 5.6 - 1.10(3) = 2.3$$

Now we can calculate a predicted score (Y') for each value of X by multiplying the slope (b) times the X score and adding the intercept (a):

$$Y' = bX + a \tag{11.4}$$

In the above example,

$$Y' = 1.10X + 2.3$$

If X is 2:   If X is 5:

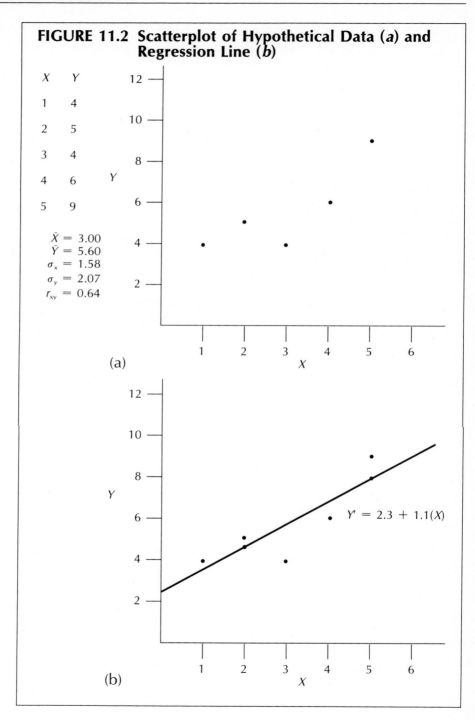

FIGURE 11.2 Scatterplot of Hypothetical Data (*a*) and Regression Line (*b*)

X	Y
1	4
2	5
3	4
4	6
5	9

$\bar{X} = 3.00$
$\bar{Y} = 5.60$
$\sigma_x = 1.58$
$\sigma_y = 2.07$
$r_{xy} = 0.64$

(a)

$Y' = 2.3 + 1.1(X)$

(b)

$$Y' = bX + a$$
$$Y' = 2.3 + 1.1(2) = 4.5$$

$$Y' = bX + a$$
$$Y' = 2.3 + 1.1(5) = 7.8$$

Because all the predicted Y' scores fall on the regression line, with these two Y' values, 4.5 and 7.8, we can draw the regression line as shown in Figure 11.2b. Recall that the regression line represents the predicted values of Y for each value of X. One can see in Figure 11.2b that the actual Y scores do not fall on the line. The discrepancy between the actual Y scores and the predicted Y' scores for a given X value represents error of estimate (e): $e = Y - Y'$. Using the regression line, one would predict a Y score of 4.5 for those with an X score of 2. But it can be seen that the actual Y score was 5. Hence, the error of estimate is $e = 5 - 4.5 = 0.5$. If one wants an index of the average error, one could just find the sum of the discrepancies overall and divide by the number of pairs of scores. But the sum of the errors is always 0; the negative discrepancies exactly balance the positive discrepancies. So, as in the calculation of standard deviation, one squares e, sums the squares (Σe^2), and divides by $n - 2$. Taking the square root of this number, one gets the standard deviation of the errors of estimate. This index, called *the standard error of estimate*, serves as an indicator of the accuracy of the prediction. The formula can be written

$$\sigma_{est} = \sqrt{\frac{\Sigma (Y - Y')^2}{n - 2}} \tag{11.5}$$

where

σ_{est} = standard error of estimate
Y = actual value(s) of Y for a given X value
Y' = predicted value(s) of Y for a given X
n = number of observations

An alternative and computationally easier formula to use for standard error of estimate is

$$\sigma_{est} = \sigma_Y \sqrt{1 - r^2} \tag{11.5a}$$

where

σ_Y = standard deviation of Y scores
r^2 = the square of the correlation coefficient between X and Y

Let us consider an example involving prediction. A supervisor of high school counselors noted that those on her staff who were diffident seemed to do a poorer job than those who were not. She decided to develop a measure of diffidence to see if that measure could be a useful predictor of counselor success.

She identified the various components of the construct diffidence and with the advice and help of other professional counselors eventually produced a diffidence measure with satisfactory construct validity and reliability. She then administered the scale to a representative sample of high school counselors. For each of the subjects she also recorded the mean client satisfaction on a scale where higher numbers indicated greater satisfaction.

The supervisor found a Pearson correlation of $-.50$ between the Diffidence Scale scores and client satisfaction. The direction of correlation told her that as diffidence scores increased, client satisfaction scores tended to decrease. The difference between the correlation and 0 indicated how strong the relationship was. This strength was indicated by the coefficient of determination (r^2). In this case r^2 was $-.5^2 = .25$, indicating that 25 percent of the variance in the client satisfaction scores was in common with the diffidence scores.

The supervisor can predict client satisfaction scores (Y') using counselor's diffidence scores (X). The first step is the calculation of b in the prediction formula. The Diffidence Scale had a mean of 20 and a standard deviation of 4, while the client satisfaction scores had a mean of 16 and a standard deviation of 3. Thus, $b = r \left(\dfrac{\sigma_x}{\sigma_y} \right) = -.5 \left(\dfrac{3}{4} \right) = -.375$

The next step is to calculate a:

$$\begin{aligned} a &= \bar{Y} - b\bar{X} \\ &= 16 - (-.375)20 \\ &= 23.5 \end{aligned}$$

The equation for predicting Y scores from X scores is thus:

$$\begin{aligned} Y' &= bX + a \\ &= -.375X + 23.5 \end{aligned}$$

A counselor with a Diffidence Scale score of 24 would be predicted to have a client satisfaction score of $(-.375)24 + 23.5 = 14.5$. For a Diffidence Scale score of 14, one would predict $(-.375)14 + 23.5 = 18.25$.[9] A useful check for the accuracy of the calculation of beta and alpha is to calculate the predicted score of Y for the mean on X. Correct calculations will yield the Y mean. In this case $(-.375)20 + 23.5 = 16$.

/ Standard Error of Estimate

Since the correlation is not perfect, some counselors will score higher on client satisfaction than would be expected given their Diffidence Scale scores, and some counselors will score lower than would be expected. The

---

[9]All predictions are precise when we are dealing with the subjects on whom the data were obtained. When we use these procedures to make predictions for subjects for whom only X scores are available, the utility of these procedures is determined by the validity of the assumption that the correlation for the new subjects will be the same as the correlation for the original subjects. For example, if our counselor supervisor uses Diffidence Test scores to help determine which applicants for counselor jobs to hire, the Diffidence Test scores will be useful if the assumption that the correlation between Diffidence Test scores among applicants would be similar to the $-.5$ found in the original study.

standard error of estimate indicates how much the actual Y scores are expected to differ from the predicted Y scores.

The standard error of estimate is essentially a measure of variability and as such can be interpreted like a standard deviation. Approximately 68 percent of the actual Y scores will fall between plus or minus one standard error of estimate (2.60), and approximately 95 percent will fall between plus or minus two standard errors (5.20) of the predicted score. For example, any counselor with a Diffidence Scale score of 10 would be predicted to have a client satisfaction score of 19.75. Using the standard error of estimate, one would expect that 68 percent of those counselors for whom we predict 19.75 will have client satisfaction scores between 17.15 and 22.35. We would expect about 95 percent to have scores between ± 2 s_{est}, or between 14.55 and 24.95.

/ Multiple Regression

In many real-life situations more than one variable is used to predict a criterion. The prediction of a criterion using two or more predictor variables is called *multiple regression*. For example, college grade-point average is typically predicted by using a combination of variables submitted by students in the admissions process. The multiple-regression equation is an extension of the simple regression equation:

$$Y' = a + b_1X_1 + b_2X_2 + \ldots b_nX_n \tag{11.6}$$

where

$$Y' = \text{criterion to be predicted}$$
$$a = \text{constant}$$
$$b = \text{regression weight for each predictor}$$
$$X_1 \text{ to } X_n = \text{predictors}$$

The statistical procedure weights each predictor so that the predictor variables in combination give the optimal prediction of the criterion (Y'). The use of multiple regression is illustrated in a study by Jacobs.[10]

Jacobs used data submitted by 4145 freshmen at a Midwestern university to predict first-semester grade-point average. The predictor values were scores on the Scholastic Aptitude Test subtests (SAT verbal and SAT quantitative), along with students' relative high school rank (RHSR). Relative high school rank, found by dividing a student's rank in the high school graduating class by the size of the class, adjusts for the variation in size of high schools. Table 11.3 shows the simple correlations between each of the predictors and the criterion.

It can be seen in Table 11.3 that none of the variables has a very high correlation with freshman GPA; the best single predictor would be relative

---

[10]Jacobs, L. C. (1985). *GPA Prediction Procedures and Normative Data for Freshmen.* Bloomington: Indiana University, Bureau of Evaluative Studies and Testing.

TABLE 11.3 Correlations of Each Predictor with the Criterion

	SATV	SATM	RHSR*
GPA	0.31	0.39	−0.42

*The negative correlation between relative high school rank and GPA is due to the way that rank in class is measured. The highest achiever in the class has a rank of 1 (the lowest number); the lowest achiever in the class has a rank equal to the size of the class (a high number). The students with the lowest *size* rank are predicted to have the highest GPA; hence, the correlation coefficient is negative.

high school rank. A multiple-regression analysis was carried out in order to determine the correlation of the best possible weighted *combination* of the three predictor variables with GPA. The multiple correlation (R) was .50. Thus 25 percent (R^2) of the variance in GPA was accounted for by SATV, SATM, and RHSR. The combination of variables had the highest correlation with GPA and thus provided the most accurate prediction. The regression equation for these data was: Y' (GPA) = 2.0813 + (−.0131)RHSR + .0014SATM + .0008SATV. The equation indicates that an individual's predicted GPA is equal to the sum of the constant (2.0813) plus the products of each of the three predictors and its respective regression weight. Assume a student has the following scores: SATV = 460, SATM = 540, RHSR = 21. The student's predicted GPA at the university would be 2.93:

$$Y' = 2.0813 + (−.0131)(21) + .0014(540) + .0008(460) = 2.93$$

The standard error of estimate was .55.

In the development of a multiple-regression or prediction equation, each case must have a score on each of the independent (X) variables (predictors) and the dependent (Y) variable (criterion). In the future, however, the equation can be used with similar groups when only the independent variables (X's) are known. SAT scores and relative high school ranks can be used to predict the as yet unknown freshman GPA for applicants to the university.

The variables should be measured on an interval scale. It is possible, however, to put categorical variables such as gender, social class, marital status, political preference, and the like into a regression equation if they are recoded as binary variables. For instance, if the variable is gender, 1's can be assigned to females and 0's to males. Such recoded variables are referred to in multiple regression as *dummy variables.*[11]

Because the computations are very complex, multiple regression is done by computer. Computer programs are available that provide not only the

[11]See J. Cohen and P. Cohen (1983), *Applied Multiple Regression: Correlation Analysis for the Behavioral Sciences* (2d ed.), Hillsdale, NJ: Erlbaum Associates, for a readable discussion of multiple regression.

multiple correlation coefficient (R) and the regression equation but also the proportion of variance in the criterion accounted for by the combination of predictors (R^2), tests of statistical significance for the R and for the contribution of each predictor. There are several procedures available for selecting the independent variables in the multiple-regression equation. The most commonly used method is called *stepwise selection*. The first variable considered for entry is the one with the largest positive or negative correlation with the criterion. An F-test of significance is performed to determine if, in the population, that variable would significantly contribute to the prediction of the criterion.[12] If the first variable meets the criterion, the variable that adds most to the prediction is selected next. The selection is based on the highest correlation after statistically controlling for the correlation between predictor 1 and the criterion (partial correlation). The third variable to enter will be the one with the next highest correlation after the first two predictors are statistically controlled. These variable-selection steps continue until no more variables meet the entry criteria. At each step, an R is computed that tells whether the variable entered would add significantly to the amount of variance in the criterion that has been predicted by the variables already entered. The researcher should consult the user's guide accompanying the computer package that will be used, for example SPSS^x, for descriptions of other approaches to the selection of variables in multiple regression.

If one wants to use the multiple-regression equation for predictive purposes, it should be validated on another sample. Because chance errors operate differently in different samples, the regression weights calculated for the original sample may not be the same in other samples. That is, the predictor that is best in the original sample may not be the best in another sample. In order to determine the validity of the multiple-regression equation, it should be *cross-validated* by trying it on another sample. In the cross validation, the multiple correlation will generally be lower than in the original sample on which the regression weights were calculated. This tendency for multiple correlations to decrease when the research is repeated with a different sample is referred to as *shrinkage*. The amount of shrinkage depends on the size of the original sample and the number of predictors (actually the ratio of predictors to sample size).[13] The larger the sample on which regres-

---

[12]To determine whether each variable is entered, the F-value is compared to an established criterion. One criterion is the minimum value of the F-statistic that a variable must achieve in order to be significant. The second criterion is to specify the probability associated with the F-statistic, such as .05. A variable enters into the equation only if the probability associated with the F-test is less than or equal to the level of significance specified.

[13]When N is small, it is recommended that one apply a shrinkage correction formula for R in order to get a better estimate. The formula is

$$R_c^2 = 1 - (1 - R^2)\left(\frac{N - 1}{N - n}\right)$$

where

R_c^2 = corrected (shrunken) R^2
N = size of sample
n = total number of independent variables

sion weights are derived, the less the shrinkage. In order to obtain stable multiple R's, it is generally recommended that a researcher have at least 30 subjects for each predictor in the regression equation. Some writers, however, recommend as many as 300 subjects for each predictor.

Multiple regression is not restricted to prediction purposes; it is widely used in different kinds of research. Because multiple regression can identify the variables that account for the variance in dependent variables, it can be used to help researchers understand complex phenomena. A researcher who wants to understand a phenomenon such as persistence in college could use multiple regression to analyze the separate and collective contributions of a number of independent variables to this phenomenon.

/ Discriminant Analysis

Discriminant analysis is a statistical procedure related to regression. It uses a number of predictor variables to classify subjects into two or more distinct groups, such as dropouts versus persisters, successful versus unsuccessful students, delinquents versus nondelinquents, and so on. The criterion in discriminant analysis is a person's group membership. The procedure results in an equation, or *discriminant function*, where the scores on the predictors are multiplied by weights to permit classification of subjects into groups. When there are just two groups, the discriminant function is essentially a multiple-regression equation with the group membership criterion coded 0 or 1. But with three or more groups as the criterion, discriminant analysis goes beyond multiple regression.

Vacc and Picot used discriminant analysis to identify predictors of success in a school of education doctoral program.[14] They wanted to find the variables that discriminated membership into one of two groups: those who successfully completed doctoral study and those who did not. They used a number of predictors: Miller Analogies Test (MAT) scores, undergraduate GPA, graduate GPA, time lapse between the master's degree and entrance into the doctoral program, doctoral major, age at entrance, gender, marital status, and race.

The variables found to be successful predictors in this study were the MAT score, gender, and the major area. The discriminant equation was

$$Z = C + .57382X_{MAT} - .44895X_{sex} + .65722X_{major} \qquad (11.7)$$

The positive sign for the coefficient for MAT indicates that students with high MAT scores were most likely to finish the doctoral program. Because the authors did not state how the variable, gender, was coded, it is impossible to determine from the equation whether males or females were

---

[14]Vacc, N. N., and R. Picot (1984). Predicting success in doctoral study. *College Student Journal, 18*, 113–116.

more likely to finish. The coefficient is negative, so the gender with the lower code number would be more likely to be successful. The authors stated that educational-administration majors were most likely to finish. The derived equation was found to be more effective in identifying successful students (95.6 percent were correctly identified) than unsuccessful students. The authors believed that there were too few unsuccessful students on which to base an analysis.

The complex computations involved in discriminant analysis require a computer. Interpretation of the results is also complex, and the beginning researcher would most likely need to consult a statistician knowledgeable in this area.

/ Factor Analysis

Another widely used procedure based upon correlation is factor analysis. This procedure analyzes the intercorrelations among a large set of measures in order to identify a smaller number of common *factors*. Factors are hypothetical constructs assumed to underlie different types of psychological measures, such as intelligence, aptitude, achievement, personality, and attitude measures. Factor analysis indicates the tests or other instruments that are measuring the same thing and to what extent, enabling researchers to deal with a smaller number of constraints. Some factor analysis studies of intelligence tests, for example, have identified underlying verbal, numerical, spatial, memory, and reasoning factors.

The first step in factor analysis involves the selection of the variables to be included in the analysis and the development of a correlation matrix that shows the correlation of each measure with every other measure. There may be a very large number of correlations in the matrix. The matrix is then subjected to computations with a factor analysis computer program that produces clusters of variables that intercorrelate highly with one another but have low correlations between the clusters. These clusters are called factors and the object is to identify a smaller number of separate factors that can account for the covariation among the larger number of variables. For example, consider the following hypothetical correlation matrix:

	1	2	3	4	5	6
1. Vocabulary	—	.80	.15	.20	.22	.25
2. Analogies	.80	—	.12	.25	.10	.28
3. Arithmetic	.15	.12	—	.75	.15	.12
4. Numerical Reasoning	.20	.25	.75	—	.20	.22
5. Picture Completion	.22	.10	.15	.20	—	.82
6. Block Design	.25	.28	.12	.22	.82	—

An "inspection" factor analysis shows three clusters where the intercorrelations are high (measures 1 and 2, 3 and 4, and 5 and 6) and then low correlations among the clusters. One would expect to find three factors underlying performance on these six measures; they appear to be verbal, numerical, and spatial. In a real factor analysis the researcher provides the computer with a criterion by which the final number of factors is determined.

Next the correlations between each of the original variables and the common factors that were identified are computed. These correlations are called *factor loadings*. The magnitude of the factor loadings indicates the importance of the factor to performance on each variable. One hopes to find that each variable will have high factor loadings with one factor and low factor loadings with other factors. This would indicate that a variable shares variance with other variables in that factor but little or no shared variance with variables loaded on other factors.

The next step involves what is called *factor rotation*. This is a simplification process designed to produce a clearer pattern of the factors and the variables on which they load. As a result, the factors are more directly interpretable. The computer program provides different methods of rotation, each with its criterion of simplicity; the user must make a decision about the method to use.

The researcher then names the resulting factors. This step involves identifying the variables that load significantly on a factor and deriving a name that would apply to all the variables. An analysis might result in a numerical factor, a verbal factor, a spatial factor, and so on.

Posner and Kouzes subjected an instrument called the Leadership Practices Inventory (LPI) to factor analysis.[15] They analyzed the responses of 2876 subjects to the 30 items of the inventory and extracted five factors that were being measured by the 30 items. Table 11.4 shows the factor structure for the LPI.

It can be seen that items 8, 18, 23, 13, 28, and 3 have high factor loadings on Factor 1 but low loadings on the other factors. These items appear to be measuring a leader's ability to enable others to act. On the other hand, items 5, 25, 15, 20, 10, and 30 have high loadings on Factor 2, and so on.

It is beyond the scope of this book to cover the computational procedures of either discriminant analysis or factor analysis. The reader is referred to books such as Kim and Mueller's *Introduction to Factor Analysis*[16] and Klecka's *Discriminant Analysis*[17] for readable discussions of these topics.

/// SUMMARY

Descriptive research methods are used to obtain information about existing conditions and have been widely used in educational research. These methods

---

[15]Posner, B. Z., and J. M. Kouzes (1988). Development and validation of the leadership practices inventory. *Educational and Psychological Measurement, 48*, 483–496.

[16]Kim, J., and C. W. Mueller (1978). *Introduction to Factor Analysis: What It Is and How to Do It*. Beverly Hills: Sage Publications.

[17]Klecka, W. R. (1980). *Discriminant Analysis*. Beverly Hills: Sage Publications.

TABLE 11.4 Factor Structure (Factor Loadings) for the Leadership Practices Inventory (N = 2876)

Item Number	Factor 1 Enabling Others to Act	Factor 2 Encouraging the Heart	Factor 3 Inspiring a Shared Vision	Factor 4 Challenging the Process	Factor 5 Modeling the Way
8	.719	.173	.096	.008	.098
18	.694	.200	.176	.088	.214
23	.680	.198	.189	.231	.273
13	.526	.169	.092	.085	.006
28	.509	.280	.206	.195	.290
3	.459	.208	.235	.069	.256
5	.111	.731	.220	.099	.109
25	.152	.725	.255	.143	.128
15	.402	.689	.102	.129	.113
20	.451	.673	.163	.148	.172
10	.400	.635	.079	.154	.189
30	.224	.532	.194	.250	.240
7	.185	.215	.709	.251	.119
2	.156	.165	.657	.276	.136
27	.223	.255	.623	.384	.239
17	.173	.225	.615	.270	.240
22	.223	.151	.506	.362	.136
12	.166	.114	.481	.345	.107
16	.180	.169	.266	.641	.233
26	.164	.185	.241	.637	.057
11	.043	.082	.184	.622	.145
1	.182	.128	.219	.648	.153
21	.354	.194	.178	.473	.145
6	.170	.049	.138	.392	.173
29	.218	.185	.144	.192	.609
9	.343	.158	.031	.107	.512
14	.164	.164	.239	.228	.509
4	.232	.142	.353	.238	.411
19	.109	.156	.334	.315	.409
24	.319	.120	.115	.227	.372

Source: Posner and Kouzes (1988), p. 493.

range from the survey, which describes the status quo of educational variables, to the correlational study, which investigates the relationship between variables. Other descriptive methods include the developmental study, follow-up study, documentary analysis, and trend analysis. Descriptive methods are not restricted to data gathering; they can also be used in studies involving hypothesis testing. Correlational studies permit one to use the known correlation to predict from one variable to another. In simple prediction, a variable, X, is used to predict another variable, Y. In multiple regression, more than one variable—X_1, X_2, X_3— are used to predict Y. One can determine the accuracy of the prediction and how much of the variance in Y is accounted for by the "best" linear combination of the predictors.

Other sophisticated statistical procedures based on correlation are discriminant analysis and factor analysis.

// Key Concepts

coefficient of correlation	factor analysis
content analysis	follow-up study
correlation matrix	intercept
correlational study	longitudinal study
cross-sectional study	multiple regression
cross validation	regression
discriminant analysis	slope
dummy variable	standard error of estimate
factor	trend analysis

/// EXERCISES

1. Identify the type of descriptive research—namely, *developmental study, follow-up study*, or *trend analysis*—indicated in each of the following items.
   a. Terman's study of adults who were intellectually gifted as children
   b. analysis of data from the past and present in order to "predict" the future

2. In developmental studies, when one wants to study how individual children change rather than what is typical at each stage of development, one would prefer the
   a. cross-sectional method
   b. longitudinal method

3. In a correlational study the investigator
   a. compares the differences within a group on one variable with differences within the same group on another variable
   b. starts with a group that is initially homogeneous on a variable being studied
   c. compares the performance of one group on a variable with the performance of a comparable group on that variable
   d. creates and then measures a difference between two groups

4. The longitudinal technique in developmental studies has the advantage of

a. more-intensive individual study
b. providing data for different age groups at the same time
c. prompt data gathering
d. no sampling errors

5. In order to compute a correlation coefficient between traits A and B, one must have
   a. one group of subjects, some of whom possess characteristics of trait A and the remainder of whom possess those of trait B
   b. measures of trait A on one group of subjects and measures of trait B on another
   c. one group of subjects, some who have both traits A and B, some who have neither trait, and some who have one trait but not the other
   d. two groups of subjects, one of which could be classified as A or not A, the other as B or not B
   e. measure of traits A and B on each subject in one group

6. An investigation finds a positive correlation between IQ scores and length of attention span among ten-year-olds. From this finding one would state that
   a. a long attention span is a cause of intelligence
   b. a high IQ is a cause of long attention span
   c. there is a high probability that a large sample of high-IQ ten-year-olds will have a shorter mean attention span than a large sample of low-IQ ten-year-olds
   d. one would predict longer attention spans for high-IQ ten-year-olds than for low-IQ ten-year-olds

7. Examine the following research topics and decide whether *experimental research*, *causal-comparative research*, or *correlational research* is the appropriate research design for each one:
   a. the effect of parents' divorce on the achievement motivation of the children
   b. the effect of a specific program of vocabulary instruction on social studies achievement
   c. the relationship between class size and student satisfaction with quality of instruction
   d. the effect of phonics instruction upon the reading grade level of fourth-grade students

8. A researcher found a correlation of $-.42$ between rank in high school class and achievement in college for a sample of 1500 college freshmen. How would you interpret this coefficient in terms of direction, magnitude, and percentage of shared variance?

9. A school administrator wants to predict achievement in foreign languages. She has available scores on an intelligence test, a language aptitude test, and a reading test; she also knows the gender of the students. How would you recommend that she proceed to predict foreign language achievement? What name would be given to your procedure?

10. Explain how it is possible for the measures of two variables to be associated in a fairly systematic way without the existence of any causal relationship between the variables?

11. A researcher is investigating the construct validity of an inventory designed to measure teacher stress. He wishes to know if the inventory is measuring a single construct or multiple constructs. What procedure would you recommend that the researcher use to answer this question?

12. A researcher wanted to predict achievement in the first year of law school. He conducted a multiple-regression analysis with a sample size of 1000 and used six predictor variables: undergraduate GPA, undergraduate major, LSAT score, a writing-test score, gender, and time lapse between undergraduate degree and application to law school. The resulting $R = .20$ was significant at the .01 level of significance. What interpretation would you make of the researcher's findings?

13. Assume there is a correlation of $+.94$ between average number of hours spent studying each day (X) and freshman students' first-semester GPA (Y) for a group of 100 subjects. Having the following information, $\bar{X} = 5.74$ $s_X = 2.31$ $\bar{Y} = 2.75$ $s_Y = .90$, calculate the predicted GPA for a student who studies 6 hours per day.

/// ANSWERS

1. a. follow-up study
   b. trend analysis

2. b

3. a

4. a

5. e

6. d

7. a. causal-comparative research
   b. experimental research

    c. correlational research
    d. experimental research

8. The r of $-.42$ indicates a moderate negative relationship between rank in high school class and achievement in college—that is, those students with a low numerical ranking would tend to have high achievement. The negative correlation is due to the way that rank in class is measured. The highest achiever in the class has a rank of 1 (the lowest number); the lowest achiever in the class has a rank equal to the size of the class (the highest number). The student with a rank of 1 in a class of 400 would be expected to have a higher GPA in college than the student with a rank of 400.

    An $r = -.42$ indicates that about 18 percent of the variance in college grades can be accounted for by achievement in high school as indicated by rank.

9. The school administrator would select a sample of students and obtain their scores on the three tests and their grades in foreign languages. Gender would be coded 0 or 1. The data would be entered into a multiple-regression analysis with the intelligence test, language aptitude test, reading test, and gender as independent variables and grades in foreign language as the dependent variable. Once the multiple-regression equation is developed, it can be used to predict foreign language achievement of similar groups of students when only the independent variables are known.

10. Even when two variables are correlated, one cannot infer that one causes the other. Correlation does not indicate causation. A third variable, unmeasured by the researcher, may account for the observed relationship.

11. The researcher should subject the inventory to factor analysis.

12. With the large sample size, it is not surprising that a coefficient of only .20 would be statistically significant. It is not large enough, however, to be useful in prediction. $R^2 = .04$; only 4 percent of the variance in law school achievement would be predictable from this combination of predictor variables.

13. $b = .37$
$a = .63$
$Y' = a + bX$
$Y' = .63 + .37(6)$
$Y' = 2.85$ (predicted GPA)

CHAPTER 12

Survey Research

INSTRUCTIONAL OBJECTIVES

After studying this chapter, the student will be able to

1. State the purpose of survey research
2. Describe the four categories of surveys classified according to their scope and subject matter
3. List the steps involved in carrying out a survey
4. Explain the importance of probability sampling in survey research
5. Use sample data to estimate the confidence interval around the population parameter
6. State the advantages and disadvantages of the interview as a data-gathering technique
7. Write both open-ended and closed questions
8. List five guidelines for conducting an interview
9. State the advantages and disadvantages of the questionnaire as a data-gathering technique
10. State ten rules for writing items for a questionnaire
11. List guidelines that one should follow relative to the format of a questionnaire
12. Explain the advantages of pretesting a questionnaire
13. Explain the follow-up procedures one should employ with a mail survey
14. Write a cover letter for a questionnaire
15. Outline procedures for dealing with nonrespondents after follow-up procedures have been used
16. Discuss the procedures for assessing the validity and reliability of questionnaires and/or interviews
17. Explain the data analyses that are appropriate for survey data
18. Discuss how a researcher can provide for control of variables

The survey is an important and frequently used method of research for sociology, business, political science, and government, as well as for education. The range of topics covered by surveys, as well as the techniques used, has increased significantly in the past 50 years. Hardly a week goes by that we are not exposed through the news media to the results of some type of survey. Surveys sample populations in order to discover the incidence and distribution of, and the interrelationships among, sociological, psychological, and educational variables.[1] The data gathered in a survey are usually responses to predetermined questions that are asked of a sample of respondents. The researcher, however, wants to generalize the findings to the total group from which the sample came, that is, the population.

According to their purpose, surveys can be classified into two broad categories: descriptive and explanatory. Descriptive surveys focus on determining the status of a defined population with respect to certain variables. They basically inquire into the status quo; they attempt to measure what exists without questioning why it exists. Some typical descriptive survey questions are: What proportion of American youth graduates from high school? What proportion of high-school graduates in Indiana enters four-year colleges? How many books per pupil do high school libraries contain? How many school systems in the country instituted AIDS education programs during the past year?

An explanatory survey is a form of causal-comparative research. It goes beyond merely describing the variables; it attempts to determine if the variables of interest covary and/or under what conditions they covary. The explanatory survey seeks to *explain* attitudes and behavior on the basis of data gathered at a point in time.

Explanatory surveys usually begin with a hypothesis that directs the data gathering. For example, a researcher who is interested in studying suicide among college students may believe that group affiliation is an important factor influencing the incidence of suicide. He hypothesizes that college students who have group affiliations will have a lower incidence of suicide than students who do not. The researcher would survey a sample of colleges and gather data on the incidence of suicide and the types and extents of group affiliation among the victims. If the survey reveals that students who belong to sororities or fraternities or to other social or religious organizations on campus do have lower suicide rates, the researcher might conclude that lack of group affiliations among college students is a contributing factor in campus suicides. The hypothesis of a relationship between group affiliation and suicide was supported in this survey.

The same problems in interpretation of findings that were discussed in causal-comparative research occur with the explanatory survey. Time or-

---

[1]Kerlinger, F. N. (1979). *Behavioral Research: A Conceptual Approach* (p. 151). New York: Holt, Rinehart and Winston.

der of occurrence and alternative explanations of the relationships must be investigated before conclusions are reached.

/// CENSUSES AND SAMPLE SURVEYS

Surveys vary in focus and in scope. A survey that covers the entire population of interest is referred to as a *census*, of which an example is the U.S. Census undertaken by the government every 10 years. In research, however, the population does not include all the people of a country. *Population* is used to refer to the entire group of individuals to whom the findings of a study apply. The researcher defines the specific population of interest. It is often difficult or even impossible for researchers to study very large populations. Hence, they select a smaller portion, a sample, of the population for study. A survey that studies only a portion of the population is known as a *sample survey*.

Surveys may be confined to simple tabulations of *tangible objects*, such as What proportion of children rides school buses? and What is the average class enrollment? The most challenging type of survey is one that seeks to measure *intangibles*, such as attitudes, opinions, values, or other psychological and sociological constructs. In such a study one must bring to bear not only the skills involved in proper sampling but also the skills involved in identifying or constructing appropriate measures and employing the scores on these measures to make meaningful statements about the constructs involved. If we classify surveys on the basis of their scope (census or sample survey) and their subject matter (tangibles or intangibles), we have four categories: (1) a census of tangibles, (2) a census of intangibles, (3) a sample survey of tangibles, and (4) a sample survey of intangibles. Each type has its own contributions to make and its own inherent problems.

// A Census of Tangibles

When one seeks information about a small population, such as a single school, and when the variables involved are concrete, there is little challenge in finding the required answers. If a school principal wants to know how many desks are in the school, how many children ride the school bus, or how many teachers have master's degrees, a simple count will provide the information. Because the study covers the entire population, the principal can have all the confidence characteristic of perfect induction. Well-defined and unambiguous variables are being measured, and as long as the enumeration is accurate and honest, the principal can say without much fear of contradiction, "On the first of September there were 647 children's desks in our school," or "Sixty-five percent of the present faculty have master's degrees." The strength of a census of this type lies in its irrefutability. Its weakness lies in its confinement to a single limited population at a single point in time. The information provided by such a census may be of immediate importance to a limited group, but typically such surveys add little to the general body of knowledge in education.

// A Census of Intangibles

Suppose the school principal now seeks information about pupil achievement or aspirations, teacher morale, or parents' attitude toward school. The task will be more difficult because this census deals with constructs that are not directly observable but must be inferred from indirect measures. The National Study of School Evaluation (NSSE) publishes an opinion inventory designed to measure attitudes and opinions about schools. There is an inventory for students, one for teachers, and one for parents. Administration of the inventory to all the students or teachers or parents in the school system would represent a census of intangibles.

Another example of this type of census is the achievement testing program carried out by most schools. All children are tested, and the test scores are used to compare their performance with national norms, their own previous performance, and so on. The principal must be knowledgeable about the nature of the measuring instruments used and their appropriateness for measuring pupil achievement in the school and so must ask how reliable the tests are, whether they measure the same construct of achievement as that defined by the goals of the school, and how well they measure that construct.

The value of a census of intangibles is largely a question of the extent to which the instruments used actually measure the construct of interest. Reasonably good instruments are available for measuring aptitude and achievement in a variety of academic areas. Many other variables remain very difficult to measure. Because we lack instruments that can meaningfully measure the constructs involved, many important questions in education have not been dealt with successfully. Such variables as teacher success, student motivation, psychological adjustment, and leadership have been difficult to define and measure operationally.

// A Sample Survey of Tangibles

When investigators seek information about large groups, the expense involved in carrying out a census is often prohibitive. Therefore, sampling techniques are used and the information collected from the sample is used to make inferences about the population as a whole. We have seen that when sampling is well done the inferences made concerning the population can be quite reliable.

A well-known example of a sample survey is the Coleman report.[2] This study was conducted in response to Section 402 of the Civil Rights Act of 1964, which directed the Commissioner of Education to conduct a survey of inequalities in educational opportunities among various groups in the United States. The sample survey included over 600,000 children in grades one, three, six, nine, and twelve of approximately 4000 schools. The schools were considered generally representative of all American public schools, although there was some intentional overrepresentation of schools with minority group populations.

From the data generated by the survey it was concluded that 65 percent of blacks attended schools in which over 90 percent of students were black and 80 percent of whites attended schools enrolling over 90 percent white. When comparisons were made concerning class size, physical facilities, and teacher qualifications, relatively little difference was found among schools serving different racial and ethnic groups. However, these variables did differ between metropolitan and rural areas and between geographical regions. Those disadvantaged in regard to these variables appeared to be rural children and those in the South, regardless of race.

// A Sample Survey of Intangibles

The public opinion polls are examples of this type of study. Opinion is not directly observable but must be inferred from responses made by the subjects to questionnaires or interviews. Opinion polling began in the 1930s and has grown tremendously. It has been estimated that 100 million survey interviews were conducted in the United States from 1971 to 1976; in 1980, 28 million people were interviewed on the telephone alone.[3] Where respondents have been willing to reveal their preferences freely before elections, the pollsters have been quite accurate in inferring public opinion from which they have predicted subsequent election results. These polls have provided excellent examples of the usefulness of sample statistics in estimating population parameters. When those who support one candidate are reluctant to reveal their preference, while those who support the other candidate feel free to say so, considerable error is introduced into the results of the poll. For example, people are more willing to say they will vote against an incumbent than for him or her. Before the 1948 presidential election several polls showed Dewey leading the incumbent, Truman, but with many people indicating that they were undecided. Truman won the election. Apparently most of those who had indicated that they were undecided actually voted for Truman. Respondents are also reluctant to reveal a choice that may

---

[2]Coleman, J. S., *et al.* (1966). *Equality of Educational Opportunity.* Washington: U.S. Government Printing Office.

[3]Winkler, K. J. (1988). Researchers told to be wary of how surveys are used. *The Chronicle of Higher Education,* Sept. 7, A10.

appear to be based on self-interest, prejudice, or lack of knowledge about the issues.

How someone is going to vote is an intangible, but what is marked on a ballot is a tangible. The television network news services have done very well in predicting how states will vote when only a few precincts have reported, but they are able to use tangible measures of a sample (that is, how some ballots have been marked) to predict the vote of a population. Therefore, the risks are only those involved in estimating population parameters from sample statistics. However, pollsters who estimate how a population will vote on the basis of how people say they will vote have the additional handicap of measuring what is intangible at the time the measurements are made. Surveys of intangibles are limited by the fact that the data we collect are only indirectly measuring the variables we are concerned about. The seriousness of this limitation depends on how well the observations measure the intangible variable.

The same survey may study tangibles and intangibles at the same time. The authors of the Coleman report asked the students to answer questionnaires and administered intelligence and achievement tests in order to make inferences about social class, ability, and achievement, as well as the relationship of these variables to each other and to tangible variables in the study.

/// THE SURVEY TECHNIQUE

Survey research involves a number of steps:

1. *Planning:* Survey research begins with a significant question that the researcher believes can be answered most appropriately by means of the survey technique. The research question typically concerns the distribution of and/or the relationships among behavioral characteristics of people as they occur in a natural setting. A clearly stated hypothesis formulated at this stage will be extremely important to guide the study. A review of the literature will reveal what other researchers have learned about the question. Decisions must be made at this time on the population to which one wants to generalize and on the methods and procedures that will be used to gather the data.

2. *Sampling:* Sampling is of major concern in surveys. The researcher must make decisions about the sampling procedure that will be used and the size of the sample to survey. If one is to generalize the sample findings to the population, it is essential that the sample selected be representative of that population. The sampling procedure that is most likely to yield a representative sample is some form of probability sampling (see Chapter 6). Probability sampling permits one to estimate how far sample results are likely to deviate from the population values.

3. *Construction of the instrument(s):* The researcher next decides on the format and writes the questions for the instrument that will be used to gather

the data from the sample. Among the data-gathering techniques used in surveys are personal interviews, questionnaires, and telephone interviews.

4. *Carrying out the survey:* This step includes pretesting the instrument to determine whether it will provide the desired data, training the users of the instrument (for example, interviewers), interviewing subjects or distributing questionnaires to them, and verifying the accuracy of the data gathered.

5. *Processing the data:* The last step includes the coding of the data, statistical analysis (done, most likely, by computer), interpreting the results, and reporting the findings.

The following example illustrates the survey method.[4]

1. *Purpose:* To survey college students concerning their attitudes about dating behaviors related to sexual activity and to examine the reported incidence of sexual aggression and coercion in college dating.

2. *Hypothesis:* Dating behavior is ambiguous and may result in physically and sexually coercive behavior by both partners.

3. *Sample:* The survey was conducted at a small Midwestern university with a student enrollment of 6000. Participants consisted of 408 students (approximately a 7 percent sample): 247 women and 161 men who were enrolled in undergraduate psychology courses. Respondents voluntarily and anonymously completed the survey during a class period. The mean age of the respondents was 21.5, and they were predominantly single.

4. *Instrument:* A questionnaire of 13 items was designed to elicit attitudes about sexual activity in a dating context, as well as respondents' experiences with sexually assaultive behavior. Items were scored on a six-point scale ranging from "never" (1) to "frequently" (6). No data were given concerning the validity and reliability of the questionnaire.

5. *Data:* Data were reported in the form of frequency distributions for the total sample and for each sex. *T*-tests were performed to determine the significance of any sex differences in responses.

6. *Results*:* Fifty-eight percent of the entire sample reported engaging in sexual activity with a dating partner, not because they wanted to, but rather because they believed it was inappropriate to refuse. There were significant differences between the responses of men and women on this item. Forty-eight percent of women and 25 percent of men reported being sexually assaulted on a date. Ten percent of women and 2 percent of men said they had been physically abused in a dating relationship. These differences between men and women were statistically significant.

7. *Conclusion:* The hypothesis of the study was supported by the findings of the survey. It was concluded that because of the serious nature and consequences of sexual assault, university personnel at all levels need to ac-

---

[4]Sandberg, G., T. Jackson, and P. Petretic-Jackson (1987). College students' attitudes regarding sexual coercion and aggression: Developing educational and preventive strategies. *Journal of College Student Personnel, 28,* 302–311.

*Not all the results of the survey are reported here.

knowledge the existence of date rape and other forms of coercive and abusive behavior in college settings and develop social policy and a program of prevention and treatment services on college campuses.

// Selection of the Sample

The reader is encouraged to look again at the section in Chapter 6 on sampling techniques and the factors that influence the size of the sample selected. Some additional discussion of sample size appears in the following section.

/ Sample Size

The size of the sample to draw is one of the early questions the researcher must answer. How does one decide on the number of people to survey? Many researchers believe they have to select a sample that is at least 10 percent of the population, but this is not necessary. Contrary to what is generally believed, the accuracy of the data is determined by the *absolute size* of the sample, rather than by the percentage its size is of the population. You may notice that the major public opinion polls in the United States do not use really large numbers. For example, a CBS News poll of registered voters prior to the 1988 election concerning their preference for a presidential candidate surveyed only 1343 people, an extremely small number relative to the size of the population.[5]

The main consideration when deciding on sample size is the degree of accuracy one wants in the estimation of population values. How much error is the researcher willing to tolerate in generalizing from the sample statistic to the population parameter? If researchers use probability sampling, they have a basis for estimating how far sample results are likely to deviate from the population values, that is, the margin of error, for a given sample size. They select a sample size that will enable them to be confident that their estimates will be correct within a small range about 95 percent of the time. Let us illustrate.

/ Estimating the Population Values

In the case of binomial variables (two values only) the binomial distribution provides a basis for estimating the proportion of the population possessing some characteristic. For example, what proportion of registered voters favor cutting the national defense budget? Or what proportion of voters support off-shore oil drilling as a way to meet our nation's energy

---

[5]A CBS News poll of 1343 people reported on November 4, 1988, showed Bush leading Dukakis by 7 percentage points. The margin of error was ± 3.

needs? We use the responses from samples to estimate population proportions. When n is large (50 or more), sample proportions are approximately normally distributed, with a mean equal to p (population proportion) and a standard deviation called the standard error that has the formula

$$\text{standard error} = \sqrt{\frac{pq}{n}}$$

where

p = proportion giving one response (e.g., yes)
q = proportion giving the other response (no)
pq = the variance of the sample
n = sample size

You recall that the standard error is a measure of the accuracy of the sample data as an estimate of the population value. The smaller the standard error, the more likely the sample represents the population. Assume we have surveyed a random sample of 500 voters and asked them if they favor cutting the national defense budget; 375, or 75 percent, say *yes* and 125, or 25 percent, say *no*. Can we consider .75 as an estimate of the true proportion of all voters who favor cutting the defense budget? How good an estimate it is can be determined by setting confidence limits for the true proportion. The closer these limits are to .75, the more accurate the estimate will be. The first step is to calculate the standard error:

$$s.e. = \sqrt{\frac{(.75)(.25)}{500}} = .0194$$

We use the standard error to set up an interval likely to contain the true population value a certain percentage of the time. At the 95 percent confidence level, which is the conventional level, the interval is the sample value ± 1.96 standard errors.

Recall from Chapter 5 that 95 percent of the area under the normal curve falls between $+1.96$ standard deviations and -1.96 standard deviations of the mean. In this case the interval for the percentage of people in the population who favor cutting the defense budget is $.75 \pm 1.96(.019) = .75 \pm .037$; that is, there is a .95 probability that the true proportion in the population favoring a lower defense budget is between 71 and 79 percent ($.75 \pm .04$). The margin of error for this survey is thus 4 percentage points. If the researcher wants a smaller margin of error, a larger sample is needed. One can see from the formula for standard error that increasing n decreases the size of the standard error. If in the above study 1500 voters had been surveyed instead of 500, the standard error would be reduced to

$$\sqrt{\frac{(.75)(.25)}{1500}} = .011.$$

The 95 percent confidence limits would then extend only $\pm.02$ [.75 $\pm$ (1.96

$\times$ .011)], giving 73 to 77 as the confidence interval likely containing the population value. The larger n increased the precision of the estimate as the margin of error went from 4 to 2 percentage points. How much must the size of n be increased in order to achieve a given level of accuracy? Assume a high school principal wants to know how the students feel about having a required AIDS education program in the school. The principal wants the estimate accurate to within 4 percentage points at the 95 percent confidence level. The formula for setting up the confidence interval ($1.96 \times s.e. = .04$) can be used to find n. The only problem is that the principal doesn't know p in the formula for standard error. The principal can do one of two things. First, he can conduct a pilot study with $n = 25$ in order to obtain a rough estimate of p. Assume that he finds that seven out of the 25 students say that they would like the program ($p = 7/25 = .28$). If $p = .28$, then $q = .72$. Substituting in the formula,

$$1.96 \sqrt{\frac{pq}{n}} = .04$$

the value of n can be found

$$1.96 \sqrt{\frac{(.28)(.72)}{n}} = .04$$

Dividing both sides by 1.96 and squaring both sides, we have

$$\sqrt{\frac{(.28)(.72)}{n}} = \frac{.04}{1.96}$$

$$\frac{(.28)(.72)}{n} = \left(\frac{.04}{1.96}\right)^2$$

$$\frac{.2016}{n} = .0004164$$

$$n = 484$$

The principal would need to sample 484 students in order to establish the 95 percent confidence interval ($.28 \pm .04$). Assume the principal surveys 484 students and finds that only 121 students say they want the program; the sample proportion is now $.25(121/484)$. He can use $p = .25$ and solve for n again.

$$1.96 \sqrt{\frac{(.25)(72)}{n}} = .04$$

This time $n = 450$, convincing the principal that the original sample of 484 students was more than enough to make the estimate that $p = .25$. The principal could say that for his population of students, $p = .25 \pm .04$ and that the probability is 95 percent that the interval contains the true population value. Thus, the principal was able to calculate the size of the sample to use to obtain the confidence and error limits desired. If the second calculation of n resulted in a value greater than 484, then it would have been necessary to increase the number of students surveyed and to recalculate.

Another procedure the principal could have used that would have eliminated the pilot study is just to assume that $p = .50$. Solving the equation

$$1.96\sqrt{\frac{(.50)(.50)}{n}} = .04$$

$n = 600$. Using $p = .50$ is always a safe way to calculate the sample size because pq is at its maximum possible value when $p = q = .50$ and the result is the largest possible estimate of the sample size needed. Then, if one finds that p is actually larger or smaller than .50, having the larger sample size calculated by assuming that $p = .50$ will provide an even more precise estimate than one expected. This procedure is the most conservative way, if not the most economical way, to arrive at sample size. Table 12.1 shows the sample size needed to have a certain margin of error for a given p. Note that the largest sample is required when the tolerable margin of error is lowest and $p = .50$. As the acceptable margin of error increases and p varies from .50, the required sample size decreases.

/ Estimating the Population Mean

Assume the survey data are in the form of means. For example, a high school principal is interested in the intelligence level of the entering freshman class. The principal selects a random sample of 100 of these students and locates their scores on the standardized intelligence test given the previous year to all students in the city. The mean score for the sample was found to be 112. The population standard deviation (σ) on this standardized test was known to be 15. The formula for the standard error of the mean is

$$\text{standard error} = \frac{\sigma}{\sqrt{n}} = \frac{15}{\sqrt{100}} = 1.5$$

TABLE 12.1 Minimum Sample Sizes Required for Various Margins of Error around the Parameter Estimation at the .95 Confidence Level. Sizes are Shown as a Function of Anticipated Sample Proportions.

Maximum Margin of Error	Value of p		
	.10 or .90*	.25 or .75	.50
1%	3462	7212	9616
2%	866	1803	2404
3%	385	802	1069
5%	139	289	385
10%	35	73	97

*The sample variance, pq, is the same when $pq = (.10)(.90)$ as when $pq = (.90)(.10)$.

Again the researcher sets up the 95 percent confidence interval for the population value by adding and subtracting 1.96 standard errors to the sample statistic. Thus, the interval for the population mean $= \bar{X} \pm 1.96$ s.e. With a mean of 112 and standard error of 1.5, the principal could be 95 percent confident that the population mean on intelligence for the entire freshman class is between 109 and 115 (112 $\pm$ 3).

The formula for standard error of the mean can be used to calculate the size of the sample needed for a specified degree of accuracy at the 95 percent confidence interval. Suppose the principal wanted a margin of error smaller than the $\pm$ 3 points in this study, say only ±2 points. What size sample would be needed to have a margin of error of 2—that is, 1.96 (s.e.) = 2?

$$\text{Substitute in the formula:} \quad 1.96\left(\frac{\sigma}{\sqrt{n}}\right) = 2$$

$$\text{Divide both sides by 1.96:} \quad \frac{\sigma}{\sqrt{n}} = \frac{2}{1.96}$$

$$\text{Square both sides:} \quad \frac{\sigma^2}{n} = \left(\frac{2}{1.96}\right)^2$$

$$\frac{\sigma^2}{n} = 1.04$$

$$n = \frac{\sigma^2}{1.04}$$

$$= \frac{225}{1.04}$$

$$= 216$$

We now have the equation for calculating n, sample size. In order to have a margin of error of two points at the 95 percent confidence level, the principal would have to increase the sample size to 216. If still greater accuracy is desired (for example, margin of error of 1), the size of the sample would have to be further increased.

Increasing the size of the sample can be expensive. Mailing of questionnaires and follow-ups is costly; interviewing is even more expensive. The researcher must consider the time and money available for the survey and select as large a sample as can be economically managed. But remember: Size alone does not guarantee a representative sample; the sampling procedure used is more important in determining whether the sample is representative of the population. The reader is encouraged to read again the section in Chapter 6 on sampling procedure and other factors to consider when deciding on sample size.

/// DATA-GATHERING INSTRUMENTS

The interview and the questionnaire both utilize the question-asking approach. These instruments can be used to obtain information concerning facts, beliefs, feelings, intentions, and so on. Although both the interview and the questionnaire make use of the question approach, there are important differences between the two methods.[6]

In an interview, data are collected through face-to-face or telephone interaction between the interviewer and the respondent. The questionnaire obtains information through the respondent's written responses to a list of questions. Each method has advantages as well as disadvantages. The researcher must decide which of the two methods is more appropriate for the needs and characteristics of a particular study.

// Interviews

One of the most important aspects of the interview is its flexibility. The interviewer has the opportunity to observe the subject and the total situation in which he or she is responding. Questions can be repeated or their meanings explained in case they are not understood by the respondents. The interviewer can also press for additional information when a response seems incomplete or not entirely relevant.

A greater completion rate is another obvious advantage of the interview. Personal contact increases the likelihood that the individual will participate and will provide the desired information. The low return rate typical for mailed questionnaires (40 percent is common) not only reduces the sample size but also may bias the results. Furthermore, the interviewer is able to obtain an answer to all or most of the questions. Missing data represent a serious problem for the mailed questionnaire.

Another advantage is the control that the interviewer has over the order with which questions are considered. In some cases it is very important that respondents not know the nature of later questions because their responses to these questions might influence earlier responses. This problem is eliminated in an interview, where the subject does not know what questions are coming up and cannot go back and change answers previously given. For individuals who cannot read and understand a written questionnaire, interviews provide the only possible information-gathering technique.

The main disadvantage of interviews is that they are more expensive and time-consuming than questionnaires.

Two basic types of questions, open-ended or closed, are used in an interview, according to the nature of the response desired from the respondent. The open-ended question permits a free response from the subject rather than restricting the response to a choice from among stated alternatives. The individual is free to respond from his or her own frame of ref-

---

[6]A worthwhile general discussion of construction and use of questionnaires and interviews as research instruments is included in D. Warwick and C. Lininger (1975), *The Sample Survey: Theory and Practice* (ch. 6–7), New York: McGraw-Hill, and D. A. Dillman (1978), *Mail and Telephone Surveys: The Total Design Method,* New York: Wiley.

erence. The interviewer simply reads the question and records the respondent's answer verbatim. An example of an open-ended question is What are the most prominent writing problems that you have observed among your freshman students?

With the closed-question format, the interviewer reads the question and presents the respondent with the various alternative response options. From the list of stated options, the individual picks the response that best represents his or her own belief or opinion. An example of a closed question is

> What type of writing assignments are typically required in your course?
> (1) reports (2) themes or essays (3) research papers (4) take-home essay examinations (5) other (please specify)

The open-ended response format permits greater freedom of expression for the respondent and provides a wider range of responses. However, open-ended questions require more time for both interviewer and respondent. It is difficult for the interviewer to record the responses verbatim and later classify and code the data for analysis. The closed question is easier and quicker for the subject to respond to and easier for the interviewer to analyze and code. A closed format also ensures that all subjects will have the same frame of reference in responding and may also make it easier for subjects to respond to questions dealing with topics of a sensitive or private nature.

A limitation of the closed question is that it does not provide much insight into whether respondents really have any information or any clearly formulated opinions about an issue. It is easier for the uninformed respondent to choose one of the suggested answers than to admit to lack of knowledge on an issue. For example, in response to the question What aspects of the president's new economic package do you think will be most helpful? the respondent without any knowledge of the president's program could easily select a reasonable answer from among those provided. On the other hand, respondents who have the information or who have well-informed opinions on the issue may dislike being restricted to simple response categories that do not permit them to qualify their answers.

Of course a combination of open-ended and closed questions may be used in a single interview. Closed questions are recommended for securing factual information or opinions on issues where it is possible to identify a limited number of alternative responses. The open-ended question is preferred for more complex questions where the researcher is interested in identifying the subject's understanding of an issue, the frame of reference used in responding, or the motivations underlying the response.

In practice, a researcher in the process of constructing an interview schedule often begins with an interview made up of open-ended questions administered to a few subjects strictly for the purpose of identifying the possible alternative responses to the questions. Then, on the basis of the results from this small sample, an interview schedule made up mainly of closed questions can be prepared.

/ Conducting the Interview

The interviewer's main job is to ask the questions in such a way as to obtain valid responses and to record the responses accurately and completely. The initial task for the interviewer is to create an atmosphere that will put the respondent at ease. After introducing himself or herself in a friendly way, the interviewer should state briefly the purpose of the interview but should avoid giving too much information about the study, which could bias the respondent.

The interviewer also has the responsibility of keeping the respondent's attention focused on the task and for keeping the interview moving along smoothly. This can best be done if the interviewer is thoroughly familiar with the questions and their sequence so that he or she can ask the questions in a conversational tone and without constantly pausing to find what question is coming next. Of course the interviewer must refrain from expressing approval, surprise, or shock at any of the respondent's answers.

If comparable data are to be obtained, the interviewer must standardize the process. Questions must be worded the same and presented in the same order for all respondents. If the respondent starts to hedge, digresses, or gives an irrelevant response, or if he or she has obviously misinterpreted the question, then the interviewer may probe by saying, "Explain your answer a little further" or "Can you tell me a little more than that?" Of course the interviewer must be careful not to suggest or give hints about possible responses.

A complete and accurate recording of the respondent's answers must be made. On the open-ended questions the respondent's exact words must be recorded verbatim while he or she is responding. This recording can be facilitated by abbreviating words and sentences or by using a tape recorder. Taping has the obvious advantage of recording the subjects' responses verbatim, along with the added advantage of freeing the interviewer to participate in the dialogue rather than having to concentrate on note taking. However, many people feel uncomfortable about having their answers taped and may become inhibited and excessively cautious about what they say. Ethics demands that the subject's permission be obtained before a tape recorder is used.

/ Training the Interviewer

It is essential that potential interviewers receive training before being sent out to use this technique. They should first spend time observing sample interviews being conducted by trained individuals and then should be required to conduct interviews under the direct supervision of the instructor. In the practice interviews the interviewees should be individuals drawn from the same population that will be used in the research study.

// Questionnaires

The direct one-on-one contact with subjects involved in the interview process is time-consuming and expensive. Often much of the same information can be obtained by means of a questionnaire. Because a questionnaire is designed for self-administration and is often mailed, it is possible to include a larger number of subjects as well as subjects in more-diverse locations than is practical with the interview.

Another advantage is that a questionnaire that can guarantee confidentiality may elicit more truthful responses than would be obtained with a personal interview. In the interview, subjects may be reluctant to express unpopular points of view or to give information that they think might be used against them later. Furthermore, the interviewer—whose personal appearance, mood, or conduct may influence the results of an interview—is not present when the questionnaire is completed, so these potential problems are avoided.

A disadvantage of the questionnaire is the possibility of misinterpretation of the questions by the respondents. It is extremely difficult to formulate a series of questions whose meanings are crystal-clear to every reader. The investigator may know exactly what is meant by a question, but because of poor wording or differential meanings of terms, a significantly different interpretation is made by the respondent. Furthermore, large segments of the population may not be able to read and respond to a mailed questionnaire. Only people with considerable education may be able to complete a very complex questionnaire.

And as mentioned earlier, questionnaires do not elicit as high a completion rate as the interview. It is easy for the individual who receives a questionnaire to lay it aside and simply forget to complete and return it. A low response rate limits the generalizability of the results of a questionnaire study. It cannot be assumed that nonresponse is randomly distributed throughout a group. Studies have shown that there are usually systematic differences in the characteristics of respondents and nonrespondents to questionnaire studies.[7] Response rate is often higher among the more intelligent, better educated, more conscientious, and more interested or generally more favorable to the issue involved in the questionnaires. The goal in a questionnaire study is 100 percent returns, although a more reasonable expectation may be 75–90 percent returns.

---

[7]Dillman, *Mail and Telephone Surveys*, p. 52.

A number of factors have been found to influence the rate of returns for a mailed questionnaire. Some of these are (1) the length of the questionnaire, (2) the cover letter, (3) the sponsorship of the questionnaire, (4) the attractiveness of the questionnaire, (5) the ease of completing it and mailing it back, (6) the interest aroused by the content, and (7) the follow-up procedures used. These will be discussed in greater detail in later sections.

/ Constructing the Questionnaire

Constructing a good questionnaire is a difficult and time-consuming task. But we know that a well-constructed questionnaire is more likely to elicit a good response than a poorly constructed one. The following are suggestions for writing items for a mailed questionnaire:

1. *Construct the instrument in such a way that it reflects quality.* A questionnaire that appears to have been thrown together quickly will not elicit high returns. During the process of constructing the questionnaire, numerous revisions may be necessary in order to eliminate ambiguous or unnecessary items.

2. *Keep the questionnaire as brief as possible so that it requires a minimum of the respondents' time.* Respondents are much more likely to complete and return a short questionnaire. The researcher must make an effort to eliminate all unnecessary items, especially those whose answers are available from other sources. All the items of a questionnaire should serve a research problem function; that is, they should elicit data needed to test the hypotheses or answer the questions of the research study. For example, a question that asks the respondent's age in a study where this information is not needed in the data analysis can be eliminated.

3. *Make sure that the respondents have the information necessary to answer the questions.* Avoid questions dealing with experiences or topics known to be unfamiliar to your sample.

4. *Phrase questionnaire items so that they can be understood by every respondent.* The vocabulary used should be nontechnical and should be geared to the least-educated respondent. At the same time, the researcher should avoid talking down to respondents or choosing words that sound patronizing. It is a good idea to have some other people, preferably ones whose background is similar to those who will be included in the study, read and give their interpretation of the content of each question. For example, questions using terms like *deficit spending, balance of trade,* and *gross national product* might not be appropriate in a survey designed for the general public. The researcher should also be careful not to use abbreviations or acronyms that might not be familiar to all.

5. *Keep individual questionnaire items as short and simple as possible.* Eliminate any words and phrases not essential to the clear meaning of the question. Carefully choosing the words to be used is even more important

if the questionnaire is to be used with a cultural or socioeconomic group other than that of the researcher.

6. *Phrase questionnaire items so as to elicit unambiguous answers.* Whenever possible, responses should be quantified. For example, instead of having respondents check *sometimes, often,* or *always,* state the alternative *number of times per week.* Words like *often* and *sometimes* have different meanings for different people.

7. *Phrase questionnaire items so as to avoid bias that might predetermine a respondent's answer.* That is, the wording of a question should not influence the respondent in a certain direction. For this reason, stereotyped, prestige-carrying, emotionally loaded, or superlative words should be avoided. Some words have such an emotional appeal in our culture that they tend to bias questions regardless of how they are used. For example, the question Have you exercised your American right and registered to vote? would undoubtedly bias the question. The simple question Have you registered to vote? would be preferable. Dillman says that words such as *freedom, equality, private enterprise, justice,* and *honesty* have a strong positive appeal in our culture. Words such as *bureaucrat, socialist, boss,* and *government planning* have a strong negative appeal. Such words should be avoided if at all possible.

8. *Avoid questionnaire items that might mislead because of unstated assumptions.* The frame of reference for answering the questions should be clear and consistent for all respondents. If any assumptions have to be made before respondents give an answer, then questions designed to inquire into these assumptions should also be included.

For example, in a survey designed for high school seniors the question Do you think your high school has adequately prepared you for college? assumes that the student is going to college and that he knows what is required in the way of preparation. The question Have you registered to vote for the upcoming election? assumes that the high school student is 18 years of age, which may not be true.

9. *Make sure that the alternatives to each questionnaire item are exhaustive, that is, express all the possible alternatives on the issue.* For example, What is your marital status? should include not only the alternatives *married* and *single,* but also *widowed, divorced, separated.*

In developing the alternatives for questionnaire items designed to identify attitudes or opinions on issues, it is a good idea first to present the questions in an open-ended form to a small sample of respondents. Their answers can then be used as alternatives in the final product. On questions for which there is a wide variety of possible responses, one should always include the alternative *other,* along with a request that the respondent explain that choice. The question What is your position in the school system? might be followed by the alternatives *administrator, teacher, librarian, other (please specify)* ——————.

10. *Avoid questions that might elicit reactions of embarrassment, suspicion, or hostility in the respondent.* Questions should not put the respondent on the defensive. For example, people often resent questions about their age, income, religion, or educational status. Instead of asking a subject's age, the researcher can ask for his or her year of birth. People seem less concerned about giving their year of birth than about giving their age. The question Do you have a high school diploma? might cause embarrasment to one who did not graduate from high school. The question might ask What grade had you completed when you left school?

11. *Avoid "double-barreled" questions that attempt to ask two questions in one.* For example, the question Do you feel that the university should provide basic-skills courses for students and give credit for these courses? is a double-barreled question. When a respondent answers a double-barreled question, the researcher doesn't know whether the answer applies to both parts of the question or to just one. A *yes* answer to the above question may mean that the respondent believes either that the university should offer basic-skills courses and should give credit for them, or that it should offer the courses but not give credit for them.

/ Types of Questions

Both open-ended and closed questions are used in questionnaires. We have already discussed in connection with interviews the advantages and disadvantages of these question formats. Questions can be structured in several ways:

1. *Completion, or fill-in, items* are open-ended questions to which respondents must supply their own answers stated in their own words. For example, What is the major weakness you have observed in your students' preparation for college?

2. *Checklists* are questions that present a number of possible answers, and the respondents are asked to check those that apply. For example, What type of teaching aids do you use in your classes? (check as many as apply)

1. BLACKBOARD
2. FILMS
3. VIDEOTAPES
4. AUDIOTAPES
5. SPEAKERS
6. BOOKS
7. OTHER (please specify)

Responses to these items are also classified into nominal categories.

3. *Scaled items* ask respondents to rate a concept, event, or situation on such dimensions as (*a*) quantity or intensity, indicating "how much," or

(*b*) frequency, indicating "how often." For example, How would you rate the students whom you are teaching this semester on writing skills? (circle number)

1. VERY POOR
2. LESS THAN ADEQUATE
3. ADEQUATE
4. MORE THAN ADEQUATE
5. EXCELLENT
6. INSUFFICIENT INFORMATION

4. *Ranking* questions ask respondents to indicate the order of their preference among a number of options. Rankings should not involve more than six options because it becomes too difficult for respondents to make the comparisons. An example of a ranking item follows.

Do your students have more difficulty with some types of reading than with other types? Please rank the order of difficulty of the following materials, with 1 being the most difficult and 4 the least difficult.

——— TEXTBOOKS
——— OTHER REFERENCE BOOKS
——— JOURNAL ARTICLES
——— OTHER (please specify)

5. *Likert-type items* that let subjects indicate their responses to selected statements on a continuum from *strongly agree* to *strongly disagree* are frequently used in questionnaires. An advantage of this type of item is that points can be assigned to the various responses and measures of central tendency, variability, correlation, and the like can be calculated.

/ Arrangement of Questions

It is recommended that special attention be given to the very first question because it may determine whether the respondents continue with the questionnaire or toss it aside. It is important the first question be interesting and easy enough for all respondents to interpret and answer. Being able to answer the first question increases the subjects' motivation and their confidence about the ability to complete the questionnaire. However, being easy does not mean that the question is insignificant. It is essential that the first question seek worthwhile information that is clearly related to the topic under consideration. For this reason, one should avoid beginning with questions relating to age, gender, education, occupation, ethnic origin, marital status, and the like. The respondents may regard these questions as irrelevant or as an invasion of privacy and may therefore not continue with the questionnaire. It is also recommended that the first few questions be of the closed type, which the respondents can complete quickly, rather than open-ended ones, which may require a long written response.

Questions that are similar in content should be grouped together. For example, in a questionnaire asking university faculty about the basic academic skills of their students, all the questions on reading would be placed together. Then questions on writing would appear together, followed later by questions related to mathematics skills. Within the content areas, the items should be grouped according to the type of question. For example, the questions requiring a simple *yes* or *no* would be placed together, as would items requiring subjects to rank or to indicate the extent of the agreement or disagreement.

Within each of the topic areas, the questions should be arranged in good psychological order. A logical or psychological arrangement contributes to better-thought-out answers on the part of the respondents. For example, one would first ascertain whether or not respondents were satisfied with working conditions before asking for changes that they would recommend. If both general and specific questions are asked on a topic, place the general questions first. Objective items on an issue or situation should precede the more subjective questions. Questions that are less likely to be objectionable should precede items that are more objectionable. People are sometimes reluctant to answer questions about attitudes, preferences, motives, behavior, personal feelings, and the like, but if objective questions can be used first to clarify and specify the situation, it may be easier for individuals to respond. For example, a researcher who wanted to survey students on the extent of marijuana usage might begin by asking more-objective questions first, such as How would you describe marijuana usage in our school: serious problem, moderate problem, slight problem, or no problem? This could be followed by the questions Do you think the frequency of marijuana smoking has increased, stayed about the same, or decreased this year? and Do you know students who use marijuana? Then perhaps Do you ever smoke marijuana? could be asked.

An implication of the above principle of placing less objectionable questions before more objectionable ones is that the items dealing with biographical data such as age, gender, and occupation should be placed at the end of the questionnaire rather than at the beginning. There will be fewer objections to giving this personal information after the individual has completed the rest of the questionnaire and can see why these kinds of data would be relevant.

/ Layout of the Questionnaire

The questionnaire should be laid out so that it is attractive, easy for the respondent to read and answer, and convenient for the researcher to code and score.[8]

---

[8]See Dillman, *Mail and Telephone Surveys,* for a detailed discussion on how to accomplish this.

1. *Number questions consecutively* throughout the questionnaire without any repetitions or omissions. Having a unique number for each question avoids confusion in coding responses.

2. *Questions can be differentiated from answer categories* by using lowercase letters for the questions and uppercase letters for the answers. Any specific directions for responding are put inside parentheses and are in lowercase. For example:

Do you favor setting standards in basic skills as a requirement for high school graduation? (circle number)

1. NO
2. YES

3. *Use numbers to identify the various answer categories.* Numbers are preferable to letters, blanks, or boxes because the numbers assigned to the options represent a form of precoding that will facilitate processing of the data.

What is the highest level of education that you have completed?
1. GRADE SCHOOL
2. SOME HIGH SCHOOL
3. COMPLETED HIGH SCHOOL
4. SOME COLLEGE
5. COMPLETED COLLEGE
6. SOME GRADUATE WORK
7. A GRADUATE DEGREE

The 5 indicates that the individual has completed college, and a count can easily be made for that category. Because of the varying lengths of the options, it is recommended that the number for the options be placed to the left of the response categories rather than at the right.

4. *Be consistent in assigning numbers to the various answer categories.* That is, always use the same number for the same answer throughout the questionnaire. It is conventional to assign low numbers to the negative responses and higher numbers to the positive responses. For example, 1 is assigned to *no* and 2 is assigned to *yes*; 1 is assigned to *unfavorable* and 2 to *favorable*. Whatever number scheme is chosen, it must be used throughout because it is confusing for a respondent to associate 1 with *no* in the first part of the questionnaire and then find 1 associated with *yes* in another part.

5. *Response categories should be arranged in a vertical rather than a horizontal format.* The vertical arrangement makes the questionnaire appear less crowded and eliminates the common error of checking the space on the wrong side of the answer.

What is your present marital status?
1 Never married   2 Married   3 Divorced   4 Separated   5 Widowed

The above confusing arrangement could be improved in the following way:

What is your present marital status? (circle number)
1. NEVER MARRIED
2. MARRIED
3. DIVORCED
4. SEPARATED
5. WIDOWED

6. *Have the questionnaire reproduced by a high-quality printing method, such as offset.* Quality printing gives the questionnaire a more professional appearance and will make a more favorable impression on respondents.

/ Pretesting

Before the final printing it is essential that the questionnaire be pretested in order to identify ambiguities, misunderstandings, or other inadequacies. First, it is a good idea to ask colleagues who are familiar with the study to examine a draft of the questionnaire and give their opinions on whether the instrument will obtain the desired data and whether there are any problems that may have been overlooked.

Next, the questionnaire should be administered personally and individually to a small group of persons drawn from the population to be considered in the study. Respondents answer the questions one at a time and provide feedback to the researcher on any difficulties they have with the items. Attention would be paid to comments like "I don't know what you mean here" and "More than one of these answers apply to me." The researcher would try to ascertain whether the questions are interpreted in the same way by all respondents.

Observations made of the respondents as they fill out the questionnaire can also be enlightening. Spending an undue amount of time on a question or leaving a question blank and returning to it later can be clues that there are problems with some of the items.

The results of pretesting can be used to clarify the items or perhaps to eliminate some. It is especially important to determine whether the questions will operate equally well in the different social classes and culture groups of the population to be studied.

Some specific questions that should be answered as a result of pretesting are

1. Do the respondents appear to be comfortable with the questionnaire and motivated to complete it?
2. Are certain items confusing?
3. Could some items result in hostility or embarrassment on the part of respondents?

4. Are the instructions clear?
5. How long will it take a respondent to complete the questionnaire?
6. Do all respondents interpret the items in the same way?

/ Distributing the Questionnaire

Researchers may find it useful to mail an introductory letter to potential respondents in advance of the questionnaire itself. This procedure alerts the subject to the study so that he or she is not overwhelmed by the questionnaire package. In any case, a cover letter addressed to the respondent by name and title must accompany the questionnaire. Figure 12.1 shows a cover letter with the important parts identified. The cover letter serves to introduce the potential respondents to the questionnaire and "sells" them on responding. The cover letter should include the following elements:

1. *The purpose of the study.* The first paragraph of the letter should explain the purpose of the study and its potential usefulness. It will be helpful to relate the importance of the study to a reference group with which the individuals may identify. A cover letter with a questionnaire for graduate students would certainly want to stress the importance of the data for improving graduate education at the university.

2. *A request for cooperation.* The letter should explain why the potential respondent was included in the sample and should make an appeal for the respondent's cooperation. Respondents should be made to feel that they can make an important contribution to the study.

3. *The protection provided the respondent.* The letter must not only assure the respondents that their responses will be confidential but must also explain how that confidentiality will be maintained. In order to facilitate the follow-up procedure necessary for a high return rate, it is recommended that identification numbers be used on the questionnaires. If there is no identification, the problem of nonresponse bias is compounded because there is no way to know who has responded and who has not and follow-up procedures become very confused. If identification numbers are used, it is essential that the respondents be told that the numbers are there simply to enable the researcher to check the respondents' names off the mailing list when the questionnaires are returned. The respondents must be assured that their names will never be placed on the questionnaires themselves; thus, there will be no way to associate particular responses with any individuals. If the researcher intends to destroy the questionnaires immediately after the responses have been rostered, this information should be conveyed in the letter in order to reassure the respondents of their anonymity.

Some researchers prefer not to use any identification system at all, especially when the topic is a sensitive one. In this case, it is necessary to include in the mail-out package a postcard that the respondent can mail separately to indicate that the questionnaire has also been mailed. The post-

FIGURE 12.1 Example of a Cover Letter for a Survey

Letterhead paper →

INDIANA UNIVERSITY
BUREAU OF EVALUATIVE STUDIES AND TESTING
Third Street and Jordan Avenue
Bloomington, Indiana 47405

Recent date →

February 15, 1989

Dear I.U. Graduate:

Purpose of survey →

The Bureau of Evaluative Studies and Testing is conducting a survey of recent graduates of Indiana University-Bloomington in order to gather data on attitudes and opinions regarding their educational experiences at I.U.B. We are interested in how well I.U.B. met your academic needs. The results of the survey will be used in reviewing and strengthening programs for present and future students.

Importance of respondent →

Request for cooperation →
Limited time for return →

Your name was drawn in a random sample of all graduates of I.U.B. from 1983 through 1987. In order that the results accurately represent all the recent graduates, it is very important that each questionnaire be completed and returned. Responding should take less than ten minutes of your time, but it will be critical to the success of the study. I would urge you to complete the questionnaire and return it in the enclosed envelope by February 24, 1989.

Confidentiality assured →

Promise of results →

You may be assured that your responses will remain completely confidential. The return envelope has an identification number that will enable us to check your name off the mailing list when the questionnaire is returned. The envelope will then be discarded. Your name will never be placed on the answer sheet or the questionnaire. If you are interested in receiving a summary of the results, please check the box on the back of the envelope and it will be mailed to you by mid-summer.

If you have questions about the study, please write or call. The telephone number is 812-855-1595.

Expression of appreciation →

Your cooperation is greatly appreciated.

Sincerely,

Lucy C. Jacobs

Lucy C. Jacobs, Ph.D.
Project Director

Signed by Project Director → rather than graduate student or staff

LCJ:nc
Enclosure

card would contain a pretyped message that the questionnaire has been returned and a place for the respondent to write his or her name. In this way, a record can be kept of the returned questionnaires.

4. *Sponsorship of the study.* The signature on the letter is important in influencing the return of the questionnaire. If the study is part of a doctoral dissertation, it would be helpful if a person well known to the respondents, such as the head of a university department or the dean of the school, signs

or countersigns the letter. Such a signature is likely to be more effective than that of an unknown graduate student. If there is a sponsor for the study, such as a foundation or some agency, this should be mentioned. A university or agency letterhead should be used.

5. *Promise of results.* An offer may be made to share the findings of the study with the respondents if they are interested. They should be told how to make their request for the results known to the researcher. One method is to provide a place for checking on the back of the return envelope, as well as a place for the respondent's name and address.

6. *Appreciation.* An expression of appreciation for their assistance and cooperation with the study should be included.

7. *Recent date on the letter.* The cover letter should be dated near the day of mailing. A potential respondent will not be impressed by a letter dated several weeks before receipt.

8. *Request for immediate return.* It is also important to urge immediate return of the questionnaire. If a time period such as 2 weeks or a month is suggested, the respondent may lay the questionnaire aside and, in spite of good intentions, forget about it. A questionnaire that fails to receive attention within a week is not likely ever to be returned.

All of the above elements should be included, but at the same time, the cover letter should be as brief as possible. One page is the maximum recommended length. Enclose the letter in an envelope along with the questionnaire. Always include an addressed, stamped return envelope for the respondent's use. This is indispensable for a good return rate.

/ Follow-ups

In order to reach the maximum percentage of returns in a mailed questionnaire survey, planned follow-up mailings are essential. Several steps are typically taken in the follow-ups:

First Reminder   If the questionnaire has not been returned in a week or 10 days after the initial mailing, a postcard should be sent to the respondent. This card serves as a polite reminder that a questionnaire was sent earlier and that the response is very important to the study. Urge respondents to complete and return the questionnaire immediately ("today"). Of course a word of thanks should be expressed to those who may have already mailed the questionnaire.

An offer can be made to send another questionnaire if one is needed by those who may have misplaced or never received it. Usually the postcard reminder will bring in a large number of responses.

Second Follow-up   This follow-up, which should be sent about 3 weeks after the original mailing, involves a letter, another copy of the questionnaire, and an addressed return envelope. The letter should first tell the nonrespondents that their questionnaires have not been received and should reiterate the usefulness of the study. The enclosure of a replacement questionnaire should be emphasized, along with a strong appeal to complete and return it. The respondents should be told not to respond a second time if they have already mailed the questionnaire.

Third Follow-up   The third and final follow-up is sent out 6–7 weeks after the initial mailing. It is similar to the second, having both a letter and a replacement questionnaire. Many researchers send this follow-up by certified mail. If a researcher has 75 to 90 percent returns after three follow-ups, he or she may be ready to terminate the survey and to declare the remaining subjects nonrespondents. The researcher must decide whether the responses obtained through additional follow-up efforts would be worth the cost and the time involved. It is sometimes suggested that the researcher include in the third follow-up a postcard on which subjects could indicate that they do not wish to participate in the survey and will not be returning the questionnaire. Such a procedure permits easy identification of nonrespondents.

/ Dealing with Nonresponse

Nonresponse is a serious problem in survey research. If, after follow-up attempts, response rate falls below about 75 percent, the researcher should try to contact the nonrespondents to learn something of their characteristics as well as to obtain their responses. Research shows that respondents tend to differ from nonrespondents in characteristics such as education, intelligence, motivation, and interest in the topic of the research. A survey with low response rate can thus be seriously biased in spite of the researcher's starting out by mailing questionnaires to a representative sample. The usual approach is to try to interview either personally or by telephone a small random sample (perhaps 10 percent) of the nonrespondents. The mean responses or proportion of responses of the respondents and nonrespondents to the items may be compared to see whether the two groups differ significantly. If no significant differences are found when the responses of the initial respondents are compared with those of the interview sample, then one could reasonably assume that the respondents represent an unbiased sample of all who received the questionnaires. But without the check, one has no way of knowing if the respondents are different and therefore biased. If there are meaningful differences, some type of weighting procedure can be applied to the nonreturns in the final analysis of data.[9] Aiken shows that the extent to which the responses of the respondents to survey items are

---

[9]Hansen, M. H., and W. N. Hurwitz (1946). The problem of non-response in sample surveys. *Journal of the American Statistical Association, 41*, 517–529.

representative of the responses of the total sample is a function of the sample size, proportion of returns, and proportion of respondents responding to items in a specified direction. He provides a formula for determining the minimum proportion of people who must return a survey in order for the researcher to feel confident that the responses of the respondents are representative of the total sample.[10]

If one finds that certain clearly identifiable subgroups did not return the questionnaire, it may be necessary to change the original research question to exclude these subgroups. For example, if secondary teachers showed a much lower rate of returns than did elementary teachers in a survey, the researcher might conclude that the questionnaire had little relevance or interest for secondary teachers and decide to restrict the study to elementary teachers. The research question would be restated to indicate the change.

/ Group-Administered Questionnaires

The self-administered questionnaire is usually used in groups assembled for a specific purpose (for example, the parents of freshmen attending pre-registration day on campus) or to gather information in a specific situation (say, in a dormitory). The administrator of the survey is present and can provide assistance if necessary. The sample is usually quite specific (parents of freshmen) and generalizable only to that population.

// The Telephone Interview

The telephone interview has become popular as a source of data. Its major advantages are lower cost and faster completion with relatively high response rates. Telephone interviews can be conducted with persons scattered over a large geographic area in a short period of time. National polling organizations often use the telephone to obtain national opinions among voters near election time. Other large-scale surveys in major cities use the telephone instead of sending interviewers into areas where they could be exposed to dangers. Another advantage of the telephone interview in a large city is that one is able to reach people who might not open their doors to an interviewer but who would be willing to talk on the telephone.

Its main disadvantage is the lack of opportunity for establishing the rapport with the respondent that is possible in a face-to-face situation. It may be difficult to overcome the suspicions of the surprised respondents, especially when personal or sensitive questions are asked. An advance letter that informs the potential respondents of the approaching call is a good way to deal with this problem. A great deal of skill is required to construct a

---

[10]Aiken, L. R. (1981). Proportion of returns in survey research. *Educational and Psychological Measurement, 41,* 1033–1038.

telephone questionnaire and carry out the interview so that good results are obtained. Another disadvantage is that households without telephones are automatically excluded from the survey, which may bias results. For an excellent discussion of the telephone interview, the reader is referred to the text by Dillman.[11]

/// VALIDITY

Some attention must be given to the validity question—that is, whether the interview or questionnaire is really measuring what it is supposed to measure. The most obvious type of validity evidence needed is content-related, which may be gathered by having some competent colleagues who are familiar with the purpose of the survey examine the items to judge whether they are adequate for measuring what they are supposed to measure and whether they are a representative sample of the behavior domain under investigation.

Some studies have used direct observation of behavior to provide criterion-related evidence of the validity of responses. After responses were obtained, observations were made to see whether the actual behavior of the subjects agreed with their expressed attitudes, opinions, or other answers. Other data sources, such as third parties, may also be used as criteria.

Some variables that influence the validity of a questionnaire are (1) How important is the topic to the respondent? We can assume more valid responses from individuals who are interested in the topic and/or are informed about it, and (2) Does the questionnaire protect the respondents' anonymity? It is reasonable to assume that greater truthfulness will be obtained if the respondents can remain anonymous, especially when sensitive or personal questions are asked.

/// RELIABILITY

Having two different interviewers interview the same individuals to check on the consistency of the results is one procedure for assessing reliability of questionnaires or interviews.

Internal consistency may be checked by building some redundancy into the instrument. That is, items on the same topic may be rephrased and repeated in the questionnaire or interview.

It is also possible to repeat a questionnaire or interview with the same individuals after a period of time or to administer two different forms of the questionnaire to the same individuals. Such procedures are often expensive

---

[11]Dillman, *Mail and Telephone Surveys*, chs. 7–8.

and time-consuming and somewhat impractical because it is not easy to find subjects willing to repeat the questionnaire or interview a second time. Another problem with this approach is that some answers to questions dealing with less stable aspects of behavior may change legitimately over time.

/// STATISTICAL ANALYSIS IN SURVEYS

Descriptive surveys don't typically require complex statistical analysis. Data analysis may simply consist of determining the frequencies and percentages for the major variables in the study. For example, a survey of library resources may report the number of volumes of fiction, the number of volumes of nonfiction, and so on—that is, simple tabulations are sufficient. A survey of people's attitudes on an issue may report the number and percentage of people falling in different response categories.

In an explanatory survey, however, there is interest in exploring the relationship between the variables of the study; that is, there is interest in knowing whether X and Y covary or under what circumstances they covary. The relationship is generally explored by setting up frequency distributions of one variable against another variable by means of cross tabulations. The simplest cross tabulation contains two variables with two categories for each variable. More-complex forms are possible, such as 2×3, 2×4, 3×4, and so on. But frequency analysis and interpretation become more difficult as the number of variables increases. A cross tabulation shows how frequently various combinations of the variables occur, from which one can "see" the relationship between the variables. In order to better show the strength of the relationship, the frequencies are usually converted to percentages. Cross tabulations can be used with almost any kind of data, but they are usually used with categorical or nominal data.

Consider the hypothetical results of a survey of attitudes toward a new library tax for improving and expanding the county library. A cross tabulation of frequency data on two variables is shown in Table 12.2.

Table 12.2 shows that 62.5 percent (150/240) of city residents favor the library tax, compared with 36.9 percent (96/260) of the county residents. One must conclude from the data in the table that there is a direct relationship

TABLE 12.2 Attitudes toward Library Tax by Residence

	City	County	Total
Favor	150	96	246
Oppose	90	164	254
Total	240	260	500

between place of residence and attitude toward the library tax. A majority of city people favor the library tax, while the majority of county residents are opposed. A more cautious observer, however, might point out that the city (the location of a major state university) has a greater proportion of educated people and that it may be educational level rather than place of residence per se that accounts for the favorable attitude toward the library tax. In other words, there may be a third variable, educational level, because the more highly educated are more likely to live in the city near their university employment and are also more likely to support the library tax.

In order to explore this alternative explanation, we would need to "control" for this third variable. In order to control for a third variable that is related to the two major variables in a survey, it is necessary to hold that variable constant and then see whether the relationship between the first two variables continues to exist when the third variable is *not* free to vary.

The simplest way to hold a variable constant is to divide the subjects into separate groups, each having a different value on that variable, and to do the same analysis with each of these groups. That is, one observes whether within each of these groups a relationship exists between the first two variables. If there is still a relationship between the variables, then it cannot be due to variation in the third variable, because within each of the groups the third variable has been held constant. To control for the third variable (educational level) in the above example, we would categorize the respondents into college-educated and non-college-educated (assuming this information is available) and look at the relationship for these two separate groups. Table 12.3 shows the data.

The data in Table 12.3 show that the alternative explanation is correct; that is, if college education is controlled by holding it constant, there is no relationship between the variables *place of residence* and *attitude toward the tax*. Among the college-educated, 80 percent (144/180) of the city residents

TABLE 12.3 Attitudes toward Library Tax Unrelated to Education

	College-Educated		
	City	County	Total
Favor	144	80	224
Oppose	36	20	56
Total	180	100	280

	Non-College Educated		
	City	County	Total
Favor	6	16	22
Oppose	54	144	198
Total	60	160	220

TABLE 12.4 Attitudes toward Library Tax Related to Education

	College-Educated		
	City	County	Total
Favor	80	20	100
Oppose	40	40	80
Total	120	60	180

	Non-College Educated		
	City	County	Total
Favor	70	76	146
Oppose	50	124	174
Total	120	200	320

[12]Several computer programs that provide cross tabulations also provide the statistics for this purpose.

favor the tax, and so do 80 percent (80/100) of the county residents. Among the non-college-educated, 10 percent (6/60) of the city residents favor the tax, as do 10 percent (16/160) of the rural residents.

Suppose the data had been as shown in Table 12.4. Even though educational level has been held constant within each table, the relationship between the variables *residence* and *attitude* is evident. Among the college-educated, 66.7 percent (80/120) of the city residents favor the tax, compared with 33.3 percent (20/60) of the rural residents. Among the non-college-educated, 58.3 percent of the city residents favor the tax, compared with 38 percent of the rural residents. In this case, there *is* something about the city and county respondents, other than their education, that leads them to feel differently about the library tax.

We may need to control for many variables in a survey study. For example, gender may need to be controlled before a relationship could be explained. In this case, one would separate the subjects into two groups, male and female, and look at the data for each of the groups separately. Social class can be controlled by categorizing subjects into separate groups on the basis of appropriate criteria and analyzing the data within each of the groups. When planning a survey, the need to control variables should be anticipated as far as possible and questions needed for such analysis should be included.

// Statistics for Cross Tabulations

The researcher will usually want to summarize the relationship shown in a cross-tabulation table with a measure indicating the extent of association between the variables or with a test of statistical significance.[12] The choice of the measure of association depends on the level at which the two variables shown in the cross tabulation were measured.

When both variables in the cross tabulation are measured at the nominal level, the chi-square test may be used to determine whether a systematic relationship exists between the two variables. (See Chapter 6 for discussion of chi square.) Chi square, however, will indicate *only* whether the variables are related or are independent. It does not tell us the extent to which they are related. For example, the value of χ^2 for the data in Table 12.4 is 16.67, which is statistically significant at the .01 level. Thus, we know that there is a significant relationship between place of residence and attitude toward the tax among the college-educated, but we do not know how strongly the two variables are related. For 2 × 2 tables such as were used in the examples in this chapter, the phi statistic (ϕ) can be used as a measure of the strength of the relationship. Phi has a value of 0 when no relationship exists and +1 when the variables are perfectly related. For tables of any size larger than 2 × 2, the appropriate measure of relationship is the contingency coefficient (C). It has a minimum value of 0, but the maximum value it can take depends on the size of the table. For this reason, C should only be used to compare tables having the same number of rows and columns.[13] If two-dimensional contingency tables are larger than 2 × 2 and the two variables are nominal, one can use Cramér's statistic, which is a mathematical generalization of phi.

If the two variables in the cross tabulation are ordinal, there are other statistics—such as gamma, Kendall's Tau B and Tau C, or Somer's D—that can be used to indicate the extent of relationship. The reader is referred to statistics textbooks for a discussion of Cramér's statistic and the above measures.[14]

/// SUMMARY

The survey is a widely used research method for gathering data ranging from physical counts and frequencies to attitudes and opinions. Surveys are classified according to their purpose, focus, and scope. They should involve careful planning, unbiased sampling of a population, development of data-gathering instruments, and careful analysis of the results.

If researchers use some type of probability sampling, they can infer population values from the sample results. The usual procedure is to set up a confidence interval that is most likely to include the population value. The width of the interval is a function of the risk they are willing to take of being wrong and the sample size. The interval narrows as the probability of

---

[13]The reader is referred to D. Ary and L. C. Jacobs (1976), *Introduction to Statistics* (ch. 9), New York: Holt, Rinehart and Winston, for a discussion of the computation of phi and the contingency coefficient.

[14]Hays, W. L. (1988). *Statistics* (4th ed.). New York: Holt, Rinehart and Winston.

being right decreases and as sample size increases. One can also use this procedure to estimate the sample size needed for any desired level of precision.

Interviews and questionnaires are the major means of data collection for a survey. Both procedures involve asking questions of selected subjects, but each has unique advantages and disadvantages. It is important that the instruments used be reliable. Various follow-up procedures have proved effective in increasing returns from mailed questionnaires.

Cross tabulations provide an excellent way to show the relationship existing between the variables in a survey.

// Key Concepts

census	Likert-type items
checklists	margin of error
cross tabulations	nonresponse
descriptive survey	open-ended question
double-barreled questions	pretesting
explanatory survey	ranking items
follow-up	response set
interview	sample survey
interviewer bias	scaled items

/// EXERCISES

1. Suggest a research question that can best be answered by means of a survey.

2. Distinguish between descriptive and explanatory surveys.

3. What are some of the factors that influence the size of the sample?

4. The evening news on television reported the following: In a recently conducted survey of the American public, 45 percent of the respondents said they approve of the president's performance. What else would you want to know before you made an interpretation of this report?

5. How would you interpret the following report? "A poll of 1000 randomly selected registered voters in Indiana found that 37 percent favored a state lottery. Figures from this poll are subject to a sampling error of ±3 percent. The confidence level is 95 percent."

6. For each of the three sample sizes below, construct the 95 percent confidence interval for the population proportion. Assume the sample proportion is .40 for each. What effect does an increase in sample size have on the width of the interval? Why?
   n of sample A $=$ 100 n of sample B $=$ 1000
   n of sample of C $=$ 10,000

7. You have developed a scale that measures "burn-out" in teachers. A random sample of 100 teachers working in the metropolitan school system has an average score of 10.5, with a standard deviation of 2.3. What is your estimate of the average burn-out score for the entire population of teachers in the school system? Use the 95 percent confidence level.

8. A national polling organization wants to be able to predict the outcome of the presidential election to within ± 5 percent. How large a random sample will be needed to achieve this level of precision? Assume 95 percent confidence level.

9. A survey had an initial response rate of 51 percent. What suggestions would you make to the researcher to deal with this low response rate?

10. Interest in a major in business has been declining at State University in the past few years. The business department wants to know if the incoming freshman class has interest in such a major. Not having the financial resources to survey all 4500 freshmen, they survey a random sample of 500. They find that 110 students report that they are interested in such a major. At the 95 percent confidence level, what is your estimate of the number of freshmen who would be interested in majoring in business?

11. Which of the following would be biased samples of the population of college students at a large university?
    a. a random sample of students entering the library on Friday evening
    b. a random sample of students registered for classes
    c. a random sample of students buying season tickets for basketball
    d. a sample composed of students who volunteered after seeing a notice in the school newspaper

12. Go to the library and locate the following research article that illustrates the survey technique: Strange, C. C., and M. R. Schmidt (1979). College student perceptions of alcohol use and differential drinking behavior. *Journal of College Student Personnel, 20,* 73–79.
    a. What was the research problem?
    b. What was the sample size, and how was the sample selected? What was the setting for the survey?
    c. Describe the instrument that was used. What type of data was the instrument designed to gather?

d. In what form were the data reported? What kind of statistical analysis was done on the data?

e. List some of the major findings from this survey.

f. Are there any flaws in the design or methodology of this survey that might affect the validity of the findings?

/// ANSWERS

1. Answers will vary.

2. Descriptive surveys attempt to determine what exists without questioning why it exists; explanatory surveys seek to explain the findings.

3. Some of the factors are the homogeneity of the population, the number of categories of observations that will be made, the type of sampling design used, and the degree of accuracy one wants in the estimation of the population parameter.

4. One would want to know the size of the sample, how it was drawn, the width of the interval around the estimated population parameter (the margin of error), and the confidence level.

5. The probability is .95 that the proportion of registered voters who favor a state lottery is between 34 and 40 percent.

6.

Sample A	Sample B	Sample C
$\text{s.e.} = \sqrt{\dfrac{(.40)(.60)}{100}}$	$\text{s.e.} = \sqrt{\dfrac{(.40)(.60)}{1000}}$	$\text{s.e.} = \sqrt{\dfrac{(.40)(.60)}{10,000}}$
$= .049$	$= .0155$	$= .005$
$\text{interval} = 40 \pm 1.96(.049)$	$= .40 \pm 1.96(.0155)$	$= .40 \pm 1.96(.005)$
$= .40 \pm .10$	$= .40 \pm .03$	$= .40 \pm .01$
$= .30 \text{ to } .50$	$= .37 \text{ to } .43$	$= .39 \text{ to } .41$

An increase in sample size decreases the width of the interval. As n increases, the sample error decreases and hence the size of the interval.

7. $$\text{s.e.} = \frac{s}{\sqrt{n}} = \frac{2.3}{\sqrt{100}} = \frac{2.3}{10} = .23$$

$$\text{estimate} = \bar{X} \pm 1.96(.23) = 10.5 \pm .45, \text{ or between } 10.05 \text{ and } 10.95$$

8. Assume $p = q = .50$

$$1.96\sqrt{\frac{(.50)(.50)}{n}} = .05$$

$$\sqrt{\frac{.25}{n}} = \frac{.05}{1.96}$$

$$\frac{.25}{n} = \left(\frac{.05}{1.96}\right)^2$$

$$\frac{.25}{n} = .00065$$

$$n = 384.6, \text{ or } 385 \text{ people}$$

9. The researcher should follow up with a postcard reminder and then another mailing or two of the questionnaire. After follow-up efforts have been completed, the researcher should try to interview some of the remaining nonrespondents to find out about their characteristics and to obtain their responses in order to determine if they differ significantly from the respondents.

10.

$$p = .22 \quad \left(\frac{110}{500}\right)$$

$$q = .78$$

$$s.e. = \sqrt{\frac{(.22)(.78)}{500}} = .0185$$

$$interval = .22 \pm 1.96(.0185) = .22 \pm .04$$

Between 18 percent and 26 percent, or between 810 and 1170, of the students could be expected to be interested in a major in business.

11. Samples (a), (c), and (d) would not be representative of the population of college students at a large university.

12. a. What are students' attitudes toward their own use of alcohol and their perceptions of drinking behavior among fellow students?
   b. A 5 percent sample ($N = 1150$) of University of Iowa students was selected on a random basis using the last four digits of their student ID numbers.
   c. A mailed questionnaire was developed to gather data on the frequency of use of alcohol, reasons for using alcohol, attitudes toward the consequences of their drinking, knowledge of the drug alcohol, and student perceptions of alcohol-abuse helping resources.
   d. Numbers and percentages were calculated for the total group and for men and women separately. A chi-square test of independence was used to test for the relationship between responses and gender and certain other variables.
   e. A large majority of students used alcohol in some form; of those, 55 percent did so at least once a week. A majority consumed 1–3 drinks in one sitting; 29 percent consumed 4–6 drinks. There were significant differences between males and females in the kind of alcoholic beverages used, frequency of use, and amount consumed. Students had limited knowledge of the drug alcohol. Over one-third of the students indicated they worried about the long-range consequences of drinking, and approximately the same number reported having a student friend whom they thought might have a drinking problem. Over three-fourths preferred an off-campus resource to go to if they thought they had a drinking problem.
   f. The return rate on the survey was rather low (57 percent). However, they did do a review of nonrespondents and found that they were very similar to the respondents with respect to gender, class standing, and kind of residence. The findings also depended on self-reported data.

13

Qualitative and Historical Research

INSTRUCTIONAL OBJECTIVES

After studying this chapter, the student will be able to
1. Distinguish between quantitative and qualitative research
2. Describe ways qualitative inquirers establish trustworthiness
3. Describe the critical aspects of qualitative research
4. Describe the nature of case studies and their advantages and disadvantages
5. Distinguish between case studies, naturalistic studies, and single-subject experiments
6. Describe the characteristics of historical research
7. Distinguish between primary and secondary sources in historical research
8. Define and give examples of internal and external criticism

The research methods described in Chapters 9–12 use numbers to answer questions. Such procedures are classified as quantitative research, as they employ such quantitative measures as counts, means, correlations, and *t*-tests. In contrast, qualitative research employs words to answer questions. Historical research is more often qualitative in nature, although quantitative methods are used when appropriate.

/// QUALITATIVE INQUIRY

The phrase *qualitative inquiry* is a generic term for a variety of approaches to educational research and evaluation variously labeled as *ethnography, naturalistic inquiry, case studies, fieldwork, field studies,* and *participant observation.*[1] These approaches can be differentiated in terms of different philosophical and analytical traditions;[2] however, they do share a common set of features that sets them apart from the quantitative approach to educational research and evaluation outlined in Chapters 1, 2, and 4 and the procedures described in Chapters 9–12.

// Distinguishing Qualitative Inquiry from Quantitative Inquiry

Qualitative inquiry differs from the quantitative approach to the study of social and behavioral phenomena in its rejection of the argument that the aim and methods of the social sciences are, at least in principle, the same as the aim and methods of the natural or physical sciences.[3] Quantitative inquirers argue that both the natural and social sciences strive for testable and confirmable theories that explain phenomena by showing how they are derived from theoretical assumptions (see the discussion of scientific theory in Chapter 1). In other words, both aim at a type of scientific explanation that includes the discovery of and appeal to laws—laws governing the behavior of the physical world, on the one hand, and laws governing human behavior, on the other.

Qualitative inquiry begins from a different methodological assumption, namely, that the subject matter of the social or human sciences is funda-

---

[1]See, for example, Y. S. Lincoln and E. G. Guba (1985), *Naturalistic Inquiry*, Beverly Hills: Sage Publications; J. P. Goetz and M. D. LeCompte (1984), *Ethnography and Qualitative Design in Educational Research*, New York: Academic Press; S. B. Merriam (1988), *Case Study Research in Education*, San Francisco: Jossey-Bass; R. C. Bogdan and S. K. Biklen (1982), *Qualitative Research for Education*, Boston: Allyn and Bacon; and J. Spradley (1980), *Participant Observation*, New York: Holt, Rinehart and Winston.

[2]Jacob, E. (1988). Clarifying qualitative research: A focus on traditions. *Educational Researcher, 17,* 16–24; and P. Atkinson, S. Delamont, and M. Hammersley (1988). Qualitative research traditions: A British response to Jacob. *Review of Educational Research, 58,* 231–250.

[3]The view that the social sciences should have the same goal and methods of investigation as the natural sciences is called *naturalism* or the *naturalistic interpretation of the social sciences.* Confusion often arises because there is a type of qualitative inquiry called *naturalistic inquiry.* In this case, the term *naturalistic* has a different meaning; it refers to the fact that qualitative studies are conducted in a "natural" (as opposed to an artifically constructed) setting. This is further explained in the section "Critical Aspects of Qualitative Inquiry," on pages 449–453.

mentally different from the subject matter of the physical or natural sciences and therefore requires a different goal for inquiry and a different set of methods for investigation. Qualitative inquirers argue that human behavior is always bound to the context in which it occurs, that social reality (for example, cultures, cultural objects, institutions, and the like) cannot be reduced to variables in the same manner as physical reality, and that what is most important in the social disciplines is understanding and portraying the meaning that is constructed by the participants involved in particular social settings or events. Qualitative inquiry seeks to understand human and social behavior from the "insider's" perspective, that is, as it is lived by participants in a particular social setting (for example, a culture, school, community, group, or institution). It is an intensely personal kind of research, one that freely acknowledges and admits "the subjective perception and biases of both participants and researcher into the research frame."[4]

Defenders of qualitative approaches argue that, in contrast, quantitative inquiry is principally concerned with the discovery of "social facts" devoid of subjective perceptions or intentions and divorced from particular social and historical contexts.

Quantitative approaches in the human sciences rely on a hypothetico-deductive model of explanation. Inquiry begins with a theory of the phenomena to be investigated. From that theory any number of hypotheses are deduced that, in turn, are subjected to a test using a predetermined procedure such as an experimental, causal-comparative, or correlational design. The ultimate goal of using this hypothetico-deductive model is to revise and support theories or lawlike statements of social and behavioral phenomena based on the results of hypothesis testing. Theories are refined and extended (and sometimes abandoned) to account for the results of testing their implications or instances (deductions).

Qualitative inquiry relies on a different model of explanation and argues for a different goal of inquiry. In general, it holds that the search for generalizations (lawlike statements or theories that are invariant over time and place) is misguided. Human behavior is always bound to a particular historical, social, temporal, and cultural context; therefore, the law-and-its-instances kind of explanation sought in a hypothetico-deductive approach is rejected in favor of a cases-and-their-interpretations kind of explanation.[5] Qualitative inquirers seek to interpret human actions, institutions, events, customs, and the like, and in so doing construct a "reading," or portrayal, of what is being studied. The ultimate goal of this kind of inquiry is to portray the complex pattern of what is being studied in sufficient depth and detail so that one who has not experienced it can understand it. When

---

[4]Goetz and LeCompte, *Ethnography and Qualitative Design*, p. 95.
[5]Geertz, C. (1980). Blurred genres: The refiguration of social thought. *American Scholar, 49*, 165–179.

qualitative inquirers interpret or explain the meaning of events, actions, and so forth, they generally use one of the following types of interpretation: (1) the construction of patterns through the analysis and resynthesis of constituent parts, (2) the interpretation of the social meaning of events, or (3) the analysis of the relationships between events and external factors.[6]

Qualitative and quantitative approaches also differ in their respective views on the role of values in inquiry. Quantitative inquirers admit that the inquirer's values may play a role in deciding what topic or problem to investigate, but that the actual investigation itself must be value-free—that is, the inquirer must follow procedures specifically designed to isolate and remove all subjective elements, like values, from the inquiry situation, so that what remains are just the "objective facts." For example, imagine an experimental study involving two different classes of third-graders in which one third-grade class is the experimental group and the other is the control group. Imagine further that observers are placed in each classroom to record interactions between teachers and students. Quantitative inquirers prefer that the observers be unaware of whether they are observing the experimental or the control group, that they be unaware of subject characteristics (their social class, IQ, previous academic achievement, and so on), and that they use highly structured observational protocols that require only low-level inferences and little, if any, interpretation about what is happening in the interactions between teacher and students. These procedures are used in quantitative inquiry to ensure that the observers' values and beliefs will not influence or contaminate the observations that they make. By following these procedures for making observations, the quantitative inquirer provides strong assurance (some might say a guarantee) that the inquiry is value-free.

In contrast, the qualitative approach argues that inquiry is always value-bound—it can never be considered value-free—and that inquirers must be explicit about the roles that values play in any given study. Qualitative inquirers argue that inquiry is value-bound in the following ways: in the choice of a problem to investigate, in the choice of whether to adopt a quantitative or qualitative approach to a problem, in the choice of methods used to investigate that problem, in the choice of a way to interpret results or findings, and by the values inherent in the context where the study takes place.[7] Qualitative inquirers believe that it is impossible to develop a meaningful understanding of human experience without taking into account the interplay of both the inquirers' and participants' values and beliefs. Furthermore, qualitative inquirers argue that human inquiry requires frequent, continuing, and meaningful interaction between inquirers and their respondents (subjects) and that inquiry must maximize rather than minimize this kind of contact.[8]

---

[6]McCutcheon, G. (1981). On the interpretation of classroom observations. *Educational Researcher, 10,* 5–10; and P. Diesing (1972). *Patterns of Discovery in the Social Sciences.* London: Routledge & Kegan Paul.

[7]Lincoln and Guba, *Naturalistic Inquiry,* pp. 160–186.

[8]*Ibid.,* p. 107.

Because qualitative inquiry openly acknowledges the role of values in inquiry and demands involvement and interaction of inquirers and respondents, it is often claimed that the findings (results) of such studies are simply a matter of opinion. To counter that charge, qualitative inquirers employ a variety of techniques to demonstrate the trustworthiness of their findings. These techniques are discussed in greater detail later.

/ Critical Aspects of Qualitative Inquiry

Although qualitative inquirers work in many different ways, they do share a common interest in a particular set of procedures for conducting an inquiry. Some of the more critical aspects of that way of proceeding include the following.[9]

Concern for Context Qualitative inquiry assumes that human behavior is context-bound, that is, human experience takes its meaning from and therefore is inseparable from, social, historical, political, and cultural influences. Thus, inquiry is always bounded by a particular context, or setting. Proponents of qualitative inquiry argue that the quantitative approach to the study of human experience seeks to isolate human behavior from its context; it engages in "context-stripping."[10]

Natural Setting The context in which human experience is studied must be naturally occurring (like a classroom, an entire school, an organization), not contrived or artificial (like those of a laboratory experiment). Thus, qualitative inquiry takes place in the field, in settings as they are found. In addition, qualitative inquiry places no prior constraints on what is to be studied. For example, it does not identify, define, and investigate or test the relationship between a particular set of independent and dependent variables; rather, it studies human experience holistically, taking into account all factors and influences in a given situation.

Human Instrument In qualitative studies, the investigator is the data-gathering instrument. He or she talks with people in the setting, observes their activities, reads their documents and written records, and records this information in field notes and journals. Qualitative inquiry relies on fieldwork methods—interviewing, nonstructured observation, and document analysis—as the principal means of collecting data, avoiding the use of paper-and-pencil tests, mechanical instruments, and highly structured observational pro-

[9]In addition to the references listed in note 1, see also R. R. Sherman and R. B. Webb (eds.) (1988), *Qualitative Research in Education: Focus and Methods,* London: The Falmer Press; and D. M. Fetterman (1988), *Qualitative Approaches to Evaluation in Education,* New York: Praeger.

[10]Mischler, E. G. (1979). Meaning in context: Is there any other kind? *Harvard Educational Review, 49,* 2–10.

tocols. The qualitative inquirer deals with data in the form of words, rather than numbers and statistics; but from time to time he or she may also collect data in numerical form. Managing the large volume of data that is generated from interviews, observations, and the collection of documents is an important consideration in qualitative studies.[11]

Qualitative investigators also typically keep a personal or reflexive log or journal in which they record accounts of their thoughts, feelings, assumptions, motives, and rationale for decisions made. This is one way in which the qualitative inquirer addresses the issue of the inquiry being value-bound.

Emergent Design   In quantitative studies, researchers carefully design all aspects of a study *before* they actually collect any data; they specify variables, measures for those variables, statistics to be used to analyze data, and so forth. This is possible because these researchers know in advance what they are looking for: They have specific hypotheses or questions in mind and can imagine what a test of the hypothesis or an answer to the question might look like. Regardless of the particular problem or phenomena being investigated, researchers insist that this careful specification of elements of a study's design is extremely important. In contrast, qualitative inquirers rarely, if ever, fully specify all aspects of a design before beginning a study; rather, the design *emerges* as the study unfolds. They adjust their methods and way of proceeding (design) to the subject matter at hand. This is necessary because the qualitative inquirer is never quite sure just what will be learned in a particular setting (the investigator has not decided in advance what he or she is looking for), because what can be learned in a particular setting depends on the nature and types of interactions between the inquirer and the people and setting and those interactions are not fully predictable, and because important features in need of investigation cannot always be known until they are actually witnessed by the investigator.

Thus, qualitative inquiry can only be characterized beforehand in a very general way that indicates how a study might unfold: It begins with a general research problem, question, or topic—for example, How do social workers cope with the stress of their jobs? How do teachers in rural schools react to distance-learning technologies? What is chronic pain? or What is the relationship of rural schools to their communities? The inquirer then seeks to gain access to a particular site or group of people in which he or she can study the topic and negotiates entry by adopting a role as either a full participant-observer, just an observer, or some combination of the two. Negotiating entry, adopting a role, and developing and maintaining trust with the participants in a study are fairly complex topics about which much has

---

[11]See, for example, H. G. Levine (1985), Principles of data storage and retrieval for use in qualitative evaluations, *Educational Evaluation and Policy Analysis, 7,* 169–186.

been written.[12] Following an initial period of becoming oriented to the site, learning about its members, and so forth, the investigator begins to focus the inquiry on salient aspects or issues by forming tentative (working) hypotheses or questions. These initial hypotheses or questions are subsequently refined (narrowed) as the investigation becomes more sharply focused. Typically, during this stage, the inquirer will conduct literature reviews on the topic to deepen his or her understanding of the phenomena being investigated. Hypotheses are eventually confirmed and tested through a variety of procedures. The final stage is exiting from the site.

Establishing Trustworthiness[13]   Qualitative inquirers use a variety of procedures to check the credibility of the data being gathered and to confirm their developing insights or hypotheses. Among these techniques are prolonged engagement at the site and persistent observation to provide sufficient scope and depth to observations. Triangulation—the use of multiple sources of data, multiple observers, and/or multiple methods—is another technique that is used to enhance the probability that hypotheses and interpretations are credible. Periodic debriefing with the inquirer's peers and member checks (submitting the inquirer's interpretations to members in a setting for their validation) are other important procedures.

To enhance the dependability (roughly equivalent to the reliability) of the study, a qualitative inquirer often maintains an audit trail of materials that documents how the study was conducted, including what was done, when, and why. The audit trail contains the raw data gathered in interviews and observations, records of the inquirer's decisions about whom to interview or what to observe and why, files documenting how working hypotheses were developed from the raw data and subsequently refined and tested, the findings of the study, and so forth. Using the audit trail as a guide, an independent, third-party auditor examines the inquirer's study in order to attest to the dependability of procedures employed and to examine whether findings are confirmable, that is, whether they are logically derived from and grounded in the data that were collected.[14]

Inductive Analysis   In most qualitative studies data collection and data analysis take place simultaneously. In other words, the inquirer does not wait until all the data are "in" before he or she begins to interpret them. From the outset of the first interview or observation, the qualitative inquirer is reflecting on the meaning of what he or she has heard and seen, developing hunches (working hypotheses) about what it means and seeking to confirm

---

[12]See, for example, W. B. Shaffir, R. A. Stebbins, and A. Turowetz (1980), *Fieldwork Experience*, New York: St. Martin's; and R. M. Emerson (ed.) (1988), *Contemporary Field Research*, Prospect Heights, IL: Waveland.

[13]Lincoln and Guba, *Naturalistic Inquiry*, pp. 289–331.

[14]Schwandt, T. A., and E. S. Halpern (1988). *Linking Auditing and Metaevaluation*. Beverly Hills: Sage Publications.

or disconfirm those hunches in subsequent interviews or observations. This process of data analysis is inductive—it proceeds from data to hypotheses to theory. As the inquirer reduces and reconstructs the data through the processes of coding and categorization, he or she aims at the development of grounded theory (theory about the phenomena being observed that is directly tied to—grounded—in the data about that phenomena).[15]

Reporting   Reports of qualitative inquiry will, of course, vary, depending on the nature of the publication in which they appear (for example, a paper prepared for the *American Educational Research Journal*[16] will differ from a monograph or book-length study), yet they are generally heavily narrative in form and contain thick descriptions of setting and context, as illustrated in this excerpt from Alan Peshkin's field study of a fundamentalist Christian school:

> Bethany Baptist Academy's remarkably clean hallways are the pride of Headmaster McGraw. The airy, spacious elementary classrooms have the stimuli-cluttered look of elementary classrooms anywhere. By contrast, the secondary classes are relatively dreary, though livened somewhat by bulletin boards displaying pinned and stapled pictures and good thoughts, an administration requirement. The gym, with a stage built to one side, doubles as an assembly hall. Opposite the stage is a small kitchen. To buy lunch, children line up against the gym wall, pick up their trays of food, and enter the lunchroom. The school library and the administrative quarters are in the elementary wing. Headmaster McGraw's well-decorated office is behind that of his secretary, who acts also as a factotum for the entire school—nurse, cheerleader consultant, piano accompanist for vocal soloists, and upholder of school rules. A decorative bookcase containing several books on Abraham Lincoln held in place by Lincoln bookends stands against the office wall; above it are two pictures of Lincoln and the Gettysburg Address framed. A waist-high barrier separates the visitor's sitting area from the offices. On the wall behind the visitor's couch hangs a picture of Theodore Roosevelt with "Thoughts of T. R." printed beneath. Surrounding this picture are plaques: the William Muller Award for high school students; the Anne Muller Award for the senior girl whose life best exemplifies the principles of the founder; the National School Choral Award, etc.[17]

Rather than presenting tables of statistics and graphic displays of numerical data, reports of qualitative studies present the natural language of the participants in a study as drawn from interview data and documents. For

[15]Strauss, A. L. (1987). *Qualitative Analysis for Social Scientists*. Cambridge: Cambridge University Press.

[16]See, for example, M. L. Smith and L. A. Shepard (1988), Kindergarten readiness and retention: A qualitative study of teachers' beliefs and practices, *American Educational Research Journal, 25*, 307–333; and J. J., Blase (1988), The everyday political perspective of teachers: Vulnerability and conservatism, *Qualitative Studies in Education, 1*, 125–142.

[17]Peshkin, A. (1986). *God's Choice: The Total World of a Fundamentalist Christian School* (p. 33). Chicago: University of Chicago Press.

example, in the same study noted above, Peshkin provides the reader with the following account in which Bethany's librarian describes her practice of censorship:

> Some of the science books, if they have too much evolution or are too slanted in certain places, but they have good qualities in them, then I take them to Mr. Kruger [the science teacher]. I let him pick out what he can use. . . .
>
> I look for evolution. That's one of the things. I look for swear words. We take those out. I found a double page of monkeys developing into man and, of course, we don't approve of that at all, so I just sealed the pages together and it didn't bother the reading on either side. Then, in the beginning, there was a section on evolution. I bracketed that in black letters and wrote EVOLUTION across it so that anybody reading knows that it is evolution, rather than destroying the whole book, because a lot of it was good. If I find a naked person, I draw a little bathing suit on them or I put a little dress on, but just in a regular book that doesn't have anything to do with art. But in art, art is art, and if you find a person without any clothes on, that's what they drew. We had one storybook where the kids were all bathing in the nude. It was not anything, so I just put bathing suits on them.
>
> We just put out twenty new books on the value of honesty and that sort of thing. I had each of the lower-grade teachers take four and read them through to see if they contained anything we should worry about. One of the books sort of made light of discipline and so we, instead of having a little frowning boy in there, you know, that had been punished and didn't accept it, we put a sticker on there with a smiling face.[18]

// Case Studies

Case studies and single-subject experiments (see Chapter 9) both study a single individual or a single, discrete social unit, such as a family, club, or gang. However, single-subject experiments focus on a single behavior or a very limited number of behaviors, whereas case studies attempt to describe the subject's entire range of behaviors and the relationship of these behaviors to the subject's history and environment. In a single-subject experiment the investigator introduces a specific treatment for the purpose of studying the effect of this treatment on the subject, whereas in a case study the investigator observes the subject's reaction to naturally occurring events.

In a case study the investigator attempts to examine an individual or unit in depth. The investigator tries to discover all the variables that are important in the history or development of the subject. The emphasis is on understanding why the individual does what he or she does and how behavior changes as the individual responds to the environment. This requires detailed study for a considerable period of time. The investigator gathers data about

---

[18]*Ibid.*, pp. 262–263.

the subject's present state, past experiences, environment, and how these factors relate to one another.

Many case studies arise from endeavors to solve problems. The well-known case studies of Freud began with his attempt to assist his subjects in solving their personality problems. As he attempted to probe deeply into the dynamics of his patients' personalities, he reasoned that the relationships that he observed between them and their environments might also be characteristic of other individuals with similar problems. He published detailed accounts of his interviews with patients and his interpretations of their thoughts, dreams, and actions, on the assumption that far-reaching generalizations could be made from these studies.

The greatest advantage of a case study is the possibility of depth; it attempts to understand the whole child or the whole adult in the totality of that individual's environment. Not only the present actions of an individual but his or her past, environment, emotions, and thoughts can be probed. The researcher attempts to determine *why* an individual behaves as he or she does and not merely to record behavior.

Case studies often provide an opportunity for an investigator to develop insight into basic aspects of human behavior. The intensive probing characteristic of this technique may lead to the discovery of previously unsuspected relationships.

On the other hand, the advantages of the case study are also its weaknesses. Although it can have depth, it will inevitably lack breadth. The dynamics of one individual or social unit may bear little relationship to the dynamics of others. In practice most case studies arise out of counseling or remedial efforts and therefore will provide information on exceptional rather than representative individuals.

The opportunities for insight in a case study are also opportunities for subjectivity or even prejudice. The preconceptions of an investigator can determine which behaviors are observed and which are ignored as well as the way in which the observations are interpreted.

The reputation of the case study approach has suffered because some investigators in the past have explained their observations in constructs that are impossible either to confirm or refute through empirical study.

Since the extent to which case studies can produce valid generalizations is extremely limited, their major usefulness is not as tools for testing hypotheses but rather in the production of hypotheses, which can then be tested through more rigorous investigation. For example, the insights Jean Piaget gained in his famous case studies on the maturation of intellect provided useful hypotheses that have since been investigated through other methods.

In those instances when case studies result from attempts to learn about individuals in order to help them, the research aspect of the study takes second place. However, case studies are also frequently conducted with the primary aim of gaining knowledge. Itard's classic case study on the Wild

Boy of Aveyron[19] was an effort to learn about the effects of civilization through studying a boy who had grown up in isolation from civilization in eighteenth-century France. Piaget's case studies were conducted in order to learn about mental growth in children rather than to benefit the subjects involved.

/// HISTORICAL RESEARCH

Historical research is the attempt to establish facts and arrive at conclusions concerning the past. The historian systematically and objectively locates, evaluates, and interprets evidence from which we can learn about the past. Based on the evidence gathered, conclusions are drawn regarding the past so as to increase our knowledge of how and why past events occurred and the process by which the past became the present. The hoped-for result is increased understanding of the present and a more rational basis for making choices.

The historian operates under different handicaps from those of researchers in other fields. Control over treatment, measurement, and sampling is limited, and there is no opportunity for replication. As in descriptive and causal-comparative research, the independent, or treatment, variables are not controlled by the researcher. All the cautions in interpreting those studies also apply to historical research. However, in descriptive and causal-comparative research, measurement can usually be controlled through deciding what measures will be administered as the dependent variable. While historians have no choice concerning what documents, relics, records, and artifacts survive the passage of time, they do have some limited control over what questions they will ask of these sources and what measures they will apply to them. When interviewing witnesses of past events and when searching the historical record, researchers can decide what questions to ask and what is to be measured. But they can measure only those things that witnesses remember or the record contains.

In descriptive and experimental research, investigators can attempt to control sampling; that is, they can decide for themselves whom they are going to study. Historians can study only those people for whom records and artifacts survive. If newspapers ignore a particular segment of a community and no other sources for that community exist, then historians are unable to assess directly the contributions that particular segment of a population made to the life of that community. Another limitation impinging upon historical researchers is that no assumption about the past can be made merely because no record can be found, nor can it be assumed that a conspiracy of silence has distorted the historical record.

---

[19]Itard, J. G. *The Wild Boy of Aveyron.* Trans. G. and M. Humphrey (1962). New York: Appleton.

// Primary and Secondary Sources

The historian classifies materials as *primary* and *secondary sources*. Primary sources are original documents, relics, remains, or artifacts. These are the direct outcomes of events or the records of eyewitnesses. Examples would be the minutes of a school board meeting, an unedited videotape of a basketball game, a collection of artwork completed by a third-grade class. In primary sources only the mind of the observer intrudes between the original event and the investigator. Note that the mind of the observer *does* come between the event and the record in each of our examples. Someone has decided what will and will not be recorded in the proceedings of the school board; when the camera is to be on or off and where it is to be focused during the basketball game; which artwork is to be kept.

In secondary sources the mind of a nonobserver also comes between the event and the user of the record. If a newspaper reporter has been present at a school board meeting, the published report is a primary source. If the reporter relies on the minutes of the meeting or an interview with a participant to prepare the report, then this report is a secondary source. Common examples of secondary sources are history books, articles in encyclopedias, and reviews of research. Historians seek to employ primary sources whenever possible.

// External and Internal Criticism

Two ideas that have proved useful in evaluating historical sources are the concepts of *external* (or lower) *criticism* and *internal* (or higher) *criticism*.

Basically, external criticism asks if the evidence under consideration is authentic and, depending on the nature of the study, might involve such techniques as authentication of signatures, chemical analysis of paint, or carbon dating of artifacts. Suppose a historian has a letter describing Massachusetts schools that is believed to have been written by Horace Mann. Using external criticism, the investigator would ask Is the paper of the right age? Is the handwriting Mann's? Are the point of view and the writing style consistent with Mann's other writings?

After the authenticity of a piece of evidence has been established, the historical investigator proceeds to internal criticism, which requires an evaluation of the worth of the evidence—for instance, whether a document provides a true report of an event. Such a question can best be answered by substantiating one piece of evidence by comparing it with others that throw light on an event or provide further information about an event and the people or circumstances surrounding it. In the example, the investigator would ask Is Mann's description of the schools unbiased? Does it agree with other contemporary descriptions of the schools?

Since historical research does have limitations, one could very well ask why it should be attempted. The fundamental reason is that there is no other way to investigate many questions. How else might one attempt to assess the effect of the Kent State shootings and other campus disorders in the spring of 1970?

An advantage of historical research, and sometimes a reason for using this approach, is that it is unobtrusive. The researcher is not physically involved in the situation studied. There is no danger of experimenter-subject interaction, nor is there any need to get the permission of school authorities for the research. The historian locates appropriate documents, gathers suitable data, and draws conclusions at a distance from the situation being studied.

In addition, historical research may provide new perspectives to a crisis situation. The uninvolved nature of historical research may make it acceptable in an emotionally charged situation where other types of research would be impossible.

Because of its limitations, caution must be exercised in generalizing the results of historical research. Students who plan to do historical study should consult appropriate bibliographies and sources on historical methodology.[20]

/// SUMMARY

Qualitative studies, including case studies, are a distinctive type of research in education and the social sciences that can produce vivid and richly detailed accounts of human experience. These studies are based on a fundamentally different approach to the study of social reality than that which underlies the standard quantitative approach to the study of education. Qualitative inquiries demand a set of skills that are not readily learned by examining textbook accounts of methods. Fieldwork experience in negotiating access to a site, developing a researcher role, establishing and maintaining trust with participants in the study, conducting and recording interviews and observations, managing data, and performing data analysis are necessary in order to become proficient in this approach to inquiry.

Noncurrent records and remains are used in historical research to generate and test hypotheses. Primary sources are employed as much as possible. The historical researcher attempts to establish the authenticity of sources through external criticism and their veracity through internal criticism. Because of the inherent weaknesses, extreme caution should be exercised in generalizing conclusions reached through historical research.

---

[20]Barzun, J., and H. F. Graff (1985). *The Modern Researcher* (4th ed.). San Diego: Harcourt Brace Jovanovich; R. E. Beringer (1978). *Historical Analysis: Contemporary Approaches to Clio's Craft*. Malabar, FL: R. E. Krieger; W. N. Brickman (1982). *Educational Historiography: Tradition, Theory, and Technique*. Cherry Hill, NJ: Emeritus; R. R. Sherman (ed.) (1984). *Understanding History of Education* (2d ed.). Cambridge, MA: Shenkman.

// **Key Concepts**

audit trail	internal criticism
concern for context	natural setting
debriefing	naturalistic inquiry
emergent design	participant observation
ethnography	primary source
external criticism	qualitative inquiry
historical research	quantitative inquiry
human instrument	secondary source
inductive analysis	triangulation

/// **EXERCISES**

1. Identify which of the following statements are characteristic of the quantitative approach and which are characteristic of the qualitative approach:
   a. Assumes that the aims and methods of the social sciences are the same as the aims and methods of the physical sciences.
   b. Argues that human behavior is always bound to the context within which it occurs.
   c. Employs hypothetico-deductive explanations.
   d. Employs triangulation to establish trustworthiness.

2. How do case studies differ from single-subject experiments?

3. A psychologist reports the happenings in a gathering of a group who expected on a given night that the planet earth would disappear. His report consists of his actual observations of the group. This investigation could be classified as
   a. qualitative research
   b. experimental research
   c. historical research
   d. causal-comparative research

4. Identify methods that qualitative researchers use to establish trustworthiness.

5. An investigator has a letter describing education in Uganda in 1977. It is supposed to have been written by President Idi Amin. What question would be asked in
   a. external criticism
   b. internal criticism

6. When is a historical document considered to be secondary?

7. What are the advantages and disadvantages of historical research as compared with other types of research?

/// ANSWERS

1. a. quantitative
    b. qualitative
    c. quantitative
    d. qualitative

2. Single-subject experiments focus on a single behavior or a very limited number of behaviors. The investigator introduces a specific treatment for the purpose of studying the effect of this treatment on the subject. A case study attempts to describe the subject's entire range of behavior as it occurs in a natural setting. The researcher observes the subject's behavior in relation to the influence of the physical, social, and psychological environment.

3. a

4. prolonged engagement at the site; persistent observation; triangulation—the use of multiple observations, sources of data, and methods; periodic debriefing; and maintenance of an audit trail

5. a. Was the letter really written by Idi Amin?
    b. Does it accurately describe education in Uganda in 1977?

6. A document is secondary if the mind of a nonobserver comes between the event and the document.

7. One advantage of historical research is the unlikelihood of researcher or experimental interaction effects confounding interpretation of findings. A historical perspective can deal with issues and past situations that cannot be handled experimentally. The main disadvantage is the lack of experimental control, which makes unequivocal interpretation of data and generalization difficult. There is also the possibility of gathering inadequate or inaccurate information that is not verifiable.

PART VI

Communicating Research

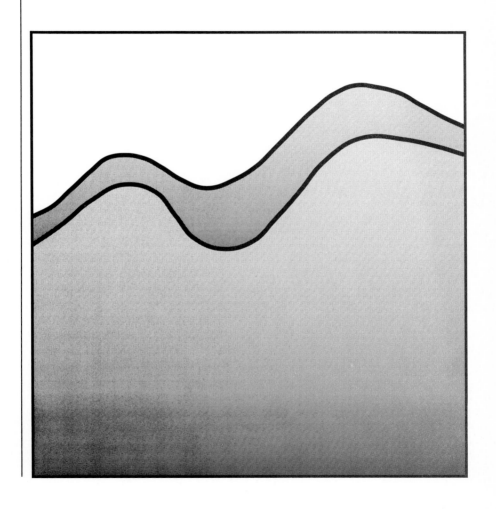

CHAPTER 14

Guidelines for Writing Research Proposals

INSTRUCTIONAL OBJECTIVES

After studying this chapter, the student will be able to

1. Describe the components of a research proposal and why they are important
2. Identify common weaknesses in research proposals
3. Critique research proposals
4. Select statistics appropriate for the questions being asked and the data involved
5. Describe ethical and legal considerations in research
6. Describe the role of an institutional review board
7. Write a research proposal that meets the guidelines

In most cases researchers will need to present their projects in organized written form at two stages: (1) the initial stage, which requires preparation of a research proposal, and (2) the final stage, a finished report of the results of the research.

/// WRITING A RESEARCH PROPOSAL

Writing the research proposal can be the most crucial and exciting step in the research process. At this stage the whole project crystallizes into concrete form. In the proposal, researchers demonstrate that they know what they are seeking and how they will recognize it and explain why the search is worthwhile. The researchers' inspirations and insights are translated into step-by-step plans for discovering new knowledge. The format may be the relatively informal outline offered by a student to satisfy the requirements of a research course, a formal thesis or dissertation proposal presented to a committee, or a funding request to a foundation or governmental agency.

The following suggested outline for writing a research proposal contains the steps essential to formulate and propose a research study:

1. Introduction
   a. Statement of the problem
   b. Review of the literature
   c. Questions and/or hypotheses
2. Methodology
   a. Subjects
   b. Instruments
   c. Procedures
3. Analysis of data
   a. Data organization
   b. Statistical procedures
4. Significance of the study
   a. Implications
   b. Applications
5. Budget and time schedule
   a. Budget
   b. Time schedule

Although it is not necessary to follow this outline rigidly, it should provide a useful guide for the writing of any proposal because all the aspects listed here must be considered.

// Introduction

A critical part of a research proposal is the introduction to the proposed study. The author should first state the research problem clearly and unambiguously, then link the problem to the body of information available in the field and establish the importance of and the need for carrying out the research. Regardless of how tightly the design of the study is formulated and how well the statistical procedures are selected, unless the introduction is written carefully and intelligently, other parts of the proposal will probably not receive serious consideration. It is not unusual for proposals to be turned down solely on the basis of a poor introduction, without much consideration being given to the proposed methodology and statistical design. It is recommended that this section be prepared with care, caution, and the aim of promoting the reader's interest in the problem.

The introduction to a research proposal should include (a) a statement of the problem, (b) a review of the literature, and (c) questions and/or hypotheses.

/ Statement of the Problem

A clear and direct statement of the problem should be made very early in the introduction, ideally at the beginning of the first paragraph, and followed by a description of the background of the question. This section of the introduction should also include a brief indication of the potential significance of the study, although it is imperative to avoid the temptation to sell the importance of the topic before stating it. Two common errors to watch for are (1) beginning the introduction with an elaborate presentation of the background of a problem before the problem itself has been clearly stated and (2) concentrating on a justification for the study at this point with the statement of the problem buried in the discussion or only vaguely brought in near the end.

Another common error is to assume that the reader knows as much about the content of the question as does the author. The problem should be stated so that it can be understood by someone who is generally sophisticated but who is relatively uninformed concerning the area of the problem.

Usually the background of the problem will be developed in the section on related literature. However, it is sometimes useful to mention in the statement of the problem those studies that have led directly to it. If the problem has arisen from the author's experience, this may be explained briefly in this section.

At an appropriate point in this section any terms that may not be familiar to the reader or those to which the author is ascribing specific meanings should be defined in the way they will be used in the study. The specific limitations of the scope of the study and a foreshadowing of the hypothesis should close this section.

/ Review of the Literature

In the section on related literature the author presents what is so far known about the problem under consideration, thus providing the setting for the questions or hypotheses of the proposed study. Include only literature relevant to the objectives of the proposed study. The literature cited does not have to be exhaustive, but it should contain the most pertinent related studies and show an awareness of promising current practices.

In this section the author of the proposal demonstrates not only how he or she proposes to proceed from the known to the unknown but also how firm the author's grasp of the field and awareness of recent developments are. This does not mean that the review should be a *tour de force* of the author's erudition. Only literature that clearly relates to the objectives of the study should be included.

The literature should be organized by topic. Topical organization serves to point out to the reader what is known about various aspects of the study. Thus, a complete picture of the background of the study is put together step by step.

A pitfall to be avoided in a related-literature section is the presentation of a series of abstracts, one per paragraph. This presents the audience with tedious reading and misses the opportunity for laying meaningful groundwork for the study. It is much better to organize by topic and to point out how the studies presented relate to the question(s).

Not all related studies need to be discussed in detail. In reviewing several similar studies, the author may describe the most important one, then simply state that the results were confirmed in similar studies that are listed but not described in detail. Enthusiastic beginning researchers often imagine their proposed study is unique and that there is no related research available. This is very rarely the case. A thorough search will almost always turn up several research papers related to at least some aspects of a proposed study. Even if there should chance to be no research in the field, there is usually literature of a theoretical or speculative nature that should be included as part of the background of a study.

Of course the author should include theories and research results contrary to the stated hypothesis as well as those in agreement with it.

The related literature section should conclude with a discussion of the findings and their implications. Here the author shares the insights gained from the review of the literature and points out the gaps in what is known about the topic, thus leading directly to the question he or she proposes to investigate.

/ Questions and/or Hypotheses

The problem, which has already been stated in a general way, should now be made specific. If the project is a survey, the problem will be stated in question form—for example, What percentage of teachers in the state of Iowa have tenure?

If the project is designed to test a theory, however, the problem will be stated in hypothesis form. Although the answer to a survey question may take any number of values, the answer in a hypothesis-testing experiment is always either yes or no.

The statement of the research hypothesis is typically determined by the implications of the related literature and the deductive logic of the study. Some authorities suggest that the hypothesis should be stated in null form because it is the null hypothesis that will be involved in the statistical test. However, we suggest that in this section of the proposal a research hypothesis be stated in terms of anticipated relationships between variables. In this way the author gives the readers a clearer indication of the intent of the study than would be conveyed if the null hypothesis were stated at this point. The use of the research hypothesis at this stage also allows the researcher to build the deductive logic underlying the study. The null hypothesis can be introduced in the analysis-of-data section.

It is a good thing if a hypothesis can be stated concisely in operational form. If this is not possible, a hypothesis stated in general terms should be followed by the definitions and stipulations necessary to define it in operational form.

// Methodology

In this part of the proposal the author shows how the study will be set up in order that the research question will be answered or the hypothesized relationships will be observed, if in fact these relationships exist. In previous chapters appropriate research designs for different types of research were introduced. The researcher should select from among these research designs, experimental or otherwise, the one that best suits the question and/or hypothesis under consideration. For example, if one is to compare two methods of teaching chemistry, one is in fact raising an experimental question. This research problem requires at least two groups of subjects: experimental and control. If one also wishes to investigate the interaction effect between methods of teaching chemistry and another variable—intelligence, for instance—the question, while still experimental, asks for a more sophisticated design than that of a two-group design. One needs, in this case, to set up a factorial design with at least four groups for such a study.

In the methodology part of the proposal the author includes all steps that will be taken to investigate the question under consideration. The proposed sampling procedures, methods of data collection, and instruments to be used are described.

A convenient way of presenting the research methodology is to categorize all information regarding the design as (1) subjects, (2) instruments, or (3) procedures, as appropriate.

/ Subjects

The first step in identifying the subjects in a study is to describe the population of interest: Is the study concerned with college freshmen, dyslexic six-year-olds, principals of elementary schools, and so forth? Then the author/researcher describes the procedure for drawing the sample from the population. If random selection is not possible, it should be explained why a particular procedure for sample selection has been adopted and how the sample used does or does not resemble the population of interest. A careful description of the subjects can help the reader of the proposal to determine if, in the reader's view, the results of the study can be generalized to the extent intended.

/ Instruments

The goal of a research project is to investigate relationships between constructs. However, since constructs are usually impossible to measure directly, we must select or develop indicators that will approximate them as well as possible. If an instrument is one already established, the proposal should include reported evidence of its reliability and also its validity for the purpose of the study. In cases where the instruments are to be developed by the researcher, it is necessary to outline the procedure to be followed in developing them. This outline should include the steps that will be taken to obtain validity and reliability data on these instruments. If the description of the reliability and validity procedures results in so much detail that it interrupts the continuity of the proposal, it is preferable to include this material in an appendix rather than in the text.

/ Procedures

In the procedures section the author describes the way in which the experiment will be set up so that the hypothesized relationships can be observed, if these relationships in fact exist. In effect, the researcher is saying, "*If* this hypothesis is true, *then* these results will be observed." By designing the study explicitly as an operation to permit the observation of the hypothesized relationships, the researcher lays the foundation for the study.

A careful description of the procedures of a study is a basic requirement of any research proposal. In survey research the writing of this section is relatively simple because the procedure merely involves sending out a questionnaire to be filled out and returned or conducting an interview. However, all the steps—that is, preparing the questionnaire or interview schedule, training the interviewers, giving them directions as to how to approach the subjects and how to perform the interview—should be listed and explained.

In experimental research the procedures may be more complex. In this section the author should list the groups, specify step by step the manipulations planned for each one, and link each treatment to the proposed questions and hypotheses. These steps should be completely designated in operational form. By basing the procedures of the experiment on the hypotheses, the author facilitates direct and unambiguous interpretation of results. The possibility of confounding variables—those variables that could account for criterion score differences that are not part of the independent variable—should also be considered here. It should be specified in the procedures section how the author/researcher proposes to control for these variables. For example, one might control for student and teacher differences by random assignment of students and teachers to the control and experimental groups. The time spent, physical setting, and facilities could also be made equivalent. This section should include all the steps that operationally define the experimental and control treatments.

Documents such as teaching or reading materials planned for an experiment need not be included in the main text of the proposal because discussion of such details usually interrupts continuity of the proposal. It is recommended that the author place these documents in an appendix, describing them briefly but clearly in the procedures section. It is, however, essential to explain in this section any differences in the presentation of these materials to the different groups involved in the experiment.

After the section on procedures has been drafted, it should be read to verify that all the steps necessary to answer every question and test every hypothesis have been described. The completeness of this section can be checked with the question Could the reader carry out this research by following the steps as described? If this question can be answered in the affirmative, this section is complete.

// Analysis of Data

The next part of the research proposal describes the methods of handling and presenting data and the statistical procedures to be used under the sections (1) data organization and (2) statistical procedures.

/ Data Organization

The presentation of the results of a research study can take different forms depending on the way the findings are organized. It is necessary to plan in advance for the arrangement of research results into an organized form. This is best done by reference to questions or hypotheses of the study. Planning in advance for the organization and presentation of data enables a researcher to determine whether the information being collected is relevant to the research questions. Those who bypass this step often find they have wasted considerable time and money in collecting irrelevant pieces of information.

Tables, figures, and charts are essential means for organizing and summarizing a whole set of data. While the research is in the planning stage, the researcher should be able to picture how the data will be organized and presented in tabular form. At this stage one should list the bits of information that will be available for each subject, decide how the information will be presented and summarized, and decide what statistical procedures shall be employed.

/ Statistical Procedures

The design of the study determines what statistical techniques should be employed, not vice versa. In other words, the researcher decides what design will permit observation of the hypothesized relationships, then selects the statistical procedure that fits the questions asked and the nature of the data involved. The researcher does not first select an appealing statistic and then design the study to fit that statistic.

The most commonly used statistical procedures have been described in earlier chapters. They are summarized for convenience in Table 14.1. (Descriptive Statistics) and Table 14.2 (Inferential Statistics). Table 14.1 is designed to help identify the indices that may be used to describe in summary form the data of a study. The appropriate statistical procedure is determined partly by the type of measurement scale characterizing the dependent variable. Therefore, the rows in the table are identified as *interval, ordinal,* and *nominal.* Columns (1), (2), and (3) list the various purposes descriptive statistics may serve. The most common uses of these statistics are

1. to provide an index to describe a group or the difference between groups (measures of central tendency)
2. to provide an index to describe the variability of a group or differences in the variability of groups (measures of variability)
3. to locate an individual in a group (indices of location)
4. to provide an index to describe the relationship of variables within a population (measures of correlation)
5. to describe how a set is divided into subsets
6. to describe the interaction among two or more variables in relation to a criterion (measures of interaction)

The required cell can be located by identifying the row and column heading appropriate to one's study. Each cell is divided, and the section to use is determined by whether the study is concerned with one group or with more than one group. (Recall that one *may* choose a procedure for a lower scale of measurement but not the reverse; for example, one may use a median or a mode to describe interval data but may not use a mean to describe ordinal or nominal data.)

TABLE 14.1 Descriptive Statistics

Type of Scale of Dependent Variable	(1) Central Tendency		(2) Variability		(3) Location	
	One Group	More Than One Group	One Group	More Than One Group	One Group	More Than One Group
Interval	mean	difference between means	standard deviation or variance	difference between standard deviations or variances	z-score, or other standard score	difference between an individual's standard score in more than one distribution
Ordinal	median	difference between medians	quartile deviation	difference between quartile deviations	percentile rank*	difference between an individual's percentile rank in more than one distribution
Nominal	mode	difference between modes	range	difference between ranges	label or categorization	label or categorization

TABLE 14.1 Continued

Type of Scale of Dependent Variable	(4) Correlation		(5) Subsets		(6) Interaction	
	One Group	More Than One Group	One Group	More Than One Group	One Group	More Than One Group
Interval	Pearson r	difference in Pearson r's for same variables in two groups			difference between observed cell means and expected cell means in factorial ANOVA (observed interaction)	differences in observed interaction among groups
Ordinal	Spearman's rho or Kendall's tau* or W*	difference in Spearman rhos for same variables in two groups				
Nominal	point biserial correlation	difference in point biserial correlations for same variables in two groups	proportion or percentage	differences in proportions or percentages	differences between observed cell frequencies and expected cell frequencies	differences in observed interaction among groups

Purpose of the Statistic

*This statistic is not described in this text but may be found in any number for statistics texts.

TABLE 14.2 Inferential Statistics

Type of Scale of Dependent Variable	Purpose of the Statistic					
	(1) Central Tendency		(2) Variability		(3) Location	
	One Group	More Than One Group	One Group	More Than One Group	One Group	More Than One Group
Interval	standard error of the mean	t-test or one-way ANOVA		Bartlett's test* or t-test for homogeneity of variance*; F-max* statistics	standard error of measurement*	standard error of difference scores*
Ordinal	standard error of median*	median test, sign test,* Kruskal-Wallis one-way ANOVA,* or Friedman's test*				
Nominal						

TABLE 14.2 Continued

Type of Scale of Dependent Variable	(4) Correlation		(5) Subsets		(6) Interaction	
	One Group	More Than One Group	One Group	More Than One Group	One Group	More Than One Group
Interval	t-test for Fisher's z transformation or F-test for linearity*	t-test for Fisher's z transformation*			F-test for multifactor ANOVA	F-test for multifactor ANOVA
Ordinal	test for Spearman's rho or Kendall's tau* or W*					
Nominal	chi-square or test for significance of point biserial*	Cochran's Q*	chi-square or binomial test	chi-square or Fisher's exact test*	information theory A*	chi-square test for information theory A*

(header: Purpose of the Statistic)

*This statistic is not described in this text but may be found in any number of statistics texts.

In determining what type of scale to use in expressing the data, the researcher should consider the advantage of all three scales on the descriptive level. Interval data typically provide more information than ordinal data, and ordinal data provide more information than nominal data. In making inferences, statistical tests of interval data are more "powerful" than tests of ordinal data; that is, one has a greater chance of rejecting a null hypothesis when interval measures are used than when ordinal measures are used. In the same manner, ordinal tests are more powerful than nominal measures. Therefore, when a choice is possible, a researcher will prefer interval data to ordinal and ordinal data to nominal.

For example, if we have interval data for the dependent variable and want an index to describe the difference between groups, the table identifies the difference between two means as an appropriate statistic. (We could, if we choose, use difference between medians or difference between modes, but these would be less powerful than the difference between means.)

If the study is inferential in nature, the researcher will proceed to test the statistical significance of the index selected. Appropriate statistics for this purpose are listed in Table 14.2. In our example the *t*-test or one-way ANOVA would be appropriate.

Remember that a statistical procedure is selected on the basis of its appropriateness for answering the question involved in the study. Nothing is gained by using a complicated procedure when a simple one will do just as well. Statistics are to serve research, not to dominate it.

In this section of the proposal a specific description of the plans for administering the instruments and collecting the data should be given. These plans should include the time schedule, procedures for replacing subjects lost during the course of the experiment, plans for counterbalancing for order effects if needed, and other necessary details. We often tell our students, "Imagine you have gotten a fantastic grant for doing your study, but you are run over by a truck the very next day. Could a colleague pick up your proposal and actually conduct the study?" If this question can be honestly answered in the affirmative, the data analysis part of the study is complete.

// Significance of the Study

Some researchers prefer to state the significance of the problem in the introduction to the proposal. Leaving this topic for a later section, however, provides the opportunity to relate it to both the background and the design of the study. This section is best handled in two stages: (1) implications and (2) applications.

/ Implications

Because the aim of research is to increase knowledge, the author of the proposal should show how his or her particular study will do this by discussing what the results will mean to theory and information in the specific area to which the research question is related, and to what extent these results will be useful in solving problems and answering questions in the general field. Finally, the author should show how the results of the study will provide grounds for further research in the area. In addition, it may be explained how the author/researcher's own experience and expertise, coupled with the facilities and goals of the institution where the study is being carried out, place him or her in a favorable position to solve the problem in question.

/ Applications

The author should be able to convince readers of the potential application of the findings to educational practice. This discussion should show how and to what extent educational practitioners could use the results in order to improve their work. To find the extent to which the study has application to educational practice, the researcher may ask Will the results of my study change anything in the field of education? Would my results help teachers, school counselors, principals, or educational planners to improve their work?

This aspect carries considerable weight in attracting research funds for carrying out the study. Many foundations evaluate research proposals on the basis of whether they will have any application to practice.

// Budget and Time Schedule

All research should be planned with regard to the feasibility of carrying out the work. A proposal should conclude with a presentation of (1) budget and (2) schedule.

/ Budget

Reviewing the previous sections of the proposal, the researcher now lists the personnel, equipment, space, and time that will be required for the project. Most universities and school systems have an office responsible for assisting in the preparation of research budgets. This office gives advice concerning the local and agency regulations and procedures and can assist in translating the needs of the proposal into dollars-and-cents figures.

/ Time Schedule

The researcher should also prepare a realistic schedule for completing the research within the time available. This information helps the reviewer of the proposal and the researcher to see how much time would be needed to complete the research, and it should provide opportunities for periodically evaluating the development of the project.

/// CRITIQUING THE PROPOSAL

After completing the draft of a proposal, the author/researcher should go through it again carefully with a critical eye. It is also profitable to have colleagues read the proposal. Often someone else can identify weaknesses or omissions that are not evident to the author.

In his work with the Research Advisory Committee of the USOE Cooperative Research Program, Smith identified six common weaknesses that the committee found in proposals submitted for funding.[1]

1. *The problem is trivial.* Problems that are of only peripheral interest to educators or show little likelihood of adding to knowledge in education are not considered to be deserving of support. Smith gives as an example a plan to study an adult education program for library trustees and comments: "Not only is it of peripheral value to education and oriented toward action rather than research, but it is, to put it bluntly, a problem of little significance."

2. *The problem is not delimited.* The classic illustration by Good and Skates is a splendid example of this weakness.[2] A letter written by a graduate student to the Commissioner of Education for Alaska indicated that the student had selected for his thesis the topic "The Teaching of English as Revealed in the Courses of Study of the English-Speaking Nations of the World." In the second paragraph he asks the commissioner, "Do you know some interesting books on Alaska: her history, her economic problems, commerce, imports, exports, human relations, religion, etc.?"

In order to produce a feasible proposal, the researcher must focus the study. This is not to say that a study should never include a number of related variables. The researcher should attack those aspects of a problem that can reasonably be handled in a single study. A cluster of related variables can, and often should, be included in a study, but unwieldy, overinclusive efforts should be avoided.

3. *The objectives, hypotheses, or questions are too broadly stated.* Proposal writers are often tempted to state their objectives, hypotheses, or questions in broad, sweeping generalizations. In such cases one finds when reading the procedures section that the actual planned study is not capable of meeting the grand objectives set forth. Sometimes the objectives or hypotheses are stated in such broad, general terms that one must go to the procedures to

---

[1]Smith, G. R. (1963). A critique of proposals submitted to the cooperative research program. In J. A. Culbertson and S. P. Hencly (eds.). *Educational Research: New Perspectives* (ch. 17). Danville, IL: Interstate Publishers and Printers.

[2]Good, C. V., and D. E. Skates (1954). *Methods of Research* (pp. 82–83). New York: Appleton.

discover what the study is really about. It seems obvious that the objectives and procedures should match; yet the Research Advisory Committee found that many proposals failed to meet this basic requirement.

4. *The procedures are lacking in detail.* Smith points out that "an investigator who omits more than he includes should not expect the committee to read procedural details between the lines. The committee lacks both the desire and the clairvoyance to do so." Remember, the procedures should be complete enough to allow for replication.

5. *A simple design is used to investigate a complex problem.* The design of a study should fit the problem. A simple comparison of the means of two groups is appropriate when a single variable is involved. More-complex studies require more-complex designs.

6. *Relevant variables are not considered or are lightly dismissed.* Failure to consider relevant extraneous variables is a serious error in a research proposal. The researcher should demonstrate that he or she is aware of such variables and explain how they will be handled in the design of the study.

/// THE IMPORTANCE OF COMPLETING THE PROPOSAL BEFORE COLLECTING DATA

A clear, well-stated, complete proposal indicates that the prospective researcher is actually ready to set the study in motion. It shows that the researcher knows what to do, why to do it, and how to do it. A prospective researcher who cannot produce a complete and coherent proposal is clearly not yet ready to proceed to the data-collecting stage of the project. Novice researchers are often inclined to say, "Let me collect my data now and decide what to do with it later." Simultaneously collecting data and writing the proposal may seem to be a time-saving procedure, but such is seldom the case. Countless work-hours and thousands of dollars have been wasted in just that way. Until the proposal is formulated, one cannot be sure exactly what data will be needed nor what will be the best way to handle this information in the light of the purpose of the study. Those working under deadlines should set for themselves a date for the completion of the proposal well in advance of the target date for completing the entire project.

This is not to say that data collection must *never* precede the proposal. A pilot study may be useful in planning a project, trying the instruments, determining the feasibility of the procedures, and so on. However, such pilots do not contribute substantive data to the study itself. They should be regarded as preliminary skirmishes and no more.

/// ETHICAL AND LEGAL CONSIDERATIONS

Strict adherence to ethical standards in planning and conducting research is most important. Researchers have obligations both to their subjects and to their profession. The ethical standards concerning research adopted by the American Psychological Association provide a useful guide for all who employ human subjects in research:

1. Only when a problem is of scientific significance and it is not practicable to investigate it in any other way is the psychologist justified in exposing research subjects, whether children or adults, to physical or emotional stress as part of an investigation.
2. When a reasonable possibility of injurious aftereffects exists, research is conducted only when the subjects or their responsible agents are fully informed of this possibility and agree to participate nevertheless.
3. The psychologist seriously considers the possibility of harmful aftereffects and avoids them, or removes them as soon as permitted by the design of the experiment.[3]

// Obligation to Subjects

When studying human subjects, one must respect their integrity and humanity. Three major areas of concern are (1) protection of the human subjects from harm, (2) respect for their right to know the nature and purpose of the study and their right to give or withhold consent to participate (the right of informed consent), and (3) respect for subjects' privacy.

/ Protection of Subjects from Harm

Subjects must be protected from physical, mental, and social harm. The use of human subjects in federally funded research has been regulated for several years, but in 1975 a substantially more expansive set of rules was adopted that covered all research performed by or under the general supervision of all institutions receiving federal research funds. As a result of these rules most colleges and universities and many school systems established Institutional Review Boards (IRBs) that required a prior review of all research plans involving the use of human subjects in virtually any manner. All educational research was covered. The implementation of these regulations was not popular, and concern about overregulation came from numerous quarters. The Congress mandated the creation of a National Commission for the Protection of Human Subjects of Biomedical and Behavioral Research, and the final report of the commission recommended a reduction in the scope of the regulations, which was implemented through new regulations issued January 26, 1981.[4]

The new regulations limit the federal regulations to those projects funded by grants from the Department of Health and Human Services and

---

[3]Ethical Standards for Psychologists (1963). *American Psychologist, 18,* 56–60.

[4]*Code of Federal Regulations 45* (1982; Part 46, pp. 100–104). Washington: U.S. Government Printing Office.

provide several broad categorical exemptions from the regulations. The five major categorical exemptions are as follows:

1. Research conducted in established or commonly accepted educational settings, involving normal educational practices, such as (i) research on regular and special education instructional strategies, or (ii) research on the effectiveness of or the comparison among instructional techniques, curricula, or classroom management methods.
2. Research involving the use of educational tests (cognitive, diagnostic, aptitude, achievement), if information taken from these sources is recorded in such a manner that subjects cannot be identified, directly or through identifiers linked to the subjects.
3. Research involving survey or interview procedures, except where all of the following conditions exist: (i) Responses are recorded in such a manner that the human subjects can be identified, directly or through identifiers linked to the subjects, (ii) the subject's responses, if they became known outside the research, could reasonably place the subject at risk of criminal or civil liability or be damaging to the subject's financial standing or employability, and (iii) the research deals with sensitive aspects of the subject's own behavior, such as illegal conduct, drug use, sexual behavior, or use of alcohol. All research involving survey or interview procedures is exempt, without exception, when the respondents are elected or appointed public officials or candidates for public office.
4. Research involving the observation (including observation by participants) of public behavior, except where all of the following conditions exist: (i) Observations are recorded in such a manner that the human subjects can be identified, directly or through identifiers linked to the subjects, (ii) the observations recorded about the individual, if they became known outside the research, could reasonably place the subject at risk of criminal or civil liability or be damaging to the subject's financial standing or employability, and (iii) the research deals with sensitive aspects of the subject's own behavior, such as illegal conduct, drug use, sexual behavior, or use of alcohol.
5. Research involving the collection or study of existing data, documents, records, pathological specimens, or diagnostic specimens, if these sources are publicly available or if the information is recorded by the investigator in such a manner that subjects cannot be identified, directly or through identifiers linked to the subjects.[5]

While these new regulations virtually exempt educational research from direct federal regulations, the IRBs remain in place, and institutions may elect to continue regulations that are more restrictive in character or broader in scope than the federal regulations. There has been some informal pressure for institutions to continue the broader regulations. Given the confusion of the present regulatory situation, the researcher should plan to consult his or her IRB to determine institutional rules and should examine the current

---

[5]*Ibid.*, p. 101.

federal regulations in the *Code of Federal Regulation* (45 *CFR* Part 46),[6] which may be found in most libraries.

For research that is funded by the Department of Health and Human Services and that involves human subjects outside the exempted categories, the federal regulations require a determination of whether the subjects will be placed "at risk" by the research procedures. If the researcher can demonstrate that the physical, mental, and social risks involved in the proposed project are no greater than those encountered "in daily life or during the performance of routine physical or psychological examinations or tests," the subjects are not considered "at risk."[7] If the subjects are "at risk," then the researcher must be able to argue that (1) the value of the knowledge that is likely to be gained exceeds the potential harms, (2) all subjects will be fully informed of the risks in the procedures, and the voluntary and written consent of each subject will be obtained, and (3) appropriate medical or other support services will be available to subjects who participate in the research. If these conditions are met, the IRB will usually give approval to the proposed work. Typically, there is no appeal procedure from an IRB.

The obtaining of informed consent from minors and other persons who are not considered capable of representing themselves is a difficult area. A number of cases involving this issue have been decided in state and federal courts in recent years, and many are pending. Researchers facing this problem are advised to consult with the chair of their IRB (if they are in an institution with one) or with the legal counsel of their institution or organization. The Office for Protection from Research Risks in the Department of Health and Human Services is usually willing to consult on these matters and may be able to provide current information on the legal ruling relevant to various groups.

/ The Issue of Informed Consent

Although federal regulations now require formal subject consent in only a limited range of cases, there are numerous nongovernmental sets of professional ethics that suggest that all subjects be fully informed of the purposes of the procedures and given a completely free choice in participation. The researcher must consider the desirability of informing the subjects about the research and obtaining formal consent from them.

In some cases, it may be argued, prior knowledge of the purposes of the study would bias the results. For cases like this it is still important to maintain the voluntary nature of participation even if the purposes are not fully or accurately presented prior to the procedures. In cases where it is important not to discuss the purpose prior to the procedure, a full explanation

---

[6]*Ibid.*, p. 102.
[7]*Ibid.*

should be provided to all subjects after the completion of the procedures. Coercion of subjects and fraudulent explanations of purpose are prohibited by virtually every professional code of ethical standards.

/ The Right to Privacy

There is broad professional agreement that all subjects have an inherent right to privacy. If it is not necessary to collect the individual's name and other identifying information, it is recommended that the information not be collected. If it is necessary to collect the data for follow-up or other purposes, then it is the responsibility of the researcher to provide secure storage for that information and to control access to it. In general, it is recommended that only the principal researcher and those staff members who must know individual data for work-related purposes have access to it. If students or colleagues are to be given access to the data or if it is to be placed in an archive, then it is the responsibility of the principal researcher to remove all personal identifying information from those files.

For research funded by the Department of Health and Human Services, the investigator must provide assurance for the secure storage and maintenance of all names and other identifying information. If the research project collects any personally incriminating or socially damaging information, this obligation is even more important. Failure to secure information of this type could lead to sanctions under the federal regulations (disqualification from further grant support) or to civil suits for personal damages.

// Obligation to the Profession

The researcher is also responsible to the consumers of research. Most research studies, in education as well as in other fields, are published in journals, monographs, books, and other media and are referred to and consumed by professionals in the field. The researcher is morally obligated to plan a study in such a way that the findings obtained would not result in offering misleading information. Even more, the researcher is obligated to report exactly and honestly what the findings were. Research must not be reported in such a way as to mislead. Reporting that misleads is a serious abuse of the researcher's responsibility to the profession.

/// SUMMARY

A research proposal is a step-by-step plan for discovering new knowledge. It is at this stage that the reseacher's inspiration and insights crystallize into concrete form. Several categories of information should be included in a research proposal.

A clear statement of the problem, accompanied by unambiguous definitions of terms, should be made early in the proposal. A review of pertinent literature should follow. A good review of literature shows what is so far known about the problem and lays the foundation for stating hypotheses regarding relationships between variables under consideration. In addition, this part should be written with the aim of providing a foundation for the interpretation of results.

In the discussion of methodology that follows the introductory section, methods for subject selection, methods of data collection, observational procedures, and measurement techniques are all described with sufficient detail so that a reader could carry out the research by following the proposed steps exactly as the original writer of the proposal would.

The next part of the research proposal describes the procedures to be used for data presentation, such as tables, figures, and charts, and introduces the statistical techniques that will be used for data analysis.

A discussion of the potential significance of the study should follow. Here the researcher should attempt to show how the findings will increase knowledge and what the results will mean to theory and research in the field of interest. A discussion of the applications of the findings to practice would be helpful to readers who wish to assess the significance of the proposed research.

The final section of the proposal contains the time schedule and estimated budget of the study. This information is useful to readers in making an overall evaluation of the proposal.

A matter of considerable importance in planning research is the observation of ethical standards. Subjects must have the right of informed consent, they must be protected from harm, and their privacy must be respected.

// Key Concepts

categorical exemptions
Code of Federal Regulations
common faults in research
   proposals
ethical considerations in research

ingredients of research proposals
institutional review boards
legal considerations in research
protection of subjects from harm
right to informed consent

/// EXERCISES

1. What are the basic components of a research proposal?

2. Why is it so important that the introduction be written carefully and intelligently?

3. At what point in the proposal should a clear statement of the problem be made?

4. Rewrite the following hypotheses, operationalizing all variables:
   a. Children who learn reading by the i/t/a method read better than those taught by a traditional approach.
   b. High school students who score above the top quartile of the XYZ Mechanical Aptitude Test make better mechanics.
   c. Scores on the math subtest of the SRA Achievement Test for smart seventh-grade students who have been instructed with the new-math approach for 1 year will exceed scores of smart seventh-grade students who have been instructed with a traditional approach.

5. What are some confounding variables that may affect differences of mean achievement scores between classes of the same grade level? How could you control for these variables in your proposed procedures?

6. What is the appropriate statistic for measuring correlation if the scale of the dependent variable is nominal?

7. What measure of central tendency is appropriate for interval data?

8. For what types of data is ANOVA appropriate?

9. What is the function of an institutional board of review?

10. How might some research results be affected by subjects' knowledge of participation? How is the requirement of informed consent met in these circumstances?

11. What precautions should be taken to ensure confidentiality of responses and subjects' privacy in research projects?

12. List some common faults that should be avoided in preparing a research proposal.

/// ANSWERS

1. introduction, methodology, analysis of data, significance of the study, and budget and time schedule

2. If the introduction is not well done, the reader will not be inclined to read the rest of the proposal.

3. in the first paragraph of the introduction

4. a. Third-graders who learned reading in first and second grade by the i/t/a method will score higher on the California Reading Test than third-graders who learned to read using a basal reading approach.

b. Juniors and seniors who scored above the top quartile of the XYZ Mechanical Aptitude Test before becoming apprentices will be rated more highly by supervisors after 1 year in a mechanics apprenticeship program than those scoring below the top quartile.

c. Scores on the math subtest of the SRA Achievement Test of seventh-graders with IQs above 115 on the WISC who have been instructed with the new-math approach for 1 year will exceed scores of similar students who have been instructed with the traditional approach.

5. Different average ability levels, physical class environments, teachers, and types and amount of materials are some factors. One can control for these variables by pretesting for ability level, selecting classes with similar environments, and training teachers to certain levels of competence. Using large numbers of classes randomly assigned to conditions offers a different type of control.

6. point biserial

7. the mean

8. nominal independent variable and interval dependent variable

9. The institutional board of review determines if the subjects in a proposed experiment are at risk under DHEW guidelines and then determines if benefits outweigh the risks.

10. Knowledge that an unusual or experimental treatment is being used can influence subjects' psychological state and/or expectancy, which may detract from or otherwise influence the actual treatment effects. The subjects in such circumstances should be told that they will be informed of the purpose of the study when it is completed.

11. Subjects should not have to identify themselves unless necessary and should not be identified as individuals in the public report of the study unless they have given their consent.

12. The problem is trivial.
The problem is not delimited.
The objectives, hypotheses, or questions are too broadly stated.
The procedures are lacking in detail.
A simple design is proposed for a complex problem.
Relevant variables are not considered.

15

Analyzing, Interpreting, and Reporting Results

INSTRUCTIONAL OBJECTIVES

After studying this chapter, the student will be able to
1. Describe the role of computers in research
2. List principles that the researcher should keep in mind when interpreting results that were anticipated
3. Distinguish between statistical significance and practical significance
4. List principles that the researcher should keep in mind when interpreting unanticipated results
5. Explain the various circumstances that might result in the retention of a null hypothesis
6. List some principles of interpretation that the researcher should keep in mind when the null hypothesis has been retained
7. Write appropriate titles for a dissertation or other research report
8. Describe the nature of the content to be included in each section of a thesis or dissertation
9. State the procedure to be followed when preparing a research article for a professional journal
10. State the procedure to be followed when preparing a paper to be read at a professional conference

Once the research data have been collected, the researcher next processes the data, analyzes the results, carefully interprets the findings, and finally writes the report of the study. A brief discussion of each of these tasks is presented in this chapter.

/// PROCESSING THE DATA

The first step in processing the data collected is to refer to the proposal in order to check the original plans for presenting data and performing the statistical analysis. It has already been decided what questions are to be answered, how the variables in these questions are operationally defined, and what research designs and statistical procedures will be used. Now all that remains is to organize the raw data, perform the necessary calculations, and interpret the results.

Today research projects in education and other behavioral sciences are often characterized by complexity and involved computational work. To achieve precision and to save time and energy, most researchers take advantage of electronic computing facilities for their data analysis. It is appropriate, therefore, to include here a brief discussion of computers and their use in the processing of data.

// The Use of Computers in the Processing of Data

The development of the computer has changed the scope of research and has made it possible to conduct research studies that one would not otherwise think of undertaking. Before the days of computers, researchers avoided studies involving several variables and large numbers of subjects because of the time and labor involved in tabulating and analyzing the data generated. Sophisticated statistical tests and complex analyses were not often undertaken. Today the computer can process large amounts of data and perform complex statistical analyses with phenomenal speed and efficiency. Therefore, researchers can choose analyses solely on the basis of what is appropriate for answering the research questions without concern for the number of variables or the complexity of the analyses.

Researchers may employ either a *mainframe computer* or a *microcomputer* at this stage. A mainframe computer is large and expensive. In most universities and other institutions a mainframe computer handles payroll, accounting, and numerous other functions, in addition to serving the needs of researchers. Advantages of the mainframe are speed, capacity, and flexibility. A major disadvantage is that a researcher must compete with other persons and agencies for access to the mainframe, which can lead to delays and inconvenience. Microcomputers are small and relatively inexpensive, and many researchers find them easier and more convenient to use. More computer programs are available for mainframes, but microcomputer programs are available for the analyses most educational researchers need, and more are becoming available as microcomputers become more powerful and more widely used.

A computer program is a set of step-by-step instructions in computer language that inform the computer of what data to use and what operations to perform on that data. Those who are knowledgeable in computer languages and programming techniques may write their own programs. Fortunately, however, numerous prepared programs are available. These are known as packages, or canned programs, and they are recommended for those with little or no programming experience. There are a number of canned statistical programs for mainframe computers. One well-known series is the *Biomedical Series* (BIMED), developed originally for use in biological and medical fields.[1] A great number of BIMED programs are available for various statistical analyses. Another series—and one of the most popular for the educational researcher—is the *Statistical Package for the Social Sciences* (SPSS-X).[2] SPSS-X contains many of the most common statistical procedures employed by social scientists. It uses a simple language that is easy to learn and requires no knowledge of how computers work. The researcher decides on the data analysis to be done and then checks the SPSS-X manual to find the appropriate program. Another series of packaged programs is *Statistical Analysis System* (SAS).[3] This series requires a somewhat higher level of user sophistication than does SPSS-X.

A version of SPSS-X is also available for use with some microcomputers. MYSTAT,[4] a microcomputer version of SYSTAT, is another useful statistical package. Greenberg's *Using Microcomputers and Mainframes for Data Analysis in the Social Sciences*[5] provides useful descriptions of microcomputer and mainframe statistical programs and how to use them.

/ Recommendations

A word of caution is in order here. The results that are produced are only as good as the information that is fed into the computer. The computer does not make computational mistakes, but if errors in the data or errors of logic are entered into the computer, the computer will blindly, but efficiently, turn out "garbage" for results. There are two kinds of errors that can be made in programming. Language errors, such as misspelled instructions, will be detected by the computer, in which case the job will not be accepted.

---

[1]*Biomedical Computer Programs* (1983). Berkeley: University of California Press.
[2]*SPSS-X User's Guide*, 3d ed. (1988). Chicago: SPSS Inc.
[3]*SAS User's Guide* (1983). Raleigh, NC: SAS Institute.
[4]Wilkenson, L. (1986). *SYSTAT: The System for Statistics*. Evanston, IL: SYSTAT, Inc.
[5]Greenberg, B. (1987). *Using Microcomputers and Mainframes for Data Analysis in the Social Sciences*. Columbus, OH: Merrill.

Errors of logic, such as incorrect instructions, will be accepted by the computer and may result in a very expensive output of meaningless results.

Finally, we want to make these recommendations in relation to computer usage:

1. Take full advantage of computers in your data processing, but make a critical evaluation of the computer's product. Though computers do not make mistakes, they also never correct mistakes made in preparing the data for processing or in programming.
2. Do not blindly use whatever program you can find in program manuals. You should already have decided what kind of statistical procedure is most appropriate for a given set of data.

/// PRINCIPLES OF INTERPRETATION

Once the research data have been collected and the statistical analysis has been made, the researcher can proceed to the challenging task of interpreting the results. Adding to knowledge has been the principal focus of the research endeavor. When the interpretation stage is reached, the researcher can show what has been learned in the project and how this knowledge fits into the general body of knowledge in the field.

// The Role of the Proposal in Facilitating Interpretation

The proper foundation for interpreting the results of a study should have been laid systematically through each stage of the development of the proposal, even before the actual research began. By bearing in mind throughout the study what their data will consist of and may tell them, researchers prepare themselves for interpreting their data and fitting those data into the body of knowledge.

A carefully thought-out plan expressed as a thorough and complete proposal can be expected to generate results that can be easily and meaningfully interpreted. If the study has been laid out in such a way that the consequences of the hypotheses will be expressed in reliable observations, then the interpretation and value of the observations should be obvious.

// The Importance of Keeping to the Original Plan

Once the proposal has been accepted and the project set in motion, the study must be carried out exactly as planned. This rule has ethical as well as practical implications.

To illustrate the ethical implications, let us suppose that Mr. Williams, a foreign-language teacher, has developed, with a great expenditure of time and effort, a system of teaching French that he believes to be greatly superior to existing methods. To test the efficacy of this method, he establishes an experimental group that is taught by his method and a control group, taught by another method. He devises a series of weekly French achievement tests to serve as the dependent variable. Suppose that he discovers in the first few weeks that the mean test scores for the two groups are almost identical. Having a big investment in his own method, he finds it hard to believe that it is no better than the other, so he decides to sit in on the two classes to see what has "gone wrong." He discovers that the experimental group seems to show much greater knowledge and appreciation of French life and culture. Because he is determined to find a difference between scores, he decides to change his dependent variable to scores on tests on French life and culture.

Such a change would be unethical. Given two random groups, one can always find a superiority in either group if one looks long enough. If the experimental group had not appeared superior on French life and culture, it might have been superior in verbal fluency, listening skills, on-task behavior, or some other variable. The language teacher *must* carry out the experiment as planned and not change the dependent variable. The investigator should report the evidence suggesting a relationship between method and appreciation of French life and culture, but it should be made clear to the readers that this was not a hypothesized relationship and therefore could easily have been a function of chance. It is unethical to abandon independent or dependent variables that do not seem to be "working out" or add promising new ones. Such changes must be left for future studies.

The addition of new variables is also unwise from a practical standpoint. Such a tactic can confuse the results of a study and obscure the meaning of the results. Researchers are often tempted to add interesting new variables that crop up in their study. However, the theoretical base for interpreting these variables has not been laid, and again the best advice to researchers is to leave them for later studies.

// Interpretation of Expected Results

Understandably researchers are pleased when the results of a study fit into the previously constructed framework and interpretation can proceed as expected. The study has "worked," and there is agreement between rationale and results.

Only a few words of caution need apply in such a case:

1. Do not make interpretations that go beyond the information. This may seem a patently obvious injunction, but researchers often get so excited when results are as expected that they draw conclusions that do not have a valid basis in the data. Even in published research one frequently finds more interpretations than the data warrant.

2. Do not forget the limitations of the study. These limitations, of course, should have been previously identified in the study—limitations inherent in the less-than-perfect reliability and validity of the instruments, limitations due to the restriction in sampling, the internal validity problems, and so forth.

3. Ethics require that the researcher report internal validity problems that could account for the results. If, despite the researcher's best efforts, the nonexperimental variables were particularly benign for the experimental group and those for the control group were particularly malign, these conditions must be reported and taken into account in interpreting results. (For example, despite random assignment of teachers to groups, the experimental group may have mostly experienced teachers and the control group may have mostly inexperienced teachers.)

4. Remember that statistical significance means only that for the appropriate degrees of freedom the results are unlikely to be a function of chance. Statistical significance does not mean that the results are significant in the generally accepted meaning of the word—that is, important, meaningful, or momentous. Do not assume that statistical significance guarantees momentous import to your findings.

Let us suppose that two equivalent groups have been subjected to two different systems of learning spelling over a 2-year period. Those using System A show a mean gain equivalent of 2.15 years of growth on standardized tests during the experiment, while those using System B show a gain of 2.20 in the same period. If the groups are large and/or if the differences within groups are small, the differences between the means would be statistically significant. But a difference of half a month over a 2-year period is relatively meaningless in practical terms. If System B is more expensive in terms of student time, teacher time, or materials, teachers would be unwise to adopt it simply because it produced statistically significantly greater gains than System A. If, on the other hand, System B is the less expensive, teachers would be inclined to favor it because its results *are* so similar to those of System A in practical terms.

The potential importance or meaningfulness of results must be established in the proposal before the study begins. A study is not important if it does not provide meaningful information to be added to the existing body of knowledge, no matter how statistically significant the results may be.

// Interpretation of Negative Results

Researchers who find results opposite to those hypothesized often develop sudden revelations concerning the shortcomings of their study. Their interpretation of results reads like a confession. The instruments were inadequate for measuring the variables involved, the sample was too small and was so unrepresentative that results cannot be validly generalized to a meaningful target population, and so on. Hindsight reveals internal validity problems that explain why the study did not come out as it "should have."

Of course any or all of these things could be true, and the shortcomings of any study should be reported no matter what the results. However, research is always a venture into the unknown, so there is no ultimate "should be." An investigator predicts the expected results of a study on the basis of theory, deduction, and the results of previous research. If these are so conclusive that there can be absolutely no doubt as to the results of this study, then the study is pointless in the first place.

When we undertake a study, we implicitly state that the outcome is a matter of conjecture, not a matter of certainty. When we complete our proposal, it is understood that we declare that we will impartially seek to determine the true state of affairs with the best instruments and procedures available to use for that purpose. Therefore, we are obliged to accept and interpret our data no matter how the data stand. When the results contradict the theoretical rationale of the study, the discussion section of our report should include a reconsideration of the original theory in light of the findings. Researchers are often reluctant to present and interpret data that conflict with previous research or with well-established theory. However, it may be that their results are right and previous results wrong. The progress of the science of education will be retarded if investigators are reluctant to report findings that do not agree with those reported in earlier studies. Contradictory results indicate that a question is not settled and may stimulate further research. Additional research or theory formation may eventually reconcile seemingly contradictory results. Theory is tentative and should not deter investigators from giving a straightforward interpretation of what was found.

The reconsideration of the theoretical base of a study belongs in the discussion section. One must *not* go back and rewrite the related literature and hypothesis sections of the report.

// Interpretation of Results When the Null Hypothesis Is Retained

Since a null hypothesis may be retained for a variety of reasons, interpreting such a result can be particularly difficult. A retained null hypothesis may occur because: (1) The null hypothesis is, in fact, true. There may be no relationship between variables. The experimental treatment may be no more effective than the control treatment. (2) The null hypothesis is false, but internal validity problems contaminated the investigation so badly that the actual relationship between variables could not be observed. (3) The null hypothesis is false, but the research design lacked the *power* to reject it.

Any of these states of affairs may be the case, but the investigator does not know which is true and therefore should not claim any one of them as the explanation for the results.

It is incorrect to present a retained null hypothesis as evidence of no relationship between variables. A retained null hypothesis must be interpreted as lack of evidence for either the truth or falsity of the hypothesis. A widely used toothpaste commercial states that tests show a particular toothpaste to be unsurpassed in reducing tooth decay. Interpreting the term *unsurpassed* to mean "no significant difference," we can imagine a test in which a very small number of subjects were used and/or numerous internal validity problems were present. If a retained null hypothesis is the desired result of an experiment, it is remarkably easy to arrange for such an outcome.

Of course if one is studying a small population and can do a complete census of that population, a retained null hypothesis can legitimately be interpreted as a lack of relationship between variables within that particular population. A retained null hypothesis also acquires credibility when a very large sample is involved. For example, the Coleman report, with over 600,000 subjects, provides such a large base that we are willing to accept an observed lack of relationships between variables as evidence of an actual lack of relationships in this case. However, in most studies the retained null hypothesis must be interpreted as a lack of evidence and no more.

There is a danger that investigators who become too enamored of their experimental hypothesis may be tempted to interpret a retained null hypothesis as if it were not there. They cite internal validity problems and declare that the results would certainly have been significant if only those unanticipated problems had not ruined the experiment. Of course one should report all internal validity problems that arise in a study, but one should not use them to explain away disappointing results. One may suggest additional research, planned in such a way as to avoid the internal validity problems encountered, but still one must report a retained null hypothesis as lack of evidence and no more.

The *power* of an experiment refers to the statistical ability to reject a null hypothesis when it is, in fact, false. This power is a function of the size of the sample, the heterogeneity of subjects with reference to the dependent variable, the reliability of the measuring instruments used, and the nature of the statistical procedure used to test the hypothesis. Researchers should take these factors into account when planning an experiment. A number of statistics textbooks explain how to plan experiments in such a way that meaningful relationships will have a high probability of producing statistically significant results. The power of an experiment should be considered in planning the study. It must not be brought in at the end of a study to explain away lack of statistical significance. For example, one should not say, "The results would have been statistically significant if the sample had been larger."

With rare exceptions the only legitimate interpretation of a retained null hypothesis is that *sufficient evidence for a conclusion has not been observed.*

// **Interpretation of Unhypothesized Relationships**

We emphasized earlier that a researcher should not abandon a hypothesis during the conduct of a study in order to pursue more-promising avenues that present themselves during the course of the study. This does not mean that any unhypothesized relationships that may be observed in the conduct of a study should be ignored. On the contrary, they should be recorded and analyzed with the same rigor that is employed in pursuing hypothesized relationships. Throughout the history of science serendipitous discoveries have often proved to be important.

However, such findings should always be viewed with more suspicion than findings directly related to the hypothesis because there is a relatively great possibility that a spurious unhypothesized relationship will appear in a study. Such relationships should be reported, but they should be considered as incidental to the main thrust of the investigation. They should be made the subject of a study specifically designed to investigate them before they can be employed as the basis for conclusions.

/// **THE RESEARCH REPORT**

The results of a research project are of little value unless thay can be communicated to others. Therefore, a knowledge of the procedures involved in writing a research report is important to all researchers. The purpose of this section is to give a general guide to the organization and presentation of a report. For specific rules on style and format a style manual should be consulted (several are listed at the end of this chapter).

In a research report the investigator communicates both the procedures and the findings of the research and also discusses the implications of the findings and their relationship to other knowledge in the field.

Because the report will be read by busy professionals, it should be as concise and as logically organized as possible. Anecdotes, stories of personal experiences, and argumentative discourses are out of place in a research report. This does not mean that the report has to be dull and pedantic. If the researcher has approached the study with a spirit of enthusiasm, this spirit tends to be conveyed between the lines.

And because the purpose of the report is to present the research rather than the personality of the author, the tone of the report should be impersonal. In keeping with this, first-person pronouns are never used. Thus, one would not write "I randomly assigned subjects to the two treatment groups," but rather "Subjects were randomly assigned to the two treatment groups." Despite a natural enthusiasm about the importance of the work, the author should not brag about it but should leave its evaluation to readers and to posterity.

A formal and uniform method of presenting research reports has evolved. Although at first glance these formalities may seem inhibiting, in practice they serve a useful purpose. It is important to have research reports arranged in such a way that readers know exactly where to find those specific parts of a report they may be seeking. In Chapter 3 you were advised to read through the summary section of a journal article first when gathering related research. If an article does not have a summary section, you are forced to spend additional time reading it through before determining whether it is relevant.

In addition, the presence of an established format eliminates the need for devising one's own. As this topic is discussed, it will be seen that the established format follows logically the steps in a research project presented in earlier chapters.

A research report may be presented as (1) a thesis or dissertation, (2) a journal article, or (3) a conference paper. A different approach is required in each of these cases.

// The Thesis or Dissertation

Most universities have a preferred manual that describes in detail the form the university requires. For those students who are free to choose, several style manuals are listed at the end of this chapter. Once a manual has been chosen, the entire report should be styled according to its recommendations.

The outline lists the sequence and general components described in most style manuals:

1. Preliminary pages
   a. Title page
   b. Acceptance page
   c. Acknowledgments or preface
   d. Table of contents
   e. List of tables
   f. List of figures
2. Text
   a. Introduction
      1. Statement of the problem and rationale for the study
      2. Objectives
      3. Definitions of terms
      4. Related literature
   b. Methods and results
      1. Subjects
      2. Procedures

3. Instruments
4. Presentation and analysis of data
 c. Discussion of results
  1. Interpretation of findings
  2. Implications
  3. Applications
 d. Conclusions and summary
  1. Conclusions
  2. Summary
3. Supplementary pages
 a. Bibliography
 b. Appendices
 c. Vita (if required)
 d. Abstract

/ 1. Preliminary Pages

The preparation of the preliminary pages is largely a matter of following the rules of the style manual. However, one aspect of these pages that needs additional explanation at this point is the title of the study itself.

The title should describe, as briefly as possible, the specific nature of the study. For example, consider (a) a study of culturally disadvantaged children that compares the reading readiness of those who have participated in a Project Head Start program with that of a matched group of children with no formal preschool experience, and (b) the title, "A Comparison of Reading Readiness Test Scores of Disadvantaged Children Who Have Attended Head Start Classes for Six Weeks or More with Similar Children with No Preschool Experience." While this title does convey what the study is about, it is too long. Such phrases as "a comparison of," "a study of," "an investigation into" are usually superfluous. Furthermore, most prospective readers will know that Project Head Start is a preschool experience designed for culturally disadvantaged children. However, to go to the other extreme by providing a title that is too brief or too vague to convey the nature of the study is a much more serious mistake. With vague or overly brief titles a prospective reader must search out the article in order to determine what it is about. Titles such as "Head Start and Readiness" or "Reading among the Disadvantaged" illustrate this shortcoming. *The title should identify the major variables and the populations of interest.* The operational definitions of the major variables and the description of the samples need not be included in the title.

Because correct titling will ensure correct indexing, a useful strategy is for researchers first to decide under what key words they want their studies to be indexed, working from there to a concise title. In our example the important key words for indexing would be *reading readiness* and *Project*

Head Start. So an appropriate title might be "Reading Readiness of Project Head Start and Non–Head Start Children." This title is reasonably brief, yet it gives the prospective reader a valid indication of what the study is about.

Emotion-laden titles, such as "We Must Expand the Head Start Program" or "Don't Let the Disadvantaged Become Poor Readers," should be avoided at all costs. The prospective reader will not expect research findings under such titles but rather armchair articles attempting to sell a point of view.

/ 2. Text

A. Introduction The introductory section includes everything that took place in laying the groundwork for the research. It typically consists of materials already prepared for the proposal with relatively minor alterations. The statement of the problem and the justification for the study remain the same, as do the statement of objectives, definition of terms and review of related research. However, here the brief account of the sources of the data and the methods used is written in the past tense rather than in the future tense used in the wording of the original proposal. The review of the related research is usually presented as a separate chapter of the introductory section.

B. Methods and Results Four categories of information are included in this part of the report:

1. *Subjects:* A detailed description of the sample should be presented. This enables the reader to judge the potential population external validity of the research. The population from which the sample was drawn should be defined, and the method of sampling should be specified. The kind of information given in the description of the sample will vary from study to study, but in general one can determine what information to include by considering what variables might influence the criterion scores in the study.

2. *Procedures:* The report on procedures of the study should be complete enough so that anyone wanting to replicate the study would find all the necessary information there. One of the characteristics of the scientific approach is the possibility of confirming findings by repeating the procedures and observational information necessary for replication. The design of the study, the number of groups (if the study is an experiment), the treatment of subjects, and other pertinent information are included in this section.

3. *Instruments:* A research report should specify all the measuring instruments and observational systems used in carrying out the study. The specifications can be brief when previously established measures have been used since the references will contain the relevant information about such instruments. If special instruments have been developed for the study, a

detailed description of these instruments must be provided along with evidence of reliability and validity and a discussion of scoring procedures.

4. *Presentation and analysis of data:* A recommended technique for the presentation and statistical analysis of data is to organize the discussion around the hypotheses; that is, to restate the first hypothesis and present findings concerning it, repeating this procedure for each hypothesis in turn.

Tables and figures may be profitably employed to present the data more clearly and more concisely than would be possible if the same information were presented in text form. Most style manuals provide examples of commonly used types of tables and figures and instructions for their construction. A well-constructed table can give the reader a concise overview of the data.

Tables constructed in the conduct of the study cannot usually be incorporated directly into the report. For example, on completion of a study one may have an alphabetical list of the subjects in one's study and their scores on criterion measures. Rather than present this list as it stands, one would construct a table of the information in summary form. (Basic raw-data tables may be included in the appendices if it is felt they can contribute to understanding.) The first table in the report usually summarizes the descriptive data, such as means, standard deviations, correlations, percentages. Later tables present the results of applying inferential statistics and tests of significance to the data. For example, a summary table would be used to present the results of an analysis of variance.

It is desirable to arrange the tables in such a way that they illustrate the relationship of the data to the hypotheses of the study. Beginning researchers are frequently tempted to include the data in both forms, and in so doing they merely make their reports longer and more tedious. A better approach is to present the data in tables and figures accompanied by sufficient text to point out the most important and interesting findings. It is especially important to relate the information in the tables to the hypotheses.

The statistical foundation of the analysis of results must be clearly stated. It is convenient to integrate statistical treatment with the presentation of data.

C. Discussion of Results   The findings are interpreted again in relation to the hypotheses (or questions), and the implications and applications of the study are discussed.

1. *Interpretation of findings:* Probably the most difficult, but also the most rewarding, part of the report, the researcher's interpretation of the results relates these findings to the theory and research in the area and to the research procedures.

2. *Implications:* The contribution of the results to knowledge in the general field of study is a matter that should also be discussed in this part. The researcher explains here how the results may modify relevant theories and suggests further studies that logically follow.

3. *Applications:* A statement regarding the application of the findings helps readers of the report to consider how the findings can be applied in practice.

The sections on implications and applications of the results are often not sufficiently developed because it is assumed that these will be as obvious to the reader as they are to the researchers. In fact, in the conduct of the study the investigators should have gained insights into the problem that are deeper than those that most of their readers can be assumed to have. Therefore, one would expect their interpretations to be more meaningful than those that readers might make for themselves.

D. Conclusions and Summary The conclusions and summary sections together form the capstone of the report.

1. *Conclusions:* The discussion of the conclusions indicated by the research findings should be limited to those that have direct support in the research findings. Researchers are often tempted to conclude too much. The hypotheses provide a convenient framework for stating conclusions; that is, researchers should indicate in this section whether the findings support the hypotheses.

It is important to distinguish between results and conclusions. Results are direct observations summarized and integrated by the statistical analysis, such as statistical analysis of two group means. A conclusion is an inference based on the results, expressed in terms of the hypothesis of the study, such as one group's treatment being more effective than the other group's. For example, a study might result in the observation that the mean spelling test scores of students taught spelling by Method A is significantly higher than the mean of students taught by Method B. The conclusion that Method A is more effective than Method B is not a direct result of the study but rather is an inference based on the results of the study.

Researchers may include a brief discussion of their ideas on the implications of their findings and recommendations for possible applications of the findings. They may also suggest any new questions for research that grew out of their study.

2. *Summary:* Because the summary will be more widely read than other sections of the report, its wording must be particularly clear and concise. The summary usually includes a brief restatement of the problems(s), the main features of the methods, and the most important findings. Upon completing a draft of this section, the author should check it carefully to determine whether it gives a concise but reasonably complete description of the study and its findings. One should also check to ascertain that no information has been introduced here that had not been included in the appropriate preceding sections. It is a good idea to have a colleague read the conclusions section to see if one is communicating as well as one intended to do.

/ 3. Supplementary Pages

A. Bibliography   The bibliography must include all sources mentioned in the text or footnotes. Most universities insist that only these be listed, but a few ask that pertinent references not specifically mentioned also be listed. The style manual previously selected will give complete details on the method of listing references. It is important to follow these rules rigorously and completely. In fact, it is a good strategy to learn them before carrying out the search through the literature for the proposal. By listing each reference in the correct form as it is encountered, one can avoid the extra time involved in finding the references again in order to have them in complete form for the bibliography. It is advisable to list them on cards or enter them in one's microcomputer so that they can be filed in alphabetical order.

B. Appendices   The appendices contain pertinent materials that are not important enough to be included in the body of the report but may be of value to some readers. Such materials may include complete copies of locally devised tests or questionnaires, together with the instructions and scoring keys for such instruments, item analysis data for measurements used, verbatim instructions to subjects, and tables that are very long or of only minor importance to the study.

C. Vita   The authors of research reports are sometimes asked to include brief accounts of their training, experience, professional memberships, and previous contributions.

D. Abstract   Most institutions require a separate abstract of the dissertation, which should include a definitive statement of the problem and concise descriptions of the research methods, major findings, conclusions, and implications. The abstract must be limited in length (typically 600 words or less). The abstract pages are numbered separately and placed either at the very beginning or the very end of the dissertation.

// The Journal Article

In preparing a research article for publication in a journal, a good first step is to look through one's bibliography to determine which journal has published the greatest amount of work in one's area of interest. Information concerning the procedure for submission of manuscripts will usually be found on the inside of a journal's front cover. Many journals will specify which style manual should be used, for example, the *Publication Manual of the American Psychological Association* or the *NEA Style Manual*. If a manual is not specified, the preferred style, method of referencing, and so on, may be determined from a study of the articles included in a recent issue of the journal.

A research article follows the same general outline as a dissertation, but it must be much shorter. A thesis or dissertation functions to demonstrate a student's competence and requires a full setting forth of the related research, complete description of the procedures, complete tabulation of results, and reflective elaboration. The journal article, on the other hand, requires only communication of the author's contribution to knowledge. For the sake of economy of journal space and readers' time, the article must be concise. The related-literature section contains only those results and arguments that provide the basis for the problem. The general statement of the problem is given in one paragraph, or possibly even omitted, in which case the article would begin with the hypothesis. The procedures section is also presented very briefly, although all the information needed to replicate the experiment should be included if at all possible. The results section will be of greatest interest to the reader and therefore will represent a greater proportion of the article than it would in a dissertation. Only the most important findings should be discussed in any detail.

A brief cover letter should accompany the manuscript. The editor will usually send the author a postcard acknowledging receipt of the manuscript and circulate copies of it among the appropriate members of the editorial board for review. From this point considerable time usually elapses before the author is informed whether the article has been accepted (6 weeks is probably typical). After an article is accepted, it is usually many months before it appears in print.

When a manuscript is rejected by a journal, the rejection notice is sometimes accompanied by a statement of the reasons for this rejection. A rejection by one journal does not necessarily mean that the article is unworthy of publication. A number of factors—such as competition for space, changes in editorial policy, or bias of reviewers—can influence the decision on publication. An article that has been rejected by one journal may be revised and submitted to another. Many articles make the rounds of several journals before finding a home. It is not ethical to submit an article to more than one journal at a time, however.

// The Professional Convention

Many researchers find that hearing papers read at professional conventions is a good way to keep up to date in their field. The reason for this is that there is a great lapse of time between the completion of a research project and its appearance in print. This time lag is often so long that professional journals have sometimes been described as being archival in nature.

Papers presented at professional meetings are prepared in much the same manner as journal articles. They are not necessarily always reports of completed research but may be progress reports of ongoing projects. A read paper is less formal than a journal article and can usually be more precisely geared to its audience. The audience can generally be expected to be familiar with details of related research and methods of measurement.

The paper will frequently be organized as follows:

1. Direct statement of the hypothesis
2. Brief description of the procedures
3. Findings, conclusions, and implications

The time allowed for reading a paper is usually quite brief, frequently less than 15 minutes. Therefore, the paper should focus on the most important aspects of one's study. A convenient rule of thumb is to allow 2½ to 3 minutes for each page of double-spaced typed copy.

If figures or tables will assist in the presentation, copies should be available for the audience. Some speakers also distribute copies of the text of their paper to the audience. However, since the audience reads the paper silently more rapidly than the author can read it aloud, there may be a gap in attention. It is preferable to have copies of a complete description of the study available for those who request it after the paper is presented.

/// STYLE MANUALS

The following are widely used manuals detailing general form and style for theses and dissertations:

American Psychological Association (1983). *Publication Manual* (3d ed.). Washington: American Psychological Association.

Campbell, W. G., and S. V. Ballou (1982). *Form and Style: Theses, Reports, Term Papers* (6th ed.). Boston: Houghton Mifflin.

The Chicago Manual of Style (1982; 13th ed., rev.). Chicago: University of Chicago Press.

Turabian, K. (1987). *A Manual for Writers of Term Papers, Theses, and Dissertations* (5th ed.). Chicago: University of Chicago Press.

/// SUMMARY

With electronic computation facilities available on almost all university campuses, many researchers are able to take advantage of these facilities in their data processing. The use of computers saves time and energy and facilitates a great degree of precision in very complex computations.

To use computers for data processing, the researcher needs to transform the data into a form that can be read into a computer and to provide instructions for the computer to act on the data by means of an appropriate program.

Writing computer programs requires training, but the researcher can often use available programs prepared for use in data analysis.

The interpretation of the results of a study is a straightforward task if, in the proposal, the researcher has laid a proper foundation for the research study. The following cautions should be kept in mind: (1) interpretation should be strictly based on the data derived from the study, (2) internal- and external-validity problems and other limitations of the study should be considered, and (3) conclusions must be presented as probability statements rather than as facts.

Negative results deserve the same respect and interpretation as do positive results. A retained null hypothesis is interpreted as the result of insufficient evidence and no more. Unhypothesized results deserve attention as sources of future hypotheses.

Formal procedures have been developed for preparing theses, journal articles, and papers. Mastering and employing these procedures assist researchers in communicating with one another and with practicing educators. Several style manuals provide details on these procedures.

// Key Concepts

canned programs
computer use
interpreting expected results
interpreting negative results
interpreting retained null
   hypotheses

interpreting unexpected results
practical *vs.* statistical significance
preparing conference papers
preparing journal articles
preparing theses or dissertations
style manuals

/// EXERCISES

1. What changes has the computer brought about in the practice of educational research?

2. Name three commercially available computer programs for statistical analysis.

3. What is the difference between results and conclusions?

4. Explain the difference between *statistical significance* of the results and the *significance of the study.*

5. What states of affairs can lead to a retained null hypothesis?

6. Decide whether each title is acceptable or unacceptable and give reasons for your choices:
   a. Grade-Point Average and Driver Education

    b. The Effects of Individualized Tutoring by Sixth-Grade Students Three Times a Week on Reading Performance of Below-Average Second-Grade Readers

    c. Children Should Be Taught the New Math!

    d. Relationship between Personality Characteristics and Attitudes toward Achievement of Good and Poor Readers

7. What are the differences in format for research reported in dissertation form, in journal form, and in a paper to be read at a conference?

8. Should one discuss research results that do not agree with one's hypothesis?

/// ANSWERS

1. The computer has made it possible to design and conduct research studies without regard for the number of variables or the complexity of the analysis. The data from studies having large numbers of subjects, using multivariate techniques, or requiring sophisticated statistics can now be analyzed with speed and accuracy.

2. The Statistical Package for the Social Sciences-X (SPSS-X), the Biomedical Series (BIMED), and the Statistical Analysis System (SAS).

3. A result is a direct observation. A conclusion is an inference based on results.

4. Statistical significance means only that the results are not likely to be a function of chance; the significance of the study is determined by the importance of the findings in regard to theory testing or practical implications.

5. A retained null hypothesis could result from the null hypothesis's actually being true in nature; or it could result from contamination by internal validity problems that obscure treatment effects, from lack of statistical power of the design used in the study, or from inability of the instruments to measure accurately the effects of treatment on the dependent variable.

6. a. unacceptable: no statement of relationship is given
    b. unacceptable: too wordy
    c. unacceptable: emotion-laden titles are not appropriate for research articles

d. acceptable: meets criteria for title

7. Dissertation form is the most formal and detailed in presentation; it follows the specifics of a particular style manual. The journal article is a more concise presentation, with a brief statement of problem, related literature, and methodology; a greater proportion of the article is devoted to major results and a discussion of their significance. A paper that is to be read at a conference is the most informal; geared to its audience, it states the hypothesis, briefly describes the procedure, and emphasizes the most important findings.

8. Yes. Results contrary to one's expectations are as legitimate as any other results and should be interpreted as such.

Appendix

TABLE A.1 Areas of the Normal Curve

(1) z	(2) Area between the Mean and z	(3) Area beyond z	(1) z	(2) Area between the Mean and z	(3) Area beyond z
0.00	.0000	.5000	0.45	.1736	.3264
0.01	.0040	.4960	0.46	.1772	.3228
0.02	.0080	.4920	0.47	.1808	.3192
0.03	.0120	.4880	0.48	.1844	.3156
0.04	.0160	.4840	0.49	.1879	.3121
0.05	.0199	.4801	0.50	.1915	.3085
0.06	.0239	.4761	0.51	.1950	.3050
0.07	.0279	.4721	0.52	.1985	.3015
0.08	.0319	.4681	0.53	.2019	.2981
0.09	.0359	.4641	0.54	.2054	.2946
0.10	.0398	.4602	0.55	.2088	.2912
0.11	.0438	.4562	0.56	.2123	.2877
0.12	.0478	.4522	0.57	.2157	.2843
0.13	.0517	.4483	0.58	.2190	.2810
0.14	.0557	.4443	0.59	.2224	.2776
0.15	.0596	.4404	0.60	.2257	.2743
0.16	.0636	.4364	0.61	.2291	.2709
0.17	.0675	.4325	0.62	.2324	.2676
0.18	.0714	.4286	0.63	.2357	.2643
0.19	.0753	.4247	0.64	.2389	.2611
0.20	.0793	.4207	0.65	.2422	.2578
0.21	.0832	.4168	0.66	.2454	.2546
0.22	.0871	.4129	0.67	.2486	.2514
0.23	.0910	.4090	0.68	.2517	.2483
0.24	.0948	.4052	0.69	.2549	.2451
0.25	.0987	.4013	0.70	.2580	.2420
0.26	.1026	.3974	0.71	.2611	.2389
0.27	.1064	.3936	0.72	.2642	.2358
0.28	.1103	.3897	0.73	.2673	.2327
0.29	.1141	.3859	0.74	.2704	.2296
0.30	.1179	.3821	0.75	.2734	.2266
0.31	.1217	.3783	0.76	.2764	.2236
0.32	.1255	.3745	0.77	.2794	.2206
0.33	.1293	.3707	0.78	.2823	.2177
0.34	.1331	.3669	0.79	.2852	.2148
0.35	.1368	.3632	0.80	.2881	.2119
0.36	.1406	.3594	0.81	.2910	.2090
0.37	.1443	.3557	0.82	.2939	.2061
0.38	.1480	.3520	0.83	.2967	.2033
0.39	.1517	.3483	0.84	.2995	.2005
0.40	.1554	.3446	0.85	.3023	.1977
0.41	.1591	.3409	0.86	.3051	.1949
0.42	.1628	.3372	0.87	.3078	.1922
0.43	.1664	.3336	0.88	.3106	.1894
0.44	.1700	.3300	0.89	.3133	.1867

TABLE A.1 Areas of the Normal Curve (cont.)

(1) z	(2) Area between the Mean and z	(3) Area beyond z	(1) z	(2) Area between the Mean and z	(3) Area beyond z
0.90	.3159	.1841	1.35	.4115	.0885
0.91	.3186	.1814	1.36	.4131	.0869
0.92	.3212	.1788	1.37	.4147	.0853
0.93	.3238	.1762	1.38	.4162	.0838
0.94	.3264	.1736	1.39	.4177	.0823
0.95	.3289	.1711	1.40	.4192	.0808
0.96	.3315	.1685	1.41	.4207	.0793
0.97	.3340	.1660	1.42	.4222	.0778
0.98	.3365	.1635	1.43	.4236	.0764
0.99	.3389	.1611	1.44	.4251	.0749
1.00	.3413	.1587	1.45	.4265	.0735
1.01	.3438	.1562	1.46	.4279	.0721
1.02	.3461	.1539	1.47	.4292	.0708
1.03	.3485	.1515	1.48	.4306	.0694
1.04	.3508	.1492	1.49	.4319	.0681
1.05	.3531	.1469	1.50	.4332	.0668
1.06	.3554	.1446	1.51	.4345	.0655
1.07	.3577	.1423	1.52	.4357	.0643
1.08	.3599	.1401	1.53	.4370	.0630
1.09	.3621	.1379	1.54	.4382	.0618
1.10	.3643	.1357	1.55	.4394	.0606
1.11	.3665	.1335	1.56	.4406	.0594
1.12	.3686	.1314	1.57	.4418	.0582
1.13	.3708	.1292	1.58	.4429	.0571
1.14	.3729	.1271	1.59	.4441	.0559
1.15	.3749	.1251	1.60	.4452	.0548
1.16	.3770	.1230	1.61	.4463	.0537
1.17	.3790	.1210	1.62	.4474	.0526
1.18	.3810	.1190	1.63	.4484	.0516
1.19	.3830	.1170	1.64	.4495	.0505
1.20	.3849	.1151	1.65	.4505	.0495
1.21	.3869	.1131	1.66	.4515	.0485
1.22	.3888	.1112	1.67	.4525	.0475
1.23	.3907	.1093	1.68	.4535	.0465
1.24	.3925	.1075	1.69	.4545	.0455
1.25	.3944	.1056	1.70	.4554	.0446
1.26	.3962	.1038	1.71	.4564	.0436
1.27	.3980	.1020	1.72	.4573	.0427
1.28	.3997	.1003	1.73	.4582	.0418
1.29	.4015	.0985	1.74	.4591	.0409
1.30	.4032	.0968	1.75	.4599	.0401
1.31	.4049	.0951	1.76	.4608	.0392
1.32	.4066	.0934	1.77	.4616	.0384
1.33	.4082	.0918	1.78	.4625	.0375
1.34	.4099	.0901	1.79	.4633	.0367

TABLE A.1 Areas of the Normal Curve (cont.)

(1) z	(2) Area between the Mean and z	(3) Area beyond z	(1) z	(2) Area between the Mean and z	(3) Area beyond z
1.80	.4641	.0359	2.25	.4878	.0122
1.81	.4649	.0351	2.26	.4881	.0119
1.82	.4656	.0344	2.27	.4884	.0116
1.83	.4664	.0336	2.28	.4887	.0113
1.84	.4671	.0329	2.29	.4890	.0110
1.85	.4678	.0322	2.30	.4893	.0107
1.86	.4686	.0314	2.31	.4896	.0104
1.87	.4693	.0307	2.32	.4898	.0102
1.88	.4699	.0301	2.33	.4901	.0099
1.89	.4706	.0294	2.34	.4904	.0096
1.90	.4713	.0287	2.35	.4906	.0094
1.91	.4719	.0281	2.36	.4909	.0091
1.92	.4726	.0274	2.37	.4911	.0089
1.93	.4732	.0268	2.38	.4913	.0087
1.94	.4738	.0262	2.39	.4916	.0084
1.95	.4744	.0256	2.40	.4918	.0082
1.96	.4750	.0250	2.41	.4920	.0080
1.97	.4756	.0244	2.42	.4922	.0078
1.98	.4761	.0239	2.43	.4925	.0075
1.99	.4767	.0233	2.44	.4927	.0073
2.00	.4772	.0228	2.45	.4929	.0071
2.01	.4778	.0222	2.46	.4931	.0069
2.02	.4783	.0217	2.47	.4932	.0068
2.03	.4788	.0212	2.48	.4934	.0066
2.04	.4793	.0207	2.49	.4936	.0064
2.05	.4798	.0202	2.50	.4938	.0062
2.06	.4803	.0197	2.51	.4940	.0060
2.07	.4808	.0192	2.52	.4941	.0059
2.08	.4812	.0188	2.53	.4943	.0057
2.09	.4817	.0183	2.54	.4945	.0055
2.10	.4821	.0179	2.55	.4946	.0054
2.11	.4826	.0174	2.56	.4948	.0052
2.12	.4830	.0170	2.57	.4949	.0051
2.13	.4834	.0166	2.58	.4951	.0049
2.14	.4838	.0162	2.59	.4952	.0048
2.15	.4842	.0158	2.60	.4953	.0047
2.16	.4846	.0154	2.61	.4955	.0045
2.17	.4850	.0150	2.62	.4956	.0044
2.18	.4854	.0146	2.63	.4957	.0043
2.19	.4857	.0143	2.64	.4959	.0041
2.20	.4861	.0139	2.65	.4960	.0040
2.21	.4864	.0136	2.66	.4961	.0039
2.22	.4868	.0132	2.67	.4962	.0038
2.23	.4871	.0129	2.68	.4963	.0037
2.24	.4875	.0125	2.69	.4964	.0036

TABLE A.1 Areas of the Normal Curve (cont.)

(1) z	(2) Area between the Mean and z	(3) Area beyond z	(1) z	(2) Area between the Mean and z	(3) Area beyond z
2.70	.4965	.0035	3.05	.4989	.0011
2.71	.4966	.0034	3.06	.4989	.0011
2.72	.4967	.0033	3.07	.4989	.0011
2.73	.4968	.0032	3.08	.4990	.0010
2.74	.4969	.0031	3.09	.4990	.0010
2.75	.4970	.0030	3.10	.4990	.0010
2.76	.4971	.0029	3.11	.4991	.0009
2.77	.4972	.0028	3.12	.4991	.0009
2.78	.4973	.0027	3.13	.4991	.0009
2.79	.4974	.0026	3.14	.4992	.0008
2.80	.4974	.0026	3.15	.4992	.0008
2.81	.4975	.0025	3.16	.4992	.0008
2.82	.4976	.0024	3.17	.4992	.0008
2.83	.4977	.0023	3.18	.4993	.0007
2.84	.4977	.0023	3.19	.4993	.0007
2.85	.4978	.0022	3.20	.4993	.0007
2.86	.4979	.0021	3.21	.4993	.0007
2.87	.4979	.0021	3.22	.4994	.0006
2.88	.4980	.0020	3.23	.4994	.0006
2.89	.4981	.0019	3.24	.4994	.0006
2.90	.4981	.0019	3.30	.4995	.0005
2.91	.4982	.0018	3.40	.4997	.0003
2.92	.4982	.0018	3.50	.4998	.0002
2.93	.4983	.0017	3.60	.4998	.0002
2.94	.4984	.0016	3.70	.4999	.0001
2.95	.4984	.0016	3.90	.49995	.00005
2.96	.4985	.0015	4.00	.49997	.00003
2.97	.4985	.0015	4.50	.4999966	.0000034
2.98	.4986	.0014	5.00	.4999997	.0000003
2.99	.4986	.0014	5.50	.499999981	.000000019
3.00	.4987	.0013	6.00	.499999999	.000000001
3.01	.4987	.0013			
3.02	.4987	.0013			
3.03	.4988	.0012			
3.04	.4988	.0012			

TABLE A.2 Table of *t*-Values

df	Level of significance for a directional (one-tailed) test					
	.10	.05	.025	.01	.005	.0005
	Level of significance for a nondirectional (two-tailed) test					
	.20	.10	.05	.02	.01	.001
1	3.078	6.314	12.706	31.821	63.657	636.619
2	1.886	2.920	4.303	6.965	9.925	31.598
3	1.638	2.353	3.182	4.541	5.841	12.941
4	1.533	2.132	2.776	3.747	4.604	8.610
5	1.476	2.015	2.571	3.365	4.032	6.859
6	1.440	1.943	2.447	3.143	3.707	5.959
7	1.415	1.895	2.365	2.998	3.499	5.405
8	1.397	1.860	2.306	2.896	3.355	5.041
9	1.383	1.833	2.262	2.821	3.250	4.781
10	1.372	1.812	2.228	2.764	3.169	4.587
11	1.363	1.796	2.201	2.718	3.106	4.437
12	1.356	1.782	2.179	2.681	3.055	4.318
13	1.350	1.771	2.160	2.650	3.012	4.221
14	1.345	1.761	2.145	2.624	2.977	4.140
15	1.341	1.753	2.131	2.602	2.947	4.073
16	1.337	1.746	2.120	2.583	2.921	4.015
17	1.333	1.740	2.110	2.567	2.898	3.965
18	1.330	1.734	2.101	2.552	2.878	3.922
19	1.328	1.729	2.093	2.539	2.861	3.883
20	1.325	1.725	2.086	2.528	2.845	3.850
21	1.323	1.721	2.080	2.518	2.831	3.819
22	1.321	1.717	2.074	2.508	2.819	3.792
23	1.319	1.714	2.069	2.500	2.807	3.767
24	1.318	1.711	2.064	2.492	2.797	3.745
25	1.316	1.708	2.060	2.485	2.787	3.725
26	1.315	1.706	2.056	2.479	2.779	3.707
27	1.314	1.703	2.052	2.473	2.771	3.690
28	1.313	1.701	2.048	2.467	2.763	3.674
29	1.311	1.699	2.045	2.462	2.756	3.659
30	1.310	1.697	2.042	2.457	2.750	3.646
40	1.303	1.684	2.021	2.423	2.704	3.551
60	1.296	1.671	2.000	2.390	2.660	3.460
120	1.289	1.658	1.980	2.358	2.617	3.373
∞	1.282	1.645	1.960	2.326	2.576	3.291

Source: Table A.2 is taken from Table III of Fisher and Yates, *Statistical Tables for Biological, Agricultural, and Medical Research,* published by Longman Group UK Ltd., London (previously published by Oliver and Boyd, Ltd., Edinburgh), and by permission of the authors and publishers.

TABLE A.3 The 5 (Roman Type) and 1 (Boldface Type) Percent Points for the F Distribution

n_1 degrees of freedom for numerator

denominator df = n_1

Each cell lists the 5% point (Roman) / 1% point (Boldface).

n_2	1	2	3	4	5	6	7	8	9	10	11	12	14	16	20	24	30	40	50	75	100	200	500	∞
1	161 / 4,052	200 / 4,999	216 / 5,403	225 / 5,625	230 / 5,764	234 / 5,859	237 / 5,928	239 / 5,981	241 / 6,022	242 / 6,056	243 / 6,082	244 / 6,106	245 / 6,142	246 / 6,169	248 / 6,208	249 / 6,234	250 / 6,258	251 / 6,286	252 / 6,302	253 / 6,323	253 / 6,334	254 / 6,352	254 / 6,361	254 / 6,366
2	18.51 / 98.49	19.00 / 99.00	19.16 / 99.17	19.25 / 99.25	19.30 / 99.30	19.33 / 99.33	19.36 / 99.34	19.37 / 99.36	19.38 / 99.38	19.39 / 99.40	19.40 / 99.41	19.41 / 99.42	19.42 / 99.43	19.43 / 99.44	19.44 / 99.45	19.45 / 99.46	19.46 / 99.47	19.47 / 99.48	19.47 / 99.48	19.48 / 99.49	19.49 / 99.49	19.49 / 99.49	19.50 / 99.50	19.50 / 99.50
3	10.13 / 34.12	9.55 / 30.82	9.28 / 29.46	9.12 / 28.71	9.01 / 28.24	8.94 / 27.91	8.88 / 27.67	8.84 / 27.49	8.81 / 27.34	8.78 / 27.23	8.76 / 27.13	8.74 / 27.05	8.71 / 26.92	8.69 / 26.83	8.66 / 26.69	8.64 / 26.60	8.62 / 26.50	8.60 / 26.41	8.58 / 26.35	8.57 / 26.27	8.56 / 26.23	8.54 / 26.18	8.54 / 26.14	8.53 / 26.12
4	7.71 / 21.20	6.94 / 18.00	6.59 / 16.69	6.39 / 15.98	6.26 / 15.52	6.16 / 15.21	6.09 / 14.98	6.04 / 14.80	6.00 / 14.66	5.96 / 14.54	5.93 / 14.45	5.91 / 14.37	5.87 / 14.24	5.84 / 14.15	5.80 / 14.02	5.77 / 13.93	5.74 / 13.83	5.71 / 13.74	5.70 / 13.69	5.68 / 13.61	5.66 / 13.57	5.65 / 13.52	5.64 / 13.48	5.63 / 13.46
5	6.61 / 16.26	5.79 / 13.27	5.41 / 12.06	5.19 / 11.39	5.05 / 10.97	4.95 / 10.67	4.88 / 10.45	4.82 / 10.27	4.78 / 10.15	4.74 / 10.05	4.70 / 9.96	4.68 / 9.89	4.64 / 9.77	4.60 / 9.68	4.56 / 9.55	4.53 / 9.47	4.50 / 9.38	4.46 / 9.29	4.44 / 9.24	4.42 / 9.17	4.40 / 9.13	4.38 / 9.07	4.37 / 9.04	4.36 / 9.02
6	5.99 / 13.74	5.14 / 10.92	4.76 / 9.78	4.53 / 9.15	4.39 / 8.75	4.28 / 8.47	4.21 / 8.26	4.15 / 8.10	4.10 / 7.98	4.06 / 7.87	4.03 / 7.79	4.00 / 7.72	3.96 / 7.60	3.92 / 7.52	3.87 / 7.39	3.84 / 7.31	3.81 / 7.23	3.77 / 7.14	3.75 / 7.09	3.72 / 7.02	3.71 / 6.99	3.69 / 6.94	3.68 / 6.90	3.67 / 6.88
7	5.59 / 12.25	4.74 / 9.55	4.35 / 8.45	4.12 / 7.85	3.97 / 7.46	3.87 / 7.19	3.79 / 7.00	3.73 / 6.84	3.68 / 6.71	3.63 / 6.62	3.60 / 6.54	3.57 / 6.47	3.52 / 6.35	3.49 / 6.27	3.44 / 6.15	3.41 / 6.07	3.38 / 5.98	3.34 / 5.90	3.32 / 5.85	3.29 / 5.78	3.28 / 5.75	3.25 / 5.70	3.24 / 5.67	3.23 / 5.65
8	5.32 / 11.26	4.46 / 8.65	4.07 / 7.59	3.84 / 7.01	3.69 / 6.63	3.58 / 6.37	3.50 / 6.19	3.44 / 6.03	3.39 / 5.91	3.34 / 5.82	3.31 / 5.74	3.28 / 5.67	3.23 / 5.56	3.20 / 5.48	3.15 / 5.36	3.12 / 5.28	3.08 / 5.20	3.05 / 5.11	3.03 / 5.06	3.00 / 5.00	2.98 / 4.96	2.96 / 4.91	2.94 / 4.88	2.93 / 4.86
9	5.12 / 10.56	4.26 / 8.02	3.86 / 6.99	3.63 / 6.42	3.48 / 6.06	3.37 / 5.80	3.29 / 5.62	3.23 / 5.47	3.18 / 5.35	3.13 / 5.26	3.10 / 5.18	3.07 / 5.11	3.02 / 5.00	2.98 / 4.92	2.93 / 4.80	2.90 / 4.73	2.86 / 4.64	2.82 / 4.56	2.80 / 4.51	2.77 / 4.45	2.76 / 4.41	2.73 / 4.36	2.72 / 4.33	2.71 / 4.31
10	4.96 / 10.04	4.10 / 7.56	3.71 / 6.55	3.48 / 5.99	3.33 / 5.64	3.22 / 5.39	3.14 / 5.21	3.07 / 5.06	3.02 / 4.95	2.97 / 4.85	2.94 / 4.78	2.91 / 4.71	2.86 / 4.60	2.82 / 4.52	2.77 / 4.41	2.74 / 4.33	2.70 / 4.25	2.67 / 4.17	2.64 / 4.12	2.61 / 4.05	2.59 / 4.01	2.56 / 3.96	2.55 / 3.93	2.54 / 3.91
11	4.84 / 9.65	3.98 / 7.20	3.59 / 6.22	3.36 / 5.67	3.20 / 5.32	3.09 / 5.07	3.01 / 4.88	2.95 / 4.74	2.90 / 4.63	2.86 / 4.54	2.82 / 4.46	2.79 / 4.40	2.74 / 4.29	2.70 / 4.21	2.65 / 4.10	2.61 / 4.02	2.57 / 3.94	2.53 / 3.86	2.50 / 3.80	2.47 / 3.74	2.45 / 3.70	2.42 / 3.66	2.41 / 3.62	2.40 / 3.60
12	4.75 / 9.33	3.88 / 6.93	3.49 / 5.95	3.26 / 5.41	3.11 / 5.06	3.00 / 4.82	2.92 / 4.65	2.85 / 4.50	2.80 / 4.39	2.76 / 4.30	2.72 / 4.22	2.69 / 4.16	2.64 / 4.05	2.60 / 3.98	2.54 / 3.86	2.50 / 3.78	2.46 / 3.70	2.42 / 3.61	2.40 / 3.56	2.36 / 3.49	2.35 / 3.46	2.32 / 3.41	2.31 / 3.38	2.30 / 3.36
13	4.67 / 9.07	3.80 / 6.70	3.41 / 5.74	3.18 / 5.20	3.02 / 4.86	2.92 / 4.62	2.84 / 4.44	2.77 / 4.30	2.72 / 4.19	2.67 / 4.10	2.63 / 4.02	2.60 / 3.96	2.55 / 3.85	2.51 / 3.78	2.46 / 3.67	2.42 / 3.59	2.38 / 3.51	2.34 / 3.42	2.32 / 3.37	2.28 / 3.30	2.26 / 3.27	2.24 / 3.21	2.22 / 3.18	2.21 / 3.16

TABLE A.3 The 5 (Roman Type) and 1 (Boldface Type) Percent Points for the F Distribution (cont.)

n_1 degrees of freedom for numerator

denominator df = n_1	1	2	3	4	5	6	7	8	9	10	11	12	14	16	20	24	30	40	50	75	100	200	500	∞
14	4.60 / **8.86**	3.74 / **6.51**	3.34 / **5.56**	3.11 / **5.03**	2.96 / **4.69**	2.85 / **4.46**	2.77 / **4.28**	2.70 / **4.14**	2.65 / **4.03**	2.60 / **3.94**	2.56 / **3.86**	2.53 / **3.80**	2.48 / **3.70**	2.44 / **3.62**	2.39 / **3.51**	2.35 / **3.43**	2.31 / **3.34**	2.27 / **3.26**	2.24 / **3.21**	2.21 / **3.14**	2.19 / **3.11**	2.16 / **3.06**	2.14 / **3.02**	2.13 / **3.00**
15	4.54 / **8.68**	3.68 / **6.36**	3.29 / **5.42**	3.06 / **4.89**	2.90 / **4.56**	2.79 / **4.32**	2.70 / **4.14**	2.64 / **4.00**	2.59 / **3.89**	2.55 / **3.80**	2.51 / **3.73**	2.48 / **3.67**	2.43 / **3.56**	2.39 / **3.48**	2.33 / **3.36**	2.29 / **3.29**	2.25 / **3.20**	2.21 / **3.12**	2.18 / **3.07**	2.15 / **3.00**	2.12 / **2.97**	2.10 / **2.92**	2.08 / **2.89**	2.07 / **2.87**
16	4.49 / **8.53**	3.63 / **6.23**	3.24 / **5.29**	3.01 / **4.77**	2.85 / **4.44**	2.74 / **4.20**	2.66 / **4.03**	2.59 / **3.89**	2.54 / **3.78**	2.49 / **3.69**	2.45 / **3.61**	2.42 / **3.55**	2.37 / **3.45**	2.33 / **3.37**	2.28 / **3.25**	2.24 / **3.18**	2.20 / **3.10**	2.16 / **3.01**	2.13 / **2.96**	2.09 / **2.89**	2.07 / **2.86**	2.04 / **2.80**	2.02 / **2.77**	2.01 / **2.75**
17	4.45 / **8.40**	3.59 / **6.11**	3.20 / **5.18**	2.96 / **4.67**	2.81 / **4.34**	2.70 / **4.10**	2.62 / **3.93**	2.55 / **3.79**	2.50 / **3.68**	2.45 / **3.59**	2.41 / **3.52**	2.38 / **3.45**	2.33 / **3.35**	2.29 / **3.27**	2.23 / **3.16**	2.19 / **3.08**	2.15 / **3.00**	2.11 / **2.92**	2.08 / **2.86**	2.04 / **2.79**	2.02 / **2.76**	1.99 / **2.70**	1.97 / **2.67**	1.96 / **2.65**
18	4.41 / **8.28**	3.55 / **6.01**	3.16 / **5.09**	2.93 / **4.58**	2.77 / **4.25**	2.66 / **4.01**	2.58 / **3.85**	2.51 / **3.71**	2.46 / **3.60**	2.41 / **3.51**	2.37 / **3.44**	2.34 / **3.37**	2.29 / **3.27**	2.25 / **3.19**	2.19 / **3.07**	2.15 / **3.00**	2.11 / **2.91**	2.07 / **2.83**	2.04 / **2.78**	2.00 / **2.71**	1.98 / **2.68**	1.95 / **2.62**	1.93 / **2.59**	1.92 / **2.57**
19	4.38 / **8.18**	3.52 / **5.93**	3.13 / **5.01**	2.90 / **4.50**	2.74 / **4.17**	2.63 / **3.94**	2.55 / **3.77**	2.48 / **3.63**	2.43 / **3.52**	2.38 / **3.43**	2.34 / **3.36**	2.31 / **3.30**	2.26 / **3.19**	2.21 / **3.12**	2.15 / **3.00**	2.11 / **2.92**	2.07 / **2.84**	2.02 / **2.76**	2.00 / **2.70**	1.96 / **2.63**	1.94 / **2.60**	1.91 / **2.54**	1.90 / **2.51**	1.88 / **2.49**
20	4.35 / **8.10**	3.49 / **5.85**	3.10 / **4.94**	2.87 / **4.43**	2.71 / **4.10**	2.60 / **3.87**	2.52 / **3.71**	2.45 / **3.56**	2.40 / **3.45**	2.35 / **3.37**	2.31 / **3.30**	2.28 / **3.23**	2.23 / **3.13**	2.18 / **3.05**	2.12 / **2.94**	2.08 / **2.86**	2.04 / **2.77**	1.99 / **2.69**	1.96 / **2.63**	1.92 / **2.56**	1.90 / **2.53**	1.87 / **2.47**	1.85 / **2.44**	1.84 / **2.42**
21	4.32 / **8.02**	3.47 / **5.78**	3.07 / **4.87**	2.84 / **4.37**	2.68 / **4.04**	2.57 / **3.81**	2.49 / **3.65**	2.42 / **3.51**	2.37 / **3.40**	2.32 / **3.31**	2.28 / **3.24**	2.25 / **3.17**	2.20 / **3.07**	2.15 / **2.99**	2.09 / **2.88**	2.05 / **2.80**	2.00 / **2.72**	1.96 / **2.63**	1.93 / **2.58**	1.89 / **2.51**	1.87 / **2.47**	1.84 / **2.42**	1.82 / **2.38**	1.81 / **2.36**
22	4.30 / **7.94**	3.44 / **5.72**	3.05 / **4.82**	2.82 / **4.31**	2.66 / **3.99**	2.55 / **3.76**	2.47 / **3.59**	2.40 / **3.45**	2.35 / **3.35**	2.30 / **3.26**	2.26 / **3.18**	2.23 / **3.12**	2.18 / **3.02**	2.13 / **2.94**	2.07 / **2.83**	2.03 / **2.75**	1.98 / **2.67**	1.93 / **2.58**	1.91 / **2.53**	1.87 / **2.46**	1.84 / **2.42**	1.81 / **2.37**	1.80 / **2.33**	1.78 / **2.31**
23	4.28 / **7.88**	3.42 / **5.66**	3.03 / **4.76**	2.80 / **4.26**	2.64 / **3.94**	2.53 / **3.71**	2.45 / **3.54**	2.38 / **3.41**	2.32 / **3.30**	2.28 / **3.21**	2.24 / **3.14**	2.20 / **3.07**	2.14 / **2.97**	2.10 / **2.89**	2.04 / **2.78**	2.00 / **2.70**	1.96 / **2.62**	1.91 / **2.53**	1.88 / **2.48**	1.84 / **2.41**	1.82 / **2.37**	1.79 / **2.32**	1.77 / **2.28**	1.76 / **2.26**
24	4.26 / **7.82**	3.40 / **5.61**	3.01 / **4.72**	2.78 / **4.22**	2.62 / **3.90**	2.51 / **3.67**	2.43 / **3.50**	2.36 / **3.36**	2.30 / **3.25**	2.26 / **3.17**	2.22 / **3.09**	2.18 / **3.03**	2.13 / **2.93**	2.09 / **2.85**	2.02 / **2.74**	1.98 / **2.66**	1.94 / **2.58**	1.89 / **2.49**	1.86 / **2.44**	1.82 / **2.36**	1.80 / **2.33**	1.76 / **2.27**	1.74 / **2.23**	1.73 / **2.21**
25	4.24 / **7.77**	3.38 / **5.57**	2.99 / **4.68**	2.76 / **4.18**	2.60 / **3.86**	2.49 / **3.63**	2.41 / **3.46**	2.34 / **3.32**	2.28 / **3.21**	2.24 / **3.13**	2.20 / **3.05**	2.16 / **2.99**	2.11 / **2.89**	2.06 / **2.81**	2.00 / **2.70**	1.96 / **2.62**	1.92 / **2.54**	1.87 / **2.45**	1.84 / **2.40**	1.80 / **2.32**	1.77 / **2.29**	1.74 / **2.23**	1.72 / **2.19**	1.71 / **2.17**
26	4.22 / **7.72**	3.37 / **5.53**	2.98 / **4.64**	2.74 / **4.14**	2.59 / **3.82**	2.47 / **3.59**	2.39 / **3.42**	2.32 / **3.29**	2.27 / **3.17**	2.22 / **3.09**	2.18 / **3.02**	2.15 / **2.96**	2.10 / **2.86**	2.05 / **2.77**	1.99 / **2.66**	1.95 / **2.58**	1.90 / **2.50**	1.85 / **2.41**	1.82 / **2.36**	1.78 / **2.28**	1.76 / **2.25**	1.72 / **2.19**	1.70 / **2.15**	1.69 / **2.13**

TABLE A.3 The 5 (Roman Type) and 1 (Boldface Type) Percent Points for the F Distribution (cont.)

n_1 degrees of freedom for numerator

df = n_1	1	2	3	4	5	6	7	8	9	10	11	12	14	16	20	24	30	40	50	75	100	200	500	∞
27	4.21/**7.68**	3.35/**5.49**	2.96/**4.60**	2.73/**4.11**	2.57/**3.79**	2.46/**3.56**	2.37/**3.39**	2.30/**3.26**	2.25/**3.14**	2.20/**3.06**	2.16/**2.98**	2.13/**2.93**	2.08/**2.83**	2.03/**2.74**	1.97/**2.63**	1.93/**2.55**	1.88/**2.47**	1.84/**2.38**	1.80/**2.33**	1.76/**2.25**	1.74/**2.21**	1.71/**2.16**	1.68/**2.12**	1.67/**2.10**
28	4.20/**7.64**	3.34/**5.45**	2.95/**4.57**	2.71/**4.07**	2.56/**3.76**	2.44/**3.53**	2.36/**3.36**	2.29/**3.23**	2.24/**3.11**	2.19/**3.03**	2.15/**2.95**	2.12/**2.90**	2.06/**2.80**	2.02/**2.71**	1.96/**2.60**	1.91/**2.52**	1.87/**2.44**	1.81/**2.35**	1.78/**2.30**	1.75/**2.22**	1.72/**2.18**	1.69/**2.13**	1.67/**2.09**	1.65/**2.06**
29	4.18/**7.60**	3.33/**5.42**	2.93/**4.54**	2.70/**4.04**	2.54/**3.73**	2.43/**3.50**	2.35/**3.33**	2.28/**3.20**	2.22/**3.08**	2.18/**3.00**	2.14/**2.92**	2.10/**2.87**	2.05/**2.77**	2.00/**2.68**	1.94/**2.57**	1.90/**2.49**	1.85/**2.41**	1.80/**2.32**	1.77/**2.27**	1.73/**2.19**	1.71/**2.15**	1.68/**2.10**	1.65/**2.06**	1.64/**2.03**
30	4.17/**7.56**	3.32/**5.39**	2.92/**4.51**	2.69/**4.02**	2.53/**3.70**	2.42/**3.47**	2.34/**3.30**	2.27/**3.17**	2.21/**3.06**	2.16/**2.98**	2.12/**2.90**	2.09/**2.84**	2.04/**2.74**	1.99/**2.66**	1.93/**2.55**	1.89/**2.47**	1.84/**2.38**	1.79/**2.29**	1.76/**2.24**	1.72/**2.16**	1.69/**2.13**	1.66/**2.07**	1.64/**2.03**	1.62/**2.01**
32	4.15/**7.50**	3.30/**5.34**	2.90/**4.46**	2.67/**3.97**	2.51/**3.66**	2.40/**3.42**	2.32/**3.25**	2.25/**3.12**	2.19/**3.01**	2.14/**2.94**	2.10/**2.86**	2.07/**2.80**	2.02/**2.70**	1.97/**2.62**	1.91/**2.51**	1.86/**2.42**	1.82/**2.34**	1.76/**2.25**	1.74/**2.20**	1.69/**2.12**	1.67/**2.08**	1.64/**2.02**	1.61/**1.98**	1.59/**1.96**
34	4.13/**7.44**	3.28/**5.29**	2.88/**4.42**	2.65/**3.93**	2.49/**3.61**	2.38/**3.38**	2.30/**3.21**	2.23/**3.08**	2.17/**2.97**	2.12/**2.89**	2.08/**2.82**	2.05/**2.76**	2.00/**2.66**	1.95/**2.58**	1.89/**2.47**	1.84/**2.38**	1.80/**2.30**	1.74/**2.21**	1.71/**2.15**	1.67/**2.08**	1.64/**2.04**	1.61/**1.98**	1.59/**1.94**	1.57/**1.91**
36	4.11/**7.39**	3.26/**5.25**	2.86/**4.38**	2.63/**3.89**	2.48/**3.58**	2.36/**3.35**	2.28/**3.18**	2.21/**3.04**	2.15/**2.94**	2.10/**2.86**	2.06/**2.78**	2.03/**2.72**	1.98/**2.62**	1.93/**2.54**	1.87/**2.43**	1.82/**2.35**	1.78/**2.26**	1.72/**2.17**	1.69/**2.12**	1.65/**2.04**	1.62/**2.00**	1.59/**1.94**	1.56/**1.90**	1.55/**1.87**
38	4.10/**7.35**	3.25/**5.21**	2.85/**4.34**	2.62/**3.86**	2.46/**3.54**	2.35/**3.32**	2.26/**3.15**	2.19/**3.02**	2.14/**2.91**	2.09/**2.82**	2.05/**2.75**	2.02/**2.69**	1.96/**2.59**	1.92/**2.51**	1.85/**2.40**	1.80/**2.32**	1.76/**2.22**	1.71/**2.14**	1.67/**2.08**	1.63/**2.00**	1.60/**1.97**	1.57/**1.90**	1.54/**1.86**	1.53/**1.84**
40	4.08/**7.31**	3.23/**5.18**	2.84/**4.31**	2.61/**3.83**	2.45/**3.51**	2.34/**3.29**	2.25/**3.12**	2.18/**2.99**	2.12/**2.88**	2.07/**2.80**	2.04/**2.73**	2.00/**2.66**	1.95/**2.56**	1.90/**2.49**	1.84/**2.37**	1.79/**2.29**	1.74/**2.20**	1.69/**2.11**	1.66/**2.05**	1.61/**1.97**	1.59/**1.94**	1.55/**1.88**	1.53/**1.84**	1.51/**1.81**
42	4.07/**7.27**	3.22/**5.15**	2.83/**4.29**	2.59/**3.80**	2.44/**3.49**	2.32/**3.26**	2.24/**3.10**	2.17/**2.96**	2.11/**2.86**	2.06/**2.77**	2.02/**2.70**	1.99/**2.64**	1.94/**2.54**	1.89/**2.46**	1.82/**2.35**	1.78/**2.26**	1.73/**2.17**	1.68/**2.08**	1.64/**2.02**	1.60/**1.94**	1.57/**1.91**	1.54/**1.85**	1.51/**1.80**	1.49/**1.78**
44	4.06/**7.24**	3.21/**5.12**	2.82/**4.26**	2.58/**3.78**	2.43/**3.46**	2.31/**3.24**	2.23/**3.07**	2.16/**2.94**	2.10/**2.84**	2.05/**2.75**	2.01/**2.68**	1.98/**2.62**	1.92/**2.52**	1.88/**2.44**	1.81/**2.32**	1.76/**2.24**	1.72/**2.15**	1.66/**2.06**	1.63/**2.00**	1.58/**1.92**	1.56/**1.88**	1.52/**1.82**	1.50/**1.78**	1.48/**1.75**
46	4.05/**7.21**	3.20/**5.10**	2.81/**4.24**	2.57/**3.76**	2.42/**3.44**	2.30/**3.22**	2.22/**3.05**	2.14/**2.92**	2.09/**2.82**	2.04/**2.73**	2.00/**2.66**	1.97/**2.60**	1.91/**2.50**	1.87/**2.42**	1.80/**2.30**	1.75/**2.22**	1.71/**2.13**	1.65/**2.04**	1.62/**1.98**	1.57/**1.90**	1.54/**1.86**	1.51/**1.80**	1.48/**1.76**	1.46/**1.72**
48	4.04/**7.19**	3.19/**5.08**	2.80/**4.22**	2.56/**3.74**	2.41/**3.42**	2.30/**3.20**	2.21/**3.04**	2.14/**2.90**	2.08/**2.80**	2.03/**2.71**	1.99/**2.64**	1.96/**2.58**	1.90/**2.48**	1.86/**2.40**	1.79/**2.28**	1.74/**2.20**	1.70/**2.11**	1.64/**2.02**	1.61/**1.96**	1.56/**1.88**	1.53/**1.84**	1.50/**1.78**	1.47/**1.73**	1.45/**1.70**

denominator

TABLE A.3 The 5 (Roman Type) and 1 (Boldface Type) Percent Points for the _F_ Distribution (cont.)

n_1 degrees of freedom for numerator

denominator df = n_1	1	2	3	4	5	6	7	8	9	10	11	12	14	16	20	24	30	40	50	75	100	200	500	∞
50	4.03 **7.17**	3.18 **5.06**	2.79 **4.20**	2.56 **3.72**	2.40 **3.41**	2.29 **3.18**	2.20 **3.02**	2.13 **2.88**	2.07 **2.78**	2.02 **2.70**	1.98 **2.62**	1.95 **2.56**	1.90 **2.46**	1.85 **2.39**	1.78 **2.26**	1.74 **2.18**	1.69 **2.10**	1.63 **2.00**	1.60 **1.94**	1.55 **1.86**	1.52 **1.82**	1.48 **1.76**	1.46 **1.71**	1.44 **1.68**
55	4.02 **7.12**	3.17 **5.01**	2.78 **4.16**	2.54 **3.68**	2.38 **3.37**	2.27 **3.15**	2.18 **2.98**	2.11 **2.85**	2.05 **2.75**	2.00 **2.66**	1.97 **2.59**	1.93 **2.53**	1.88 **2.43**	1.83 **2.35**	1.76 **2.23**	1.72 **2.15**	1.67 **2.06**	1.61 **1.96**	1.58 **1.90**	1.52 **1.82**	1.50 **1.78**	1.46 **1.71**	1.43 **1.66**	1.41 **1.64**
60	4.00 **7.08**	3.15 **4.98**	2.76 **4.13**	2.52 **3.65**	2.37 **3.34**	2.25 **3.12**	2.17 **2.95**	2.10 **2.82**	2.04 **2.72**	1.99 **2.63**	1.95 **2.56**	1.92 **2.50**	1.86 **2.40**	1.81 **2.32**	1.75 **2.20**	1.70 **2.12**	1.65 **2.03**	1.59 **1.93**	1.56 **1.87**	1.50 **1.79**	1.48 **1.74**	1.44 **1.68**	1.41 **1.63**	1.39 **1.60**
65	3.99 **7.04**	3.14 **4.95**	2.75 **4.10**	2.51 **3.62**	2.36 **3.31**	2.24 **3.09**	2.15 **2.93**	2.08 **2.79**	2.02 **2.70**	1.98 **2.61**	1.94 **2.54**	1.90 **2.47**	1.85 **2.37**	1.80 **2.30**	1.73 **2.18**	1.68 **2.09**	1.63 **2.00**	1.57 **1.90**	1.54 **1.84**	1.49 **1.76**	1.46 **1.71**	1.42 **1.64**	1.39 **1.60**	1.37 **1.56**
70	3.98 **7.01**	3.13 **4.92**	2.74 **4.08**	2.50 **3.60**	2.35 **3.29**	2.23 **3.07**	2.14 **2.91**	2.07 **2.77**	2.01 **2.67**	1.97 **2.59**	1.93 **2.51**	1.89 **2.45**	1.84 **2.35**	1.79 **2.28**	1.72 **2.15**	1.67 **2.07**	1.62 **1.98**	1.56 **1.88**	1.53 **1.82**	1.47 **1.74**	1.45 **1.69**	1.40 **1.62**	1.37 **1.56**	1.35 **1.53**
80	3.96 **6.96**	3.11 **4.88**	2.72 **4.04**	2.48 **3.56**	2.33 **3.25**	2.21 **3.04**	2.12 **2.87**	2.05 **2.74**	1.99 **2.64**	1.95 **2.55**	1.91 **2.48**	1.88 **2.41**	1.82 **2.32**	1.77 **2.24**	1.70 **2.11**	1.65 **2.03**	1.60 **1.94**	1.54 **1.84**	1.51 **1.78**	1.45 **1.70**	1.42 **1.65**	1.38 **1.57**	1.35 **1.52**	1.32 **1.49**
100	3.94 **6.90**	3.09 **4.82**	2.70 **3.98**	2.46 **3.51**	2.30 **3.20**	2.19 **2.99**	2.10 **2.82**	2.03 **2.69**	1.97 **2.59**	1.92 **2.51**	1.88 **2.43**	1.85 **2.36**	1.79 **2.26**	1.75 **2.19**	1.68 **2.06**	1.63 **1.98**	1.57 **1.89**	1.51 **1.79**	1.48 **1.73**	1.42 **1.64**	1.39 **1.59**	1.34 **1.51**	1.30 **1.46**	1.28 **1.43**
125	3.92 **6.84**	3.07 **4.78**	2.68 **3.94**	2.44 **3.47**	2.29 **3.17**	2.17 **2.95**	2.08 **2.79**	2.01 **2.65**	1.95 **2.56**	1.90 **2.47**	1.86 **2.40**	1.83 **2.33**	1.77 **2.23**	1.72 **2.15**	1.65 **2.03**	1.60 **1.94**	1.55 **1.85**	1.49 **1.75**	1.45 **1.68**	1.39 **1.59**	1.36 **1.54**	1.31 **1.46**	1.27 **1.40**	1.25 **1.37**
150	3.91 **6.81**	3.06 **4.75**	2.67 **3.91**	2.43 **3.44**	2.27 **3.14**	2.16 **2.92**	2.07 **2.76**	2.00 **2.62**	1.94 **2.53**	1.89 **2.44**	1.85 **2.37**	1.82 **2.30**	1.76 **2.20**	1.71 **2.12**	1.64 **2.00**	1.59 **1.91**	1.54 **1.83**	1.47 **1.72**	1.44 **1.66**	1.37 **1.56**	1.34 **1.51**	1.29 **1.43**	1.25 **1.37**	1.22 **1.33**
200	3.89 **6.76**	3.04 **4.71**	2.65 **3.88**	2.41 **3.41**	2.26 **3.11**	2.14 **2.90**	2.05 **2.73**	1.98 **2.60**	1.92 **2.50**	1.87 **2.41**	1.83 **2.34**	1.80 **2.28**	1.74 **2.17**	1.69 **2.09**	1.62 **1.97**	1.57 **1.88**	1.52 **1.79**	1.45 **1.69**	1.42 **1.62**	1.35 **1.53**	1.32 **1.48**	1.26 **1.39**	1.22 **1.33**	1.19 **1.28**
400	3.86 **6.70**	3.02 **4.66**	2.62 **3.83**	2.39 **3.36**	2.23 **3.06**	2.12 **2.85**	2.03 **2.69**	1.96 **2.55**	1.90 **2.46**	1.85 **2.37**	1.81 **2.29**	1.78 **2.23**	1.72 **2.12**	1.67 **2.04**	1.60 **1.92**	1.54 **1.84**	1.49 **1.74**	1.42 **1.64**	1.38 **1.57**	1.32 **1.47**	1.28 **1.42**	1.22 **1.32**	1.16 **1.24**	1.13 **1.19**
1000	3.85 **6.66**	3.00 **4.62**	2.61 **3.80**	2.38 **3.34**	2.22 **3.04**	2.10 **2.82**	2.02 **2.66**	1.95 **2.53**	1.89 **2.43**	1.84 **2.34**	1.80 **2.26**	1.76 **2.20**	1.70 **2.09**	1.65 **2.01**	1.58 **1.89**	1.53 **1.81**	1.47 **1.71**	1.41 **1.61**	1.36 **1.54**	1.30 **1.44**	1.26 **1.38**	1.19 **1.28**	1.13 **1.19**	1.08 **1.11**
∞	3.84 **6.64**	2.99 **4.60**	2.60 **3.78**	2.37 **3.32**	2.21 **3.02**	2.09 **2.80**	2.01 **2.64**	1.94 **2.51**	1.88 **2.41**	1.83 **2.32**	1.79 **2.24**	1.75 **2.18**	1.69 **2.07**	1.64 **1.99**	1.57 **1.87**	1.52 **1.79**	1.46 **1.69**	1.40 **1.59**	1.35 **1.52**	1.28 **1.41**	1.24 **1.36**	1.17 **1.25**	1.11 **1.15**	1.00 **1.00**

Source: Reprinted by permission from _Statistical Methods_, 7th ed., by George W. Snedecor and William G. Cochran. Copyright © 1980 by Iowa State University Press, Ames, Iowa 50010.

TABLE A.4 Table of χ^2

Degrees of Freedom	P = .99	.98	.95	.90	.80	.70	.50	.30	.20	.10	.05	.02	.01
1	.000157	.000628	.00393	.0158	.0642	.148	.455	1.074	1.642	2.706	3.841	5.412	6.635
2	.0201	.0404	.103	.211	.446	.713	1.386	2.408	3.219	4.605	5.991	7.824	9.210
3	.115	.185	.352	.584	1.005	1.424	2.366	3.665	4.642	6.251	7.815	9.837	11.341
4	.297	.429	.711	1.064	1.649	2.195	3.357	4.878	5.989	7.779	9.488	11.668	13.277
5	.554	.752	1.145	1.610	2.343	3.000	4.351	6.064	7.289	9.236	11.070	13.388	15.086
6	.872	1.134	1.635	2.204	3.070	3.828	5.348	7.231	8.558	10.645	12.592	15.033	16.812
7	1.239	1.564	2.167	2.833	3.822	4.671	6.346	8.383	9.803	12.017	14.067	16.622	18.475
8	1.646	2.032	2.733	3.490	4.594	5.527	7.344	9.524	11.030	13.362	15.507	18.168	20.090
9	2.088	2.532	3.325	4.168	5.380	6.393	8.343	10.656	12.242	14.684	16.919	19.679	21.666
10	2.558	3.059	3.940	4.865	6.179	7.267	9.342	11.781	13.442	15.987	18.307	21.161	23.209
11	3.053	3.609	4.575	5.578	6.989	8.148	10.341	12.899	14.631	17.275	19.675	22.618	24.725
12	3.571	4.178	5.226	6.304	7.807	9.034	11.340	14.011	15.812	18.549	21.026	24.054	26.217
13	4.107	4.765	5.892	7.042	8.634	9.926	12.340	15.119	16.985	19.812	22.362	25.472	27.688
14	4.660	5.368	6.571	7.790	9.467	10.821	13.339	16.222	18.151	21.064	23.685	26.873	29.141
15	5.229	5.985	7.261	8.547	10.307	11.721	14.339	17.322	19.311	22.307	24.996	28.259	30.578
16	5.812	6.614	7.962	9.312	11.152	12.624	15.338	18.418	20.465	23.542	26.296	29.633	32.000
17	6.408	7.255	8.672	10.085	12.002	13.531	16.338	19.511	21.615	24.769	27.587	30.995	33.409
18	7.015	7.906	9.390	10.865	12.857	14.440	17.338	20.601	22.760	25.989	28.869	32.346	34.805
19	7.633	8.567	10.117	11.651	13.716	15.352	18.338	21.689	23.900	27.204	30.144	33.687	36.191
20	8.260	9.237	10.851	12.443	14.578	16.266	19.337	22.775	25.038	28.412	31.410	35.020	37.566
21	8.897	9.915	11.591	13.240	15.445	17.182	20.337	23.858	26.171	29.615	32.671	36.343	38.932
22	9.542	10.600	12.338	14.041	16.314	18.101	21.337	24.939	27.301	30.813	33.924	37.659	40.289
23	10.196	11.293	13.091	14.848	17.187	19.021	22.337	26.018	28.429	32.007	35.172	38.968	41.638
24	10.856	11.992	13.848	15.659	18.062	19.943	23.337	27.096	29.553	33.196	36.415	40.270	42.980
25	11.524	12.697	14.611	16.473	18.940	20.867	24.337	28.172	30.675	34.382	37.652	41.566	44.314
26	12.198	13.409	15.379	17.292	19.820	21.792	25.336	29.246	31.795	35.563	38.885	42.856	45.642
27	12.879	14.125	16.151	18.114	20.703	22.719	26.336	30.319	32.912	36.741	40.113	44.140	46.963
28	13.565	14.847	16.928	18.939	21.588	23.647	27.336	31.391	34.027	37.916	41.337	45.419	48.278
29	14.256	15.574	17.708	19.768	22.475	24.577	28.336	32.461	35.139	39.087	42.557	46.693	49.588
30	14.953	16.306	18.493	20.599	23.364	25.508	29.336	33.530	36.250	40.256	43.773	47.962	50.892

Source: Reprinted with permission of Macmillan Publishing Co. from *Statistical Methods for Research Workers*, by R. A. Fisher. Copyright © 1970 by the University of Adelaide, Australia.

TABLE A.5 Critical Values of the Pearson Product Moment Correlation Coefficient

	Level of significance for a directional (one-tailed) test				
	.05	.025	.01	.005	.0005
	Level of significance for a nondirectional (two-tailed) test				
$df = N - 2$	.10	.05	.02	.01	.001
1	.9877	.9969	.9995	.9999	1.0000
2	.9000	.9500	.9800	.9900	.9990
3	.8054	.8783	.9343	.9587	.9912
4	.7293	.8114	.8822	.9172	.9741
5	.6694	.7545	.8329	.8745	.9507
6	.6215	.7067	.7887	.8343	.9249
7	.5822	.6664	.7498	.7977	.8982
8	.5494	.6319	.7155	.7646	.8721
9	.5214	.6021	.6851	.7348	.8471
10	.4973	.5760	.6581	.7079	.8233
11	.4762	.5529	.6339	.6835	.8010
12	.4575	.5324	.6120	.6614	.7800
13	.4409	.5139	.5923	.6411	.7603
14	.4259	.4973	.5742	.6226	.7420
15	.4124	.4821	.5577	.6055	.7246
16	.4000	.4683	.5425	.5897	.7084
17	.3887	.4555	.5285	.5751	.6932
18	.3783	.4438	.5155	.5614	.6787
19	.3687	.4329	.5034	.5487	.6652
20	.3598	.4227	.4921	.5368	.6524
25	.3233	.3809	.4451	.4869	.5974
30	.2960	.3494	.4093	.4487	.5541
35	.2746	.3246	.3810	.4182	.5189
40	.2573	.3044	.3578	.3932	.4896
45	.2428	.2875	.3384	.3721	.4648
50	.2306	.2732	.3218	.3541	.4433
60	.2108	.2500	.2948	.3248	.4078
70	.1954	.2319	.2737	.3017	.3799
80	.1829	.2172	.2565	.2830	.3568
90	.1726	.2050	.2422	.2673	.3375
100	.1638	.1946	.2301	.2540	.3211

Source: Table A.5 is taken from Table VII of Fisher and Yates, *Statistical Tables for Biological, Agricultural, and Medical Research*, published by Longman Group UK Ltd., London (previously published by Oliver and Boyd, Ltd., Edinburgh), and by permission of the authors and publishers.

TABLE A.6 Table of Random Numbers

Row	00000 01234	00000 56789	11111 01234	11111 56789	22222 01234	22222 56789	33333 01234	33333 56789
				1st Thousand				
00	23157	54859	01837	25993	76249	70886	95230	36744
01	05545	55043	10537	43508	90611	83744	10962	21343
02	14871	60350	32404	36223	50051	00322	11543	80834
03	38976	74951	94051	75853	78805	90194	32428	71695
04	97312	61718	99755	30870	94251	25841	54882	10513
05	11742	69381	44339	30872	32797	33118	22647	06850
06	43361	28859	11016	45623	93009	00499	43640	74036
07	93806	20478	38268	04491	55751	18932	58475	52571
08	49540	13181	08429	84187	69538	29661	77738	09527
09	36768	72633	37948	21569	41959	68670	45274	83880
10	07092	52392	24627	12067	06558	45344	67338	45320
11	43310	01081	44863	80307	52555	16148	89742	94647
12	61570	06360	06173	63775	63148	95123	35017	46993
13	31352	83799	10779	18941	31579	76448	62584	86919
14	57048	86526	27795	93692	90529	56516	35065	32254
15	09243	44200	68721	07137	30729	75756	09298	27650
16	97957	35018	40894	88329	52230	82521	22532	61587
17	93732	59570	43781	98885	56671	66826	95996	44569
18	72621	11225	00922	68264	35666	59434	71687	58167
19	61020	74418	45371	20794	95917	37866	99536	19378
20	97839	85474	33055	91718	45473	54144	22034	23000
21	89160	97192	22232	90637	35055	45489	88438	16361
22	25966	88220	62871	79265	02823	52862	84919	54883
23	81443	31719	05049	54806	74690	07567	65017	16543
24	11322	54931	42362	34386	08624	97687	46245	23245

Column Number

TABLE A.6 Table of Random Numbers (cont.)

2nd Thousand

Row	00000 01234	00000 56789	11111 01234	11111 56789	22222 01234	22222 56789	33333 01234	33333 56789
00	64755	83885	84122	25920	17696	15655	95045	95947
01	10302	52289	77436	34430	38112	49067	07348	23328
02	71017	98495	51308	50374	66591	02887	53765	69149
03	60012	55605	88410	34879	79655	90169	78800	03666
04	37330	94656	49161	42802	48274	54755	44553	65090
05	47869	87001	31591	12273	60626	12822	34691	61212
06	38040	42737	64167	89578	39323	49324	88434	38706
07	73508	30908	83054	80078	86669	30295	56460	45336
08	32623	46474	84061	04324	20628	37319	32356	43969
09	97591	99549	36630	35106	62069	92975	95320	57734
10	74012	31955	59790	96982	66224	24015	96749	07589
11	56754	26457	13351	05014	90966	33674	69096	33488
12	49800	49908	54831	21998	08528	26372	92923	65026
13	43584	89647	24878	56670	00221	50193	99591	62377
14	16653	79664	60325	71301	35742	83636	73058	87229
15	48502	69055	65322	58748	31446	80237	31252	96367
16	96765	54692	36316	86230	48296	38352	23816	64094
17	38923	61550	80357	81784	23444	12463	33992	28128
18	77958	81694	25225	05587	51073	01070	60218	61961
19	17928	28065	25586	08771	02641	85064	65796	48170
20	94036	85978	02318	04499	41054	10531	87431	21596
21	47460	60479	56230	48417	14372	85167	27558	00368
22	47856	56088	51992	82439	40644	17170	13463	18288
23	57616	34653	92298	62018	10375	76515	62986	90756
24	08300	92704	66752	66610	57188	79107	54222	22013

TABLE A.6 Table of Random Numbers (cont.)

Column Number

Row	00000 01234	00000 56789	11111 01234	11111 56789	22222 01234	22222 56789	33333 01234	33333 56789
				3rd Thousand				
00	89221	02362	65787	74733	51272	30213	92441	39651
01	04005	99818	63918	29032	94012	42363	01261	10650
02	98546	38066	50856	75045	40645	22841	53254	44125
03	41719	84401	59226	01314	54581	40398	49988	65579
04	28733	72489	00785	25843	24613	49797	85567	84471
05	65213	83927	77762	03086	80742	24395	68476	83792
06	65553	12678	90906	90466	43670	26217	69900	31205
07	05668	69080	73029	85746	58332	78231	45986	92998
08	39302	99718	49757	79519	27387	76373	47262	91612
09	64592	32254	45879	29431	38320	05981	18067	87137
10	07513	48792	47314	83660	68907	05336	82579	91582
11	86593	68501	56638	99800	82839	35148	56541	07232
12	83735	22599	97977	81248	36838	99560	32410	67614
13	08595	21826	54655	08204	87990	17033	56258	05384
14	41273	27149	44293	69458	16828	63962	15864	35431
15	00473	75908	56238	12242	72631	76314	47252	06347
16	86131	53789	81383	07868	89132	96182	07009	86432
17	33849	78359	08402	03586	03176	88663	08018	22546
18	61870	41657	07468	08612	98083	97349	20775	45091
19	43898	65923	25078	86129	78491	97653	91500	80786
20	29939	39123	04548	45985	60952	06641	28726	46473
21	38505	85555	14388	55077	18657	94887	67831	70819
22	31824	38431	67125	25511	72044	11562	53279	82268
23	91430	03767	13561	15597	06750	92552	02391	38753
24	38635	68976	25498	97526	96458	03805	04116	63514

TABLE A.6 Table of Random Numbers (cont.)

	Column Number							
Row	00000 01234	00000 56789	11111 01234	11111 56789	22222 01234	22222 56789	33333 01234	33333 56789
				4th Thousand				
00	02490	54122	27944	39364	94239	72074	11679	54082
01	11967	36469	60627	83701	09253	30208	01385	37482
02	48256	83465	49699	24079	05403	35154	39613	03136
03	27246	73080	21481	23536	04881	89977	49484	93071
04	32532	77265	72430	70722	86529	18457	92657	10011
05	66757	98955	92375	93431	43204	55825	45443	69265
06	11266	34545	76505	97746	34668	26999	26742	97516
07	17872	39142	45561	80146	93137	48924	64257	59284
08	62561	30365	03408	14754	51798	08133	61010	97730
09	62796	30779	35497	70501	30105	08133	00997	91970
10	75510	21771	04339	33660	42757	62223	87565	48468
11	87439	01691	63517	26590	44437	07217	98706	39032
12	97742	02621	10748	78803	38837	65226	92149	59051
13	98811	06001	21571	02875	21828	83912	85188	61624
14	51264	01852	64607	92553	29004	26695	78583	62998
15	40239	93376	10419	68610	49120	02941	80035	99317
16	26936	59186	51667	27645	46329	44681	94190	66647
17	88502	11716	98299	40974	42394	62200	69094	81646
18	63499	38093	25593	61995	79867	80569	01023	38374
19	36379	81206	03317	78710	73828	31083	60509	44091
20	93801	22322	47479	57017	59334	30647	43061	26660
21	29856	87120	56311	50053	25365	81265	22414	02431
22	97720	87931	88265	13050	71017	15177	06957	92919
23	85237	09105	74601	46377	59938	15647	34177	92753
24	75746	75268	31727	95773	72364	87324	36879	06802

TABLE A.6 Table of Random Numbers (cont.)

			Column Number					
Row	00000 01234	00000 56789	11111 01234	11111 56789	22222 01234	22222 56789	33333 01234	33333 56789
				5th Thousand				
00	29935	06971	63175	52579	10478	89379	61428	21363
01	15114	07126	51890	77787	75510	13103	42942	48111
02	03870	43225	10589	87629	22039	94124	38127	65022
03	79390	39188	40756	45269	65959	20640	14284	22960
04	30035	06915	79196	54428	64819	52314	48721	81594
05	29039	99861	28759	79802	68531	39198	38137	24373
06	78196	08108	24107	49777	09599	43569	84820	94956
07	15847	85493	91442	91351	80130	73752	21539	10986
08	36614	62248	49194	97209	92587	92053	41021	80064
09	40549	54884	91465	43862	35541	44466	88894	74180
10	40878	08997	14286	09982	90308	78007	51587	16658
11	10229	49282	41173	31468	59455	18756	08908	06660
12	15918	76787	30624	25928	44124	25088	31137	71614
13	13403	18796	49909	94404	64979	41462	18155	98335
14	66523	94596	74908	90271	10009	98648	17640	68909
15	91665	36469	68343	17870	25975	04662	21272	50620
16	67415	87515	08207	73729	73201	57593	96917	69699
17	76527	96996	23724	33448	63392	32394	60887	90617
18	19815	47789	74348	17147	10954	34355	81194	54407
19	25592	53587	76384	72575	84347	68918	05739	57222
20	55902	45539	63646	31609	95999	82887	40666	66692
21	02470	58376	79794	22482	42423	96162	47491	17264
22	18630	53263	13319	97619	35859	12350	14632	87659
23	89673	38230	16063	92007	59503	38402	76450	33333
24	62986	67364	06595	17427	84623	14565	82860	57300

Source: Kendall, M. G., and B. B. Smith (1938). Randomness and random sampling numbers. *Journal of the Royal Statistical Society, 101,* 164–166. Reproduced by permission of the Royal Statistical Society, London.

/// INDEX